# COUNTRIES AT
# THE CROSSROADS

# COUNTRIES AT THE CROSSROADS

## A Survey of Democratic Governance

Sarah Repucci

Christopher Walker

EDITORS

FREEDOM HOUSE

NEW YORK • WASHINGTON, D.C.

ROWMAN & LITTLEFIELD PUBLISHERS, INC.

LANHAM • BOULDER • NEW YORK • TORONTO • OXFORD

ROWMAN & LITTLEFIELD PUBLISHERS, INC.

Published in the United States of America
by Rowman & Littlefield Publishers, Inc.
A wholly owned subsidary of The Rowman & Littlefield Publishing Group, Inc.
4501 Forbes Boulevard, Suite 200, Lanham, Maryland 20706
www.rowmanlittlefield.com

PO Box 317
Oxford
OX2 9RU, UK

British Library Cataloguing in Publication Information Available
**Library of Congress Cataloging-in-Publication Data**

Countries at the crossroads : a survey of democratic governance / Sarah Repucci,
Christopher Walker, editors.
    p. cm.
Includes bibliographical references and index.
ISBN 0-7425-4971-2 (hardcover : alk. paper)—ISBN 0-7425-4972-0 (pbk. : alk. paper)
1. Democracy—Case studies. 2. Representative government and representation—Case
studies. I. Repucci, Sarah, 1976– II. Walker, Christopher, 1964–
    JC423.C7196 2005
    320.3—dc22                                                    2005016339

Printed in the United States of America

The paper used in this publication meets the minimum requirements of American
National Standard for Information Sciences—Permanence of Paper for Printed Library
Materials, ANSI/NISO Z39.48-1992.

# CONTENTS

# COUNTRIES AT THE CROSSROADS
## 2004–2005

| 2004 COUNTRIES | 2005 COUNTRIES |
| --- | --- |
| Afghanistan | Algeria |
| Armenia | Angola |
| Azerbaijan | Bangladesh |
| Bahrain | Bhutan |
| Cambodia | Bolivia |
| East Timor | Burkina Faso |
| Georgia | China |
| Guatemala | Colombia |
| Haiti | Ecuador |
| Indonesia | Egypt |
| Jordan | Eritrea |
| Kazakhstan | Ethiopia |
| Kenya | Honduras |
| Kyrgyzstan | Iran |
| Malaysia | Laos |
| Morocco | Libya |
| Nepal | Mauritania |
| Nicaragua | Mozambique |
| Nigeria | Paraguay |
| Pakistan | Peru |
| Qatar | Philippines |
| Sierra Leone | Russia |
| Sri Lanka | Rwanda |
| Uganda | Swaziland |
| Ukraine | Syria |
| Uzbekistan | Tajikistan |
| Venezuela | Thailand |
| Vietnam | Tunisia |
| Yemen | Turkey |
| Zimbabwe | Zambia |

# ACKNOWLEDGMENTS

*Countries at the Crossroads* is the product of the collective contributions of numerous Freedom House staff members and consultants. This study was also made possible by the generous support of the Bureau of Democracy, Human Rights, and Labor at the U.S. Department of State.

Country report authors made an outstanding contribution to this effort, working to produce 30 clear, informed analyses of a highly diverse group of countries. The report authors are: Adam Albion, Martin Edwin Andersen, Michele Penner Angrist, Carolyn Bull, Jeffrey Clark, Daniel Connell, John Daniel, Bradford Dillman, Stephen Fairbanks, Joseph Fewsmith, Michael Gold-Biss, Rounaq Jahan, Cédric Jourde, Harvey Kline, Peter Lambert, David Lesch, Robert Lloyd, Augustin Loada, Duncan McCargo, Michael McFaul (with Sanja Tatic), Andrés Mejía-Acosta, Gabriella Montinola, Alison Pargeter, Imogen Parsons, Sara Rakita, Sarah Repucci, David Simon, Denis J. Sullivan, Donna Lee Van Cott, and Richard Whitecross.

A group of distinguished regional experts served on the advisory committee, providing valuable input on the narratives and scores. They are: Morton Abramowitz, Joel Barkan, Linda Beck, Daniel Brumberg, John Carey, John Entelis, Bernard Haykel, Jeffrey Herbst, Michael Hutt, Nina L. Khrushcheva, Thomas Lansner, Thomas Melia, Amit Pandya, Robert Rotberg, Michael Shifter, Peter Sinnot, Bridget Welsh, Elizabeth Wishnick, and Coletta Youngers.

The *Countries at the Crossroads* methodology was originally developed with the expert contribution of a group of senior advisers, including Larry Diamond, Hoover Institution; Paul Martin, Columbia University; Rick Messick, World Bank; Ted Piccone, Open Society Institute; Louise Shelley, American University; and Ruth Wedgwood, Johns Hopkins University. Jay Verkuilen of the University of Illinois, Urbana-Champaign, provided invaluable guidance, in addition to his participation in the methodology committee.

Freedom House staff devoted extensive time and energy to launch this pilot effort. Sarah Repucci, researcher, and Christopher Walker, director of studies, edited the survey. Arch Puddington, director of research; Adrian Karatnycky, counselor and senior scholar; and Jennifer Windsor, executive director of Freedom House, provided overall guidance and support for the project, in addition to serving on the survey's internal review committee. Research assistant Amy Phillips supplied important research and editorial support, as did staff members Sanja Tatic and Mark Rosenberg and interns Alex Taurel and Ana Jelenkovic. Nancy van Itallie copyedited the volume. Ida Walker was the proofreader, and Beverly Butterfield designed and typeset the volume.

# EXPERT ADVISORY COMMITTEE

# MEETING THE DEMOCRATIC GOVERNANCE CHALLENGE

*Sarah Repucci and Christopher Walker*

Democratic governance has taken a central place in the international policy debate as the business community, foreign assistance providers, and world leaders have come to recognize its indispensability in facilitating political development and economic growth. With this heightened interest has come greater demand for relevant and effective tools to monitor and measure sound governance. By providing a clear and wide-ranging analytical instrument, *Countries at the Crossroads* strives to help meet this demand.

Through its systematic and comprehensive review of core issues relating to democratic governance—covering the thematic areas of Accountability and Public Voice, Civil Liberties, Rule of Law, and Anticorruption and Transparency—*Crossroads* provides policymakers and analysts alike a single source of information and analysis that can meet a multiplicity of needs. *Crossroads'* numerical ratings and the extensive country essays that accompany them are intended to promote increased understanding of the progress states must make if they are to attain honest, transparent, and democratically accountable governance rooted in justice and the rule of law.

In 2005, the *Crossroads* analysis highlights two critical components of democratic governance in particular: free media and an independent judiciary. The *Crossroads* analysts identified these themes as among the most pressing priorities for regimes struggling with inadequate governmental accountability, weak rule of law, and pervasive corruption. As pillars on which strong and stable governance can be built, free media and independent judges should be primary goals for the countries covered in this volume.

*Crossroads* examines a unique group of countries: by and large those in the messy middle, perched between full democratic freedom and total repression. The survey offers an independent, external evaluation of the state of the rule of law, transparency, anticorruption efforts, governmental

1

accountability, and respect for fundamental civil liberties in countries where democracy is absent or has not been securely consolidated. Moreover, the volume provides a clear and detailed assessment of the reform steps these countries must take if they are to join the community of stable, free, and democratic nations.

The 2005 edition is the second in the *Countries at the Crossroads* series. It examines 30 countries distinct from those in the first, 2004, edition. *Crossroads* is designed to evaluate this same set of 60 countries biennially, with the 2004 countries covered in each even-numbered year and the 2005 countries covered in odd-numbered years. In this way, *Crossroads* will cover the most extensive set of countries possible while creating a body of work that offers its readership useful time series data, as well as comprehensive narrative analysis that monitors progress or backsliding in the countries covered.

Freedom House publishes a range of analytical surveys, among them *Freedom in the World: The Annual Survey of Political Rights and Civil Liberties; Freedom of the Press: The Annual Survey of Global Media Independence; Nations in Transit: Democratization in East Central Europe and Eurasia;* and *Citizenship and Justice: A Survey of Women's Rights in the Middle East and North Africa.*

*Countries at the Crossroads* is unique among Freedom House's publications in that it is the only such project to focus exclusively on government performance.

## Crossroads Findings and the Importance of Government Performance

By focusing on government performance, *Countries at the Crossroads* places primary responsibility for the protection of basic rights and good governance on governments. Government performance has taken on a higher profile in the international assistance community due to the establishment by the U.S. government of the Millennium Challenge Account (MCA). The MCA's conceptual foundation is based on the idea that economic development flourishes when it is linked to democratic and free market policies. The MCA emphasizes rewarding countries that rule justly, invest in their own citizens, and foster economic freedom.

At root, the MCA seeks to reward sound policies, something on which both international assistance providers and the business community place high value. In order to help identify specific areas where improved policies are most urgently needed, the *Crossroads* survey contains targeted recommendations for priority action by the governments examined. These recommendations are designed to focus attention on different dimensions of public policy challenges. In some instances the recommendations provide guidance for the passage of specific legislation or regulatory steps to be taken by governments. In others, recommendations set forth basic principles that must be observed. In the 2005 *Crossroads* recommendations, the need for improvement is emphasized in two particularly critical areas: fostering independent media and enabling the independence of the judiciary.

### Media and Judicial Independence as Linchpins of Democratic Governance

In more than half of the reports in the 2005 *Crossroads* edition, experts cited in their recommendations defense of news media and judicial independence as top priorities. The *Crossroads* findings suggest that by dominating the flow of information and the legal apparatus, regimes are able to exert thorough control over a country's political and economic life; the media and legal spheres function as keystones for maintaining an effective monopoly on power.

Under the most repressive regimes, the constriction of the flow of information has quashed a valuable channel for the expression of societal discontent. It has constrained the enabling environment for debate of alternative policy options to meet complex societal challenges. It has also allowed incumbents to employ state broadcasting and print resources to deny opposition forces the opportunity to reach a competitive threshold. Independent news media can also serve as a crucial mechanism for building popular political will for reform. By educating the public, informing them of unlawful or unethical behavior, and sharing information on possible best practices, the news media help facilitate policy improvement. Autocratic leaders are well aware of independent media's power and therefore seek to deny unfettered airing of issues. In so doing, they deny their own citizens the opportunity to improve their circumstances.

Meanwhile, an independent judiciary serves as a country's legal backbone, providing safeguards and guarantees that cut across other sectors of society. Executive dominance of judges and courts leads to unchecked power. Under such conditions, incumbents are at liberty to use the judicial system as an instrument to reward cronies and eliminate political competition. The lack of an independent judiciary is directly related to the problem of corruption. It should therefore come as no surprise that vested interests within the regime, or forces aligned closely with it, have a large stake in preventing the emergence of an independent institution that is capable of rendering decisions that promote public welfare rather than distribute spoils to narrow, corrupt interests. The misuse of public power for private or political profit flourishes when corrupt officials have little accountability for their actions. In these settings, an indispensable check on abuse of power—an independent judiciary—is suppressed in favor of judicial compliance and even affirmation.

The impact of such shortcomings can be seen in the example of Syria, covered in this volume by analyst David Lesch. Syria's Bashar al-'Asad was the only presidential candidate in 2000 after the death of his father, Hafiz al-'Asad, who had ruled unchallenged since 1970. A few powerful families in or connected to the government control the country's wealth, and the ruling Ba'ath party keeps a tight grip on political institutions. Criticism is stifled in the local media, which are state run, thus depriving Syrians of the opportunity to voice opposition through the mainstream press. Meanwhile, both the president and the minister of justice participate in the council that appoints and promotes judges, ensuring executive influence in judicial proceedings. Authorities rarely face court proceedings, whether for corruption—which is rampant—or other abuse of power, leaving systemic problems unchecked. With avenues for debate in the media suppressed and regime opponents targeted by the courts, the Syrian system offer little space for political change.

Thus, this *Crossroads* volume suggests that independent media and an independent judiciary are fundamental components of any efforts at reform. Without these two mechanisms in place, other sectors and institutions are likely to face insurmountable obstacles to advancement.

### Combating the Scourge of Corruption

Of course, both independent media and the judiciary are vitally important institutions for combating corruption, a subject that begs attention in virtually all of the countries examined in this volume.

Denial of free expression and fair and independent judicial practice serves to immunize regimes and other powerful interests aligned with the authorities from meaningful scrutiny and accountability. By allowing corrupt practices to continue unchecked, such repression helps institutionalize them. Without meaningful exposure in the media and punishment through the courts, corruption is free to pervade society. As many of the states covered in this volume have ambitions of joining or more deeply integrating into the global economy, corruption is an issue that rightfully captures the attention of policymakers and businesspeople alike.

*Crossroads* does not attempt to measure corruption in a given country per se but instead evaluates the existence of laws and standards to prevent and combat corruption, the enforcement of such measures, and governmental transparency. Of the four main thematic areas addressed in the survey, the measure for anticorruption and transparency is the one in which the 30 governments on the whole received the lowest scores. The average score for this thematic area is 2.57, which reflects the implementation of few to very few standards and guarantees to prevent and root out corruption and ensure governmental transparency. The lowest score in this area—Libya at 0.19 out of 7—is the lowest in any area in the survey. The highest that any government scores in this area is just 3.88 (Colombia); this is considerably short of a score of 5, which is the threshold for a basic standard of effective performance.

These findings suggest that corruption is most likely a considerable problem for all of these governments. This is particularly true given that, of the four subsections covered in this thematic area, the one that addresses the environment for preventing corruption receives the lowest score for half of the 30 governments.

Within the sphere of corruption, the *Crossroads* experts highlighted several priority steps for reform:

- an end to impunity for crimes of corruption;

- the creation of an independent office to investigate and prosecute corruption-related crimes; and

- enhanced access to government information.

## Country Review

*Countries at the Crossroads* examines a wide spectrum of polities: multiparty systems with competitive elections that meet the minimum criteria of electoral democracy; dominant-party states in which multiparty systems have been usurped by a leadership that suppresses genuine electoral competition; one-party, authoritarian states; and monarchies. To a greater or lesser degree, all have some shortcomings in the fields of democracy, human rights, and accountable government. Many also confront considerable poverty: Of the 30 countries, 21 have gross national incomes per capita of less than $1,500; only one country (Libya) has a gross national income per capita of more than $3,000.

Of the 30 countries covered in the 2005 edition of *Crossroads*, six are struggling democracies (Bangladesh, Honduras, Mozambique, Paraguay, Thailand, Turkey). Five more are democratic governments facing popular unrest (Bolivia, Peru, Ecuador) or violent insurgencies (Philippines, Colombia). One country has in recent years experienced significant erosion in democratic practice (Russia), and three other states possess electoral systems with strong influence from the ruling party (Burkina Faso, Ethiopia, Zambia). Two are monarchies (Bhutan, Swaziland), and eight are authoritarian regimes (Algeria, Angola, Egypt, Iran, Mauritania, Rwanda, Tajikistan, Tunisia). Finally, this edition includes five countries that are among the world's worst performers with respect to freedom (China, Eritrea, Laos, Libya, Syria).

Colombia is the only country in the survey to achieve a score of 5 or above in any category; its score is 5.02 in Accountability and Public Voice. Colombia clearly faces serious governance challenges in regions affected by insurgent activity. However, the central government has nevertheless managed to afford considerable guarantees for free and fair elections, accountable government, and civic engagement in other parts of the country.

### Four Pivotal Countries: China, Egypt, Iran, and Russia

Among the 30 countries covered in this edition of *Crossroads*, four are of particular strategic concern. China, Egypt, Iran, and Russia play pivotal roles in their respective regions while also influencing political, economic, and security affairs on the wider world stage. Given these countries' relative importance, their ability to implement comprehensive reforms successfully will affect an exceptionally wide range of interests and actors, including multinational companies, neighboring states, and international institutions.

### China

China is at once economically dynamic and politically unaccountable. The Chinese leadership is attempting an ambitious and wide-ranging economic reform effort that holds considerable promise as well as risks. Among the most vexing challenges confronting China is the scope and depth of that country's corruption. China's tradition of secrecy is as strong as its tradition of transparency is weak. China's controlled media and restricted judiciary prompt serious questions about whether the leadership will be able to calibrate its airing of the corruption issue in a sufficiently deft manner to meet its larger economic reform ambitions. More fundamentally, China's authorities have asserted the need for vastly improved governance if the country is to join the ranks of advanced, modern states. Whether it can achieve this goal in the absence of meaningful political reform is the seminal and, as yet, unanswered question.

Joseph Fewsmith, author of the *Countries at the Crossroads* China report, observes that

> neither the demands for political reform that emerged in the 1980s nor economic growth have led to democratic transition [in China]. The government's defenders point to gradual improvements in governance and the avoidance of the sort of chaos that might be expected to emerge in such a populous country undergoing rapid change and experiencing growing differences in income. Its critics, however, point to continuing abuses of power, including the stifling of dissent, to argue that China should embark on a program of political reform to bring democratic rights—not just improved standards of living—to its citizens.

Among the principal recommendations for the Chinese authorities is that they recognize the public's right to information by allowing the media to report on all topics, including corruption by officials. In addition, the courts should be separated from the supervision of party committees.

## Egypt

Egypt is the Middle East's pivotal state. Egyptian President Hosni Mubarak, who is 77 years old and has not faced electoral competition during a quarter century in power, is confronted with an increasingly restive civil society and frustrated wider population. The Egyptian authorities have yet to embark on a path of democratic reform that could help ameliorate the increasingly difficult challenges confronting them to improve the country's economic performance and ease political tensions. The nascent public expression of these difficulties has come in the form of public protests from the *kifaya* (enough) movement. Kifaya represents a part of a larger community of civic activists in Egypt that the authorities should allow to help advance Egypt's democratic reform process. However, the regime has actively worked to curb efforts by civil society actors to move reform forward.

Denis Sullivan, author of the Egypt report, writes that

> [Egypt's] law-making process, along with political and security institutions, is used more to thwart political opposition and civil liberties than to protect (let alone expand) them. [President] Mubarak keeps Egypt an authoritarian system, far from the democracy that he claims it to be. . . . Egypt has a vibrant civil society and an array of political institutions that could promote democracy. However, the president has not abided by his own promise, made repeatedly since he came to power, to allow democracy to function. Egyptian politics thus remain both restricted and promising.

Among the chief recommendations for Egypt in *Countries at the Crossroads* is that the government should amend the Press Law to end crippling fines and imprisonment for journalists who commit slander. In the judicial sphere, the government should allow judges to be promoted within their own ranks, not from executive branch agencies such as the ministry of justice. The emergency court system should be disbanded to allow for fairer and more accountable trials.

## Iran

The Iranian leadership faces a restive citizenry that has clearly expressed its desire for more accountable and effective governance. However, the clerical dictatorship that wields power in Tehran has shown little inclination toward democratic reform.

Stephen Fairbanks in his *Countries at the Crossroads* report portrays a country in which a select group of high-ranking clergy has

> proved intolerant of those who seek to broaden political participation, attempting to cap dissent with tough restrictions on freedom of expression. They have not hesitated to use their monopoly on juridical authority to keep critics and rivals under control. Political dissidents and journalists have no protection from arbitrary arrest or interrogations under torture. Corruption and bribery are pervasive, bred by the exclusive access to power open to supporters of the ruling clerics.

Among the main recommendations in the Iran report is that the authorities should permit unfettered freedom of expression by releasing journalists, Web site operators, and other individuals imprisoned for peacefully expressing their opinions. Moreover, the regime should allow the media to investigate all forms of corruption without fear of retaliation.

## Russia

Under the leadership of President Vladimir Putin, Russia's governance has taken a sharp turn toward more highly concentrated rule. The Kremlin's tightening grip has increasingly marginalized key societal institutions, including the press, the judiciary, and civil society. This in turn has raised genuine questions about the durability of the rule of law in Russia and whether Moscow's economic modernization ambitions can be realized in such a stultifying environment.

The author of the *Countries at the Crossroads* Russia report, Michael McFaul, writes that

> although the formal institutions of Russian democracy remain in place, the actual democratic content of these institutions has eroded considerably in the last few years. President Putin has systematically weakened or destroyed every check on his power, while at the same time strengthening the state's ability to violate the constitutional rights of individual citizens. He has weakened the power of Russia's regional leaders, the independent media, the business community or oligarchs, both houses of parliament, the Russian prime minister and his government (as opposed to the presidential administration), independent political parties, and genuine civil society.

Among the key recommendations to the Russian authorities is that the state broadcasters should be privatized or supervised by an independent board to help safeguard against political interference. State control over the judiciary must end as well.

## Conclusion

Recent events in Georgia, Ukraine, Kyrgyzstan, and Lebanon demonstrate the ability of popular resistance to effect change in corrupt and unresponsive political leadership. These advances have been spurred in part by the information revolution, which allows news of transformations in any corner of the globe to be transmitted across borders with a speed unimaginable even a generation ago. However, in many of the countries covered in this survey, citizens paradoxically face considerable hurdles to obtaining information about their own government's performance. While transparency has taken a high place on the international agenda, it remains an aspiration in many of the countries under review here.

In countries where corruption and cronyism have become entrenched, average citizens are becoming more frustrated with their leadership's inability to deliver political goods and to promote public welfare. The directing of public resources under these mismanaged regimes into a relatively small circle of private hands creates an untenable governance atmosphere for average citizens. Over the long haul, such arrangements will lead neither to stable political environments nor to sound and reliable business environments. Key international stakeholders—national governments, relevant multilateral organizations, and the business community—all have a genuine interest in encouraging improved governance in these countries.

Sound governance cannot be achieved by decree. Consensual decision making is required, in which leaders are chosen through free and fair elections and institutions such as the media and the judiciary are permitted to share information and hold the authorities accountable. Open channels between the government and civil society—operating under the rule of law—can contribute to strengthening regime legitimacy. Regimes that claim to rely on self-reform or self-policing, without the benefit of independent institutions and their own citizens' voices, will be at a severe—perhaps fatal—disadvantage in managing the challenges and opportunities of the 21st century.

# COUNTRY SCORES

| | Accountability and Public Voice | Civil Liberties | Rule of Law | Anticorruption and Transparency |
|---|---|---|---|---|
| Algeria | 2.90 | 2.90 | 2.49 | 2.55 |
| Angola | 1.79 | 2.81 | 2.22 | 2.10 |
| Bangladesh | 3.63 | 4.05 | 3.42 | 2.64 |
| Bhutan | 2.40 | 3.36 | 4.23 | 3.34 |
| Bolivia | 3.54 | 4.12 | 3.52 | 3.12 |
| Burkina Faso | 3.44 | 3.88 | 3.32 | 3.12 |
| China | 1.08 | 1.61 | 1.76 | 2.18 |
| Colombia | 5.02 | 4.39 | 4.21 | 3.88 |
| Ecuador | 3.92 | 4.12 | 3.33 | 3.42 |
| Egypt | 2.31 | 2.18 | 3.19 | 1.76 |
| Eritrea | 0.67 | 1.54 | 1.03 | 1.71 |
| Ethiopia | 1.88 | 2.83 | 2.06 | 2.76 |
| Honduras | 3.81 | 3.88 | 3.35 | 2.96 |
| Iran | 1.75 | 1.89 | 2.70 | 1.73 |
| Laos | 1.19 | 2.16 | 1.63 | 1.51 |
| Libya | 0.56 | 1.17 | 1.12 | 0.19 |
| Mauritania | 2.00 | 2.39 | 2.12 | 1.97 |
| Mozambique | 4.13 | 4.49 | 3.39 | 2.78 |
| Paraguay | 4.10 | 4.06 | 3.92 | 3.28 |
| Peru | 4.65 | 4.64 | 3.84 | 3.21 |
| Philippines | 4.46 | 3.92 | 3.30 | 3.50 |
| Russia | 2.88 | 3.72 | 3.41 | 2.79 |
| Rwanda | 1.48 | 2.21 | 1.22 | 1.97 |
| Swaziland | 1.85 | 2.98 | 1.45 | 1.85 |
| Syria | 1.29 | 2.04 | 2.13 | 1.70 |
| Tajikistan | 1.77 | 2.74 | 2.84 | 1.40 |
| Thailand | 4.04 | 3.72 | 4.22 | 3.48 |
| Tunisia | 1.65 | 3.08 | 2.79 | 3.53 |
| Turkey | 4.35 | 3.98 | 4.18 | 3.43 |
| Zambia | 3.85 | 4.57 | 4.26 | 3.39 |

# ACCOUNTABILITY AND PUBLIC VOICE

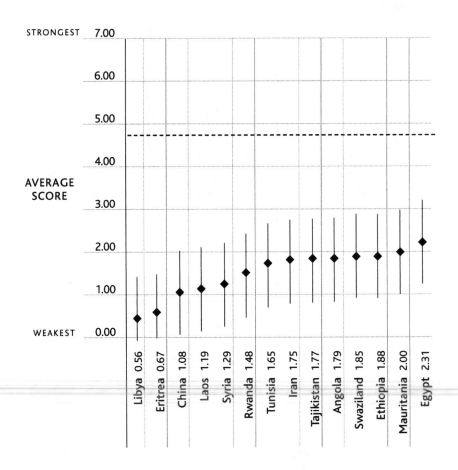

Note: Horizontal bars represent margin of error. Margin of error = 0.69, which is derived from an approximate 95 percent confidence interval based on using ±2* (standard error of measurement).

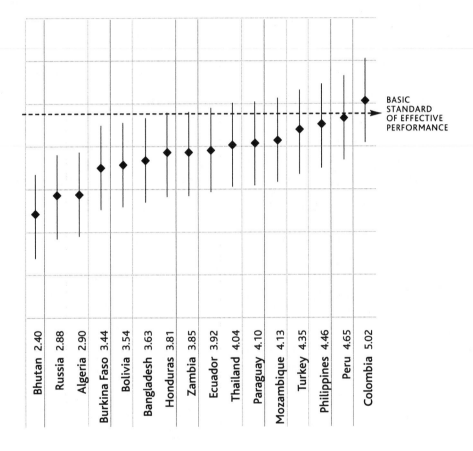

BASIC
STANDARD
OF EFFECTIVE
PERFORMANCE

Bhutan 2.40
Russia 2.88
Algeria 2.90
Burkina Faso 3.44
Bolivia 3.54
Bangladesh 3.63
Honduras 3.81
Zambia 3.85
Ecuador 3.92
Thailand 4.04
Paraguay 4.10
Mozambique 4.13
Turkey 4.35
Philippines 4.46
Peru 4.65
Colombia 5.02

# CIVIL LIBERTIES

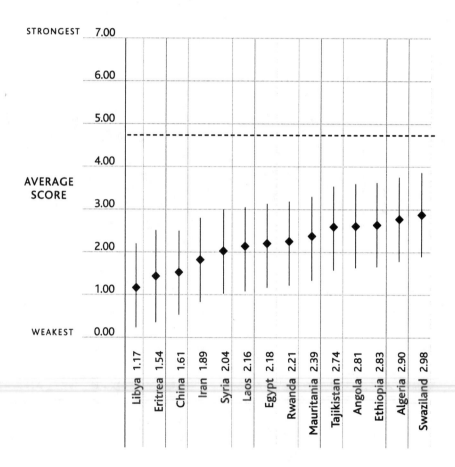

Note: Horizontal bars represent margin of error. Margin of error = 0.82, which is derived from an approximate 95 percent confidence interval based on using ±2* (standard error of measurement).

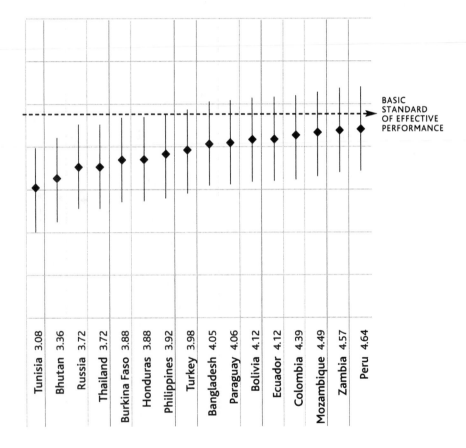

BASIC
STANDARD
OF EFFECTIVE
PERFORMANCE

Tunisia 3.08
Bhutan 3.36
Russia 3.72
Thailand 3.72
Burkina Faso 3.88
Honduras 3.88
Philippines 3.92
Turkey 3.98
Bangladesh 4.05
Paraguay 4.06
Bolivia 4.12
Ecuador 4.12
Colombia 4.39
Mozambique 4.49
Zambia 4.57
Peru 4.64

# RULE OF LAW

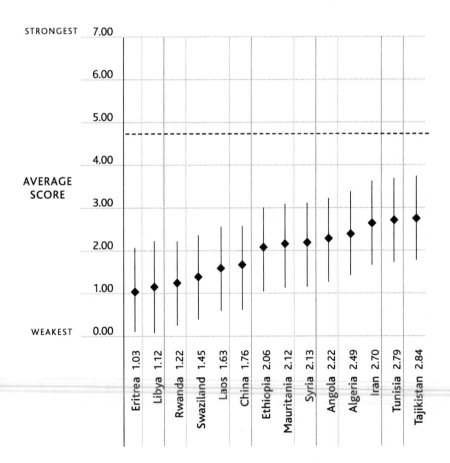

STRONGEST 7.00

6.00

5.00

4.00

AVERAGE
SCORE 3.00

2.00

1.00

WEAKEST 0.00

Eritrea 1.03
Libya 1.12
Rwanda 1.22
Swaziland 1.45
Laos 1.63
China 1.76
Ethiopia 2.06
Mauritania 2.12
Syria 2.13
Angola 2.22
Algeria 2.49
Iran 2.70
Tunisia 2.79
Tajikistan 2.84

Note: Horizontal bars represent margin of error. Margin of error = 0.69, which is derived from an approximate 95 percent confidence interval based on using ±2* (standard error of measurement).

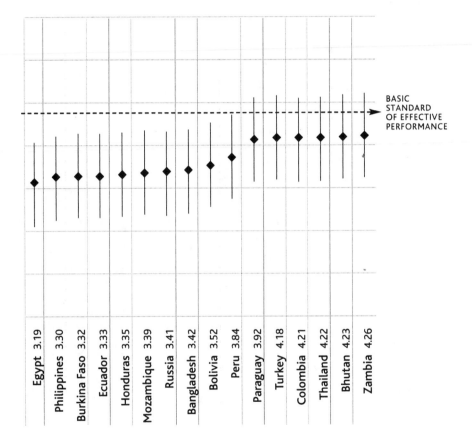

BASIC STANDARD OF EFFECTIVE PERFORMANCE

Egypt 3.19

Philippines 3.30

Burkina Faso 3.32

Ecuador 3.33

Honduras 3.35

Mozambique 3.39

Russia 3.41

Bangladesh 3.42

Bolivia 3.52

Peru 3.84

Paraguay 3.92

Turkey 4.18

Colombia 4.21

Thailand 4.22

Bhutan 4.23

Zambia 4.26

# ANTICORRUPTION AND TRANSPARENCY

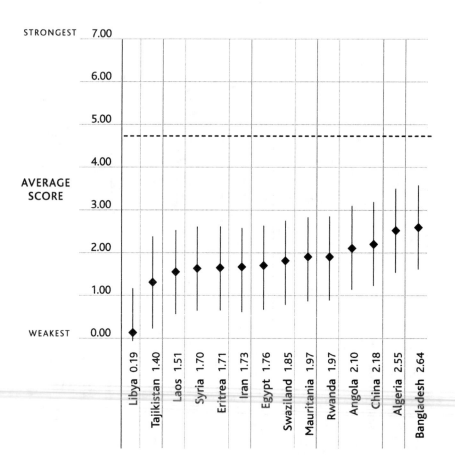

Note: Horizontal bars represent margin of error. Margin of error = 0.54, which is derived from an approximate 95 percent confidence interval based on using ±2* (standard error of measurement).

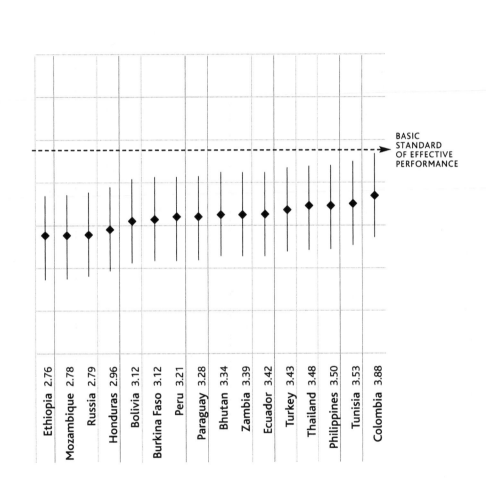

BASIC
STANDARD
OF EFFECTIVE
PERFORMANCE

Ethiopia 2.76
Mozambique 2.78
Russia 2.79
Honduras 2.96
Bolivia 3.12
Burkina Faso 3.12
Peru 3.21
Paraguay 3.28
Bhutan 3.34
Zambia 3.39
Ecuador 3.42
Turkey 3.43
Thailand 3.48
Philippines 3.50
Tunisia 3.53
Colombia 3.88

# INTRODUCTION TO COUNTRY REPORTS

The *Countries at the Crossroads 2005* survey contains reports on 30 countries. Each report begins with a section containing basic political and economic data arranged in the following categories: **capital, population,** and gross national income (GNI) **per capita.** In addition, numerical ratings are provided for **Accountability and Public Voice, Civil Liberties, Rule of Law,** and **Anticorruption and Transparency.**

The **capital** was obtained from the CIA *World Factbook 2004.* Population data were obtained from the Population Reference Bureau's *2004 World Population Data Sheet* for all countries except Bhutan, whose population figure is from the Bhutan National Statistical Authority. Data on **GNI per capita** were obtained from the World Bank World Development Indicators database (www.worldbank.org) and from Internet World Stats (www.internetworldstats.com).

The **Accountability and Public Voice, Civil Liberties, Rule of Law,** and **Anticorruption and Transparency** categories contain numerical ratings between 0 and 7 for each country, with 0 representing the weakest performance and 7 representing the strongest performance. For a full description of the methods used to determine the survey's ratings, please see the chapter on Survey Methodology.

Following the political and economic data, each country report is divided into five parts: an introduction, and analyses of **Accountability and Public Voice, Civil Liberties, Rule of Law,** and **Anticorruption and Transparency.** The introduction provides a brief historical background and a description of major events. The **Accountability and Public Voice, Civil Liberties, Rule of Law,** and **Anticorruption and Transparency** sections summarize each government's degree of respect for the rights and liberties covered in the *Countries at the Crossroads* survey. Each section contains a set of recommendations highlighting the specific areas of most immediate concern for the government to address.

# ALGERIA

CAPITAL: Algiers
POPULATION: 32.3 million
GNI PER CAPITA: $1,720

**SCORES**

ACCOUNTABILITY AND PUBLIC VOICE: 2.90
CIVIL LIBERTIES: 2.90
RULE OF LAW: 2.49
ANTICORRUPTION AND TRANSPARENCY: 2.55
(scores are based on a scale of 0 to 7, with
0 representing weakest and 7 representing
strongest performance)

*Bradford Dillman*

## INTRODUCTION

Civil violence in Algeria has diminished significantly since Abdelaziz
Bouteflika was elected president in April 1999. There are far fewer
reports of police and security forces committing arbitrary arrests, torture, "disappearances," and extrajudicial killings. Nevertheless, the government has failed to reinstate the rule of law since the military coup of
1992, and the military still intervenes in government decision making
and remains unaccountable to elected civilian leaders. Multiparty elections are not completely free, and there were credible accusations of pre-
election unfairness, irregularities, and fraud in the 2002 parliamentary
elections and the 2004 presidential election. Although the Algerian
media are among the most open in the Arab world, the government
since 2003 has attacked freedom of expression in newspapers through
a variety of legal and economic sanctions.

**Bradford L. Dillman** is assistant professor of international political economy at the University of Puget Sound. He is the author of numerous publications on Algeria, including *State and Private Sector in Algeria: The Politics of Rent-seeking and Failed
Development* (Boulder, CO: Westview Press, 2000).

Authorities do not adequately protect citizens from torture, police harassment, and long-term detention without trial. Small armed opposition groups and criminal gangs continue to attack citizens, although the government now has a better ability to prevent non-state actors from threatening people and property. Women face significant discrimination in divorce, marriage, employment, and inheritance despite government steps in 2004 to reform the retrograde 1984 family code. While the constitution recognizes the right to freedom of association, authorities frequently limit civic associations, political parties, and trade unions through bans on demonstrations, police harassment, and rejection of applications for legal recognition.

The executive branch interferes extensively in the operations of the judiciary. The civilian government cannot effectively subject police, military, and internal security forces to regular control and accountability. Although an ad hoc commission appointed by the president in 2003 to investigate thousands of disappearances in the 1990s has proposed compensating families of the disappeared, no perpetrators of these crimes have been brought to justice. Corruption is a growing, systemic problem within the public administration, state enterprises, and the private sector. The pace of economic reforms has slowed significantly since 2001.

Since his reelection in April 2004, President Bouteflika has reshuffled some of the higher ranks of the military in order to reduce their influence in political affairs. He has publicly emphasized the importance of restoring the authority of the state, reforming the judiciary, and strengthening human rights. In addition, he has emphasized a plan for national reconciliation that many believe will result in a general amnesty for any Algerian who committed crimes during the period of civil conflict since 1992. Many of these reforms are positive steps toward strengthening civilian control and rebuilding state institutions. However, it is too soon to predict whether they will be successfully implemented and whether they will expand civil liberties and government accountability to the public.

## ACCOUNTABILITY AND PUBLIC VOICE – 2.90

Algeria experienced a period of rapid democratization from 1988 to 1991. During that time, the opposition Islamic Salvation Front (FIS) won more than half of the seats in communal assemblies in 1990 elections and 188 of the 231 National Assembly seats determined in the first round of 1991 parliamentary elections. However, the military staged a coup in January 1992 to forestall a second round of voting that probably would have given the FIS a two-thirds majority in the Assembly. Since then, senior officers in the armed forces—often referred to as *le pouvoir*—have played an important role in Algerian politics, particularly on security and terrorism issues. Algeria has held local, parliamentary, and presidential elections with varying degrees of fraud and unfairness since 1995. The military and the presidency have circumscribed political competition by banning the FIS, refusing to officially authorize some parties, and limiting the role of legal political parties in government decision making.

During parliamentary elections in May 2002—which determined seats in the current National Assembly—turnout was officially only 47 percent, the lowest in Algeria's history. Turnout in Algiers was only 32 percent, and most voters in the Berber region boycotted the elections altogether. The National Liberation Front (FLN) emerged as the biggest winner, taking 199 seats in the now 389-seat National Assembly. Opposition parties denounced fraud, including a large discrepancy between the number of valid votes for independents and small parties initially announced by the interior minister and the number later confirmed by the Constitutional Council.[1]

Algeria's current electoral laws create a proportional representation system for the National Assembly in which voters choose candidate lists in multi-member districts. The number of seats in each district corresponds to the district's percentage of the population. Voting is based on universal suffrage, and the minimum voting age is 18. Campaign spending limits are rarely enforced.

The executive, legislative, and judicial branches of government do not practice effective oversight of one another. A constitutional amendment in 1996 strengthened the powers of the president over the prime minister. The National Assembly has limited powers to hold the executive, security forces, or the judiciary to account. The upper house of parliament, the National Council, has 144 seats, 96 of which are chosen through indirect elections by local assemblies within each of the country's 48 provinces (*wilayas*). Another 48 members are appointed by the president. In the most recent indirect elections, the National Democratic Rally won 82 percent of the 96 seats and the opposition FLN won

13 percent, demonstrating that opposition parties are effectively shut out of the upper house. Three-fourths of the members of the National Council must approve bills passed by the National Assembly before they can become laws. Elected municipal councils (APCs) and regional assemblies (APWs) have little power in comparison to *walis* (prefects) appointed by the national executive. The Algerian press reported in September 2004 that a technical commission tasked with proposing revisions of the constitution is recommending elimination of the post of prime minister, whose powers would be assumed by the president; elimination of the National Assembly's power to censure the government; and extension of the presidential mandate to seven years with a limitation of two terms.[2] If adopted, these revisions would significantly strengthen the role of the president.

In the run-up to the April 2004 presidential election, the government carried out a number of measures that reduced the overall fairness of the process and hampered campaigning by rivals of incumbent Abdelaziz Bouteflika. Using methods such as challenging signatures on candidacy petitions, freezing opposition party accounts, and minimizing opposition press coverage, the government was able to neutralize much of the opposition. Islamist former foreign minister Ahmed Taleb Ibrahimi and secularist former prime minister Sid Ahmed Ghozali were prevented from running, and former prime minister and FLN leader Ali Benflis was forced to run as an independent. Former prime minister Mouloud Hamrouche withdrew his candidacy in protest at fraudulent electoral practices.

Some aspects of the election were an improvement over previous elections. All six legally certified candidates were entitled to state-provided campaign funds and television access in March. The military announced its neutrality. The government amended the electoral law in January 2004 to prevent active-duty soldiers from voting in barracks on election day—a procedure that in the past had been a source of fraud. Candidates were allowed to post representatives in polling stations. Nearly 120 international monitors from the Arab League, the African Union, the European Parliament, and the OSCE observed voting on election day.

Incumbent Abdelaziz Bouteflika was reelected with 85 percent of the vote in universal, secret, direct suffrage. Ali Benflis and Abdallah Djaballah received only 6 and 5 percent of the votes, respectively, which many Algerians believed were suspiciously low figures. International observers and the National Political Commission for the Supervision of the Presidential Election—a government-appointed body—concluded that the election was transparent and there was no evidence of fraud that would have changed the outcome.[3] Despite the apparently clean election, four opposition candidates issued statements after results were announced condemning massive fraud and "falsification."[4] Police brutally dispersed several hundred Benflis supporters who gathered in Algiers on the evening of election day. Algerian press reported that many polling stations in Kabylia were wrecked or unable to operate, and abstention in that region was high.

The 1996 revised constitution forbids political parties from being formed on the basis of religion, ethnicity, gender, and regionalism. In order to gain legal status—and thus the right to participate in elections—political parties need approval from the minister of the interior, who determines whether a party's platform and membership, among other things, are consistent with requirements in the 1997 party law. Since 1997, the FLN, the military-backed National Democratic Rally (RND), and the moderate Islamist Movement of Society for Peace (MSP) have dominated the National Assembly in a loose alliance. The government refuses to formally authorize the Movement for Fidelity and Justice (Wafa), an Islamist-nationalist party headed by Ahmed Taleb Ibrahimi, and the secular Democratic Front. Thus, both these parties have difficulty opening bank accounts, renting space, and recruiting staff. Authorities have repeatedly stated that they have no intention of allowing the FIS—banned in 1992—to regain legal status. Ali Benhadj and Abassi Madani—two leaders of the FIS—were released from prison in June 2003 after 10 years of incarceration. Madani has since been living outside Algeria. Benhadj is barred from making public statements or participating in political activities; he has been subject to constant surveillance and frequent summoning by the police.

Although Algeria has a wide range of vocal civic associations and business organizations, various laws and government policies restrict the ability of these groups to organize and influence legislation. The interior ministry refuses formal authorization to a number of nongovernmental organizations (NGOs) that are critical of government policies. The government consults on an ad hoc basis with a national association representing public sector executives and with several organizations of private business owners (*le patronat*), but most of these actors complain that officials fail to implement policies that address their demands.

Although the constitution guarantees freedom of expression, journalists face significant restrictions. The 1990 information code states that freedom of speech must respect "individual dignity, the imperatives of foreign policy, and the national defense." Newspapers are not supposed to print security-related information unless it has been released by the government. The penal code—amended in 2001—mandates large fines and prison terms of up to two years for journalists found guilty of insulting or libeling the president, the National Assembly, the National Popular Army, or other state institutions.

Since early 2003, the government has carried on a campaign of harassment and intimidation against journalists and publishers deemed critical of the regime. A number of journalists have been brought to court, fined, or imprisoned for alleged violations of the information code and other laws. Many repeatedly face harassment from public authorities and questioning by the police.[5] In June 2004, Mohamed Benchicou—director of the anti-Bouteflika newspaper *Le Matin*—was sentenced to two years in prison for alleged violation of a law governing capital transfers and foreign exchange controls.[6] Benchicou had accused the minister of the interior of involvement in corruption and had authored a book in early 2004 that accused the president of embezzlement. *Le Matin* was closed in June 2004 and its headquarters was sold. Ahmed Bennaoum, director of *Er-Rai al-Aam*, was jailed on libel charges in June 2004. Hafnaoui Ghoul—a journalist and member of the Algerian League for the Defense of Human Rights—was jailed in May 2004 on defamation charges following his publication of several articles denouncing corruption and misappropriation of funds. Authorities later subjected him to numerous libel suits.

Some newspapers critical of the government have been suspended or threatened with shutdown for failure to pay taxes. In August 2003 six newspapers were temporarily closed for failure to make payments owed to five public printing companies. ANEP—a public company that monopolizes all advertising for public companies and the administration—often penalizes outspoken newspapers by withholding advertising placements in them. The government owns a number of important daily newspapers as well as the country's five main printing companies, and it retains a monopoly over radio and television broadcasting.

*Recommendations*

- The government should cease its campaign of prosecuting journalists for alleged defamation of officials and state institutions. The penal code should be amended to eliminate onerous penalties such as imprisonment and heavy fines on journalists and newspaper directors who are found to have slandered or insulted public officials.
- The government should grant legal registration to all political parties and civic organizations that meet basic regulatory requirements.
- A truly independent, politically balanced electoral commission needs to be established with broad powers to oversee election campaigns, balloting, and vote tabulation.

## CIVIL LIBERTIES – 2.90

Since 1992, an estimated 150,000 people have died as a result of widespread civil violence between armed Islamists and government forces in Algeria. Tens of thousands bear physical and psychological wounds. At least 1 million are thought to have been displaced from their homes since 1992.[7] At the height of the violence, from 1994 to 1999, antigovernment groups committed massacres, rapes, kidnappings, bombings, and thefts against the civilian population. Military and security forces and state-armed militias also engaged in gross human rights violations, including torture, extrajudicial killings, arbitrary arrest, and prolonged detention without trial.

Since 1999, reports of severe human rights abuses have markedly decreased, but violence by state and non-state actors remains significant. The government estimates that in 2003 nearly 900 people died as a result of civil conflict.[8] Armed opposition groups and criminal gangs continue to operate in parts of the country, and bombings, banditry, assassinations of police officers, and massacres of civilians still take place. State-armed militias—including the Groupe de Légitime Defense and the communal guards—continue to carry out counterinsurgency operations and law-enforcement activities, often without adequate supervision by authorities. The estimated 200,000 members of these self-defense groups—many of whom receive stipends from the ministry of defense—are accused of numerous abuses and extrajudicial killings.[9] The government has initiated steps to disband some groups and recuperate some of the tens of thousands of small arms distributed to them in the 1990s, but the process is haphazard and limited.[10]

Victims of terrorism accuse the government of failing to punish insurgents who have perpetrated severe human rights violations. President Bouteflika promulgated a Law of Civil Concord in July 1999 offering exemption from prosecution to members of armed groups who had not committed serious crimes and who surrendered to authorities within six months. Militants who had committed serious crimes were offered reduced sentences. In January 2000 Bouteflika signed an amnesty decree exempting militants from prosecution if they voluntarily surrendered to government authorities. Hundreds of members of the Islamic Salvation Army, the armed wing of the FIS, are believed to have benefited from the amnesty, which human rights groups have deplored.

In October 2003, Algeria-Watch—an independent human rights group based in Germany—published a report accusing high-ranking military, police, and security officials of condoning systematic torture and extrajudicial killing. It documented 300 specific cases of torture since 1992—most of which occurred between 1993 and 1997.[11] Algeria-Watch also published in April 2003 a detailed—but non-exhaustive—list of more than 1,100 cases of summary executions carried out by government forces since 1992.[12]

Preventive detention is still widely practiced. The code of penal procedure empowers authorities to detain a suspect for up 48 hours before arraignment by an examining magistrate. Suspected terrorists or subversives can be held in pre-arraignment detention up to 12 days before seeing a magistrate, and those accused of the most serious crimes can be legally held from 20 to 60 months in pretrial detention while a magistrate investigates their case. In 2004 approximately 4,000 people were held in long-term preventive detention, according to the minister of justice.[13] Algeria has taken steps to amend its laws and penal code to place them in conformity with international human rights conventions. It has not carried out capital punishment since 1994 and has indicated its intention to eliminate the death penalty and to define torture as a crime.

The ministry of defense's Department of Information and Security (DRS)—also known as Military Security—is accused of carrying out many acts of torture in its detention centers. DRS agents function as law-enforcement officers, often arresting citizens without warrants or identification, holding detainees in secret locations, and holding suspects longer than the legal limit. With no apparent accountability to the judiciary or civilian authorities, DRS agents have never been brought to justice for human rights violations perpetrated in the line of duty.[14] Fear of retribution discourages most victims of torture from reporting violations to authorities. While in theory victims of judicial errors are entitled to compensation, no victims have been indemnified.

Poor conditions prevail in Algeria's grossly overcrowded prisons. An administrative investigation into a series of prison uprisings and fires in 2002—in which more than 50 prisoners died—had still not been completed by September 2004. In December 2003 a commission was established to examine prison reform, and by June 2004 the ministry of justice had prepared a draft law that would increase the use of parole and release on bail, expand visitation rights, and allow increased access to prisoners by national and international NGOs.[15]

Although serious investigations into past human rights abuses are rare, the government has taken some steps recently to account for thousands of individuals who disappeared in the 1990s and who are presumed to have been killed by security forces. In 2001 President Bouteflika created a nominally independent National Consultative Commission for the Promotion and Protection of Human Rights (CNCPPDH). In September 2003 Bouteflika issued a presidential decree establishing an ad hoc commission within CNCPPDH to identify cases of alleged disappearances and to determine the whereabouts of those who have disappeared. The ad hoc committee has an 18-month mandate and will submit a final report to the president in March 2005.

Attorney Farouk Ksentini, who now heads the ad hoc commission, estimated in November 2002 that the security forces and their allies are responsible for the disappearance of 7,000 to 12,000 individuals.[16] Ksentini acknowledged in 2004 that the state collectively is responsible for some disappearances but argues that the state itself is not guilty: Offenses by local commanders were not authorized by those higher up in the chain of command.[17] Other government officials assert that many of those who have disappeared were killed by armed insurgents or are evading arrest. The commission has made little progress in identifying the circumstances of the disappearances or holding any officials accountable. It has no statutory power to compel testimony by government officials or force them to release documents.[18] The government has offered compensation to families of the disappeared but shows no willingness to pursue justice for the victims. The CNCPPDH has been hostile to three autonomous, non-authorized organizations representing families of the disappeared. Police have broken up demonstrations by organizations representing families of the disappeared who demand prosecution of those who killed their relatives.

The government has in the past sporadically allowed representatives of international NGOs such as Amnesty International, Human Rights Watch, and the International Federation for Human Rights (FIDH) to visit the country, but it currently denies access to these organizations. The Algerian League for the Defense of Human Rights (LADDH) and the Algerian League for Human Rights (LADH) actively report on a variety of human rights violations. Several other associations also address their concerns to authorities. Most domestic NGOs have faced harassment, and it is illegal for them to receive funding from abroad. Salah Eddine Sidhoum, an Algeria-Watch leader who had been condemned in absentia in 1997 for membership in a terrorist group, surrendered to authorities and was jailed at Serkhadji prison in September 2003. The criminal court of Algiers acquitted him of the charges in October 2003.

The state of emergency—in effect since the 1992 coup—requires political parties and organizations to seek formal authorization to assemble and to stage demonstrations. Authorities regularly refuse to permit demonstrations or meetings, often without offering justification. There are numerous reports of gendarmes, riot-control police, and security forces using excessive force to break up both legal and unauthorized demonstrations. Public demonstrations in the Algiers region have been banned since 2001. Protesters are regularly detained and then released or sentenced on public order charges. In May 2004, gendarmes put down rioting in the village of T'kout east of Algiers, and some who had demonstrated in support of local autonomy were assaulted or tortured while in custody.[19] Some members of self-styled citizens' groups were charged with membership in criminal associations and sentenced to prison in 2004. In the last several years, the government has introduced more stringent measures in recruitment of police officers and has bolstered training programs. According to authorities, the government now annually expels 300 to 400 police officers from the force for violations of the discipline code or other unspecified shortcomings.[20]

"Petitioning in the streets" has been most widespread in the Berber region of Kabylia. Berbers demonstrated and rioted in favor of greater political, cultural, and linguistic rights there in April and May 2001, and security forces killed as many as 100 unarmed civilians. In May 2001 President Bouteflika ordered the creation of an ad hoc National Commission of Inquiry into the Events in Kabylia. A preliminary report in July 2001 found the gendarmerie responsible for using excessive force. The commission's final report in December 2001 noted that many witnesses were afraid to testify.

The constitution was revised in April 2002 to recognize the main Berber language—Tamazight—as a national language. Berbers continue to demand recognition of Tamazight as an official language that can be used in public administration on a par with Arabic. The government has offered to put the issue to a national referendum. Talks with the government over the issue collapsed in early 2004, and many Berbers boycotted the presidential election. Many citizens' movements ('arush) are active in Kabylia but are not legally registered as associations. There is no significant discrimination against Berbers on the basis of their identity, even though many express collective economic and political grievances.[21] Berbers serve in influential positions in the military, media, and political elite.

The constitution guarantees the right of workers to form and join labor unions. However, workers must obtain government approval to establish a union, and unions may not affiliate with political parties or receive funding from foreign sources. Officials regularly consult the largest national labor union—the General Union of Algerian Workers (UGTA). The UGTA has been a prominent critic of privatization of state-owned enterprises and has had some success in slowing down the privatization process. Since 1990 civil servants and public sector workers have formed some 50 autonomous unions, but the ministry of labor has in most cases refused to authorize them formally.

Since 1992, a number of women have faced significant threats to their personal security. In April 2004 the national gendarmerie reported that violent acts against women—including rape, beating, and kidnapping—have increased in recent years.[22] In the first quarter of 2004 there were 354 reported abductions of women. According to the gendarmerie, an estimated 4,000 children born of rape have been abandoned by their mothers since 1997. Women's organizations deplore the fact that women raped by men in armed groups are not entitled to compensation from the government because they are not legally defined as victims of terrorism. In September 2004, a government minister announced that beginning in October the government would make monthly payments of approximately $35 to all single mothers with children.[23] In August 2004, the government drafted a bill to amend the Code of Algerian Nationality with the intent of allowing Algerian mothers married to non-Algerian fathers to pass their nationality on to their children.

The 1984 Family Code prevents women from enjoying equal rights with men. Some of its discriminatory stipulations include: that a woman has a legal obligation to obey her husband, an adult women is under the legal guardianship of her husband or a male relative, women have weaker rights than men to initiate divorce, and women inherit less than men. In August 2004, the government approved a long-overdue draft bill to amend the Family Code. Although still subject to approval by the National Assembly, the draft bill would, among other things, establish equal rights and obligations between spouses, make it easier for women to initiate divorce proceedings, and strengthen custody and financial rights of women following divorce.[24]

By international standards, a relatively low percentage of women work outside the home. According to the National Economic and Social Council (CNES), women constituted 55 percent of all university students but only 14 percent of the workforce—not counting the informal sector. Of the women in the workforce, 43 percent have jobs in the public sector, and of these, the vast majority are employed in the education and health sectors.[25] In 2004 the government indicated it would seek to amend the penal code to make sexual harassment in the workplace a crime. Few women have reached positions of influence within political institutions, although in 2002 women won 6 percent of the seats in the National Assembly.

Algeria passed legislation in 2002 to protect the rights of persons with disabilities. The government provides them social assistance, prosthetic centers, and vocational training. Companies that employ people with disabilities are eligible for a 50 percent reduction in social security payments. There is a National Council for Disabled Persons within the ministry of social protection. However, public buildings and government services are not easily accessible to the disabled.

Islamic movements played an important role in Algeria's war of liberation from French rule, and post-independence governments have catered to conservative Muslims by vigorously promoting Arabization in education and public administration and by passing a Family Code based on conservative Islamic principles, among other things. However, since the rise of the FIS and the resort to violence by Islamist groups calling for an Islamic republic, government officials have sought to restrict the use of religion for partisan purposes and to prevent all political activities within mosques. The constitution declares Islam the state religion. Although there are few de facto restrictions on the practice of religion by Algeria's small population of non-Muslims, proselytizing by non-Muslim groups is illegal. Religious organizations must register with the government. Most imams in mosques are appointed by the government and paid by the ministry of religious affairs. The government has a legal right to pre-screen public sermons. The government keeps close watch on sermons during Friday prayers and monitors mosques for potential security-related offenses. Imams can be imprisoned for three to five years for engaging in any activity that is contrary to the mission of the mosque or that undermines national cohesion. The penal code also allows for imprisonment of three to five years for anyone denigrating Islam or insulting the Prophet Mohammed.

*Recommendations*
- The state of emergency declared in 1992 should be officially repealed.
- The government should amend the 2001 penal code to reduce the length of time during which citizens can be held in pre-arraignment and long-term preventive detention and sanction police and judicial officials who flout detention procedures.
- An independent truth-and-reconciliation commission should be established with the power to investigate and publicly disclose human rights abuses committed since 1992.
- The government should provide a full accounting of disappearances and compensation to family members of the disappeared, while imposing criminal sanctions on those responsible for these killings.
- The government should take steps to ensure that women receive equal protection under the law. The Family Code should be amended to create equal divorce and inheritance rights, better protect women from domestic violence and marital rape, eliminate male guardianship over adult women, and suppress polygamy.

## RULE OF LAW – 2.49

Algeria has no Sharia courts. A Constitutional Council—three of whose nine members are appointed by the president—rules on the constitutionality of laws adopted by the National Assembly. A Council of State—created in 1998 under the auspices of the president—regulates administrative courts. A Supreme Court handles appeals cases. The president of the Supreme Court stated that in 2003 the Supreme Court was able to deal with only 17,100 of the 32,700 appeals cases brought before it, and in the first nine months of 2004 the court was overwhelmed with more than 70,000 appeals cases.[26]

Algeria's judiciary is not independent from the executive branch. The lack of impartiality and independence of judicial authorities is widely criticized—even by the government itself. The Supreme Judicial Council (CSM), headed by the president, is constitutionally responsible for assigning, promoting, and transferring judges. In practice, the ministry of justice plays a leading role in determining the career paths of judges. Thus, judges, prosecutors, and magistrates are averse to making judicial decisions contrary to government expectations for fear of imperiling their careers. Judges who criticize political manipulation of the judiciary have in some cases been sanctioned, suspended, or transferred. The CSM meets on a regular basis to impose sanctions on individual judicial officials who abuse their power.

The judiciary's serious deficiencies weaken the rule of law. Public perception of corruption and bribery in the judicial system is widespread. Examining judges liberally use—and abuse—their power to commit suspects to prison pending trial. Magistrates typically overlook judicial irregularities such as summary investigations or suspects' statements made under duress. Magistrates are overwhelmed by large caseloads. New judges receive adequate general training at the National Judicial Institute, but they frequently lack specialized training, particularly in the rising body of international agreements to which Algeria is a signatory.

President Bouteflika announced his intention to reform the system of justice after he was first elected in 1999. The National Assembly approved a bill in 1999 to redefine the statutes governing judges, but for three years the upper house refused to approve the bill. The Constitutional Council in 2002 rejected as unconstitutional a revised judicial reform bill, and the government in June 2004 introduced two draft bills to reorganize the judiciary that addressed the technical concerns of the court. Among other things, the bills reportedly would strengthen the independence of the CSM, allow judges the right to form unions, and require magistrates to submit financial disclosure statements every five years.[27] President Bouteflika has stressed his goal of expanding the number of well-trained magistrates.

The constitution states that anyone charged with a crime is presumed innocent until proven guilty. It also recognizes the right of the accused to a lawyer and guarantees the right to defense in penal matters. However, the right to a fair trial is frequently undermined by the use of confessions under duress to produce convictions. Detainees suspected of serious crimes are routinely denied access to a lawyer, often held incommunicado, and prevented from contacting family members—all in violation of the penal code. Many lawyers are loath to accept cases involving accused terrorists for fear of retribution. Large caseloads give strong incentives for magistrates to accept the state's version of events in order to avoid long trials.

Since his reelection in April 2004 President Bouteflika has sought to reassert the power of the civilian presidency over the military, but current and retired officers—often referred to as *le pouvoir*—remain important decision makers. Major-General Larbi Belkheir, a former interior minister and organizer of the 1992 coup, has been Bouteflika's cabinet director since 1999. Major General Smail Lamari has been head of the Direction of Counter-Espionage since 1990. Another important decision maker for more than a decade is Major-General Mohamed "Tewfik" Médiène—head of military security. General Muhammad Lamari—a coup ringleader and army chief of staff since 1993—resigned in July 2004, a move some observers believe may allow Bouteflika to assert some control over the largely autonomous military. In August 2004 Bouteflika—who retains the post of minister of defense—nominated new commanders for military regions. He also issued a presidential decree creating the position of general secretary within the ministry of defense.

The Algerian constitution guarantees the right to own private property. However, poorly defined land-ownership statutes make it difficult for many citizens to enforce their property rights and to gain access to property. The most valuable land in Algeria is considered property of the state, which has controlled it since abandonment by French colonists during the independence movement. A 1987 law grants collectivized groups of farmers long-term usufruct rights on state-owned land—and ownership of buildings and machinery—but it bars farmers from selling the land.

In the face of a proliferation of illegal transactions and illegal housing construction on this state-owned land, President Bouteflika in September 2004 indicated his government would press for a new law granting long-term land concessions to newly created farming enterprises. Concession shares could be bought by outside investors, but the state would still own the land and ensure it is only used for agricultural purposes.[28] While the government is reluctant to privatize agricultural land and industrial real estate fully, it issued an executive decree in August 2003 that allows the occupants of more than 600,000 state-owned apartments and 44,000 state-owned commercial properties to purchase their units from the state.

### Recommendations

- To ensure the protection of judicial officials from executive interference, the Supreme Judicial Council should be composed of a majority of magistrates who are elected by their peers, granted financial autonomy from executive control, and empowered to nominate and assign judges free from executive interference.
- A new statute should be enacted to permit judges and lawyers to form autonomous trade unions with the legal right to negotiate professional matters with officials in the executive branch.
- Steps must be taken to reassert civilian authority over the military, including by the appointment of a civilian minister of defense and sanctioning of officers who interfere in judicial proceedings.

## ANTICORRUPTION AND TRANSPARENCY – 2.55

Despite nearly 15 years of economic reform, Algeria has yet to make the transition to a stable market economy. The state maintains a leading role in the economy as an employer, investor, and regulator. Although the private sector has significantly increased its contribution to gross domestic product, particularly in the retail, construction, and transportation sectors, it still accounts for less than one-fourth of total industrial production (excluding the oil sector).[29] Bureaucratic regulations pose a major impediment to the efficiency of the market, and laws governing economic activities are piecemeal, poorly implemented, and largely inconsistent with the demands of a market economy.

The government does a poor job of disseminating economic information and has a weak statistical collection capability. Public access to information involving legal proceedings is limited. Citizens face serious impediments when seeking information about government operations, and petitions to gain access to information from agencies rarely succeed. Budget formation is largely monopolized by the executive branch with little formal input from civic groups. The annual budget law is subject to review by the National Assembly—which typically presses for amendments—but legislators have little ability to oversee executive spending once a budget is passed. An audit court is responsible for controlling a posteriori the finances of the state and the public services. Its reports—sent annually to the president—are not published.

The International Monetary Fund (IMF) reports that the pace of reforms in Algeria has slowed markedly since 2001.[30] Dramatically higher oil revenues in the past two years—permitting an accumulation of more than US$37 billion in foreign exchange reserves by September 2004—have dampened enthusiasm for structural economic reforms.[31] The government's current emphasis on expansionary fiscal policies will complicate efforts to increase transparency in the budget process and to enhance parliamentary oversight of government accounts.

Only a small portion of the largest public enterprises have been privatized in the past decade. Full or partial sales of state-owned enterprises ground to a halt in 2003. Poorly managed public banks continue to dominate the financial system, holding 90 percent of long-term loans and more than 80 percent of banking deposits. The treasury has repeatedly recapitalized these banks, which continue to provide huge lines of credit to unprofitable state enterprises. Auditing and accounting practices for public banks and state enterprises are generally poor and nontransparent.[32]

Data from the World Bank's Investment Climate Surveys reveal broad governance problems in the economy. One 2003 survey of more than 500 Algerian enterprises revealed that nearly 45 percent of respondents indicated that interpretation of regulations is unpredictable, and one-fourth lacked confidence that courts would uphold property rights.[33] More than one-third of the businesses indicated that tax administration was a major constraint. A separate World Bank database, the

Doing Business Project, indicates that Algerian businesses face significant barriers to starting up, hiring and firing workers, getting credit, and enforcing contracts.[34]

Corruption is pervasive in Algeria. International reports and newspaper accounts point to a systemic problem that stems from ineffective enforcement of laws, over-bureaucratization, and the breakdown of some government controls during civil conflict in the 1990s. Algeria's score in Transparency International's 2004 Corruption Perceptions Index, 2.7 out of 10, puts it among the five most corrupt countries in the Middle East and North Africa.[35] Algerian businesspeople acknowledge the necessity of bribing officials to obtain licenses and administrative approvals. They frequently accuse the judiciary of failing to protect their legal rights.

It is widely believed that military officers have abused their authority by controlling a wide range of economic activities. They are accused of forming alliances with civilians to control the importing and distribution of foodstuffs and medicine, to siphon off the output of public enterprises, and to steal public funds. The expression "political-administrative mafia" is often used to describe officials who utilize their public offices for private economic gain. Government officials and military officers are believed to use sanitary inspections, customs regulations, and their influence with magistrates to harass private companies that compete with their clientelistic economic networks.[36]

The Algerian media regularly report on alleged corruption. The private Association to Fight Corruption has been active in calling for investigations of corruption and the strengthening of laws against it. However, whistle-blowers in the public sector face harassment, and several journalists who reported on corruption in 2004 were put on trial for libel and defamation (see "Accountability and Public Voice"). Ex-government officials sometimes raise allegations of malfeasance, but they have little power to compel investigation of the charges. In the face of widespread accusations of favoritism in the granting of public contracts, the president in 2002 issued a decree requiring the government to publish provisional awards of contracts so that unsuccessful bidders may appeal government decisions.

The belief is widespread that those convicted of economic and administrative crimes are low-level operatives and that truly guilty high-ranking officials are immune from prosecution. In the past 15 years, the government has formed a number of commissions of inquiry to investigate a variety of administrative and financial scandals, but reports of these commissions are almost never released to the public, and few people are found guilty. For example, no indictments have resulted from an inquiry launched in 2003 into official responsibility for damage and loss of life during an earthquake that year, even though a commission appointed by the housing ministry found that the state had failed to enforce building codes.[37]

Since 2003 the government has shown some dynamism in investigating one of the worst financial scandals in Algerian history. Investigators in that year found that the privately owned Khalifa Group had committed serious financial irregularities and fraudulent practices that may have resulted in the transfer of several billion dollars out of the country. There are accusations that government officials illegally bestowed favors on the group in exchange for bribes and kickbacks. A number of officers and employees of Khalifa Bank and the Khalifa Group have been charged, and the government continues to pursue indictments and convictions in the affair.[38] In September 2004, Algerian newspapers reported that an Algerian court had charged Abdelouhab Keramane, a former governor of the Central Bank, with involvement in the Khalifa affair.[39] He is the first high-ranking government official to be charged. In another response to the scandal, Prime Minister Ouyahia in August 2004 issued instructions stipulating that public funds could be held only in public banks.[40]

*Recommendations*
- The government should accelerate privatization of public banks and state enterprises with full public disclosure of sales and with provision of a social safety net for displaced workers.
- Increased enforcement of anticorruption provisions in existing laws should proceed in tandem with enhancement of judicial independence, protection of freedom of expression for civic organizations, and creation of an independent anticorruption office capable of monitoring the performance of the executive branch.
- The government should consult more systematically with private sector associations during drafting of economic laws and administrative decrees. Commercial laws and real estate laws should be streamlined to enhance property rights and reduce bureaucratic impediments to private investment.

- The government should take steps to enhance its data-collection capacity and significantly expand public access to economic and administrative data.

## NOTES

[1] "Diminishing Returns: Algeria's 2002 Legislative Elections" (Brussels: International Crisis Group, 24 June 2002).

[2] Youcef Brahimi, "Fin des travaux de la commission technique de revision de la Constitution," *Le Jeune Indépendant,* 19 September 2004.

[3] Olivier Pierre-Louveaux, "The Presidential Elections of the 8th April 2004 in Algeria," in *Security in the Mediterranean and Beyond: A Collection of Essays,* ed. Bruce George, 2004, http://www.rthonbrucegeorgemp.co.uk.

[4] Ibid.

[5] "Algeria – Annual Report 2004" (Paris: Reporters without Borders, 2004), http://www.rsf.org/article.php3?id_article=9921.

[6] "Mohamed Benchicou, Le Matin; Legal Action, Imprisoned" (New York: Committee to Protect Journalists [CPJ], 14 June 2004), http://www.cpj.org/cases04/mideast_cases04/algeria.html.

[7] "Profile of Internal Displacement: Algeria" (Geneva: Norwegian Refugee Council/Global IDP Project, 2004).

[8] "Algeria" (New York: Amnesty International [AI], 2004), http://web.amnesty.org/web/web.nsf/print/2004-dza-summary-eng.

[9] Jeanne Kervyn and François Gèze, "L'organisation des forces de répression" (Paris: Comité Justice pour l'Algérie, September 2004), http: www.algerie-tpp.org/tpp/pdf/dossier_16_forces_repression.pdf.

[10] Souhila Hamadi, "L'Etat veut disarmer les Patriotes en Algérie," *Liberté,* 17 May 2004.

[11] "Algérie: La machine de mort" (Paris and Berlin: Algeria-Watch [AW], October 2003), http://www.algeria-watch.org/fr/mrv/mrvtort/machine_mort/machine_mort.htm.

[12] "1100 Exécutions Sommaires" (AW, April 2003), http://www.algeria-watch.org/mrv/2002/1100_executions/1100_executions_A.htm.

[13] "L'appareil judiciaire mis en cause," *L'Expression,* 9 December 2004.

[14] "Algeria: Steps Toward Change or Empty Promises?" (AI, 16 September 2003), http://web.amnesty.org/library/Index/ENGMDE280052003?open&of=ENG-DZA.

[15] Samia Lokmane and Souhila Hammadi, "La liberté conditionnelle favorisée," *Liberté,* 6 September 2004.

[16] "Time for Reckoning: Enforced Disappearances in Algeria" (New York: Human Rights Watch [HRW], February 2003).

[17] Mohamed Abdoun, "À coeur ouvert avec L'Expression: Farouk Ksentini," *L'Expression,* 6 September 2004.

[18] "Truth and Justice on Hold: The New State Commission on 'Disappearances'" (HRW, December 2003), http://www.hrw.org/reports/2003/algeria1203/algeria1203.pdf.

[19] "T"Kout, Tizi-Ouzou, Serkadji, Châteauneuf . . . La torture au coeur du système de pouvoir en Algérie" (AW, 5 June 2004), http://www.algeria-watch.de/fr/aw/aw_tkout.htm.

[20] "Le directeur général de la police dresse le bilan de la situation sécuritaire," *La Tribune*, 18 December 2004.

[21] "Algeria: Unrest and Impasse in Kabylia" (Brussels: International Crisis Group, 10 June 2003).

[22] Samar Smati, "À l'épreuve des violences contre la femme," *Le Quotidien d'Oran*, 20 September 2004.

[23] "Algerian single mothers get aid," BBC News, 28 September 2004, http://news.bbc.co.uk/go/pr/fr/-/1/hi/world/africa/3697836.stm.

[24] "Communiqué du Conseil de Gouvernement," 18 August 2004, http://www.cg.gov.dz/dossiers/communiques/Conseil%20GVT/com-cg-18-08-2004.htm.

[25] Younes Hamidouche, "La femme algérienne et le marché du travail," *La Tribune*, 7 December 2004.

[26] "Bouteflika favorable à la révision du code de la famille," *El Watan*, 11 October 2004.

[27] "Le statut des magistrats et le Conseil supérieur de la magistrature débattus hier à l'APN," *La Tribune d'Algérie*, 28 June 2004.

[28] Boudedja Nora, "Avant projet de loi sur le foncier relevant du domaine privé de l'état," *El Watan*, 12 October 2004.

[29] "Algeria: Financial System Stability Assessment, Including Reports on the Observance of Standards and Codes on the Following Topics: Monetary and Financial Policy, Transparency and Banking Supervision" (Washington, D.C.: International Monetary Fund [IMF], May 2004), 9.

[30] "Algeria: 2003 Article IV Consultation—Staff Report; Staff Statement; Public Information Notice on the Executive Board Discussion; and Statement by the Executive Director for Algeria" (IMF, February 2004), 26.

[31] "Benachenhou: "40 milliards de dollars à fin 2004," *Liberté*, 30 October 2004.

[32] "Algeria: Financial System Stability Assessment" (IMF, May 2004), 10.

[33] *World Development Report 2005: A Better Investment Climate for Everyone* (Washington, D.C.: World Bank, 2004), 246–47.

[34] Ibid., 248–49.

[35] "Corruption Perceptions Index" (Berlin: Transparency International [TI], 2004).

[36] Omar Benderra and Ghazi Hidouci, "Algérie: économie, predation et Etat policier" (Comité Justice pour l'Algérie, May 2004), http://www.algerie-tpp.org/tpp/pdf/dossier_14_economie.pdf.

[37] "Conclusions de l'enquête sur le séisme du 21 mai 2003," *Liberté*, 23 March 2004.

[38] Salima Tlemçani, "L'affaire Khalifa en déballage," *El Watan*, 5 September 2004.

[39] "Affaire Khalifa Bank," *Le Quotidien d'Oran*, 7 September 2004.

[40] "Ahmed Ouyahia justifie l'instruction sur les banques publiques," *Le Quotidien d'Oran*, 5 September 2004.

# ANGOLA

CAPITAL: Luanda
POPULATION: 13.3 million
GNI PER CAPITA: $710

**SCORES**
ACCOUNTABILITY AND PUBLIC VOICE: 1.79
CIVIL LIBERTIES: 2.81
RULE OF LAW: 2.22
ANTICORRUPTION AND TRANSPARENCY: 2.10
(scores are based on a scale of 0 to 7, with
0 representing weakest and 7 representing
strongest performance)

*Imogen Parsons*

## INTRODUCTION

Angola's 27-year-long civil war ended in April 2002, after Jonas Savimbi—leader of the armed rebel movement National Union for the Total Independence of Angola (UNITA) since its creation in 1966—was killed in a government ambush. A peace agreement was signed in 1991 and multiparty elections held in 1992; UNITA lost, claimed fraud, and returned the country to war. A further agreement signed in 1994 (the Lusaka Protocol) was similarly unsuccessful in halting the war. While the war was not primarily fought for profit but for power, Angola's exceptionally vast natural resources (primarily oil and diamonds) funded the military efforts of both sides and has kept Angola on the global political radar.

Peace has brought a gradual easing in the general political climate. Over the period 2003–2004, these trends have continued in most areas. Antigovernment protests and demonstrations are increasingly widespread,

**Imogen Parsons** is a PhD candidate at the London School of Economics and Political Science. She has conducted extensive fieldwork in Angola and has previously published works on the subjects of peace-building, demobilization and reintegration, and post-conflict reconstruction in Angola.

and the media are wide-ranging in their criticisms. The number of cases of detention and abuses of journalists and opposition figures has decreased, although incidents continue to be reported. Economic and financial transparency has broadly increased and Angola has signed on to international initiatives including the Kimberley Process and the African Union Peer Review Mechanism.

At the same time, the ruling Popular Movement for the Liberation of Angola (MPLA) has tightened its grip on power and is unlikely to concede much to opposition parties in the next elections. State institutions remain heavily politicized; the judiciary is not completely exempt from MPLA pressure and influence. At the local level the party and state are in many places virtually indistinguishable, even though Angola made the transition from a one-party state under Marxist-Leninist rule to a free-market, multiparty democracy in 1991. The MPLA often takes credit for state functions such as healthcare provision and distribution of humanitarian aid; the latter has in some areas been made conditional on recipients joining or already being members of the MPLA. Political violence allegedly stirred by MPLA militants against UNITA ex-combatants and families has become increasingly common. State media retain a pro-MPLA line, and independent media are still effectively prevented from expanding beyond Luanda.

Government accountability to the Angolan population remains weak. Citizens have few opportunities for legal redress against perceived injustice or abuse, and localized corruption is still endemic. The legitimacy of the government itself remains questionable because elections have not taken place since Angola's first democratic vote, in 1992. The ending of the war, which should lead to a decrease in currently high levels of military expenditure, has not yet been followed by increased dedication of resources to broad socio-economic development. Angola ranked 166th out of 175 countries in the UNDP's 2004 Human Development Index, falling two places since 2003. NGOs and international organizations continue to provide health services, food, and agricultural support to large segments of the population, with around 1 million people (of a total of around 13 million) still deemed vulnerable by the World Food Programme.[1]

Finally, the ongoing separatist conflict in the province of Cabinda has still not been resolved, with persistent allegations against the Angolan Armed Forces of human rights abuses including torture, disappearances, and killings. The government has attempted to replicate its military win over UNITA with disastrous results for the local population. Cabindan rebel movements are divided and weakened, militarily incapable of mounting a serious challenge to the government. Although rebels and civil society organizations now appear more willing to begin a negotiation process, the government has not yet accepted the offer. A situation of "no war, no peace" prevails.

## ACCOUNTABILITY AND PUBLIC VOICE – 1.79

Government accountability remains weak in Angola, with public voice increasingly tolerated but little heeded. Although the constitution provides for the separation of powers, stating that "the President of the Republic, the National Assembly, the Government and the Courts shall be sovereign bodies" (Article 53), this division has not been effectively realized. Power remains concentrated in the hands of the president, who appoints the prime minister and government, provincial governors, the governor of the national bank, members of the High Council of the Judicial Bench, and the majority of the Council of Ministers. The National Assembly, whose representatives are elected by proportional representation, is, in practice, largely subordinate to the executive. The executive (the Council of Ministers) also enjoys some legislative power. Governmental accountability is limited. Citizens are able to present complaints through a commission at the National Assembly, but prosecutions are rare.

The powers of the presidency have increased in recent years, through legislation including the Law on State Secrecy and the Law on National Security, passed in 2002. Intelligence services and the presidential guard report directly to the office of the president. Parallel structures of power are frequently more important than formal institutions of government. The MPLA, of which President José Eduardo dos Santos is head, exercises tight control over many state institutions. The civil service is highly politicized.

Presidential and legislative elections were last held in 1992, and thus the legitimacy of the government remains questionable. The United Nations declared the last elections "generally free and fair," but UNITA contested the MPLA's victory, returning the country to civil war. As a result, second-round presidential elections, required since dos Santos failed to gain an outright majority, were never held. President dos Santos himself has been in power since 1979, and the MPLA has ruled since independence was declared from Portugal in 1975. President dos Santos had said in 2001 that he would step aside for the next elections; however, in 2003 he indicated that he would respect the wishes of his party, effectively retracting the promise.

The Government of National Unity was formed in 1997, following the signing of the Lusaka Protocol; it was composed of MPLA and opposition representatives in proportions reflecting the 1992 election results. However, where a UNITA representative holds a ministerial position, the MPLA vice minister is more powerful. By the end of 1998, Angola had returned to war, which lasted until 2002. Following intense pressure on the MPLA to set a date, an electoral timetable was approved in September 2004, anticipating elections in 2006. New electoral laws are planned that will regulate party registration and financing, campaigning opportunities, and access to broadcast time, along with constitutional revision and compilation of a new voter register.

The opportunities for rotation of power are limited, as most political parties are weak and fragmented. More than 130 parties formed post-1992, but few are genuinely active politically and only 11 opposition parties are represented in the National Assembly. Provision for state financing of registered parties exists. Opposition parties have tried to organize into coalitions such as the Angolan Civil Opposition Parties (POC), which in October 2003 organized the first authorized anti-government demonstration in Luanda since the end of the war, calling for elections.

UNITA has reorganized itself as a political party, but its leadership appears disorganized and fractured, and it does not currently represent a significant challenge to the MPLA's power. Thousands of former UNITA supporters and ex-combatants are reported to have joined the MPLA as party members (some say in order to access humanitarian aid and other benefits).

Universal suffrage is provided for in the constitution, but many Angolans do not currently have identification papers, and a new voters' register is needed. Efforts to rectify this are, albeit gradually, under way. As in 1992, the prospect of elections has already begun to give rise to localized conflicts and tensions, with complaints from UNITA that its party members and officials have been harassed and intimidated by members of the MPLA, JMPLA (the youth organization of the MPLA), and the Civil Defense Force (local militia groups armed by the government during the war).[2] A joint party commission was formed to investigate the allegations, although with few results so far.

Civic monitoring of government has increased in recent years, with more government willingness to consult on legislation, although its impact remains limited. For example, the recently approved Land Law was much debated, with civil society and NGOs actively lobbying the National Assembly and government, but the law was subsequently passed with only minor changes. The draft new constitution was published in print and on the Internet in 2004.

Criticism of government by media, civil society groups, and churches is increasingly common in Luanda, although far less tolerated in other provinces. Onerous registration requirements allow the government to retain some control over civil society groups and NGOs. Regulation of international NGOs in particular has tightened since 2002, with government officials criticizing donor interference in domestic affairs. Registration has been denied or continually deferred for some groups.

Overall, journalists report an increase in media freedom since the war ended. Restrictions still exist, however, particularly outside Luanda. The government takes a paternalistic attitude toward the independent media. In May 2004 the president criticized *pasquins* (a derogatory term for unreliable newspapers) for their abuse of press freedom.[3] Also in May, independent journalists complained at being excluded from a government press conference held in Benguela. State media, which are rarely, if ever, critical of the government, remain dominant outside Luanda. Private radio is limited to three largely uncritical provincial stations; the (often critical of government) Catholic-backed station Radio Ecclesia has been prevented from broadcasting nationally despite a statement by dos Santos in May that there was no legal impediment.[4] Private newspapers are rare; in any case, few have access to newspapers due to their high cost. Dos Santos stated in December 2003 at the MPLA congress that the state monopoly on television broadcasting would end, but few have access to television in any case. Financial support promised to private media in 2002 has been retracted.[5] A new press law has been promised for a number of years but is still pending.

Although the constitution (Article 35) provides for freedom of the press, the Press Law restricts that freedom. Specific libel and defamation laws effectively protect government officials and the president from statements deemed offensive and contrary to the dignity of public office, even if true.[6] These are rarely invoked, but a story published by the independent newspaper *Angolense* in January 2003 on the multimillion-dollar fortunes of the Angolan elite has resulted in cases brought by five prominent officials against journalist Graça Campos. Editors of *Angolense* have reported anonymous threats and intimidation.

For fear of reprisals, many journalists continue to exercise self-censorship. Arbitrary detentions of journalists continued in 2002–2003,[7] although they were less common than before, and no cases were reported in 2003–2004. However, Luanda authorities in September 2004 seized independent newspapers.[8] The amended Press Law provides for seizure of periodicals by police in cases where "timely intervention" by a competent magistrate is impossible.[9]

Broader freedom of expression is also limited. In December 2003, a Luanda car-washer was killed by members of the presidential guard for singing lyrics from a popular antigovernment rap song. The perpetrators were arrested and are still in jail.

*Recommendations*
- Greater separation of the executive and legislative branches of government should be effected, with the latter given increased power. Efforts should be made to strengthen the neutrality and competence of the civil service and state institutions at both central and local levels. Increased investment in intermediate and higher education within Angola will be needed to train such personnel.
- The government should strengthen efforts to incorporate concerns and recommendations expressed by civil society about impending legislation into the revision process. Consultative mechanisms should be created to ensure participation of community-based organizations and traditional authorities in the provinces.
- Locally elected government, anticipated in the draft new constitution, would greatly revitalize and legitimize the state at the local level by granting it greater financial and political autonomy. This reform should incorporate traditional authorities and representatives of civil society.

- Laws relating to freedom of the press should be revised to eliminate excessively punitive statutes on defamation and libel. Domestic independent media should not be prohibited from expanding nationally. Ensuring media freedom will be especially important in the run-up to elections and may require formation of an independent commission or board to regulate and ensure, inter alia, access to state media (especially radio) by opposition parties for campaigning purposes.
- An independent electoral commission should be established as soon as possible to participate in the revision of electoral laws; it should have the power to oversee a comprehensive and universally accessible voter registration process and to investigate complaints relating to that or any other aspects of the electoral process.

## CIVIL LIBERTIES – 2.81

Virtually all basic civil rights and protections are guaranteed by the Angolan constitution. While Angola is not a party to some important international treaties,[10] specific provisions in the constitution and Angolan law provide for many of the rights covered by them.

The government has no independent human rights monitoring body with overall competence, although one is provided for by the draft new constitution. Currently the ministry of justice has a human rights unit, and the National Assembly has a human rights commission. In 2004 provincial human rights commissions were reactivated and a National Human Rights Action Plan was drafted.

A precondition for access to basic civic rights—such as state education—is the possession of a valid *cedula* (birth/civil registration). Many lack this document due to constraints including physical access to registration and inability to pay, although the government has made important progress with the implementation of a national free birth registration campaign for children.[11]

The government is beginning to tackle the problem of trafficking in children. It established a juvenile court in 2003, and the first trafficking investigation opened in March 2004.[12] No specific laws against trafficking exist, although laws prohibiting forced labor and kidnapping, for instance, may be used to prosecute cases.

Specific ethnic groups do not appear to be discriminated against by the state. The major ethnic groups in Angola, estimated to make up some 75 to 80 percent of the population, are (in order of size) the Ovimbundu, Mbundu, and Bakongo. They are represented in government, some linked historically with specific political parties (for example, MPLA has been associated with Mbundu support, UNITA with Ovimbundu). Parties are not strictly ethnically defined or representative, however, and smaller and nonrepresented ethnic groups do not appear to be significantly excluded as a result.

The UNHCRC has drawn attention to potential discrimination against smaller ethnic minorities in Angola, the San and Kung in particular, but the size of these groups is negligible and little is known about them.[13] More worrying is apparent persecution of Bakongo "regressados" (returned refugees), who were targets of violence in 1992, during police operations against illicit diamond miners in predominantly Bakongo areas in 2004,[14] and of Ovimbundu associated (sometimes incorrectly) with UNITA.

Angola is one of the most heavily mined countries in the world as a result of the war; recent estimates of unexploded munitions vary from around 500,000 to 2 million. The government estimates there are at least 80,000 disabled landmine victims in Angola, along with large numbers of amputees and war-disabled. These groups face considerable hardship due to lack of adequate social services and a weak and unaccommodating job market. Other disabled people face similar challenges. The needs and interests of people with disabilities are not obviously represented by the government. The Ministry for Social Assistance and Reintegration and the Ministry of Health both have relevant responsibilities, but they do not have great power in relation to other ministries. Most support is provided by international NGOs.

The rights of women are well protected constitutionally. However, although the constitution takes precedence over customary law in Angolan courts, women's lack of access to formal justice systems undermines this. Societal attitudes frequently lag behind the provisions of the constitution. Despite broadly equitable labor laws women are still predominantly confined to the informal sector and face discriminatory attitudes in the workplace.[15] No specific laws exist against domestic violence, and sentencing of men convicted of violence against women is frequently lenient.[16] The problem appears to have intensified in the postwar period. Participation of women in the state is higher than in many other African countries, although they still form a minority at around 10 percent in the central government and 3 percent in local government. A Ministry of Family and the Promotion of Women was created in 1997, and the MPLA women's group has been active in promoting women's rights.

Freedom of association, assembly, demonstration, and expression are guaranteed under the constitution, but impediments still exist. The state may prevent creation of groups for security reasons or if they exhibit "racist, fascist or tribalist ideologies" and has effectively prevented registration of some organizations (see "Accountability and Public Voice"). The MPLA has been accused of trying to coerce and co-opt media figures, state employees, and former UNITA combatants into joining the party, often using financial and material inducements.[17] Trade unions exist and are active, although non-MPLA ones are weak.

Religious belief, practice, and association are generally unimpeded by the state, although religious organizations must be registered and colonial-era statutes forbidding non-Christian groups still technically exist. Religious groups and churches in Cabinda have reported some interference from the government, such as being prohibited from holding religious meetings in homes; such meetings are illegal and moreover often include antigovernment protest.

Direct harassment of activists, political opponents, and media figures is far less commonly reported than in the past, but fears and accusations among the opposition persist. The charismatic leader of opposition party PDP-ANA, Mfulumpinga Lando Victor, was fatally shot in Luanda in July 2004. It is unclear who was behind the shooting. Even less freedom exists outside Luanda. For example, in July 2004 up to 80 houses of returning refugees and others alleged to have links to UNITA were torched in Mexico Province.[18]

Protests and demonstrations are permitted under Angolan law, subject to notification and authorization. Although increasingly tolerated by the government, opposition and civil society groups have complained at being denied authorization for or being physically prevented from holding demonstrations. Police involvement at organized protests has generally been nonviolent, although in some cases intimidation and repressive measures have been reported. In February 2004 civilians were killed when people at a demonstration in Cafunfo attempted to enter a police station and police allegedly opened fire indiscriminately.[19]

The constitution (Article 23) prohibits torture and other cruel, inhuman, or degrading treatment or punishment, and arbitrary detention and arrest are prohibited under Angolan law. Yet a 30-page report released in November 2003 catalogued cases of disappearances, extrajudicial killings, arbitrary detention, rape, and torture committed by the Angolan Armed Forces after 40,000 troops were sent to Cabinda in 2002 to combat insurgents following the end of the war with UNITA.[20] Reports continued to emerge into 2004 but no formal investigation has been launched and no visible moves made to punish those responsible.

Under the constitution, as well as a number of the international treaties to which Angola is party, the right of habeas corpus is protected, unlawful arrest and detention prohibited, and maximum detention periods clearly stipulated. Lack of resources and of trained judges again means these provisions are regularly denied, however, with lengthy detentions and pretrial waits common. The situation improved in 2004 as the government made efforts to monitor and regularize pre-trial detention periods through implementation of a computerized database; some politically motivated cases may persist, however. Prison conditions are poor, with pervasive overcrowding and prisoners dependent on food brought by friends and relatives.

Human rights workshops with the national police were held in early 2004. Citizens can denounce police abuse of power at these sessions, and in Huambo there is a free telephone line. However, many Angolans will require proof that such complaints are heeded and properly investigated before they will make use of such provisions.

*Recommendations*

• Mechanisms permitting citizens to report cases of abuse, repression, and excessive use of force by state security services and armed forces should be expanded into all areas of Angola, including free and anonymous phone lines for reporting purposes. The government should ensure that any abuses reported are promptly and impartially investigated and punished and that those making such complaints are protected from reprisal.

- A full and impartial investigation should be launched into abuses of human rights by state security services and armed forces documented by NGOs and civil society organizations, particularly (but not limited to) those related to the conflict in Cabinda.
- Efforts to ensure civic registration of all Angolan citizens should be increased, with free registration extended to adults. This should be accompanied by civic education, including information on the rights and responsibilities of citizens. It should be carried out by neutral parties, such as civil society organizations and churches.
- The government should not inhibit nongovernmental defenders of human rights and activists promoting awareness of civic rights from carrying out their work.
- Legislation on registration of civic, political, and religious organizations should be equally and transparently applied to all groups, with applications processed promptly. Authorization of protests and demonstrations should also be handled evenly, with permission granted or denied on a politically neutral basis.

## RULE OF LAW – 2.22

Lack of accessibility is the most serious impediment in Angola's justice system, which is out of reach to an estimated 80 percent of Angolans.[21] The president has the power to appoint and dismiss judges of the Supreme Court, the general prosecutor and his/her deputies, and three members of the magistrates supreme council. Judges are subject to monitoring and disciplining by the high council of the judicial bench, and the attorney general also has the power to rule on the legality of judges' acts.

The 2003 International Bar Association (IBA) delegation to Angola failed to find any specific case in which the court's independence had been compromised. Courts have ruled against the Angolan government in cases involving media freedom and political freedom of expression. In 2004, the Supreme Court brought charges against a former provincial governor for acts committed during his time in office. The question of the political affiliation of judges is less certain. The IBA delegation's report cites contradictory sources: One states that judges are not allowed to belong to political parties, while another claims, more plausibly, that in practice most appointees must also be MPLA party members.[22]

As of September 2004, the judicial proctorate (ombudsman) post remained empty, with functions assumed by the attorney general. This office is designed to defend citizens' rights, "ensuring by informal means the justice and legality of the public administration."[23] It will be able only to recommend corrective action and not to enforce it, although the draft new constitution states that public bodies have a duty to comply with its recommendations. The Constitutional Court has not been created.

Although all Angolan citizens are constitutionally guaranteed the right to legal aid and counsel, lack of resources in the judicial system limits implementation. Of the approximately 600 lawyers in the entire country, 90 percent are in Luanda.[24] As of June 2004, nine municipal courts were in operation.[25] Court employees are underpaid, in some cases accepting bribes in order to expedite a case, and state-provided defenders are often inexperienced, with little knowledge of the law.[26] Efforts to train judges and lawyers and to promote rights of prisoners and detainees are ongoing, led especially by the Angolan Bar Association (ABA).

The Angolan military, which is among the largest forces in southern Africa (some 140,000 troops), as well as the police, are subject to civilian control. Security forces and armed forces are subordinate (and loyal) to the government and presidency and are not substantially influenced by non-state actors, nor do they interfere in the national political system themselves. However, some reports have linked them, particularly the Civil Defense Force, to the local-level political harassment of opposition party members.

Army generals are frequently reputed to have private business interests, in the diamond industry in particular. One of the major activities of the army since 2002 has been the expulsion of illegal diamond miners from Angola (see "Civil Liberties"), which may have caused some conflict of interest. In December 2003 Radio Ecclesia broadcast an interview with a government official claiming that soldiers had been intervening in diamond areas to protect *garimpeiros* (informal diamond miners) working for their superiors.[27]

The protection of property rights is a major problem in Angola, and it is as yet unclear whether the new land law passed in August 2004 will improve the situation or worsen it. Provision is made in the new law for regularization of informal land tenure. However, the period for submission of requests for registration was limited to one year, which civil society groups have claimed is impractical, if not impossible, for most. In addition, even if tenure is established, all land still legally belongs to the Angolan state; individuals have the right to surface usage only. The bill allows for expropriation of land for "public utility" purposes or in cases where land is not usefully exploited by tenants. The system for the awarding of development contracts remains opaque and open to corruption. As in the early 1990s, individuals with strong connections to the regime may again benefit.

The government has made attempts to close down informal settlements and markets in Luanda, for which it has been widely criticized. Accusations have emerged of private business interests influencing government actions and decisions and of police brutality during evictions. Viana market was closed in March 2004, and forced removals led to violence between police and traders (see "Civil Liberties"). Populations were forcibly removed from Boavista in 2001 and Bem Fica in 2003 without provision of adequate alternative housing.[28] The shopping center due to replace Kinaxixi market is to be built by a company run by one of dos Santos's closest allies.[29] Such cases show no signs of diminishing, especially with the postwar increase in construction and development projects.

*Recommendations*

- The constitutional court should be created, with greater efforts made to revise Angolan statutes in order to ensure they are compatible with the constitution and with international law and conventions to which Angola is a party. Of particular concern are those related to government ability to curtail civil liberties, freedom of expression, and association, and the protection of the rights of women and children.
- The judicial proctorate post should be filled. The incumbent should be given adequate resources and complete political autonomy in undertaking investigations and should have power to oblige public bodies to comply with its recommendations.
- Access to the judicial system should be extended by further increasing the number of lawyers and judges, reactivating courts in all municipalities, and reinforcing the legal aid system. The government should support efforts by the ABA in this direction—for instance, placing lawyers in police stations—without compromising the ABA's independence. Court procedures should be simplified

and/or support be provided to complainants/defendants so that low levels of literacy do not exclude people from justice systems.

- Cases of bribe-taking by court officials must be investigated and punished and any forms of political interference in judicial processes ended. Particular efforts must be made in this area in the provincial and municipal courts.
- The land registration and regularization period should be extended. All land appropriation, coerced expulsions, and relocations of populations must be suspended during this time, and support should be given to communities and individuals throughout the process.

## ANTICORRUPTION AND TRANSPARENCY – 2.10

Corruption and lack of transparency are the major problems besetting the Angolan state. Angola scores 2.0 out of 10 in Transparency International's 2004 Corruption Perceptions Index, indicating "rampant corruption." This represents a slight improvement on previous years however: In 2003 it scored 1.8, and in 2002 it received 1.7.[30]

The change reflects a gradual move toward transparency in the oil sector in particular. Previously the government had insisted on tight secrecy clauses in contracts signed with international oil companies. In 2004, by contrast, the Angolan government disclosed that it was receiving a $300 million signature bonus from ChevronTexaco.

An IMF report leaked in 2002 suggested $1 billion per year went missing from Angolan state coffers.[31] The government has claimed the discrepancy reflects miscalculations due to changing kwanza/dollar exchange rates and high rates of inflation. In response to criticism, in July 2003 the government released the KPMG Oil Diagnostic Executive Summary and in May 2004 the full report. While falling short of a full audit, the Oil Diagnostic did reveal a number of discrepancies in the government records of oil revenues.[32]

On July 21, 2004, the IMF issued a statement pointing to "significant progress . . . made towards macroeconomic stability over the last year." This followed a similarly complimentary statement issued on April 27 that stressed the progress made by the Angolan government and specifically its "readiness to share with staff some critical financial information on the current and prospective management of oil revenues."[33] However, NGOs and civil society continue to push for a full independent audit of the government's oil accounts and changes in Angolan law to enshrine greater transparency of revenues.

Accusations against Angolan officials relating to illicit international arms deals and embezzlement of funds have been made in European courts; the government has attempted to block these, at times using oil contracts as leverage.[34] In 2003 the government attempted openly and unapologetically to protect French-Brazilian businessman Pierre Falcone from prosecution by nominating him Angolan representative to UNESCO, thereby granting him diplomatic immunity.[35] In January 2004 a French magistrate nevertheless issued an international arrest warrant against him; the Angolan government has since been accused of refusing to renew French company Total's oil contracts in a further attempt to have charges dropped.[36]

Insufficient guards against corruption exist within the state at national and local levels, and public and private spheres are inadequately separated. Currently, although some restrictions exist (for instance members of the National Assembly cannot be employed by foreign or international businesses), it is common for government officials and civil servants to operate private businesses alongside their official posts. This frequently creates conflicts of interest, particularly as international firms investing in Angola are required to be partnered with Angolan companies, many of which are front organizations involving prominent government figures.

Awarding of concessions and contracts is opaque and open to abuse. Government contracts are frequently granted to allies, associates, and relatives of government and MPLA officials. The draft new constitution provides for the separation of public and private sectors and political neutrality of the public sector,[37] but it is sufficiently vague that it is unlikely to threaten to any great extent the economic system. Members of government are not required to disclose details of their financial assets and incomes. When the independent newspaper *Angolense* published details of personal fortunes of the elite, a number of them resorted to legal action (see "Accountability and Public Voice").

Lower-level, small-scale corruption is also endemic, in part due to the heavily bureaucratic nature of Angolan administration and the inadequacy of government salaries. Angolan National Police are prone to extortion and petty corruption. Payment and acceptance of bribes is common practice.

Foreign assistance is often used as a tool for political purposes, with distribution of food and other aid taking place under the banner of the MPLA. Awarding of contracts has also been opaque, with, in extreme cases, credit (and payment) taken by Angolan subcontractors for work actually done by NGOs.

Mechanisms for independent monitoring of government activities and prevention of corruption are limited. The Tribunal de Contas (the accounting court) has the power to monitor the national budget in order to prevent corruption and misuse of funds. It has been active only since 2001, with its first ruling in 2003, but has prosecuted a number of cases since. Several high-profile officials have been charged with misappropriation of public funds, including (among others) a UNITA member of parliament, the Angolan ambassador to South Africa, and the former director of the National Institute of Scholarship. The draft new constitution provides for a High Authority against Corruption, to be elected by the National Assembly.

The attorney general provides for impartial investigation of alleged corruption by government officials. However, in 2004 opposition party PADEPA protested at the attorney general's failure to investigate allegations of attempted corruption by Deputy Prime Minister Aguinaldo Jaime. The attorney general has himself been accused of improper land appropriation in a Luanda district.[38]

State secrecy laws are weighted in favor of the government and not the public. Citizens do have a right to request information from the government; however, such requests are generally treated with suspicion. This is particularly true in the case of any data deemed potentially sensitive or critical of the government. Some moves toward greater openness have occurred through publication of draft legislation and government financial data, but these are generally limited to newspaper and Internet sources to which the majority of the population do not have access.

*Recommendations*

- The government should revise Angolan law so as to incorporate moves toward transparency, such as the regular publication of data relating to oil revenues, audits, and other external reports. A full and independent audit of Sonangol (the state-owned oil company) should be carried out and the results published.

- Angola should sign on to international initiatives such as the Extractive Industries Transparency Initiative and adhere to their provisions. Companies that sign up to and implement such initiatives and move to disclose data relating to oil payments should not be punished by the Angolan government.
- Potentially repressive laws (including the State Secrets Law) should be revised or repealed, especially those created in or justified by wartime expediencies. Greater freedom of access to government data and information by citizens and civic organizations should be permitted and greater attempts be made to publish and publicize data related to government expenditures, revenues, and policies.
- The awarding of economic concessions and contracts should be open and transparent. Public officials should be required to disclose private interests and incomes.
- The handling of foreign assistance and related sub-contracts must be made more transparent. Where appropriate, a separate financial management unit should oversee funds.

## NOTES

[1] "Humanitarian Situation in Angola Quarterly Analysis: July–September 2004" (Luanda: UN, October 2004).

[2] For reports of political harassment, see William Tonet and Antonio Setas, "Reconciliation Is Not What It Used to Be," *Folha* 8 (5 June 2004): 14–15; "Acts of political intolerance promoted by the MPLA between 23 February and 8 April 2004," (UNITA Memorandum), April 2004; "Actos de Aliciamento," (UNITA statement), September 2004. On the nature and activities of the ODC, see Suzana Mendes, "Are the Civilian Defense Forces a cover for MPLA security forces?" *A Capital,* 10 July 2004.

[3] Eduardo dos Santos (Washington, DC: Voice of America, press conference, 14 May 2004).

[4] Ibid.

[5] Finance Ministry Press Adviser Bastos de Almeida, cited in "Producing newspapers in Angola costs seven times more than anywhere else," *A Capital,* 21 August, 2004.

[6] *Unfinished Democracy: Media and Political Freedoms in Angola* (New York: Human Rights Watch [HRW], 14 July 2004), 16.

[7] "Attacks on the Press 2003: Angola" (New York: Committee to Protect Journalists [CPJ], 2004), http://www.cpj.org/attacks03/africa03/angola.html.

[8] "Luanda verification authorities confiscate private weekly publications," *A Capital,* 11 September 2004.

[9] Amended Press Law, August 2000, Article 25 (2): Arrest of Publication. See http://www.angola.org.uk/law_press.htm.

10  *Angola: Promoting Justice Post-conflict* (London: International Bar Association [IBA], July 2003), 19.

11  "Multiple indicator cluster survey on women and children in Angola at the start of the millennium: an analysis" (Luanda: National Statistical Institute/UNICEF, 2003); "Consideration of Reports Submitted by States Parties Under Article 44 of the Convention. Initial reports of State parties due in 1993. Angola" (New York: United Nations Committee on the Rights of the Child, Report CRC/C/3/Add.66, 10 August 2004).

12  *Trafficking in Persons Report* (Washington, DC: U.S. Dept. of State, 14 June, 2004), 42.

13  "Consideration of Reports . . . Angola" (New York: UN Committee on the Rights of the Child, Report CRC/C/3/Add.66, 10 August 2004), 21; "Consideration of Reports . . . Angola. Concluding Observations" (New York: UN Committee on the Rights of the Child, Report CRC/C/15/Add.246, 1 October 2004), 5.

14  "Angola Semi-Annual Risk Assessment: June to November 2004" (Berne: Swisspeace FAST Update, December 2004), 3.

15  "Combined Initial through Third Periodic Report on Angola: Concluding Observations" (New York: United Nations Division for the Advancement of Women, Convention on the Elimination of All Forms of Discrimination Against Women [CEDAW], Report A/59/38 part II, October 2004), point 129; "Combined Initial through Third Periodic Report on Angola" (New York: UN Division for the Advancement of Women, CEDAW, CEDAW/C/AGO/4-5, 31st Session, 7 November 2002), 16.

16  "UN Recommends Special Focus on Women's Rights in Angola," UN Integrated Regional Information Networks (IRIN), 13 July 2004.

17  "Unfinished Democracy: Media and Political Freedoms in Angola" (New York: HRW, 14 July 2004).

18  "Violence in Cazombo as Houses Torched," UN Integrated Regional Information Networks (IRIN), 20 July 2004.

19  "Angola: Riot over generator leaves unknown number dead," IRIN, 26 February 2004.

20  "A Year of Pain" (Cabinda: Ad-hoc Commission for Human Rights in Cabinda, 3 November 2003); see also earlier report from same source, "Terror in Cabinda," 10 December 2002.

21  "Annual Appeal 2004: Overview of Activities and Financial Requirements" (New York: UN, Office of the High Commissioner of the United Nations for Human Rights, 2004), 50.

22  *Angola: Promoting Justice Post-conflict* (IBA, July 2003), 33.

23  Constitutional Law, Article 142 (1). Similar provision is made in the draft new constitution.

24  Ibid., 23.

25  *Mid-Year Review of the Consolidated Appeals Process (CAP): Humanitarian Appeal 2004 for Angola* (New York: UN, Office for the Coordination of Humanitarian Affairs [OCHA], June 2004), 8.

26  *Angola: Promoting Justice Post-conflict* (IBA, July 2003), 32, 37.

27  "Angolan Official Says Army Involved in Diamond Trafficking," AFP, 18 December 2003.

[28] *Mass forced evictions in Luanda: a call for a human rights based housing policy* (London: Amnesty International, November 2003).

[29] *Country Report 2004: Angola* (London: Economist Intelligence Unit, June 2004), 14.

[30] "Corruption Perceptions Index" (Berlin: Transparency International, 2002, 2003, 2004).

[31] See Justin Pearce, "IMF: Angola's 'missing millions,'" BBC News, 18 October 2002, referring to "Angola: Staff Report for the 2002 Article IV Consultation" (Washington, DC: International Monetary Fund [IMF], 18 March 2002); "Angola: Selected Issues and Statistical Appendix" (IMF, 11 July 2003). See also, *Some Transparency, No Accountability: The Use of Oil Revenue in Angola and Its Impact on Human Rights* (New York: HRW, A1601, 13 January 2004).

[32] See *Some Transparency, No Accountability: The Use of Oil Revenue in Angola and Its Impact on Human Rights* (New York: HRW, A1601, 13 January 2004), 16–31.

[33] "IMF Staff Statement on Angola," IMF Press Release No. 04/88, 27 April 2004.

[34] See *All the President's Men: The Devastating Story of Oil and Banking in Angola's Privatised War* (London: Global Witness, March 2002).

[35] "Presidential Aide Defends Appointment of French National to UN Post," unpublished text of recorded telephone interview with Angolan presidential adviser Carlos Belli Bello by Radio France Internationale (RFI) correspondent Antonio Garcia.

[36] *Country Report 2004: Angola* (London: Economist Intelligence Unit, June 2004), 15.

[37] Draft New Constitution, published at www.angolapress-angop.ao/especiais/leiconstituicaao/imagens/Versao%20Final%20Constitui%E7%E3o%20segunda%20leitura.pdf.

[38] "Attorney General said involved in fraud involving piece of land," *Angolense*, 31 July 2004.

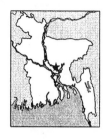

# BANGLADESH

CAPITAL: Dhaka
POPULATION: 141.3 million
GNI PER CAPITA: $380

**SCORES**

ACCOUNTABILITY AND PUBLIC VOICE: 3.63
CIVIL LIBERTIES: 4.05
RULE OF LAW: 3.42
ANTICORRUPTION AND TRANSPARENCY: 2.64
(scores are based on a scale of 0 to 7, with
0 representing weakest and 7 representing
strongest performance)

*Rounaq Jahan*

## INTRODUCTION

In December 1990 a people's movement toppled 15 years of military rule in Bangladesh. Since 1991, the country has witnessed three national parliamentary elections held at regular five-year intervals that on the whole have been assessed as free and fair by national and international election monitors. The elections resulted in rotation of power between the two major political parties.

The elections were organized under a neutral non-party caretaker government, which was institutionalized by a constitutional amendment in 1996. In 2004, the Awami League (AL), the main opposition party at that time, started demanding reforms of the caretaker government system, alleging that the ruling Bangladesh Nationalist Party (BNP)–led coalition government was trying to manipulate the leadership of the next caretaker government (CG). The contention over the neutrality of the caretaker government has raised doubts about the smooth organization of the next parliamentary election, scheduled for 2006. The year 2004

**Rounaq Jahan** is Senior Research Scholar, Southern Asian Institute, School of International and Public Affairs, Columbia University, New York.

also saw continued confrontations between the election commission (EC) and the government over the conduct of elections.

In 2004, repeated bomb and grenade attacks on political and cultural events, assaults on prominent individuals, illegal arms shipments, and the growing violence of Islamist and other extremist groups shook public confidence in the government's ability to maintain law and order. The legislative and judicial branches of government were rather ineffective in holding the executive branch accountable. Parliament hardly functioned because the main opposition party, the AL, boycotted most parliamentary sessions, alleging government repression and denial of opportunities to debate critical issues of public concern. In the absence of separation of powers between the executive and the judiciary, the lower judiciary in particular remained largely under the control of the executive branch. A worrisome development was the increasing politicization of the civil bureaucracy.

The Bangladesh constitution guarantees fundamental rights and civil liberties. But over the years the government has also formulated some laws that limit civil liberties. Women and ethnic and religious minorities often face discrimination.

Civil society and the media have emerged as the two most effective instruments of accountability and public voice in Bangladesh. But civil society groups themselves face government harassment and repression. Many have become politicized along party lines. The media have also come under strong pressure from state and non-state actors. Hundreds of journalists have faced intimidation and assaults, and five were killed in 2004.

## ACCOUNTABILITY AND PUBLIC VOICE – 3.63

In December 1990 a people's movement ended 15 years of military rule in Bangladesh, and the contending political parties reached a consensus that in the future, winning free and fair elections would be the legitimate means of gaining and continuing in state power. Since 1991, three national parliamentary elections have been held at regular five-year intervals; the elections were judged to be largely free and fair by national and international election monitors. The losing party in each election complained of vote rigging, but in all cases it finally accepted the election results and agreed to serve as the opposition in parliament. The elections resulted in rotation of power between the two major political parties: The BNP won the 1991 and 2001 elections and the AL won in 1996.

Each of the three elections was organized under a neutral non-party CG, and all political parties enjoyed equal campaigning opportunities. Voter turnout has sharply increased from 56 percent in 1991 to 75 percent in 1996 and 2001.[1]

The first CG in 1991 was an ad hoc arrangement; the next two, in 1996 and 2001, were institutionalized by a constitutional amendment that stipulates that at the end of five years the government stands dissolved and a non-party CG is formed whose main task is to organize a free and fair parliamentary election within 90 days. According to the constitution, the non-party CG is headed by the most recently retired chief justice or, if he or she is not available, the previous one.

The AL had launched a two-year-long mass campaign for the institutionalization of a non-party CG between 1994 and 1996, and the party again raised questions about the neutrality of the CG of 2001. In 2004, the AL yet again started demanding reforms of the CG system, alleging that the ruling BNP-led coalition government was trying to predetermine the leadership of the next CG by increasing the retirement age of Supreme Court judges to 67; this would ensure that the last retired chief justice, K. M. Hasan, would become the leader of the CG in 2006. The AL alleged that Justice K. M. Hasan is a BNP sympathizer.[2] The BNP-led coalition government has so far refused to enter into any dialogue with the AL over the issue of CG reforms. The contention over the neutrality of the CG has raised doubts about the smooth organization of the next parliamentary election as the ground rules for free and fair elections have again been opened up for debate. The future of electoral democracy in Bangladesh appears to be uncertain in the absence of a negotiated consensus between the two major political parties on the rules of the political game.

The year 2004 also saw continued friction between the election commission (EC) and the government over the conduct of elections. The opposition political parties made persistent allegations that the ruling coalition was rigging votes. The most notable case was that of a by-election in the Dhaka 10 constituency, where a vacancy occurred in March when a ruling BNP member of parliament, Major Mannan, resigned to join a newly formed opposition party, Bikalpa Dhara Bangladesh (BDB). In the ensuing by-election, Major Mannan was twice denied the electoral symbol chosen by the BDB until a high court ruled in his favor.[3] The voting on July 1, 2004, ended with the victory of the ruling coalition candidate, Mosaddak Ali Falu. Major Mannan and the election monitoring bodies alleged massive vote rigging and appealed to the EC to cancel the election. The media widely reported on cases of vote fraud.[4] The EC admitted that the election was unsatisfactory but argued that it was legally powerless to cancel the election or challenge the result.[5] The EC's autonomy is compromised by its dependence on the government for funding, recruitment and posting of officers, and control over the machinery of law enforcement during elections.

The future of free and fair elections was also jeopardized by the increasing criminalization of politics and use of money and *mastaans* (hoodlums) to capture votes, not just in parliamentary elections but also in local elections. The electoral laws stipulating a ceiling on campaign spending and other electoral guidelines have been regularly violated with impunity over successive elections, continuing throughout 2004. Innumerable public discussions have put forward recommendations for strengthening the EC to make it independent of executive pressure, but these debates, largely limited to civil society and minor political parties, receive very little attention or support from the major parties.

Civil society, the media, and the international community have for some years been registering their growing concern about the deteriorating state of governance in Bangladesh. These concerns were fully captured in the statement on the topic by the vice president of the World Bank at the meeting of the Bangladesh Development Forum in Dhaka in May 2004.[6] The media and civil society remained proactive in pointing out governance failures and demanding accountability from the government. But the legislature and judiciary, who are in theory mandated to hold the executive branch accountable, have proved inadequate in discharging their responsibilities.

Although Bangladesh has had a parliamentary system since 1991, in practice, parliament hardly functions as an effective accountability mechanism. Regardless of which party is in power, the main opposition party has boycotted most parliamentary sessions, alleging government repression and impediments in parliament to voicing its views. The year 2004 saw no exception to this practice; the AL for the most part refrained from participating in parliament. The AL also boycotted parliamentary committees due to controversies over their composition. In the absence of scrutiny and oversight by the legislative branch, the executive continued to function like the vice-regal system of the British and Pakistani colonial days, with few checks on its actions.[7]

The increasing politicization of the civil bureaucracy is a serious cause for concern. Although the civil service is, in principle, recruited on merit and inherited a tradition of neutrality from colonial days, over the years there has been a growing tendency to apply partisan criteria in its selection and promotion. One of the instruments used to compromise the political autonomy of the bureaucracy has been the extension of senior civil servants' service on contract after they have passed the compulsory retirement age. There have also been allegations of partisan influence in recruitment and promotion of various officials.

In the absence of an effective parliament or other accountability mechanisms, civil society and the media have emerged as effective instruments of accountability and public voice in Bangladesh. A large and proactive civil society, including numerous nongovernmental organizations (NGOs), has gained an international reputation both in delivering services and in advocacy. Government regulations for NGO registration remain time-consuming. Government approval is required to receive donor funds, although donors have been relatively free of state pressure in funding NGOs registered with the government. NGOs have been vocal in protesting violations of human rights and providing critiques of public policies and legislation. For example, civil society, particularly human rights organizations, led protests against the government's ban on the publications of the Ahmadiyya community on January 7, 2004.[8] Ahmadiyya, a small Muslim minority sect, has come under attack by extremist Sunni groups who have been increasing pressure on the government to declare the Ahmadiyyas as non-Muslim. Islamic Oikkya Jote (IOJ), one of the two Islamist parties in the ruling coalition, has tacitly supported this demand. Throughout the year civil society groups repeatedly mobilized to defend the Ahmadiyya mosques against pre-announced attacks by Islamist extremists.[9]

Civil society groups were equally vocal in protesting extrajudicial killings of various individuals by the Rapid Action Battalion (RAB), an elite anti-crime force drawn from the police, army, navy, and air force that was launched in June 2004. The government labeled these killings as "crossfire" deaths. In addition, several rights groups filed public-interest litigation in the high court challenging the mass arrests that took place in April 2004 (see "Civil Liberties").[10]

Civil society groups themselves have faced harassment and repression from the government. Proshika—one of the largest NGOs, with involvement in both micro-credit and social advocacy—and a few like-minded NGOs were targeted in particular for their alleged pro-AL sympathies. Several officials and workers of Proshika, including its chief, Kazi Faruque Ahmed, were imprisoned on charges of corruption. Kazi Faruque Ahmed was later charged with sedition. Ahmed and his colleagues were finally freed after months of legal battles.[11] Donors funding Proshika had refused to accept the government's allegations of corruption and instituted their own audits, which cleared Proshika. Unfortunately, as with other elements of civil society, the NGO community has become divided along partisan lines, weakening their ability to speak with a united voice.

The media have also come under strong pressure from state and non-state actors. Five journalists were killed, 111 were injured, and cases were filed against 63 others in 2004. A further 263 journalists received death threats from various fundamentalist or criminal organizations.[12] Editors of four leading newspapers faced libel suits. Despite these risks, privately owned media, both print and electronic, reported freely on governance failures and human rights violations. Privately owned newspapers and television channels largely determine their own media content free of government control. However, threats and attacks as well of fear of incurring official displeasure result in a degree of self-censorship on the editorial content of some private media. Individual citizens were on the whole free to express their opinions. Government-owned radio and television tend to be constrained in their freedom of expression, but threats to freedom of expression came more from non-state extremist groups than from the state. Nevertheless, by widely publicizing extrajudicial killings as well as the atrocities of Bangla Bhai and other extremist groups, election fraud, political repression, and assassinations, the media remained an important instrument for holding the government accountable before the court of public opinion. For example, as a result of media publicity, the government was finally compelled to take action against Bangla Bhai.

*Recommendations*

- A system of co-chairmanship should be introduced in parliamentary committees so that both the ruling and the opposition political parties feel equal ownership and participate in the work of the committees.
- The election commission should be made fully independent of the executive branch. To this end, it should have an independent budget and freedom to recruit its own staff. It should also be able to exercise control over the machinery of law enforcement before and during elections. It should be fully empowered to punish violations of electoral rules.
- Campaign finance and other electoral reforms should be introduced and enforced.
- The existing government regulations controlling NGOs should be changed to ensure greater autonomy from government control. A joint government–NGO body should be set up to oversee the conduct of the NGOs.
- The state should protect journalists from harassment and attacks by non-state actors by applying the full force of the law against those who threaten or attack journalists.

## CIVIL LIBERTIES – 4.05

The Bangladesh constitution guarantees fundamental rights and civil liberties. Political, cultural, and religious freedoms for all groups are protected. All citizens are recognized as equal irrespective of their ethnicity, gender, or religion. The constitution also mandates affirmative action measures to promote gender, racial, and social equality and eliminate discrimination. Notwithstanding the law, in practice women and ethnic and religious minorities often face discrimination. Over the years Bangladesh has also formulated some laws that limit civil liberties.

In 2004, the newspapers reported many incidents of state terror. The most prominent examples were extrajudicial killings by law enforcement officers, who killed a total of 238 people in 2004. Some of these killings were carried out by newly constituted special forces—with names such as RAB, Cheetah, and Cobra—who were specifically empowered and equipped to combat the escalating crime rates. In addition, these forces killed approximately 147 people in what were presumed to be staged encounters with people the government referred to as criminals.[13] Newspapers also reported police torture of people in detention.

Odhikar, a human rights group, reported 522 people killed in political violence in 2004. The state not only failed to protect against these political killings, it resorted to arbitrary arrests of political opponents and even innocent citizens. For example, police and members of the Bangladesh Rifles, a paramilitary force under the Home Ministry, arrested 8,500 people in the run-up to the April 30 deadline given by the AL to oust the government. From September 23 to 29, ahead of the AL's planned October 3 mass rally, police arrested 5,748 people.[14] Citizens had no redress against such human rights violations beyond petitioning the courts.

Repeated bomb and grenade attacks on political and cultural events, assaults on prominent individuals, illegal arms shipments, and the growing violence of Islamist and other extremist groups shook public confidence in the government's ability to maintain law and order. On January 12, 2004, five people were killed by bomb blasts at Hazrat Shahjalal Shrine in the northeastern city of Sylhet. On May 21, again at the Shahjalal Shrine, an attempt was made to assassinate the British High Commissioner, Anwar Choudhury, in a grenade attack that injured him and killed two other people.[15] On August 7 a car bomb killed AL leader Mohammad Ibrahim.[16] The year's biggest grenade attack, on August 21 at an AL rally in the capital city, Dhaka, killed 23 people, including senior AL leader Ivy Rahman, and maimed and injured hundreds. The AL Chief Sheikh Hasina was targeted but miraculously escaped with minor injures.[17] The government sought the assistance of Interpol, the FBI, and Scotland Yard in investigating the grenade attacks on the UK High Commissioner and the August 21 AL rally, but these investigations have so far failed to identify the culprits.

In 2004, human rights groups and the media also reported increasing killings, abductions, ransom-seeking, and rape by non-state actors. According to these groups, 866 women and children were raped and, of them, 116 were killed.[18] Furthermore, the government has yet to take any step to fill the office of the ombudsman, which was created by an act of parliament in 1980 but has never been filled. The government also made no progress in creating a human rights commission. A draft bill had been prepared but has yet to be tabled in parliament.

Throughout 2004, newspapers widely publicized the spate of killings and abductions carried out by an Islamist militant organization, Jagrata Muslim Janata Bangladesh (JMJB), in the northern region. However, top government officials persisted in denying the existence of its leader, Siddiqual Islam, alias Bangla Bhai, until the prime minister issued a directive for his arrest. However, Bangla Bhai remained at large for a long time, reportedly due to immunity from the local agents of law enforcement.[19] [*Editor's note:* Bangla Bhai was arrested in 2005.]

The Bangladesh constitution guarantees freedom of association and assembly, yet these rights were repeatedly violated by the state in 2004. Partisan supporters of the ruling coalition disrupted the meetings of the newly formed political party, BDB, and rallies and protest marches of the AL.[20] In addition, law enforcement agencies tended to apply excessive force in dealing with peaceful demonstrations and public protests.

The organized trade union movement in Bangladesh remains weak, politically fragmented, and in many cases subject to control by individual leaders or employers. As a result, rates of trade union membership in Bangladesh remain among the lowest in the world. In the principal export industry—ready-made garments—most owners severely discourage unionization of their workers and prefer to treat them as casual labor with few legally enforceable rights. Formation of trade unions in the export processing zones is illegal, and unions affiliated with the political opposition tend to face repression. In the past decade, many professional and business organizations have also become politically factionalized.

The year 2004 also witnessed state actions in restricting some religious freedoms. As mentioned above, one of the partners of the ruling coalition, IOJ, started a mass agitation to put pressure on the government to declare the Ahmadiyya community to be non-Muslims. The government resisted the pressure from its coalition partner, and the police protected Ahmadiyya mosques from the attacks of the extremists. However, the government eventually succumbed to the pressure of the religious extremist groups and their colleagues in the coalition and banned Ahmadiyya publications on January 8, 2004. As with the Ahmadiyya mosques, the government also took steps to provide police protection for the religious festivals of other minorities, most notably the Hindus. No major incident of Hindu–Muslim communal violence was reported in the media in 2004. However, over the past few decades Hindus have faced continual discrimination. For example, immediately following the 2001 elections, the Hindus were subjected to various forms of violence including killing, assault, rape, ransom-seeking, and loss of property.

The state continued to take some proactive measures, such as an employment quota and free education for girls up to the secondary level, to promote gender equity. Special measures have also been taken to protect rights of excluded groups, such as the disabled. Since independence, Bangladesh has adopted several laws and policies to advance women's empowerment. Laws relating to age at marriage, dowry, and violence against women have been formulated to modify and abolish discriminatory social customs. The government also adopted a law and action plan to ensure equal access to opportunities for people with disabilities. Nevertheless there remains a wide gap between the laws and policies and their actual implementation and practice.

Two issues relating to gender equity gained prominence in 2004. Despite a persistent demand by women's organizations for a quota of seats reserved for women in parliament based on direct election, and despite consensus among all women's groups that women should be permitted to contest the reserved seats directly, in 2004 the government introduced a constitutional amendment (14th Amendment) stipulating women's reserved seats in parliament on the basis of indirect election. Women's rights groups protested against the 14th Amendment on the streets as well as through filing a petition in the high court against the amendment, arguing that it violates the principles of the constitution. But the government nevertheless used its two-thirds majority in parliament to pass the 14th Amendment.[21]

The other issue relating to gender that gained international publicity was the blacklisting of Bangladesh by the U.S. Department of State on June 15, 2004, on the ground that the government has failed to take adequate steps to curb the high rate of trafficking in women and children. The State Department report maintained that an estimated 10,000 to 20,000 women and young girls are trafficked annually from Bangladesh.[22] The Bangladesh government contradicted this figure, claiming that only 708 women and children had been trafficked in 2004. The U.S. government warned Bangladesh of economic sanctions if it failed to take measures to improve the situation within 60 days.[23] After the U.S. threat, the Bangladesh government moved quickly to introduce several concrete measures to constrain trafficking: revival of the police anti-trafficking unit, appointment of a special prosecutor for dealing with trafficking cases in expedited courts, institution of a referral mechanism for the victims to avail themselves of services offered by NGOs, speedy disposal of 17 pending cases relating to trafficking, and a listing of traffickers.[24] Once the government of Bangladesh made public announcement of these specific steps, the U.S. government withdrew the threat of economic sanctions.

*Recommendations*

- The state should rescind all laws and directives that limit fundamental rights of citizens guaranteed by the constitution.
- An independent and bipartisan commission should be established to investigate the acts of terror by state as well as non-state actors and recommend actions.
- Extrajudicial killings by law enforcement officials should be promptly investigated, and the culprits should be tried and punished.
- The state should take measures such as female scholarship programs to provide incentives for the implementation of laws to promote gender equity. It should also provide equal access to opportunities by other marginalized groups such as people with disabilities and religious and ethnic minorities.

## RULE OF LAW – 3.42

Historically Bangladesh has prided itself on a relatively independent, impartial, and nondiscriminatory judiciary. However, this proposition has remained more valid for the upper judiciary, which consists of the high court and appellate divisions of the Supreme Court, than for the lower courts—the district courts and magistracy. Appointments to the lower judiciary and career advancement remain within the direct control of the executive, which has increasingly compromised the courts' independence. In theory judges in the lower judiciary are recruited on the basis of competitive examinations, but their career advancement remains exposed to politicization and patronage. The judgments of the lower judiciary are not only subject to political and administrative interference from the executive but tend to be amenable to financial inducements to influence their decisions. In practice, this has meant that political opponents of the regime who have been arbitrarily taken into custody on flimsy legal grounds can be denied bail by the lower courts and kept in custody until bail is obtained from the higher courts. Thus, political figures, journalists, and NGO executives who have been victimized by the government have been subject to arbitrary arrest and exposed to torture and denied due process until their lawyers can work their way through the lower judiciary to appeal to the Supreme Court.

The upper judiciary was until recently relatively immune from political patronage. However, in the last few years appointments to the high court division of the Supreme Court have been exposed to political influences. Appointments to the appellate division, the highest tier of the judiciary, have tended to be above controversy largely because such appointments follow a seniority principle for elevating judges from the high court to the appellate division. However, successive governments have occasionally interfered with the seniority principle, apparently on political grounds. This has applied, in particular, to the appointment of the chief justice (see "Accountability and Public Voice"). Recently, the appointment of the chief justice has become politically contentious because after his retirement he may head the CG.

Judicial appointments became quite controversial in 2004. In August, the government appointed 19 judges to the high court simultaneously. However, the Supreme Court Bar Association (SCBA), the principal representative body of the bar, deemed a number of these appointees professionally incompetent; their promotion was seen to be largely an act of political patronage. The SCBA appealed to both the government and the chief justice to rescind some of the more egregious appointments. Failure to respond to the request led a segment of the SCBA to boycott the courts of the more unacceptable of the judicial appointees.[25]

The training of the lower judiciary tends to be shallow; lawyers complain of some judges' poor comprehension of certain points of law and the resulting weakness of their judgments. This complaint now extends to the upper judiciary, where deterioration in professional quality has been observed. This owes in some measure to the fact that the best lawyers practicing in the Supreme Court rarely choose to make themselves available for judicial appointment because of the severe loss of income involved. As a result, relatively less successful lawyers are now being elevated to the bench.

Public prosecutors are very much creatures of the government and are largely appointed according to their political affiliation. The question of independent action by such prosecutors therefore hardly arises, particularly when political opponents are in the dock.

The legal system of Bangladesh works on the presumption of innocence until a person is proven guilty. However in practice many people, particularly the poor, are exposed to arbitrary arrest and can be held for long periods in custody without trial. A fair and timely hearing, based on access to independent counsel, is a fundamental right enshrined in the constitution, but the exercise of this right is severely circumscribed by the financial means of the citizen. The government has taken no practical measures to provide independent counsel to the poor. NGOs have attempted to provide legal aid, but the capacity of such organizations is severely limited by their narrow resource base.

The government generally complies with judicial decisions. However, in practice, executive enforcement of judicial decisions often takes a long time, which is particularly problematic in judgments involving commercial and financial issues. In response to written petitions by NGOs and private citizens during 2004, the courts issued stay orders on a number of government decisions. Yet the executive branch delayed their implementation by counter-petitions and other tactics. In one instance, the executive branch distorted and misinterpreted a court order about the separation of the judiciary from the executive branch.[26] The Supreme Court issued several contempt orders against the executive branch including one against the chief of police, forcing his early retirement.[27]

The prosecution of ruling-party actors for abuse of power is rare. In some cases criminals with ruling party affiliations are detained for particular criminal acts, but this too is infrequent, and such persons rarely spend any extended time in custody. In these circumstances, treatment by the lower courts is influenced by the political orientation of the person involved, although the upper judiciary is more likely to be politically neutral in its judgments.

According to the constitution, civilian authorities control the police, military, and internal security forces. In practice, these forces sometimes overstep the bounds of law under the political direction of the ruling party. A recent and disturbing manifestation of law enforcement without accountability has been the creation of the RAB (see "Accountability and Public Voice"). The RAB's main task is to track down and apprehend criminal elements who have created an atmosphere of insecurity throughout the country. The RAB since its inception has pursued an aggressive strategy against criminal gang members that has led to a large number of killings in so-called crossfire after people have been arrested. These crossfire custodial deaths are viewed by human rights groups as a form of extrajudicial execution arising from lack of civilian oversight of the RAB. These extrajudicial executions have generated serious disquiet within the political opposition as well as among civil society and have now drawn the attention of the international community as well. However, arbitrary action by law enforcement agencies can still be subject to the rule of law through reference to the higher judiciary, who have frequently intervened to curb arbitrary behavior.[28]

The military, by and large, tend to be free of the influence of non-state actors and have in the post-1991 situation attempted to avoid being drawn into the political disputes of the major political parties. The internal security services also tend to be immune from outside political influence. The police, on the other hand, are known to build alliances with both commercial and criminal interests.

Although the military was involved in the seizure of power from an elected government in 1975 and then again in 1982 and ran the country under martial law after these interventions, since 1991 the country has been ruled by elected governments. In recent years the military and internal security forces have not overtly interfered in politics/government. However, periodic allegations have arisen that the ruling party has used the military to serve the party's immediate political interests. For example, in the last election in 2001, the AL claimed that the military had exercised a political bias against them in the discharge of their duties during the campaign and election. But no concrete proof to support this charge has been forthcoming.

Every citizen is entitled to own property individually as well as in association with others. The state enforces property rights and contracts, and laws protect citizens from unjust deprivation of property. However, in practice the right is constrained for minority groups, the poor, women, and those exposed to illegal actions by people enjoying political patronage or with sufficient financial and coercive power at their disposal to influence administrative and judicial decisions and to intimidate those vulnerable groups.

*Recommendations*

- The government should take immediate steps to separate the judiciary from the executive branch of the government and enact measures that will insulate the judiciary from partisan political influence.
- Training of judicial as well as law enforcement agencies should stress professional standards and human rights norms.
- The government should initiate a process of dialogue with all political parties to eliminate armed cadres and criminal elements from the ranks of the parties.
- A public judicial enquiry should be initiated into the extra-judicial crossfire deaths of detainees under Rapid Action Battalion custody. RAB should be abolished.

## ANTICORRUPTION AND TRANSPARENCY – 2.64

In 2004, Transparency International (TI)'s Corruption Perceptions Index listed Bangladesh as the most corrupt country of those surveyed, a notoriety the country has earned every year since 2001.[29] The TI report called for the establishment of a truly independent anticorruption commission (ACC). On February 17, 2004, the parliament passed an anticorruption commission bill. In May 2004, the government set up a search body to select members of the proposed commission. [*Editor's note:* In December 2004 three members of the ACC were appointed.[30]]

Combating corruption was a major campaign theme of the ruling coalition government. However, since assuming office in 2001, it has done very little besides establishing the ACC, and this was mostly due to donor pressure. The state is encumbered by unnecessary bureaucratic regulations, registration requirements, and other controls. The government has not taken any measure that would require public officials to make financial disclosures of their assets for public and media scrutiny. Nor are there clear rules or standards to protect against conflicts of interest in the private sector.

Public and private sector officials work in an environment that does little to prevent or punish use of official position to pursue personal interests. Indeed over the years, using official positions to seek personal gains has become the norm rather than the exception. While all agencies of the government have become corrupt, according to the TI surveys, tax administration and the law enforcement agencies are particularly noteworthy. No effective internal audit system exists to ensure the accountability of tax collection. An office of the auditor-general regularly reports to parliament on inappropriate use of public funds, but little action is taken against public officials pursuant to these reports.

Allegations of corruption receive wide and extensive airing in the news media,[31] but the allegations are rarely investigated or prosecuted without prejudice. The government generally does not move to file anticorruption cases against high-ranking members of the government or the ruling party. However, one corruption case that drew major media publicity in 2004 involved a high court judge accused of taking bribes and fixing bail. For the first time in the country's history, such a case was referred to the Supreme Judicial Council. After the council's report the judge was removed by the president on April 24, 2004.[32]

Over the last decade, the government has increasingly used anticorruption laws to pursue partisan interests. High-profile corruption cases have been lodged against members of the political opposition for actions taken during their tenure in office; these cases have been dropped when the same opposition came to power after winning an election. The legal system is not conducive to independent investigation and prosecution nor does it protect anticorruption activists.

Lack of governmental transparency has contributed to corruption. No freedom of information law entitles citizens to access to government information. Some information, particularly information relating to the budget and expenditures, is increasingly available to citizens, often through government Web sites. However, ordinary citizens still have difficulty obtaining navigating the system. The government is particularly responsive to international donor sentiments and provides an enabling environment for the legal administration and distribution of foreign assistance. However, the government has not been transparent in ensuring open bidding or effective competition in the awarding of government contracts. Partisan considerations and corruption have reportedly influenced such awards.

## Recommendations

- The state should investigate and prosecute high-ranking government and ruling party officials for corruption when charges are leveled against them.
- The government should strengthen and empower the anticorruption commission to function independently.
- The government should enact and implement a freedom of information act.
- The state should remove unnecessary bureaucratic regulations, registration requirements, and other controls that can be used by public officials to extract bribes.

## NOTES

[1] "Bangladesh Electoral System: FPTP" (Stockholm: International IDEA, 18 April 2005), http://www.idea.int/vt/country_view.cfm?CountryCode=BD.

[2] Shakhawat Liton and Shimeen Mahmud, "The Chief Advisor Should be Appointed Through Consensus," *The Daily Star,* 14 January 2005.

[3] Shahnaz Parveen, "The Year of Living Dangerously," *The Daily Star,* 1 January 2005.

[4] "Observers Tell of Massive Rigging" and Star Report, "An (S)Election It Really Was," *The Daily Star,* 2 July 2004.

[5] "High Court Order Was Violated Says EC," *The Daily Star,* 2 July 2004.

[6] "Donors Concerned at Politically Linked Violence," *The Daily Star,* 9 May 2004.

[7] Rounaq Jahan, "Why Are We Still Continuing with a Viceregal Political System," *The Daily Star,* 14 January 2003.

[8] "Ban on Ahmadiyya Books Infringement of Rights," *The Daily Star,* 10 January 2004.

[9] Shahanaz Parveen, "The Year of Living Dangerously," *The Daily Star,* 1 January 2005; "Ahmadiyya Complex Capture Plan Foiled," *The Daily Star,* 28 August 2004.

[10] "Mass Arrests Challenged," *The Daily Star,* 28 April 2004.

[11] "Proshika Chief Qazi Faruque Arrested," *The Daily Star,* 23 May 2004; "Proshika Boss Charged with Sedition," *The Daily Star,* 21 June 2004; Mustafa Zaman, "Proshika: A Case Gone Sour," *Star Weekend Magazine,* 14 May 2004.

[12] Zayadul Ahsan and Shamim Ashraf, "Long List of Violence as Cross Fire Crosses Line," *The Daily Star,* 1 January 2005.

[13] "238 Killed in Hands of Law Enforcers Last Year," *The Daily Star,* 1 January 2005.

[14] Ibid.

[15] Sylhet, "Blast at Shahjalal Shrine Injures British HC, Kills 2," *The Daily Star,* 22 May 2004.

[16] Sylhet, "Car Bomb Kills Sylhet AL Leader, Mayor Unhurt," *The Daily Star,* 8 August 2004.

[17] "Assassination Attempt on Hasina," *The Daily Star,* 22 August 2004.

[18] "238 Killed in Hands of Law Enforcers Last Year," *The Daily Star*, 1 January 2005.

[19] Eliza Griswold, "The Next Islamist Revolution?" *The New York Times Magazine*, Bangladesh Media monitoring for 1/24/2005. World Bank Group Media Monitoring.

[20] "BNP Men Attack B Chy, Cops Join to Foil Rally," *The Daily Star*, 12 March 2004.

[21] "Rights Activists File Writ Against 14th Amendment," *The Daily Star*, 21 June 2004.

[22] *Trafficking in Persons Report* (Washington, DC: U.S. Dept. of State, June 2003), http://www.state.gov/g/tip/rls/tiprpt/2004/.

[23] Ibid.

[24] "6 Steps Suggested to Curb Crime," *The Daily Star*, 28 June 2004.

[25] Shahiduzzaman, "Judiciary Blues," *New Age*, New Year Special, January 2005.

[26] Ibid.

[27] Ibid.

[28] Ibid.

[29] Shahiduzzaman, "Judiciary Blues," *New Age*, January 2005.

[30] "Search Body Formed for Anti-Graft Commission," *The Daily Star*, 10 May 2004.

[31] "Govt Obliged to Protect People from Criminals," *The Daily Star*, 10 May 2004.

[32] Shahiduzzaman, "Judiciary Blues," *New Age*, January 2005.

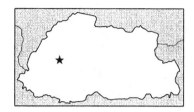

# BHUTAN

CAPITAL: Thimphu
POPULATION: 764,000
GNI PER CAPITA: $590

**SCORES**

ACCOUNTABILITY AND PUBLIC VOICE: 2.40
CIVIL LIBERTIES: 3.36
RULE OF LAW: 4.23
ANTICORRUPTION AND TRANSPARENCY: 3.34
(scores are based on a scale of 0 to 7, with
0 representing weakest and 7 representing
strongest performance)

*Richard W. Whitecross*

## INTRODUCTION

Bhutan lies in the eastern Himalayas, south of China and north of India. With a population of about 764,000 and a territory approximately the size of Switzerland, it is a traditional monarchy in the process of becoming a parliamentary democracy.

Bhutan is unique in its character as the last remaining Himalayan Buddhist state. In 1616, the Zhabdrung, Ngawang Namgyal, came to the region from Ralung in southern Tibet.[1] Following an active policy of consolidating his authority in Bhutan, the Zhabdrung unified the territory under the Drukpa (a religious sect) theocracy. The system of government introduced by the Zhabdrung took its definitive form in the 1640s and continues to influence the political administrative structures of contemporary Bhutan. Furthermore, the Zhabdrung introduced *driglam namzha*, a code of conduct and etiquette based on Buddhist concepts and monastic practice, to Bhutan.[2]

---

**Richard W. Whitecross** is a lawyer and lecturer in the School of Social and Political Studies, University of Edinburgh. His doctoral thesis, *The Zhabdrung's Legacy: State Transformation, Law and Social Values in Contemporary Bhutan* (2002) examined local-level understandings of legal change and law in Bhutan.

The monarchy was established in 1907. The third king, Jigme Dorje Wangchuk (reigned 1952–72), introduced wide political, social, and economic reforms that have continued to shape contemporary Bhutan. In 1953 the king established the National Assembly with 150 members. In 1965, a Royal Advisory Council was created. Acknowledging the importance of international recognition, especially after the occupation of Tibet by Chinese forces in 1950, Bhutan eventually joined the United Nations in 1971.

The physical geography of the country, where steep mountains separate valleys, until quite recently limited communication and movement of peoples. It was only with the assistance of India beginning in the early 1960s that road building began in Bhutan, thereby permitting communication and movement of people and goods. As a result, the rate of change in the country has increased exponentially during the past 40 years. However, Bhutan remains primarily a rural society shaped by traditional norms and networks. Many communities are still several days' walk from the nearest road, and, accordingly, all political changes must be set against the considerations of Bhutan's geography and the traditional Buddhist social organization, which remains largely intact throughout the country.

The fourth and current king, Jigme Singye Wangchuk, ascended the throne in 1972 at age 17. The king has inaugurated political changes as part of a determined drive to establish a constitutional monarchy in conformity with international norms. The king transferred his royal powers to an elected council of ministers by royal edict in 1998, and the chairman of the council of ministers, a position that rotates among the cabinet ministers, now acts as prime minister and head of the government. However, although royal powers have been transferred, the king retains a high degree of personal authority due to the deep respect the population accords him. The king has worked very hard to promote change in Bhutan while recognizing the country's vulnerability to negative outside influences (for example, consumerism, the breakdown of the extended family, and youth delinquency).

At present, there is no written constitution. In November 2001, the king announced that the first written constitution should be prepared for Bhutan. A drafting committee was appointed and a draft submitted to the king and cabinet in 2002. The draft constitution underwent further revision with the advice of an Indian constitutional law expert, and has been circulated for public discussion throughout the 20 *dzongkhags* (administrative districts) prior to debate in the National Assembly.[3] [*Editor's note:* The finalized draft of the constitution was made available publicly in March 2005.[4] The 34 articles formally recognize a wide range of human rights for the Bhutanese, including freedom of expression, equal access to state services and opportunity, freedom of religion (Article 7). In addition, it sets out the basis for the development of registered political parties (Article 15) and provides that the majority party forms the government (Article 17).] If ratified, the constitution will provide for greater political openness and opportunity for change in the country. However, fully effective governance in Bhutan will require a major transformation in attitudes toward political participation, including an acceptance of criticism from the public by officials of all ranks.[5]

In December 2003, the kingdom launched a successful and relatively bloodless campaign against Indian insurgents from the United Liberation Front of Assam, the National Democratic Front of Bodoland, and Kamtapur Liberation Organization, who had established camps in southern Bhutan during the 1990s, thereby preventing development in these areas. The military action was undertaken after the king and government had made repeated attempts to resolve the situation peacefully. The action was taken partly as a result of increased pressure by India on Bhutan to expel the insurgents, who were involved in a range of guerrilla activities in the northeastern states of India. The speed with which military action was taken was noteworthy, although in September 2004 a bomb blast in the southern border town of Gelephu raised the specter of ongoing terrorist attacks by these insurgent groups.

## ACCOUNTABILITY AND PUBLIC VOICE – 2.40

At present there are no officially recognized political parties in Bhutan. [*Editor's note:* The draft constitution allows for the establishment of political parties so long as they "promote national unity." Parties based on "region, sex, language, religion, or social origin" are forbidden, and parties may be banned by the Supreme Court or the parliament if their dissolution is deemed in the national interest. Elections are to be publicly funded, and only the top two political parties may participate in each general election (Article 15).] Various opposition groups such as the Bhutan People's Party, Bhutan National Democratic Party, Bhutan

Gorkha Liberation Front, and the Bhutan Communist Party have emerged outside the country and draw their support from people living in refugee camps in eastern Nepal.[6]

The National Assembly was established in 1953 as part of the reforms introduced by the third king. The main function of the National Assembly is to enact legislation for the country, review the five-year development plans and programs initiated by the government, and preserve Bhutan's unique national identity by protecting and promoting its customs and traditions.[7] The legislature has oversight of government budgets and elects the cabinet ministers. At present the National Assembly has 150 members; 105 representatives (*chimi*) are elected from the individual dzongkhags, 10 members are nominated by the Central Monk Body, and 35 are nominated by the government.

The elected representatives are chosen either by secret ballot (as in the case of *gups*—the heads of local government) or by consensus of the gups and the head of each household (for chimis).[8] Any Bhutanese citizen irrespective of gender can stand for election provided he or she is above 21 years of age. Although the representatives criticize some policies, most have only a modest understanding of politics and economics and are more locally than nationally focused.[9] The annual reports of the National Assembly suggest a conservative stance on the part of its members. Although criticism of aspects of government policies or questions concerning draft legislation are permitted, many Bhutanese voice concerns that the National Assembly representatives lack the education and experience necessary to debate the increasing complexity and volume of draft legislation.

In 2002 the country made a major move toward deepening democratic participation in local government. Under a law enacted by the Gewog Yargye Tshogchung Chatrim (National Assembly), direct universal election of gups was introduced. Elections for gups in 199 of the 201 *gewogs* (the smallest administrative unit in Bhutan, comprising several villages) were held in November 2002. It was the first secret ballot election held with universal suffrage in Bhutan; each adult over the age of 21 (males and females enjoying equal rights), rather than a representative from each village household, was eligible to vote.

This experience of direct participation in the electoral system raises important issues that will affect future elections in Bhutan. First, there are concerns about the application of inconsistent eligibility criteria at some of the polling stations. For example, in one gewog nearly 40 percent of the potential voters were denied the opportunity to vote because they could not produce their national identity cards.[10] Second, the voter turnout throughout the country was low. Third, practical issues concerning the location of the polling booths need to be addressed; for example, many voters walked considerable distances to cast their votes, and this may indicate why turnout was low. Finally, an independent election authority is needed to oversee all future elections to ensure consistency throughout the country in the presentation of ballots and the physical layout of polling stations and to help educate the public about the process of voting. The election authority is being established, but it is unclear when it will be operational.[11]

In addition to the constitution, a draft election bill has been prepared, but it is unclear how it will address the shortcomings of the 2002 election process. The draft election bill may contain provisions concerning election campaign finances, or these may be regulated by a separate piece of legislation. However, at present elections are small-scale and localized; it may not be until the constitution is implemented and political parties emerge that detailed provisions regulating campaign finances will be introduced.

A major official policy document published in 1999 stresses the separation of each branch of government.[12] Significant political reforms of 1998 effectively passed royal powers to a council of ministers who are elected through a secret ballot by the National Assembly representatives. The National Assembly has become increasingly critical of ministries, and recent debates have raised serious concerns over policy issues. However, there is still a widespread belief that the National Assembly is not yet fully independent of external private influences (business concerns, social networks), and reports of the National Assembly debates indicate that it remains strongly conservative.

The civil service was until very recently the main employer for young graduates in Bhutan. Selection is based on academic qualifications; for many this meant being given further training before entering their respective ministry. The current head of the Royal Civil Service Commission, a progressive, has been emphasizing the need for civil service matters to be dealt with efficiently and openly rather than being delayed. Some Bhutanese complain about the inefficiency and the contradictory advice provided by low-level officials—for example, in explaining how to obtain a business license or submit a contract tender.[13] As a result, such reform has widespread popular support.

While the Bhutanese researcher Lham Dorji comments that "the use of the term [civil society] within western contexts creates room for confusion in identifying civil society within our own context," civil society in Bhutan is limited.[14] A few nongovernmental organizations (NGOs) are emerging that focus on gender, education, environmental issues, and providing training for people with disabilities, but as yet there is no formal mechanism for the involvement of civil society organizations in the decision-making process. Outside Bhutan, mainly in Nepal and India, a variety of groups and organizations established by Nepalese refugees focus on critical human rights issues. Once Bhutan's constitution is formally enacted, it is possible that it will create new opportunities for civil society to emerge by engaging the people more fully in the political process and enabling them to develop new networks of association: For example, the emergence of parents' groups to voice concerns over educational matters or access for children with disabilities to special needs education. This may be enhanced if the Office of Legal Affairs evolves into a fully fledged ministry of justice with, as suggested by the European Union, "a Human Rights Unit to both promote human rights as well as interact with external agencies." This reference appears to foresee civil society developing and new nongovernmental organizations being established in the country.[15]

There is no diversity of independently run media in Bhutan. *Kuensel* is the only national newspaper; it is available in English, Dzongkha, and Nepali. Originally government owned, *Kuensel* was privatized in 1992. In general it is not very critical of government policy or officials. However, editorials questioning government efforts toward good governance are increasing and are positive signs of a change in the media. Although there are rumors of various individuals being offended by the tone of certain editorials, it appears the authors are able to continue publishing without interference.

The Bhutan Broadcasting Service is government run and similarly does not offer the public any critical assessment of government policies.[16] The Internet is available and has been unrestricted in Bhutan since a second Internet provider was introduced in 2004. Access is gradually being introduced throughout the country. One positive contribution to freedom of speech in Bhutan has been the introduction by

*Kuensel* of KuenselOnLine. The section "From the Readers" provides a forum for the public to raise topics and engage in online discussion. Although analysts have acknowledged that some comments from readers are screened out, the range of topics is wide, and government policies and officials (though rarely named) are openly debated and criticized. This, however, is a forum in which opinions are expressed with a degree of anonymity. There remains a deeply ingrained reluctance to criticize officials openly because such criticism is viewed as disrespectful.

*Recommendations*
- The requirement for the national identity card for voters should be dropped until the Department of Registration is able to issue national identity cards more efficiently.
- Ballot boxes must be standardized, with visual and verbal instructions displayed on the boxes in order to make the electoral process simpler for voters. The location of polling stations should be reconsidered in light of the low turnout for the 2002 gup elections.
- Bhutan Broadcasting Service should be placed under an independent broadcasting board. News media sources should be diversified and not solely under government control.
- Grassroots civic education programs should be developed to ensure public engagement and understanding of the democratic reforms being introduced.

## CIVIL LIBERTIES – 3.36

At present no separate bill of rights sets out the civil liberties of Bhutanese citizens. Although there has been some recent questioning of traditional values, a general consensus, even among young educated Bhutanese, maintains the significance of traditional patterns of social interaction and respect toward elders and social superiors.[17] [*Editor's note:* The draft constitution enumerates for the first time the civil liberties to be granted to Bhutanese citizens, including equality before the law, freedoms of assembly and religion, and freedom from torture or cruel punishment. (Article 7) It also establishes that Bhutanese citizens have a duty to preserve the nation's cultural heritage and to act in aid of the laws by reporting crimes, including those committed by government agents (Article 8)]. There are no reports of the arbitrary or unlawful deprivation of life by the government or its agents. In March 2004, the death penalty was formally abolished. Prison conditions in Bhutan have improved significantly since visits by the International Committee of the Red Cross (ICRC) in the mid-1990s. According to Amnesty International, 11 possible prisoners of conscience from eastern Bhutan are currently serving prison sentences. Four had completed their sentences but had not been released. There were a further 50 political prisoners from southern Bhutan. One such prisoner was sentenced to life imprisonment because he was formerly a member of the Druk National Congress, which is banned.[18] Concern over the treatment and welfare of prisoners has been taken into account in recent structural changes in the design of new court buildings, police, and criminal procedures. Torture is officially prohibited.

There have been no recent murders or extrajudicial killings of political opponents or peace activists in Bhutan. Although there are unverified reports of abuse by the armed forces and the police, mainly toward Southern Bhutanese, no arbitrary arrests have been reported recently. Rather, there are unconfirmed reports of police checking Southern Bhutanese papers and withholding important certificates, without which the individuals are placed in a potentially vulnerable position. The introduction of a computerized charge sheet and the requirements of the civil and criminal court procedure code in 2001 make arbitrary arrest very difficult.

The 2001 civil and criminal court procedure code ensures that all detainees are brought before the court as swiftly as possible. Recent reforms have significantly increased the speed with which trials are heard by the courts (see "Rule of Law"). Abuses by non-state actors are not tolerated. However, Bhutanese women privately acknowledge that it is only recently that the Royal Bhutan Police have begun to take cases of domestic violence seriously. The Royal Bhutan Police have undergone training on human rights and are aware of the importance of following the correct procedures when detaining and charging individuals. However, the process of education will have to be ongoing in order to change ingrained attitudes.

There is a right of petition and appeal through the formal court process up to the king. However, it is unclear to what extent ordinary Bhutanese, especially those in rural areas, understand this system. The High Court has carried out various workshops to increase understanding, and several district court judges have toured their respective districts to explain the role and use of the courts. Yet issues of distance and a social disinclination to approach high officials may hamper effective and meaningful access to and use of the right of petition and appeal.

Compared to those in other parts of South Asia, Bhutanese women enjoy greater freedom and equality with men. The right to inherit often passes property to women rather than men. However, in some respects Bhutanese women are still not equal with their male counterparts. Gender inequalities remain in school enrollment as well as functional literacy. Women still do not receive equal pay with their male counterparts. In August 2003, the National Assembly formally enacted legislation to prevent trafficking in women and children, and this was underscored in the penal code enacted in 2004. There is no reported problem of trafficking in women or children in Bhutan.[19]

The government recently established a National Commission for Women and Children designed to monitor implementation of women's and children's human rights. Eventually the commission will also be empowered to receive and investigate complaints of human rights violations. Given its early stage of development, it is unclear how effective the commission will be in its role. Its legitimacy will depend on how truly independent it is from government and it effectiveness on whether it is adequately staffed and resourced.[20]

Although some women have been appointed to higher positions in the government and NGOs, including the first female district court judge in 2003, a strong need remains to enhance women's access to and active participation at all levels of government. The NGO RENEW has noted that "a traditional lack of education for girls has resulted in significantly lower levels of achievement for Bhutanese women, who continue to be highly underrepresented in higher-skilled and higher-paid professions." It also notes women continue to be subject to "indirect forms of gender bias" in both home and workplace.[21] The number of women in the National Assembly is gradually increasing, although women are still notably reluctant to stand for election. In the gup elections of 2002, there were no women candidates in any of the gewogs, and the proportion of women who voted compared to the number eligible to vote was significantly lower than for male voters.[22]

The government recognizes the importance of freedom of religion and conscience and is seeking to balance that fundamental right with a desire to preserve Bhutan's own religious traditions. Bhutan is officially a Buddhist country. [*Editor's note:* The draft constitution maintains the role of Mahayana Buddhism as the official religion in Bhutan and requires all religious institutions to act "to promote the spiritual heritage of the country." (Article 3)] At present, the state formally supports the Central Monk Body of the Drukpa Kagyu sect. The state does not interfere in the appointment of religious or spiritual leaders. To a lesser degree, state funds are made available for Nyingma monasteries and temples. The Nyingma sect is more prominent in central and eastern Bhutan, and relations between the two sects are generally positive.

A significant Hindu population lives chiefly in the southern districts, although not all Southern Bhutanese are Hindu, and many would describe their religious practices as syncretic (in particular, those descended from Tamang and Gurung migrants may be Buddhist from birth).[23] Buddhists do not view the Hindu deities as separate from those of the Buddhist pantheon, and Hindus sometimes worship in Buddhist temples. Hindu festivals are recognized by the state and are openly celebrated. Information on the amount of state support for Hindu religious sites or teachers is unavailable. Until 1990 five *pathshalas* (religious teaching institutions) operated in Bhutan, but they were closed following disturbances in southern Bhutan. By 1999, two pathshalas had been reopened to provide Sanskrit training for the performance of Hindu rituals. *Sadhus* (Hindu holy men) are not uncommon sights in Thimphu and the southern districts, and are treated respectfully by all communities.

The small and gradually increasing Christian population is drawn primarily, though not exclusively, from among the Southern Bhutanese. Various reports suggest official moves to prevent freedom of worship in the late 1990s and early 2000. The general trend is tolerance toward the Christian community. However, Christians are still not permitted to proselytize actively. Employers are aware of Christian employees, but there is no active discrimination against them.[24]

In all parts of society, the majority of Bhutanese are respectful toward other religions. However, at present no specific legislation in Bhutan prohibits discrimination on the basis of religion. While the majority of Bhutanese view the choice of religious belief as a private matter, one does encounter occasional skepticism over the reasons for conversion. Conversion to certain evangelical forms of Christianity among those residing in the refugee camps and Kathmandu has politicized religion. This is in turn linked to a deep concern among educated Bhutanese over the targeting of Bhutan by evangelical missionaries and the use of financial incentives to gain converts. [*Editor's note:* The draft constitution ensures that all Bhutanese will enjoy religious freedom, although there is a prohibition on "inducement" to change religions, which may restrict proselytizing (Article 7).]

No one ethnic or linguistic group dominates in Bhutan. The Ngalong, Sharchop, and Bumthaps, together with the smaller linguistic groups and nomads of Laya, Lingzhi, and Merak Sakteng, share a common religion and have been treated as part of one nation since the 17th century. In particular, Buddhism is central to the identity of the Ngalong, Sharchop, and central Bhutanese and unites these populations with a shared cultural heritage. The monarchy has its historical roots in central and northeastern Bhutan, and these links serve to unite the various linguistic and ethnic groups. Cross-marriage between ethnic and linguistic groups has been increasing.

The Druk National Congress (DNC) sought in the early 1990s to gain support in the east of Bhutan by arguing that the Sharchop (Eastern Bhutanese) were being marginalized by the central government and that the DNC would be better placed to provide for the Sharchop. In contemporary Bhutan, Sharchop are not marginalized, and indeed they are active at all levels of government, the judiciary, and private enterprise. However, in addition to the eastern prisoners of conscience noted above, Amnesty International has noted discrimination against Southern Bhutanese in terms of access to employment and higher education. Amnesty has also cited difficulty among Southern Bhutanese in obtaining security clearance certificates, which are issued by the police and required for activities such as acquiring a passport and gaining admission to school.[25] The smaller groups, for example the Doyas and the nomadic peoples of Merak Sakteng, are supported by the government in maintaining their cultural identities within Bhutan. All ethnic groups are represented in the National Assembly, although no official figures on representation are available.

Nepali settlers have been arriving in the southern region since the late 19th and early 20th centuries. The settlers came from a range of ethnic and linguistic groups from primarily eastern Nepal. These groups are collectively referred to by the Bhutanese as "the people of the southern border" or Lhotshampa. The majority are Hindu, although some are Buddhist.[26] Since the 1980s Bhutanese from the central region have been settling in urban centers that have been developed in the south as well.

In the late 1980s, people of Nepalese descent claimed that the Citizenship Act of 1985, the manner in which the 1988 census was conducted, and other new government policies discriminated against them. For example, they objected to the re-emphasis of *driglam namzha* and specifically the requirement to wear traditional Bhutanese costume when entering public offices and temples, closure of Sanskrit schools, and the promotion of Dzongkha language teaching. According to the government of Bhutan, the emphasis on Bhutanese cultural traditions and language was designed to promote a cohesive national identity in face of mounting external pressures that were perceived to be eroding Bhutan's unique cultural tradition.[27] The disagreement led to a series of public protests in the southern dzongkhags and serious confrontation with the army and police in the early 1990s.[28] Since that time, a significant number of people of Nepali descent claiming Bhutanese citizenship have resided in refugee camps established by United Nations High Commissioner for Refugees (UNHCR) in eastern Nepal.

In 1994 the governments of Nepal and Bhutan established a joint verification process. Under the terms of this agreement, two teams of Bhutanese and Nepalese officials would examine each of the refugees' claims to Bhutanese citizenship, and those deemed to be genuine Bhutanese would be permitted to return and settle in Bhutan. The verification exercise carried out in Khudunabari camp categorized 70.55 percent as having emigrated from Bhutan voluntarily and only 2.4 percent as genuine refugees.[29] However, the joint verification process was disrupted when frustrated residents violently assaulted Bhutanese officials on a visit to the Jhapa camp in December 2003.[30] To date, there are no reports of the process resuming.

No legislation prohibits discrimination on the grounds of disability. Two institutions educate and train students with disabilities. However, although disability has been recognized as a separate issue, it is still treated mainly as a health concern. Access to employment is very difficult, with little provision for physical access and equality of opportunity. There is no provision to ensure that information about government services and decisions is made available in formats and settings accessible to people with disabilities. This reflects the fact that educational facilities for a range of disabilities are still being established and developed in the country rather than an intentional oversight.

At present the government is the largest employer in Bhutan through the civil service and education. Currently, no antidiscrimination legislation applies to employment and occupation. There is a Labor Act, and a draft of new labor laws has been prepared. However, employment laws and, more particularly, antidiscrimination laws have not been seen as a priority. At present, no legal provisions permit the formation of trade unions. This is due primarily to the small-scale agricultural nature of most of the Bhutanese economy, the use of foreign labor on various large-scale projects, and the only gradual emergence of private enterprise. People are not forced to join any organizations in the country.

At present, protests and demonstrations are prohibited. However, there is a right to assemble provided that it does not contravene the provisions of the civil and criminal court procedure code 2001 and penal code 2004. Under these codes, it is lawful to assemble provided that those assembling do not to engage in violent conduct "deleterious to the public order and tranquility."[31] Associations of laypeople who raise money for religious institutions are commonplace, and public events are held without any interference. As the majority of Bhutanese do not live in urban centers, large groups of people are unusual apart from during religious festivals or other celebrations.

*Recommendations*

- Human rights training should be provided to the army and police force on a regular basis.
- New labor laws establishing the rights of workers and duties of employers should be enacted, in particular with regard to preventing discrimination against workers with disabilities and ensuring gender equality.
- The human rights of all people residing within Bhutan, not only those officially recognized as Bhutanese, must be clearly set forth in the new constitution and enforced following its enactment.
- Media and government campaigns should promote public awareness of the problems experienced by children and adults with disabilities, and antidiscrimination laws should be enacted for workers with disabilities.

- Policies should be developed and implemented to enhance women's access to political forums. More research needs to be done into what is preventing Bhutanese women from participating fully as candidates and voters.

## RULE OF LAW – 4.23

A modern code of law was enacted in Bhutan in 1959. These Supreme Laws cover land, marriage, inheritance, weights and measures, and criminal matters. The laws present the first recognizably modern law text in Bhutan. Importantly, in the opening statement they contain a declaration that all Bhutanese are equal before the law, although many Bhutanese feel that there is still an inequality in treatment. For example, some Bhutanese have complained about cases settled by judges who are connected to a socially more influential party.[32] However, it is unclear whether these comments might simply reflect personal dissatisfaction with judicial verdicts. Since their enactment, the Supreme Laws have been modified and separate acts based on the original chapters of the Supreme Laws passed.

Government records indicate that the home ministry used to interfere with the High Court on a regular basis. However, during the last 12 years, the High Court has asserted its independence, notably in the acquittal of five Southern Bhutanese suspected of being "anti-nationals" (terrorists): The decision was opposed by the home ministry, but the High Court emphasized the correctness of the acquittals.[33] The separation of powers was reaffirmed in Section 2 of the civil and criminal court procedure code 2001 and re-emphasized at the beginning of the 80th session of the National Assembly in 2002.

The judges at district and High Court level are free from interference by both the executive and the legislature. The National Assembly does have the right to ask the High Court to send a representative to explain the latter's draft legislation. Recently, the chief justice appeared before the National Assembly to explain and clarify aspects of the draft penal code, which was under debate. As the legislative body, the National Assembly has the remit to scrutinize all legislation, and the High Court must comply with its decisions. The National Assembly discusses judicial practices, notably sentencing policies, but only on a consultative basis.[34] For example, in some cases in which the death penalty was mandated by law, many representatives called for the death penalty to be used, but the High Court maintained its practice of passing life sentences. On March 20, 2004, the king abolished the death penalty.

The gups and chimis are responsible for communicating the resolutions of the National Assembly and new laws to their constituents. In a recent initiative, district court judges have started to conduct educational tours of their districts in an attempt to ensure that ordinary, remote villagers are aware of how the contemporary legal system operates. The response to these tours has been very positive. However, it is unclear how successful this process is in practice. The volume of legislation has significantly increased, and other methods of informing the people at the local level are required to ensure that all people are able to understand the new laws affecting them and how to use those laws as required.

In September 2003, a National Judicial Commission was established to coordinate legislation and judicial appointments. Accordingly, judicial appointments are confirmed by the king based on the recommendation of the chief justice and the National Judicial Commission. Appointment and promotion are based on ability rather than on length of service or social connections. Legal education in Bhutan has significantly developed over the past 12 years.

Previously, judges were typically trained by working as bench clerks before being appointed. The lack of formal legal education was noted by senior members of the judiciary as a major drawback to the development of an efficient and, more important, independent judiciary. As a result, a National Legal Course was established in 1994. Since 1994, 74 young lawyers with LLB and National Legal Course certificates have graduated and entered the judiciary and various government ministries. A number of the young lawyers have undertaken advanced studies abroad. This young cadre of lawyers is enabling the judiciary to overcome public misgivings regarding the independence of the courts and the quality of justice being provided by the courts.

During the 1990s, the High Court established itself as fully independent of the executive; this marks one of the main steps toward the current process of political transformation in Bhutan. However, as stated in the civil and criminal court procedure code 2001, "any party having fully exhausted the judicial appeal process and still aggrieved by the decision of the Court may appeal to His Majesty." The retention of the traditional right of appeal to the king is important for maintaining continuity in tradition and acts as a reminder of the pivotal role of the monarchy in Bhutan, even as it is transformed into a constitutional monarchy. All appeals are heard by the Royal Advisory Council, which examines cases on behalf of the monarch. The Royal Advisory Council has limited powers in order to preserve the independence of the High Court.[35]

Contrary to what some writers suggest, rules and court procedures have been in place since the inception of the contemporary legal system in the 1960s, and the civil and criminal court procedure code 2001 represents recognition of the importance of constantly monitoring and amending procedural rules as required.[36] Among its detailed provisions are a clear statement of the presumption of innocence until proven guilty, the right to a *jabmi* (independent legal counsel), and a reiteration of the opening section of the Supreme Laws that all Bhutanese, irrespective of rank and status, will be treated equally by the court.[37] Legal aid is provided to those requiring it. The monitoring of procedures appears to be working well.[38] However, in some instances litigants feel that the court did not treat them fairly or equally.[39] There remain traces of hesitancy about engaging in formal court procedures, in part based on a lingering mistrust of officials in general. A draft evidence bill is pending that will set out in more detail the rules of evidence to be applied in the courts. Ordinary Bhutanese remain ill-informed of their current rights, the national laws, and the operation of the court system. However, sections of Bhutanese society have resorted to the courts recently to challenge policies of, for example, the City Corporation of Thimphu and its land-restructuring policies for the capital.

At present, although one can purchase copies of some of the current legislation, not all legislation is readily available. Copies of the laws are provided to all gups, but it is not clear how able the gups are to interpret the laws and thereby provide advice to ordinary villagers. Some analysts have raised doubts about the literacy of gup and *mangmi* (assistant to the gup).[40]

The Office of Legal Affairs was established in 2000. In effect, this office acts on behalf of the Bhutanese state in civil and criminal matters. It is separate from the High Court and, more important, from the ministry for home affairs. One area that the office is actively tackling is public corruption, as demonstrated in the recent election bribery case in

Chukha (see "Accountability and Public Voice"). However, the office is understaffed and requires more trained prosecutors.

The police and military do not interfere in the political process. However, the Royal Bhutan Police still remain under the supervision of the armed forces, and it is far from clear how effective civilian state control is of the military.[41] Although it is difficult to obtain information from both the military (army) and police about incidents concerning internal discipline and possible abuse by officers, reports of abuses do appear periodically in the national newspaper.[42]

Private ownership of land is generally respected. During the National Assembly sessions in both 2003 and 2004, debates arose concerning discrepancies in land holdings as revealed by a more accurate cadastral survey still being completed. Using the current land-surveying techniques, a significant percentage of holdings have been found to be larger than what was recorded on land titles based on the previous survey. There was deep concern that the government would repossess the excess land (under the Land Act 1979 the maximum landholding is 25 acres). However, the assembly accepted a five-point proposal submitted by the cabinet under which a payment for "genuine excess" can be made up to June 30, 2007. No details are provided as to how genuine excess will be demonstrated.[43]

Many Bhutanese are either receiving grants of land from the government or acquiring land by private purchase, particularly in the agriculturally more productive southern districts, notably Gelephu. In part this highlights the increased mobility of the Bhutanese population, allowing them to leave their original settlements and pursue new lives and careers in other parts of the country. However, concerns have been expressed that it will be difficult for refugees returning under the terms of the Joint Verification Process to reclaim their former property if it has been transferred to a new owner. It is unclear whether substitute land of equivalent value will be provided in the event that the original holdings have been reallocated.

### Recommendations

- Wider education of the general public, not only of local and district level officials, about the legal system and individual rights under law should take place.
- The public should have wider access to legal texts through government offices and district courts.

- The army and police force should be made accountable to the civilian government by being placed under the home ministry.

## ANTICORRUPTION AND TRANSPARENCY – 3.34

The Bhutanese government is actively streamlining its business and commercial regulations and registration requirements using forms that are available online. However, ordinary Bhutanese find many of the regulations confusing and the processes cumbersome and time-consuming. The economy is heavily controlled by the government, although this should be understood as reflecting the state-led process of modernization since the 1960s.

The state is seeking to encourage the development of private enterprise, in part in recognition of the need to generate wider employment opportunities for the growing educated population. Foreign aid and overseas assistance constitute a significant percentage of the Bhutanese government's own budget and fund many development and social welfare programs run mainly by the government. These funds are, according to aid providers, well managed and carefully administered by the government. Public disclosure of the interests of public officials is limited and is not subject to media scrutiny. No list of interests or income is available for either members of the executive or the National Assembly. Although the state seeks to prevent conflicts of interest in the private sector, it is generally recognized that conflicts do exist.

The auditing provisions that review the spending of government funds are clearly directed at preventing the misappropriation of funds by government officials, as well as reprimanding those who fail to perform their duties properly. The Royal Audit Commission and the auditor general exercise very strong scrutiny of public sector financial management, raising concerns over weaknesses and making recommendations for their remedy. In the "Auditor General's Advisory Series 2003," he directly draws attention to everything from minor oversights to gross irregularities, which the relevant ministry or public body is instructed to address. Furthermore, the advisory contains critical comments on the failure by various ministries and even the cabinet to follow correct tendering procedures. The Royal Audit Authority also urges "that where the instances of lapses are considerable" instant administrative or disciplinary actions be taken "for the overall national interest."[44]

Penalties are imposed for noncompliance with reporting and other requirements. Internal audits are increasingly effective as indicated by the downward trend in fiscal irregularities. Project accounting and financial management are improving gradually, although at present skilled chartered accountants are reported to be in short supply in Bhutan.[45]

Allegations of corruption by government officials are investigated and prosecuted without prejudice. The Office of Legal Affairs is responsible for investigating and prosecuting those officials charged with corruption. Press reports reveal a strong determination by the government and the judiciary to send out a clear message that corruption by public officials will be taken seriously and will be prosecuted. However, although the media do report allegations of corruption, media debate is limited. After the recent royal advisory council elections, the Chukha district court sentenced 16 people to prison for bribery.[46] Karma Dorji, a businessman who stood for election, publicly declared that he paid 12 members of the Dzongkhag Development Committee 5,000 Nu ($110) each to vote for him. Those sentenced included three private business men, four gups (and one former gup), five mangmi, and one National Assembly representative. The sentences were upheld on appeal by the High Court of Justice.[47]

The apparent acceptability of bribery in the Chukha case has worrying implications. Although corruption is not endemic in Bhutan in comparison to other countries in the region, the issue does deeply concern government officials, the judiciary, and ordinary citizens. It is difficult to distinguish between popular myths of corruption and actual acts of corruption. Those who discussed the Chukha verdict believed that the verdict was just and appropriate, while some Bhutanese suggested that payments by potential candidates were not unusual. Indeed, it has been suggested that bribery is commonplace in the tender award system.[48] Accordingly, the Bhutanese authorities are preparing a prevention of corruption bill that will specifically address public corruption. Currently, whistleblowers have no specific legal protection. However, the Office of Legal Affairs does investigate all cases of bribery and corruption reported to it.

Access to government information is gradually improving, especially as Web sites are developed and information made available through them. However, at present it remains quite difficult to gain access to a full range of information on government policies, audits, and expenditures.

The legislature has limited control over the budget-setting process of the executive, although National Assembly members do challenge the budget. A lack of skilled personnel makes it difficult to ensure that the budget-making process is clear and that government accounts are published in a timely fashion. There is a tendering process, with advertisements appearing in *Kuensel* and the necessary documentation available on a Web site. However, as the auditor general notes, lapses have occurred in the tendering process that need to be addressed.

Education is free from corruption, notably the payment of bribes for good grades, as the examination board is located in India and the examination papers are marked outside the country. Although competition for entry to certain senior high schools in the country is now increasing, there are no reports of bribery to gain admission.

## Recommendations

- Public access to routine documents, including draft legislation, should be enhanced through their provision either to all gups or to local government offices.
- Civil service salaries should be increased to minimize the possible temptation to accept or seek bribes.
- The contract tendering process should be simplified and strengthened. The process of award should be transparent to discourage corruption.
- Additional skilled financial auditors should be trained to further strengthen the Royal Audit Authority.

### NOTES

[1] The title Zhabdrung literally means "at the feet of" or "in the presence of" and is the title given to the lineage of spiritual rulers of Bhutan.

[2] *Driglam namzha* is often referred to as a dress code and is "the path to maintain harmonious behavior" (*Driglam Namzha [Bhutanese etiquette]: A Manual* [Thimphu: National Library of Bhutan, 1999]). It includes various elements: observing religious practices; conducting certain ceremonies linked to Bhutanese national identity; maintaining trust and respect; proper behavior in the presence of superiors; and how to eat, walk, and present oneself in society; as well as the appropriate form of dress for visiting public offices and temples. See also Dasho Khadro, *dPal ldan 'Brug pa'i khrims kyi lhan khag nang rgyun skyong 'bad dgo pa'i sgrig lam* [The Code of Conduct to Be Diligently Maintained in the Court of Justice of the Glorious Drukpa] (Thimphu: Royal High Court of Justice, 1997). Karma Phuntsho, a Bhutanese Buddhist scholar, presents a short

critique of *driglam namzha* in his article "Echoes of Ancient Ethos: Reflections on Some Popular Bhutanese Social Themes," in K. Ura and S. Kinga, eds., *The Spider and the Piglet* (Thimphu: Centre of Bhutan Studies, 2004), 564–80.

3 "His Majesty presents the draft Constitution to the lhengye zhungtsho," *Kuensel*, 27 November 2004, http://www.kuenselonline.com/article.php?sid=4745.

4 Constitution Drafting Committee, "Draft Constitution of the Kingdom of Bhutan," 2005, http://www.constitution.bt/draft_constitution_en.pdf

5 Karma Ura, *The First Universal Suffrage Election at County (Gewog) Level in Bhutan* (Chiba: Institute of Developing Economies, discussion paper, 2004). Also Karma Ura, *Bureaucracy and Peasantry in Decentralization in Bhutan* (Chiba: Institute of Developing Economies, discussion paper, December 2004).

6 A fuller discussion of the causes of the refugee issue is beyond the scope of this paper. For various perspectives on this issue see M. Hutt, *Bhutan: Perspectives on Conflict and Dissent* (Gartmore: Kiscadale Press, 1994; in particular, the articles by Jigme Thinley and Kinley Dorji, which present the Bhutanese perspective on the issue) and M. Hutt, *Unbecoming Citizens: Culture, nationhood and the flight of refugees from Bhutan* (Delhi: Oxford University Press, 2003).

7 C. Hainzl, *The Legal System of Bhutan: A Descriptive Analysis* (Vienna: Ludwig Boltzmann Institute for Human Rights, 1998), 9; and "Bhutan Civics" (Thimphu: Royal Government of Bhutan [RGOB], 1999), 44–45.

8 T. Mathou, *Bhoutan: Dernier Royaume Boudhhiste de l'Himalaya* (Paris: Kailash Editions, 1998), 187.

9 T. Mathou, "Bhutan: Political Reform in a Buddhist Monarchy" *Journal of Bhutan Studies*, 1 (1): 1999, 114–44.

10 Ura, *The First Universal*; Ura, *Bureaucracy and Peasantry in Decentralization in Bhutan*.

11 Karma Ura, *The First Universal* (2004), has provided a detailed consideration of the 2002 gup elections with recommendations that should be carefully considered by the Election Authority once it is functioning.

12 *Enhancing Good Governance: Promoting Efficiency, Transparency and Accountability for Gross National Happiness* (Thimphu: RGOB, 1999).

13 These were some of the examples provided during various conversations with a range of Bhutanese during a recent visit to Bhutan.

14 "Bhutanese Perspective on Civil Society," Kuensel, 13 January 2005, http://www.kuenselonline.com/article.php?sid=4929.

15 "Bhutan and the European Community Co-operation Strategy 2002–2006" (Brussels: European Commission, 21 March 2003), 9, http://europa.eu.int/comm/external_relations/bhutan/csp/index.htm.

16 *Bhutan – 2004 Annual Report* (Paris: Reporters Without Borders, 2004), http://www.rsf.fr/article.php3?id_article=10153&var_recherche=Bhutan.

17 Karma Phuntsho, "Echoes of Ancient Ethos: Reflections on some popular Bhutanese social themes," in K. Ura and S. Kinga, eds., *The Spider and the Piglet* (Thimphu: Centre of Bhutan Studies, 2004), 564–80.

18 "Bhutan" (London and New York: Amnesty International [AI], 2004), http://web.amnesty.org/report2004/btn-summary-eng.

[19] Author interviews with women in Bhutan between 2001 and 2004.

[20] "Gender equality guaranteed,"Kuensel, 8 May 2004, http://www.kuenselonline.com/article.php?sid=4039.

[21] *RENEW, Respect Educate Nurture Empower Women* (Thimphu: Kuensel Corporation, 2004), 4.

[22] Karma Ura, *The First Universal* (2004), 12.

[23] See M. Hutt, *Unbecoming Citizens,* 101.

[24] Author interviews; F. Pommaret, "Himalaya: la colonisation des ames," in C. B. Lavenir, ed., *Missions: Cahiers de Mediologie.* (Paris: Fayard, 2004), 140–47.

[25] See "Bhutan" (AI, 2004), http://web.amnesty.org/report2004/btn-summary-eng and earlier reports.

[26] For greater detail see F. Pommaret, "Ethnic Mosaic: Peoples of Bhutan," in C. Schiklegruber and F. Pommaret, eds., *Bhutan: Mountain Fortress of the Gods* (London: Serindia, 1997), 43–59. On the linguistic groups of Bhutan see G. Van Driem, Dzongkha (Leiden: Research School of Asian, African and Amerindian Studies [CNWS], 1998), ch. 1.

[27] See Jigme Thinley, "A kingdom besieged," and Kinley Dorji, "Bhutan's Current Crisis: A View from Thimphu," in M. Hutt, ed., *Bhutan: Perspectives* (1994), 43–76 and 77–95.

[28] For a discussion of the complex background leading up to the flight of the refugees and the various perspectives, see Jigme Thinley, "A kingdom besieged," and Kinley Dorji, "Bhutan's Current Crisis: A View from Thimphu," in M. Hutt, ed., *Bhutan: Perspectives* (1994), 43–76 and 77–95. The refugees' perspective is set out in M. Hutt (2003) *Unbecoming Citizens.*

[29] "Bhutan" (AI, 2004), http://web.amnesty.org/report2004/btn-summary-eng.

[30] "Bhutanese JVT officials attacked in Jhapa," *Kuensel,* 23 December 2003, http://www.kuenselonline.com/article.php?sid=3572.

[31] Penal Code 2004, Sec. 436, based on the National Security Act 1992, Sec 12.

[32] Kuenselonline "From the Readers" has threads entitled "Drangpon: a change in name only" and "Justice delayed is justice denied," http://kuenselonline.com/phorum/read.php?f=2&i=30982 and http://kuenselonline.com/phorum/read.php?f=2&i=30867.

[33] B. Shaw, "Aspects of the 'Southern Problem' and Nation-Building in Bhutan," in M. Hutt, ed., *Bhutan: Perspectives* (1994), 141–64, 149.

[34] Death Penalty News (AI Index: ACT 53/001/2004, 1 June 2004), http://web.amnesty.org/library/Index/ENGACT530012004.

[35] C. Hainzl, *The Legal System of Bhutan* (1998).

[36] See, for example, A. Sinha, *Himalayan Kingdom Bhutan: Tradition, Transition and Transformation* (New Delhi: Indus Publishing Company, 2001).

[37] *Civil and Criminal Procedure Code* 2001, Sections 3–7, 32–33. Supreme Laws refer to the Thrimzhung Chenmo, the first modern law code, in 17 chapters, passed by the National Assembly in 1959.

[38] Author interviews with ordinary Bhutanese, police, and lawyers.

[39] See *Strategy for Danish Development Co-operation,* http://www.um.dk/Publikationer/Danida/English/CountriesAndRegions/Bhutan.bhutan.De.

[40] Karma Ura, *The First Universal* (2004).

[41] Some suggest that the military and police are under the home ministry. However, various diagrams of the Bhutanese system of government depict the armed forces (which include the Royal Bhutan Police) as separate. *Enhancing good governance* (RGOB, 1990); "Window on Bhutan" (RGOB 2000, 2002).

[42] "Officer shot dead by constable," *Kuensel,* 4 September 2004, 1.

[43] "Assembly endorses excess land rule proposed by lhengye zhungtso," *Kuensel,* 25 July 2004, http://kuenselonline.com/article.php?sid=3100.

[44] "Auditor General's Advisory Series 2003," (RGOB), http://www.raa.gov.bt/contents/papers/agadvisory-series2003.htm.

[45] "Strengthening financial auditing," *Kuensel,* 5 July 2004, http://www.kuenselonline.com/article.php?sid=4244.

[46] For further details, see "16 Prosecuted for Bribery in Chukha Election," *Kuensel,* 22 May 2004, http://www.kuenselonline.com/article.php?sid =4090; "16 Imprisoned for Three to Five Years in Chukha," *Kuensel,* 5 June 2004, http://www.kuenselonline.com/article.php?sid=4140.

[47] "Chukha judgement upheld," *Kuensel,* 7 August 2004, http://www.kuenselonline.com/article.php?sid=4367.

[48] A recent thread on *Kuenselonline* entitled "corruption" reflects the general concern about corruption, whether real or imagined; see http://www.kuenselonline.com/phorum/read.php?f=2 &i=31742&T=31742.

# BOLIVIA

CAPITAL:  La Paz (administrative),
Sucre (judicial)
POPULATION:  8.8 million
GNI PER CAPITA:  $900

**SCORES**

ACCOUNTABILITY AND PUBLIC VOICE: 3.54
CIVIL LIBERTIES: 4.12
RULE OF LAW: 3.52
ANTICORRUPTION AND TRANSPARENCY: 3.12
(scores are based on a scale of 0 to 7, with
0 representing weakest and 7 representing
strongest performance)

*Donna Lee Van Cott*

## INTRODUCTION

Between January 2003 and November 2004 Bolivia underwent more tumultuous changes than any other country in Latin America apart from Haiti. On October 17, 2003, President Gonzalo Sánchez de Lozada fled the country following five days of violent conflict between government security forces and a broad array of civil society groups in the capital and its outskirts. The violence—stemming from opposition to the president's decision to export the country's natural gas through a port in Chile— left an estimated 59 to 82 persons dead and hundreds injured.[1] Sánchez de Lozada's use of excessive military force against mostly unarmed indigenous protesters cost him the support of the *mestizo* (mixed-race) middle class, coalition partners, his vice president, and, ultimately, the U.S. embassy.

The uprising followed a violent revolt against an IMF-mandated income tax increase in February 2003, widespread popular mobilizations against government economic policies in 2001 and 2000, and a

**Donna Lee Van Cott** is assistant professor of political science and Latin American studies at Tulane University. She recently completed a book on indigenous political parties in South America.

longstanding struggle between coca growers and drug eradication forces. Sánchez de Lozada and his predecessors had responded to these acts of resistance with increasingly brutal force, blaming them on isolated groups of troublemakers. Meanwhile, the country's democratic institutions were showing increasing signs of strain.

Constitutional order was preserved when Vice President Carlos Mesa, a well-regarded journalist and historian, assumed the presidency and promised to address swiftly the principal demand of the opposition: constitutional changes that would allow a popular referendum on the unpopular gas plan and the convocation of a constituent assembly. Although the main leaders of the radical opposition promised to renew violent protests if their demands were not met within 90 days, Mesa defied expectations and fulfilled his most important commitments. On February 20, 2004, he promulgated a law to reform the constitution, which the congress approved with uncharacteristic speed. Among the reforms was the legalization of binding or consultative referenda and legislative initiatives, a constituent assembly, and a measure allowing "citizens' groupings" and indigenous peoples to stand for election. The referendum on the gas issue took place on July 18, and the constituent assembly is scheduled for 2005. Moreover, Mesa made these bold moves while maintaining high popularity ratings: His approval rating was above 80 percent at the beginning of 2004; it dropped to above 60 percent the following August after 10 months of battles with the traditional political party elite and militant social movement leaders.[2]

The fragile government still faces a number of hurdles. Municipal elections in which civil society groups and indigenous peoples will compete for the first time are scheduled for December 2004; new hydrocarbon and petroleum laws must be negotiated with a fractured congress;[3] and the National Constituent Assembly must address the demands of the excluded indigenous majority and heal a widening rift between the four departments of the western highlands, where political power traditionally has resided, and the five departments of the lowland crescent, where an increasingly confident new economic elite seeks greater autonomy. Support for this and future democratic governments will depend on their ability to address the high levels of inequality and poverty that affect 70 percent of the population in the context of an economic climate that has worsened in recent years: As Mesa took office unemployment stood at 12 percent, the fiscal deficit reached

8 percent of gross domestic product, and economic growth had slowed to between 2 percent and 3 percent, down from 4 percent in the 1990s. The external debt stood at US$4.5153 billion in May 2004, equivalent to 55 percent of GDP.[4]

## ACCOUNTABILITY AND PUBLIC VOICE – 3.54

Bolivia has held regular, free, and fair elections since 1979. There are six major political parties, but no party has ever won a majority of votes. For years this led to a system in which, in the absence of an absolute majority, coalitions of parties in congress effectively chose the president. Although coalition-formation has facilitated governance at the beginning of each presidential term, the coalitions, built on patronage, are fragile and prone to erosion, leaving presidents with slim bases of support. After 18 years of relative stability, Bolivia's democratic institutions showed increasing signs of strain.

This system was challenged in October 2003, when President Sánchez de Lozada was forced to flee the country amid violent conflict over new national energy policies. Vice President Carlos Mesa assumed the presidency as provided for in the constitution.

Before the 2004 constitutional reform, only political parties were allowed to participate in elections, under rules that often set high barriers to new vehicles sponsored by popular sectors. Since 1979, parties failing to meet a 3 percent vote threshold have been subject to fines and the loss of their registration, a problem that plagued numerous indigenous parties. In addition, a politically manipulated National Electoral Court has disqualified aspiring parties owing to small and often falsified infractions. For example, the indigenous party Instrumento Político para la Soberanía de los Pueblos (IPSP) competes under the label Movement toward Socialism (MAS) because its registration repeatedly has been denied under its own name. In 2002 MAS leaders complained bitterly that the registration of rival indigenous party Indigenous Pachakutik Movement (MIP) was accepted notwithstanding numerous irregularities; they blamed the major parties, which stood to benefit from splitting the indigenous vote.

On February 20, 2004, President Mesa promulgated a law to reform the constitution that included the legalization of binding or consultative referenda and legislative initiatives and the creation of a national constituent assembly. As of September 2004 a law regulating the assembly's convocation was expected by the end of November, and elections were planned for December.

The national constituent assembly will provide unprecedented access to real decision-making power for heretofore underrepresented groups through new provisions allowing citizens' groups and indigenous peoples to put forward candidates for elected office. These groups will receive state resources for campaigning in subsequent elections in proportion to the votes they win, just like political parties, and will be allowed to form alliances with political parties. Indigenous peoples will not need to collect signatures in order to register candidates, while citizens' groups will need 2 percent of the municipal electoral registration list. As of September 2004, some 800 citizens' and indigenous groups had registered their intention to participate in the December 2004 municipal elections. However, the majority was not likely to be able to collect sufficient signatures and have them verified before the October 6 deadline, due to the lack of resources available to the electoral court.[5]

President Mesa has sponsored efforts to increase civic engagement in policymaking. For example, the July 18 gas referendum, which posed five questions, was preceded by a campaign to promote citizen awareness and involvement through more than 550 informational events throughout the country, although it is unclear whether this dialogue led to substantive policy changes. Trade union leaders criticized the referendum for not including an option authorizing nationalization of the hydrocarbon sector, and business leaders objected to the possibility of altering existing contracts. More objective observers noted that the questions were phrased to the president's best advantage. They ask voters to approve of Mesa's abrogation of his predecessor's Hydrocarbon Law and of the general thrust of Mesa's policy: to recuperate Bolivian state ownership of hydrocarbons and enhance the role of the state oil company, which had been privatized; to "use gas as a strategic resource for the achievement of a useful and sovereign outlet to the Pacific ocean"; and to use the proceeds of hydrocarbon exportation to fuel the domestic market and invest in education, healthcare, roads, and employment. Most Bolivians agree with these general principles. But the wording skirts the volatile question of nationalization of hydrocarbon production, which opponents had specifically wanted to include. Ultimately, all of the questions received support—that is, a vote of "yes"—exceeding 55 percent of votes cast, and on three of questions more than 80 percent of voters voted "yes."[6] Approximately 60 percent of eligible voters participated in the referendum.

Nongovernmental organizations (NGOs) with international funding often are able to influence policy because the government relies on international agencies for funding and technical support on many social policy issues. It is not uncommon to find the offices of international development organizations, such as Harvard's Institute for International Development, inside government ministries.

Congressional approval is required for major legislative changes, but this is typically difficult to achieve given the fragmentation of the party system. Presidents have either formed and maintained governing coalitions through patronage appointments or allowed major issues to stagnate while addressing minor issues through supreme decree. For example, the appointment of high judicial officers has been delayed for a decade, while the president has implemented indigenous peoples' rights under International Labour Organization Convention 169 by supreme decree. Thus, legislative oversight is lacking.

In August 2004, the Bolivian media exposed the high degree of political hiring and nepotism in the congress, where more than 1,000 political appointments are distributed among the political parties. In response to public outcry, congressional leaders promised to crack down on nepotism.

The government discriminated against dissenting news media when allocating state advertising funds and applied pressure for the dismissal of critical reporters. Reporters without Borders cited telephone threats, confiscation of newspapers from newsstands, and destruction of transmitters, primarily carried out by the military intelligence services.[7] For example, on October 15, 2003, two hooded men blew up the transmitter serving a Catholic radio station and a university-based television station that had criticized the government for using excessive force against demonstrators. More seriously, Reporters without Borders reported numerous abuses of journalists by Bolivian authorities during 2003, including 17 physical attacks, mainly in connection with coverage of civil unrest. Several anti-government media outlets were accused of treason during the uprising against President Sánchez de Lozada, but no prosecution resulted. In October 2003 several journalists at the state-owned television station resigned in protest over pressure not to show images of government violence.[8] Although reported abuses and harassment of journalists have declined since October 2003, in September 2004 a *La Razón* reporter was briefly denied entrance to Congress following an exposé by his newspaper on legislative nepotism and corruption.[9] Journalists are wary of a current proposal to establish a regulatory agency to monitor the press, and they often practice self-censorship. However, despite the harassment, journalists continue to publish analyses critical of the government, and diverse media outlets do function. Given the small size of the population and the low level of literacy, the number of distinct news sources available at newsstands in major cities is impressive.

*Recommendations*
- The 2005 constituent assembly should address pending issues with broad public support: the direct election of departmental governors, the elimination of immunities protecting government officials from criminal prosecution, and the creation of political institutions that incorporate indigenous authorities and values.
- The president and his anticorruption prosecutor, themselves professional journalists, should improve relations between the state and Bolivia's independent media, including by consulting journalists when drafting legislation affecting access to public information.
- The ability of political parties to influence the National Electoral Court must end. The National Electoral Court should be accountable only to unaffiliated professionals and independent governmental investigative agencies.
- Fines on political parties failing to meet vote thresholds should be eliminated.
- Rules for choosing representatives for the constituent assembly must facilitate adequate representation of politically underrepresented regions and demographic groups.

## CIVIL LIBERTIES – 4.12

Bolivia has ratified the major UN human rights conventions. The constitution, revised in 1995, 2002, and 2004, protects a wide range of civil and political rights, including liberty in religious teaching, the free expression of ideas and opinions, and association with others for legal purposes.

Nevertheless, violence against civilians is a problem. According to the nongovernmental Bolivian Permanent Assembly for Human Rights (APDHB), state-sponsored human rights violations led to the deaths of at least 120 Bolivians between September 2002 and October 13, 2003.[10] Amnesty International and Human Rights Watch expressed concern with respect to the excessive force used by the army and police in October 2003, noting that the majority of those killed were protesters who were shot when armed mainly with sticks and stones. Violent confrontations between police and protesters were common before this as well.[11] According to the APDHB, since 1985 social conflicts pitting the government against civilians have led to the deaths of 350 people and injuries to 7,000 more, while at least 12,000 have been unjustly detained. In none of these cases has a member of the police or the military been prosecuted.[12]

Reports of human rights violations declined markedly after the change in government. Mesa exercised more restraint toward protesters and relaxed the coca eradication policy, which had been linked to confrontations between police and civilians. However, human rights advocates complain that investigations of government abuses are handled internally and do not result in appropriate disciplinary action. In December 2003 Human Rights Watch complained that a "lack of cooperation by the Bolivian Armed Forces put at risk the investigation of the events of September and October" and that "military tribunals lack independence and impartiality."[13] Human rights workers complain of harassment and even attack by government officials and assert that the judicial system is too weak, inefficient, underfunded, and subject to political pressure to pursue cases properly. For example, the prosecutor general's office never received Senate-approved funds to investigate the February 2003 incidents. Arbitrary arrests and detentions continue, particularly among coca growers and trade union leaders, notwithstanding improvements in the code of criminal procedure. Prisons are severely overcrowded and underfunded, rendering them unable to meet inmates' basic health requirements. Bolivia ratified the UN Convention against Torture and Other Cruel, Inhuman or Degrading Treatment or Punishment in 1999, yet beatings and torture by inmates and prison officials are common.[14]

In 1995, the congress passed Law 1674 Against Intrafamily Domestic Violence, and regulations for its implementation were established by supreme decree in 1998. Among its most important provisions is the requirement that government officials and nongovernmental professionals providing services to victims report abuse to the police, family protection brigades (special units in the police created in all provincial capitals), the prosecutor general's office, or integrated legal services offices in municipal governments, which handle concerns regarding women and the family in more than 64 offices throughout the country. Procedures for filing complaints also have been made simpler. The first defendant prosecuted under the law, using a new oral justice forum for domestic violence, was sentenced to eight years in jail in 2002.[15]

Efforts to secure women's rights are hampered by the fact that many Bolivian women are not aware that they have rights, and significant social discrimination means that widespread education about legal equality is lacking. Although the minimum wage law protects men and women equally, most urban women are employed in the informal sector, which is not protected. The labor code restricts the proportion of female personnel at a business to 45 percent except where a particular enterprise requires more, and national labor law limits a woman's workday to one hour less than a man's and prohibits her from working at night. However, such discriminatory labor laws are rarely enforced. Employers are required by law to contribute to social insurance for family leave benefits for families with young children, and as the payments are higher for female workers, some say this leads to discrimination in hiring.[16]

Policy issues affecting women have been treated since 1993 in a special government office, the title and location of which tends to change with administrations. These offices typically are located at a low level within government ministries. Women's access to public office has improved somewhat since the mid-1990s. The first female cabinet member was appointed in 1997, but the 2000 cabinet had no female members, and Sánchez de Lozada appointed only one in 2002. Since 1997, political parties have been required to reserve 30 percent of their congressional lists for female candidates for the one-half of congressional seats elected from party lists. The quota law and increasing demands by female members of the major parties led to an unprecedented number of female candidates in the 2002 national elections. Of these, 30 were elected to the congress (out of 157 seats), up from 16 in 1997.[17]

A law against trafficking in boys, girls, and adolescents became law in November 2003. Nevertheless, the U.S. State Department classifies Bolivia as "a source country" for adults and children "trafficked for labor and sexual exploitation" to other Latin American countries, the United States, and Europe. Bolivians are particularly susceptible because of their greater poverty compared to neighboring countries and the large number of Bolivians who emigrate illegally in search of employment. Despite government efforts, resources are insufficient to enforce existing norms.[18]

Indigenous peoples—including a 30,000-member Afro-Bolivian population that the government treats as indigenous—comprise approximately 60 percent of the population. The majority are either Aymara (1,549,320) or Quechua (2,298,980) and live in the western highland departments. Approximately 286,000 lowland Indians inhabit the eastern departments. Bolivia codified a limited array of rights for indigenous peoples in the 1994–1995 constitutional reform, including recognition of the juridical personality of indigenous communities as public collective actors, the right to bilingual education, and the right of indigenous authorities to exercise administrative functions and to resolve internal conflicts. The UN Committee on the Elimination of Racial Discrimination received reports in 2003 that the police had threatened and harassed human rights workers assisting indigenous peoples and that the right to equal treatment and nondiscrimination was being denied to Afro-Bolivians. However, the Mesa government issued a supreme decree implementing International Labor Organization (ILO) Convention 169 with respect to indigenous communities' territory and the use of natural resources, which rural elites had obstructed for years. ILO Convention 169 requires that indigenous peoples be consulted prior to government or private exploitation of natural resources located within their territories. Implementation of indigenous peoples' constitutional right to bilingual education also has progressed. For example, the Mesa government provided training in classroom teaching, produced educational materials in indigenous languages for more than 5,000 teachers, and produced and distributed primary school educational materials in Spanish, Aymara, Quechua, and Guarani.[19]

Indigenous participation in government increased dramatically after the implementation of the 1994 Law of Popular Participation. Those identifying themselves as indigenous won 28.6 percent of seats available in the first nationwide municipal elections, in 1995. Representation at the national level was scant until the formation of two new indigenous political parties in 1995 (the Assembly for the Sovereignty of the Peoples, or ASP) and 2001 (the Indigenous Pachakutik Movement, or MIP). The ASP elected four Indians to Congress in 1997. In 2002, an offshoot of the ASP (Political Instrument for the Sovereignty of the Peoples [IPSP]), registered as MAS, won 35 seats and the MIP won six, requiring the congress to hire translators for the first time. An additional 8 to 17 indigenous representatives entered congress with the traditional parties depending on the source consulted (there is no consensus on how to define "indigenous" identity). President Mesa appointed two indigenous cabinet members.

Bolivians with disabilities are protected under the 1995 Persons with Disabilities Act. However, enforcement agencies are not active in many parts of the country, and no penalties exist for noncompliance with nondiscrimination and accommodation laws. The definition of disability used by national surveys is very limited, thus causing undercounts that allow the government to withhold additional resources. The Ministry of Education estimates that between 74 percent and 97 percent of disabled children are excluded from public schools. The unemployment rate for people with disabilities is estimated at 60 percent to 85 percent, compared with approximately 12 percent in the general population. The Rehabilitation Bureau of the Ministry of Health, which provided health care to people with disabilities, was closed in 1994, leaving many disabled Bolivians without access to medical treatment. Government forms, including ballots, are not printed in Braille, nor are Braille texts available in national libraries. Barely any public buildings are considered fully accessible. Post offices, public transportation, and other government services are not wheelchair accessible and do not provide assistance for people with disabilities.[20]

The Bolivian constitution recognizes Roman Catholicism as the official national religion but guarantees religious freedom to all other groups. The Catholic Church receives some monetary support from the state, and the Bolivian Bishops' Conference has some influence over Bolivian political life. The bishops were vocal in calling for government intervention to prevent bloodshed during the riots under the previous government. Non-Catholic religious groups must register with the government in order to engage in political or proselytizing activity, but no such registrations have been denied since the 1980s.

The constitution and the General Labor Law provide for the right of all Bolivians to form trade unions for lawful purposes, and both employers and employees are guaranteed the right to freedom of association. In practice, however, a large segment of the population, especially in rural areas, works in the informal economy and is thus unprotected. Freedom of association and political assembly are generally respected, although the military and police used violence against demonstrators under previous governments. NGOs are allowed to operate freely so long as they register with the government, and such registrations are granted freely and without bias.

### Recommendations

- The responsibilities of the military and police in controlling civil unrest must be clarified and regulated to prevent violence such as that which marked 2003. Civil society organizations must be involved in the process of setting and enforcing limits on security forces in order to establish public trust.
- Full implementation of existing indigenous constitutional rights should be a priority, particularly with respect to recognition of land and resource rights.

## RULE OF LAW – 3.52

Bolivia's justice system is characterized by underpaid, poorly trained judges and administrative officials who are overly susceptible to financial and political pressure; inefficiency that generates long delays and the violation of defendants' rights; and user fees, transportation costs, and often the necessity for bribes to ensure prompt attention and favorable outcomes, which place civil proceedings beyond the reach of the majority of Bolivians. As a result, Bolivians seek justice through appeals to the executive branch, particularly local politicians, and through informal dispute-resolution mechanisms.[21]

A major restructuring and de-politicization of the judicial system has been under way since the 1994–1995 constitutional reform. That reform created a judiciary council to professionalize and regulate judges, a constitutional tribunal to handle constitutional questions, and a people's defender to protect citizens from abuses by public officials. A host of reforms to the criminal, civil, and administrative codes followed. Final approval and implementation of those reforms continued during the second Sánchez de Lozada administration. However, their realization was continually delayed by the lack of professionalism and training among the country's judiciary and the resistance of political party leaders, who want to maintain control over judicial appointments for patronage purposes and to be able to manipulate the outcome of sensitive cases. During the aftermath of the 2003 energy riots, prosecutors faced political pressure not to investigate charges of abuse against members of the military and police, and the government made it known that if judges ruled against them in criminal cases, such cases might be transferred to more friendly military tribunals.[22]

Among the most important judicial reforms was the creation of a new code of criminal procedure, which went into effect on May 31, 2001. It shifted Bolivia from a written, inquisitorial, and mostly secret model to one that is adversarial, is more transparent, and allows for oral proceedings—an important change in a country with high illiteracy. The new code requires that translators or interpreters be made available to non-Spanish-speakers and that defense attorneys be provided to the indigent without charge. However, public defenders are poorly trained, underpaid, and stretched too thin, leaving legal assistants, who lack the legal standing to protect defendants and intervene in official proceedings, to substitute for them. Police routinely deny them access to vital information about their investigations. Still, the code makes legal proceedings more efficient: In its first year the duration of criminal proceedings was reduced by at least 75 percent.[23]

Beginning in December 2003, USAID's judicial reform program provided technical assistance, training, physical infrastructure, and information technology to support implementation of the new criminal code. It also set up a criminal records registry, a case liquidation/dismissal system, and a system to randomly select registered voters to participate in oral trials as citizen judges. However, despite a massive public education campaign and training for justice officials, implementation of the code is hampered by the lack of knowledge of its provisions among the public and officials charged with its implementation.

The code does implement indigenous peoples' constitutional right to exercise customary forms of dispute resolution and community justice. Indigenous justice enjoys higher legitimacy and levels of satisfaction within indigenous communities than the formal justice system, which is typically more expensive, geographically remote, and culturally insensitive.[24] Conversely, lack of political will in the congress and the executive has delayed the Community Justice Law—which would facilitate and institutionalize the coordination of indigenous and state justice systems—for years, and in mid-2003 the justice ministry specifically prohibited activity on the law. President Mesa addressed problems of coordination between the systems through a supreme decree regulating the Law of Arbitration and Conciliation.[25]

A new Law of Execution of Penalties and Supervision regulating the prison system entered into force in 2002, and reforms of the customs code and the Law of Responsibilities, which holds government officials accountable, also were initiated. Work on the Law of Responsibilities was suspended in July 2002 because of what a USAID report called "political obstacles to serious reform."[26] It was taken up again a year later with respect only to the judicial branch and passed into law on December 22, 2003.[27]

Justice became much more accessible to the poor majority with the creation of neighborhood Integrated Justice Centers, which provide free legal services to the indigent. The centers offer community and indigenous judges, who seek to resolve civil, family, and criminal conflicts peacefully. Six pilot centers opened in El Alto in September 2004; the government plans to replicate them throughout the country.[28]

On July 31, 2004, President Mesa appointed 13 men and 4 women to the Supreme Court and Judicial Council, as well as 9 departmental prosecutors, filling long-standing vacancies that followed 10 years of congressional inaction. The interim appointments allow the Supreme Court to achieve a quorum so that it can undertake a backlog of work. In a break from the standard practice of political appointments, the independent consulting firm Price Waterhouse chose Mesa's designees. Under the constitution, the congress was supposed to make the original nominations; Mesa's move was intended to provoke them into action. Congressional leaders responded with outrage, and leaders of the Movimiento Nacional Revolucionario (MNR) and Movimiento de la Izquierda Revolucionaria (MIR) delegations prepared their own list of nominees.[29] In a separate development, a new system to evaluate and dismiss incompetent judges was introduced in September 2004.[30]

Full civilian control of the military is lacking. The military high command challenged the supremacy of civilian leaders and the constitution when it rejected a May 2004 Constitutional Court ruling. That ruling overturned a February 16 military court verdict that acquitted four officers accused of the murder of two civilians during the February 2003 tax revolt. At the time, Bolivia's prosecutor general was pursuing 16 additional lawsuits against the army and police for related incidents, as well as the alleged use of excessive force during the October 2003 uprising. The military has refused to let officers testify and has impeded the prosecutor's access to evidence collected by the military tribunal. After a week of tense private discussions with the president, the military prevailed: On May 13 the Senate approved a law banning appeals of military court rulings and expanding the jurisdiction of these courts.[31] In August 2004 President Mesa promised to propose a law to the congress to regulate the intervention of the military in the control of civil disturbances like those of February and October 2003. In the meantime, a supreme decree regulates such situations.[32]

Legal protection of private property in Bolivia is enshrined in the constitution but is quite weak in practice, as the government has few resources to protect it. Because of extensive corruption in the judicial system, it is difficult for Bolivians to seek restitution for theft of physical or intellectual property. The October 2003 energy policy centered on the distribution of property rights over the country's extensive energy reserves. The new policies had a disproportionate negative impact on indigenous Bolivians, who in many places had previously asserted group property rights over resource-rich land. Many of the oil rights granted to foreign interests by the Sánchez de Lozada government were on lands traditionally held by indigenous groups, and those groups are asking President Mesa to help them reclaim their land.[33]

## Recommendations

- The government should make the Community Justice Law a priority in order to fulfill commitments in the 1994 constitution and to reduce the demands on the formal justice system.
- Accessibility of justice in underserved geographic areas and social groups must be improved.
- Efforts should continue to professionalize judicial and investigative offices.

- Military leaders must be made accountable to civilian institutions by ensuring that civilian courts have ultimate jurisdiction over the armed services and civilian officials have ultimate authority over military personnel.

## ANTICORRUPTION AND TRANSPARENCY – 3.12

Bolivia received a score of 2.2 out of a possible 10 (no corruption) in Transparency International's 2004 global corruption index, placing it at 122 out of 146 countries.[34] Moreover, Bolivians "ranked fighting corruption as the country's first priority" in an August 2004 survey.[35]

After assuming office in 2002, Sánchez de Lozada created an anticorruption office in the vice presidency and appointed journalist Lupe Cajías as presidential anticorruption delegate (DPA) to head the office. In its first year the office handled several high-profile cases involving senior government officials. Between October 19, 2003, and August 6, 2004, according to Cajías, the DPA received 497 complaints and handled 29 important criminal proceedings, "nine of which have already been settled."[36] In general, the office is developing standard operating procedures that will reduce the autonomy of individual government officials and, thus, reduce opportunities for corruption. As of September 2004, in consultation with civil society groups and with funding and technical support from USAID and the Inter-American Development Bank, Cajías was drafting a new law regulating public purchases, hiring, and the awarding of government contracts, a law holding political parties accountable for the corruption of their members, a law protecting people who denounce public corruption, and a law creating a special national prosecutor to fight corruption. In 2004 the DPA created specialized anticorruption teams throughout the country.[37]

However, critics point out that the DPA has undertaken no investigations or denunciations of the government since Mesa took office and has shifted its focus to municipal corruption. Most of the investigations are awaiting prosecution in the backlogged courts or in the congress. Cajías herself complained that many positions in the Public Ministry are vacant and the majority are filled by interim appointments due to lack of congressional action.[38] In the most high-profile case prosecuted in 2004, President Mesa pardoned Sánchez de Lozada's minister of government after his conviction for misuse of funds. Ironically, exactly one year earlier Sánchez de Lozada had intervened to protect his defense minister from a DPA investigation, angering then Vice President Mesa. There is a public perception that the anticorruption office and its "czarina" have lost influence and autonomy.[39]

A 2004 report assessing Bolivia's implementation of the Inter-American Convention against Corruption, ratified in 1997, applauded the country's efforts in enacting pertinent standards and promoting citizen participation in monitoring corruption. However, it criticized the absence of a firm timeframe for public agencies to adopt ethics standards as well as the lack of provisions against conflicts of interest and provisions ensuring public officials' registration of their and family members' income and assets. The report also decried the lack of protections for witnesses and whistleblowers participating in anticorruption cases and the persistence of laws punishing those who insult public officials, which discourage citizens from coming forward.[40]

Bolivia has been trying to modernize and professionalize the civil service since 1990, when the Government Administration and Control Law was enacted. In addition to an entrenched culture of government corruption, a main obstacle is the lack of resources for undertaking investigations, training personnel, and offering salaries that support professional careers. In August 2004, the Public Ministry, which has primary responsibility for investigating crime and regulating, investigating, and prosecuting corruption, had a deficit of more than US$37 million. The ministry lacks investigators knowledgeable about criminal procedures and has no legal norms for hiring them. That month Prosecutor General Oscar Crespo was replaced after nearly 20 years of overseeing the ministry, opening up the possibility for genuine change. The newly appointed prosecutor general immediately declared vacant 740 jobs in the Public Ministry and fired 30 investigators. Aspirants for these jobs will have to take competency exams.[41]

An unprecedented terrorist attack occurred on February 27, 2004, when a car bomb killed anti-drug prosecutor Mónica von Borries. Authorities suspect that fugitive Marco Marino Diodato, whom von Borries had investigated for corruption and drug trafficking, was behind the murder. They arrested a Brazilian citizen, who allegedly confessed his participation on Diodato's orders. Others blame landowners whom von Borries was investigating.[42]

In September 2004 a corruption scandal involving the top leaders of the national police, which received extensive media coverage, led to the replacement of the commander in charge.[43]

The anticorruption office is working with the Carter Center on new access to information and transparency laws and the implementation of a transparency policy with respect to public information. After work was delayed on both laws, Mesa issued a supreme decree on January 31, 2004, covering both access to information and transparency. The decree has created controversy because of broad exemptions for some government officials and agencies, restrictions on the type of information available to citizens, and a lack of clear guidelines on implementation, which leaves too much to the discretion of public officials.[44] In addition, public officials are reluctant to share information, government offices are disorganized, and it is unclear who will pay the costs of providing information. Despite a 2004 constitutional amendment protecting the privacy of individuals with respect to their personal information held by the government, it is unclear how privacy rights will be harmonized with the right to information. Government Web pages have been created providing a variety of important legal and policy information to citizens, including information on government expenditures and contracts. On August 6, 2004, President Mesa posted on his Web site a detailed report of government activities and expenditures since he took office.[45] However, fewer than 300,000 Bolivians have access to the Internet.[46]

The Bolivian government, in cooperation with the WTO, has set up a financial transparency portal to make current and past budgets and other financial information public. According to WTO reports, the portal contains relevant budget information but is not user-friendly and should be directly linked to the government financial system.[47]

*Recommendations*
- In order to encourage citizens to come forward, laws punishing slander or insult of public officials should be abolished and norms should be created to protect whistleblowers and witnesses involved in cases of public corruption.
- The government should actively continue to involve civil society groups in the design and implementation of its anticorruption and access-to-information strategies.

- The transparency of government decision making, particularly with respect to economic policy, should be improved by involving a wider array of civil society representatives in policymaking above the municipal level.
- More mechanisms are needed to enable civil society groups to monitor government performance at all levels. For example, the successful vigilance committee model could be expanded from municipal governments to other areas and levels of government oversight.

## NOTES

[1] The People's Defender gives the lower figure; the Bolivian Permanent Assembly for Human Rights gives the higher estimate. Three soldiers also were killed. Both sources quoted in "Counting the human cost of protests," *Latin American Weekly Report,* 11 November 2003, 8.

[2] José Antonio Aruquipa, "Terrorism intensifies: Anti-drug prosecutor dies in attack," *Latinamerica Press* 36, 5 (10 March 2004): 3; "La aprobación de Mesa cae ocho puntos; la gente pide otra agenda," *La Razón,* 30 August 2004, http://www.la-razon.com/el_evento/agosto/eve040830a.html.

[3] Bolivia has an estimated 900 million barrels of oil and 54 trillion cubic feet of natural gas. Raúl Vasquez, "Bolivia: Social Movements in Trouble?" *NACLA Report on the Americas* 38, 1 (July/August 2004): 43.

[4] "Optimism from central bank," *Latin American Economy and Business* (June 2004): 17; "Primary economy outperforms services," *Latin American Andean Group Report* (6 January 2004): 10; *World Factbook 2004,* Bolivia (Springfield, Va.: U.S. Central Intelligence Agency, 2004); Carlos D. Mesa Gisbert, *Mensaje–Informe de Gestion,* 17 October 2003–6 August 2004.

[5] "Los grupos recibirán subsidios y pueden aliarse a los partidos," *La Razón,* 18 August 2004, http://www.la-razon.com/politica/Agosto/pol040818a.html; "Ajustes legales para las municipales," *La Razón,* 11 August 2004, ea.gmcsa.net/2004/08-Agosto/20040810/Editorial/notas/Editorial.html; "La participacion de agrupaciones en las municipales sera escasa," *La Razón,* 9 September 2004, http://www.la-razon.com/politica/septiembre/pol040909a.html.

[6] Mesa, *Mensaje–Informe;* "Mesa unveils tailor-made referendum," *Latin American Andean Group Report* (8 June 2004): 10; "La mayoría aprueba al Gobierno y cree que las petroleras ayudarán," *La Razón,* 13 August 2004.

[7] *Bolivia–Annual Report 2004* (Paris: Reporters without Borders, 2004), http://www.rsf.org/article.php3?id_article=10233& Valider=OK.

[8] "Bolivia, Attacks on the Press 2003" (New York: Committee to Protect Journalists, 2004), http://www.cpj.org/attacks03/americas03/bolivia.html.

[9] Ibid.; "2003 World Press Freedom Review," (Vienna: International Press Institute, 2004), http://www.freemedia.at/wpfr/Americas/bolivia.htm; "Cossío y Vaca Díez comprometen acciones en contra del nepotismo," *La Razón,* 2 September 2004.

[10] "A la comunidad internacional y al pueblo Boliviano" (La Paz: Bolivian Permanent Assembly for Human Rights [APDHB], press release, 15 October 2003), web.entelnet.bo/apdhdb/docs/doc33.htm; in comparison, during the 2000 "Water War" and contemporaneous protests 20+ people were killed and hundreds injured; confrontations in 2001 left an estimated 17 dead, in Willem Assies, "David Fights Goliath in Cochabamba: Water rights, neoliberalism and the renovation of social protest in Bolivia," *Latin American Perspectives* (2003): 14–36; "Bolivia: Chapare—Human rights cannot be eradicated along with the coca leaf" (New York: Amnesty International, 25 October 2001), http:/web.amnesty.org/library/ print/engamr180102001.

[11] *Informe de la Organización de los Estados Americanos (OEA) sobre los hechos de febrero del 2003 en Bolivia* (Washington, DC: Secretaría General de la OEA, Mayo del 2003); *2004 Annual Report,* "Bolivia" (New York: Amnesty International, 2004), http://www.amnestyusa.org/countries/bolivia; "Se debe ejercer mesura al responder a las protestas" (New York: Human Rights Watch, 15 October 2003), hrw.org/spanish/press/2003/bolivia_manifestaciones.html; "Bolivia" (New York: Amnesty International, 2003).

[12] "Legal consequences: Human rights organizations sort out the consequences of October protest and press for prosecutions," *Latinamerica Press* 2 (28 January 2004): 11.

[13] Author's translation, "Fortalecer la investigación por muertes de manifestantes" (New York: Human Rights Watch, 22 diciembre 2003), hrw/org/spanish/press/2003/bolivia_fortalecer_investigacion.html.

[14] *Latin American Weekly Report,* 25 November 2003, 12; "Bolivia," 2003 and "Bolivia," 2004 (New York: Amnesty International, 2003 and 2004).

[15] Jarmila Moravek de Cerruto, "Domestic Violence, Legislation and Health in Bolivia," paper presented at symposium "Gender Violence, Health and Rights in the Americas," Cancun, Mexico, 4–7 June 2001, 2; "Ocho años de Cárcel por pegar a su mujer," *Actualidad,* 23 May 2002, http://www.bolivia.com/noticias/autonoticias/detallenoticia6307.asp.

[16] "Social Security Throughout the World: The Americas 2003" (Washington, DC: U.S. Social Security Administration, March 2004), http://www.ssa.gov/policy/docs/progdesc/ssptw/2002-2003/americas/bolivia.html.

[17] "Algunas caracteristicas del próximo Parlamento," *La Razón,* 7 July 2002; interviews by author in Bolivia, April–July 1997, June 2002; Mala N. Htun, *Advancing Women's Rights in the Americas: Achievements and Challenges* (Washington, DC: Inter-American Dialogue, 2001).

[18] *Trafficking in Persons Report* (Washington, DC: U.S. Dept. of State, 14 June 2004), http://www.state.gov/g/tip/rls/tiprpt/2004/33198pf.htm.

[19] Mesa, *Mensaj –Informe.*

[20] "2004 International Disability Rights Monitor," Bolivia (Chicago: Center for International Rehabilitation, 2004), http://www.cirnetwork.org/idrm/reports/americas/countries/bolivia.html.

21  *Advancing Judicial Reform: An Environmental Case Study in Bolivia* (New York: Human Rights First [formerly Lawyers Committee for Human Rights], n.d.), http://www .uoregon.edu/~caguirre/bolivia/html; interviews by author, La Paz, March–June 1997, December 1998.

22  "Bolivia: Strengthen Investigation into Protest Deaths" (New York: Human Rights Watch, 22 December 2003), hrw.org/english/docs/2003/12/22/bolivi6847.htm.

23  "Bolivia," *Report on Judicial Systems in the Americas 2002–2003* (Santiago, Chile: Centro de Estudios Judiciales de las Americas, n.d.), 88, http://www.cejamericas.org/report; Daniel Mogrovejo, *Informe sobre la Implementación de la Reforma Procesal Penal en Bolivia (Ciudad de La Paz)* (Santiago: Centro de Estudios de Justicia de las Americas, n.d.).

24  "Bolivia: Judicial reforms underway," *Report of the Justice Study Center of the Americas (2003)* (Santiago: Centro de Estudios de Justicia de las Americas, 2003), http://www .cejamericas.org/reporte.html.

25  *USAID-Bolivia Administration of Justice Program (BAOJ)-phase III, Final Report,* August 2001–December 2003 (Washington, DC: U.S. Dept. of State, Agency for International Development, n.d.), 7; Mesa, *Mensaje – Informe.*

26  *USAID-Bolivia Administration of Justice Program,* 6.

27  Nardy Suxo, "La necesidad de un derecho a la información en Bolivia," in *La Promoción de la democracia a través del acceso a la información: Bolivia* (Atlanta: Carter Center, 2004), 11–12; *USAID-Bolivia Administration of Justice Program,* 1–2.

28  "La justicia sale de los palacios a los barrios populares," *La Razón,* 17 September 2004, ea.gmcsa.net/2004/09-septiembre/20040915/seguridad/septiembre/seg040915a.html.

29  "El Presidente da el primer paso para renovar la justicia en el país," *La Razón,* 1 August 2004, ea.gmcsa.net/2004/08-Agosto/20040801/El_Evento/Agosto/eve040801a. html; "La designación de Mesa no es legal, según Crespo," *La Razón,* 1 August 2004, ea.gmcsa.net /2004/08-Agosto/20040801/El_Evento/ Agosto/eve040801c.html; "Los políticos pretenden retomar el control de los cargos judiciales," *La Razón,* 13 August 2004, http://www.la-razon.com/El_evento/Agosto/ eve040813a. html.

30  "Las acefalías en el Poder Judicial serán cubiertas hasta octubre" and "Los malos jueces serán alejados de sus cargos," *La Razón,* 11 August 2004, both at http://www.la-razon.com/El_evento/Agosto/eve040811a.html.

31  "Rebellion succeeds, then fades from sight," *Latin American Weekly Report,* 18 May 2004, 5.

32  "Las FFAA acusan a la justicia civil de afectar su integridad," *La Razón,* 8 August 2004, ea.gmcsa.net/2004/08-Agosto/20040808/Seguridad/Agosto/seg040808b.html; "Mesa promete a los militares una ley de protección especial," *La Razón,* 8 August 2004, ea .gmcsa.net/2004/08-Agosto/20040808/Seguridad/Agosto/seg040808a.html.

33  Juan Forero, "Where the Incas Ruled, Indians Are Hoping for Power," *New York Times,* 17 July 2004.

34  "Corruption Perceptions Index 2004" (Berlin: Transparency International, 2004), http://www.transparency.org/cpi/2004/cpi2004.en.html.

35  "La aprobación de Mesa cae ocho puntos."

[36] Guadelupe Cajías de la Vega, "Certezas y dudas en el debate de una nueva norma," in *La promoción de la democracia a través del acceso de la información: Bolivia* (Atlanta: Carter Center, 2004), 85.

[37] Unpublished report by Plan de Trabajo, Programa de Apoyo a la Lucha Contra la Corrupción, Casals/USAID, November 2004–November 2005.

[38] Lupe Cajías, "Bolivia" (Washington, DC: Organization of American States [OAS], 2004).

[39] "Lupe Cajías no ve corrupción en el Gobierno y se fija en las alcaldías," *La Razón*, 16 August 2004, http://www.la-razon.com/info_lunes/agosto/inf040816a.html; confidential interview by author, October 2004.

[40] *Mechanism for Follow-up on Implementation of the Inter-American Convention against Corruption*, Sixth Meeting of the Committee of Experts (Washington, DC: OAS, 26–30 July 2004).

[41] "El nuevo Fiscal hace planes y pide dinero para ejecutarlos," *La Razón*, 13 August 2004, http://www.la-razon.com/el_evento/Agosto/eve040813b.html; "Fiscalía General declarará 740 cargos en vacancia," *La Razón*, 11 August 2004, ea.gmcsa.net/2004/08-Agosto/20040810/Seguridad/Agosto/seg040810a.html.

[42] Aruquipa, "Terrorism Intensifies," 3–4.

[43] "Los partidos revelan cómo se cuotean el Parlamento," *La Razón*, 31 August 2004, http://www.la-razon.com/politica/Agosto/po1040831a.html; "Los escándalos en la Policía frenan los deseos de cambio," *La Razón*, 17 September 2004, http://www.la-Razon.com/seguridad/septiembre/seg040917c.html.

[44] Antonio Birbuet Días, "Administración pública y acceso a la información," in *La Promoción de la democracia a través del acceso a la información: Bolivia* (Atlanta: Carter Center, 2004), 20–22.

[45] Mesa, "Mensaje–Informe."

[46] Cajías, "Certezas y dudas," 87.

[47] Miguel Solana, *Portales de Transparencia: Delivering Public Financial Information to Citizens in Five Latin American Countries* (Manchester, UK: University of Manchester, December 2003), http://www.e-devexchange.org/eGov/laportals.htm.

# BURKINA FASO

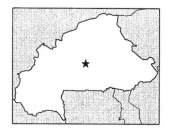

CAPITAL: Ouagadougou
POPULATION: 13.6 million
GNI PER CAPITA: $250

**SCORES**
ACCOUNTABILITY AND PUBLIC VOICE: 3.44
CIVIL LIBERTIES: 3.88
RULE OF LAW: 3.32
ANTICORRUPTION AND TRANSPARENCY: 3.12
(scores are based on a scale of 0 to 7, with
0 representing weakest and 7 representing
strongest performance)

*Augustin Loada*

## INTRODUCTION

After four years of revolutionary regime ended in a bloody coup led by Captain Blaise Compaoré on October 15, 1987, Burkina Faso entered a process of liberalization. At the end of the 1980s, internal and external pressures resulted in further democratic reforms. The adoption of a new constitution in June 1991 was a major step in this process. Many opposition parties, however, raised criticisms about the new constitution, which they claimed invested too much power in the executive and unfairly gave the incumbent president the right to manage the transition to the constitutional regime. Therefore, they urged President Compaoré to convene a national conference—a constituent assembly with sovereign power to amend the new constitution—and form a government of national unity to manage the democratic transition. Confronted with President Compaoré's steadfast refusal to satisfy their demands, all major opposition parties boycotted the December 1991 presidential elections,

**Augustin Loada** is a professor of public law and political science. He is the dean of the faculty of law and political science at the University of Ouagadougou and director of the Center for Democratic Governance, an independent NGO based in Burkina Faso.

resulting in an easy victory for the president, although voter turnout was less than 25 percent. His party also won the May 1992 and May 1997 legislative elections, in which the opposition participated but accused the ruling party of fraud. The opposition largely chose to boycott the November 1998 presidential elections, although political leaders from two small parties challenged President Compaoré, who was nevertheless reelected with 88 percent of the total votes.

The murder of the well-known journalist Norbert Zongo on December 13, 1998, launched the country into a deep sociopolitical crisis. A movement led by civil society groups and opposition parties protested the failure to bring Zongo's assassins to justice. The crisis, which shook the regime to its foundations, paved the way for a reinforcement of the democratic process. Political and electoral reforms adopted in 2000 and 2001 introduced significant changes following intensive consultations among political parties.[1] This made possible the reestablishment of a minimum of confidence between political parties and the introduction of more transparent and effective electoral rules. The result of this was a significant gain in the May 2002 legislative elections for opposition parties, which combined won 54 out of 111 seats.

Despite progress, democratization in Burkina Faso is far from complete.[2] In spite of the electoral reforms implemented since 2001, the people's will is not fully expressed due in part to electoral corruption and the absence of equal campaigning opportunities for all candidates. The excessive power of the executive and the ruling party disrupts the balance of power among the branches of government.

In contrast, freedom of expression and civil society groups are relatively well protected, with thousands of associations and a pluralist and sometimes critical press in operation. Civil liberties are generally guaranteed, although torture continues and often goes unpunished. The principles of equality and nondiscrimination are legally ensured, but in practice some groups, such as women, have suffered from inequalities. The rule of law is also constitutionally guaranteed but undermined by the judiciary's lack of independence and credibility and the weak democratic control over the police and military forces. An arsenal of laws intended to ensure transparency and to fight corruption lacks effectiveness, and in practice, corruption continues to increase because the political will to tackle it remains weak.

## ACCOUNTABILITY AND PUBLIC VOICE – 3.44

The constitution states that government authority is based on the will of the people as expressed through elections. These elections are organized by the Independent National Electoral Commission (CENI) on the basis of universal and equal suffrage and are open to a variety of political parties and candidates. However, although administration of elections in Burkina Faso has steadily improved, there is still much to be done to achieve free and fair voting. Indeed, elections are still undermined by corruption, and the electoral law somewhat favors the ruling party.

In October 2003, 16 people were arrested and charged with attempting to overthrow the Compaoré government. Among them were two civilians—a pastor whose church was attended by the majority of the arrested people, and a party leader well known for his radical opposition to the regime—and several soldiers formerly of the regiment in charge of President Compaoré's safety. The government claims the plot began three years earlier and involved financial support from Cote d'Ivoire and Togo.[3] However, the majority of the opposition and the public believe that the regime invented the charges as a pretext to neutralize its radical opposition.

According to the constitution (Article 167), any regime that does not derive its power from the constitution, such as a regime that comes to power via a military coup, is not legitimate. In the event that an illegitimate regime does come to power, the constitution invites citizens to revolt against it. Yet the government's announcement of the 2003 coup attempt did not result in widespread indignation among the population. The tepid popular response points to the deficiency in the consolidation of democracy in Burkina Faso.

Unlike the 2001 electoral reforms, which were affirmed by wide consensus, the revised electoral code of April 2004 has been questioned by some opposition parties and by many members of civil society. The ruling party has been accused of redrawing electoral districts and revising the system of proportional representation to its advantage. In addition, the ministry of territorial administration and decentralization, which was in effect excluded from the administration of the 2002 elections because it was viewed as partisan, was tasked in the 2004 electoral code with certain electoral functions, such as voter registration, at the request of the

CENI. This led the opposition to question the independence of the CENI. Free elections in Burkina Faso have also been hindered by widespread electoral fraud, the electorate's weak civic awareness, and the dominance of religious and traditional leaders, who influence the votes of their followers and—in exchange for compensation from the regime—often encourage them to support the ruling party.

During electoral campaigns, the High Council for Information ensures that all political parties and candidates have equal and free access to the state-owned media, which have a monopoly on election coverage. In general, the High Council fulfills its responsibilities, guaranteeing equal access to the national media during electoral campaigns. However, aside from the ruling party and a handful of larger opposition parties, most parties have trouble filling the time or space provided for them in the media, mainly due to organizational shortcomings such as a lack of professionalism, means, and qualified staff.

The opposition has two main criticisms of tactics used by the ruling party to manipulate reporting by the state-owned media. First, the state-owned media tend not to cover opposition political activities outside electoral campaigns. Second, in election years the government and ruling party typically organize a thinly veiled pre-electoral campaign of media coverage endorsing government activities—the organization of cultural activities and sports events, for example, or the unveiling of infrastructure and community facilities—which clearly influences the mobilization and vote of the electorate. The High Council does not regulate media coverage before the campaign, and the opposition has no effective way to counterattack. In addition, no rules regulate the funding of political parties or candidates, and there is no limitation on campaign spending. The ruling party thus has an advantage in campaign funding because it can easily generate funds from its members and supporters as well as from outside the party and the country.

These obstacles to democratization are heightened by the fragmentation of the opposition. According to the ministry of territorial administration and decentralization, which is in charge of civil liberties, as of September 2004, 103 political parties were officially registered.[4] This quasi-anarchic situation complicates the formation of an opposition capable of posing a credible alternative to the ruling party. In addition, the ruling party has frequently been accused of actively encouraging dissidents and defectors within the main political opposition parties. Thus, given its difficulty in unseating the ruling party, the opposition considers the enforcement of a two-term limit for the presidency of great importance to its success, as it would reduce the incumbent advantage. The two-term limit, which was eliminated in 1997 but contested by civil society groups and opposition parties, was reinstated in 2000 during the crisis sparked by the murder of Norbert Zongo. But since January 2004, adherents of the ruling party have made clear their view that the provision is not retroactive and that therefore President Compaoré is eligible for two more consecutive presidential terms.

A May 2000 law allocates funds for non-electoral-campaign activities to political parties that took part in the previous election, with higher levels for parties that received at least 5 percent of the total votes—currently three political parties.[5] However, no law addresses private funding or funds from foreign donors, both of which are increasingly sought by political parties.

The constitution of Burkina Faso is based upon the separation of powers between the executive, the legislature, and the judiciary. However, the checks and balances system does not function as it was designed. The president possesses exorbitant powers; the parliamentary check is not sufficient due to parliament's weakness combined with pressure from the ruling party, which expects parliament to be supportive rather than critical of the government.

In principle, recruitment for civil service jobs is by competitive examinations based on merit. But in practice, some competitive examinations have been subject to corruption. In addition, access to strategic posts appears to be conditional on membership in the ruling party rather than on intrinsic qualifications. The government also uses controversial methods to recruit and promote senior civil servants, such as the so-called psychotechnical tests that were added to the August 2004 examination for entrance to the master's level of the Ecole Nationale des Régies Financières. These tests are meant to evaluate certain psychological factors that might affect a candidate's eligibility for a job, but opponents charge that they are manipulated to favor the government's preferred candidates.

Under Article 8 of the constitution, associations and civic groups can testify or comment on pending government policy or legislation. However, for many adherents to the ruling party, democracy is understood as rule by the majority. The government does not want to give the impression of weakness in the face of pressures from civil society or the press. Unless it is constrained by popular opinion, the political leadership rarely changes course as a result of peaceful demonstrations or strikes. For example, the ruling party adopted the April 2004 electoral reform in the face of strong resistance from civil society.

The institutional framework regulating nongovernmental organizations (NGOs) is not restrictive. The government imposes no onerous requirements for registration, and funders of civic organizations are free from state pressures. As a result, thousands of associations and NGOs operate in Burkina Faso. Still, the activities of human rights groups are sometimes impeded by the government or local authorities.

Freedom of the press and media pluralism are relatively ensured. However, the government sometimes pressures the state-owned media to revise their editorial positions when they are too critical of the regime or if it seems to favor the opposition. The private media are relatively independent and often critical of the government and the opposition, and the government makes no direct attempt to control them. However, investigative journalists are sometimes intimidated when they try to report on corruption or human rights abuses committed by powerful people. For example, Newton Ahmed Barry—a well-known journalist who investigated the credibility of official reports on the 2003 coup attempt and who later questioned the independence of the president of the military court of Ouagadougou—was summoned repeatedly by the police or the general prosecutor in 2003 and 2004.

The press code is generally unrestrictive. However, it does include some repressive clauses, notably with respect to defamation, which is punishable by imprisonment. This year only one dispute, which was solved by mediation, arose with a journalist. The government protects and promotes the freedom of cultural expression through the ministry of culture.

The government allocates public funds to private media. However, this financial assistance is insufficient given the large number of recipients, and many financially struggling organizations are vulnerable to indirect pressures. Some private media are allied with the ruling party while others are aligned with opposition parties, although all claim to be independent. Intimidation by the police and journalists' fears of the regime lead to self-censorship, resulting in a failure to publish stories examining official corruption. Moreover, journalists themselves are not free from corruption, with some being paid to promote partisan opinions in their reporting.

*Recommendations*

- The government should invest more in civic education to promote awareness of the right to free expression and to inform the public about proper electoral procedures as a means to combat electoral fraud.
- The law on funding of political parties should be reformed to include regulation of private funding and to limit electoral expenditure.
- Regulation of the media should ensure equal access to public media by all political parties, including outside electoral campaign periods.
- The parliament should empowered to provide a check on the actions of the executive. Parliamentarians should be trained to assume this role.

## CIVIL LIBERTIES – 3.88

Burkina Faso's constitution forbids torture, and the country has ratified the International Convention against Torture. But in practice, citizens are subject to torture and inhumane or degrading treatment when in police or military custody. Only when deaths in custody are denounced in the media do judicial authorities intervene, although authorities have never officially acknowledged torture as a cause of death. Rather, suicide or natural death is given as the cause. For example, in May 2004, a citizen died inside Baskuy state police barracks in Ouagadougou. His family referred the matter to the authorities, but as of September 2004 no one has been arrested for the death. In addition, human rights activists have often accused the security forces of killing criminals,[6] although the authorities have claimed that they were acting in self-defense.

Prison conditions do not support the human dignity of prisoners due to overpopulation and lack of hygiene, infrastructure, and staff. In September 2004, a disruption in the water supply at the central prison of Ouagadougou caused a rebellion that resulted in the deaths of several prisoners and the escape of at least 100 others.

Since the assassination of the journalist Norbert Zongo in December 1998, no members of the political opposition or human rights defenders have been killed. However, justice has been very slow in Zongo's case. Citing the separation of powers, the government has not taken responsibility for this delay and has instead maintained that it has given the justice system the necessary means to clear up the issue. In reality, the government has not acted on the findings of an independent investigative commission, and it is unlikely that the case will move forward in the near future.

When political tensions are high, there is little protection against arbitrary arrest. Policemen often harass citizens to intimidate them. In September 2004, in spite of his parliamentary immunity, Hermann Yaméogo, a vocal opponent of President Compaoré, was arrested at the airport and had his passport seized before later being released. He was accused of giving false information to Ivorian and Mauritanian authorities on the involvement of Burkina Faso in the rebellion in Côte d'Ivoire and in the unsuccessful attempt to overthrow the Mauritanian president. Yaméogo, who the ruling party characterizes as a traitor and stateless, is being prosecuted for having secret dealings with Cote d'Ivoire and Mauritania, whom the Burkinabe government considers to be the country's enemies. The ruling party appears intent on discrediting him nationally and pushing him out of the running for the 2005 presidential elections. Opposition politician Noël Yaméogo, Hermann's cousin, was also detained in September 2004.

There is very little protection against long-term detention without trial. Detention is initially limited to 72 hours, with a possible extension by 48 hours at the request of the prosecutor or examining magistrate, but in practice it often extends beyond that. Frequently, the reason given is that the police do not have adequate means to collect the necessary information to permit release or to indict. The Burkinabe Movement for Human Rights, the country's largest human rights organization, intervened at a police station in Ouagadougou at the beginning of 2004 to obtain the release of a citizen who had spent 21 days in detention. Following her participation in the 35th session of the African Commission of Human and Peoples' Rights, the minister of human rights said in an interview in June 2004 that the government is open to a debate on this problem and to ideas about how to resolve it.[7] However, no steps have yet been taken.

When state authorities violate citizens' rights, the latter can refer the matter to the justice system or to the national ombudsman, the Mediator of Faso. These mechanisms tend to work slowly and often decide in favor of the state authorities. Indeed, citizens who report abuse are far more likely to receive compensation in cases involving non-state entities, such as private businesses, than in those involving state authorities. However, the involvement of civil society organizations on behalf of a citizen can often lead to prompt compensation.

Abuses are sometimes committed by traditional chiefs and their relatives, who still consider the members of their community to be their subjects. These traditional leaders grant themselves the right to hand out punishments to subjects who fail to uphold traditional values. That said, traditional chiefs have appeared more reluctant to exercise this right since 2000, when a prominent traditional chief, who had ordered one of his subjects to be beaten to death, was put under house arrest. Nevertheless, in 2004, the guards of another important traditional chief, the king of Yatenga, manhandled one of his subjects. The affair was settled out of court through traditional procedures of mediation.

Most laws state the principle of nondiscrimination and specifically condemn discrimination based on sex, race, ethnic group, region, skin color, language, religion, caste, political opinions, wealth, and birth. The government addresses women's rights and has carried out some awareness campaigns among the general population. However, women's rights are not always guaranteed in practice because of traditional values that view women as inferior, leading to discrimination against them. There is no legislation specifically on gender discrimination. Instead, the law punishes certain social practices and backward customs that discriminate against women. For example, excision on young girls is punishable under the penal code. Several people found guilty of excision were jailed in 2004. With the support of the national commission for control of excision and the ministry for women's affairs, positive discrimination is practiced by the state and by some civil society organizations to increase girls' access to education by offering free schooling and scholarships. Still, much remains to be done to achieve genuine equality between men and women in Burkinabe society.

Officially, the labor code and the laws on employment and civil servants forbid any discrimination in access to employment. In practice, however, women are not treated equally to men during the recruiting process and in their compensation. Women are often reluctant to complain for fear of losing the opportunities they do have.

In recent years, the government has been taking steps to prevent the trafficking in women and children. In September 2004, the government adopted a plan of action to control trafficking in children. The ministry for women's affairs has created the national committee for control of trafficking in children and sponsored volunteer groups to monitor the problem. Security forces are on alert and have been given sensitivity training. Still, the country's, and individual families', poverty seems to ensure that the problem will persist.

Burkina Faso's population is composed of more than 60 ethnic groups. The most prominent is the Mossi, who constitute an estimated 6 million people—half of the total population of Burkina Faso. Muslims, who represent half of the population, are the main religious group. However, they are less politically influential than Christians, who represent only about 10 percent of the population but are better organized and have played a prominent role in the education of state elites. Despite the inequality of influence on politics, all ethnic and religious groups completely and effectively exercise their rights and basic freedoms without any discrimination and with full equality before the law. Mechanisms are in place to ensure social cohesion and tolerance within the Burkinabe society. The government deliberately avoids promoting policies that favor one ethnic or religious group, in accordance with the principle of nondiscrimination established by the constitution. Ethnicity and religious affiliation are not significant factors in political life in Burkina Faso. Nevertheless, negative stereotypes exist about certain groups, a problem the government does not consider a priority or its responsibility and does not usually take steps to combat.

The government does little to ensure the rights of people with disabilities. Many services available to the general public, such as post offices, are not accessible to people with disabilities, a fact that is denounced by many NGOs. The government does not strive to provide information on government services and decisions in forms accessible to people with disabilities, in spite of a 1986 provision ensuring access to public buildings for the disabled. In addition, there are no efforts to promote access to education and employment for people with disabilities. Few policies promote their rights.

Freedom of religious belief is acknowledged in the constitution (Article 7) and respected by the government, which imposes only one limitation: respect for law, order, and standards of good behavior. The government does not generally interfere in the appointment of religious or spiritual chiefs or in the internal activities of religious groups. However, due to the disorganization of the Muslim community and offenses committed in the past, the government has in the past few years participated in arrangements for travel to Mecca for the annual Muslim pilgrimage through a commission composed of representatives of the government and the Muslim community. In 2004, the government disbanded an organization that was similarly involved in arranging pilgrimages but had failed to present sufficient safety guarantees for participants and was disturbing the work of the government-sponsored commission. Most Muslims would prefer that sole responsibility for arranging the pilgrimage be returned to their community.

Freedom of association is recognized in the constitution (Article 21), and the law related to freedom of association is unrestrictive. Many associations form freely and are recognized by the authorities. However, while the government acknowledges the rights of these groups, it dislikes most of them, as they frequently criticize the government's record on human rights and democracy. The government often accuses these groups of partisanship and sometimes resorts to excessive force in response to public demonstrations and protests. In February 2004 security forces opened fire during a public meeting of the traders and vendors of Ouagadougou's central market, resulting in many injuries and violent demonstrations in the following days.

Trade unions are permitted to operate, and workers can freely join. However, in practice, direct and indirect sanctions are often inflicted on workers who strike. Judicial decisions in favor of workers are not always respected. In September 2004, a new labor code was adopted that forbids sympathy strikes and strikes for political reasons. The code also requires the labor tribunal to endorse all arbitration agreements established by factory inspectors before implementation. These provisions are contested by labor unions, which criticize the resulting decline in civil liberties and the lengthening of procedures. Only a minority of workers are employed in the formal state-owned and private sectors. Unregistered workers or those in the informal sector have difficulty turning to the state to report abuse.

*Recommendations*

- The government should reinforce human rights training for the police and military forces, especially on the prohibition of torture and inhuman, cruel, and degrading treatment.
- The government should promote training for the security forces and civil society organizations on the peaceful management of public demonstrations to help avoid violence.
- The government should promote awareness among the general population, traditional authorities, and the police about women's and children's rights.
- The government should improve prison conditions by building new facilities and providing prisoners more and better food, health care, and legal assistance.

## RULE OF LAW – 3.32

In Burkina Faso, judicial independence is maintained in legal texts, and judges are instructed to make impartial decisions, respecting only the law and their inner conviction. Judges and prosecutors benefit from statutory guarantees that in theory ensure their independence. But the reality is mixed. Judicial appointments and promotions are determined by the executive, which can therefore influence judges' decisions. The head of state, assisted by the minister of justice, presides over the High Magistrate Council, which manages magistrates' careers and is dominated by members appointed by the executive. Magistrates considered loyal and accommodating move quickly up the ranks and are put in charge of important cases, such as those implicating people in power. In contrast, independent-minded magistrates are typically posted far from the capital.

Prosecutors are part of the hierarchy headed by the minister of justice. They can express themselves freely during trials, but their written addresses must be in accordance with the prescriptions of the hierarchy. In addition, they can be removed from their positions at any time. This system allows for unity and coherence in the government's judicial policy. But the main consequence is that members of the executive use prosecutors to meddle in judicial decisions; prosecutors can exert strong influence over the presiding magistrate.

Judges are susceptible to bribery, especially given their modest remuneration. The High Magistrate Council set up a commission to consider the problem of bribery among judges and how to combat it, but the commission has yet to issue its recommendations. As a result of magistrates' economic vulnerability and fears of executive reprisals, many try to avoid any confrontation with the executive. Judges have adequate legal training before assuming the bench, but this initial training could be reinforced and improved by continued education.

Public officials can be sued for abuse of power and other inappropriate actions. The leaders of the ruling party, however, are rarely subject to such measures. In general, only public officials who are disloyal to those in power face suits, granting most politicians de facto immunity. Thus, public authorities tend to comply with judicial decisions. However, some plaintiffs complain of delays in the execution of these decisions, especially when the cases concern administration officials or certain powerful private actors.

According to the constitution, accused persons are presumed innocent until proved guilty. In practice, accused criminals are often subject to condemnation in the media, which challenges the presumption of innocence of the accused. The practice of detaining accused persons for long stretches of time before trial also undermines this principle. This point is illustrated by the case of the president of one of the opposition parties, who was released by a military court in April 2004 after having been detained for six months while awaiting trial related to an attempted coup.

Citizens with financial means have access to the services of an independent lawyer of their choice. The state provides counsel when those accused of serious crimes cannot afford it. But funds to provide assistance to persons accused of lesser crimes are lacking.

According to the constitution, citizens are entitled to have their cases heard by an independent, impartial, and public tribunal. However, for the poor, the right to a fair and speedy trial exists mostly in theory. In contrast, in cases in which the accused are members of the political opposition, justice moves very swiftly, thus indicating some orchestration by the ruling power. Justice is perceived by the majority of the population as not very credible, partly because it favors the politically and economically powerful.

President Compaoré controls most of the military apparatus. Democratic oversight of the security and military forces is negligible. For example, the constitution states that the military can be sent to a foreign country only if the action is approved by the parliament (Article 106); in reality, the parliament is often informed of such actions after the fact or is not informed at all. Officially, military and security services abstain from all interference in the political process. But ties between some members of the military and the ruling party are well known. Members of the military are sometimes appointed to strategic positions in the government or to head important projects. Security forces are occasionally used for partisan purposes, such as to intimidate opponents or investigative journalists. In September 2004, the director of police was a former deputy of the ruling party.

Property rights—individual or in association with others—are guaranteed by the constitution (Article 15). In general, the state adequately respects and enforces property rights and contracts. If the state does not respect its contractual commitments, it can be sued. The constitution states that land can be expropriated only for the public good and with just and prior compensation, except in the case of an emergency. The current government generally respects these conditions. However, there is not always agreement between the government and the victim of expropriation on what constitutes just compensation.

There are contradictions between traditional customs and the 1996 land and agrarian act, which establishes a national land domain defined by the law as comprising all lands of the national territory and all lands acquired abroad by the state. The state has basically made no effort to find solutions to these contradictions. In practice, the land continues to be managed by traditional authorities according to the customs of the community, particularly in rural areas, although these customs have been legally abrogated since 1985. Only in areas managed by the state and in urban districts does the state impose its will. Even in towns, land is sometimes controlled by no one or ruled by traditional authorities whose power has officially been abolished. In face of this legal dualism, the state seems powerless. Thus, land conflicts are sometimes irremediable.

### Recommendations

- The High Magistrate Council and the public prosecutor's office should be reformed to allow for greater independence from undue interference from the executive.

- To improve accountability and reduce human rights violations, parliament should have oversight of the security forces and the military.
- Human rights transgressions committed by the security forces and military must be thoroughly investigated and punished.
- Legal aid for the poor should be reinforced with more funding.
- Traditional and modern rights of land management must be reconciled through the revision of the state land law to involve traditional authorities in land management and through awareness campaigns for law enforcement personnel.

## ANTICORRUPTION AND TRANSPARENCY – 3.12

Since the beginning of the economic liberalization process in 1990, Burkina Faso, with the support of the IMF and the World Bank, has implemented multiple economic reforms to simplify procedures, privatize public enterprises, and break up the monopolies that generated corruption. The state considerably reduced its involvement in the economy through the process of economic liberalization. It has disengaged from most sectors of production, now considered the basis for economic growth. However, the state remains the main actor of economic development because of the embryonic nature of the formal private sector.

Many laws and institutional arrangements aim at ensuring the separation of the public domain from the personal interests of government officials. For example, during their time in office, members of the government cannot directly or indirectly buy or lease anything that belongs to the state unless a waiver is granted by law. In addition, under the constitution (Article 77), members of the government must submit a list of their property holdings to the constitutional council when they take and leave office. In reality, these constitutional provisions are not observed. The purchase of state property by members of the government is common in Burkina Faso. The president of the constitutional council revealed during a press conference in December 2003 that very few officials were in compliance with Article 77 and that he has no means to enforce the law.[8] The journalist Norbert Zongo, before his murder, found that the written declarations of state officials' assets received by the constitutional chamber of the Supreme Court (today the constitutional council) were still sealed because there was no authorization for a judge to read the content.

The state is not sufficiently protected against conflicts of interest in the private sector because of the close relationships between private economic actors and government authorities. The most important businessmen and -women of the country are either supporters of the ruling party or friends or family members of top state officials. They survive economically because of public contracts and could not prosper without political favors. The state justifies this by asserting that these actors are the pillars of economic growth and must therefore be supported.

Although normative and institutional mechanisms for the prevention and punishment of corruption are in place, they are not at all effective due to the lack of political will. The state does not rigorously apply the legislative and administrative procedures designed to ensure integrity and to prevent, detect, and punish corruption by public officials. State authorities downplay corruption, pointing out that the situation in Burkina Faso is better than in other countries in the region. Public corruption is used as a way to gather support and reward and maintain loyalty. Similarly, ruling party followers can divert public resources with impunity, provided that they remain loyal. According to the High Authority to Combat Corruption, several reports from the state general inspector revealed cases of incompetent management or embezzlement of public funds, with no subsequent action taken. Only people who do not belong to the ruling party are subject to judicial action.

Citizens who are victims of corruption have the right to sue. The results of these suits vary, with more successful outcomes generally achieved by those with higher social, economic, or political status.

Several cases of fraud in university examinations or in professional civil servant exams were widely publicized in August 2003. This led the government to cancel 14 professional exams, which were rescheduled in December 2003.[9] Less is known about corruption in higher education than in secondary education; in the latter, teachers or headmasters do not hesitate to ask for money or favors in exchange for providing admission to schools or advance copies of tests. The government does attempt to contain this practice. Teachers and headmasters have been sued since July 2004 in a case of leaked exams. The prosecutor has pursued very severe penalties in order to set an example.

The fiscal administration has in place systems to verify accounts for tax collection purposes. But these systems are not always efficient, as the fiscal administration is among the most corrupt sectors of the government.[10] To reinforce the control mechanisms, the government plans to set up an integrated tax collector's office that will computerize the collection of customs money and government finances.

An audit office verifies public accounts, punishes management errors, and assists the National Assembly in the execution of finance laws. The audit office is an independent institution whose members benefit from statutory guarantees recognized by the judiciary. Unfortunately, the office is ineffective due to the insufficient human, financial, and material resources at its disposal. It has yet to publish a report. Moreover, no measures are in place for monitoring results or guaranteeing the effective application of those recommendations it might issue.

Many government bodies have been set up to address the prevention or suppression of corruption. However, these bodies, other than the audit office, are under the control of the executive and subject to political pressure. The executive is the primary instigator of court cases against government officials and primarily targets opposition party members. In practice, few allegations of public corruption are fully investigated and prosecuted.

Some allegations of corruption are widely publicized, mainly in the private media. Investigative journalism plays an important role in combating corruption in Burkina Faso. However, journalists face difficulties because of the culture of secrecy that prevails in the state apparatus. The work of media, civil society, and anticorruption advocates is also hampered by the lack of a legal environment to protect them. The impunity in the case of Zongo's murder and also the intimidation of journalists and activists of the National Network to Fight Corruption (RENLAC), an independent NGO, create insecurity that endures today.

No law provides for freedom of information. Reports from auditing bodies are not made public. Secrecy continues to hold back the administration, and civil servants maintain the ability to withhold information from the public.

The executive budget-making process is comprehensive, and parliament has the right to amendment. However, the constitution (Article 120) prohibits any amendment to the budget that would decrease public revenues or resources or increase public expenditures unless a corresponding increase in revenue or reduction in expenditures is proposed simultaneously. This provision reduces the ability of the deputies to influence the process. The government has adopted several reforms and improved budget transparency in recent years. However, many expenditures are classified as interdepartmental and miscellaneous, thus making them difficult to track. Documents relating to the budget process are not generally available to the public, much less simplified in order to make them accessible to average citizens. Moreover, the parliament and audit office have no means to execute an efficient verification of public expenditures. In recent years the government has improved the management of public expenditures through an integrated system of tax collection and review. It also attempts to submit draft laws on the regulation of public accounts to the National Assembly for a vote within a reasonable amount of time, but these bills have been subject to considerable delays.

Several reforms have been implemented in recent years to improve laws regulating public contracts. However, the state still does not ensure effective transparency, openness, and full competition. In principle, full competition is required for public procurement except in an emergency. In fact, this principle is frequently bypassed on the pretext of emergency. This leads to abusive recourse (about half of public procurement, according to RENLAC) to particular procedures (private contracts) that sometimes mask cases of corruption. Official corruption, which is often very difficult to prove, results in some public contracts going to less worthy enterprises or entrepreneurs.

Foreign aid constitutes 75 percent of state development investments. Conditions placed on aid by donors lead to the lawful administration and distribution of foreign aid. However, some grants are not mentioned in the state budget. They are managed in a parallel structure and thus open to corruption.

*Recommendations*
- The government should adopt a law ensuring the publication of the assets of public officials, verification of these declarations, and monitoring of changes in their assets over time.
- The capacity of control mechanisms should be reinforced through institutional reform, more human and financial resources, and

autonomy or independence. These institutions should be given the power to pursue violations and publish their reports in a timely manner.

- Protection for anticorruption activists against intimidation of all kinds should be reinforced through a law banning such practices.
- A new law should codify citizens' rights to information and to access to government documents.

## NOTES

[1] "La réforme du système électoral burkinabè" (Stockholm: International Institute for Democracy and Electoral Assistance [IDEA], 1999).

[2] "Report on democracy in Burkina Faso" (Stockholm: IDEA, 1998).

[3] "Defence Minister Sacked after Questioning over Coup Attempt," *IRIN News,* 18 January 2004, http://www.irinnews.org/report.asp?ReportID=38987&SelectRegion=West_Africa&SelectCountry=BURKINA_FASO.

[4] "Liste des organisations et partis politiques légalement reconnus" (Ouagadougou: Ministère de l'Administration territoriale et de la décentralisation, 9 September 2004).

[5] For 2004, 250 million CFA are registered in the national budget.

[6] "Rapport 1996–2002 sur l'état des droits humains au Burkina Faso" (Ouagadougou: Mouvement Burkinabè des Droits de l'Homme et des Peuples, 2003).

[7] *Sidwaya,* 5020, 9 June 2004, 4–5.

[8] *Le Pays,* 3020, 9 December 2003, 5.

[9] *L'Observateur-Paalga,* 28 October 2003, 11.

[10] "Burkina Faso Human Development Report 2004: Corruption and Human Development" (Ouagadougou: United Nations Development Programme, 2004).

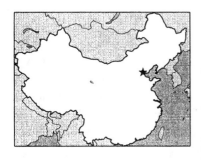

# CHINA

CAPITAL: Beijing
POPULATION: 1.3 billion
GNI PER CAPITA: $960

**SCORES**

ACCOUNTABILITY AND PUBLIC VOICE: 1.08
CIVIL LIBERTIES: 1.61
RULE OF LAW: 1.76
ANTICORRUPTION AND TRANSPARENCY: 2.18
(scores are based on a scale of 0 to 7, with
0 representing weakest and 7 representing
strongest performance)

*Joseph Fewsmith*

## INTRODUCTION

In the late 1980s and early 1990s, as socialism disappeared from large parts of the globe and as the Soviet Union itself broke into its constituent units, the People's Republic of China (PRC) defied expectations, first by crushing popular demonstrations in Beijing as well as many other cities throughout the country, and then by resuming a course of economic reform that has led to extraordinary growth. But neither the demands for political reform that emerged in the 1980s nor economic growth have led to democratic transition. The government's defenders point to gradual improvements in governance and the avoidance of the sort of chaos that might be expected to emerge in such a populous country undergoing rapid change and experiencing growing differences in income. Its critics, however, point to continuing abuses of power, including the stifling of dissent, to argue that China should embark on a program of political reform to bring democratic rights—not just improved standards of living—to its citizens.

Joseph Fewsmith is professor of international relations and political science at Boston University. His most recent books are *China Since Tiananmen* (Cambridge University Press, 2001) and *Elite Politics in Contemporary China* (ME Sharpe, 2001).

In broad terms, one can identify three trends that have characterized China's governance in recent years. First, there has been a substantial withdrawal of the Chinese Communist Party (CCP) and state from the day-to-day lives of the Chinese people. No longer are citizens subjected to long harangues and study sessions. Entertainment and leisure activities have expanded greatly. The range of information available to citizens has grown substantially—despite government control of the media—in part because of the emergence of new media, such as the Internet, in part because of commercial pressures to sell newspapers and books, and in part because the state has enlisted the media in an effort to monitor the worst abuses in the Chinese system. Thus, for citizens who do not confront the state, the role of government in their lives has shrunk and the scope of their private lives has enlarged and improved.

Second, at the same time, China's political life remains monopolized by a single party, the media continue to be the voice of the party, the judicial system is still supervised by the political system (that is, the CCP) and government officials (most of whom are members of the CCP) who rule the country, and the interpenetration between the political system and the economy is substantial. These features have generated corruption and abuses of power that have undermined the legitimacy of the government, threatened social stability, and deprived citizens of their right to hold the government accountable. Efforts to create opposition political parties are suppressed, voices that are overly critical of the government are gagged, and citizens and even journalists who seek to protest or expose wrongdoing are frequently silenced, sometimes violently. Legal protections of citizens' rights remain inadequate, and abuse of prisoners, including the use of torture, continues to be common. Freedom of religion is severely restricted, with frequent arrests of leaders of house churches and other clergy. The suppression of religious freedom and minority populations tends to be blurred together in areas such as Tibet and Xinjiang where Buddhists and Muslims seek greater autonomy from Han Chinese rule.

Finally, there is a trend toward institutionalization. The CCP has repeatedly called for ruling through law and for building institutions that will curb abuses of power and prevent corruption. The past year has seen some substantial steps in this direction, including some innovations in local electoral practices. Such institution building, while still in its early stages, could improve governance. Nevertheless, its intent is clearly to enhance the control and legitimacy of the state, not to bring about democratic governance. Therefore, it is unlikely that the sorts of reforms China needs in order to bring about popular supervision of government will take place any time soon.

## ACCOUNTABILITY AND PUBLIC VOICE – 1.08

As a Leninist system, the PRC has never made the holding of free and fair elections a goal; on the contrary, the government has repeatedly stated that it would never copy Western-style democracy, believing that to do so would lead to political disintegration and social chaos. Under China's Communist system, the leadership continues to be selected at party conclaves. Theoretically, the top leadership is chosen by a party congress—a meeting of party delegates representing lower levels and such functional groups as the People's Liberation Army (PLA)—which convenes in Beijing every five years and ratifies the selection of a Central Committee. In practice, the selection of party delegates is carefully controlled from the top. There has been some moves toward democratic choice in recent years as the number of people nominated for the Central Committee has exceeded the number named to the Central Committee by a small number (usually five—the current Central Committee is made up of 198 full and alternate members). The Central Committee then ratifies the Politburo, which in turn names the Politburo Standing Committee—the core of the political system—including the general secretary of the CCP (currently Hu Jintao) and the membership of such critical organs as the Secretariat, which oversees much of the day-to-day functioning of the political system, and the Central Military Commission, which oversees the PLA.

The legislative branch of government, the National People's Congress (NPC), is composed of about 3,000 delegates chosen by local people's congresses (though vetted by the CPP). The NPC promulgates important laws, although important policies can be conveyed directly by the CCP or by executive order of the State Council. Although the NPC has long had a reputation as a rubber-stamp body that consistently ratifies the policies of the central government, in recent years it has begun to express itself in the law-making process (in which its committees can have considerable input): questioning the reports of ministers, offering resolutions, and showing through its vote totals which nominees for office are more popular (although no one nominated for a position by the government has yet lost an election). Still, when the government wants the NPC to pass particular legislation, it always complies.

The State Council is the government side of the political system. Although most members, including all top leaders, are members of the CCP and are responsible to it, the State Council and its subordinate organs are not formally part of the structure of the CCP. Rather, the CCP rules through the government. The State Council is headed by the premier, currently Wen Jiabao.

The Chinese People's Political Consultative Conference (CPPCC) is a so-called united front body that brings together the CCP with the eight democratic parties that are a legacy of China's civil war period (members of the non-Communist parties can, but do not necessarily, hold dual membership in the CCP). The CPPCC, particularly its Standing Committee, is a body that is often used to acknowledge the contributions of social notables in various fields, from politics to science and culture. In this sense, it is a body that co-opts some of China's best and brightest.

Although there is no intention to permit Western-style democracy (which the CCP distinguishes from socialist democracy, which they consider to mean rule by the party in the long-term interests of the Chinese people), the party has found it desirable to allow some degree of democracy at the village level. According to China's constitution, villages are below the formal government structure and are supposed to be self-governing, although in fact they are ruled by the village party secretary. The township (the form of government above the village) is considered the lowest level of state administration. The breakup of the commune system in 1983 created a substantial political vacuum at the local level as the relationship between the village party secretary and the village head (the government side of the local political system) became less than clear and relations between local cadres and villagers began to worsen. In response, the government began to introduce elections at the village level in the late 1980s. Such elections were limited in scope—only the village government leaders, not the party leaders, could be elected through popular voting. But the elections increased tension between village government leaders (primarily the village head) and the village party secretary, with the former claiming authority based on his (or, very rarely if ever, her) being popularly elected while the latter claimed authority by virtue of representing the CCP at the local level. Scholars vary in their estimation of how competitive such elections are and what percentage of villages hold such competitive elections. For some years Chinese reformers and foreign observers hoped that the competitive electoral mechanism introduced at the village level could be raised to the township level (and, eventually, to yet higher levels). Unfortunately, these hopes have not yet been realized.[1]

Over the past year or so, some interesting breakthroughs in elections for local people's congresses have taken place at the township level. People's congresses are the legislative arm of government, corresponding to the NPC at the national level. Nominations are normally closely guarded by the CCP and voters generally vote through their *danwei* (work unit) or residence, making elections formalistic and easy to control. But the election law allows for candidates to be nominated through the petition of ten or more people and allows for representatives to be elected through write-in campaigns. This has opened the way for several novel elections for local posts around the country.[2] These innovations are obviously extremely limited in a country the size of China, and sometimes elections are negated after the fact.[3] However, they do bespeak a changing political environment and citizen awareness.

China still has a very long way to go to establish a system of accountability through checks and balances, either among branches of government or through monitoring of government by citizen groups. In 2002, the Shenzhen Special Economic Zone in southeast China did begin an experiment in separating the powers of policy making, policy implementation, and supervision, but recent reports suggest that this limited reform has withered in favor of what officials refer to as streamlining and efficiency.[4] In some areas, there seems to be real retrogression. For instance, whereas previously China's provincial people's congresses were headed by senior, often retired, cadres, today about three-quarters are headed by the provincial party secretary, thus concentrating political power.

Over the past decade and more, China has made substantial efforts to upgrade the quality and competence of its civil service. In the 1980s, efforts focused on developing and implementing a retirement system, and this has been increasingly effective over the years. Retired officials no doubt still play a role, but it is much reduced by comparison with years past. Also in the 1980s, a substantial effort brought in younger, better educated, and more professional cadres. Judging by the educational characteristics of the Central Committee and ministerial-level cadres, these efforts have been very successful. Still, the role of the CCP makes criteria for promotion as much political as professional.[5]

There has been a rapid development of nongovernmental organization (NGOs) in recent years (see "Civil Liberties"). NGOs are legally required to register with the government, but not all do. There have also been some experiments recently with a type of hearing system in which affected sectors of the public are allowed to comment on impending policy changes, but such a system is far from being universalized and NGOs have not been a part of this process.

China has long been characterized by tight control over the media, and this continues to be true, although the extent of the control varies with the type of media. All media are either owned directly by the CCP or government or are controlled by them through the governmental affiliations that every media outlet is required to establish. There is some ambiguity about what can be published and what cannot (for instance, if the government opposes corruption, can a publication expose it without seeking prior approval from higher-level authority?); in general, editors are trusted to know where the lines are. However, the job of knowing what to report and how to report it has become more complicated in recent years because the prevalence of the Internet, cell phones, and text messaging have made the former practice of simply not reporting incidents more difficult, especially when there is a major public safety issue involved.

The textbook case in this regard was the Severe Acute Respiratory Syndrome (SARS) crisis in 2003. In that instance, media silence, then mendacity, clearly made SARS a more serious threat to public health than it otherwise would have been. Finally, in April 2003, the minister of health and the mayor of Beijing were dismissed, and the media were told to report the facts of the epidemic accurately. They did so, but the propaganda apparatus continued to set the themes in the campaign against SARS. The crisis did popularize a term, *zhiqingquan* (the right to know), which has reverberated through public discourse in the months since.

As government concerns have changed, the media have been enlisted to support the new agenda. For instance, in recent years, abuse of power and corruption, particularly at lower levels, have become major concerns, in part because they have led to the rapid growth of social disturbances. The official news weekly *Liaowang* recently reported that the number of what they called mass incidents (protests and demonstrations) in 2003 had increased by 14.4 percent over the previous year to some 58,500, involving more than 3 million people.[6] Accordingly, the government has tasked the media with exposing corruption and the abuse of power, which allows the central government to be portrayed as caring about the welfare of the common people as well as to monitor the behavior of local officials. A large number of journalists have high professional ethics and hope to use their journalistic abilities to bring about a more just society. In some instances, such zealousness coincides with the desires of government—and sometimes it does not, leading to various forms of suppression of journalists.

Some notable instances of media repression took place in 2003–2004. A hard-hitting investigative report on corruption and abuse of power in the countryside was banned after it became a surprise bestseller in late 2003. The authors were sued for libel by Zhang Xide, a former county CCP secretary who was criticized in the book and whose son is a local judge, raising concern that the authors would not receive a fair trial. In the south of China, the editor-in-chief of *Nanfang dushi bao* (Southern Metropolitan News), one of the most daring newspapers in the country, was arrested and charged with corruption in March 2004, and two other editors were sentenced to prison terms, allegedly for embezzlement and bribery. Only one was released as of September 2004. In May 2004, freelance journalist Liu Shui was sentenced to two years' administrative detention, allegedly for soliciting prostitution, but more probably for writing essays commemorating the June 4, 1989, Tiananmen Square crackdown, advocating the release of political prisoners, and calling for political reform. In September 2004, Huang Jinqiu, an Internet essayist, was sentenced to 12 years in prison for "subversion of state power." In addition, a news assistant for the *New York Times* was detained and charged with "providing state secrets to foreigners," charges the *New York Times* has vigorously denied.

One trend in recent years that does not bode well for the expansion of journalistic freedom has been the extent of violence perpetrated against journalists by private actors. In the past, journalists were protected by their status as employees of the state. In recent years, as the media have become more competitive, as journalists have developed a professional commitment to social justice, and as crime and corruption have emerged as big stories, those being exposed by journalists have retaliated, sometimes violently. *Zhongguo Qingnian Bao (China Youth News)* listed 19 journalists who had been beaten in 2003, although the reality went well beyond this documented few. The All-China Journalists Association reported in 2004 that it had been contacted more than 350 times since 1998 by journalists requesting protection. In addition, by the end of September 2004, 42 journalists were in jail in China, more than in any other country. Thus, as much as the Chinese government has tried to enlist journalists in its efforts to root out crime, corruption, and abuses of power, journalism has become a dangerous profession, the third most dangerous profession after police work and coal mining.[7]

*Recommendations*

- It is important to expand the role of elections, preferably to the township level. Those elected must be protected against arbitrary dismissal.
- Open hearings should be held on all pending legislation.
- The government should reduce the ability of leading cadres to promote subordinates by institutionalizing civil service procedures and enlarging the number of people who participate in promotion decisions.
- The public's right to know, which is increasingly recognized, needs to be institutionalized by allowing the press to report on corruption and abuses of power at higher levels as well as at lower levels.
- A press law protecting reporters from reprisals should be passed.

## CIVIL LIBERTIES – 1.61

The CCP and the Chinese state have gradually withdrawn from control of the day-to-day lives of the average citizen as consumerism and leisure activities have become more important. As the state has retreated, arbitrary intervention in the lives of most people has been substantially reduced. Nevertheless, abuse of power and the arbitrary and harsh administration of law remain substantial problems. Those who are arrested have no presumption of innocence, are frequently detained for long periods of time (exceeding the limits prescribed by PRC law), face harsh treatment (including torture), and have little access to legal counsel. Indeed, lawyers who are known to be too aggressive in the defense of their clients face intimidation and sometimes arrest.

Although the Chinese legal system has many shortcomings, perhaps the biggest problem lies in the attitude of low-rank law-enforcement personnel. One legal writer claimed that "the vast majority *(jueda duoshu)* of people's police who handle cases" believe that "torture is a fast and effective interrogation technique," and therefore "torture has existed for a long time on a large scale."[8] As a result of such attitudes, according to official Chinese sources (which are usually understated), 241 persons were tortured to death over the two-year period from 1993 to 1994 (no more recent figures are available). If there is an upside in this picture of police brutality, it is that the law-enforcement community in China has begun to criticize such attitudes and practices in an effort to professionalize police work.[9]

Although China removed the crime of counterrevolution from the criminal code in 1997, the crime of endangering state security is almost as vague. Moreover, there are many problems with the administration of justice. Suspects are frequently held for long periods of time, much longer than the two and a half months the Criminal Procedure Law calls for. To China's credit, the public media carried out a campaign in 2003 to eliminate illegal detentions. In March 2004, the Supreme People's Procuratorate stated that it had handled some 30,000 cases of extended detention, clearing up most cases. This statement may have exaggerated the reality, but even critics concede the sincerity of the efforts.[10]

As a one-party state, China has harshly repressed political opposition. The crackdown in June 1989 is well known, as is the jailing of the organizers of the China Democracy Party (which was formed in 1998). Although some of the organizers of that party have been released recently—Xu Wenli in 2002 and Wang Youcai in 2004—others, including Qin Yongmin, remain in jail. Still others who are viewed as potentially causing problems, or even just embarrassment, for the government are detained or removed from Beijing during sensitive periods, such as the anniversary of the Tiananmen crackdown. For instance, Jiang Yanyong, the doctor who blew the whistle on the SARS cover-up in April 2003 and again challenged the government in 2004 by writing a letter calling for a reevaluation of Tiananmen, was one of those detained in June 2004 as the 15th anniversary of Tiananmen approached.[11]

One bright spot in the area of civil liberties is the use of the administrative litigation law, by which citizens can sue the government. Although it is written narrowly—courts cannot overturn the validity of regulations issued by the government—citizens have turned increasingly to the administrative litigation law. Since it took effect in 1990, some 730,000 cases have been filed. In 2004, 114,900 cases were concluded. Moreover, citizens win a healthy 31 percent of the time.[12] The law appears to provide at least some incentive for better governance, although abuses remain widespread.

Gender equality has been elusive in China. Women suffer obvious discrimination in the political arena; currently only 5 of the 198 full members of the Central Committee are women. Women constitute 38.6 percent of the workforce. In a period of industrial restructuring, women are often the first to be laid off and the last to be re-hired.

Suicide is surprisingly common in China; although estimates vary, it is about 20 per 100,000 population, about twice the rate in the United States and neighboring Chinese populations in Hong Kong and Taiwan. Suicide is gender biased. Young rural women are particularly vulnerable, accounting for 20 percent of all suicides. As Sing Lee and Arthur Kleinman note, "China is one of the very few countries in the world to report higher rates of completed suicide in women than in men,"[13] usually because women are forced into marriages they do not want.

China's religious policy reflects both its history and the practices of post-1949 China, with the government working to bring religious observances under the purview of the state or, failing that, repressing heterodox religions that the state sees as a potential threat.[14] The Chinese state recognizes five religions: Buddhism, Taoism, Islam, Protestantism, and Catholicism. Each is headed by an official patriotic organization, supervised by the State Administration for Religious Affairs (SARA), which is, in turn, under the CCP Central Committee.

Religious observances are required to take place in officially recognized churches or temples, although the 1997 PRC White Paper on Religious Freedom does state that "There is no registration requirement for, to quote from Chinese Christians, 'house services,' which are mainly attended by relatives for religious activities such as praying and Bible reading."[15] Larger house churches, involving more than a family and its relatives, are expected to register, although many do not. In practice, such non-official house services have come to dominate Christian religious practices. For instance, there are about 4 million registered and an estimated 8 million unregistered Catholics in China.[16] Similarly, there are some 13 million registered Protestants but perhaps 50 million who worship in illegal house churches.[17] The relations between these official and unofficial forms of worship are often complex, for frequently unregistered Protestants will worship in officially sanctioned churches and registered Protestants will worship in illegal ones. Although relations between Beijing and the Holy See are frequently strained, the Chinese government in January 2004 nevertheless permitted the consecration of Feng Xinmao, who had been approved by the pope, as bishop of the Hengshui diocese in Hebei province.[18]

Religious repression appears to come in waves. In 1999, the Falungong religious movement challenged the government by rallying some 10,000 practitioners to stage a silent protest outside CCP headquarters in Beijing. This demonstration showed the government that a large number of Falungong practitioners were well organized and spanned across county and provincial boundaries. The demonstration came only weeks before the very sensitive 10th anniversary of the Tiananmen student protests, but Falungong was nevertheless able to stage it without the security forces knowing in advance. This ability scared the CCP, and in July 1999 it launched an extensive and harsh crackdown on Falungong. The crackdown continues, although it is less active since Falungong appears to have been effectively suppressed on the mainland.

Following this crackdown and the general prohibition of cults that accompanied it, other religious practices were repressed as well. For instance, in late 2000 and early 2001, hundreds of Buddhist temples, Daoist shrines, and Christian churches were demolished in the city of Wenzhou, Zhejiang.[19] Similarly, 2003–2004 witnessed another wave of repression. For instance, in March 2004, Wei Jingyi, the bishop of Qiqihar, Heilongjiang, was arrested.[20] In April, the government began cracking down on the Three Class Servants Church—a Protestant house church in Heilongjiang—seizing its leader and allegedly holding him for ransom.[21] In August 2004, the government in Inner Mongolia seized a Buddhist temple that had been under renovation. Police seized 70 lamas and arrested the spiritual leader.[22]

Freedom of religion faces special difficulties in the minority areas of Tibet and Xinjiang, where religion, national culture, and politics are intertwined. Both Tibet and Xinjiang are organized as autonomous

regions, which in theory recognizes the special role of religion and ethnicity in these areas. The Chinese government recruits local ethnic minorities into the autonomous regional governments, but in reality, power
is tightly controlled by the central government, including the use of various police and security forces. Both Tibet and Xinjiang are represented
on the Central Committee, but because that body does not meet in regular session it is not an effective forum for voicing concerns or demands.
A Nationalities' Affairs Commission under the State Council has the
difficult task of attempting to reconcile the concerns of nationalities,
including Tibetans and Uighrs (the dominant group in Xinjiang), with
Chinese political control.

The Chinese government has continued tough measures to prevent
Tibetan independence, including jailing many monks and nuns. According to the Tibetan Information Network (TIN), instances of political
imprisonment in Qinghai and Gansu provinces have fallen to low levels, but arrests of Tibetans in Sichuan province have risen. About 75
people are believed to be imprisoned in Tibet.[23] In September 2004,
representatives of the Dalai Lama visited China, the third such delegation to do so in recent years, suggesting some easing of tensions between
the Tibetan community and the Chinese government.

Tensions between the Chinese government and the Muslim population (mostly Uighur) of Xinjiang Autonomous region have been high
for a number of years. The Chinese government prohibits private ma-
drassas and mosques, and it imposes strict travel restrictions on imams
in Xinjiang. The state-controlled China Islamic Association attempts
to impose interpretations of the Koran that are acceptable to the party.
Separatist movements have been known to carry out bombings in
Beijing and elsewhere, and state authorities have cracked down harshly.
In the wake of the September 11 attacks in the United States, the Chinese government has repressed religious activities in the name of opposing terror, although many outside observers believe that repressive
measures have gone far beyond what is needed to curtail separatist or terrorist activities.[24]

[*Editor's note:* The Regulations on Religious Affairs issued by the Chinese government in December 2004 appeared to mark a step backward.
Under the regulations, the state protects "normal" religious activities,
but the definition of normal appears to be subject to state interpretation. The regulations evince great state concern about religion being

used to subvert state control. They appear to tighten restrictions on religious activities, although they may prove difficult to implement given the burgeoning of religious sentiment in China today.]

A 1991 law mandates equal treatment for the approximately 60 million disabled Chinese and provides for penalties against discrimination. State organizations must fill hiring quotas for the disabled, and collective economic organizations are given bonuses for hiring and training disabled employees.[25] The state has made efforts to provide medical assistance and access to government services to the disabled, but progress has been slow in rural areas. Disabled people are often hindered by traditional attitudes, which view congenital disability and disabling illness as shameful or blameworthy.

Although China has seen an unprecedented growth in the number of NGOs, most—and the most important in terms of membership and dissemination of government policy—remain either an arm of the government (such as the All-China Federation of Trade Unions) or attached to some governmental organ (which is what the Ministry of Civil Affairs requires). Some 130,000 NGOs in China have registered with the government, but many if not most of these should be considered government-organized nongovernmental organizations (GONGOs). Despite legal requirements to register, perhaps as many as 300,000 NGOs in China are unregistered. But most of these are small-scale, local NGOs that play little role in government. Some people argue that the important issue is not whether China's NGOs have registered but the social capital they create in society. Collectively, these groups do seem to have an impact on state–societal relations.

Particularly since the 1999 Falungong protest, the government has cracked down on organizations that it feels would challenge the state. Thus, while small-scale, informal organization is allowed to exist outside the control of the state, particularly at the local level, NGOs are not permitted to be vehicles for organizing political or religious movements. Demonstrations have been increasing in recent years and are now a common occurrence. However, force is used if these grow to a scale that, in the eyes of the government, appears to threaten social order or the government.

China has long had labor unions, organized by the party-state and coordinated by the All-China Federation of Trade Unions. In recent years, officials of China's labor unions have been critical of state policy.

But the voice of China's labor unions is limited, and their role ultimately is to support state policy. As a result, workers frequently see the labor union as opposed to their interests, making it more difficult for labor unions to bridge the gap between the state and the workers. As China's private economy has expanded, there has been even less of a role for labor unions to play. Efforts to form independent unions are repressed by the state.

*Recommendations*
- There must be legal penalties when cases of torture occur. Even the Chinese legal community recognizes that torture is wrong.
- Courts must penalize local police in violation of the law against long-term detention, and the media should publicize violations of the law.
- Freedom of religious belief, already guaranteed by the Chinese constitution, should be enforced.
- Freedom of association, including labor unions, must be recognized.

## RULE OF LAW – 1.76

China has come a long way since the days when Mao Zedong declared that he was like a "monk holding an umbrella," unrestrained by "law or heaven." Building a legal system in China has been a slow and difficult process, and it has a long way to go. It was something of a breakthrough when, in 1997, the 15th Party Congress called for ruling the country through law. And since being appointed general secretary of the CCP in 2002, Hu Jintao has repeatedly emphasized the importance of law and building institutions. Nevertheless, the distinction between "rule of law" and "rule by law" is not very clear in China, in theory or in practice. There is no question that the government has favored "rule by law," seeking to keep itself above the law.

China has an authoritarian system, one that has explicitly rejected "checks and balances," including judicial independence. At all levels of the system, courts are subordinate to the political power at the same level—this power appoints the judges and allocates operating funds. Politically important and sensitive cases are also considered by the party Political and Legal Commissions and Discipline Inspection Commissions at different levels, further reducing the independence of judges.

The fact that judges are frequently under-trained—many being demobilized military officers—and corrupt makes the administration of justice difficult at best. The implementation of judicial decisions, particularly outside the jurisdiction in which they are made, is also problematic.

Another problem in the administration of justice is the tendency to carry it out through campaigns. Specifically, China implements periodic strike-hard campaigns, including one in 2003–2004. Such campaigns are organized at times when the crime rate goes up, and they put pressure on local police and judges to arrest and convict more people. These campaigns are generally popular with the public, which favors cracking down on crime, but they frequently result in higher rates of prisoner abuse, including torture, and miscarriages of justice. In 2003, Chinese courts handled 735,535 criminal cases and investigated 43,490 officials for abuse of power and dereliction of duty.[26]

Perhaps the most pervasive abuse of citizens' rights occurs through the re-education through labor system. Individuals can be sentenced to up to three years of labor, with the possibility of a one-year extension, without a court trial. Although this system is much criticized, in China and abroad, its use has actually expanded in recent years. Whereas the number of detainees was 150,000 to 200,000 in the mid-1990s, the figure now has risen to about 300,000. It has been estimated that 2 percent to 10 percent of these detainees are political prisoners.[27]

One encouraging sign is the end of the custody and repatriation system. Under this system, migrants without the proper residence permit could be detained by the local police and sent back to their home village. This system was already controversial when Sun Zhigang, a college student who had forgotten to carry his ID, was detained and beaten to death in Guangzhou in 2003. This case, which was widely publicized on the Internet, led to the repeal of the custody and repatriation system, as well as the conviction of those responsible for his death.

Naturally, one difficulty in trying to build a legal system that is transparent and fair is that important sectors of society are effectively off-limits to public scrutiny. Although there is a tradition of the party controlling the gun (as the party puts it), the military and security forces tend to be independent arenas. The party can and at times does exert its will over the military—as when the party felt it had to curtail corruption in the military and therefore decided to get the military out of business (many in the military agreed)—but in general the military is supposed to supervise itself. The military is a clear component of the political system. Representatives of the military sit on the Politburo, and 22 percent of members of the Central Committee are from the military. In recent years, the military budget has increasingly come under the control of the State Council, but that, too, is subject to negotiation.

Private property is a relatively new phenomenon for China. Since the early 1990s, people in the cities have been encouraged to buy their own housing, and now some 70 percent of Beijing residents own their own apartments. Such rapid privatization (the word still cannot be used in the media) in China has brought many conflicts as new property owners try to hold property developers accountable for promises made or for repairs. Such conflicts have ballooned in recent years. At least one lawyer has been jailed for his vigorous defense of displaced householders. He was charged with leaking state secrets, but he appears to have been arrested primarily because of his efforts to help people evicted by Zhou Zhengyi, a powerful land developer in Shanghai, since convicted of corruption. In a positive development, revisions to the Chinese constitution passed in March 2004 now recognize the inviolability of private property.

In the rural areas, farmers own the plots on which their houses are built and a small amount of land suitable for raising vegetables and chickens or pigs. However, the land they cultivate for rice or wheat is owned by the collective and assigned for long periods of time (30 years) to individual households.

In recent years, the private economy has been the fastest-growing sector of the Chinese economy. There are currently about 2.5 million private enterprises and another 46 million individual entrepreneurs (small-scale enterprises with fewer than eight people). Private entrepreneurs have become increasingly active in local politics, taking up positions in local people's congresses and especially local CPPCCs. This group, however, has not supported democracy, preferring to work through close personal relations with local political authorities. Between 20 and 30 percent of China's private entrepreneurs are members of the CCP, most joining the party before going into business.[28]

### Recommendations

- The courts must be separated from the supervision of party committees at the same level and their judgments made applicable in other jurisdictions.

- The training of judges, while improving, needs to be further upgraded.
- Defendants need ready access to lawyers, and lawyers who defend clients must not be subject to harassment or arrest on trumped-up charges.
- Chinese law should extend a presumption of innocence.
- The re-education through labor system should be abolished.

## ANTICORRUPTION AND TRANSPARENCY – 2.18

For many years, corruption has been recognized as a serious problem by observers both within China and without. Causes of corruption include the power given to party and government, the lack of transparency, the continued involvement of the state in the economy (both public and private), the lack of clear disclosure regulations, the restrictions on the media that prevent independent disclosure of high-level corruption, and the absence of an electoral mechanism that would allow voters to punish perceived violators of the public trust. Although the problem of corruption has long been recognized, the issue has continued to worsen in recent years. In 2003, Qinghua University professor Hu Angang gave a widely quoted estimate of corruption costing some 15 percent of gross domestic product every year from 1999 to 2001.[29] Such an estimate can only be a guess, but it suggests the severity of the problem.

In the edition of the annual *Blue Book* on social conditions that the Chinese Academy of Social Sciences published in early 2004, Wen Shengtang of the Supreme People's Procuratorate wrote that the problem of corruption continues to worsen. In the first nine months of 2003, the people's procuratorate at various levels investigated 32,759 cases, of which 905 involved sums of over 1 million yuan (approximately US$120,000). According to Wen, some new tendencies in official corruption are particularly noteworthy. First, the number of cases involving the *yibashou* (number-one person) has increased notably, presumably because they have become more corrupt. For instance, in the past 10 years, Guizhou province has prosecuted 103 people at the *ting* (prefecture/office) level and above; 54 (52 percent) of these were number-one leaders. Second, the length of time during which corruption goes undiscovered has been growing longer. Of the seven cases involving corruption at the vice ministerial level or above between 1980 and 1988, the average length of time corruption continued before discovery was 1.43 years. In the 16 similar cases in the 1998 to 2002 period, the average length of time was 6.31 years—with the longest case continuing undetected for 14 years. Third, the illegal selling of office has been increasingly concealed behind a facade of correct procedure.[30] According to official figures, between 1998 and 2002, 846,000 CCP members were disciplined and 137,700 expelled from the party, of whom 28,996 were officials at the county level, 2,422 at the bureau level, and 98 at the provincial level.[31]

In 2003–2004, there was evidence both of the continuing scale of corruption and of serious efforts to combat it. In the first six months of 2004, 24,247 people were questioned in regard to 21,164 cases of corruption, about 4 percent of which involved sums of more than 1 million yuan (US$120,000). About 1,700 of those being investigated were officials at the county level or higher.[32]

In June, the director of the national audit office, Li Jinhua, gave a report on the implementation of the 2003 budget that revealed extensive problems in the misuse of funds and the lack of oversight. He told China's legislature that embezzlement of public funds occurred in 55 ministries and commissions of the State Council. Some of the abuses noted were: the amount of central government subsidies to localities was understated by 77.5 percent in the provincial budgets surveyed by the audit office (a sum of 321.3 billion yuan, or about US$38.7 billion); the State Forestry Administration Survey, Planning and Design Institute and four other units drafted or altered seven false "Forestation to Prevent Desertification" projects to misappropriate 4.15 million yuan (US$500,000); the former State Power Corporation had losses of some 7.84 billion RMB yuan (US$945 million).[33] Among those convicted of corruption was Wang Zhonglu, who was said to have taken bribes of 390,000 yuan (US$47,100). Wang is a former deputy governor of Zhejiang province who was also president of Zhejiang International Trust and Investment Corporation, where he reportedly cost the company over 44 million yuan (US$5.3 million) in losses. This suggests an endemic problem of public officials holding simultaneous positions in economic institutions.[34] In addition, the Chinese press reported in 2004 that some 4,000 corrupt officials had fled abroad with more than 5 billion yuan (US$600 million) over the past 20 years.[35]

As an unusually explicit and detailed report by Auditor General Li Jinhua suggests, 2004 witnessed a new openness in discussing corruption as well as new and apparently more vigorous efforts to combat it. For instance, the national audit administration has worked to build a national auditing system to fight corruption, touted as the first of its sort in the country. At the same time, the CCP has adopted a number of new regulations that aim to improve cadre selection and prevent corruption in the party. These regulations include Provisional Regulations on the Public Selection of Party and Government Leading Cadres, Provisional Regulations on Contested Appointment in Party and Government Organs, and the Regulations on Inner-Party Supervision of the CCP (for Trial Implementation). Such regulations, at a minimum, reflect a desire in the CCP to regularize the cadre system, to make the selection and promotion of cadres more subject to rules and less subject to personal favoritism, and to improve relations between the cadres and the public. However, the CCP has adopted other regulations in the past in an effort to curb corruption; whether these new ones prove any more successful remains to be seen.

There has been an effort in recent years to inject more transparency into government. Most municipal and provincial governments maintain Web sites, as does the central government and ministries of the State Council. Policies and laws are generally given wide publicity, although a few years ago local governments tried hard to stop the circulation of regulations governing the taxation of peasants. New laws and regulations are also intended to increase transparency, at least to some extent. These efforts face considerable resistance, both because of the nature of the political system and deeply embedded habits. For instance, although the decisions of the CCP are widely disseminated, the process by which those decisions were reached, including different perspectives on what should be done, are not revealed to the public. The media is not allowed to probe such issues. Alternative forms of media, particularly the Internet and cell phones, allow information to circulate more freely (although these too are subject to being blocked by the state), but this has not led to significant transparency of government operations.

*Recommendations*
- The press must have more freedom to report on the corruption of officials.

- Government officials should be required to make public financial disclosure statements to improve transparency and reduce corruption.
- Whistle-blowers should be protected by law.

## NOTES

[1] Li Lianjiang, "The Politics of Introducing Direct Township Elections in China," *China Quarterly,* no. 171 (September 2002): 704–23.

[2] Li Fan, ed., *Zhongguo jiceng minzhu fazhan baogao [Grassroots democracy in China]* (Beijing: Falüchubanshe, 2004).

[3] Huang Guangming and He Hongwei, "Striking Dilemma in Grassroots Administration in Dianjiang [sic, Qianjiang] Village [sic, City], 187 Elected Village Officials Dismissed in Three Years," *Nanfang zhuomo,* 12 September 2002, trans. FBIS CPP-2002-0916-000029; Dang Guoying, "The Reality and Future of Villagers' Autonomy," *Nanfang zhuomo,* 30 September 2002, trans. FBIS CPP-2002-1008-0000051.

[4] "China Said to Allow 'Limited' Political Reform in Shenzhen," *Hong Kong Daily Mail,* 23 January 2002; and Chow Chung-yan, "Shenzhen 'Still the City of Tomorrow,'" *South China Morning Post,* 28 June 2004.

[5] John P. Burns, "Governance and Civil Service Reform," in Jude Howell, ed., *Governance in China* (New York: Roman and Littlefield, 2003), 37–57.

[6] "Economic Reform Causing Social Unrest and Crime in China: Report," Agence France Presse (AFP), 9 June 2004.

[7] Sophie Beach, "In China, New Journalism and New Threats" (New York: Committee to Protect Journalists [CPJ], 24 August 2004), http://www.cpj.org/Briefings/2004/China_8_04/China_8_04.html.

[8] Du Jingji, "Qianlun xingxun bigong de chansheng ji qi duice [A superficial discussion of the sources of tortured confession and policies to deal with it]," as quoted in Murray Scot Tanner, "Torture in China: Calls for Reform from within China's Law Enforcement System" (Washington, DC: U.S. Congress, prepared statement to accompany testimony before the Congressional-Executive Commission on China [CECC], 26 July 2002).

[9] Murray Scot Tanner, "Torture in China," prepared statement to accompany testimony before the China-Executive Committee on China, 26 July 2002, http://www.chinaaid.org/English/Advocacy/CAA%20PRESS%20RELEASE%20ON%20100%20CHUR H%20LEADERS%20ARREST%20In%20TONGXU%20HENAN%2008-6-04.htm.

[10] *Congressional Executive Commission on China 2004 Annual Report* (Washington, DC: U.S. Congress, 5 October 2004), 16.

[11] Jim Yardley, "China Hides Dissidents for Tiananmen Anniversary," *New York Times,* 4 June 2004.

[12] Hu Hong, "Empower Administrative Litigation," *China Daily,* 14 November 2004, http://www.chinadaily.com.cn/english/doc/2004-11/14/content_391269.htm.

[13] Sing Lee and Arthur Kleinman, "Suicide as Resistance in Chinese Society," in Elizabeth J. Perry and Mark Selden, eds., *Chinese Society: Change, Conflict and Resistance,* 2nd ed. (London and New York: Routledge, 2000), 292–93.

14 Anthony Yu, *State and Religion in China* (Peru, Ill.: Open Court Publishing, 2005); Pitman Potter, "Belief in Control: Regulation of Religion in China," *The China Quarterly* 174 (June 2003): 317–37.

15 "White Paper—Freedom of Religious Belief in China" (Washington, DC: Chinese Embassy, 1997), http://www.china-embassy.org/eng/zt/zjxy/t36492.htm.

16 *CECC 2004 Annual Report*, 327–28, fn 326.

17 "Remarks by Paul Marshall, Senior Fellow, Center for Religious Freedom, Freedom House, Before the Congressional-Executive Commission on China, Roundtable on Religious Freedom in China" (CECC, 25 March 2002), http://www.cecc.gov/pages/roundtables/032502/marshallRmks.php?mode=print&PHPSESSID=9.

18 On Feng Xinmao see, "First Bishop Ordained in Decades with Graduate Degree," *AsiaNews*, 8 January 2004, http://www.asianews.it.

19 John Fisher, "China: Official Press Confirms Wenzhou Destruction Campaign," Keston News Service, 31 May 2001, http://www.starlightsite.co.uk/keston/kns/2001/010531CH.htm.

20 Magister, "The Bishop of Xi'an's Long March."

21 "China Moves to Crush Millions-Strong Christian House Church" (Washington, DC: Center for Religious Freedom, 19 May 2004), http://www.Freedomhouse.org/religion/news/bn2004/bn-2004-05-19.htm.

22 Jim Yardley, "In Crackdown, China Shuts Buddhist Site and Seizes Catholic Priests," *New York Times*, 19 August 2004, 7.

23 "New Cases of Tibetan Political Imprisonment," Tibet Information Network [TIN], 8 July 2004.

24 Dru Gladney, "Cyber-Separatism and Uyghur Ethnic Nationalism in China" (Washington, DC: Center for Strategic and International Studies [CSIS], Forum on The Role of Xinjiang in China-Central Asia Relations, 5 June 2003), http://www.csis.org/china/030605.cfm.

25 Center for International Rehabilitation, *International Disability Rights Monitor*, China 2003 Compendium Report http://www.cirnetwork.org/idrm/reports/china.cfm

26 *CECC 2004 Annual Report*, 12.

27 Ibid., 17.

28 Bruce Dickson, *Red Capitalists in China* (Cambridge: Cambridge University Press, 2003).

29 *Shanghai Star*, 19 June 2003, http://app1.chinadaily.com.cn/star/2003/0619/fe21-1.html.

30 Wen Shengtang, "2003 nian de fanfubai douzheng [The struggle against corruption in 2003]," in Ru Xin, Lu Xueyi, and Li Peilin, eds., *2004 nian: Zhongguo shehui xingshi fenxi yu yuce* [China's Social Situation: Analyses and Forecasts, 2004] (Beijing: Shehui kexue wenxian chubanshe, 2004).

31 "Hu Warns Against Aping Western Politics," *The Straits Times*, 16 September 2004.

32 Cao Zhe, "Prosecutors Confirm Big Graft Cases Increase," *China Daily*, 9 August 2004.

33 "Li Jinhua shenjizhang zuo 2003 niandu shenji gongzuo baogao," 24 June 2004, http://www.xinhuanet.com/zhengfu/2004-06/24/content_1543949.htm.

34 "Former Official Sent to Prison for Corruption," *China Daily*, 3 September 2004.

35 "Corrupt Officials Flee China," BBC News, 19 August 2004, http://news.bbc.co.uk/go/pr/fr/-/hi/world/asia-pacific/3579992.stm.

# COLOMBIA

CAPITAL: Bogota
POPULATION: 45.3 million
GNI PER CAPITA: $1,820

**SCORES**

ACCOUNTABILITY AND PUBLIC VOICE: 5.02
CIVIL LIBERTIES: 4.39
RULE OF LAW: 4.21
ANTICORRUPTION AND TRANSPARENCY: 3.88
(scores are based on a scale of 0 to 7, with
0 representing weakest and 7 representing
strongest performance)

*Harvey F. Kline*[1]

## INTRODUCTION

Democracy in Colombia is affected by three major characteristics of the country—endemic violence, poverty, and a tendency not to enforce laws that have been passed. These three factors combine to produce a democratic regime that at times appears very advanced but which with more careful study demonstrates many weaknesses.

All dimensions of democracy in Colombia are affected by the rampant violence that the country suffers, especially outside Bogotá and a few other major cities. When Álvaro Uribe Vélez became president on August 7, 2002, the country had been suffering from violence for nearly 40 years. It can be traced to the 1960s, when two major Marxist guerrilla groups emerged: the Armed Forces of the Colombian Revolution (Fuerzas Armadas Revolucionarias de Colombia, FARC) and the Army of National Liberation (Ejército de Liberación Nacional, ELN). Both groups have called for revolutions to end capitalism, redistribute income,

**Harvey F. Kline** is professor of political science at the University of Alabama–Tuscaloosa. He has taught on three occasions at the Universidad de los Andes in Bogota with grants from the Fulbright-Hayes Commission. He has published five books on Colombian politics

and improve the lives of the poor. As the Colombian government had never established a national police force that was effective in all parts of the country, landowners set up self-defense or paramilitary groups to defend themselves from the guerrillas. These were approved by law between the early 1960s and the late 1980s. In the 1980s drug dealers joined many of them, making the paramilitary groups even more powerful. In 1997 the paramilitary groups organized nationally as the United Self-Defense Groups of Colombia (Autodefensas Unidas de Colombia, AUC) under the leadership of Carlos Castaño. Common crime added to the picture, with the result that Colombia has one of the highest indexes in the world of both homicides and kidnapping.

The National Planning Department gave a statistical picture of the Colombia that Uribe inherited in a comparison of the last two years of the presidency of Ernesto Samper (1996–1998) with the four years of the presidency of Andrés Pastrana (1998–2002). Murders rose from 25,039 a year during the Samper presidency to 26,891 under Pastrana, while kidnappings increased from 2,068 to 3,106. Terrorist attacks increased from 744 to 944, and attacks on towns went from 90 to 130. The number of massacres likewise went up, from 114 to 176, and the number of victims of those mass murders increased from 607 to 1,013. Most dramatically, the number of internal refugees increased from 3,907 a year during the last two years of the Samper government to 41,355 a year during the four-year Pastrana presidency.[2]

Uribe rejected the peace approach of his predecessor, who had granted a demilitarized zone the size of Switzerland to the FARC. Instead, Uribe announced that his government would negotiate with any insurgent group that declared a cease-fire with the goal of demobilizing and turning in its weapons. At the end of 2002 the government signed a cease-fire with AUC, although its implementation was still not complete by September 2004, despite verification of the effort by the Organization of American States. Although 2,624 paramilitary troops demobilized during 2004,[3] much remained to be done in the effort.

Uribe's policies also included a strengthening of the Colombian military, with the assistance of aid from the United States. Indexes of violence have gone down, while tourism within the country has become less dangerous. Colombians have started having more positive attitudes about their country.

Colombia is a poor country, with a per capita income in 2003 of US$1,810.[4] Furthermore, income is very inequitably distributed, with many people at the bottom living on less than US$1 a day and without government medical insurance, social security or unemployment benefits, or any kind of welfare. Politics are dominated by individuals of the middle- and upper-income groups, with poor people having only the right to vote for candidates chosen by the upper-income groups.

Formally the Colombian constitution specifies a long list of human rights, but in practice many of the rights are violated. In addition, international humanitarian rights are breached by guerrilla and paramilitary groups. Women and ethnic minorities have even more difficulty in securing their constitutional guarantees. While the Colombian government does not often interfere with press freedom, that liberty is seriously affected by the violence of the country. Until 2004, when only one journalist was killed, Colombia had one of the highest numbers of deaths of journalists in the world.[5] Journalists here regularly exercise self-censorship as a way to protect themselves.

Corruption remains a serious problem in Colombia. The Uribe government has made noises about being tougher on this issue; however, to this point few actions have been taken. An independent judiciary exists, but it is inadequately staffed and often spends time in disputes over jurisdiction. Elections are generally free and without fraud, although guerrillas maintain that the lack of real choice makes the voting meaningless.

## ACCOUNTABILITY AND PUBLIC VOICE – 5.02

Colombians pride themselves on having one of the more democratic governments in Latin America. Indeed there were only three short dictatorships during the 19th century (only one of which was military) and only four years of military government during the 20th century. Nevertheless, before 1953 the regime was far from truly democratic, and repeated periods of violence culminated in a partisan conflict between the two political parties between 1946 and 1964. As a way to end the partisan violence, party leaders proposed a National Front government. After this was approved by the people in a plebiscite and by the congress as a constitutional amendment, between 1958 and 1974 power was shared equally by the two parties. The presidency alternated every four years between the parties, and all elective bodies and appointed positions not part of the civil service were divided equally between them. While this clearly was not a democracy, it did lead to the end of the violence between the parties.

Since 1974 Colombia has come closer to the ideal of a democracy. Presidential elections have been held every four years, as have those for the Senate and since 1991 for the lower house of the national congress. Every election does include charges of fraud and intimidation of voters, but both major parties have seen their candidates elected to the presidency. Members of other parties are also elected to the national and departmental legislatures. Although the executive is clearly the strongest branch of government, Colombia's traditional democratic checks and balances have functioned more effectively than those in most other Latin American countries.

Political parties are granted government funds according to the number of votes received in the previous election, as well as private funds. The controls on the latter are weak; these funds allegedly include contributions from drug dealers, most notably in the 1994 election of Ernesto Samper. The lower house of congress debated Samper's impeachment as a result of these funds, but no vote took place, in part because so many of its members had also received monies from drug groups.

With increased democratization since the 1980s, including popular elections of governors and mayors, insurgent groups have expanded their power at the local level. There have been accusations that many politicians, including members of the national congress, are elected with the aid of paramilitary squads, drug dealers, or guerrilla groups.

President Uribe has proposed that the constitution be changed to allow immediate reelection of the president. Under the 1991 constitution, the president can serve only one term. This constitutional amendment passed the Colombian congress in the 2003 sessions and is being considered in 2004 (passage by congress in two consecutive years is one way to amend the constitution). Uribe's approval ratings have been very high—at 70 percent in mid-2004—and it seems likely that, should the amendment pass, he will be a strong candidate in 2006. [*Editor's note:* The amendment passed on November 30, 2004, and the Constitutional Court considered its constitutionality in January 2005.]

The government publishes a daily record of pending legislation, laws passed, and new regulations. Since the constitution of 1991 the civic sector is less hampered by governmental regulation than before. However, there are accusations that some civic sector organizations are fronts for insurgent groups, hence affecting the climate in which all organizations can influence policy and causing at least tacit pressure on them. During the presidency of Andrés Pastrana, for example, civic sector groups opposing his demilitarized zone for the ELN were charged with being fronts for paramilitary organizations.

The constitution provides for media freedom in Colombia. Recent Colombian governments, including that of Uribe, have done little to limit such freedom. Current laws allow journalists to criticize the government. Libel cases seldom go beyond the obligation to rectify a statement and rarely include a fine, although the Uribe government has proposed a law that would define libel so as to give more latitude to the government.

The media are private, without undue government influence on content. However, while some individuals could be imprisoned for stating their views, the greater fear is murder by groups opposing them. The Committee to Protect Journalists reported that in the 10 years between 1994 and 2003, Colombia was second in the world (after Algeria) in the number of journalists killed (31),[6] although only one was killed in 2004. In addition, media ownership concentration among business people with ties to the government forces journalists to refrain from criticism of the government.[7] Hence, self-censorship is common.

In April 2004 a delegation of press-freedom organizations visited the northeastern city of Barrancabermeja, site of the largest oil refinery in Colombia and battleground between paramilitary and guerrilla groups. The delegation met with journalists, prosecutors, the local ombudsman's office, police and army commanders, and civilian authorities and concluded that a climate of intimidation existed for journalists. Reporters were threatened and in some cases attacked, most often with little protection from the police.[8]

*Recommendations*

- The Colombian government should do more to prevent fraud and intimidation of voters in elections, including providing for better protection of election sites.
- The government should afford increased police protection for at-risk journalists.

- The Colombian electoral commission should disqualify candidates with close ties to insurgent groups when there is no doubt of the connection.
- The Colombian political establishment should take steps to counteract the advantages of incumbency before the next presidential election.
- Libel laws, which currently require only that untrue statements be corrected, should not be changed, as this would hamper the freedom of the media.

## CIVIL LIBERTIES – 4.39

The Colombian constitution grants many fundamental rights, including protection against disappearances, torture, and cruel, inhumane, or degrading punishment. However, in practice these rights are formal but not real. Human rights groups allege that the Colombian government violates human rights. According to Human Rights Watch, Colombia has more reported human rights and international humanitarian law violations than any other country in the hemisphere.[9]

The government denies these allegations, questioning the methodology of the human rights groups. It charges that guerrilla and paramilitary groups are the ones that violate rights in the country, and it alleges that, as human rights groups do not point out this fact, they are tacitly helping the insurgent groups.

In May 2004 Amnesty International (AI) charged that human rights violations were worsening in "security areas" of Colombia (those areas that the government has designated as having an especially high level of violence). While acknowledging that both kidnappings and the number of internal refugees were declining, AI added that government forces, paramilitary groups, and the armed opposition were guilty of massacring civilians. More than 3,000 civilians were murdered for political reasons and at least 600 disappeared in 2003. Despite government charges, the report did point out that both paramilitary and guerrilla groups were responsible for violations of international humanitarian law.[10]

Each year many Colombians are wounded, killed, or forced to flee their homes because of the violence of guerrilla and paramilitary groups. In 2003 some 250,000 citizens were displaced by the violence, bringing the number of displaced people in the country to 2.73 million, a total third-largest in the world behind the Sudan and Congo.[11] Still, improvements have taken place under Uribe. In July 2004 the Ministry of Defense reported that homicides were down 14.5 percent in the first two years of the Uribe government as compared to the last two of the Pastrana presidency, in addition to decreases in the number of victims of massacres and the number of terrorist acts.[12] Another Ministry of Defense report showed a significant drop in kidnappings in the first two years of the Uribe government.[13]

The Colombian state punishes military officers who violate human rights, including those who use torture. In the first half of 2004 some 500 officers were purged, not only for human rights violations but also for corruption and for connections to paramilitary groups.[14] The National Prosecutor's Office indicts officers for many offenses but without doubt does not detect all cases. Many officers have connections to the paramilitary groups, although it is unknown what proportion of the officer corps is so involved.

Arbitrary arrests occur. In February 2004 the Colombian non-governmental organization (NGO) Permanent Assembly for Peace investigated the mass arrests that had been taking place. Using figures from the Defender of the People, the National Prosecutor's Office, and the media, the NGO found that 6,038 people were arrested in 203 cases between September 2002 and December 2003. Of those, 4,846 were arrested in the mass operations, of whom 3,750 were not indicted.[15]

Formally, Article 30 of the constitution grants individuals the right of habeas corpus, which is supposed to be resolved within 36 hours. The penal process guarantees trial within a set time period after legal arrest, and if the limit is not met, the individual has the right to be released. Drug dealers and white collar criminals take advantage of this right more than poor people do, as the latter are poorly educated and often are unaware of this right. Prison conditions are not humane, with inmates in some cases required to pay for basic needs such as food, clothing, and linens.

Colombians have the right to sue anyone who violates their human rights. The Constitutional Court reportedly had 600,000 such cases between 1999 and 2003, relating to heath, education, nutrition, and protection from violence.[16]

Formally the Colombian constitution prohibits discrimination on the basis of gender. Colombian women have the same literacy rate as men do (92 percent),[17] and their participation at all levels of the educational system is equal to that of males, including university education. Yet that equality does not extend to employment opportunities in either the public or private sector. Unemployment is higher for women, and those employed tend to be in inferior positions. As Senator Piedad Zuccardi has said, in Colombia, "formally there are laws, decrees, and norms in favor of women. Nevertheless, in real life one is not given an opening of spaces. That's why many women still think they are discriminated against."[18]

Law 581 of 2000 created mechanisms so that women might have adequate and effective participation in government. In maximum decision-making posts and other directive posts at the national, departmental, and municipal level, women have the right to a minimum of 30 percent of the positions.[19] Yet this law is not complied with in all parts of Colombia. In Cali, for example, of the 19 posts named by Mayor Apolinar Salcedo, only 3 were filled by women. The mayor's excuse was that, if he were to comply with the law, "it will fall to me to kick some men out of their jobs."[20]

The government has set up a Presidential Council for Women's Equity, within which is an Observatory of Matters of Gender (OAG). The OAG reported that while 53 percent of Colombian adults were female, women occupied only 46 percent of national ministries, 6 percent of departmental ministries, and 7.5 percent of municipal ministries in 2002–2004. Women held 12 percent of the national senate seats and 11 percent of the national house seats. In the private sector the unemployment rate for women was higher than it was for men. The report concluded, "Sexual stereotypes and roles assigned to women as well as to men still persist. They reinforce and reproduce ways of thinking, in the public sector as well as the private one."[21]

Colombian women are more affected than men by the violence in the country. AI alleges that all sides of the conflict—government troops, guerrillas, and paramilitary squads—have sexually abused and oppressed women. Women are targeted for a number of purposes, including to sow terror within communities, to force people to flee their homes, to take revenge on adversaries, and to accumulate "trophies of war." Rape and sexual mutilation are frequent.[22] Despite the gravity of the crimes against women, the perpetrators enjoy almost complete impunity.

Colombia has formal means to control the trafficking of children, such as a minor's needing the permission of both parents to leave the country or the permission of a judge when that of one parent is lacking. However, child prostitution remains a problem. Trafficking of women is much more difficult to detect as they can legally leave the country. Information campaigns attempt to prevent the acceptance of fraudulent contracts.

The Colombian people include mixtures of three racial strains. In the census of 1960, the first in which race was a question, 14 percent replied that they were white, 5 percent that they were Afro Colombian, and 1 percent Indian, while an additional 40 percent said they were mulatto and another 40 percent said they were tri-ethnic. No Colombian census since that time has included this variable. One contemporary expert estimates that 80 percent of Colombians are of mixed heritage.[23] The Colombian constitution of 1991 recognized Colombia as a multiethnic society for the first time. It gave indigenous people two seats in the Senate, to be filled by them as they see fit, and Afro-Colombians two members of the lower house of congress.

The situation of the indigenous people (defined in Colombia as individuals of indigenous ethnic background who still speak an indigenous language and dress in a traditional way) is dire. The 8 percent of the national population who live on reservations, which make up 30 percent of the national territory, have been devastated by both indiscriminate and selective murders, massive displacement, the forced recruitment of young people by insurgent groups, rape of the women, and the seizure of their land.[24] In September 2004, indigenous groups responded with a "Great Meeting for Dignity and Life," sponsored by the National Indigenous Organization of Colombia (ONIC), and a "March for Dignity" in the southern department of Cauca, which had some 45,000 participants.[25] However, neither demonstration had the desired positive effects of encouraging government involvement to lessen adverse conditions.

Traditionally, members of the Afro Colombian community were defined as descendants of escaped slaves who had moved to isolated communities. Today, especially with the displacement of many Afro Colombians to the large cities because of the rampant violence, those descendants are found in all parts of the country, along with other people of similar ethnic background who have never lived in remote areas. They are estimated at about 10 million people, spread out across the country but concentrated in the major cities. While there is no legal discrimination against them and they have had some representatives in high levels of politics, Afro Colombians typically are of lower income, education, and social class.[26]

Over the last six years more forceful laws and regulations have been developed to enable a larger number of people with disabilities to gain equal access to education, public spaces, and the health and social security systems. However, these efforts have not had their full potential effect as they receive insufficient funds and are not high among the government's priorities.

The Colombian constitution states that citizens have liberty of conscience, freedom of religion, and freedom of expression. These rights are generally respected. While Colombia was traditionally a Roman Catholic country, in the past 20 years large numbers of citizens have joined other religions, including as many as 600,000 who have become evangelical Christians. While the Roman Catholic hierarchy is not controlled in any way by the government, and divorce has existed since the 1991 constitution, Colombians still observe numerous church holidays.

The constitution likewise recognizes freedom of association, including the right to form labor unions or associations as well as the right to form political parties, movements, and political groups and to publicize their ideas and programs. Generally speaking, labor union activities have been unfettered by the government, although laws limit the right to strike. Unions have been legally punished when they violate those laws. Union members are occasionally subjected to violence. However, generally speaking, the government does not use excessive force against worker demonstrations, and freedom of association is generally respected.

*Recommendations*
- The government should continue to curb violence through expansion of constabulary forces, while at the same time increasing the protection of civil liberties through a stronger court system.
- The government should do more to ensure that the human rights that are listed in the constitution are a reality in the country through more effective protection of life and property for all Colombians, regardless of race or background.

- The government should publicize women's employment rights in the private sector more effectively.
- The government should protect women and children better from trafficking by increasing penalties and providing citizens with information on protecting themselves.
- The government should do more to protect the indigenous communities from violence by providing greater protection for their rural settlements.

## RULE OF LAW – 4.21

The rule of law has never applied in all of Colombia. Even in early 2004, of the 1,096 municipalities in the country, more than 180 had no police. The major theme of the Uribe presidency has been to bring the rule of law to all parts of the country. After his election, Álvaro Uribe formulated an "integral strategy to win the war" in Colombia. A government-appointed commission prepared a "Report on Human Development Concerning Security and Justice" whose first major conclusion was that the war and justice are too serious to leave in the hands of generals and lawyers. Therefore, it stated, the government should manage security and justice. That demanded coordination among the entities that make up the system.

The report's insistence that the government should concentrate on fighting the armed groups, capturing the perpetrators of the worst crimes, and judging them, resulted in a change in the previous concentration of troops on combating illicit drugs, protecting hydrocarbons, and protecting highways. In the justice system, judges were to spend less time on cases having to do with the financial sector.

The Uribe policy was centered on two axes. The first was to regain control of the national territory through the creation of high mountain battalions (professional soldiers trained in special skills), of patrols of peasant soldiers (volunteers recruited by regional commanders in small towns) to assist the military and police, and of networks of cooperating individuals, based on rewards to informers. The second was a legal offensive with a declaration of internal disturbance, under which the government decreed a property tax (falling most heavily on businesses) and created two rehabilitation zones in which violence was particularly severe, necessitating greater military efforts and funds for recovery. The

Constitutional Court approved the first declaration of internal disturbance but found its prolongation unconstitutional.

Some Colombians worried that the peasant soldiers would be no more than the newest incarnation of state-sponsored paramilitary groups. In the 1960s the Colombian government assisted paramilitary, or self-defense groups, to fight the guerrillas. While officially the government assistance ended in the late 1980s, human rights groups and others argue that a close connection remains. The government's response is that the peasant soldiers would not be allowed to maintain control of their weapons and they would always work under the orders of an officer from the military or police.

The security policy led to important qualitative achievements, such as travel for citizens during holidays in military-guarded caravans. A July 2004 Ministry of Defense report found dramatic increases in the number of paramilitary squads, guerrillas, and drug traffickers captured.[27] However, experts are divided about whether the FARC has in fact been defeated or if it has simply carried out a tactical retreat. In addition, some rights groups have reported that President Uribe has not managed to cut the ties between members of the security forces and paramilitaries.[28]

Colombia has both civil and military court systems. The Constitutional Court is the final step in judicial review of laws, while the Supreme Court judges public officials who are accused of misbehavior. The Council of State rules on the constitutionality of decrees, as well as being the last appeal for cases of administrative law.

The Colombian legal system is impartial and generally nondiscriminatory. However, the system has a class bias, with a greater likelihood of adjudication against members of lower-income groups than against the middle and upper strata. Likewise, security services have traditionally favored the rich. Police patrols are disproportionately more common in urban areas, particularly surrounding elite neighborhoods. In addition, the private security system that protects these people is larger than the public one, with no effective structure to supervise it.[29]

The judiciary is independent from the executive and legislature, and funding is not used to control them. Historically, judicial review has led to the upending of laws passed by the congress and decrees of the president; in fact, according to a communiqué signed by Supreme Court president Silvio Fernando Trejos, "It is very well known that the Constitutional Court makes pronouncements that overturn the legitimate functions of the executive and the legislature."[30] Judges at the higher level are elected by the congress in a fair manner. Lower-level judges, however, are often recent law school graduates who lack adequate training and experience.

The legal system suffers from both disagreements over functions and the inability to adjudicate all criminal cases. For example, in early 2004 the Supreme Court announced in a communiqué that it thought it necessary to "warn about the dangers to juridical order" if the Constitutional Court did not limit itself to its "specific functions." While the tensions between the two courts were not new, they reached a boiling point in March when the Constitutional Court declared that Supreme Court decisions could be appealed to the Constitutional Court. That was a "usurpation" according to Supreme Court justices.[31]

There is no doubt that many criminal cases in Colombia do not lead to arrest, indictment, trial, and verdict. In 2004 there were 923,000 unresolved cases from previous years. The Supreme Council of the Judiciary has said that between November 2001 and October 2002, 87.5 percent of the cases that entered the prosecutor's office were resolved, while that figure rose to 97.5 percent during the same months a year later.[32]

The prosecutorial system took new form with the constitution of 1991. Abandoning the Napoleonic law method, Colombia based the new system more on the U.S. model. However, the lack of adequate funding, as well as the wealth of some lawbreakers (notably the drug dealers), has made the complete implementation of the system difficult. Although a lawyer is appointed for defendants who are not able to afford one themselves, for minor offenses this is only a senior law school student who is uncompensated, thus being generally ineffective. The system is slightly more effective in the case of major offenses.

The right to private property is included in the Colombian constitution, and governments have expressed pride that the state has never nationalized property. However, during the current conflict the state is unable to protect individual rights to property, especially land in rural areas, from seizures by guerrilla and paramilitary groups. This is especially the case with the lands of indigenous people.

As part of his policy, in March 2004 Uribe proposed an "Antiterrorist Constitutional Reform." The reform had three parts. The first contained measures to prevent terrorism, including the ability of national prosecutors and officers of the police, National Security Department, and military to carry out searches without a warrant from a judge. The second part of the proposal created "Special Units of Judicial Military Police" that would operate in those areas of the country where there was no judicial authority and also could carry out searches without prior approval. The third part of the proposal stated that all inhabitants of Colombia would have to declare where they lived. The Uribe proposal was approved by the national congress but found unconstitutional by the Constitutional Court due to procedural irregularities.

### Recommendations

- The Colombian government should intensify its efforts to sever all relationships between the armed forces and paramilitary groups.
- The functions of the different judicial organizations should be made clear so resources are not lost in jurisdictional disputes.
- Every effort should be made to lessen the backlog of criminal cases through allocating additional funds to the judicial system.
- Special care should be taken so that the government's security policy does not lead to the loss of individual rights, including those of due process. Searches without prior judicial approval should be avoided.

## ANTICORRUPTION AND TRANSPARENCY – 3.88

The Uribe government has established a four-tier plan to fight corruption: inter-institutional coordination among the executive branch, the comptroller, the national procurator, and the national prosecutor; a regional strategy to include departmental and municipal governments in the same campaign; citizen control through transparency committees that ensure the legality and fairness of government operations (especially in bid awarding); and the promotion of a culture of legality.[33] While Colombian government documents demonstrate that intricate organizations and regulations have been set up in this campaign, actual results are not apparent.

The Colombian government is characterized by excessive bureaucratic regulations and, in many cases, low salaries that increase the probability of corruption. Furthermore, adequate protection against conflicts of interest is lacking. Hence it is not surprising that in 2003 the Organization of Economic Cooperation and Development ranked Colombia the 59th most corrupt country of the 133 they rated.[34]

All government employees must make a notarized declaration of property and income. Laws against bribes exist, and there are frequent arrests, most of which are well reported in Colombian newspapers. While the procurator and the comptroller are charged with investigating corruption, the quantity of allegations overwhelms their abilities. Comptrollers also exist at departmental and local levels, but in many cases politicians have placed political friends in those posts, making this one of the most corrupt parts of the state apparatus. There are no adequate mechanisms for victims to pursue their rights. More positively, corruption does not affect higher education.

The magnitude of the problem was shown in a 2004 survey carried out by the Chamber of Commerce of Bogotá. Among the findings of this questionnaire were that 50 percent of those who contracted with the government responded that the contracting process lacked transparency. In addition, 36.5 percent thought that the process favored the formation of a monopoly of contractors, and 32.1 percent believed that conditions of the bidding were changed to favor some bidders. While 47.4 percent thought that corruption was lower in the national government in 2003 than it had been in 2002, 63 percent believed that corrupt practices had increased in departmental and municipal governments. Finally, 34.1 percent affirmed that, in cases of bribery, it was the government official who suggested the payoff.[35]

At a meeting of top officials held in Bogotá in August 2004, commendable statements were made, for example, about increasing internal controls and improving disciplinary action.[36] Unfortunately, to this point those words have not been accompanied with actions.

Sufficient transparency is lacking in public access to government information. Article 23 of the constitution guarantees the right to obtain information about the acts of the state. The government must reply to such petitions unless the information is classified for reasons of national security or for the confidentiality of judicial processes. Article 15 guarantees the right to know the personal information that data banks have collected about one. Legislative review takes place at some points of the budget-making process but is not comprehensive.

The administration and distribution of foreign assistance is handled by a state organization called the Colombian Agency of International Cooperation (Agencia Colombiana de Cooperación International). However, the United States distributes aid directly through the Agency for International Development. In addition, the Solidarity Network (Red de Solidaridad) administers special assistance in the case of natural disasters.

## Recommendations

- The contracting process with the government should be more transparent.
- The government should devise an enforceable policy to identify and punish all government officials who violate anticorruption laws.
- Through better identification, adjudication, and punishment, the government should strengthen and enforce laws that punish private individuals who participate in corruption.
- The Colombian government should increase transparency in its activities, with open-meeting laws that allow the people to know more about its operations.

## NOTES

[1] I would like to thank Armando Borrero, Mónica Varela, and Julio Pérez for their assistance in gathering information for this paper. Responsibility for the content, however, is mine.

[2] *Cifras de violencia 1996–2002,* Vol. 0, No. 1 (Bogota: Dirección de Justicia y Seguridad, Departamento Nacional de Planeación, 2003), http://www.dnp.gov.com.

[3] "Informe de balance desmovilizaciones colectivas 2004" (Bogota: Alto Comisionado para la Paz, 2004), http://www.altocomisionadoparalapaz.gov.co/desmovilizaciones/2004/balance.htm?PHPSESSID=2c08682c32ba1e3d9c50c722d80b7fe0.

[4] "Colombia, Data Profile" (Washington, DC: World Bank, n.d.), http://devdata.worldbank.org/external/CPProfile.asp?SelectedCountry=COL&CCODE=COL&CNAME=Colombia &PTYPE=CP.

[5] "Journalists Killed in 2004" (Paris: Reporters without Borders, n.d.), http://www.rsf.org/killed_2004.php3.

[6] "Journalists Killed in the Line of Duty: Statistics for 1994–2003" (New York: Committee to Protect Journalists [CPJ], 2004), http://www.cpj.org/killed/Ten_Year_Killed/stats.html.

[7] "Colombia: Attacks on the Press, 2003" (CPJ, 2004), http://www.cpj.org/attacks03/americas03/colombia.html.

[8] "Colombia: Delegation finds climate of intimidation in Barrancabermeja" (CPJ, 28 July 2004), http://www.cpj.org/cases04/americas_cases04/colombia.html.

[9] "Colombia" (New York: Human Rights Watch [HRW], January 2004), http://hrw.org/english/docs/2004/01/21/colomb6978.htm.

[10] "Amnistía Internacional insiste en empeoramiento de DD.HH.en 'áreas de seguridad' en Colombia," *El Tiempo*, 26 May 2004, http://eltiempo.terra.com.co.

[11] "En el 2003, 250 mil colombianos fueron desplazados por la violencia, revelan en E.U.," *El Tiempo*, 28 May 2004, http://eltiempo.terra.com.co.

[12] "Mindefensa rindió un parte positive," *El Colombiano*, 7 August 2004, http://www.elcolombiano.terra.com.co.

[13] "Secuestro extorsivo bajó 53 por ciento," *Semana*, 9 August 2004, http://www.Semana.com.

[14] "Silenciosa purga de militares en 2004 ha sacada de filas a medio millar de uniformados," *El Tiempo*, 11 July 2004, http://eltiempo.terra.com.co.

[15] "Polémica por capturas masivas," *El Colombiano*, 19 February 2004, http://www.elcolombiano.terra.com.co.

[16] "25% de tutelas resueltas por la Corte Constitucional desde 1999 son por desatenciones en salud," *El Tiempo*, 3 August 2004, http://eltiempo.terra.com.co.

[17] "Colombia, Data Profile" (World Bank), http://devdata.worldbank.org/external/CPProfile.asp?SelectedCountry=COL&CCODE=COL&CNAME=Colombia&PTYPE=CP.

[18] "Mujeres se sienten todavía discriminadas," *El Tiempo*, 26 August 2004, http://eltiempo.terra.com.co.

[19] Margarita María Peláez Mejía, "La ley de cuotas: un mecanismo para democratizar la democracia" (Universidad de Antioquía, Medellín, Colombia, n.d.), http://webs.uvigo.es/pmayobre/textos/margarita_pelaez/ley_de_cuotas.doc.

[20] "No se cumple la ley que exige un 30 por ciento de la participación femenina en los cargos públicos," *El Tiempo* (Bogota), 26 January 2004, http://eltiempo.terra.com.co.

[21] "Participación política de la mujeres en Colombia," *Observatorio de asuntos de género*, May–August 2004, http://www.presidencia.gov.co/equidad/documentos/boletin_1.pdf.

[22] "Colombia: Women's bodies a battleground" (New York: Amnesty International [AI], 13 October 2004), http://web.amnesty.org/actforwomen/stories-12-eng.

[23] "Manuel Zapata Olivella describe realidades de los afrocolombianos, la etnia más sufrida en el país," *El Tiempo*, 28 May 2004, http://eltiempo.terra.com.co.

[24] "'La situación de los indígenas es dramática': ONU," El Espectador, 17 March 2004, http://www.elespectador.com.

[25] "Así fueron los primeros 20 kilómetros de la marcha indígena por la dignidad, en el Cauca," *El Tiempo*, 14 September 2004, http://eltiempo.terra.com.co.

[26] "La comunidad afrocolombiana," El Tiempo, 3 June 2004, http://eltiempo.terra.com.co. It is not clear how the newspaper arrived at these figures, as "race" is not a census question.

[27] "Mindefensa rindió un parte positive," *El Colombiano*, 7 August 2004, http://www.elcolombiano.terra.com.co.

[28] "Colombia" (HRW, January 2004), http://hrw.org/english/docs/2004/01/21/colomb6978.htm.

[29] "Seguridad democrática," *Semana*, 17 October 2004, http://semana.terra.com.co.

[30] "Continúan choque entre Cortes," *Semana*, 3 March 2004, http://www.Semana.com.

[31] Ibid.

[32] "Judicatura, Contraloría y Fiscalía presentan balances distintos de esta entidad," *El Tiempo,* 3 June 2004, http://eltiempo.terra.com.co.

[33] "Programa Presidencial de Lucha contra la Corrupción" (Bogota: Presidencia de la República, 2002), http://www.anticorrupcion.gov.co/cultura_legalidad.htm.

[34] Eduardo Pizarro Leongómez, "Contrastes frente a la corrupción: Dignidad e indignidad," *El Tiempo,* 24 October 2004, http://eltiempo.terra.com.co.

[35] Eugenio Marulanda Gómez, Presidente de Confecamaras, "Encuesta de percepción empresarial sobre corrupción" (Bogota: Cámara de Comercio de Bogotá—PBEC, Foro, Corresponsabilidad del sector privado en la lucha contra la corrupción, 4 May 2004), http://216.239.39.104/search?q=cache:HKm14EfI69QJ:www.confecamaras.org.co/ PROBIDADIII.pdf+%E2%80%9CENCUESTA+DE+PERCEPCI%C3%93N+ EMPRESARIAL+SOBRE+CORRUPCI%C3%93N%E2%80%9D,+FORO,+ CORRESPONSABILIDAD+DEL+SECTOR+PRIVADO+EN+LA+LUCHA+ CONTRA+LA+CORRUPCI%C3%93N%22&hl=en.

[36] "Plan de choque contra corrupción," *El Tiempo,* 20 August 2004, http://eltiempo .terra.com.co.

# ECUADOR

CAPITAL: Quito
POPULATION: 13.4 million
GNI PER CAPITA: $1,490

**SCORES**
ACCOUNTABILITY AND PUBLIC VOICE: 3.92
CIVIL LIBERTIES: 4.12
RULE OF LAW: 3.33
ANTICORRUPTION AND TRANSPARENCY: 3.42
(scores are based on a scale of 0 to 7, with
0 representing weakest and 7 representing
strongest performance)

*Andrés Mejía Acosta*[1]

## INTRODUCTION

In August 2004 Ecuador celebrated 25 years of democratic rule, the longest period of uninterrupted civilian government since independence from Spain in 1822. During this period, the electoral authority has guaranteed free and fair competition in 7 presidential and 10 legislative elections. Women have gained significant representation in political office; indigenous people have consolidated one of the best-organized political parties in the Americas, gaining several congressional seats, mayoral offices, and cabinet positions in the government.

In contrast to the resilience of electoral democracy, civil liberties, human rights, and more generally the rule of law have been consistently deteriorating over the past decade. Political crises and widespread social discontent abruptly ended the mandate of presidents in 1997 and 2000. Although the military resisted the temptation to assume power, elected leaders crafted quasi-constitutional interpretations to restore democratic continuity. The government has ignored repeated reports of police violence and military interference in civilian matters. State and non-state

---

**Andrés Mejía Acosta** is a Killam Research Fellow at the Department of Political Science, University of British Columbia, Canada.

189

actors have infringed on freedom of the press. Violent crime is widespread and remains unpunished given the weakness of law enforcement and judicial institutions. Courts remain politicized and largely ineffective, especially for solving and prosecuting controversial government corruption scandals. Survey polls show that this sense of crisis reflects the citizens' eroding trust in existing democratic institutions: the congress, the political parties, and the judiciary.

Over the past two years, the government and political parties have adopted some legislation to promote or ensure judicial reform, government accountability and transparency, freedom of the press, access to information, and anticorruption laws. The success of such reforms, however, is limited by the contentious dynamics of shifting political coalitions. In a context in which presidents lack a single partisan majority in congress, they must constantly seek support from opposition parties by attracting cooperation through the distribution of pork, patronage, and other particularistic goods. This has opened the doors for political corruption. Successful anticorruption initiatives need to acknowledge that corrupt political behavior is often caused by the inherent congressional weakness of Ecuadorian presidents and that corruption often goes unpunished due to the politicization of the judiciary branch.

The armed conflict in Colombia is an extremely disruptive influence for domestic politics in Ecuador. The Ecuadorian armed forces do not have the capacity to control and prevent a growing number of incursions of Colombian guerrilla and paramilitary groups into Ecuadorian territory. The adoption of the dollar as Ecuador's national currency in 2000 has provided an unintended haven for money laundering and the trafficking of arms and drugs. The requests for refugee status from Colombian citizens increased exponentially from 413 in the year 2000 to more than 10,000 at the end of 2003. The Ecuadorian state is able to accept only 30 percent of those but without making any legal commitments to improve the refugees' livelihood. The spread of Colombian violence coupled with the weakness of the Ecuadorian judicial institutions creates a breeding ground for additional government corruption, violent crime, human rights violations, illegal immigration, and growing unemployment. Articulating a concise national security plan and procuring the necessary resources from the international community should be the government's prime concern for facing this imminent challenge to the Ecuadorian state and its democratic institutions.

## ACCOUNTABILITY AND PUBLIC VOICE – 3.92

Ecuadorian democracy, especially during the past decade, has survived major social and political upheaval. Corruption scandals contributed to the resignation of Vice President Alberto Dahik in 1995 and the congressional dismissal of President Abdalá Bucaram in 1997. President Jamil Mahuad was ousted in January 2000, 18 months after his inauguration, by a coalition of indigenous groups and middle-range army officers who opposed his economic policies. Two years later, the same indigenous-military coalition put Lucio Gutiérrez, the leading conspirator, in the presidency. This cycle of chronic political instability results from a complex combination of both regional and economic power struggles of the Ecuadorian elite and popular expressions of social discontent. Political alliances are short lived and ad hoc in nature, thus affecting the sustainable implementation of economic policies. Poor economic performance has in turn eroded citizens' trust in democratic institutions.

The Ecuadorian congress has one of the largest numbers of effective parties in the region.[2] Members are elected for four-year terms with no term limits. The use of a proportional representation formula for the legislature combined with lenient electoral registration thresholds has made possible the proliferation of parties representing the ethnic and regional diversity of the country, but also individual schisms of the political elite. Presidents are elected according to a majority run-off formula; since 1979 there have been 10 presidents from 9 different political parties (only the Christian Democrat [DP] party has put two presidents in office). No president has obtained a single-party majority in Congress; presidents have had to resort to distributing pork, patronage, and policy concessions to cement the loyalty of congressional allies and avoid deadlock.

Elections in Ecuador have generally been considered free and fair since the country's transition to democratic rule in 1979. Electoral participation is mandatory for all Ecuadorian adults, with the exception of the military, who do not have the right to vote (see "Rule of Law"). The Supreme Electoral Tribunal (TSE)—the election monitoring body—is composed of seven members appointed by congress from the political parties that received the most votes in the last election. Through the TSE, the government allocates fixed campaign funds to all parties, as well as additional campaign funding in proportion to the votes obtained by the party in previous elections.[3] According to Transparency International's 2004 Global Corruption Report, Ecuador has a low level of public campaign finance disclosure, granting partial access to financial reports filed.[4] Campaign financing laws have not prevented excessive campaign spending and the disproportionate influence of specific economic interests. Local watchdogs such as Participación Ciudadana-Ecuador (PCE) have had moderate success in monitoring and demanding the effective application of campaign financing laws. PCE has successfully pushed for establishing legal sanctions for violations of campaign finance caps, while obtaining public access to some campaign expenditure reports disclosed by parties and their presidential candidates during the 2002 campaign.[5] By September 2004, however, the TSE had not collected the penalty for excessive electoral spending from all parties that exceeded finance limits. According to the law, collected fines should be transferred to public hospitals, but as of September 2004, the accused populist Roldosista Party (PRE), the caudillo-based PRIAN party, and the president's Patriotic Society Party (PSP) have not shown proof of having met their legal obligations.[6]

The Ecuadorian constitution allows for adequate oversight mechanisms to ensure the appropriate checks and balances across government branches. With a simple majority, congress appoints the prosecutor general (Procurador General) from a pool of three presidential nominees. Congress appoints the attorney general (Ministro Fiscal General) upon the nomination received from the Consejo Nacional de la Judicatura (CNJ), an administrative body within the judiciary (see "Rule of Law"). The general comptroller (GC), Ecuador's top auditing authority, is nominated by the president but appointed with a qualified (two-thirds) majority of the members of Congress.

In practice, however, the fragmented and volatile nature of political coalitions has turned mechanisms of oversight and control into instruments of political blackmail or has simply rendered them ineffective. Since his inauguration in January 2003, President Gutiérrez has been unable to propose a suitable candidate for GC that has the support of a qualified congressional majority due to conflicting political interests between the main political parties (see "Rule of Law"). In the meantime, the lack of a GC has opened multiple spaces for irregularities, as the president and the rest of government officials remain unchecked in their actions.

Conflicting political forces have thwarted the effectiveness of government control agencies. One example is the sudden dismissal of Wilma Salgado, the head of the Deposit Guarantee Agency (AGD)—a government banking insurance bureau—by its board of directors in March 2004. Salgado was appointed to the AGD as a political concession made to the indigenous Pachakutik movement by the newly elected president Gutiérrez. In office, she played an active role in trying to seize assets from influential bankers who benefited from a government bailout during the 1999 banking crisis. But with the split of the indigenous from the government in August of 2003, the president's new political ally, the Social Christian party (PSC) party—closely linked with banking interests—perceived Salgado to be a liability. In an alleged attempt to preserve his new coalition and to avoid alienating key political and economic interests, President Gutiérrez stacked the AGD board that sacked Salgado a few hours later.[7]

Economic lobbies, mostly tied to powerful regional elites, play an influential role in the policy-making process. The son of a banana tycoon in the Guayas province, Alvaro Noboa, ran against President Gutiérrez in the run-off to the 2002 presidential election, and Noboa's own PRIAN party remains a pivotal actor in the making of policy coalitions in congress. Changing political alliances combined with the influence of powerful business lobbies have resulted in frequent cabinet reshuffles and political volatility. This is especially true in the economic realm, where finance ministers, central bank governors, and other economic authorities have lasted only an average of 12 months in office.[8]

There is no clear criterion for promotion or dismissal of government bureaucrats in Ecuador. In complex technical sectors such as the finance ministry and the central bank, seasoned public officials carry out operations. But the bureaucracy in other national and sub-national government agencies is populated with political appointees who tend to reflect political quotas of the relevant congressional coalition. The lower bureaucratic ranks comprise a mix of poorly paid career officials, with limited incentives and mostly static ambitions, and temporary employees (public contractors) within the agency, who are largely dependent on patronage.[9]

Government efforts to adopt progressive legislation and strengthen institutions that promote gender equality are reflected in the creation of the National Women's Council (CONAMU) in 1997.[10] The Ecuadorian government has ratified the Convention on the Elimination of All Forms of Discrimination against Women (CEDAW), and the 1998 constitution grants significant civil and political rights to protect and ensure more equal participation of women in politics, at home, and in the workforce. According to Consejo Nacional de la Mujer, in the 2000 municipal elections nearly 25 percent of elected public officials were women.[11] Women have also gained significant representation in the national government, the cabinet, Congress, and other elected and non-elected local and provincial government posts. The government has also made possible the political participation of indigenous groups, first by granting voting rights to the illiterate in the 1979 constitution and second, by recognizing in the 1998 constitution the multiethnic and pluricultural nature of the Ecuadorian state. Indigenous people—who constitute less than 30 percent of the total population—formed their own political movement, Pachakutik, in 1995 and have gained several congressional seats, mayorships, and cabinet positions since.

In recent years, Ecuador has witnessed the mushrooming of civic groups aimed at influencing and monitoring the policy-making process in many areas, including the defense and promotion of indigenous rights, campaign spending, environmental protection, and fiscal budget implementation. The state imposes no significant restrictions on or legal impediments to the creation and funding of such initiatives. Although in many cases these groups lack the legal and material means to implement their policy recommendations—partly due to government inactivity—they have significantly contributed to raising policy awareness among the population.

The government owns radio frequencies, but it does not control media content. All the media are privately owned and generally outspoken. No conglomerate has monopoly control, and all political parties enjoy some access to state-funded airtime for campaigns. According to the 2004 Reporters Without Borders annual report, however, "press freedom has deteriorated since President Gutiérrez took office and his relations with the media are very tense."[12] In October 2003, President Gutiérrez joined other heads of state from the Americas to sign a declaration proposed by the Inter American Press Association promising to respect 10 principles of press freedom.[13] Yet, when faced with widespread public criticism and disclosure of alleged corruption scandals at home, the government moved toward the promotion of libel laws. At the end of 2003, President Gutiérrez announced the introduction of a law that would "severely punish" those who "defamed people, spread rumors, who lied and were despicable." Confronted by the media, the president's press secretary clarified a few days later that the president meant not a law but a "campaign" against such things.[14]

Repeated cases of intimidation of journalists, both by government and clandestine organizations, indicate a serious erosion of freedom of the press in Ecuador in 2004. The president requested the prosecutor's office to initiate a preliminary investigation of Diego Oquendo, a journalist who asked a government official about campaign donations made by Colombian guerrillas to the Gutiérrez campaign. Gutiérrez announced that the journalist's remarks were inflammatory and undermined public order.[15] Another journalist, Rodrigo Fierro, was sentenced to six months in prison for criticizing former president Febres Cordero. The prison sentence was not imposed as Fierro is over 70 years old and has had no previous convictions. Threats and intimidation have also come from an allegedly extremist, and clandestine, organization called Legion Blanca. Marco Pérez Torres, a news director at Radio Tarqui, received death threats in September and December 2003 as a result of his critical reporting on the government's policies.[16] Amnesty International (AI) and other human rights watchdogs have expressed concern about the possible hardening of state and non-state actors against the press.

In contrast to the delicate situation of press freedom in Ecuador, the government has established effective provisions to guarantee freedom of cultural expression, including the recognition and promotion of indigenous languages. The constitution establishes that the state "will promote intercultural exchange, would base its policies and integrate its institutions according to the principles of equality and equity of cultures" (Article 62).

*Recommendations*
- The government should promote legislation that requires widespread disclosure of campaign financing and not limit legislation to media spending only. With the help of existing civil watchdogs, the government must design and enforce specific sanctions to punish campaign finance violations.
- The government must observe international commitments to allow freedom of the press at home and refrain from adopting libel laws that directly or indirectly curtail citizens' freedom of expression.

It should also adopt a proactive role to investigate, confront, and eliminate clandestine organizations that have repeatedly threatened the freedom of expression and even the lives of individuals.

- The government must expedite the appointment of the country's general comptroller and ensure that public officials in charge of government control agencies are properly appointed and removed. The appointment process should define specific criteria of service and professionalism to protect the agency from political influences.

- The government should promote civil service reform to protect the bureaucracy from shifting political coalitions and improve its technical capacity, professionalism, and remuneration.

## CIVIL LIBERTIES – 4.12

The Ecuadorian constitution and penal legislation contemplates a wide array of provisions to prevent unjustified imprisonment, torture, and abuse by private/non-state actors and allows citizens the power to petition when their rights are violated by state authorities. In practice, the Gutiérrez government has failed to address in any effective way numerous reports of police brutality and military misconduct. Despite the adoption of some legal reforms in recent years, these problems are likely to worsen due to the spillover of neighboring Colombia's civil conflict, which could well increase violent crime and affect public safety in Ecuador.

In October 2003, a delegation from AI that visited Ecuador released a report entitled: "With no independent and impartial justice there can be no rule of law."[17] The head of the national police assured AI that the police have not committed human rights violations and that cases of disappearance, extrajudicial execution, and torture were things of the past. Nevertheless, since their 2003 visit, AI has released an average of one "Urgent Action" report per month containing information about grave human rights violations allegedly committed by members of the police.[18] Such reports address two types of problems: alleged death threats against social organizations and political activists and impunity of police forces in alleged cases of mistreatment and disappearance of prisoners.

There is an environment of threats and political intimidation against those who oppose government policies, especially some indigenous leaders. On February 1, 2004, an assassination attempt was made on Leonidas Iza, the President of the Confederation of Indigenous Nationalities of Ecuador (Confederacion de Nacionalidades Indígenas del Ecuador [CONAIE]). According to an AI report, two unknown individuals shouting, "We are going to kill you," opened fire against Iza. He escaped unharmed, but four of his family members were injured and later taken to a hospital.[19] President Gutiérrez condemned the attack and called for an investigation. According to AI, the attack on Iza took place in a context of threats and intimidation against indigenous and community leaders who oppose government policies.[20] Only two months before the attacks, in December 2003, the police detained another indigenous leader, Humberto Cholango, for a few hours following a critical statement he made against President Gutiérrez. These two cases illustrate the deteriorating relationship between the government and some of the more vocal indigenous leaders.

AI has also expressed concern about developments in the Fybeca case, a controversial police operation following an alleged robbery in November 2003 at a pharmacy belonging to the Guayaquil-based company of the same name. Eight people, including two civilians, died during the operation. Forensic reports suggested that some might have been executed.[21] Three men (Jhonny Gómez, Cesar Mata, and Edwin Vivar) were arrested for the robbery attempt, but no one has seen them since. According to some family members, the prisoners called a few days later to say that their lives were at risk.[22] However, the head of the Judicial Police in Guayas province told a lawyer from the ombudsman's office that there was no record of the men being detained at the Judicial Police Headquarters.[23] In the words of Nuria García, author of the AI country report, the "Fybeca case is just one more example of the pattern of impunity that persists in Ecuador. The use of police courts in crimes against human rights is the cornerstone which upholds this pattern."[24] AI and other human rights organizations have unsuccessfully campaigned against the government use of police courts in cases of alleged human rights violations. Holding police trials away from public scrutiny increases the likelihood of police impunity. Currently, there are no signs that the case will be investigated by civil authorities. AI continues to receive reports of human rights violations by the police, including torture, deaths in custody, extrajudicial executions, and disappearances.

The problems of law enforcement are aggravated by the situation in the country's jails, including overcrowding up to two times beyond capacity, lack of resources, poor nutrition and health, and frequent violence between inmates and jail authorities.[25] Inmate riots demanding fair trials and sanitary conditions broke out in April 2004, shortly after a prolonged strike by jail workers who demanded better working conditions. Two inmates died, and several civilians and two reporters were taken hostage during the riots. Jail overcrowding is not likely to improve, as recently approved antidrug legislation calls for long-term detention without trial (*Prisión en firme*) even for minor drug offenders (see "Rule of Law").

The escalating conflict in Colombia has amplified problems of law enforcement and human rights violations along the Ecuadorian border. Various sectors of Ecuadorian society have expressed xenophobic sentiments toward Colombian immigrants as they are blamed for rising crime levels. Some irregularities have been found in the detention and trial of foreigners, who in many cases have been denied access to diplomatic representation.[26]

The government has made some efforts to improve the situation of women and children. Women have gained access to jobs traditionally reserved for men, such as positions in the police and armed forces, but much remains to be done to end job and salary discrimination in the workplace. More generally, existing legislation and civil society groups have worked together to give women a more independent and improved status in Ecuadorian society. Media concern is growing regarding alleged cases of trafficking of children, mostly for adoption purposes, but the government has not allocated material or investigative resources to address these accusations effectively.

The rights of ethnic minorities are ensured by the 1998 constitution, which recognizes the multiethnic and pluricultural nature of the Ecuadorian state. This declaration has had the effect of granting legal recognition to indigenous languages and the right to apply indigenous justice, as long as it does not conflict with existing constitutional provisions. Gradually, the indigenous—and to a lesser extent the Afro-Ecuadorian groups—have gained recognition and tolerance from a mostly mestizo Ecuadorian society. The 1998 Ecuadorian constitution grants extensive rights to people with disabilities, including preferential access to public services, tax exemptions, and nondiscrimination. In practice, the Ecuadorian society needs to play a more proactive role to fully incorporate people with disabilities into the family, the workplace, and the public sphere.

The Ecuadorian constitution upholds freedom of conscience and belief, as long as their expression does not conflict with the fundamental principles and individual rights established by the constitution. The Ministry of Interior is in charge of official recognition and legal registration (*personería jurídica*) of the diverse religious orders in Ecuador. These groups must submit a declaration of principles and a statement of their beliefs and fulfill other procedural requirements. To this date, religious orders have not been obstructed or interfered with by state entities, nor has the state had to preserve or protect the individual liberties of its citizens from illegal actions or violations of religious orders. Quite to the contrary, Ecuador has witnessed the proliferation of religious organizations, movements, and creeds of the most diverse ideological orientation throughout its territory.

Freedom of association is guaranteed by the state. Labor unions have the right to strike, although public-sector strikes are banned by the labor code. One case of concern is the recent campaign of intimidation and defamation against the Sarayaku indigenous community in the Pastaza province, which actively opposed oil-drilling concessions granted to foreign companies. The Sarayaku claim that oil extraction will damage their environment and way of life and have refused to abandon their territory. Instead, they have proposed alternative and sustainable development mechanisms to preserve their culture. During the second half of 2003, the Inter-American Commission of Human Rights (IACHR)—part of the Organization of American States (OAS)—ordered Ecuador to protect the Sarayaku community, because some of their leaders had received death threats; and some of their members were physically and verbally assaulted during a demonstration in December 2003. The government has paid little attention to these claims and human rights recommendations.[27]

*Recommendations*

- The government must adopt a more proactive role to enforce existing legislation in order to protect women's rights. It should investigate accusations of child trafficking and enact sanctions if accusations are proven to be correct. The government should also promote legislation to ensure equal gender conditions in the workplace.

- Existing legislation that allows for indefinite imprisonment without sentence must be immediately reviewed and adjusted according to the severity of cases and to existing international norms.
- The government must address the problem of jail overcrowding by expediting pending trials and giving differential treatment to dissimilar types of offenders.
- The government should fully investigate alleged violations of human rights, torture, and disappearances by police forces and punish those responsible. The government also needs to reinforce and target police-training efforts to interact with civil society in the protection of individual liberties.

## RULE OF LAW – 3.33

Ecuador's judicial system gained formal independence from political influence when constitutional reforms adopted in 1997 took away the legislative power to appoint Supreme Court (CSJ) magistrates. Currently, CSJ magistrates are appointed for life with the favorable vote of two-thirds of its members. Potential judges are nominated by representatives of different social and political sectors including the Bishops Conference, former CSJ presidents, human rights groups, and indigenous organizations. Candidates are required to have basic legal training and some years of experience before assuming the bench. The Consejo Nacional de la Judicatura (CNJ), an administrative and disciplinary body of the Judiciary, may dismiss CSJ magistrates due to incapacity, inability, or disciplinary sanctions. The CNJ is chaired by the president of the CSJ and composed of seven members appointed from outside the court with the favorable vote of two-thirds of CSJ members.

Traditionally, the selection of Supreme Court judges has resulted from intense political bargaining reflecting political, economic, and regional divides. Despite current constitutional provisions for judicial independence, powerful political interests influence the appointment process of CSJ members and their rulings. A recent example of political meddling is the judicial investigation of former president Gustavo Noboa (no relation to the leader of PRIAN) for alleged financial mismanagement. Noboa's political rival, Leon Febres Cordero—with the support of his PSC party—allege that irregularities in Noboa's foreign debt negotiations cost the country $9 billion. Many agreed that the investigation expressed a personal quarrel between the two leaders. In August 2003, Noboa sought and obtained political asylum in Dominican Republic, claiming that he did not enjoy the judicial guarantees to defend himself in the Ecuadorian court system.[28]

The politicization of the judiciary has affected its ability to prosecute and try other former government officials for alleged cases of wrongdoing. This includes former president and PRE leader Abdala Bucaram and former president and former Christian Democrat Jamil Mahuad, who face corruption charges, and pending extradition cases of several Ecuadorian bankers—some associated with the PSC party. As of September 2004, the CSJ was unable to appoint two new magistrates to the Second Criminal Chamber, which has jurisdiction over these cases. Conflicting political interests between the PSC and PRE parties over the defense of the above-mentioned cases have permeated the judiciary and impeded the formation of the qualified CSJ majority required to appoint these judges.

The constitution guarantees a fair trial and grants the accused access to independent counsel when it is beyond their means. In practice, the effective application of these rights is seriously undermined by the dramatic shortage of defense attorneys. Compared to other Andean countries, Ecuador has the lowest ratio of defense attorneys to the population, with 0.3 for every 100,000 habitants.[29] Considering this dramatic disadvantage, people with few resources or no political connections have difficulty obtaining a fair trial in the Ecuadorian judicial system. When judges recruit the services of private lawyers as defenders, these generally have little incentive to defend assigned cases effectively because they are insufficiently compensated and stand little chance of success. Prosecutors are not independent of political direction and control either.

The presumption of innocence until proven guilty is upheld by the constitution. In recent years, increased international pressure to focus attention on the war on drugs has led to the adoption of harsh antidrug legislation; this includes norms like the Law of Narcotic Drugs and Psychotropic Substances (Law 108), which contravene the presumption of innocence and allow for indefinite pretrial detention (*prisión en firme*).[30] The conservative PSC successfully sponsored this legislation in January 2004 primarily because accused drug offenders were using their right to habeas corpus to claim release from prison if they had not been tried or sentenced within a year of being detained.[31] This principle, however, has been applied equally to both minor users and mules.

The Constitutional Tribunal (TC), created in 1997 but operating since 2001, is the legal court of judicial review. The TC is composed of nine members nominated by the president, the congress, the CSJ, and civil society and appointed by a legislative majority. The TC may decide on most constitutional matters with a vote of at least five of its nine members. Over the past year, the influence of political parties is believed to have played a decisive role in the rulings of some TC members. One such example is the role played by the TC when it reopened a congressional inquiry into an influence-peddling scandal against congressman Renán Borbúa, a relation of the president. A government-friendly majority in Congress had previously stalled the process that would have stripped Borbúa of his legislative immunity, thus allowing a judicial investigation against him. The PSC challenged the congressional decision before the TC, and it is believed that PSC-friendly tribunal members played a crucial role in the decision to return the case to Congress. Ultimately, the scandal was not resolved as Borbúa resigned from Congress.

The armed forces remain a moderating force (*poder moderador*) in democratic politics in Ecuador. They played a key role during the fall of the last two presidents, and they were also pivotal in making possible the appointment of those presidents' successors. Although legislation establishes the accountability of the police and armed forces to civilian leaders, it is weakly enforced due to the politicization and weakness of the judiciary. Despite legal provisions to the contrary, the police and armed forces in Ecuador enjoy de facto independence to rule over certain areas that remain outside the control of the CNJ or CSJ. This has generated a sort of parallel justice system in which judges and prosecutors—subject to the ranks and hierarchy of these institutions—process cases of reported human rights violations or accusations of police brutality.

The military enjoys earmarked and off-budget allocations for the purpose of national security, as well as significant government subsidies and tax exemptions. These concessions appear to have become more frequent during the Gutiérrez administration as a way to cement military support for the president. The military has considerable policy-making influence through the National Security Council (COSENA). Member of the military participate on the boards of major state corporations and business enterprises, they control the customs administration, and they receive a share of petroleum revenues for military requirements. Civil-military relations have been further confounded since several former officers were appointed to top government offices. Recent proposals to extend the vote to the military have not crystallized into the political agenda, as there is a shared concern, even within the military, that votes for members of the armed services could contribute to their further involvement in politics.

Given the proximity of the Colombian conflict, the police and the military are playing an ever-growing role in preserving national security, controlling drug trafficking, and combating terrorism. However, they lack the resources, training, and capacity to face such challenges effectively, thus becoming susceptible to corruption and pressures from organized crime. Furthermore, the government lacks an autonomous doctrine of national security, choosing instead to react to war dynamics and military priorities of Plan Colombia.

The Ecuadorian constitution protects the right to private property, while acknowledging that private property must play a social role (CPE Article 30). The constitution also recognizes intellectual property, as well as collective property with agricultural or residential purposes (*cooperativas*). Property may be confiscated by the state only if its private possession conflicts with a social purpose and the individual who holds it is compensated by the state. Tensions between the traditional and the formal forms of property are no longer a source of conflict, mainly because of effective land reform in the 1970s. In addition, the 1998 constitution recognized the pluricultural and multiethnic nature of the country, thus accepting traditional claims to land property within existing law.

[*Editor's note:* In December 2004, a fragile progovernment majority violated the constitutional principle of judicial independence and, based on a simple congressional resolution, dismissed most of the 31 Supreme Court justices. The coalition, centered around the PRE and PRIAN parties, replaced the purged justices with its own partisan allies. Some weeks earlier, congress had also stacked the members of the Constitutional Court and Electoral Tribunal in its favor, thus severely impairing the separation of powers in Ecuador. It is perceived that the goal of such political realignment is to dismantle the PSC's control over the courts and to facilitate the return of the PRE's leader and former president

Abdalá Bucaram, who lives in exile in Panama and whose trial for government embezzlement is pending.]

*Recommendations*

• The government should uphold constitutional provisions for judicial independence and separation of powers. To ensure greater impartiality of CSJ magistrates, the government should adopt explicit requirements of service and professionalism for the selection and appointment of justices.

• The government should devote more political and monetary resources to strengthening and developing profesional training and advancement of justices at the national levels, thus ensuring that the career paths of justices are independent from political influences.

• The government should work with civil society and professional organizations to improve judicial transparency through the effective use of information systems to facilitate effective monitoring of cases and rulings in the Ecuadorian court system.

• Decisive government action is needed to ensure that cases concerning the violation of civil liberties in the hands of military or police personnel be tried in a civil, not a military court.

## ANTICORRUPTION AND TRANSPARENCY – 3.42

Ecuador is perceived to be a highly corrupt country, ranking 112 out of 145 countries worldwide according to Transparency International's 2004 Corruption Perceptions Index.[32] The 2004 score of 2.4 out of 10 is a negligible improvement over previous years' scores (2.3 in 2001 and 2.2 in 2002 and 2003). In principle, the state protects against conflicts of interest by requiring asset declarations of public officials and by prohibiting judges, members of the armed forces, and government officials from taking part in any private lucrative activities while in office. Since taking office, President Gutiérrez has made significant efforts to pass additional anticorruption legislation and other auxiliary norms. He set up an anticorruption system (SAE) that strengthened existing anticorruption watchdogs such as the Comisión Cívica para el Control de la Corrupción (CCCC).

Yet, corruption remains a significant problem in Ecuadorian politics. An important role has been played by the president himself, who has been accused of packing the government administration with family members, political cronies, and retired military officers. According to Jim Wesberry, director of Proyecto Si Se Puede, an independent anticorruption watchdog, the government has established the legal framework but "has not yet taken concrete measures to fight corruption."[33]

Independent investigative and auditing bodies are not fully effective because of political logrolling and legal weaknesses. Under the constitution, several agencies are in charge of auditing the government, the most important of which is the GC. As explained earlier however, the political process has stalled the appointment of the GC for nearly two years (see "Accountability and Public Voice"). The Internal Revenue Service of Ecuador (SRI) had done significant work on auditing and oversight of businesses and their tax declarations, but the sacking of its director in August 2004 for political reasons is likely to drastically undermine efforts to ensure accountability of tax collection. The government monitors and controls universities and institutions of higher education through the Consejo Nacional de Educación Superior (CONESUP); no significant problems are reported in this sector. The state is not excessively involved in the economy, although the perception of government corruption deters the formation of new businesses and foreign investment.

The creation of the SAE and the proactive role of the CCCC in facilitating the submission of corruption complaints have achieved little success in the fight against corruption. This is partly due to the absence of legal sanctions. Although corruption is a crime in the penal code, the CCCC plays only an investigative role and is not a sanctioning body. The public prosecutor (*Fiscalía*) has been accused of responding too slowly to cases brought by the CCCC.[34] Perhaps most important, presidents who lack adequate congressional support have traditionally offered to make particularistic concessions, allocate public office, and distribute side payments for personal benefit to potential political allies in congress to facilitate policy coalitions. The civil service is the key recipient of this patronage to political cronies. High turnover of government officials reflects the short-term logic of political coalitions. No corruption watchdogs have been set in place to monitor legislative activity. The lack of roll-call voting in the Ecuadorian congress shields legislators from constituency pressures and enables them to form clandestine alliances to exchange political favors for different political goals.

Although formally in place, protections for whistle-blowers and investigators of cases of bribery and corruption are sparse. In January 2004, three men assassinated Patricio Campana, an employee of the state-run oil company Petroecuador, who was investigating a case of fuel theft from the country's pipelines along the Colombian border. According to the president of oil workers, the scandal was likely to implicate government officials selling stolen fuel to proprietors of powerboats and tankers at below-market prices.[35] In general, people refrain from lodging complaints for fear of retaliation. The privately owned media have played a very active role in reporting corruption scandals, but there are few instances in which thorough investigative journalism units have uncovered and followed alleged corruption scandals to their ultimate conclusions. A related problem is the lack of judicial capacity to process an avalanche of corruption cases, as new corruption cases eclipse the previous ones.[36] There is no government agency or nongovernmental organization (NGO) that keeps track of all pending corruption scandals.

The adoption of an Organic Law for Transparency and Access to Public Information in May 2004 is an important step toward legally empowering citizens and civil society watchdogs to monitor government activity, although it is too soon to forecast its potential success in curbing government corruption. Another piece of legislation, the organic Law of Fiscal Responsibility, Stabilization, and Transparency, allows for a more comprehensive and transparent budget process. Since its approval in June 2002, a UN initiative, the Fiscal Policy Observatory, has become a de facto watchdog for monitoring government spending and acting as a proactive agent linking society's demands for social spending with policymakers' actions. This effort is partially facilitated by online reporting of government budgetary expenses every three months. A third initiative is the recent approval of a Public Contracts Law that regulates most government contracting. Most government bidding, allocation, and contracting are reported online through a newly established system (Contratanet). The government, however, has not yet disclosed contracting and bidding information in the energy and oil sectors, two areas that concentrate most of government contracting resources and thus offer the greatest opportunities for corruption.

The government channels most non-refundable bilateral and multilateral aid through the Ministry of Foreign Relations, but there are also external funds that are allocated directly to private hands and non-governmental organizations. The distribution of external funds appears to favor government-friendly authorities or districts.

## Recommendations

- The government should enforce disclosure of public contracting in all areas of government activity, including oil and energy.
- The government should consider granting the CCCC more resources to investigate alleged cases of corruption and sanction those responsible. It could also help the CCCC extend the number of branches that receive and process corruption complaints throughout the Ecuadorian territory.
- The government must promote efforts to install a congressional watchdog that effectively monitors legislators' voting patterns by keeping a record of roll calls and disseminating them to constituents.
- The government should promote a structural judicial reform to increase the courts' capacity to investigate, prosecute, and sanction reported cases of corruption.
- The government should show a commitment to improving the rule of law by trying alleged corruption cases against former presidents and bankers.

## NOTES

1. I acknowledge the research assistance and comments of Santiago Basabe Serrano and thank all the colleagues who provided valuable information for writing this report: Diego Araujo, Romel Jurado, Paulina Larreátegui, César Montúfar, Michel Rowland, and Norman Wray.
2. J. Mark Payne, Daniel Zovatto, Fernando Carrillo Flórez, and Andrés Allamand Zavala, *Democracies in Development: Politics and Reform in Latin America* (Washington, DC: InterAmerican Development Bank, 2002).
3. Law of Political Parties, Article 61.
4. Gene Ward, "The role of disclosure in combating corruption in political finance," in *Global Corruption Report 2004* (Berlin: Transparency International[TI], 2004), 46, http://www.globalcorruptionreport.org.
5. Ibid., 52.
6. "Evaluación del Gasto Electoral" (Quito: Participación Ciudadana, 2004), http://www.participacionciudadana.org/contenido.php?idContenido=258&idTema=22&idSubTema=77.
7. "Manjarrez, en la Gerencia de la AGD" (Madrid: Iberoamérica Empresarial, 2004), http://www.iberoamericaempresarial.com/edicion/noticia/0,2458,466487,00.html.

[8] Andrés Mejía-Acosta, Caridad Araujo, Aníbal Pérez Liñán, Sebastián M. Saiegh, and Simón Pachano, "Political Institutions, Policymaking Processes, and Policy Outcomes in Ecuador" (Quito: Facultad Latinoamericana de Ciencias Sociales [FLACSO], Inter-American Development Bank, 2004).

[9] Ibid.

[10] Created by Presidential Decree No. 764, 24 October 1997.

[11] Consejo Nacional de la Mujer, "Mujer: la constitución te da derechos" (Quito: CONAMU, 2004), http://www.conamu.gov.ec/index.htm.

[12] "Ecuador: Annual Report 2004" (Paris: Reporters sans frontieres, 2004), http://www.rsf.org/article.php3?id_article=10267.

[13] Ibid.

[14] Ibid.

[15] "Ecuador" (Miami: Inter American Press Association, 2004), http://www.sipiapa.org/pulications/report_ecuador2004o.cfm.

[16] "Ecuador: Death Threats/Intimidation/Fear for Safety" (Amnesty International [AI], 9 February 2004), http://web.amnesty.org/library/Index/ENGAMR280042004?open&of=ENG-ECU.

[17] "Ecuador: With No Independent and Impartial Justice There Can Be No Rule of Law" (AI, 30 October 2003), http://web.amnesty.org/library/index/engamr280102003.

[18] Ibid.

[19] "Ecuador: Fear for Safety" (AI, 3 February 2004), http://web.amnesty.org/library/Index/ENGAMR280022004?open&of=ENG-ECU.

[20] Ibid.

[21] "Ecuador: Police Courts Permit Impunity" (AI, 18 November 2004), http://web.amnesty.org/library/Index/ENGAMR280212004?open&of=ENG-ECU.

[22] Ibid.

[23] "Ecuador: Fear for Safety/Possible 'Disappearance'" (AI, 24 November 2003), http://web.amnesty.org/library/index/ENGAMR280142003?open&of=ENG-ECU.

[24] "Ecuador: Broken Promises—Impunity in the Police Courts System Continues" (AI, 2004). http://web.amnesty.org/library/index/engamr280182004.

[25] Romel Jurado, expert consultant for Fundación Regional de Asesoría en Derechos Humanos: personal communication.

[26] Gabriela Rodríguez Pizarro "Specific Groups and Individuals: Migrant Workers" (Geneva: United Nations Commission on Human Rights, 18 February 2002), E/CN.4/2002/94/Add.1.

[27] In January 2004, Ecuador's Minister of Energy and Mines reportedly responded to the IACHR's precautionary message by stating that "the OAS does not give orders here" ("la OEA no manda aquí"). Sarayacu, "Afirmaciones del Ministro de Energía y Minas ponen en grave peligro el Estado de Derecho en el Ecuador" (Quito: Sarayacu, 27 January 2004), http://www.sarayacu.com/oil/news040127.html.

[28] "Ecuador Ex-Head Goes into Exile" (London: BBC, 24 August 2003), http://news.bbc.co.uk/1/hi/world/americas/3177147.stm.

[29] Ibid.

[30] Sandra G. Edwards, "Ecuador. Illicit Drug Policies and Prisons: The Human Cost" (Washington, DC: Washington Office on Latin America, 2003), 6, http://www.wola.org.

[31] Ibid.

[32] The Corruption Perception Index (CPI) measures survey responses of business people, academics, and risk analysts and ranges from 10 (highly clean) to 0 (highly corrupt). *Global Corruption Report 2004* (TI), 286.

[33] "Wesberry: Trabajo del SAE puede ayudar en lucha contra la corrupción," *El Universo,* 24 October 2004.

[34] Michel Rowland, expert consultant for Proyecto Si Se Puede; personal communication.

[35] "Trabajador Petrolero Asesinado por Sicarios" (Quito: Centro de Medios Independientes, 2004), http://www.ecuador.indymedia.org/es/2004/02/4638.shtml.

[36] Michel Rowland, expert consultant for Proyecto Si Se Puede; personal communication.

# EGYPT

CAPITAL: Cairo
POPULATION: 73.4 million
GNI PER CAPITA: $1,470

**SCORES**
ACCOUNTABILITY AND PUBLIC VOICE: 2.31
CIVIL LIBERTIES: 2.18
RULE OF LAW: 3.19
ANTICORRUPTION AND TRANSPARENCY: 1.76
(scores are based on a scale of 0 to 7, with
0 representing weakest and 7 representing
strongest performance)

*Denis Sullivan*

## INTRODUCTION

The "Egyptian Regime"—established by Gamal Abdel-Nasser (1954–70), sustained by Anwar Sadat from 1970 until his assassination in 1981, and since led by Hosni Mubarak—is one that has prevented freedoms of speech, assembly, and association and has especially denied democracy and other political rights. The law-making process, along with political and security institutions, is used more to thwart political opposition and civil liberties than to protect (let alone expand) them. Mubarak keeps Egypt an authoritarian system, far from the democracy that he claims it to be. Like Nasser's before him, Mubarak's primary target in many of these efforts is the Muslim Brotherhood, the oldest and most popular opposition movement in Egypt. But Mubarak also has his sights on other Islamists (or politically motivated Muslims), including militant groups. His government and the parliament he controls have established laws on a wide array of issues to prevent human rights organizations, women's groups, and other nongovernmental organizations (NGOs) from forming, fund-raising, and providing social welfare services

**Denis J. Sullivan** is Professor of Political Science and Director of the Middle East Center at Northeastern University.

that seek to treat socioeconomic problems and other symptoms born of poverty and political exclusion.

Alongside these laws is an array of procedures and policies that have made Egypt an under-performer across the spectrum, from accountability and public voice to civil liberties, rule of law, and anticorruption and transparency. One of the most obviously offending laws, which also is a policy decision of the president and his near-rubber stamp parliament, is the Emergency Law, which effectively suspends Egypt's 1971 constitution. Compounding Egypt's poor performance is its deficient record on torture, political imprisonment, and the use of military courts to expedite convictions of civilians, which allows the government to accelerate executions of those it seeks to crush and denies the accused any recourse to judicial review.

While Egypt is not a military dictatorship in technical terms (as the president is officially a civilian now), it is a military-backed authoritarian system. Mubarak is a former air force officer who rules with the support of the military as well as the security services, led by the *mukhabaraat* (secret police). Like Sadat and Nasser before him, Mubarak can always count on these security services when he needs them. For example, as elections for parliament approached in 1995 and 2000, the security forces rounded up "hundreds"[1] of Muslim Brothers who were candidates for office.

Mubarak knows that the single most popular opposition movement in the country is the Muslim Brotherhood, established in 1928 and prominent ever since. Although Mubarak's dictatorial regime is not as brutal as others in the Arab world (such as Hafez al-Asad or Saddam Hussein), he perpetuates authoritarian rule with few effective limitations to his power.

Alongside these elements of authoritarianism, Egypt has a vibrant civil society and an array of political institutions that could promote democracy. However, the president has not abided by his own promise, made repeatedly since he came to power, to allow democracy to function. Egyptian politics thus remain both restricted and promising.

Fifty years after Nasser established the current regime, the president still determines the actual degrees of freedom in Egyptian society. Hosni Mubarak has now served 24 years as president, longer than either Anwar Sadat (11 years) or Gamal Abdel-Nasser (16 years). All three spoke of serving the Egyptian people; none served with a popular mandate won through competitive elections. All three have perpetuated a system that tolerates torture, represses political opponents, denies full equality before the law for women,[2] and undermines the notions of rule of law and of political and legal limitations to the power of the executive. And still, somehow, Egyptian citizens continue to assert their rights (often at great personal risk to themselves and their families) to attain greater power— the power to vote, the power to have a voice in government, the power to assemble, to a free press, to expression and belief. Egyptians continue to organize, as best they can under repressive conditions, in NGOs, syndicates, and political parties. However, there is much more for them to do in order to realize their rights more fully.

## ACCOUNTABILITY AND PUBLIC VOICE – 2.31

The authority of government in Egypt is not based upon the will of the people. While Egypt can boast of regular and perhaps also free elections, they are not fair elections under fair electoral laws. There is universal and equal suffrage, open to multiple parties (approximately 16 are legally registered), with elections conducted by secret ballot. In 2000, for the first time in the Nasser-Sadat-Mubarak regime, the parliamentary elections were monitored by independent electoral authorities—namely, the judiciary. While the government of Egypt does not allow international observation of elections, judicial oversight of the elections of 2000 is likely to have included a more honest tabulation of ballots and was probably freer of fraud and intimidation than any other election in the 50-year history of the current regime.

The president is not elected freely. The *Magles al-Sha'b* (People's Assembly or Parliament), controlled by the president, chooses one name to put before the electorate in a referendum. The people have the right to vote yes or no. Thus, presidents have been reelected with anywhere from 96 percent to 99.9 percent of the vote since the time of Nasser. Opposition candidates have no real opportunity to put their names before the electorate. Since 1952, no rotation of power has taken place between the ruling party (which has had four different names between Nasser's time and now) and any opposition party. Nasser and Sadat each chose their own successor; while Mubarak has yet to name his intended successor, speculation has been rife for the past several years that he is grooming his son Gamal for the position.

In the 1980s, Egypt moved toward pluralism and a more representative political system. In 1987, opposition and independent candidates controlled 30 percent of the seats in the People's Assembly. The ruling National Democratic Party (NDP) won only 69.3 percent of the vote that year, its poorest showing ever. By 1995, however, the NDP held 94 percent of the seats in the People's Assembly.

Irregularities clearly occur in elections, and the 1995 vote was particularly weak in this regard. However, patronage also plays an important role in keeping the ruling party in power. Government supporters benefit from government jobs, which dominate the economy. The ruling party wins in large part because it is the only party with something to offer its supporters.[3]

The elections of 2000 posed a challenge to the government. Public displeasure with the Mubarak regime was high leading up to the elections; internal political problems within the ruling party had also surfaced. The ruling party chose old-guard candidates to run in mostly safe districts (i.e., districts it was sure it would win), prompting younger-generation candidates to run as independents. Ultimately, while the NDP did win 388 seats (around 85 percent of the 444 elected to parliament), only 175 of those were the official (usually old guard) candidates. The others ran as independents and then rejoined the NDP after they won. Thus, voters had expressed their frustration and elected a majority of non-NDP candidates, including 54 true independents (who either were never part of the NDP or chose to break completely from it) and members of opposition parties. These 54 included 17 Muslim Brothers (the largest bloc of any opposition group), who ran as independents. Although the Brotherhood is an outlawed organization, there is enough openness in Egyptian society and enough defiance of the government's political parties law so that identities of Muslim Brotherhood candidates are well known. Besides the 444 elected members, parliament contains 10 members appointed by the president.[4] He usually chooses people from minorities (e.g., Copts) or other groups (women or politically important but under-represented groups) to demonstrate his attempt to balance the results.

Beneath the surface, an array of laws and procedures belies the appearance of free, fair, regular elections. A government-controlled parties committee has the power to deny parties the right to register and operate openly. This committee regularly asserts its power, especially against leftist and Islamist parties. Moreover, the government uses election laws to ensure greater or lesser majorities. For example, the single-member-district voting system in place of proportional representation allows the government to use its vast patronage system, control of security forces, and control of the airwaves and other media to generate votes. In the months leading up to local and national elections (as occurred in 1990, 1995, and 2000), the government rounds up and imprisons hundreds of primarily Islamist candidates. On election day itself, police are usually out in large numbers, and there is considerable intimidation of voters, especially in Islamist strongholds. In 1995, according to some accounts, police intimidation resulted in as many as 87 deaths and 1,500 injured on election day; in 2000, 10 were reportedly killed and around 60 injured.[5]

Egypt has no campaign finance restrictions. In fact, would-be politicians frequently donate their own wealth to the ruling party in order to be put on the ballot, thus ensuring their victory in the parliamentary elections.[6]

Although the executive is not accountable to the legislature, the judicial branch has a degree of independence from both the legislative and executive branches. Courts have issued rulings that have made the executive branch change policies or laws and even overturned elections (as in 1987 and 1990). Egypt's civil service also has some degree of independence through its recruiting procedures, which tend to reward the merit of the individual applicant rather than that person's *wasta* (personal connections). Nevertheless, wasta continues to be used when merit fails to secure someone a place in the ever-expanding bureaucracy. In the late 1980s, a study found that the vast majority of state employees received their jobs based on graduation from university (41 percent) and through competitive entrance examinations (45 percent); only about 11 percent attained their positions due to wasta.[7] While these statistics are dated, they indicate a major achievement for the Nasserist state, which inherited a system that was primarily driven by wasta or favoritism.[8]

Civil society is both restricted and overly regulated but is active and engaged in spite of government restrictions. NGOs work to advance specific causes, primarily for local development needs. On rare occasions, the government will allow NGOs to comment on legislation (such as environmental issues). However, the government applies a very effective (if unwritten) policy of divide and conquer that has kept Egypt's vibrant NGOs from working together as a unified community. NGOs have had to endure decades of government restrictions, control, harassment, and even political and legal campaigns against them.

Law 32 of 1964 was always a restrictive law of associations, providing the government of Egypt with significant tools to control, manage, and generally stifle civil society institutions. Under substantial pressure from civil society organizations within the country as well as from outside Egypt, the government attempted for several years to respond to demands for reform while not actually improving the situation. In June 2002, parliament passed an even more restrictive Law of Associations, Law 84.[9] This latest law places nearly insurmountable restrictions on accepting foreign funding and continues to provide the president and his security institutions with extensive powers to dissolve NGOs not to the executive's liking. Under Law 32 the government used this power to shut down operations of NGOs it considered political opponents— for example, it shut down the Arab Women's Solidarity Association when its leader, Dr. Nawal al-Sa'dawi, criticized President Mubarak for his support for the United States during the 1990–91 Gulf War.[10]

Egypt is awash in periodicals, weeklies, monthlies, and daily newspapers—government-owned and semi-official as well as opposition papers. However, few are independent. Under Nasser and Sadat, and to a great degree under Mubarak, government-appointed editors are expected to self-censor their product and can be removed if they do not.[11] The Mubarak government actively pursues journalists who criticize his sons or himself. In such cases, censorship, and even retribution including attacks, is well demonstrated. Circulation of the main government dailies is not widespread, and most opposition papers are weeklies with limited distribution.

Under the Press Law of 1995, the government can impose hefty fines and prison terms on journalists convicted of slander (a charge that the government itself can define). This law was put on the books after the opposition and Labor Party newspaper *Al-Sha'b* published reports critical of sitting ministers and appeared ready to investigate the alleged shady business practices of Mubarak's sons. The newspaper was closed in 2000.[12] However, the court ruled that *Al-Sha'b* could resume publication, saying it was unconstitutionally banned.[13]

*Recommendations*

- The government should again allow the judiciary to monitor and otherwise supervise parliamentary elections, and international monitors should be allowed in all future elections.
- The government should return to a proportional representation system for parliamentary elections.
- Direct elections for the president should be established.
- Law 84 should be abolished, and the government should engage in a meaningful dialogue with civil society leaders and international human rights/legal rights organizations to develop a new Law of Associations.
- The government should suspend the Press Law and allow the next legislative session to review and revise it; only the judiciary, not the executive, should be authorized to determine when slander has taken place.

## CIVIL LIBERTIES – 2.18

Egypt has a long record of torture by officers of the state against prisoners, and the state has not had a consistent or otherwise committed record of punishing the perpetrators of such crimes. In mid-2004, the Egyptian Organization for Human Rights (EOHR) published a report revealing that torture is a common practice in police stations, detention centers, and prisons. They found controls against torture to be weak, and legal repercussions for perpetrators rare. Torture has been revealed in nearly all of Egypt's governorates and affects all social classes. Its use is not limited to the detainee but can extend to the detainee's family. Between 1993 and April 2004, EOHR recorded 412 torture cases, 120 of which resulted in the death of the victim. The government began prosecuting perpetrators of torture in 2000; however, under Egyptian legislation, sentences for torture are light.[14]

Beyond torture, the government has engaged in state violence and mass arrests aimed primarily at Islamist militants—Islamic Jihad and *al-Gama'a al-Islamiya* (the "Islamic Group")—but also against nonviolent Muslim Brothers and many other nonmilitant opponents of the regime;[15] completely innocent and apolitical groups, notably homosexuals, also fall prey to government repression. The government of Egypt has been roundly and consistently criticized throughout the 1990s and early 2000s, both internally and by international organizations, for its use of unjustified imprisonment, mass arrests, torture, and other elements of state terror. Prison conditions in Egypt are abysmal, according to most human rights organizations both inside and outside Egypt.[16]

In June 2004, the government admitted that a member of the Muslim Brotherhood had died while in police custody. The ministry of interior said that Akram Zuheiri's "pelvic bone had been broken while he was being transported between detention facilities, and that he had died while being treated at the hospital, most likely from internal bleeding exacerbated by his diabetes."[17] Given the relationship between the Muslim Brotherhood and the government, Zuheiri's death was immediately the subject of speculation. Allegations were made that Zuheiri had in fact died as a result of torture at a police station. Zuheiri and 53 other Brotherhood members had been arrested on May 16, 2004, as part of the government's ongoing crackdown on the group. All were charged with sending the group's members abroad for training, with the ultimate aim of toppling the Egyptian government; the suspects denied the charges.[18]

The government has promulgated a string of laws and acts to limit personal freedoms and further consolidate state control over Egyptian society. The Emergency Law, which effectively suspends Egypt's 1971 constitution, has been in full effect in Egypt since 1981. The Antiterrorism Law of 1992 gives the government sweeping powers in determining who is a terrorist and allows execution for the crime of simply *belonging* to what it deems to be a terrorist organization. According to Amnesty International, the government has also increased use of the death penalty in the decade since 1994. The death penalty is invoked for security crimes (terrorism) but also cases of rape, murder, and drug crimes.[19]

In one of the most celebrated and publicized accounts of government repression of a democracy advocate, Saad Eddin Ibrahim was convicted—along with 27 associates—by a state security court in May 2001 of violating military decree No. 4, prohibiting the receipt of funds from abroad. Ibrahim was released temporarily in February 2002 by Egypt's highest appeals court, the Court of Cassation, which overturned the conviction and called for a retrial. It was unclear whether this release was due to repeated but quiet American pressure. Ibrahim's lead defense lawyer, Ibrahim Saleh, denied that there was international pressure, saying that Egypt's judicial system is completely independent.[20] The courts do enjoy a reputation for their relative independence from the executive branch, but the state's charges against Ibrahim were not dropped at that point. Saad Eddin was retried twice and on March 18, 2003, was finally acquitted on all charges by Egypt's Court of Cassation.[21]

Men and women are nominally equal under Egyptian law. In practice, men's rights predominate through personal status laws. These laws govern marriage, divorce, custody, and inheritance and are based on a traditional model of the family in which men are treated as superior to women. For example, as Human Rights Watch argues, the Egyptian government has created separate divorce systems for men and women. Men have a unilateral and unconditional right to divorce without going to court. Women must enter the court system, where procedural and evidentiary hurdles discriminate against them.[22]

Still, the government of Egypt has taken measures, including legislation, to improve laws and regulations to lessen if not end discrimination against girls and women. In 2000, Egyptian women won the right to file for no-fault divorce (*khula*). But to exercise that right, they had to agree to forfeit their financial rights, including having to repay the dowry given to them by their husbands upon marriage. While khula was adopted as a way to speed up the divorce process, it still requires women to petition the court to terminate their marriages (which men do not need to do). [*Editor's note:* In October 2004, the Egyptian government established family courts; however, these courts still fail to counteract structural discrimination against women.]

The government of Egypt has also worked to protect the physical rights of girls and women through its strong stance against female genital mutilation (FGM). In 1996, the government banned all medical and nonmedical practitioners from performing FGM. And in December 1997, the Court of Cassation upheld that ban. Anyone caught performing FGM is subject to the loss of his/her medical license and criminal punishment. If a girl or young woman should die at the hands of such a person, that person is subject to a charge of manslaughter.

Egypt is a transit country for women and girls trafficked from Eastern Europe and the former Soviet Union into Israel for forced prostitution. The government of Egypt does not fully comply with minimum international standards for the elimination of trafficking. In early 2004 the ministry of justice initiated an effort to enact comprehensive anti-trafficking legislation to meet these standards. However, complicating such efforts are the terms of the 1979 peace treaty with Israel, under which Egyptian border security forces are restricted in their operations along the Sinai border with Israel, where many trafficking victims transit.[23]

Egypt's population is about 90 percent Muslim; between 6 percent and 10 percent are Coptic Christian. Still, the government refuses to acknowledge that minorities exist in Egypt—and in particular refuses to consider Copts a minority population. The government delays or prevents investigations into alleged mistreatment of Copts (e.g., by the state or its security forces as well as by militant Muslims) because, according to the government, the Copts are part of the Egyptian family, and thus they are not a minority. Yet, Copts have suffered from discrimination for decades; the Coptic pope was imprisoned by Sadat, and Copts face government resistance, even rejection, when seeking to renovate or construct their churches.

Some militant Muslims seek to transform Egypt into a fundamentalist Islamic state or to transform Egyptian society into a more pious one. These include Islamic *Jihad* (*Gehad,* in Egyptian dialect) and *al-Gama' al-Islamiya* (the Islamic Group). However, most politically motivated Muslims in Egypt are non-violent, including the leadership and vast majority of the still-outlawed Muslim Brotherhood. In an effort to rein in Islamist militancy, the government issued an executive order in 1992 to nationalize tens of thousands of *sha'bi* (private) mosques. However, the effort has fallen far short of its objective of forging a single, government-controlled voice of Islam in Egypt.

In 1994, Saad Eddin Ibrahim and his Ibn Khaldun Center for Development Studies (ICDS) organized a conference on "Minorities in the Arab World." The Egyptian government, including through its control of the media, launched a campaign against the organizers and implicitly threatened to undermine it should they attempt to continue to host it in Cairo. As a result, about one-third of the invitees declined to attend. The government-controlled media then published articles denying that minorities faced problems in Egypt and attacking the conference.[24] Ultimately, the conference was held in Cyprus.

Investigating the human rights of Copts has landed scholars and activists in prison, including Hafez Abu Sa'ada, Secretary General of the Egyptian Organization for Human Rights (EOHR). Abu Sa'ada was arrested in December 1998 and charged in February 2000 (along with

EOHR's lawyer) for "taking money from foreign sources [a British Parliamentary human rights association] without permission" and for "defaming Egypt"—i.e., for conducting investigations into violence against Christians. The government eventually agreed not to pursue the trial but did not drop the charges.[25]

Egypt's emergency state security courts have been used to judge whether people of various faiths, beliefs, and even sexual orientations are guilty of "extremist ideas," "debauchery," and other crimes. Emergency courts deny the accused most rights, including the right to appeal to a higher court. Beyond the infamous arrest and subsequent trial in May 2001 of more than 60 men whose only "crime" was their homosexuality, scores of others have been similarly arrested and tried for their religious beliefs and membership in Islamist political movements.

In 2001–02, Amin Yussif (a 51-year-old civil servant), his wife, Amal Mahmud, and six others were detained in emergency court under charges of "exploiting religion for extremist ideas," which carry up to five years' imprisonment. The group was "accused of having held private religious gatherings and advocating modifications to basic Islamic rules, including rules for prayers and pilgrimage."[26] Amnesty International has noted an increase in arrests and trials of those exercising their right to freedom of religion. At the end of 2001, more than 50 prisoners of conscience were incarcerated in Egypt. Between January and April 2001 more than a dozen alleged members of the Baha'i faith were arrested and detained for several months. In February 2001 the UN Special Rapporteur on religious intolerance noted that "Baha'is are not allowed to meet in groups, especially for religious observances, and their literature is destroyed."[27] In general, the government does not permit non-Muslim proselytizing.

Egypt's Law 39 (1975) on Rehabilitation of Disabled Persons mandates assistance through government-sponsored job training, quotas requiring larger companies to hire a minimum number of disabled workers, and job protection. There is no specific protection against discrimination of people with disabilities.[28]

The Syndicates Law of 1993 was enacted after several syndicate elections were won by Islamist candidates. This law gives the government power to appoint governing boards to unions and syndicates and declare syndicate elections invalid.[29] Should demonstrations occur by syndicate members, the government can "direct" them (e.g., confine them to a university campus, where they can be contained). The government also frequently uses excessive force against demonstrators.

*Recommendations*

- The government of Egypt should suspend the Emergency Law and return to the 1971 constitution as the law of the land.
- The government must embrace international standards on prisoners' rights by amending and adopting legislation to bring it in line with international standards, thus allowing for better public monitoring as well as the independent and impartial review of complaints.
- The government of Egypt should ensure freedom of belief, thought, conscience, and religion by complying with international treaties to which it is a state party. Accordingly, the government must foster a culture of inclusion and non-discrimination through manifest state behavior and the encouragement of public dialogue.
- The government should review and repeal discriminatory provisions in the family and penal laws to promote a single standard of divorce for men and women.
- Torture must end and its perpetrators must be punished.

## Rule of Law – 3.19

Egypt's constitution guarantees the independence of the judiciary (Articles 165 and 166). Judges in the regular court system are appointed for life by the president upon recommendation of the Higher Judicial Council; they may not be dismissed without serious cause. The Higher Judicial Council is headed by the president of the Court of Cassation and is composed of senior judges and the attorney-general. However, in practice the executive authority has considerable influence over the judiciary through judicial appointments. Judges are employees of the ministry of justice, which administers and finances the court system. Thus the executive is the de facto head of the judiciary.[30]

Egypt has a dual system of security courts. Permanent state security courts have two levels and draw their judges from the regular court system; the state security court–emergency section (emergency courts) has much more direct executive involvement in its composition and jurisdiction. The permanent state security courts allow some basis for appeal;

the emergency section permits no judicial appeal, but the military governor (under the state of emergency) is allowed to affirm the verdict or order a retrial.

The president may also invoke the Emergency Law to refer any criminal case to the emergency courts, in which the accused does not receive most of the constitutional protections of the civilian judicial system. The government asserts that referral to emergency courts usually has been limited to terrorism or national security cases, as well as major cases of drug trafficking; however, the government also has occasionally used emergency courts to prosecute homosexuals, heterodox religious groups, and political dissidents. Government authorities have ignored judicial orders in some cases.

In June 2003, parliament passed several reforms introduced by the NDP's policy secretariat, headed by Gamal Mubarak.[31] The reform package included a law abolishing the state security courts. The courts had been used to deliver swift justice on national security issues, but they also tried ex-ministers, businessmen, and democracy advocates (including Saad Eddin Ibrahim), among others. After their abolishment, a number of cases referred to the state security courts were transferred to regular criminal courts. However, as long as the government retains and uses emergency courts, abolishing the state security courts will not improve human rights or rights of the accused in any meaningful way.[32]

Military courts, which are part of the military hierarchy, also continue to be used by the government for swift justice. Military courts are generally intended to try those cases involving the armed forces, but during a state of emergency the president is authorized to transfer crimes to them. Under military courts, civilian defendants have no due process before an independent tribunal. There is no appeals process; instead, verdicts can be reviewed by other military judges and confirmed by the president.[33] The authority of military courts to try civilians has been supported by Egypt's Supreme Constitutional Court (SCC).

And yet, in the ordinary court system, there is growing independence and impartiality. Judges increasingly assert and defend their authority to secure constitutional rights for all Egyptians. Increasingly, though far from consistently, the legislative and executive branches do comply with judicial decisions. Judges are among the best-trained professionals in government. They have expanded the scope of press freedom by dismissing libel suits of government ministers against the opposition press and have widened the scope of labor rights by dismissing charges against strikers.[34]

One of the most impressive demonstrations of judicial independence occurred in July 2000, when the Supreme Constitutional Court ruled that the upcoming parliamentary elections must have complete judiciary supervision. The government reacted favorably, passing amendments by presidential decree to establish full judiciary supervision for all future parliamentary elections. Even the opposition press praised the president for working within the constitution.[35]

Still, the regime ignores the courts when it can. For example, the ministry of interior continues to exercise sweeping powers of arrest and detention of dissidents and frequently ignores court decisions. Reliance on the Emergency Law allows the government to ignore the rule of law, the courts, judicial review, and other areas where it would have to subject itself to monitoring by the two other branches of government. What is less visible, and more sinister, is Mubarak's quiet yet persistent efforts to undermine judicial independence. In August 2001, Mubarak appointed a chief justice and five judges to the SCC from the ministry of justice, in defiance of the court's tradition of self-selecting its chief justices from its own ranks.[36]

While the constitution provides a platform for the rule of law in civil and criminal matters, it is suspended under the Emergency Law. Constitutionally, people are innocent until proven guilty; they have the right to an attorney; and they should be considered equal before the law and the courts. However, the "security state" of Egypt mistreats people generally, and some more than others—especially Islamists and other opponents of the state. Prosecutors are agents of this security state and thus have no effective independence from the government or its security forces. Prosecution of public officials and ruling party actors for corruption and other abuses of power is selective, depending on when the government decides it wants to punish someone by removing them from power in a public fashion.

There is neither effective nor democratic civil state control over the police or military; both are powers unto themselves, and the military is the supreme power of the Egyptian state. One of the most visible measures of this is the fact that the military budget has since Nasser's time been a secret; there is no parliamentary oversight of the military's budget, and thus no public awareness of the degree of the economic power of the military. What is well known, on the other hand, is that the military owns, runs, and profits from a significant portion of the Egyptian economy—from agriculture to manufacturing to certain tourism services. While Egypt is not a military dictatorship per se, as the president takes off his uniform to assume the civilian post, the governments of Nasser, Sadat, and Mubarak all have secured their power first and foremost through the military; power comes second from the secret police apparatus (the *mukhabaraat*), and third from the civilian institution of the ruling party, currently the NDP.

While Egypt has made some progress in ensuring property rights, there has also been stubborn resistance by both governmental and private stakeholders to promoting equality before the law. Most recently, in May 2002, Egypt passed a comprehensive intellectual property rights (IPR) law to comply with World Trade Organization regulations. However, the law may not adequately protect rights, to the extent that some in the scientific community worry that the legislation, as written, may actually deter the transfer of technology and investment from abroad.[37]

Most Egyptians live in illegal dwellings with limited infrastructure. Those who can afford legal property and a building permit face years of bureaucracy to acquire them.[38] Another arena of progress is in the government's willingness to promote (although as yet with no measurable success) ownership of property for the majority of Egyptians), an extremely difficult objective given the significant level of poverty in Egypt (some estimates say more than 50 percent of the population live in poverty). In June 2001, Egypt passed Law 148, the Home Mortgage Law, allowing many Egyptians an important vehicle to purchase a private home. Even with the new option of a private mortgage, the initial down payment still remains beyond the means of most people. Nevertheless, the law is a step in the right direction toward liberalizing the financial institutions and providing greater access to them for all Egyptians.

*Recommendations*

- The government must more consistently respect the rulings of the regular court system.
- The government should return to the time-honored tradition of promoting judges within their own ranks, not from executive branch agencies such as the ministry of justice.
- The emergency court system should be disbanded.

- The military court system should be used only for military cases.
- The military's budget should go before the parliament for public debate.

## ANTICORRUPTION AND TRANSPARENCY – 1.76

Egyptian governments, under both the current regime and its historical predecessors, are notorious for excessive bureaucratic regulations, registration requirements, and other controls that feed corruption. Whenever Egyptians face such controls, money is what ultimately triggers the requisite signature or relevant approval. Compounding the normal bureaucratic culture is the state ownership of many or most of the primary economic levers—banking and financial institutions, tourism, oil, the Suez Canal, manufacturing, the media, and so on. Furthermore, government employees receive insufficient pay, while a decreasing minority of Egyptians achieve increasingly vast wealth, thus creating a growing income gap between the classes and causing the supposed middle class to be squeezed to the smallest minority between the rich and the poor. Corruption has remained a significant problem under Sadat and Mubarak. Both promised to do much, but in fact neither has done anything significant to tackle it effectively.

That said, on November 16, 2002, President Mubarak made a clear statement that his government's new anticorruption campaign was going to last. In a speech before both houses of parliament marking the opening of their legislative session, he said, "the rule of the law is a basic necessity for combating corruption and fighting favoritism." Parliament opened that week with the NDP firmly in control; Fathi Sorour was re-elected by his colleagues as speaker of parliament for the 13th year in a row, as were his deputies and committee chairmen. However, the one major exception was Abdallah Tayel, formerly the powerful head of the economic committee, who was in jail on corruption charges. In September 2002, Tayel had his parliamentary immunity lifted and soon afterward was charged with corruption for giving out loans as the head of the joint-venture Misr Exterior Bank.[39]

In 2002–2003, parliament passed a number of proposals aimed at promoting transparency of governance and at attacking corruption. First, in September 2002 the NDP announced the creation of a new secretariat for ethics, headed by a retired judge, to confront widespread corruption among NDP members. In November 2002, the government appointed new chief executives to the four major public-sector banks and required that each establish an audit committee. In May 2003 parliament passed the Unified Banking Law, governing the Central Bank of Egypt (CBE), the banking system, and foreign exchange bureaus. The law was designed to give the CBE greater oversight powers by entitling its governor to appoint senior banking officials. This came in response to several bad loans by public-sector banks to tycoons who then defaulted and in many cases fled the country.[40]

While the government of Egypt, led by Hosni Mubarak, has made headlines and some strides in attacking corrupt government officials (prosecuting a number of them in 2002 and 2003) and suggesting structural reforms to promote transparency, many political analysts suspect that the reforms are simply another tool in the hands of an authoritarian leader determined to pave the way for his son to succeed him. The timing of the anticorruption campaign has been indicative. The campaign's near-total focus on senior officials in President Mubarak's NDP has been concurrent with the political rise of his son, leading to speculation that the crackdown is simply clearing a path for an increasing public role for Gamal. Most strikingly, the anticorruption campaign is completely government-run and managed, without any input from NGOs or other civil society groups. Although the government has expressed a desire to forge coalitions to combat graft, it has kept firm unilateral control over the anticorruption campaign.[41]

Egypt has a number of agencies that could, if properly empowered by the president, promote transparency and fight corruption. A central auditing agency, working out of the prime minister's office, is engaged in privatization of government assets and strives for financial transparency.[42] The Administrative Control Authority is Egypt's primary anticorruption watchdog,[43] although it does not have jurisdiction to investigate accusations of corruption against certain categories of state employees. All of these agencies are directly tied to the executive branch and thus the presidency; therefore, reform (with public accountability and transparency as part of that overall agenda) is only possible if the president wants it.

If the Administrative Control Authority uncovers corruption in the public sector, it refers its allegations to the supreme state security courts for prosecution. In 2002, these courts did convict several businessmen and officials, including a former finance minister, a former attorney-general, the former governor of Giza, and some members of parliament. In these cases, defendants received long prison sentences and large fines.

A branch of Transparency International functions in Egypt. Egypt's score on Transparency International's Corruption Perception Index continues to improve, from 1.1 out of 10 (10 = no corruption) in the late 1990s to 3.2 in 2004.[44]

Only the government decides which corrupt officials may be exposed and punished. The draconian 1995 press law and the restrictive NGO Law of Associations stifle civil society and leave nongovernmental democracy advocates susceptible to arrest, trial, and fines if they speak out against corrupt officials. Thus, even if opposition press and NGO leaders were correct that corruption is rampant, the government still wields the power to muzzle them.

Complicating the efforts by NGOs and others to combat corruption is the fact there is little public access to government information. With the military budget beyond scrutiny, the budget-making process is primarily closed to meaningful legislative and public inspection. While foreign assistance is overseen by the donors and is therefore administered in a reasonably fair manner, it is not immune from the country's overall corruption.

*Recommendations*
- The government should maintain its proclaimed campaign against corruption and look to independent judicial reformists to head up the effort. Judicial procedures should be revised so that instances of alleged corruption are tried in regular courts, rather than state security courts.
- The government should assist its own corruption and transparency watch-dog agencies in operating independent of the executive, for example through a more transparent and accessible budget process and new freedom of information laws.
- The government should accept NGOs and the press as partners in the campaign against corruption, while establishing mechanisms (such as the equivalent of an office of the ombudsman, responsible for overseeing anticorruption efforts, or anonymous telephone tip lines) to enable government employees and citizens to report instances of bribery, corruption, and misuse of government funds.

## NOTES

[1] In 1995, the numbers were not known exactly, but Amnesty International and other human rights groups used the term "hundreds"; in the 2000 elections, the number was "more than 200" Muslim Brothers detained. "Egypt: Muslim Brothers on Trial Must Be Released" (New York: Amnesty International [AI], 27 July 2000), http://web.amnesty.org/library/index/engmde120242000?open&of=ENG-2MD.

[2] Salwa Sha'rawi Gomaa points out that Egypt ranked 68 out of 70 countries studied in the UNDP's "Gender Empowerment Measure" (GEM) in 2003. *Progress of Arab Women, 2004* (Cairo: UN Development Fund for Women [UNIFEM], Arab States Regional Office, 2004), 273.

[3] Michael Collins Dunn, "Egypt's Parliamentary Campaign Begins," *The Estimate: Political and Security Intelligence Analysis of the Islamic World and Its Neighbors* XII, 19, 22 September 2000, http://www.theestimate.com/public/092200.html.

[4] The numbers quoted here add up to 452 seats; 2 districts in Alexandria were hotly contested and the results were not validated until a final round or by-election was held after the 2000 election.

[5] Michael Collins Dunn, "Egypt's Parliamentary Elections: An Assessment of the Results," *The Estimate* XII, 23, 17 November 2000, http://www.theestimate.com/public/111700.html.

[6] For a fictionalized discussion of this process, see Alaa al-Aswany, *The Yacoubian Building,* translated by Humphrey Davies (Cairo: American University in Cairo Press, 2004; originally published in Arabic, 2002).

[7] Monte Palmer, Ali Leila, and El Sayed Yasin, *The Egyptian Bureaucracy* (Syracuse: Syracuse University Press, 1988), 59–61.

[8] Nazih N. M. Ayubi, *Bureaucracy and Politics in Contemporary Egypt* (London: Ithaca Press, 1980), 157, 469.

[9] "Civil Society in Egypt Under Attack," *Media Alert* (New York: Human Rights First, 5 June 2002), http://www.lchr.org/media/2002_alerts/0605.htm.

[10] Interview with Dr. Nawal Saadawi; see also Denis J. Sullivan and Sana Abed-Kotob, *Islam in Contemporary Egypt: Civil Society vs. the State* (Boulder, Colo.: Lynne Rienner Publishers, 1999), 25.

[11] *Egypt: The Political Role of the Media* (Washington, DC: U.S. Library of Congress, n.d.), http://www.country-studies.com/egypt/the-political-role-of-the-media.html.

[12] Mona El-Ghobashy, "Egypt," *Global Corruption Report, 2004* (Berlin: Transparency International [TI], Country Report, 2004), 186, http://www.globalcorruptionreport.org.

[13] Michael Collins Dunn, "Egypt's Parliamentary Campaign Begins," *The Estimate* XII, 19, 22 September 2000, http://www.theestimate.com/public/092200.html.

[14] "Torture in Egypt: An Unchecked Phenomenon" (Cairo: Egyptian Organization for Human Rights [EOHR], n.d.), http://www.eohr.org/report/2004/re3.htm.

[15] "Terrorism: Questions and Answers—Jamaat al-Islamiya, Egyptian Islamic Jihad" (New York: Council on Foreign Relations, 2004), http://cfrterrorism.org/groups/jamaat.html.

[16] See, for example, "Tuberculosis . . . The Slow Deaths in the Prisons of El Wadi El Gadeed and Damanhour" (EOHR, 23 January, 2001), http://www.eohr.org/ press/2002/ 1-23.htm.

[17] Jailan Halawi, "Deadly Negligence: The Recent Death of a Muslim Brotherhood Detainee Has Cast an Unequivocal Light on Prisoners' Rights," *Al-Ahram Weekly*, 17–23 June 2004, http://weekly.ahram.org.eg/2004/695/eg4.htm.

[18] Ibid.

[19] "Egypt: Continuing executions while use of death penalty decreases worldwide" (London and New York: AI, 10 August 2004), http://www.amnestyusa.org/countries/egypt/ document.do?id=7C880A661C3C0C0A80256F260052A740.

[20] Quoted in Jailan Halawi, "Going Home," *Al-Ahram Weekly*, 7–13 February 2002.

[21] For extensive background on this case, see "Egypt's Best Known Activist on Trial" (New York: Lawyers Committee for Human Rights, n.d.), http://www.humanrightsfirst.org/ middle_east/egypt/ibrahim/hrd_ibr_more.htm.

[22] "Divorced from Justice: Women's unequal access to divorce in Egypt" (Human Rights Watch, December 2004), http://www.hrw.org/reports/2004/egypt1204.

[23] "Trafficking in Persons Report" (Washington, DC: U.S. State Department, 14 June 2004), discussed in "Human Trafficking and Modern Day Slavery," http://gvnet.com/ humantrafficking/Egypt.htm.

[24] Saad Eddin Ibrahim, "An Arab Culture of Denial," *bitterlemons-international.org*, edition 2, vol. 43, 9 December 2004, http://www.bitterlemons-international.org/ inside.php?id=261.

[25] "Human Rights Defenders in Egypt" (Human Rights First: Middle East Initiative, n.d.), http://www.humanrightsfirst.org/middle_east/egypt/hrd_egypt.htm.

[26] "Egypt: Ongoing Violations of the Right to Freedom of Belief," (AI, International Secretariat, 4 March 2002), http://www.hrea.org/lists/hr-headlines/markup/msg00224.html.

[27] Ibid.

[28] "Egypt: Rights of People with Disabilities" (Chicago: Center for International Rehabilitation, 2003) http://www.cirnetwork.org/idrm/reports/compendium/egypt.cfm.

[29] See especially, Carrie Rosefsky Wickham, "Islamic mobilization and political change: The Islamic trend in Egypt's professional associations," in Joel Beinin and Joe Stork, eds., *Political Islam* (Berkeley: University of California Press, 1997), 120–35.

[30] "Egypt: Attacks on Justice, 2002" (Geneva: International Commission of Jurists [ICJ], 27 August 2002), http://www.icj.org/news.php3?id_article=2658&lang=en.

[31] For an extensive treatment on the speculation, see Denis J. Sullivan, "The Struggle for Egypt's Future," *Current History* (January 2003).

[32] Mona El-Ghobashy, "Egypt," *Global Corruption Report*, 2004 (TI), 184–89, http://www .globalcorruptionreport.org.

[33] "Egypt: Attacks on Justice, 2002" (ICJ), http://www.icj.org/news.php3?id_ article=2658&lang=en.

[34] *Egypt: The Judiciary, Civil Rights, and the Rule of Law* (Washington, DC: U.S. Library of Congress, n.d.), http://countrystudies.us/egypt/115.htm.

[35] Mona Makram-Ebeid, "Abstract: Egypt's 2000 Parliamentary Elections," *Middle East Policy Council Journal* VIII, 2 (June 2001), http://www.mepc.org/public_asp/ journal_vol8/0106_ebeid.asp.

[36] Mona El-Ghobashy (TI, 2004), 187.

[37] Wagdy Sawahel, "Technology transfer centres to be set up in Egypt," *SciDev.Net*, 11 November 2004, http://www.scidev.net/gateways/index.cfm?fuseaction=readitem& rgwid=2&item=News&itemid=1730&language=1.

[38] Maria Golia, *Cairo: City of Sand* (Cairo: American University in Cairo Press, 2004), 18.

[39] "Egypt's Anti-Corruption Campaign" (Istanbul and London: Oxford Business Group, 11 November 2002), http://www.mafhoum.com/press4/121S71.htm.

[40] Mona El-Ghobashy (TI, 2004), 184–85.

[41] Ibid., 185.

[42] "Financial Management: Egypt" (Beirut: UNDP, Programme on Governance in the Arab Region [POGAR], n.d.), http://www.pogar.org/countries/finances.asp?cid=5.

[43] "Egypt: Falling Star," *Al-Ahram Weekly*, 26 September–2 October, 2002, http://weekly .ahram.org.eg/2002/605/eg4.htm.

[44] "Corruption Perceptions Index, 2004" (Berlin: TI, 22 October, 2004), http://www .transparency.org/cpi/2004/cpi2004.en.html#cpi2004.

# ERITREA

CAPITAL: Asmara
POPULATION: 4.4 million
GNI PER CAPITA: $190

**SCORES**
ACCOUNTABILITY AND PUBLIC VOICE: 0.67
CIVIL LIBERTIES: 1.54
RULE OF LAW: 1.03
ANTICORRUPTION AND TRANSPARENCY: 1.71
(scores are based on a scale of 0 to 7, with
0 representing weakest and 7 representing
strongest performance)

*Dan Connell*

## INTRODUCTION

Eritrea won its de facto independence in May 1991, capping a 30-year war against successive U.S.- and Soviet-backed Ethiopian governments that had laid claim to the former Italian colony after forcibly annexing it in the early 1960s. Two years later, Eritreans voted overwhelmingly (99.8 percent) for sovereignty in a UN-monitored referendum in which 98.5 percent of the 1,125,000 registered voters participated.[1] This was the first and last national ballot independent Eritrea ever held; thereafter the Eritrean People's Liberation Front (EPLF), which had already decimated its nationalist rivals or driven them out of the country before defeating the Ethiopian army, moved to institutionalize its monopoly on power.

Early in 1994, the EPLF changed its name to the People's Front for Democracy and Justice (PFDJ) and confirmed its former commander, Isaias Afwerki, as the head of the re-christened political movement and the interim president of the new country, in what was cast as a four-year transition to democratic governance. Over the next three years, the PFDJ

Dan Connell, the author of six books and numerous articles on Eritrea, teaches journalism and African politics at Simmons College, Boston.

established new state institutions, including executive, legislative, and judicial branches presiding over a three-tiered administration (national, regional, local); a streamlined civil service; professional armed forces; and new police and security forces. However, no other political parties were permitted, nongovernmental organizations (NGOs) were sharply curtailed, and there was no independent press until 1997, when print media—but not broadcast—were allowed to publish under a strict new press law.

Between 1995 and 1997, a constitution commission whose members were named by the president oversaw a national education campaign on democratic values and options for governance that drew tens of thousands of Eritreans at home and abroad into a dialogue over the nation's political future. The finished document was ratified at a national conference in May 1997. However, the president has declined to implement the constitution ever since, citing tensions with Eritrea's neighbors, with which the country has experienced a continuing cycle of violent confrontations.

A bloody three-year border war with Ethiopia beginning in 1998 ended with a tense truce in which UN peacekeepers were brought in to keep the combatants apart. Its outbreak triggered a behind-the-scenes power struggle among EPLF/PFDJ leaders over the president's conduct of the war, his hard-line approach to peace negotiations, and his resistance to democratization. These disagreements spilled into public view in the spring of 2001 through both the private press and the Internet after the president refused to allow the party's Central Council or the National Assembly to convene. As he marshaled his supporters through closed-door PFDJ sessions in January and August 2001 from which his critics were excluded, a systematic crackdown on all public dissent got under way.

On September 18 and 19, 2001, the government arrested 11 of 15 top government officials and former liberation movement leaders—the Group of 15, or G-15—who had signed a petition that charged the president with illegally suppressing debate and called for the implementation of the constitution and the democratization of the political arena. Of the remaining four, one recanted and three were out of the country when the arrests took place. Next, the government shut down the private press and arrested many of its leading editors and reporters. In the years since, there have been numerous, less publicized arrests—

elders who sought to mediate on behalf of the detainees, more journalists, mid-level officials, merchants, businessmen, young people resisting conscription, and church leaders and parishioners associated with minority Christian denominations, among others. Some were held for short periods and discharged. Others—like the G-15 and the journalists—have been held indefinitely with no charges leveled and no visitors allowed. Some who were taken and released claim they were tortured, but no executions have been reported.

The overriding problem in Eritrea today is the concentration of power in the hands of one man—Isaias Afwerki. President Isaias and the PFDJ maintain an absolute monopoly on all forms of political and economic power. They control what few media there are in the country and have fenced off the population from the outside world while fostering a xenophobic hostility to foreigners to distract the citizenry from the privations of daily life and the persistent denial of basic rights and liberties. The complete suppression of civil society precludes the development of a legal opposition within the country—or of any organized public discussion of what such an opposition might look like were it to be permitted. Under these conditions, national elections, if conducted, can only serve to ratify those already in power.

## ACCOUNTABILITY AND PUBLIC VOICE – 0.67

Eritrea's political culture has long been authoritarian, predicated on secrecy and the arbitrary exercise of absolute power. Throughout the 1970s and 1980s, the EPLF was led from within by a clandestine Marxist core, the Eritrean People's Revolutionary Party (EPRP), chaired by Isaias Afwerki. The EPRP met in secret to draft the EPLF's program prior to its three general congresses (1977, 1987, 1994); to select slates for leadership prior to elections; and to manage its affairs on a day-to-day basis. Although the EPRP ceased to function as a political organization in 1989 and was officially disbanded in February 1994, this pattern of rule by a behind-the-scenes cabal held true during the construction of the state in the 1990s and continues today.

A provisional National Assembly was established in 1992 with the addition of 75 delegates chosen in PFDJ-run regional elections to the party's 75-member Central Council. This body confirmed Commander Isaias as the acting president in an uncontested ballot that was closed to the media and the public, as are all National Assembly meetings. President Isaias then personally selected cabinet ministers, regional governors, upper-echelon judges, an auditor-general, the governor of the national bank, new ambassadors, top military commanders, and many mid-level officials and civil authorities. He also presides over all meetings of the PFDJ Central Council and the National Assembly.

Although the government has the appearance of embodying a separation of powers—an executive office with a cabinet of ministers, an interim National Assembly, and a nominally independent judiciary—this is largely an illusion. The cabinet does not provide a forum for debate or decision making. Instead, it serves as a clearinghouse to determine how policies hammered out by the president's inner circle are to be put into practice. The National Assembly is a creature of the ruling party and does not initiate policy or legislation; nor does it meet in open session.

Eritrea's constitution, ratified by a 527-member constituent assembly on May 23, 1997, guarantees citizens "broad and active participation in all political, economic, social and cultural life of the country," but it also says that these rights can be limited "in the interests of national security, public safety or the economic well-being of the country, health or morals, for the prevention of public disorder or crime or for the protection of rights and freedoms of others."[2] Government officials have said the constitution will go into effect once national elections are conducted, but such elections, first scheduled for 1998 and delayed with the outbreak of war, rescheduled for 2001 and then delayed again by the political crisis that engulfed the ruling party, have yet to be set.

Over the past decade, Eritrea has conducted regional and local elections with balloting open to men and women of all religious and ethnic backgrounds, but no forms of new political organization have been permitted, including independent parties and even caucuses within the PFDJ. Nor has the state permitted the formation of politically oriented civil society groups, think tanks, policy organizations, or other independent NGOs. All voting for local public office has been conducted in town-meeting–style sessions presided over by PFDJ cadres. Thus, organizational sectarianism, not ethnic or religious affiliation, has set the parameters for Eritrea's highly constrained political discourse.

Campaigns are not permitted, as there are no legal organizations to put them together, apart from those run by the government. Individuals are not allowed to set up organized political operations during PFDJ-run elections. Public discussion prior to such elections centers on the character of the candidates and their loyalty to the ruling party. It is extremely rare to find debate over policy options or initiatives in public forums, and there are no media in which new proposals or critiques of existing policies and programs can appear unless they are prepared by party functionaries. The only substantive exchanges over political issues take place behind closed doors at party-run seminars or leadership meetings. However, even these are strictly controlled, as the arrest and subsequent disappearance of dissident former leaders who spoke up in such meetings in 2001 demonstrated to the party faithful.

As there are no legal parties in Eritrea apart from the PFDJ, and as there have been no national elections of any kind, no rotation of power has been possible. A special parliamentary commission in 2001 drafted a party law that legalizes multiple parties and lays the groundwork for national elections, but the president has withheld it. Several opposition parties exist outside Eritrea, however. Chronic turmoil over four decades within the country's original independence movement, the Eritrean Liberation Front (ELF), has produced numerous splinters, including at the extremes both the ruling EPLF/PFDJ and the Sudan-based Eritrean Islamic Jihad.

In 2004, more than 18 externally based factions opposed the PFDJ. Some define their separate identity by ideological orientation, but most are differentiated by their links to external powers, their regional or ethnic base, or the personalities who lead them. Most seek the ouster of the Isaias Afwerki regime by extralegal means and maintain military bases or offices in neighboring Ethiopia or Sudan. Among them are the ELF group led by Adbella Idris (the largest of the former ELF factions), the ELF-Revolutionary Council, the pro-Ethiopia Eritrean Revolutionary Democratic Front (whose name mimics that of the ruling party in Ethiopia), and several smaller regional groups.[3] In 2004 13 such groups were affiliated with the Ethiopia-based Eritrean National Alliance (ENA), which is committed to the armed overthrow of the Isaias government. Its adherents are drawn mainly from among former ELF fighters and from refugees in Sudan and Ethiopia.

The government crackdown on dissent since 2001 has also given rise to a breakaway faction of former EPLF/PFDJ members that favors a nonviolent political transition—the Eritrean Democratic Party (EDP), led by EPLF founder and G-15 member Mesfun Hagos. Its stated goal is the establishment of "a constitutional system in accordance with the democratic principles laid down in the ratified Constitution of Eritrea."[4]

The civil service is based on a mix of merit and political loyalty. There are no published guidelines or legal recourse in the event of dismissal, and there is no transparent competitive process for securing civil service positions or gaining advancement. Ministerial portfolios are frequently shuffled to keep rivals from developing power bases of their own. High-ranking officers and government officials who question the president's judgment over minor issues often find themselves subjected to the Chinese practice of *midiskal* (freezing) in which they are removed from their posts and kept on salary but not permitted to work, then abruptly brought back into the fold when they are perceived to be "rehabilitated." Meanwhile, hundreds of poorly paid conscripts fill lower-level posts left open by the steady drain of military call-ups and by the flight of many young people since Eritrea went onto a war footing with Ethiopia in 1998 (see "Civil Liberties").

The only media in Eritrea today are those controlled by the state: EriTV, which began broadcasting in Asmara in 1993; Dimtsi Hafash (Voice of the Masses radio), broadcasting in six languages with a transmission power of 1,000 kilowatts; three newspapers, one published in Tigrinya (*Hadas Eritrea*), one in Arabic (*Eritrea al-Hadisa*), and one in English (*Eritrea Profile*), all of which carry roughly the same information and opinion; and a government-run press service, the Eritrean News Service (EriNA). The Ministry of Information, headed by Ali Abdu Ahmed, uses the media to propagandize without permitting opposing views to be published or broadcast.

A 1996 Press Law guarantees the freedom of the press but prohibits, among other things, the dissemination of material that "promotes the spirit of division and dissension among the people" or that contains "inaccurate information or news intentionally disseminated to influence economic conditions, create commotion and confusion and disturb the general peace." These vague proscriptions left the state broad discretion to harass the country's feisty new newspapers in 2001 after they began publishing critiques of the president. The law also bans foreign funding of indigenous press, the contravention of which was the government's unofficial rationale for the press closures in 2001.[5] The National Assembly created a committee in February 2002 to assess and, if needed, revise the Press Law, but no new proclamation has been announced since then, and the independent press remains closed. Amnesty International reported that 14 journalists remained in prison without charge in December 2003, including Aklilu Solomon, a reporter for Voice of America, who was detained the previous July after reporting adverse public reaction to the government's announcement that soldiers had been killed in the border war with Ethiopia.[6] Eritrea expelled the last resident foreign reporter, Jonah Fisher (BBC, Reuters), in September 2004 after he reported on human rights issues. Questioned by a local stringer about the country's continued incarceration of indigenous reporters and editors, Information Minister Ali Abdu Ahmed characterized the jailed journalists as "agents of the enemy" who "were not journalists, either professionally or ethically."[7]

What information and independent analysis of domestic and international issues reaches Eritreans does so largely through radio and Web-based media originating abroad. Three political parties—the EDP, the ELF-RC, and the ENA—beam weekly shortwave radio programs to Eritrea via satellite. These and other opposition groups also maintain active Web sites, as do several unaffiliated groups in Eritrea's very active diaspora, most of them highly critical of the Isaias regime. The most prominent of those opposed to the current government are Awate.com and Asmarino.com. Government supporters in the diaspora also maintain a number of sites, the most prominent of which is Dehai.org.

Eritrea has seen an explosion of Internet connectedness, particularly among young people in the main towns and cities. The four private Internet service providers are all monitored by the state, although not directly controlled, and numerous Internet cafes are open to the public. [*Editor's note:* On October 19, 2004, the Ministry of Information announced new controls on Internet cafes and on public libraries, ostensibly to limit access to pornography. Many view this as an effort to block links to the proliferating independent Web sites based outside Eritrea.[8]]

*Recommendations*
- Eritrea's already-ratified constitution should be implemented without further delay.
- The government should approve the party law legalizing multiple parties and laying the groundwork for national elections.
- The government should grant amnesty to members of opposition political movements based outside the country and allow these

organizations to renounce violence and enter the political process as legal entities competing on a level playing field with the ruling PFDJ.

- An independent commission should be established to organize Eritrea's first national elections, with adequate safeguards for competing parties and open campaigns and with extensive international monitoring throughout the process.
- The 1996 Press Law should be rescinded and constitutional protections for free media respected by permitting the re-establishment of independent newspapers and the creation of independent broadcast media.

## CIVIL LIBERTIES – 1.54

The as-yet-unimplemented constitution bans torture (Article 16), but former detainees claim to have been routinely subjected to it.[9] Amnesty International reported in May 2004 that torture of prisoners is "widespread and systematic" and that it is the "standard form" of military interrogation and punishment.[10] No public officials have ever been prosecuted for torturing or abusing prisoners.

Conditions for many current political detainees are impossible to ascertain, as the prisoners are denied all access to visitors. Even the sites where many political prisoners are kept are secret. Arrests for political infractions are frequent and arbitrary, rarely accompanied by formal charges, although Eritrea's constitution guarantees the right of habeas corpus (Article 17), and the Eritrean penal code limits detention without charge to 30 days. Estimates of the number of political prisoners detained since 1991 run from the high hundreds to the thousands, but it is impossible to get an accurate count as no charges have been filed against any of them or formal trials held. Reports are widespread of members of opposition groups such as the ELF held under detention since the early 1990s. At least one of the G-15 is thought to have died of what one government official told a visiting journalist in 2003 were natural causes, but there are no confirmed reports of executions of dissidents.[11]

Numerous governments, multilateral organizations, and human rights organizations, including the U.S. Department of State, have called for the release of Eritrea's political prisoners, particularly those arrested in September 2001. However, the Asmara government insists that it holds no prisoners for political reasons, claiming those who are incarcerated are criminals or security risks. In March 2004, the African Commission on Human Rights issued an advisory ruling that the continued detention of the 11 former high-ranking government officials taken in September 2001 was illegal.[12]

More than 220 Eritreans who were forcibly deported from Malta in 2002 remained in detention in 2004, most in secret prisons on the island of Dahlak Khebir. At Eritrea's request, some 100 Eritrean nationals were forcibly repatriated from Libya on July 21, many of them draft-age men and women who fled Eritrea through Sudan in the hope of reaching Italy once they arrived in Libya. They were reportedly detained upon arrival in Eritrea and have not been seen since. On August 27, a plane carrying another 76 Eritreans from Libya to Eritrea made a forced landing in Khartoum, where 15 were accused of hijacking the plane and sentenced to five years in prison in Sudan. The others have petitioned the UN High Commissioner for Refugees for protected status. UNHCR has recommended that even rejected asylum seekers should not be forcibly repatriated.[13]

All Eritreans between the ages of 18 and 45 are required by law to perform 18 months of national service in the armed forces or in government-run public works projects. Since the outbreak of war with Ethiopia in 1998, however, conscripts have been kept in service on a continuous basis, many serving in low- or no-paying jobs in state and party-controlled enterprises. There have been frequent, often brutal, house-to-house round-ups to identify, induct, or detain evaders. Re-induction for those who have already served has been used as political punishment for members of the press and others who have expressed public criticism of government policy.[14] A steady flow of refugees into neighboring Sudan is one by-product of this policy.

Women played a central role in Eritrea's independence war, constituting more than 30 percent of the 95,000-strong liberation army and playing a wide range of non-traditional roles. Their post-independence participation in public life presents a mixed record, as conservative social values have reasserted themselves and destructive traditional practices such as female circumcision, child marriage, and virginity testing have become increasingly common. The constitution prohibits discrimination based on race, ethnic origin, color, and gender and mandates the

National Assembly to legislate measures designed to eliminate such inequality (Article 14). Although this has yet to be put into effect, the state has already acted to diminish oppressive cultural practices and has effectively blocked trafficking in children or women. The government has declared International Women's Day an official holiday and ratified the Convention on the Elimination of All Forms of Discrimination against Women (CEDAW).

Women held three ministerial portfolios in 2004—Justice, Tourism, and Labor and Social Affairs—and in local elections in 2002, women won more than a fifth of the posts. However, gender-related changes in the public sphere are not woman-led, and women, like other social groups, are prohibited from forming their own organizations apart from the party-sanctioned National Union of Eritrean Women.

The government has increased educational opportunities for girls and opened schools in remote areas of the country for children of minority groups, offering primary education in all nine of the country's indigenous languages. Elementary school enrollment rose 270 percent from 109,087 in 1991 to 295,941 in 2001, with that for boys reaching 53 percent of the school-age population and that for girls 49 percent. However, retention and drop-out rates were high, especially for girls.[15] Secondary and post-secondary education is state-subsidized and free to students, who are accepted largely on merit, though the poorly performing economy tends to limit the number of children subsistence farm families can afford to send to school. Social pressures weed out many of the female students as sons are given priority within the family.

The society as a whole is ethnically and religiously diverse. Tigrinya-speakers, mostly Christian sedentary farmers and urban dwellers concentrated on the highland plateau, make up nearly half the population. Tigre-speaking Muslims, many of them agro-pastoralists living in the western lowlands and the coastal plains, are the second largest group, making up close to a third of the population. The remaining fraction is comprised of six, mostly Muslim, minorities, plus the Kunama, who practice traditional religious beliefs. There is no official language, although Tigrinya, Arabic, and English prevail in business and commerce.

This ethnic potpourri is almost evenly divided between Sunni Muslims and Christians (most of whom are Orthodox, along with Catholic and Protestant minorities tracing to the pre-colonial period), with a small minority (2 percent) who practice traditional beliefs. There is little institutional discrimination based on faith among these historically present groups, although Orthodox Christians of the Tigrinya-speaking ethnic group dominate the economy and hold most high-level political posts. However, the government has taken to actively suppressing evangelical Protestant denominations that have made recent inroads. The as-yet-unimplemented constitution guarantees all citizens "the freedom to practice any religion and to manifest that practice" (Article 15). However, the government has banned what it terms new churches—minority evangelical Christian denominations and mission groups, which have experienced rapid growth over the past decade.

In May 2002, the government proscribed all religious denominations but Islam, the Eritrean Orthodox Church, the Roman Catholic Church, and the Evangelical Church of Eritrea (Lutheran). Members of the prohibited denominations—less than 2 percent of the population but with growing influence among Eritrea's youth—were forbidden from worshipping anywhere in Eritrea, even in private homes. Twenty-seven girls and 30 boys were held in metal shipping containers in harsh conditions and pressed to abandon their evangelical Christian faith.[16] On January 24, 2004, police arrested 38 members of a Jehovah's Witnesses congregation worshipping in a private home in Asmara, including children and a 90-year-old man. In February and March, nearly 100 members of evangelical churches in Asmara, Mendefera, and Assab were reportedly arrested for praying in private homes, and some were held as long as one month.[17] In an April 2004 meeting, the government's Department of Religious Affairs ordered pastors of banned Christian churches to "not inform anyone outside Eritrea of your problems" and forbade them from inviting Christian speakers from abroad without government permission. The pastors at the meeting reportedly rejected these demands and insisted they would continue to inform the outside world of the threats made against them until their constitutional rights to freedom of worship were restored. The following month, three prominent evangelical leaders were arrested. Singer Helen Berhane, who had recently released an album of Christian music, was also jailed and reportedly held in a shipping container at the Mai Serwa military camp. Several evangelicals who were later released showed evidence of severe physical maltreatment.[18]

Meanwhile, the Eritrean government has come under increasing attack from Islamist terrorists based in neighboring Sudan, chiefly the

Eritrean Islamic Jihad Movement (EIJM, recently changed to the Eritrean Islamic Party for Justice and Development). EIJM was founded in Sudan in 1988 and was affiliated with Osama bin-Laden's terrorist network when it was based there in the 1990s. It is blamed for a rash of land-mine incidents, ambushes, and bombings over the past decade, including a May 25, 2004, bombing in the western town of Barentu that injured 90 people.[19] This rising confrontation has led to increasingly stringent, and often repressive, government controls over the mostly Muslim inhabitants of the western and coastal lowlands.

With no outlet for political protest in Eritrea, the Islamist resistance has become by default the channel for the rising popular dissatisfaction among Eritrean Muslims. Issues that feed its growth include a litany of perceived cultural slights: the government's refusal to accept Arabic as an official language; government interference in the selection of leader-ship in Islamic religious institutions, including the appointment of the Grand Mufti in Asmara; the virtual colonization of the lowlands by Tigrinya-speaking Christian entrepreneurs, who own most of the shops, businesses, hotels, and other urban enterprises and control most com-merce and trade there; the denigration of pastoralism as a way of life, reflected in government policies and services favoring settled farmers; resentment over a post-independence trend toward unequal representa-tion for Muslims in state and party leadership; fears that the official (but haphazardly implemented) land reform will impinge on traditional graz-ing rights, a concern that has been reinforced by the recent resettlement of war-displaced civilians and refugees returning from Sudan in the fer-tile western plains; and, most important, outrage over the conscription of women into an army where they reportedly suffer extensive abuse. These trends have politicized religious identity and augur ill for the future.

The only nonreligious membership-based organizations permitted to operate in Eritrea today are those under the party's direct control—the National Confederation of Eritrean Workers (with an estimated 20,000 members in five federations), the National Union of Eritrean Women (with 200,000 members), and the National Union of Youth and Students (with 170,000 members).[20] The trade unions are not per-mitted to organize any segment of the workforce without state and party permission, nor are strikes permitted under any circumstances. No in-dependent trade union organizing is allowed by individuals or groups outside these party-controlled structures. The women's and youth organizations are largely service providers and do not engage in policy advocacy or protest. Donations to these organizations are closely monitored by the state, which bans unrecognized organizations from accepting foreign funds. The PFDJ pre-selects the leadership slates and sets the priorities for these organizations, which are then confirmed at periodic organizational congresses.[21] With few exceptions—Planned Parenthood is one—international groups are not permitted to establish local chapters in Eritrea, and global human rights organizations have been blocked from carrying out local investigations.[22]

No group larger than seven is permitted to meet without government permission, and no organized public protest is tolerated.[23] On July 30, 2001, the president of the University of Asmara Student Union, Semere Kesete, was arrested after criticizing the forced labor imposed on students during the summer months. When University of Asmara students protested his arrest the next day outside the High Court in Asmara, they were rounded up and sent to a summer work camp, where at least two died from extreme climate conditions. In the aftermath, the university's Student Union was disbanded by the authorities and replaced by a chapter of the PFDJ-controlled National Union of Eritrean Youth and Students.[24]

All other instances of public remonstration since independence—by liberation front fighters upset over the lack of pay in May 1993, by disabled veterans protesting their banishment from major urban centers in 1994, and by young National Service conscripts in 2004—have been forcibly put down, with their leaders detained without trial for lengthy periods.

*Recommendations*
- The government should either release or bring to public trial all political prisoners, including but not limited to the former liberation front leaders and government officials identified with the Group of 15.
- Allegations of state torture should be investigated promptly and fully, and the government should ensure appropriate prosecution and punishment of perpetrators.
- A law on religion should be adopted that provides legal protections for all religious groups, and prompt legal action should be taken against those who attack members of minority faiths.

- The national service program should be depoliticized and restructured and not be used as a vehicle for coerced, underpaid labor for state and party operations.
- Full and unfettered freedom of public assembly should be permitted, as guaranteed by Eritrea's as-yet-unimplemented constitution.

## RULE OF LAW – 1.03

The judiciary functions as an arm of executive authority, with judges appointed or sacked at the discretion of the president's office. In some cases, panels of military and police officers have sentenced offenders in secret proceedings that flout basic international standards of fair trial. Detainees are not informed of the accusations against them, have no right to defend themselves or to have legal counsel, and have no recourse to independent judges to challenge abuses of their rights.[25]

The president created a system of secret military tribunals (Special Courts) in 1996 to hear cases of corruption and other unspecified abuses by government and party officials. These courts are directly accountable to his office. Hundreds have been sentenced by them, and they are closed to the public. The trials are conducted by largely untrained military judges without legal representation for the accused or any right of appeal. Prisoners are sent to secret security prisons and military camps scattered around the country, which are not open to public scrutiny or even family visits. In July 2001 the chief judge of the High Court, Teame Beyene, was removed from his post after complaining of executive interference in judicial proceedings and calling for the dismantling of the Special Courts.

The military remains under the president's personal control, as he exercises direct command over the four theater-operation generals—the most powerful figures in the country after the president—while ignoring his minister of defense, General Sebhat Ephrem. The country's national security forces are nominally headed by an Isaias Afwerki loyalist, Abraha Kassa, but, like the armed forces, they remain under the president's personal control.

All land is the property of the state under a land reform proclaimed in 1995. This guaranteed usage rights to all citizens for agricultural and residential land but has been incompletely implemented since then. Prior to this, most land in Eritrea was communally controlled under tenure arrangements that varied widely from one ethnic group to another (and within them, as well). After the sharp decline in Eritrea's economy following the outbreak of war in 1998, the government began offering long-term leases for cash payments and threatened to strip citizens living abroad of their right to land if they involved themselves in dissident political activities or failed to fulfill their tax obligations. With exports extremely low and new investment not forthcoming, the economy survives largely on remittances from the diaspora, whose members are required to pay a 2 percent asset tax in order to maintain rights to purchase land, secure inheritances, and take advantage of other privileges within Eritrea.

*Recommendations*

- Executive interference in the judiciary should be halted and judges permitted to function independently.
- The Special Courts should be abolished immediately and their functions taken over by civilian bodies.
- Those accused of any crime—political or otherwise defined—should be informed of the accusations against them, have access to legal counsel, and be able to appeal.
- Access to residential and agricultural land should not be subject to political conditions. All land transactions should be open and transparent, with conditions for lease or extended use spelled out and adhered to by both parties.

## ANTICORRUPTION AND TRANSPARENCY – 1.71

Throughout the post-independence years, the economy has been dominated by the state and the PFDJ, which share ownership of the country's major financial and commercial institutions, agricultural and industrial enterprises, utilities, services, communications facilities, and transport companies. The PFDJ itself holds dozens of businesses in banking, trade, construction, shipping, metal-works, auto repair, road surfacing, and well drilling, among other industries, and it holds controlling stakes in a number of joint ventures with foreign investors for other large-scale undertakings, such as mining.[26] These, set up in the 1980s and 1990s, had been operated by the liberation front, and the PFDJ has expanded them since then with state favor. While the state has divested itself of some large and medium-size enterprises, it continues to play a commanding role in the economy. Privatization has gone slowly, in part out of would-be investors' fear of party interference in economic ventures and in part due to the precarious security situation since 1998.

Personal corruption among individuals has historically been low in Eritrea—and severely punished when uncovered—but the state and the ruling party have made extensive use of economic levers for political ends, often acting in concert. It is common, for example, for the PFDJ to pressure enterprises to include it as a partner in new ventures and to exact payment or a percentage of profits for its cooperation. Meanwhile, in recent years, strict controls on travel—both within the country and abroad—have generated a lucrative business in such documents as highly prized exit visas and, in the process, fostered a growing practice of graft and corruption among state bureaucrats. Largely on this basis, Transparency International rated Eritrea 102nd of 146 nations in its Transparency International Corruption Perceptions Index 2004, scoring the country only 2.6 on a scale of 1 to 10.[27]

Brigadier General Estifanos Seyoum, a high-ranking member of the PFDJ and a veteran of the independence war, was relieved of his post in the ministry of finance in August 2001 after questioning the equity of tax collection from PFDJ-owned enterprises. A signatory of the May 2001 "Open Letter to the PFDJ," he was detained with the other members of the G-15 in September 2001 and has not been heard from since.[28] No public questions about tax collection or government expenditure have been raised in public forums since then. Nor is there any independent auditing body with authority to take up such issues. Under the constitution, the president appoints an auditor general, but this position has not been functional. There is no public record of the party's economic operations, no published line-item national budget for the state, no detailed accounting for tax collection or remittances—no fiscal transparency of any kind for either state or party finances. In fact, the line items for the national budget remain a well-guarded secret—not only from the general public but from most members of the cabinet and the ruling party.[29]

With an executive-dominated government running a one-party state that prohibits independent media, quashes non-party NGOs, and detains without trial or recourse to appeal those who dissent individually, there are no whistleblowers for misconduct of any kind.

*Recommendations*

- The financial affairs of the state and the People's Front for Democracy and Justice should be fully disentangled and made transparent.
- A comprehensive line-item national budget for revenue and expenses (operational and capital expenditures) should be prepared, published annually, and made easily accessible to the public.
- Tax policies and procedures should be open and transparent and subject to independent review.
- The practice of requiring exit visas to leave the country should be ended. Collection of bribes and favors for issuing government permits and documents should be thoroughly investigated and laws should be passed to prevent it in the future.
- The government should implement safeguards to protect whistle-blowers on institutional and personal corruption from retributive action by those whom they expose.

## NOTES

1. *Eritrea: A Country Handbook* (Asmara: Ministry of Information, 2002), 23–24.
2. Eritrea Constitution, Articles 7 and 26, http://unpan1.un.org/intradoc/groups/public/documents/CAFRAD/UNPAN00464.pdf.
3. On May 2, 2003, Hiruy Tedla Bairu, general secretary of the Eritrean National Alliance, told the BBC that its military wing would attack strategic targets such as television and radio stations. See the ENA Web site: http://www.erit-alliance.org.
4. The EDP's founding program (February 2002) can be retrieved from http://www.eritreaone.com/Docu/publication.htm.
5. "Eritrea: Assembly session 'conservative but not regressive,'" Integrated Regional Information Network [IRIN] News (UN Office for the Coordination of Humanitarian Affairs, Nairobi), 4 February 2002, http://www.irinnews.org/report.asp?ReportID=20331&SelectRegion=Horn_of_Africa&SelectCountry=ERITREA.
6. "Eritrea 2004" (New York: Amnesty International [AI], January 2004), http://web.amnesty.org/report2004/eri-summary-eng.
7. "Eritrean report on imprisoned journalists still pending: minister," Agence France Presse [AFP], 6 October 2004, http://dehai.org/archives/dehai_news_archive/sept-oct04/0588.html.
8. "Internet Cafes Place [sic] under Educational & Research Centers and Libraries," Shabait.com (Asmara: Ministry of Information, October 19, 2004), http://www.shabait.com/articles-new/publish/article_2468.html.
9. Interview with former detainee, Asmara, 6 September 2002.
10. "Torture is Rife in Eritrea," *The Wire* (AI, July 2004), http://web.amnesty.org/wire/July2004/Eritrea.

[11] Telephone interview with Australian Broadcasting Corporation journalist, 3 December 2003.

[12] See, "AU's Human Rights Ruling against Eritrea Documented," *Afrol*, 17 September 2004, http://www.afrol.com/articles/14148.

[13] "Libya/Eritrea" (AI, 6 September 2004), http://web.amnesty.org/library/index/ENGMDE190142004.

[14] "Eritrea: Government resists scrutiny on human rights and calls to end torture and arbitrary detention" (AI, 19 May 2003), http://news.amnesty.org/index/ENGAFR64004 2004.

[15] *Eritrea: A Country Handbook*, 99.

[16] "Eritrea 2004" (AI, January 2004).

[17] "International Religious Freedom Report 2004" (Washington, D.C.: U.S. Dept. of State, 15 September 2004), http://www.state.gov/g/drl/rls/irf/2004/35354.htm.

[18] Testimony of Dr. Paul Marshall, Senior Fellow, Center for Religious Freedom, Freedom House, before the U.S. House International Relations Committee, 6 October 2004, http://wwwc.house.gov/international_relations/107/mars0213.htm.

[19] "Sudan: Peace and the Region," IRIN (Nairobi), 2 April 2004, http://www.plusnews.org/S_report.asp?ReportID=40388&SelectRegion=East_Africa.

[20] *Eritrea: A Country Handbook*, 50–52.

[21] Numerous interviews with leaders and members of NUEW, NCEW, NUEYS, Asmara, 2001, 2002.

[22] Amnesty International delegates were refused visas in July 2002 and have not been permitted to enter Eritrea since then. Neither Human Rights Watch nor the Committee to Protect Journalists had representatives in Eritrea in 2003 or 2004.

[23] "Eritrea: January 2004" (New York: Human Rights Watch [HRW], 2004).

[24] Interviews with Asmara University students and members of NUEYS, Asmara, October 2001, February 2002; Boston, November 2003.

[25] "Eritrea: 'You have no right to ask'—Government resists scrutiny on human rights" (AI, 19 May 2004), http://www.amnestyusa.org/countries/eritrea/document.do?id=14FA0F5364535E3480256E67005A4F30.

[26] Interview with Hagos Gebrehewit, responsible for economic affairs in the PFDJ Secretariat, Asmara, 9 March 1996.

[27] "Corruption Perceptions Index 2004" (Berlin: Transparency International, 20 October 2004), http://www.transparency.org/cpi/2004/cpi2004.en.html#cpi2004.

[28] "Another Critical Official Sacked," IRIN, 7 August 2001, http://allafrica.com/stories/200108070236.html.

[29] Interviews with Eritrean government officials, Asmara, August–September 2001, February–March 2002.

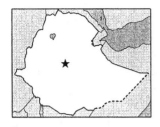

# ETHIOPIA

CAPITAL: Addis Ababa
POPULATION: 72.4 million
GNI PER CAPITA: $100

**SCORES**
ACCOUNTABILITY AND PUBLIC VOICE: 1.88
CIVIL LIBERTIES: 2.83
RULE OF LAW: 2.06
ANTICORRUPTION AND TRANSPARENCY: 2.76
(scores are based on a scale of 0 to 7, with
0 representing weakest and 7 representing
strongest performance)

*Jeffrey Clark*

## INTRODUCTION

May 2005 marks the 14th anniversary of the toppling of the Derg regime—a brutal military junta headed by Mengistu Haile Mariam and aligned with the Soviet bloc—the end of its 17-year reign of terror in Ethiopia, and the concurrent assumption of power by the Ethiopian People's Revolutionary Democratic Front (EPRDF) coalition.[1] It is a milestone offering considerable disappointment: Despite early economic gains, per capita income has started to fall;[2] the specter of famine still looms as basic food security has eroded; and hopes for democratic advancement have been thwarted by a ruling party that stubbornly monopolizes political space. The opposition is harassed and intimidated, civil society suppressed, the media tightly controlled, and independent voices stifled. The government brands those who propose alternative

**Jeffrey Clark** is an independent international development consultant with long involvement in Ethiopia through his tenure with the Congressional Select Committee on Hunger during the famine crises of the 1980s and his efforts to bolster the nongovernmental sector in the country following the collapse of the Derg. He has undertaken assignments in Ethiopia for USAID, the World Bank, and various civil society groups.

251

policy approaches as illegitimate, if not terrorists. It labors to reverse the acute poverty that afflicts millions of citizens but quells aspirations of increasingly competent nongovernmental entities poised to facilitate the development process. The government constructs systems meant to appease donors and their demands for broader participation, then uses them to extend control.

In Ethiopia today, the government's accountability to the people is minimal, as is the ability of citizens to register a voice as public policies are being considered and programs implemented. Civil liberties are respected on a haphazard basis. Rule of law is more rhetorical than real. The country benefits from the fact that large-scale corruption has not become ingrained, but the lack of transparency threatens that advantage.

The government of Ethiopia fares well in any comparison to the predecessor regime, as its officials boast. That, of course, is not much of an achievement. The country's strategic role in the fight against international terrorism allows the government to avoid donor-government scrutiny that would reveal the disappointingly meager steps toward genuine democratization that have characterized EPRDF's tenure in office.

May 2005 will also bring the third round of parliamentary elections since the end of Mengistu's brutal dictatorship. If these elections can be more participatory than previous rounds, hope will remain in play for the nation's transition from autocracy to nascent democracy. Fair elections would almost certainly see retention of power by the EPRDF— albeit at lower levels of dominance of Parliament but with significant gains in perceived legitimacy. Less fair elections have the potential to drown hopes for participatory government and national progress, perhaps even to fan the flames of resistance.

## ACCOUNTABILITY AND PUBLIC VOICE – 1.88

Few structures hold government officials accountable to citizens in Ethiopia, and no innate sense of such responsibility tempers arbitrary decision making. The media are closely controlled, the judicial system barely functions, civil society is constricted, and the executive branch of government issues decrees against political opponents and arrests them on dubious charges of corruption or supporting armed rebels. Journalists, academics, and others who question government policies are intimidated and sometimes jailed.[3] Incidents tend to be resolved with an eye more to avoidance of donor-government displeasure than adherence to consistent and transparent systems and procedures.

Under the EPRDF, citizens of Ethiopia have been able to vote in successive rounds of local, regional, and national elections for the first time in the country's history. Interest in these elections has been high, and some positions have been genuinely contested in vigorous campaigns. However, elections held to date have seen the crass manipulation of electoral processes to the advantage of the ruling party. Charges of voter intimidation have been frequent, and opposition rallies and voter education efforts have been disrupted. In some cases, the government does not certify opposition parties or candidates as being eligible to participate. Cumbersome election rules have led to self-defeating boycotts by various parties and candidates and their marginalization.

While the choice of candidates has been heavily restricted, people have been able to vote by secret ballot for the most part. Some independent monitoring of elections has taken place, and voting tabulation has been generally fair. Thus, a foundation has been laid for more genuinely competitive and participatory elections. If recent accords between the ruling party and the opposition regarding the 2005 elections hold, then that foundation will expand.

Writing in 1998, the journalist Marina Ottaway stated that the regime had conducted "three supposedly multiparty elections" in which "political participation has narrowed rather than widened."[4] One consequence was that Ethiopia's dramatic and fundamental transformation into a federation based on ethnicity was not subject to public debate; it simply was imposed by the EPRDF. That reality has left scars and fissures on the political landscape that have not yet healed.

Since 1998, participation has widened slightly as the EPRDF has been forced into new alliances to counter internal division.[5] More dissenting views can be heard in policy debates and on radio and television, as well as in newspaper columns—at least in Addis Ababa. Still, the EPRDF and its satellite parties control over 90 percent of all seats in Parliament. Reflections on the improved legitimacy that could be realized through more participatory elections were summarily dismissed.

Campaigning opportunities have not been equal for various contestants in past elections. Access to print and broadcast media has been widely uneven; permits for campaign events have been issued prejudicially; and access to public facilities has been skewed in favor of the

EPRDF and its allies. Few processes are in place that guarantee a more even playing field for the elections slated for 2005. A recent African Development Forum study ranked the independence and credibility of Ethiopia's electoral processes as being exactly half that of the average of the 16 African countries surveyed.[6]

Prospects for genuine rotation of political power in Ethiopia through the electoral process are dim due to the commanding position of the ruling party atop the machinery of government and the multiple weaknesses of the splintered opposing parties. Aspirations of the Oromo population (the largest ethnic group in the country) are thwarted by the branding of the Oromo Liberation Front (OLF)—a former partner in the struggle against the Derg that many now consider to be the main political opponent of the EPRDF—as a terrorist organization and the designation of any dissenting Oromo voice as that of an OLF collaborator. The Oromo People's Democratic Organization (OPDO) affiliation with the EPRDF does not mask growing alienation of large parts of the Oromo population from the government.

Rotation of political power is in fact contrary to the views of national evolution held by the EPRDF hierarchy. At one recent EPRDF congress, members embraced the concept of a 20-year party monopoly on power until the country is ready for democracy.

The ruling party governs with certainty that its insights on policy justify its hold on state power. Ethiopia does not have any effective campaign finance laws or other measures to prevent undue influence of privileged interests, although ideologues pose more danger than oligarchs.

Progress has been realized since 1991 in defining separate branches of government that will at some point allow for checks and balances required to hold the executive, legislative, and judicial branches accountable to each other and to the public. Nevertheless, today both the judiciary and Parliament are subservient to the executive branch. Legislators are handed bills drafted by the executive branch and told to enact them, which they do. Parliament does not defy the Council of Ministers, which is selected by the prime minister and approved by the House of People's Representatives (the lower chamber of Parliament) and which serves as the senior cabinet of the government.

Civil service positions in government ministries are largely filled through open competition. However, low skill levels and antiquated bureaucratic machinery preclude effectiveness. The abysmal salaries paid civil servants all but require many to occupy second jobs—jobs that keep them away from their government desks for several hours of their nominal workday. A dysfunctional bureaucracy (record keeping is largely not computerized, few civil servants have technical training for the positions they occupy) serves to undermine the public's faith in government and to encourage a rise in petty corruption as officials rely on bribes to subsidize paltry salaries.

Until recently, the registration process for nongovernmental organizations (NGOs) was particularly onerous and consumed vast amounts of time and energy. The legal and regulatory framework that defines the operating space for NGOs and other civil society entities dates primarily from the 1960 civil code,[7] when no indigenous NGOs existed in Ethiopia. The law's silence on the rights of NGOs combined with the government's general hostility and bureaucratic burdens clearly hamper NGO operations. The executive director of one Addis Ababa–based NGO reports that 70 percent of his professional time is devoted to satisfying bureaucratic demands from various government agencies.[8] The Ministry of Justice, responsible for registration, has made considerable strides in streamlining the process and lengthening the validity of registration. Complaints by NGOs on the registration process have diminished noticeably. However, governance, democracy, and human rights groups face enormous problems with registration and becoming operational. The Ministry of Justice retains the right to dissolve an organization that it feels is carrying out business unrelated to the purposes specified upon registration. There is little evidence of governmental pressures on local funders of civic organizations, whose contribution is still very small, but the government quite openly tries to steer international resources toward pro-government civil society actors.[9]

Forums convened by various nongovernmental entities, the World Bank, and other players allow limited discussion on public policy by civic groups. Such sessions are not regularized, and the record is mixed in terms of any discernible influence that the civic groups might have. A long-discussed NGO law is indicative: The first draft of the proposed legislation surfaced in 2000, and four years later various drafts were being circulated that reflected some of the changes advocated by the NGO sector while other concepts remained absent. No bill has made it to Parliament, and no hearings before legislators had been scheduled as of September 2004, although current prospects for the introduction of updating legislation are encouraging. Groups undertaking advocacy or lobbying work are subject to harsh treatment by the government and certainly do not enjoy any assumed right to present their case to government officials.

Media outlets are small, weak, and short on professionalism and therefore easily intimidated. There are perhaps 150 print outlets in the country, one national television broadcaster (a government entity), and only one private radio station and one private news agency. The latter are controlled by the EPRDF through a corporate front. All printing presses are owned by the government, and those presses are periodically unavailable—ostensibly for technical reasons—to newspapers thought to be publishing objectionable stories.

There is no legal protection for the media against government control or censorship. The Broadcast Law enacted in 1999 established a Broadcasting Agency with authority to issue, suspend, and revoke broadcasting licenses. This supposedly autonomous entity, however, reports to the prime minister. And, as of October 2004, it had not issued a single new license.

Various laws allow a high degree of government control over both print and broadcasting media. Vague legal phrases in the constitution and Press Law offer no objective standards for what is prohibited. Moreover, those affected by these laws have no effective recourse to the courts, which are insufficiently independent in any case. The government's interpretation of libel is such that any journalist offering virtually any criticism of government policies or officials is subject to arrest. In April 2003, the editor of *Ethiop* was arrested on a libel charge after earlier printing a story dealing with alleged embezzlement by a public hospital administrator.[10] The paper's deputy editor was detained the next month and charged with libel over an article criticizing the country's former ambassador to France. Even newspaper vendors on the streets of Addis Ababa have been harassed and detained.[11]

The government tolerates a modest degree of unfiltered reporting but largely succeeds at controlling the slant of the news reported to the public through its direct and indirect ownership of facilities and its intimidation of writers, editors, and publishers. The extremely low level of professionalism—the president of Addis Ababa University uses the term "glaring incompetence"[12]—found in the media leaves reporters prone to reporting government press releases as documented news. In contrast, free cultural expression is generally respected in Ethiopia.

In 2003, four Ethiopian journalists were imprisoned and the Ethiopian Free Press Journalists' Association was closed.[13] In April 2004, police arrested two Oromo-language journalists.[14] While the situation is less dire than a decade ago, when 32 journalists were thought to be in jail at one time, it is clear that government control over the media remains firmly entrenched. Journalists have expressed concerns for personal safety due to their reporting.[15]

### Recommendations

- The government must commit itself to a process for the May 2005 parliamentary elections that will be seen as fair and free by all participants and observers. This requires certification of all legitimate opposition parties, provision of equal access to public facilities by all participating parties, and the end of intimidation of opposition candidates by law enforcement officials.
- Legal reforms must be undertaken to guarantee a free press and freedom of expression; specifically, a press law that is *enabling* of a free press must be put into place.
- A public information campaign should be launched to publicize the role of civil society and a free press in achieving democratization and economic progress.

## CIVIL LIBERTIES – 2.83

There is no state terror in the form that took place under the Derg's rule. Unjustified imprisonment is common, and torture, while less frequent, does happen. Protections against such state actions are woefully inadequate in Ethiopia. The entire judicial structure is extremely weak and insufficiently independent from the executive branch. Police forces are poorly trained on the constitutional rights of individuals. Prosecutors are not accountable.

Few human rights monitors are in place to expose or confirm violations, and the government does not permit international groups to operate in the country. A small delegation of officials from Amnesty International (AI) was allowed to visit in March 2004. AI has reported on six individuals accused of having links with the OLF who were arrested in August 2004 and were allegedly being held incommunicado without charge or trial and were subject to torture.[16] In 2002 AI reported "harsh prison conditions with inadequate medical treatment" for inmates.[17] Human Rights Watch also reported poor prison conditions, torture, and impunity of offenders.[18] Parliament has been considering the establishment of an independent human rights ombudsman since 1998 without taking final action.

Human rights and international news reports are replete with examples of arbitrary arrests. Political activists and journalists operate on the assumption that arrest without charge or for bogus charges is possible. One human rights group claims that more than 10,000 individuals have been detained, then denied due process by the EPRDF government; some allegedly have spent up to 11 years in jail before being offered a trial, only to have the charges dropped due to lack of evidence.[19] A September 8, 2004, letter to the prime minister from Human Rights Watch refers to the re-arrest of four dissenting Oromos one week after their release from jail as ordered by the Federal High Court. It also refers to the mistreatment of one of the detainees.[20]

Abuses are less widespread than under the Derg's rule due to processes and procedures that, while weak, offer some minimal degree of protection from abuse. This is more pronounced in Addis Ababa than elsewhere. Abuse by non-state actors is rare.

Since coming to power, the EPRDF has emphasized the rights of women, people with disabilities, people who are vulnerable, and ethnic minorities. For the most part, that stance is sincere, and there have been modest gains, especially in regard to women. Women are theoretically protected under the laws of the country, but in reality they have insufficient guarantees of such protection. Violent behavior directed at them by male family members is common. Women face social prejudice against their participation in public life, although a few women do hold seats in Parliament and in the Cabinet of Ministers. One encouraging sign is the increasing cooperation between the Addis Ababa city government and the Ethiopian Women Lawyers' Association (EWLA) in providing legal counseling services to abused women in the capital area.[21]

In general, laws to protect women and children are more forcefully adhered to than in past years. The government is taking steps to prevent trafficking in women and children, and the rape of children is far more likely to lead to an arrest than previously. Policewomen are assigned to each police district in Addis Ababa. However, beyond the major cities, customary laws addressing such issues as inheritance for women remain in place. Worse, the custom of marriage by abduction continues without significant interference by authorities.[22]

Ethiopia's primary ethnic groups are the Oromos, the Tigray, and the Amharas. The premise of the ethnic-based system of federation is to ensure that all groups in the country receive equal rights and recognition under the law in order to counter some of Ethiopia's historical inequities. In practice, these guarantees have fallen short due to ingrained social prejudices, the weak judicial system, and underperforming government social assistance agencies. The government's heavy-handed dismissal of the political agenda of large segments of the Oromo population is seen as ingrained bias by many. Tensions between the government, both federal and in Oromia, and the population are increasing. Given demographics—the Oromo constitute over 40 percent of the population—such alienation clearly is not sustainable. The government itself seems less interested in the rights of people in the Somali regions of the country, and there is a deep-seated if unspoken animosity between the people of Tigray and the Oromos. There has been considerable violence and bloodshed between different ethnic groups in the Gambella region of the country in the past few years.

People with disabilities largely fend for themselves in Ethiopia, although those in urban centers receive some assistance from various NGOs with the blessing of the government. Facilities that accommodate the access requirements of people with disabilities are extremely rare—which is not surprising given the acute poverty of the country—and none are required by law. Virtually no effort is made to provide government information to individuals with disabilities. In general, the free practice of religious beliefs is not a major issue in Ethiopia. It is estimated that 45 percent to 50 percent of the population is Muslim and 35 percent to 40 percent is Ethiopian Orthodox, with the remaining population divided among other religions. The rights of Muslims, Orthodox, Catholics, Protestants, and those of other faiths are respected, as are the rights of those without faith. The government does strive to ensure that the leader of the Ethiopian Orthodox Church is not likely to become an opponent of government policies.

Article 31 of the Ethiopian constitution protects fundamental human rights and freedoms and specifically guarantees freedom of association. However, those guarantees are less ironclad in practice. The state exerts subtle pressure for citizens to support various associations, such as the official development associations attached to the various political parties that form the EPRDF. These groups sponsor official fund-raising drives each year to which civil servants and others are expected to contribute; the state-controlled media engage in efforts to boost these fund-raising efforts.

A few civic and private-sector organizations are emerging that demonstrate strength and capacity not witnessed in prior years. The Addis Ababa Chamber of Commerce and the EWLA are perhaps the best examples. These groups have been allowed to organize, mobilize members, and advocate for certain policies and programs. But advocacy is a suspicious activity in Ethiopia and is therefore difficult. In spring 2004, three staff members of HUNDEE, a community development NGO that operates in Oromia, were held in jail nine weeks for allegedly inciting unrest and hatred and for exceeding the stated objectives of the NGO.[23] A number of individuals in Addis Ababa active in promoting human rights or policy alternatives have been in jail at least once since the EPRDF assumed power.[24]

Labor unions were among the many societal associations co-opted by the Derg regime. Only a small fraction of the workforce is affiliated with any union, as not many individuals are involved in formal-sector wage employment. Unions remain weak but do play a small role as the country struggles with economic development. Their leaders are sometimes intimidated.

The police and other governmental agencies frequently use excessive force in response to demonstrations and protests. Reports from human rights groups bulge with details of individuals being killed or wounded while protesting various issues. For example, in 2002 as many as 200 demonstrators were shot dead in the town of Teppi, in the southwest of the country, while protesting administrative boundary changes; more than 300 others were detained.[25] Protests at Addis Ababa University from December 2003 through May 2004 resulted in the deaths of several students. Human Rights Watch reported that state officials acknowledged the deaths of five high school students and the wounding of a dozen more during protests against educational and economic policies in March and April 2003 in Oromia. The state parliament "justified the police tactics by asserting that the police had no funds to purchase non-lethal crowd control equipment."[26] In August 2004, scores of people were arrested in the town of Agaro, in Oromia, for alleged links to the OLF.[27] When American and British diplomats traveled to Oromia in the spring of 2004 to investigate charges of political suppression and violence against citizens by the police, the people interviewed by the diplomats were called in for police interrogation—a clear act of intimidation.[28]

*Recommendations*

- Training of police across the country must be upgraded with an emphasis on protection of the constitutional rights of all citizens.
- The long-delayed creation of an independent human rights ombudsman position must be realized.
- Human rights groups must be accepted by the authorities as valid monitors of adherence to international standards of protection.
- Efforts must be redoubled to ensure the rights of Oromo, Somali, and other ethnic groups on the fringes of power and influence.
- Beyond enactment of an NGO law, the government should put into place measures to encourage the growth and empowerment of labor unions and professional associations. A clear signal from the government respecting the right of association established in the constitution is the necessary first step. Authorizing professional associations to act as certifiers of sector (i.e., health, education) standards is also essential.

## RULE OF LAW – 2.06

Rule of law is a concept with only tenuous hold in Ethiopia. While the country has made genuine strides over the past 14 years, it lags considerably behind comparable African nations. The African Development Forum survey finds the country falling short in the respect for the rule of law and adherence to human rights principles—its score is approximately half of the average for the 16 countries studied.[29] Due process is virtually nonexistent. The court system is used to harass political opponents of the EPRDF and to protect its officials from public scrutiny.

The greatest weakness of the system is its inadequate capacity. Poorly trained judges and court administrators, the large number of vacancies, inadequate physical facilities and information management systems, and the threat of impeachment to officials asserting independence from the executive branch preclude impartiality. There is a critical shortage of skilled prosecutors who understand the nature of their job and the fair application of the law. Especially in rural areas, these low-paying positions cannot attract enough qualified individuals. A 1999 Ethiopian governance assessment found an insufficient number of judges, who had been given only limited training covering only basic legal concepts. It added that many of those appointed through this process were ultimately dismissed for petty corruption.[30]

Inadequacies in the court system serve to facilitate interference by executive-branch officials in the application of laws. Judges are subject to pressure from local administrators to reflect political views in rendering judgments, particularly at the lower levels of the judiciary. Outright politicization of criminal cases is more common at the local level than the federal. Judges bent on independence are subject to arbitrary dismissal or even the leveling of charges against them. Criminal cases are brought before courts that are predominantly political in nature.[31]

The inadequacies seen in the court system are mirrored in the governance of the *woredas* (the local units of government), in which the administrators frequently have little or no training for the tasks they are asked to perform. The problems associated with these administrators' lack of skill will become more pronounced as governmental decentralization places ever more responsibility for the implementation of the national development agenda in the woredas.

A long-term enhancement effort has been supported by the government and funded by various donors. The establishment of the Ethiopian Civil Service College is one manifestation of the attempt to improve the capacity of the judicial system. This entity has basically quadrupled the national output of trained individuals seeking careers in the system.[32] However, the starting point is so low in the Ethiopian judiciary and the gaps so wide that significant progress is years away.

Thousands of individuals accused of crimes suffer long periods of incarceration prior to trial without bail and in many cases without indictment for specific crimes. Those accused of crimes can linger in jails years on end without going to trial. Caseloads are overwhelming relative to the number and the skill of court personnel, procedures are outmoded, there is little delegation of authority, and information management systems are poor. Meanwhile, conditions in the country's jails are deplorable, with inadequate food and medical attention. Families of those jailed are expected to cover their needs.

Adherence to judicial decisions is uneven. The issuance of a court order or a verdict in a case is no guarantee of compliance. Arbitrary administrative decisions can effectively negate rulings from the bench. Court personnel have insufficient training and understanding of the rights of the accused. Presumption of innocence is a concept that has not taken root in Ethiopia. Those accused do have the right to engage independent counsel, and there is a public defenders service, but its small size and lack of facilities severely limit its impact. The treatment of individuals before the courts and tribunals varies widely.[33]

Public officials and ruling party actors are frequently prosecuted for alleged wrongdoing in Ethiopia. Former prime minister Tamirat Layne is in jail, as is Seye Abrah, a former defense minister. However, in truth what brings an official before a judge is almost always a political misstep rather than an abuse of power or some other wrongdoing. Tamirat Layne is in jail on corruption charges that may very well be accurate; there is some evidence linking him to bank accounts in Switzerland. But in general, officials are charged with corruption or other crimes only when they have crossed the EPRDF leadership.

The police, military, and internal security forces of Ethiopia are tightly controlled by the government and largely do not operate outside the mandates given them under the law. The police and internal security forces are used by the ruling party to stifle dissent and to harass opponents. A number of peaceful demonstrators have been killed in recent years by various police forces. The police as well as prosecutors are clearly involved in the arrest of dissidents and other critics on trumped-up corruption charges. The police force is also subject to petty corruption. The military is more professional and disciplined in nature, with a focus over the past six years on tensions along the border with Eritrea.

With the major exception of land, citizens of Ethiopia are allowed to own property both individually and in association with others. Land is commonly owned by the people at large; individuals may obtain long-term leases for the use and occupancy of particular tracts of property. The land-ownership question is highly controversial, with critics of the current policy asserting that it all but excludes modernization of the agricultural sector and with government officials insisting it is necessary to prevent speculators from taking advantage of peasants.

Like many questions in Ethiopia, the issue of arbitrary deprivation of property is highly complex. So much private property was confiscated by the Derg that rightful ownership is often hard to prove. The lack of transparency and government officials' addiction to secrecy leads many citizens to assume that revoking of titles of businesses or other property is political in nature. This is true in some cases, but not all. Individuals affiliated with what the government sees as the political opposition are more vulnerable to problems with property titles than others. Most citizens of the country are able to assume and retain title to properties of whatever nature if they can muster the resources for purchases or leases and the wherewithal to deal with government bureaucracies to obtain permits and licenses. The malfunctioning judicial system precludes fair and reliable enforcement of contracts, which impedes growth in the business sector and national development.

The Ethiopian constitution gives official standing to pre-existing customary and religious courts and authorizes their recognition by government agencies. The various customary courts, valid only in civil cases, handle multitudes of minor property disputes across rural areas.

*Recommendations*
- Orientation in the basic tenets of rule of law will have to be ingrained in the woreda administrators, who are destined to play an ever larger role in the country's administration given the emphasis on decentralization.
- The judicial system enhancement program already in place must be strengthened.
- Opportunities for educating and training judicial system personnel—judges, prosecutors, administrators—must be expanded considerably through greater donor investment.
- The public defenders program should be expanded substantially.
- Unduly long periods of pretrial detention must be eliminated.

## ANTICORRUPTION AND TRANSPARENCY – 2.76

Small-scale corruption is found throughout virtually the entire bureaucratic framework that defines the average citizen's interaction with government: Bribes are paid in court cases, in the obtaining of permits and licenses, for the installation of telephones, and in having traffic tickets voided. Structures to ensure transparency in official transactions are almost entirely missing, and there is a strong tradition of secrecy in the conduct of governmental affairs. Thus the possibilities of significant growth in corrupt practices loom. Yet, the belief is common that official corruption in Ethiopia is low in comparison to many other developing countries. Certainly, the pervasive corrupt practices that characterized the Moi regime in neighboring Kenya are simply not found in Ethiopia.

Excessive bureaucratic regulation provides opportunity for the bribery of government officials in attempts to obtain routine permits, licenses, and import authorizations. The Heritage Foundation's 2004 Index of Economic Freedom states that "Ethiopia's cumbersome bureaucracy deters investment. Much of the economy remains under state control, and the evidence suggests that businesses also must contend with political favoritism."[34] Thus, the regulatory system is skewed both to provide benefits to enterprises promoted by the ruling party and ample opportunities for the demanding of bribes to secure official approval of routine requests. The Index of Economic Freedom ranks Ethiopia 101st in the world at present on a scale that has North Korea in last place at 167th. The categorization of such a score is "mostly unfree."

The government struggles with reforms and a privatization process that would cut back its excessive involvement in the economy, but it has considerable distance to go to overcome historical legacies and its own ideological inclinations. The government prohibits the ownership of agricultural land, the country's banking system is state owned, and the media are largely government owned. Parastatals control a number of markets. In 1999, according to International Monetary Fund statistics, the government received 17.49 percent of its total revenue from state-owned enterprises and property.[35]

Guarantees in place to ensure transparency and effective, open bidding on government contracts are weak at best. However, vast corruption is not involved in such processes, as massive corruption is not ingrained in the culture of the country or in the conduct of official business.

There is some semblance of separation of public office from the personal interests of officeholders in Ethiopia. The blatant gorging at the trough found in many other countries is not in play, and a number of officeholders have been removed for presumably valid accusations of corruption. But a party spoils system allows officials to serve on various boards, on commissions, and in parastatals that effectively subsidize salaries.

No adequate financial disclosure procedures are in place to prevent conflicts of interest on the part of officeholders. The public is not privy to such information, and most journalists would never endanger their careers (or freedom) by pursuing such questions unless the individuals in question had clearly lost political favor in the ruling circles. Although some protection against conflicts of interest in the private sector is offered, it is inadequate and haphazardly enforced. An entrepreneur who has run afoul of the EPRDF is more likely to be investigated for any alleged conflicts than one who has not.

While imperfect in implementation, the processes in place to prevent the corruption of public offices are enforced. The case of former prime minister Tamirat Layne is one example (see "Rule of Law"). Victims of corruption have the right to seek redress in the court system. The underperforming status of the judicial system, however, lowers the prospects for fair adjudication.

Salaries of educators are notoriously low, and working conditions are bleak. In a number of rural areas, community associations and/or individual families attempt to subsidize teachers' salaries, which can create distortions in the attention paid students. There are numerous reports deemed reliable but not immediately verifiable of instructors at the university level demanding sexual favors from female students for the granting of positive grades.[36]

Internal audit rules do not ensure fairness and accountability in the tax collection system. The auditing system is neither effective nor free from political influence. Allegations of corruption are investigated somewhat haphazardly. Few citizens feel secure about reporting cases of bribery or extortion on the part of government officials.

The press in Ethiopia is low on standards and high on sensationalism. Thus, allegations of corruption—assuming they are not leveled at those clearly in favor of the ruling circles—are given extensive airing in the media. Insistence upon ascertaining the truth of the charges is limited. For example, a number of years ago, when tensions between the government and the NGO sector were especially strained, the press felt little hesitation in printing wild accusations of corruption among NGO leaders that were for the most part entirely imagined.[37]

Officials have only the most limited commitment to government transparency. Ethiopia has no freedom of information law or process, and official information is tightly held. Like officials around the world, Ethiopian officeholders prefer the laxity afforded by secrecy to the accountability and competence forced through transparency, and there is limited pressure on them to alter that mindset. The right and the means to obtain official information largely do not exist in the country.

The budgeting process in Ethiopia is dominated by the executive branch with only cursory engagement on the part of legislators. Nor is the actual expenditure of funds subject to meaningful legislative scrutiny. The government publishes vast volumes of statistics on public expenditures, but the timeliness of such publications is more problematic.[38]

The Ethiopian government, which is inordinately dependent on international assistance, does not interfere in donor programs and funding expenditures. The country has fought waves of famine and food insecurity over the past three decades and has received literally billions of dollars in food aid, relief supplies, and long-term development project funding from governments, international development organizations, and NGOs.[39] In the past, the government signaled a rather naive preference that donor countries should channel the funds generated by international NGOs into its own accounts. That effort has receded in the face of common resistance.

### Recommendations

- Freedom of information legislation must be enacted to open official processes to public scrutiny. Before a freedom of information law can be implemented, the government must acknowledge that access to information is a right enshrined in the Universal Declaration of Human Rights.
- The news media must enjoy genuine independence in order to shine light on corruption. Equally needed, however, is extensive training for journalists to end the sensationalism and lack of

verification of accusations or identification of sources commonly observed in the Ethiopian news media.

• Addressing day-to-day corruption citizens experience in the government bureaucracy should be facilitated by civil service and judicial reform. Currently dysfunctional anticorruption systems need to be made to work.

## NOTES

[1] Derg is an Amharic word with the literal meaning of *committee* and is the common reference to the military junta that ruled the country from 1974 until it was overthrown by EPRDF forces in May 1991. EPRDF is a coalition of political parties with origins in the armed struggle against Mengistu's dictatorship.

[2] Asserted separately in private interviews with the author by economists from the World Bank and the Ethiopian Economic Policy Research Institute; June 2004.

[3] A September 2004 letter from Human Rights Watch (HRW) to Meles Zenawi, the Ethiopian prime minister, raises questions on the violation of the right to bail in two cases involving political dissidents and journalists. The cases cited are typical of many other such incidents detailed in various human rights reports. Peter Takirambudde, "Letter to Ethiopian Prime Minister Meles Zenawi" (New York: HRW, 8 September 2004), http://hrw.org/english/docs/2004/09/07/ethiop9320.htm.

[4] Marina Ottaway, "Africa's 'New Leaders': African Solution or African Problem?" *Current History* 97 (May 1998): 210–11.

[5] In 2001, there was a purge of the "hardliners" within the TPLF (Tigrayan People's Liberation Front), the core of the EPRDF, that forced Meles Zenawi to expand his dealings with other ethnic and political groups, specifically Amharas—long dominant in the affairs of state of Ethiopia prior to 1991.

[6] "Perspectives on Governance with Recommendations and a Plan of Action: East Africa Sub-region" (Addis Ababa: African Development Forum, October 2004).

[7] Beyond the civil code, NGOs are governed by the constitution, tax laws, the Press and Broadcasting laws, and the DPPC (Disaster Prevention and Preparedness Commission) Proclamation of 1995.

[8] "Report on the Enabling Environment for the NGO Sector in Ethiopia" (Addis Ababa: Pact/Ethiopia, November 2004).

[9] Ibid.

[10] "Country Profile 2004: Ethiopia" (London: Economist Intelligence Unit), 25.

[11] Ibid.

[12] Interview with the author, June 2004.

[13] "Country Profile" (Economist Intelligence Unit).

[14] September 2004 letter from Human Rights Watch to the prime minister.

[15] Interviews by the author in June 2004.

[16] "Ethiopia: Fear of torture/Unlawful detention/'Disappearance'" (New York: Amnesty International [AI], 28 September 2004), http://web.amnesty.org/library/Index/ENGAFR250102004?open&of=ENG-ETH.

[17] "Report 2002" (AI).

[18] "World Report 2003: Africa: Ethiopia" (New York: HRW, 2003).

[19] Ibid.

[20] September 2004 letter from Human Rights Watch to the prime minister.

[21] "Report on the Enabling . . ." (Pact/Ethiopia, November 2004).

[22] "UNICEF Supports Fight to End Marriage by Abduction in Ethiopia" (Addis Ababa: UNICEF, 21 January 2004).

[23] "Report on the Enabling . . ." (Pact/Ethiopia, November 2004).

[24] Interviews with the author. The two were charged with inciting students at Addis Ababa University to violence; their cases are pending in the court system.

[25] Author interview, June 2004.

[26] "World Report 2003: Africa: Ethiopia" (New York: HRW, 2003).

[27] "Ethiopia" (AI, 28 September 2004).

[28] According to off-the-record comments by the diplomatic officers involved.

[29] "Perspectives on Governance . . ." (African Development Forum).

[30] "Ethiopian Governance Assessment" (London: UK Department for International Development [DFID], November 1999).

[31] Ibid.

[32] Ibid.

[33] Ibid.

[34] "Index of Economic Freedom 2004" (Washington, DC: Heritage Foundation).

[35] Ibid.

[36] This information provided to the author through an interview by a journalist long resident in Ethiopia.

[37] See the series of "Enabling Environment" reports published by Pact/Ethiopia between 1998 and 2004 for a discussion on press treatment of the NGO sector.

[38] "Ethiopian Governance Assessment" (DFID).

[39] "Ethiopia: Threat of Large Emergencies Still Looming" (Addis Ababa: UN Integrated Regional Information Networks [IRIN], 19 October 2004).

# HONDURAS

CAPITAL: Tegucigalpa
POPULATION: 7 million
GNI PER CAPITA: $930

**SCORES**
ACCOUNTABILITY AND PUBLIC VOICE: 3.81
CIVIL LIBERTIES: 3.88
RULE OF LAW: 3.35
ANTICORRUPTION AND TRANSPARENCY: 2.96
(scores are based on a scale of 0 to 7, with
0 representing weakest and 7 representing
strongest performance)

*Michael Gold-Biss*

## INTRODUCTION

Honduras has held six national elections since the armed forces left power in 1982. Each of these elections has been certified as fair and for the most part procedurally clean. It is thus possible to claim that Honduras has successfully consolidated civilian rule. The armed forces are not likely to intervene directly in politics by staging a coup, although they continue to be an important national actor. These are significant accomplishments, at both national and regional levels. Furthermore, considerable progress has been made since 1990, when the municipalities began to be allowed a significant level of self-governance; 1993 saw the direct election of mayors on separate individual ballots, and in 1997 the direct election of local government candidates on separate ballots began. Local governance, even if limited in terms of resources and expertise, has produced impressive improvements in some areas of community life.[1] Especially significant is the relative autonomy of the mayors, who do not always run on party platforms and whose accountability is

**Michael Gold-Biss** is professor of national security affairs at the Center for Hemispheric Defense Studies, National Defense University, in Washington, DC.

to their immediate constituents. However, Honduras is not yet a success story beyond the procedural level. Citizens do not enjoy the full range of rights, freedoms, and responsibilities.

Having been spared the worst of the civil war destruction of the 1980s, Honduras nonetheless suffered continuing physical devastation as one natural disaster hit after the other. Hurricane Mitch, whose aftereffects are still palpable, hit in 1998, followed by extensive damage and flooding from Hurricane Michelle and a subsequent and destructive drought in 2001. The 1999 Stockholm donors' conference following Hurricane Mitch forced an opening of dialogue between the government and nongovernmental organizations (NGOs), as well as the conditioning of assistance on more transparency, citizen participation, and improved government efficiency.[2] Unfortunately, much of public life, and especially government performance, is deeply affected and distorted by institutionalized dishonesty, corruption, fraud, and levels of impunity that are almost completely due to the lack of effective prosecutions and convictions, among other shortcomings of the judicial system.

An estimated 60 percent of the population lives in poverty, and 36 percent of children suffer from malnutrition.[3] Furthermore, overlapping waves of violence since the 1980s have overwhelmed Honduras. In the mid-1990s there was an almost anarchic explosion of *mara* (gang) violence. The violent are rarely, if ever, prosecuted and convicted, and the high profits of drug trafficking have become ever more alluring. Meanwhile, the legal economy is limping along, offering few good employment opportunities to youths with minimal educational skills. Thus, Hondurans feel besieged by violence and insecurity.

In response, the government of Ricardo Maduro Joest was elected in 2002 on a platform of zero tolerance for violent crime. His two-pronged response to the increase in violent behavior has been the passing of the *Ley Antimaras* (Antigang law), a revision of Article 332 of the penal code, and a community policing–style program called *Comunidad Mas Segura* (More Secure Community). While popular with most people for the absolute decline in the most extreme forms of gruesome violence coming from the maras, his policies have not been free from controversy. They appear to trample on civil and human rights and have unintended consequences. At times these can be horrifying, such as overcrowded prisons with inadequate prisoner safety, which twice have led to high numbers of lost lives in prison fires. President Maduro's persistently low popularity ratings, recently hovering at 37 percent, come not from his security measures or his zero-tolerance policies but from the measures he has undertaken to meet international lending agencies' demands. His backing for the U.S.–Central America Free Trade Area has also made him unpopular.[4]

Honduras's plight of being caught between the very real violence of maras, drug-traffickers, and vigilantes underscores the weakness of the governance abilities of the state, especially in the area of the rule of law. Honduras has been plagued by extrajudicial violence against those perceived to be social undesirables such as street children, prostitutes, and openly homosexual persons; much of this activity appears to be carried out by off-duty police, although civilians are also involved. As in many countries, political will is lacking to promote substantive changes that will inevitably undermine the traditional hold on power of political and economic elites. This is principally true between the two main parties, the National Party of Honduras (PN) and the Liberal Party (PL), but also in the three smaller parties, which exist primarily due to the political establishment's commitment to the status quo. In effect, the slow nature of political and social change in Honduras can be attributed to the recognition by these parties' leaders and militants that change is necessary but should be accomplished at an incremental and manageable pace. The country is slowly, but surely, creeping along the road from being a failing state with damaged governance to becoming a failed state with the fig leaf of periodic elections that fail to conceal the breakdown and atomization of public life.

## ACCOUNTABILITY AND PUBLIC VOICE – 3.81

The Honduran political system is open, with regularly scheduled free and fair elections among accepted political actors, although the Latinobarometro poll has found a sharp decline in support for democracy in Honduras since 2003.[5] The two major parties, the PN and the PL, have traditionally alternated in power in the unicameral National Congress. These parties tend to represent the interests of a single economic elite and are therefore very similar ideologically.[6] Three minor parties also have a regular presence in Congress. While no formal obstacles exist to the formation of other parties or to independent candidates' running for office, this is not common, and few succeed in being elected.

The law of elections and political organizations passed in 1981 has been amended at least 10 times. Although it is supposed to regulate all aspects of the elections, it is not uniformly enforced. For example, there are limits on how parties can finance campaigns, but the national tribunal of elections, which regulates elections, does not demand that financial reports be submitted. In May 2004 Congress approved new reforms of the electoral laws intended to increase transparency in the existing law. They include limiting the length of primary electoral campaigns to 90 days and general election campaigns to 120 days. Financing of campaigns is subject to more stringent disclosure requirements, especially donations of over 300,000 lempiras (US$16,500). The 2005 national tribunal of elections will have representation from the two major and three minor parties. Advertising restrictions have already been rendered moot as pre-presidential candidates carry out unofficial campaigns through the media, which in some cases they own.

The typical congressional deputy is a party stalwart who can deliver votes, money, or both to his party. In the Honduran electoral system, citizens vote for party ballots and not individuals; as a result, in many instances deputies do not know their constituents and feel no loyalty or responsibility to them. As in many Latin American countries, Honduras has a strong presidential system. The significant powers of the incumbent, who cannot be reelected, prevent a realistic balance of power among the branches of government. Many civil service appointments, made based on party loyalty and not expertise, are subject to significant turnover when the party in office changes. Ultimately, the economic elites have been able to use the two main parties to exert control over both the electoral process and governmental institutions. They use the law for their own benefit at the expense of the most vulnerable members of the population.[7] Those actors, be they rural laborers or the urban middle classes, with substantive agendas for change that diverge from the security program and economic plan of the president make little progress. This is likely to be the case under the rule of any of the leading current political parties.

Civic groups, NGOs, and interest groups of all kinds have become vibrant parts of Honduran civil society. After the Stockholm 1999 conference of donors, the government learned to sit down with these groups to discuss problems and their solutions. However, for the most part, this has not led the government to take action based on a public consensus and with the participation of these organizations in the implementation of policies. The best that can be said is that political leaders will allow donor cooperation with reformers in civil society. Farmer cooperatives and unions, in particular, have become more vocal and have been relatively successful in having their grievances aired and even some of their complaints addressed.

Honduras has four major newspapers, two radio stations with national reach, three television channels with national reach, and four television stations with local reach. Of these outlets, among other influential individuals, Jaime Rosenthal, three-time PL candidate for the presidency, owns a newspaper and a TV channel, and Carlos Roberto Flores, an ex-president of the PL, owns a newspaper. The government has direct influence over the media through the placement of public announcements and advertisements, and it is common to hear of journalists being paid for stories. It is not surprising that some observers have concluded that media owners use their news outlets to further their own business and political purposes.[8] The government does not interfere with satellite or cable television or radio, nor does it limit access to the Internet.

Honduran media have traditionally been intimidated by threats of prosecution with heavy prison terms and have thus practiced self-censorship, but they have for the most part been spared physical threats. It was therefore a shock when German Antonio Rivas, head of the Corporacion Mayavision-Canal 7 TV station, was shot dead upon arriving at work in November 2003. The station had recently aired stories of coffee and cattle smuggling, as well as cyanide pollution in the Lara River.[9] To date there has been no resolution of this crime, the first murder of a journalist in Honduras in 20 years. Several other journalists have been physically attacked. For example, Eduardo Irais of TV station Canal 66 was attacked in front of parliament on October 8, 2003, while covering a student protest, and Carlos Mauricio Flores of the *El Heraldo* daily was attacked on October 21, 2003, by a Colombian implicated in arms smuggling.[10] Article 345 of the criminal procedures code (CPC) imposes a two- to four-year prison sentence on those guilty of "threats, calumny, insults, or other offenses against the dignity of public authorities exercising their public duties."[11] Television presenter Renato Alvarez was given a two-year, eight-month prison sentence, suspended for five years, and deprived of his right to vote, management of his property, and other rights after being found guilty of slander in the questioning of a government minister about drug smuggling on his program, "Frente a Frente" (Face to Face), in June 2003.[12]

While there is some control over sexual imagery in movies and publications, primarily under the influence of the Roman Catholic Church, most cultural expressions are uncensored and free from government oversight. However, as Honduras is a poor society in which most forms of cultural expression are luxuries, challenges to the establishment in the form of politicized art beyond that found at universities and art institutes are rare.

### Recommendations

- Provisions of the Electoral Law and Law of Political Organizations should be strictly and publicly enforced, especially regarding the regulation of the campaign process and funding.
- A ballot system should be adopted that allows for the election of representatives accountable to constituents, not party militants selected for their ability to deliver votes or money.
- The civil service should be fully professionalized, with appointment and promotion separated from the political process.
- Laws restricting journalistic independence with threats of prosecution for slander and related offenses must be revised to guarantee freedom of speech and expression. A first step would be the elimination of libel provisions in the criminal procedures code.

## CIVIL LIBERTIES – 3.88

During the many years of military government in Honduras there were disappearances, murder, torture, and the whole host of human rights abuses associated with military governments at the time. Many of these continue to be unresolved, although President Maduro, in an act of public contrition unprecedented in the region, made a public apology for the political violence of the 1980s that resulted in the deaths of hundreds of left-wing activists at the hands of military death squads.[13] It has been difficult to prosecute and convict suspected human rights abusers partly due to the corrupt and at times incompetent nature of the criminal justice system but also due to the suppression of evidence and heavy-handed intervention of local elites. In March 2004 Lt. Marco Tulio Regalado, the first military officer convicted for a human rights violation—the killing of Honduran Communist Party activist Herminio Deras in 1983—was acquitted by a court because the evidence against him was not "irrefutable."[14]

The extent and intensity of past abuses are rapidly being overshadowed by two new and overlapping crises. The first is the execution of street children and young adults in a publicly semi-sanctioned "cleansing" of undesirables, along with the persecution of *mareros* (gang members), through both murder and "cleansing." The second is the draconian and indiscriminate application of the 2003 Ley Antimaras or *Mano Dura* (Heavy and Hard Hand) policy. The numbers of victims, the impunity of those committing the human rights abuses—which range from torture to disappearance and death—and the popular support for these policies contribute to an environment in which the rule of law is subordinate to the firepower and repressive abilities of the state.

The legal maneuver that allows for the criminalization of mara membership is the rewriting of Article 332 of the penal code in August 2003. The Honduran Congress amended Article 332 to make association in a street gang illegal. Congress modeled the reform on European laws used to combat violent Nazi gangs. In Honduras, gang members can receive 6 to 9 years in jail and leaders can receive 9 to 12. Specifically, membership in a gang is criminal, whether or not a crime has been committed. Most of the gang members are residents of the United States convicted of crimes there and deported to their country of origin after serving their U.S. prison sentences. After the first wave of 7,000 criminal deportees had been released into the streets—bringing with them guns, drugs, and gangs—murders increased in Honduras from 1,615 in 1995 to 9,214 in 1998. In most cases the deportees had left Honduras years before, had grown up in the United States, had joined gangs on the streets or in prison, and had at most extended family to turn to once back in the country. They reverted to the skills they had learned in the streets or prisons of the United States—drug dealing, theft, and even murder—to survive in what were otherwise to them entirely foreign surroundings.[15]

In practice, the evidence used to convict the gang members of their "illicit association," is based mostly on the physical evidence found on them: tattoos. Significantly, local experts of the Honduran National Police claim that the larger the tattoo, the more important the gang member is.[16] This may be accompanied by photographs of the suspect making some of the hand signals used by gangs to identify and communicate and possibly a homemade weapon or assault gun (in 2003 President Maduro signed a decree making "weapons of war" such as assault weapons of the AK-47 type illegal).[17] Honduras has the largest number of mareros in Central America, at 36,000.[18] Despite claiming that this is not an intended consequence of his anti-gang policies, President Maduro recognizes that up to 2,000 mareros have left the country since the crackdown began.[19]

Most Hondurans are breathing a sigh of relief as gang-related violence appears to abate.[20] Other programs introduced by President Maduro, such as Comunidad Mas Segura, have produced lower petty crime rates and increased a sense of security among the public. However, principled individuals and groups in society are concerned with the human and civil rights price Honduras is paying in semi-arbitrary arrests and almost indefinite incarceration. The respected NGO Casa Alianza (Alliance House) has declared that the "measures are not tackling the source of the problem: poverty and lack of opportunities."[21] Amnesty International, the U.S. Department of State, and Honduras's National Commission for Human Rights have reported cases of kidnapping, torture, and killing of gang members, carried out by secret security forces and private groups similar to those responsible for the hundreds of disappearances of suspected leftists during the civil war.[22] Government statistics indicate that between January 1998 and January 2004 there were at least 2,170 unsolved deaths of people under the age of 23.[23] Berta Oliva, director of the Committee of the Relatives of the Disappeared, has said, "It seems to me that this country is losing, in great measure, the democratic advances that have cost us so much. . . . In the 80's, this country said it was O.K. to kill off political enemies because they were antisocial. We say the same today about gang members."[24] Ramon Custodio, the National Commissioner for Human Rights, and Ms. Oliva have opposed the Ley Anti-Maras as unconstitutional, prompting the government to declare it will defend the law to protect the citizenry.[25] Human rights advocates are themselves at risk; Amnesty International noted that "in Honduras several environmentalists and one human rights lawyer were killed between 2001 and 2003."[26]

Respected NGOs, such as the Committee of Families of the Detained and Disappeared in Honduras (COFADEH), have maintained extensive records of indictments and cases without convictions and other instances in which the legal system has failed effectively to prosecute and convict human rights violators, even when evidence of involvement or fault is available. In 2003 Director of the Internal Affairs Unit of the Ministry of Security Maria Luisa Borja indicated that police agents had been involved in 20 or more summary executions and then ordered the weapons used to be destroyed. Subsequently, Borjas was demoted and transferred.[27]

Throughout the system, Honduras's prisons are overcrowded and antiquated. In April 2003, 68 inmates died in a fire at the El Porvenir prison in La Ceiba. A second prison fire took place on May 17, 2004, at the San Pedro Sula Prison. Most of the dead in both incidents were mareros. The report commissioned by President Maduro after the 2003 fire concluded that "51 of those who died were in fact shot, beaten, or burned to death by a force of the prison guards working with state police, soldiers, and other prisoners." No one has been brought to justice in that case.[28] The National Commissioner of Human Rights indicated that the crime scene of the first fire was altered and contaminated, giving reason to believe that the security forces could be covering up an execution of gang members.[29]

In 1999, prisons held more than 10,000 inmates, 90 percent of whom had been waiting for their trials for an average of 22 months; a number had waited more than five years, and some had served the maximum sentences before appearing for trial for the crime of which they were accused.[30] In 2004, the country had 26 prisons built to hold 5,500 inmates but in fact held over 13,000 prisoners, according to government statistics.[31] A new criminal procedures code (CPC), passed in 1991, entered into effect in 2002, incorporating "guarantees of individual rights, freedom from arbitrary or lengthy detentions, oral and public hearings, transparency, and other fundamental elements of due process."[32] The practical effects of the revised system may be felt in Tegucigalpa and San Pedro Sula, the largest cities, but for most of the rest of the country the old processes and procedures are still in place. In some parts of the country there is no effective police presence, much less that of the judicial system. The chief justice of the Supreme Court has emphasized the fragile nature of the judicial reforms by characterizing the new system as "a crawling baby that still needs to be fed and helped to reach maturity and walk on its own."[33] Citizens do not trust the justice system to protect them and are often wary of police, leading many to take the law into their own hands. As a result, much of rural Honduras is effectively lawless. Perhaps thinking that President Maduro's policies are not draconian enough, or to position himself better for the November 2005 presidential elections, in 2004 congressional president Porfirio Lobo Sosa proposed the reintroduction of the death penalty for murderers, kidnappers, and rapists. Few proposals have received such unanimously unfavorable reception by most political, religious, and civic leaders in the country. The death penalty is opposed largely on religious and moral grounds but is also seen to be an inappropriate solution to the root causes of violence, including poverty and social injustice.[34] Honduras has ratified the American Human Rights convention, which declares that states that have abolished the death penalty may not reintroduce it.

For both women and indigenous minorities, life can be difficult, if not outright dangerous. Women and children have been targets of violence aimed against marginalized populations perceived to be disposable or of extreme forms of domestic violence in such numbers as to attract international attention. Civilian vigilante groups or off-duty security personnel torture and murder as a form "social cleansing" of social outcasts, including street children and prostitutes, perceived to be parasites; the body of one of these victims was found in San Pedro Sula with the words *"limpiando la ciudad"* ("cleaning the city") written on his shoulder with a pen.[35] Only 8 women are among the 128 *diputados* (deputies) and their 128 designated substitutes in Congress. Indigenous and black leaders have been targeted for execution, with at least 70 having been murdered since 1970; not a single case has led to a conviction.[36] Furthermore, Amnesty International has asserted "indigenous people are subjected to human rights violations, including torture."[37] Neither women nor other marginalized groups have effective means to enforce individual rights or seek redress for rights violations. Hondurans in general are not tolerant of sexual diversity and have made targets of lesbian, gay, bisexual, and transgender people with the same virulence as they have against other groups subject to "social cleansing."[38]

People with disabilities are one of the most disadvantaged groups in Honduras. Their needs are addressed by charity rather than through a human rights approach. Their rights are not well protected in Honduran law, and no central agency addresses human rights violations against them.[39]

The Roman Catholic Church plays a significant role in Honduran political life. While not partisan, it frequently makes public announcements that emphasize the importance of good governance and the role of ethics in public life. Other faiths are free to practice and face little if any overt discrimination, and certainly none from the state. Nevertheless, only the Roman Catholic Church has the requisite public legitimacy and proximity to the state to render public pronouncements on policy matters. For example, the church hierarchy has frequently questioned the large number of prisoners held in the overcrowded prisons. Auxiliary Bishop Romulo Emiliani of the San Pedro Sula diocese, who is active in the effort to rehabilitate gang members, called for an investigation into why the prisoners who had died in the 2004 fire had not been released so that they could flee the fire. The hierarchy has also been vocal in its criticism that President Maduro's economic policies do not address the problems of the country's poor.

Honduras has a lively and vibrant union environment that frequently takes to the streets in paralyzing strikes to call for better benefits or try to roll back government price hikes. Recent examples of their activism include a transportation strike that President Maduro was able to avert by negotiations, in part by sending the presidential airplane for the strike leaders in San Pedro Sula, and a teacher's strike that he was unable to prevent, which blocked roads across the country.[40] While the government responds vigorously to strikes and protests and at times uses excessive force, there is some restraint on the force employed by security personnel.

*Recommendations*

- The government should revisit and revise the 2003 Anti-Gang Law. Safeguards to ensure due process and protection of the rights of individuals accused, prosecuted, and convicted under this law must be adopted and enforced.
- The Comunidad Mas Segura programs of community policing should be enhanced and expanded to help prevent criminal activity.

- The government must stop the practice of social cleansing, which has continued to plague children and those considered undesirable such as gang members and prostitutes, through a more active police presence and the effective prosecution of those engaged in these practices. As a first step, the government must denounce publicly these acts and carry out an educational campaign to instruct Hondurans on their constitutional rights.
- The prison system should be modernized and expanded to provide a minimum of protections for inmates and ease the overcrowding. Those who have already served maximum possible sentences for crimes they are accused of, but have not been tried for, should be released. Implementation of the new criminal procedures code should be expedited throughout the country.

## RULE OF LAW – 3.35

Traditionally, the weakest part of the Honduran state has been the judicial system. The judiciary was subordinate to, and dependent upon, both the executive and legislative branches of government. In 2001 the Congress ratified 200 constitutional amendments designed to restructure the judicial branch, such as increasing the size of the Supreme Court. Opposition was strong within Congress to some elements of these reforms, including the establishment of a constitutional court to interpret and rule on the constitutionality of legislation. No action has been taken to establish a constitutional court and currently the Supreme Court makes decisions in this area. Nevertheless, the whole process received broad popular support. Among important changes was the separation of the appointment of Supreme Court justices from the four-year electoral cycle, extending the term of each justice to seven years. Congress now selects the 15 justices from a list of 45 names prepared by a judicial selection commission that includes members of civil society. The first time around, in 2002, a politicized selection process, characterized by extreme partisanship, tainted the result, with a court almost evenly split between the two major parties.[41] Nevertheless, the process itself has been opened to public scrutiny and is much more transparent, incorporating important elements of fairness.

Much remains to be done to professionalize the rule of law and administration of justice. In particular, the appointment of judges in general has traditionally been highly politicized and characterized by extreme forms of patronage, including a significant turnover of judges with every change in government. The judiciary to some degree depends on the goodwill of Congress for its funding.

However, progress in modernizing the criminal system has also taken place. The new CPC (see "Civil Liberties") has replaced the former inquisitorial system with a more open adversarial system, including provisions such as plea-bargaining, restitution, and community service. The multiple advantages of such a flexible system include the ability to prioritize and process cases in an expedited yet fair manner, allowing for discretion over the prosecution of an infraction depending on its severity and nature. The new CPC provides for criminal investigation and prosecution as a responsibility of the public ministry. The defense of those who cannot afford their own—the majority of criminal defendants—is the responsibility of a small and under-funded public defender's office that operates under the auspices of the Supreme Court.[42] An important caveat is that for these changes to bear fruit and work effectively over the long term, significant resources and time must be invested in them. Until then—and there is no precise time-line for such changes to mature—people of wealth or influence will continue routinely to undermine the judicial system by expecting and receiving special treatment. Meanwhile, the civil procedures code remains antiquated and unwieldy, impeding the timely resolution of civil litigation, including commercial disputes.[43]

Since the armed forces formally left government in 1982, their power has gradually diminished. They are now effectively subordinated to civilian rule under the president as commander in chief and a civilian minister of defense.[44] The most significant moves to limit the power of the military were taken by President Carlos Roberto Reina (1994–1998), who ended conscription and made military service voluntary, thus greatly reducing the public role of the armed forces as a unifying factor with a national presence. Reina also drastically reduced the size of the military and established a civilian police force and the public ministry, analogous to the office of the attorney-general of the United States. The ministry of defense, today headed by a civilian, is responsible for the armed forces, while the ministry of security is responsible for the police forces. The armed forces have been sidelined from active participation in the country's political life and pursue institutional activities concerned with national security, the environment, combating drug trafficking, and fighting the illegal arms trade. Although some of the latter functions are traditionally the responsibility of domestic law enforcement agencies, the institutional and professional deficiencies of the security services, as well as the nature of the tasks involved, have led to the armed forces playing a leading role in these areas, a phenomenon common to the region as a whole.

While in theory all property rights are guaranteed by the constitution, the reality is that the economically advantaged have firmer property rights than do the poor. Title is allegedly held to lands in excess of 100 percent of the total national territory, the result of a lack of cadastres and enforceable property rights. Indeed, personal property rights are tenuous due to elite manipulation of the law, including contracts.[45] The vulnerability and corruption of the judicial system, along with the traditional weakness of the national state, has made it difficult to introduce modern economic practices, including the ability of municipalities to assess and levy property taxes accurately.[46] As the legal system cannot be relied upon to rule fairly and justly in a dispute, local and international investments are subject to high levels of uncertainty and also higher risk premiums.

The Honduran constitution provides for the protection of the lands of indigenous people. However, the situation remains poor. Although some land has been adjudicated to indigenous communities, no special land regime has been designed to address traditional landholding practices and give indigenous groups autonomy to manage their land. Serious contradictions between agrarian reform laws and regulations such as those governing forests and environmental issues have delayed progress toward a genuine policy recognizing indigenous territorial rights.[47] Furthermore, environmental activism related to land claimed by these communities has led to persecution and even death among indigenous protesters. While some individuals have been prosecuted in these cases, the economic interests behind such abuses, such as landowners' and loggers', have not been pursued.[48]

## Recommendations

- The 2001 constitutional changes enhancing the power of the Supreme Court must be fully implemented and the process of separating the selection of justices from the political process must continue. Standards of professional performance qualifying candidates for service on the court should be established, and the public, especially NGOs, should provide testimony in favor of or against the nominees.

- A constitutional court should be established to provide for the impartial and legal adjudication of constitutional issues, including changes to the constitution or controversial laws (e.g., the Anti-Gang Law).

- Property rights must be fully guaranteed, partly through the full implementation of existing laws but also through modernization of the legal system to ensure impartiality and minimize manipulation by economic and political elites.

- The antiquated civil procedures code, which is based on involved and time-consuming written procedures requiring considerable resources, should be replaced with a modern civil procedures code based on oral proceedings.

## ANTICORRUPTION AND TRANSPARENCY – 2.96

Honduras has traditionally fared poorly when it comes to the international evaluation of efforts to reduce corruption and increase transparency. The 2004 Transparency International Corruption Perceptions Index places Honduras 114 out of 145 countries, with a score of 2.3 out of 10.[49] Transparency International points out that "there is a direct relationship between high levels of corruption and low levels of economic productivity. The lack of transparency that tends to go hand in hand with government corruption leads to a level of uncertainty that effectively discourages foreign investors."[50] Honduras has yet to make substantive progress in the area of honest public policy and less opaque government dealings. Deficiencies in the rule of law seriously affect the ability to conduct business in Honduras. Funds for social programs and public works are regularly diverted. Tax evasion is routine and endemic, leading tax revenues to fall below levels required to provide essential services while maintaining macroeconomic stability.[51]

President Maduro has frequently deplored the ranking of Honduras among the world's most corrupt nations. Yet, his government's policies, effective in dealing with multilateral financial organizations such as the IMF, have not increased the confidence of the global community in better governance under his leadership. The government's only efficiency and transparency effort has been the Program of Efficiency and Transparency in the Purchases and Contracts of the State (UPET), announced in March 2004. Financed by the Inter-American Development Bank and cooperating donors, the program will be worth $23.4 million over four years.[52] The advantage of this system is the simultaneous audits of ongoing transactions. The government proposed training 350 government employees and others in the process. However, the office of the presidency did not follow up on the plan. Moreover, while such programs undoubtedly build important capacity among officials and others, they cannot address the ongoing theft of state and public resources that takes place outside this limited level of scrutiny.

In February 2004 the vice president of Transparency International, Ines Ospina, visited Honduras at the invitation of President Maduro. Her assessment of the progress being made in the country was mixed. She praised the government for undertaking actions such as delegating to the UN Development Program the purchase of medicines to ensure the transparency of the transactions, as well as to reduce the cost of the purchases.[53] On the other hand, when she met with representatives of the private sector she protested that she had not seen that sector's commitment to combat corruption and stressed that much work remained to be done to make them aware of the need to cooperate with the struggle against corruption.[54]

In general, government largess benefits political allies through legal means. For example, public resources are used to bail out government-friendly banks with bad debt, thereby encouraging more poor investments and hurting the economy through increased cost of credit.[55] The state does little if anything to enforce rules governing conflict of interest that may arise for public office holders (see "Accountability and Public Voice"). While requirements are on the books, elected officials do not offer financial disclosures to identify, much less address potential conflicts of interest. The state does nothing to regulate conflicts of interest in the private sector either, which is left pretty much to its own devices and to its ability to pay off or intimidate inquisitive officials or journalists. The high incidence of corruption and lack of transparency mean that public interest in good governance, sustained economic growth, and justice is not served.

No major government official or politician has been successfully prosecuted and forced to pay appropriate penalties, be they monetary or in terms of prison time, for corruption. The overwhelming nature of official impunity is reinforced by the legal immunity enjoyed by politicians serving in Congress (and in the Central American Parliament, an international representative body established to promote regional integration). Thus, the effectiveness of going after the "small fish" is diminished as the "big fish" continue to feed from public monies.

A case in point involved the Honduran chief prosecutor, Ovidio Navarro, who dismissed 10 public prosecutors and transferred 6 others after they criticized his controversial decision to put a number of corruption cases on hold, including some involving former President Rafael Callejas (1990–1994). As a result, prosecutors staged a strike and a large public demonstration in November 2004. The press and the general public challenged the vigorous defense Navarro mounted for his actions. The appearance of having favored former President Callejas—seven of the postponed cases were against him—reflects poorly on the prosecutor's office and the state.

The increasing availability of the Internet to the middle and upper classes of the region has led to an effort to place increasing amounts of information about the government online. This effort is a good way for governments to reach NGOs and journalists, who can redistribute information to the wider public. Information on the national budget and expenses incurred are made available by the state. Unfortunately, the information is primarily general and does not allow for reconciliation of accounts making use of generally accepted accounting rules. To some extent the government actually does not know how much money comes in and goes out. The complex nature of the different sources of revenue coming to the state, ranging from domestic taxes and export duties to international aid, is matched by various mechanisms for official expenditures including payrolls, rebates, and direct aid. Presidential and legislative budgets can differ significantly, and the reconciliation of differences usually does not take place in public. Primarily as a result of the 1999 Stockholm donors' conference, the disbursement of foreign aid related to Hurricane Mitch was for the most part free of major incidents of corruption. This transparency and accountability was partly ensured by the close scrutiny that international donors placed on the Honduran government, inspection that has eased over time as the funds associated with that particular tragedy were disbursed.

Anticorruption and transparency are very low on the priority list of the current Honduran government, and in the foreseeable future there is little hope that much will change in this area. The politics of continuing to support a restrictive political system, with few possibilities for innovation and change, offer little hope for a timely, or even eventual resolution to many of the country's almost intractable problems: "poor governmental performance providing services, bad economic policy decisions, misuse and waste of tax revenues, corruption, an uncompetitive investment environment, low growth, increased poverty, unreliable and inconsistent law enforcement, inadequate dispute resolution, poor public security, and human rights violations."[56] Globalization and the erosion of national jurisdictions, along with national solutions to regional problems, exacerbate this already cloudy and troublesome scenario.

### Recommendations

- Existing legislation regarding corruption in the state apparatus must be enforced and relevant laws should be passed to address conflicts of interest in the public sector effectively.
- Existing legislation should be enforced to protect whistle-blowers and others who expose corruption from retaliation.
- Selected government purchases and transactions should be outsourced, insofar as is possible, to international organizations that have more effective transparency and oversight.
- High-level public officials involved in corrupt practices must be fully investigated, prosecuted, and punished if found guilty.

### NOTES

[1]  Evidence of the importance of municipal empowerment in the provision of services and the improvement of quality of life can be found in a technical report by Glenn Pearce-Oroz, "Local Institutions Matter: Decentralized Provision of Water and Sanitation in Secondary Cities in Honduras" (Washington, DC: World Bank, Urban Research Symposium, 2003).

[2]  "Central America: Meeting of Central American Governments in Stockholm," *TI Newsletter* (Berlin: Transparency International [TI], September 1999), http://www.transparency .org/newsletters/99.3/reforms.html#9; *Honduras: Democracy and Governance Assessment* (Burlington, VT: ARD, Inc., January 2003), 11 (submitted under U.S. Agency for Inter-

national Development, Center for Democracy and Governance, Contract No. AEP-I-00-99-00041-00).

3  *Honduras: Amnesty International Report 2004* (London and New York: Amnesty International [AI], 2004), http://www.amnestyusa.org/countries/honduras/document.do?id=C41620B4CF489A5880256E9E005A95FA.

4  "Opposition fails to capitalize on government's woes," *Latin American Caribbean & Central America Report* RC-04-06, 22 June 2004, 11; "Economic and institutional weakness blights Central America," *Latin American Caribbean & Central America Report* RC-03-8, 16 September 2003, 1–2.

5  "Democracy's low-level equilibrium; The Latinobarometro poll," *The Economist,* 14 August 2004.

6  *Honduras: Democracy and Governance Assessment* (ARD, Inc.), 6.

7  "Honduras politics: Electoral reforms are passed," Economist Intelligence Unit (EIU) *ViewsWire,* 26 July 2004, i, 7.

8  *Honduras: Democracy and Governance Assessment* (ARD, Inc.), 16.

9  "Journalist murdered near border with Guatemala" (Paris: Reporters Without Borders [RSF], 27 November 2003, http://www.rsf.org/article.php3?id_article=8642.

10 *Honduras – Annual Report 2004* (RSF, 3 May 2004), http://rsf.org/print.php3?id_article=10234.

11 *Honduras: Democracy and Governance Assessment* (ARD, Inc.), 16.

12 *Honduras – Annual Report 2004* (RSF); "Reporters Without Borders protests against TV journalist's jail sentence" (RSF, 20 February 2004), http://rsf.org/print.php3?id_article=9321.

13 "Honduras: Politics" (sidebar), *Latin American Caribbean & Central America Report* RC-04-11, 16 November 2004, 4.

14 "Absuelven a oficial por crimen de Herminio Deras" (Officer Absolved for Crime of Herminio Deras), *La Prensa* (Honduras), 27 March 2004, http://www.laprensahn.com/policiales.php?id=1405&tabla=March_2004&fecha=20040327; "The Quest for Justice: Efforts to Prosecute Honduran Human Rights Abusers," *May I Speak Freely? Media for Social Change,* n.d., http://www.mayispeakfreely.org/index.php?gSec=doc&doc_id=35.

15 Randall Richard, "AP Investigation: 500,000 criminal deportees from America wreak havoc in many nations," The Associated Press, 25 October 25, 2003. The U.S. deportation law applies to anyone receiving a sentence of one year or more, even if it is suspended; it is retroactive; and it is virtually automatic as there are almost no grounds for appeal.

16 Ibid.

17 "Presidente sanciona decreto de ley que prohibe tenencia de las AK-47" [President signs decree making ownership of the AK-47s illegal] (Tegucigalpa: Presidency of the Republic of Honduras, press release, 10 July 2003), http://www.casapresidencial.hn/2003/07/10_1.php.

18 "Summit Rejects Salvador-Honduras Antigang Plan," *Latin America Weekly Report,* WR-03-50, 23 December 2003, 16; "Guatemala: Berger Slims Army, Slashes Spending," *Latin American Weekly Report,* 6 April 2004, http://web.lexis-nexis.com/universe/printdoc; "Shuttling between Nations, Latino Gangs Confound the Law," *New York Times,*

26 September 2004, 1; W.E. Gutman, "Gangs: The Fatal Compulsion to Belong," *Honduras this Week*, 26 March 2004, http://americas.org/item_14520.

[19] Mark Stevenson, "AP Enterprise: War on Central American street gangs brings violence to Mexico," The Associated Press, 10 December 2003.

[20] Raphaele Bail, "Marked men with no place to hide," *Christian Science Monitor*, 18 August 2004, in *Latin American Post*, http://www.latinamericanpost.com/index.php?mod=seccion&secc=4&conn=3674.

[21] "Region Wide Campaign Targets Street Gangs," *Latin American Caribbean & Central America Report*, 20 July 2004; http://web.lexis-nexis.com/universe/printdoc.

[22] "Shuttling between Nations, Latino Gangs Confound the Law," *New York Times*, 26 September 2004.

[23] Freddy Cuevas, "Comisionado derechos humanos denuncia ejecuciones en Honduras [Human Rights Commissioner Denounces Executions in Honduras]," *El Nuevo Herald*, 3 March 2004, http://www.miami.com/mld/elnuevo/8095439.htm.

[24] "Shuttling between Nations, Latino Gangs Confound the Law," *New York Times*, 26 September 2004.

[25] "Gobierno defendera Ley Antimaras para proteger a la ciudadania [Government will defend Anti-Mara law to protect citizenry]" (Presidency of the Republic of Honduras, press release, 6 January 2004), http://www.casapresidencial.hn/2004/01/06_2.php.

[26] "Americas: Human Rights Defenders: Persecution reaches emergency proportions" (AI, press release, 10 November 2003), http://news.amnesty.org/index/ENGAMR010112003.

[27] "Situacion de los Derechos Humanos en Honduras, Resumen 2004 [Situation of Human Rights in Honduras, Summary 2004]" (Tegucigalpa: Committee of Families of the Detained and Disappeared in Honduras [COFADEH], 2004), http://www.cofadeh.org/html/documentos/situacion_derechos_humanos.2004.html.

[28] "Maduro faces rap after 104 die in prison inferno," *Latin American Caribbean & Central American Report* RC-04-05, 25 May 2004, 6–7.

[29] "Situacion de los Derechos Humanos en Honduras, Resumen 2004 [Situation of Human Rights in Honduras, Summary 2004]" (COFADEH).

[30] Douglas Payne, *Honduras: Update on Human Rights Conditions* (Washington, DC: INS Resource Information Center, Perspective Series, September 2000), cited in The Center for International Policy's Central America Program, http://ciponline.org/central_america/humanrights.htm.

[31] "Prison director investigated for role in jail fire," *Latinnews Daily*, 12 August 2004.

[32] *Honduras: Democracy and Governance Assessment* (ARD, Inc.), 25.

[33] Ibid., 26.

[34] "Death penalty proposal provokes rare unanimity," *Latin American Weekly Report*, 21 September 2004.

[35] Duncan Campbell, "Murdered with Impunity," *The Guardian* (UK), ZNET, 29 May 2003, http://www.zmag.org/content/print_article.cfm?itemID=3692&sectionID=54.

[36] Figure provided by Confederation of Indian Peoples of Honduras (COMPAH) and cited in "Pech Indian Leader Killed in Olancho," EFE, 14 July 2004, http://www.americas.org/item_15571.

37 *Honduras: Amnesty International Report 2004* (AI), http://web.amnesty.org/report2004/hnd-summary-eng.

38 *Honduras: Human rights violations against lesbian, gay, bisexual and transgender people* (AI, AI Index: AMR 37/014/2003, September 2003), 1.

39 "Honduras," in *International Disabilities Rights Monitor: 2004 Regional Report of the Americas* (Washington, DC: Center for International Rehabilitation, August 2004), http://www.cirnetwork.org/idrm/reports/americas/countries/honduras.html.

40 "President Maduro summons urgent meeting to stop transportation strike," *Central America: Political press review,* BBC Worldwide Monitoring, 6 January 2004; "Teachers Block Roads in Honduras Demanding Higher Pay," EFE, 24 July 2004, http://www.americas.org/item_15399.

41 *Honduras: Democracy and Governance Assessment* (ARD, Inc.), 25.

42 Ibid., 26.

43 Ibid., 26, 43.

44 Ibid., 4.

45 Ibid., 8; *2005 Index of Economic Freedom* (Washington, DC: Heritage Foundation, 2005), http://www.heritage.org/research/features/index/country.cfm?id=Honduras.

46 *Honduras: Democracy and Governance Assessment* (ARD, Inc.), 8.

47 Roque Roldan Oritiga, *Models for Recognizing Indigenous Land Rights in Latin America* (Washington, DC: Inter-American Development Bank, Biodiversity Series, Paper 99, October 2004), 11.

48 "Pech Indian Leader Killed in Olancho" (EFE).

49 "Corruption Perceptions Index 2004" (TI), http://www.transparency.org/cpi/2004/cpi2004/cpi2004.en.html.

50 "Corruption spreads," *Latin American Caribbean & Central America Report* RC-04-11, 16 November 2004, 4.

51 *Honduras: Democracy and Governance Assessment* (ARD, Inc.), 43.

52 "Eficiencia y transparencia: Nueva formula en compras y contrataciones del estado [Efficiency and transparency: New formula for state purchases and contracts]" (Presidency of the Republic of Honduras, press release, 26 March 2004), http://www.casapresidencial.hn/politica_social/transparencia.php.

53 "Honduras esta tomando medidas transcendentales en la lucha contra la corrupcion [Honduras is taking significant measures in the fight against corruption]" (Presidency of the Republic of Honduras, press release, 25 February 2004), http://www.casapresidencial.hn/2004/02/25_2.php.

54 "International Transparency: Businessmen uncommitted to fight against corruption," *Central America: Political press review,* 27 February 2004, http://web.lexis-nexis.com/universe/printdoc. The story was quoted from the San Pedro Sula Tiempo (Time) at http://www.tiempo.hn_8.

55 *Honduras: Democracy and Governance Assessment* (ARD, Inc.), 9.

56 "Corruption spreads," *Latin American Caribbean & Central America Report,* ii.

# IRAN

CAPITAL: Tehran
POPULATION: 67.4 million
GNI PER CAPITA: $1,720

**SCORES**

ACCOUNTABILITY AND PUBLIC VOICE: 1.75
CIVIL LIBERTIES: 1.89
RULE OF LAW: 2.70
ANTICORRUPTION AND TRANSPARENCY: 1.73
(scores are based on a scale of 0 to 7, with
0 representing weakest and 7 representing
strongest performance)

*Stephen C. Fairbanks*[1]

## INTRODUCTION

In 1979, Ayatollah Ruhollah Khomeini led an Islamic revolution that promised freedom and justice to its millions of supporters. Freedom meant deliverance from autocracy, and the masses who followed the revolutionary clerics believed the solution lay in Islamic government, a new form of rule they eagerly anticipated but only vaguely understood. Millions hoped that Iran's long legacy of corruption and arbitrary application of law would be relegated to the past. They saw the revered clerics of Iran's dominant Shiite sect as the interpreters and implementers of the rule of law, applying Islamic law in place of the flawed laws of men.

Freedom and justice have turned out to be elusive. The new constitution of 1979 in effect guaranteed that its principal authors, a select group of high-ranking clergy, would be able to perpetuate a grip on power that could be broken only with their consent. They have proved intolerant of those who seek to broaden political participation, attempting to cap dissent with tough restrictions on freedom of expression. They

Stephen C. Fairbanks was the political analyst for Iran in the U.S. Department of State's Bureau for Intelligence and Research from 1986 to 1998 and director of Radio Free Europe/Radio Liberty's Persian Service ("Radio Azadi") from 1998 to 2002.

have not hesitated to use their monopoly on juridical authority to keep critics and rivals under control. Political dissidents and journalists have no protection from arbitrary arrest or interrogations under torture. Corruption and bribery are pervasive, bred by the exclusive access to power open to supporters of the ruling clerics.

Democracy has an uncertain status in the Islamic Republic of Iran. As the regime is a theocracy, its legitimacy derives from God, or at least the interpretations of God's will by senior clerics of the official Shiite Islam state religion. But Khomeini encouraged mass participation, and so the Islamic Republic depends on the popular will as an additional source of legitimacy. The uneasy coexistence of a democratic tendency within a theocratic framework has resulted in an amalgam of elected and non-elected institutions, both dominated by senior clerics.

The underlying justification for clerical domination is Ayatollah Khomeini's innovative theory of *velayat-e faqih,* meaning rule by a supreme religious jurist, which holds that highly qualified experts on Islamic law are the most suitable rulers. It is the principle that empowers the current head of state, Ayatollah Ali Khamenei, in his position as supreme leader. The loyalty that candidates for elective office must express to the principle of velayat-e faqih helps keep political development within the confines of clerical domination.

The 12-member Guardians Council, half of whom are appointed directly by Supreme Leader Khamenei and the other half by the judiciary chief (appointed by Khamenei) with the approval of the Majlis (Iran's parliament) has been the most blatant instrument for maintaining the ruling clerics' grip on power. Charged with determining that all laws comport with Islamic law and Iran's constitution, it was able to block most legislation passed by the 2000–2004 reformist-dominated Majlis, including legislation proposed by President Khatami.

The reform movement of political activists led by President Mohammad Khatami, elected by landslides in 1997 and 2001, aimed to establish a rule of law that would replace the arbitrary application of Islamic law and restore people's faith in the possibilities of Islamic government. But the movement has faltered, unable to resist the backlash of the conservative holders of the reins of power. Most of the reform legislation introduced by Khatami and his allies in the Majlis was vetoed by the conservative jurists and lawyers of the Guardians Council as incompatible with Islamic law. Since the election of conservative candidates to a majority of seats in the Majlis in 2004, fears have risen that the regime will become even more exclusive and repressive. It is widely anticipated that a conservative president will be elected to replace Khatami in June 2005.

## ACCOUNTABILITY AND PUBLIC VOICE – 1.75

The separation of the executive, legislative, and judicial branches of the government is stipulated in the constitution, but the supreme leader, chosen by the body of senior clerics known as the Assembly of Experts, ranks above all three and is responsible to none of them. In theory, he resolves disputes among the three powers and thereby guarantees their separation. He has no constitutional accountability, however, and that carries the danger of potential despotism. The constitution states that the Assembly of Experts could dismiss him for incompetence, but that is unlikely given that candidates for election to the Assembly must be approved by the Guardians Council, whose members are chosen directly and indirectly by the leader.

The supreme leader's office—itself a large bureaucracy with its own intelligence and foreign affairs functions—the Guardians Council, and the Expediency Council regularly set the agenda for the executive and parliamentary branches. These non-elective bodies, which in recent years have increasingly usurped powers from the three government branches, constitute a serious impediment to accountable government.

Popular participation in the regularly scheduled elections of the president, parliament, and local councils presents a semblance of democracy, albeit one often at odds with the nondemocratic authority of the supreme leader and the judicial and non-elected organs that support him. Elections enable the clerical regime to claim legitimacy based on the will of the people, despite the reality of the limitations of their choices. Suffrage is universal and equal. Balloting is secret, and is monitored by electoral authorities from the interior ministry. Reports of voter fraud are remarkably few for a country of 67 million people.

Political campaigning opportunities are ostensibly equal for all vetted candidates, at least regarding such activities as putting up posters and holding public speeches (although reformist candidates have complained to the contrary). Equal opportunity in airing views is lacking, however, as the state-run radio and television are controlled by the office of the supreme leader and air the views primarily of the candidates of the favored, conservative side of the political spectrum. Those reformist newspapers that have not yet been closed down are able to promote pro-reform viewpoints, although they reach a much more limited audience than radio and television. There is a one-week limit on campaigning. This minimizes campaign expenses and may obviate the need for campaign finance laws, although the powerful clerical and bazaar merchant interest groups have no difficulty in choosing and backing their own favored candidates.

Political parties in Iran are rudimentary.[2] The country's constitution provides for the formation of parties, and a 1981 law stipulates what constitutes a political party and how it can function. However, some of the more influential political groups, such as the conservative Militant Clergy Society, are not registered as parties. Most groups that do call themselves parties are little more than narrowly based political or economic interest groups or associations lacking nationwide organization or membership. The dominant, conservative side of Iran's political spectrum remains distrustful of broad-based political parties that would open up the political system beyond conservative clerical control. They wish to keep political participation open only to those most loyal to Supreme Leader Khamenei and the principle of velayat-e faqih. One conservative columnist, for example, asserted that many reformists deserved to be disqualified from running for Majlis seats in 2004 because of their "indifference and disobedience" to velayat-e faqih "in favor of the principles of Western democracy."[3] The Freedom Movement of Iran, a liberal Muslim party that supports the Islamic Republic, is banned from elections because it rejects the necessity of clerical rule. No strictly secular party is granted permission to function.

Iran's Islamic regime is far from monolithic, and competition between the two broad factions of conservatives and reformists has allowed for some degree of political dynamism. Conservatives, who sometimes refer to themselves as the fundamentalist, or principled, faction, include most of the ruling clergy and older bazaar merchants. They have some appeal to traditional Iranians, including many in the provinces, who oppose the rapid cultural changes wrought by modernity and seek a return of what they understand to be the values of Islam and the revolution. Reformists, who include more progressive clergy, less religious technocrats, and socialistic Muslim activists, seek reforms in the political system that would facilitate democracy, greater freedom of expression, an easing of repressive Islamic social strictures, and less confrontational foreign relations. Both reformists and conservatives comprise numerous, loosely allied political groupings that run the gamut of political and economic opinion. The two major factions have enjoyed a limited degree of rotation of power, resulting from sometimes fiercely contested elections. However, interference by non-elective institutions has kept the factional rivalry from effectively presenting significant policy options.

The conservatives have regained the dominance they had before the enormously popular reformist Mohammad Khatami won the presidency in 1997 and 2001 and reformists won control of the Majlis in 2000. Taking advantage of popular disappointment with the reformists for their failure to effect significant change, and benefiting from the favoritism of the Guardians Council, the conservatives won many local council elections in 2003, most Majlis seats in 2004, and are expected to take the presidency in 2005. The February 2004 Majlis elections culminated a conservative counterattack against the reformists, who they feared threatened Islamic and revolutionary values and, more important, the grip on power of Supreme Leader Khamenei and the conservative clerics. The interference of the Guardians Council finally guaranteed a conservative majority in the new parliament. The Guardians vet political candidates for presidential and parliamentary office, a practice that has regularly constricted Iranians' political choices. For the Majlis elections of February 2004 the Guardians rejected 44 percent of prospective candidates, nearly all of them affiliated with the reformist faction, including some 80 sitting legislators and the two reformist deputy speakers.[4] Numerous constituencies had no reformist candidates to compete against the favored conservatives. For some, no reason was given for their disqualification, but for many others, according to a reformist newspaper, "the reason [given] for their disqualification is that they do not believe in Islam and velayat-e faqih."[5]

The Guardians Council was able to expand its abilities to supervise elections and vet candidates considerably when the conservative-controlled Expediency Council in 2003 authorized a greatly expanded budget for the Guardians to establish supervisory offices in the provinces. The conservative-controlled Expediency Council is a non-elected institution empowered to resolve impasses between the Guardians and the Majlis. The interior ministry protested that the supervisory offices were illegal, but to no avail.[6] President Khatami in 2002 introduced a bill that aimed to reduce or eliminate the Guardians Council's role in vetting candidates, but over the course of the next year the bill was rejected several times by the Guardians Council.

The executive branch is generally responsive to parliamentary inquiries, and ministers can be impeached and ousted, the most recent case having been in the summer of 2004 when the minister for roads and transport was impeached. Despite a doctrine of parliamentary immunity, the overwhelmingly reformist deputies have been summoned to court for offenses that include speeches made in the Majlis; in March 2004 at least 11 parliamentary deputies, all reformists, were summoned, prompting a public but ineffective protest by President Khatami to judiciary chief Ayatollah Shahrudi.[7]

The perpetuation of the Shiite clerical hierarchy's domination is proof that the state system of Iran is incapable of guaranteeing that people's political choices are free from domination by the specific interests of power groups. In 2003–2004, following the increased empowerment of the Guardians Council and the return to power of conservatives in the Majlis, the clerics' grip on power tightened, while the reformists' hopes for opening the system have diminished greatly. Clerical domination extends even into the civil service, where graduates of the seminaries are given preference for jobs.[8]

Civic engagement improved in 2003–2004. More than 8,000 nongovernmental organizations (NGOs) are now operating in Iran, primarily working on social, environmental, and cultural issues.[9] Faced with a repressive political system in which reformists were stymied, many Iranians, particularly women and young people, have turned to NGOs as the only arena for social activism. President Khatami, an advocate for institutions of civil society, has encouraged the growth of the NGO sector, but some NGO activists complain that the laws on founding NGOs are often restrictive, and, more important, the government is unresponsive to the protests or suggestions of NGOs. They say that they are usually unable to engage in constructive dialogue with legislators or executive branch officials.

Nonetheless, the NGO movement "to a great extent, has found its way," according to Shiva Dolatabadi, cofounder, along with Nobel Peace Prize laureate Shirin Ebadi, of the Society for Protecting the Rights of Children. According to Dolatabadi, the rise in the number of NGOs indicates that the initial problems with registration and organizations' charters that had made it difficult to enter the sphere of NGO activity have lessened.[10]

Iran's limitations on freedom of expression have worsened in recent years. The 1997 election victory of President Khatami had produced a vibrant press scene with numerous reformist dailies, but since 1999 more than 100 papers and magazines have been shut down, and numerous journalists, overwhelmingly reformist, have been arrested and jailed.

While some reformist newspapers in 2003–2004 still coexisted with the hard-line, pro-Khamenei ones—allowing for debate between the two major factions to continue in the press—the state imposes strict rules of press censorship. No media can criticize the supreme leader, the doctrine of velayat-e faqih, or the idea of an Islamic Republic. The Islamic guidance ministry and the intelligence ministry closely monitor all written material, and each week the Supreme National Security Council, controlled by hardliners, sends all newspapers a list of banned subjects, such as student demonstrations or Iran's nuclear programs.[10] The office of the supreme leader, through an institution known as the Islamic Republic of Iran Broadcasting (IRIB), constitutionally controls all Iranian radio and television. Because Iran's constitution stipulates that "the mass-communication media, radio and television, must serve the diffusion of Islamic culture in pursuit of the evolutionary course of the Islamic Revolution,"[11] the broadcast media only present official points of view on domestic and foreign affairs. Vague libel laws are enforced if conservative clerics or politicians are "insulted," and even vaguer charges of insulting Islamic sanctities are used, principally by Tehran's press court, to suspend or permanently shut down reformist papers. Reporters Without Borders calls Iran "the biggest prison for journalists in the Middle East," citing the arrests of 43 journalists in 2003.[12]

Iranian radio and television are biased in favor of the conservative faction. This was evident when they barely covered Mohammad Khatami's campaign for the presidency in 1997, compared to the coverage they gave to the establishment candidate at the time. In October 2003 and January 2004 the supervisory board that monitors state broadcasting criticized the IRIB's partiality, particularly in its coverage of parliament, saying that it was lobbying for the conservative faction.[13] These complaints resulted in no meaningful changes, and criticism of the IRIB intensified in the run-up to the February 2004 parliamentary elections.

Even President Khatami was not exempt from the IRIB's censorship, as a Tehran daily noted that remarks he made on January 31 that efforts by the government to reach a compromise with the Guardians Council were at a dead end were "left entirely unreported by the state radio and television."[14]

An undetermined but significant number of Iranians turn to satellite television broadcast from abroad, although the regime has banned satellite dishes since 1994. Foreign radio broadcasts are important sources for news and information. Iran has increasingly directed its censorship activities toward Internet Web sites, which for more than 3 million users have become an important medium for news and discussion on political and social affairs otherwise censored in the press. Nearly 10,000 sites, deemed un-Islamic or threatening to the state, reportedly are blocked from inside the country, and several cyber-dissidents have been harassed and imprisoned.[15] Censorship has reportedly increased since the victory of hard-liners in the February 2004 parliamentary elections, and much of it has been aimed at pro-reform sites such as the popular Emrooz.com. The Iranian authorities are also trying to shut down weblogs, which have become phenomenally popular in recent years as an outlet for Iranians to express their political convictions. Between 10,000 and 15,000 Iranians regularly contribute to blogs. Many of the blogs are hosted outside Iran, making it difficult for the authorities to trace participants.

In August 2004 the conservative majority bloc in the Majlis made revisions to the government's five-year development plan so that authority for the Internet would go to the state broadcasting organization, which is under the control of the office of the supreme leader, rather than to government ministries.[16] It appears that Iran is considering the creation of a national Intranet—an Internet service just for Iran—that would be separate from the World Wide Web. If successfully implemented, it would deprive Iranians of one more outlet for free expression and keep their Internet activities under the watchful eye of the authorities.[17]

The state imposes strict censorship on cultural expression in literature and film, which must accord with Islamic standards set by the ministry of Islamic guidance and the judiciary. Censorship standards have become stricter following the conservative victories in the 2004 parliamentary elections. Iran's internationally renowned film director Mohsen

Makhmalbaf complained of a new censorship strategy emerging in 2004 when the government stopped him from making a film about what he called the suffering of the Iranian people.[18] In May, *Marmoulak (The Lizard)*, a film satirizing Iran's clergy that had made it past the censors and become a box office sensation, was withdrawn from public showing after conservative clerics, led by Guardians Council secretary Ayatollah Jannati, complained.[19]

*Recommendations*

- Iran should end the role of the Guardians Council in vetting candidates for presidential and parliamentary elections and by no longer requiring allegiance to the principle of velayat-e faqih.
- The interior ministry and other relevant institutions should lift restrictions on the formation of political parties. The government should facilitate the democratic process by allowing the people to organize according to their own criteria and to appeal freely to the public.
- The increasingly autocratic institution of the supreme leader should be abolished or removed from the political realm. A constitutional amendment commission, intervention by the Assembly of Experts, or a popular referendum should be implemented to ensure that the leader is non-partisan, above Iran's factional disputes rather than consistently siding with the conservatives' faction.
- Iran should permit unfettered freedom of expression by releasing journalists, Web site operators, and other individuals imprisoned for peacefully expressing their opinions; ending direct regime control of the broadcast media; allowing political debate and free expression of criticism through an end to vague laws that make insulting public officials and Islamic sanctities criminal offenses; and ceasing the review and prior censorship of books and films.

## CIVIL LIBERTIES – 1.89

Article 38 of the constitution of the Islamic Republic of Iran forbids "all forms of torture for the purpose of extracting confession or acquiring information" and states that "any testimony, confession, or oath obtained under duress is devoid of value and credence."[20] However, torture and forced confessions remain a problem. In 2004, after considerable media attention, legal means to address it were initiated. On April 27, 2004, judiciary chief Ayatollah Shahrudi issued a directive to the country's judicial, law enforcement, and intelligence departments proscribing the use of torture to obtain confessions. The circular appeared to be an admission of the existence of such practices, but it was nevertheless an encouraging step to correct the problem. Shahrudi initially denied that his directive was occasioned by actual abuses, but he subsequently admitted that there had been offenses at interrogation centers, which he attributed to insufficient supervision due to the judiciary's great workload.[21]

The Majlis on May 4 took Shahrudi's circular a step further by passing a bill banning torture. It specified unlawful physical and psychological pressures, banned arbitrary arrests, and gave some guidelines on searching houses.[22] The reformist press welcomed the bill, saying it would help protect citizens.[23] The bill became law after its approval the following day by the Guardians Council, a surprising development considering the Guardians' routine vetoes of reform legislation.

But whether the state has the necessary means to implement the law's guidelines is questionable, as jailed dissidents have continued to report being tortured. Human Rights Watch (HRW) called the bill an empty gesture.[24] On June 4, 2004, HRW issued a comprehensive account of the treatment of political detainees in Tehran's Evin Prison and in secret prisons around the capital, documenting systematic abuses against political detainees, including arbitrary arrest, detention without trial, torture to extract confessions, prolonged solitary confinement, and physical and psychological abuse.[25] Critics are concerned that Iran's Islamic penal code—which is based on Islamic law and has numerous articles that allow for stoning, honor killing, and physical punishment—still stake primacy over the new law.

There is little protection against long-term detention without trial. One of the best-publicized cases of such abuse is that of three religious nationalist dissidents, Reza Alijani, Taqi Rahmani, and Hoda Saber, who in July 2004 entered their second year of "temporary detention" without trial for alleged involvement in disturbances in Tehran the year before.[26]

Peaceful activists, journalists, and intellectuals continue to be arrested in Iran. One of the most notorious cases is that of ailing 75-year-old Siamak Pourzand, a well-known journalist and husband of exiled human-rights activist Mehrangiz Kar. Arrested for alleged anti-state activities in November 2001, he remains imprisoned despite suffering a heart attack in March 2004. Reportedly, Tehran's public prosecutor has told him he will not be released.[27]

In the summer and fall of 2004, some deputies of the new conservative majority proposed introducing a bill that would transfer counterintelligence investigative functions from the ministry of intelligence and security, which is accountable to the Majlis, to the judiciary, which is not. Reformists fear that would mean that accountability would be lost in the investigation of dissidents and oppositionists. Nevertheless, they admit that units of the judiciary that operate parallel to the appropriate units of the intelligence ministry have already been investigating and arresting dissidents.

The authorities often deny the existence of any political prisoners. Judiciary chief Shahrudi on May 1, 2004, explained that Iran has no political prisoners because it has no law defining political crimes (the Majlis has been unable to pass a bill to define political crimes because of unresolved disputes with the Guardians Council).[28] However, on April 27, 2004, President Khatami told an assembly of university students that Iran does have prisoners jailed because of their opinion. He put the number at 26, although regime opponents believe the number to be higher.[29]

Citizens have little recourse to redress for such abuses, although there have been some signs of improvement. In April 2004, in reaction to the domestic and international concern over Iran's imprisoned newspaper journalists and political activists, Sa'id Mortazavi, the Tehran public prosecutor who gained international notoriety for his judgments against newspapers and journalists when he headed Tehran's press court, visited renowned political prisoners Abbas Abdi, Akbar Ganji, Reza Alijani, Taqi Rahmani, and Akbar Mohammadi and ordered they be given home leave for a week.[30] Mortazavi's order can be dismissed as a public relations gesture. However, a more encouraging development took place on June 1, 2004, when the judiciary revoked the death sentence of Hashem Aghajari, a university professor and member of a reformist political organization, who was convicted of blasphemy in November 2002 for a speech that conservatives viewed as a direct challenge to clerical rule.[31]

Iran's Islamic legal system assures a basic inequality between men and women. Article 20 of the constitution asserts that men and women enjoy equal protection under the law, but only in accordance with Islamic criteria.[32] Legal discrimination against women occurs in such matters as strictly imposed dress codes: the requirement for headscarves and long sleeves or the all-enveloping *chador* contrasts with relatively few restrictions, such as a ban on wearing shorts, for men. Crackdowns by morality police against women who flout the codes increased following the February 2004 parliamentary victories of hard-liners, who warned they would not tolerate "social corruption."[33] In court proceedings, a woman's testimony is valued at only half of a man's. Women do not enjoy equality with men in divorce, blood money, or inheritance rights. The reformist-dominated Majlis of 2000–2004 introduced several bills to improve women's rights, but the Guardians Council rejected them. On the plus side, women enjoy equal voting rights, have several representatives in parliament, and are active in several political organizations. There are at least 45 women's NGOs.[34]

President Khatami on March 7, 2004, called for an end to negative views about the role of women in society, pointing to discrimination against them in policy making, economics, and family affairs. Unfortunately, the following day baton-wielding personnel of Iran's Basij militia attacked women commemorating International Women's Day in Tehran.[35]

Iranian law defines a person as disabled based on the degree to which the person's prospects for employment and self-sufficiency are limited, and the protections Iran offers reflect this definition. Since 1955, Iran has provided vocational training for disabled citizens and has mandated equal pay and equal treatment for disabled workers.[36] The Iran-Iraq War, which greatly increased the number of disabled citizens, brought additional attention to issues of access and participation in public life, and in major cities, many public buildings have been made wheelchair accessible. Iran stated in its 1996 report to the United Nations that it provides free medical care, housing assistance, transportation, and other aid to people with disabilities,[37] but these services appear largely to be limited to urban areas. There is no law protecting the individual civil rights of disabled people more generally, but they appear not to be any more restricted than those of non-disabled citizens

Religious freedom is limited in Iran, where Shiite Islam is the state religion and 89 percent of the population is Shiite. Even the large, 10 percent Sunni minority experiences some discrimination. Sunni parliamentarians in April 2004 wrote to Supreme Leader Khamenei to complain about the low number of Sunnis in the executive and judicial branches and in academia, anti-Sunni bias in the state-run mass media, and the authorities' rejection of a Sunni request to build a mosque in Tehran.[38]

The constitution recognizes Zoroastrians, Jews, and Christians as religious minorities and allows them to worship. A set number of parliamentary seats is reserved for them, but they are barred from senior government positions. Equality for these minorities took a significant step forward on December 27, 2003, when the Expediency Council approved a parliamentary bill, previously rejected by the Guardians Council, that would make blood money—paid by a perpetrator for killing or wounding someone—equal for Muslims and non-Muslims; previously, the amount for killing a non-Muslim male had been half that for a Muslim male. Blood money for non-Muslim women remains half that of men.[39]

The state can still make life difficult for non-Muslim minorities. On September 9, 2004, 80 members of the Assembly of God church, in Karaj for an annual meeting, were arrested in a sudden police raid. All but 10 pastors were released later that day, and 9 of those were released on September 12, with warnings to have no further contact with church members. The last one, Hamid Pourmand, a Muslim convert, has remained incarcerated incommunicado.[40] Muslim converts to Christianity or other religions can face the death penalty.

The Baha'i faith is not constitutionally recognized as a religion. The estimated 300,000 members of the religion, which originated in Iran in the 19th century, have endured persecution since the foundation of the Islamic Republic. They cannot practice their religion openly, open their own religious schools, or have access to higher education. Their cemeteries and holy places have been desecrated. The release of two Baha'is from prison on February 17, 2004, after they had served 15 years for "association with Baha'i institutions," was a rare positive development.[41]

Iran's ethnic minorities, particularly the Kurds and Baluchis—most of whom are also Sunnis—experience discrimination. Kurdish legislators in November 2003 wrote to President Khatami to complain that the central government has neglected the Kurdish provinces except for an increase in security crackdowns. They petitioned Khatami to attend to the region's economic underdevelopment and high youth unemployment, remedy the lack of adequate university facilities, and reduce the harsh security measures.[42]

Freedom of association is guaranteed in the constitution (Article 26). The state does allow organizations to mobilize and advocate for peaceful purposes, providing they have prior permission from the interior ministry. However, vigilante groups, plain-clothes intelligence officers, and the Basij militias harshly attack demonstrations—even ones with prior approval—if they stray into what could be interpreted as anti-government messages. Trade unions are little more than pro-regime professional organizations with little ability to organize strikes.

### Recommendations

- Iran should uphold its constitutional prohibition against torture and ill treatment and vigorously enforce the 2004 law banning torture, arbitrary arrests, and forced confessions.
- Iran should end long-term detention without trial and prolonged solitary confinement, and it should inform families about the location and status of their relatives.
- Iran should enact and enforce legislation that would grant equal rights to women in such matters as divorce, blood money, inheritance rights, and value of legal testimony.
- Iran should grant constitutional recognition to the Baha'i faith and allow its members rights equal to those of other Iranians and should end religious discrimination that prevents equal opportunities in employment and political participation for Sunnis and non-Muslim minorities.

## RULE OF LAW – 2.70

When President Khatami was swept into power in 1997 he promised to establish the rule of law, putting an end to the seemingly arbitrary application of law by the ruling clerics. But though constitutionally empowered (Article 113) to implement the constitution, the president lacks power to stop violations of it.

The judiciary is independent but only in the sense that the executive and legislative branches cannot influence it. The supreme leader, Ayatollah Khamenei, appoints the head of the judiciary, which is thus an integral part of the power structure that supports the supreme leader. During the sixth, reformist-dominated parliament of 2000–2004, the judiciary regularly summoned deputies for statements made in parliament, ending their longstanding immunity. It appears unlikely that the seventh parliament, dominated by allies of the judiciary and supreme leader, will be subject to such interference.

The judiciary, very much a part of the conservative clerical establishment, is neither impartial nor nondiscriminatory in the administration of justice. It applies Islamic law as interpreted by senior Shiite clerics, and judges are constitutionally (Article 163) appointed in accordance with religious criteria. As such, the judiciary chief and the judiciary as a whole have regularly applied their own version of the rule of law against reformist politicians, activists, and journalists in recent years. Members of the ruling conservative political hierarchy are rarely, if ever, prosecuted for abuse of power.

Key prosecutors are under the control of the conservatives. This applies perhaps most of all to Tehran's public prosecutor, Said Mortazavi, who was appointed in 2003 in apparent reward for his many decisions against newspapers and journalists as head judge of Tehran's press court. Now he is in charge of prosecuting nearly all political cases, including those of journalists and student protesters.

The Article 90 Commission, a parliamentary body stipulated by Article 90 of the constitution to investigate complaints by citizens against any of the three branches of government, is ignored by the judiciary. Public Prosecutor Mortazavi has told the Article 90 Commission it has no right to interfere in judicial matters.[43]

Citizens have the right to counsel, to be provided by the state if the defendant cannot afford one. However, political dissidents are regularly discouraged from retaining counsel. Many are told that any decision to retain counsel will reflect unfavorably on their cases. HRW reports that many former prisoners who did obtain counsel were never allowed to meet privately with their attorneys nor were their attorneys given access to their files. Several well-known attorneys who acted as defense counsel in cases relating to journalists or editors have themselves been arrested and detained.[44] The constitution (Article 165) specifies that trials must be public and that press offenses are to be tried in the presence of a jury (Article 168); however, HRW reports that in most of the cases it investigated, prisoners faced a judge and the complainant (usually a government official) without a jury or the public present.

The military and security forces are accountable to civilian authorities. The supreme leader is commander-in-chief of the armed forces and directly controls the Islamic Revolutionary Guard Corps. Augmented by the Basij militias, the guards have a domestic security role in protecting the regime against civil unrest, but since Khatami's election in 1997 the guard leadership has stood squarely on the side of the conservative faction. Guard commanders expressed a clear preference for the conservatives in the February 2004 parliamentary elections. While Iran's election law stipulates that armed forces personnel must leave the military at least two months before registering as candidates, a guard general asserted on October 3, 2003, that having guard personnel in parliament would be good for Iran.[45] Reflecting concerns about military political activity, in November 2003 the Majlis—then dominated by reformists—approved a bill banning military personnel from membership in political organizations and from engaging in election activity.[46] The winning slate of conservative candidates, advertised as approved by Supreme Leader Khamenei, included several former guard personnel.[47]

The executive branch controls other security forces, including the investigative officers of the ministry of intelligence and security and the police and law enforcement forces under the interior ministry. The investigative units of the judiciary and counter-intelligence units of the Revolutionary Guards are subservient to the conservative factions, while such vigilante groups as the Ansar-e Hezbollah do the bidding of certain hard-line clerics. The vigilantes' interference in the political process, in attacking student demonstrators and others seeking peaceful political change, has been particularly evident since Khatami became president.

Property rights normally are inviolable in Islam. With the exception of properties expropriated during the revolution from supporters of the previous regime, the registering and administration of ownership deeds is carefully attended to by legions of seminary-trained experts.

## Recommendations

- Iran should enforce its own constitutional guarantees regarding the fair and impartial administration of justice. The Guardians Council should support, rather than impede, the president in fulfilling his duty to implement the constitution.
- Judicial reform should be implemented by making the judiciary accountable to the parliament and making the judiciary responsive to citizens' complaints registered with the parliament's Article 90 Commission.

- Iran should provide for fair trials by ensuring that detainees are informed of the charges against them, giving all detainees access to counsel, and ensuring that all trials be conducted in public.
- Vigilante groups such as Ansar-e Hezbollah that are used to attack dissident citizens should no longer be tolerated, and their activities should be investigated by an independent commission.
- Iran should vigorously ensure that the Revolutionary Guards refrain from involvement in the political process.

## ANTICORRUPTION AND TRANSPARENCY – 1.73

Excessive bureaucratic regulations and a poorly paid bureaucracy produce an environment in Iran prone to corruption. The bloated bureaucracy gives preferential hiring treatment to graduates of theological seminaries, veterans of the Iran–Iraq war, and Basij militiamen rather than to candidates based on their skills and merits. Nearly every procedure can be speeded up with a little extra payment, which bureaucrats see as a necessary source of income rather than an immoral bribe.[48]

State ownership of major sections of the economy, including the petroleum sector, banking, heavy industries, and various companies seized from fleeing industrialists in the wake of the 1979 revolution, means management positions are awarded only to loyal supporters of the regime. The regime's on-again, off-again attempts to privatize state-owned industries provide abundant opportunities for crony capitalism. That has made family members of some of the revolutionary leaders, notably Expediency Council Chairman Ayatollah Ali Hashemi-Rafsanjani, phenomenally wealthy: One son holds a key position in the oil ministry, another heads the Tehran Metro project, a cousin dominates Iran's pistachio export business, and other family members control automobile assembly plants, oil engineering companies, and a private airline.[49]

Many of the assets that the 1979 revolution expropriated from Iran's wealthiest families were given to Islamic charitable foundations, known as *bonyads,* controlled by clerics. These foundations account for 10 percent to 20 percent of Iran's gross domestic product and own factories, hotels, farms, mines, and vast tracts of land. They have changed from the social welfare organizations they were in the early years of the revolution to become huge commercial conglomerates. The bonyads fall under the jurisdiction of the supreme leader and, as vehicles for rewards, are an integral part of the support structure that keeps the ruling clerics loyal to him and firmly in power. They have little more than rudimentary financial disclosure procedures and are closed to public and media scrutiny. There is no effective outside auditing body.

The regime does not enforce anticorruption laws when it comes to its loyal supporters or their relatives. A recent example is the case of Norway's Statoil, which allegedly paid a bribe to Mehdi Hashemi-Rafsanjani, son of the Expediency Council chairman. While Statoil was issued a stiff penalty notice in Norway in June 2004 for bribing Mehdi Hashemi and others who were influential in Statoil's commercial activity in Iran,[50] Mehdi Hashemi was left untouched in Iran.

On August 25, 2004, President Khatami announced that the judicial and executive branches, particularly the ministry of intelligence and security, are taking steps to deal with economic corruption, which he said would cause discomfort for those with vested interests.[51] Supreme Leader Khamenei declared the Iranian year 1383—March 20, 2004, to March 20, 2005—the "year of accountability" for the government, in which combating corruption was to be a major goal. But after six months, a conservative newspaper reported that no important step had been taken in this area. The paper noted that the ministries had failed to form mandated "accountability staffs," both the executive and judicial branches had scaled back or eliminated weekly press conferences, and the Majlis had taken no new steps toward accountability. One Assembly of Experts member, the paper noted, concluded that "unfortunately until today none of our organizations has carried out accountability that is worthy of the exalted leader's order."[52]

Admitting to problems is a good start, but Iran has a long way to go before allegations of corruption by high government officials can be aired in the news media and investigated and prosecuted without prejudice. Governmental operations and services, the budget-making process and accounting of expenditures, the awarding of government contracts and similar issues all remain opaque. None of the government branches regularly shares information on these matters with the press.

### Recommendations

- Iran should allow its press and broadcasting media to investigate all forms of corruption and to investigate the transactions of high officials and their families without fear of retaliation.

- Iran should investigate and prosecute violations of existing anti-corruption laws without concern for the violators' family status or government position.

- The bonyads, accounting for a large but unreported share of the Iranian economy, should be subjected to internationally accepted financial disclosure procedures.

- Iran should increase the transparency of its official institutions, particularly the judiciary, which should be open to parliamentary investigations of bribery and economic corruption.

- Iran should address the endemic corruption of the government bureaucracy by basing government hiring on merit, streamlining procedures in order to eliminate red tape and many of the redundant civil servants, and improving bureaucrats' pay scales in order to reduce the levels of petty bribery.

## NOTES

[1] The author wishes to thank Dr. Rasool Nafisi for his generous assistance in this project.

[2] Stephen C. Fairbanks, "Theocracy versus Democracy: Iran Considers Political Parties," *Middle East Journal* 52, No. 1 (Winter 1998)

[3] Mehdi Bostanabadi, "How Were Extremists Who Call Themselves Reformists Isolated?" *Resalat*, 21 February 2004.

[4] "Iran Report" (Prague and Washington, DC: Radio Free Europe/Radio Liberty [RFE/RL], 12 January 2004), http://www.rferl.org/reports/iran-report/2004/01/2-120104.asp.

[5] "The Wide Wave of Disqualifications, the Trigger of a Crisis," Towse'eh, 12 January 2004, p. 1

[6] Abbas William Samii, "Dissent in Iranian Elections: Reasons and Implications," *Middle East Journal* 58, 3 (Summer 2004).

[7] "Iran Report" (RFE/RL, 22 March 2004), http://www.rferl.org/reports/iran-report/2004/03/11-220304.asp.

[8] Christopher de Bellaigue, "Who Rules Iran?" *The New York Review of Books*, 27 June 2002.

[9] Golnaz Esfandiari, "Iran: Growing NGO Community Offers Political Activism Where Government Does Not" (RFE/RL, 16 February 2004), http://www.rferl.org/features article/2004/02/202f2c48-84ae-4ef0-b6e9-b16ad3b6ed42.html.

[10] Ibid.

[11] Iranian Constitution, Preamble, translated in A. Tschentscher, ed., "International Constitutional Law" (last modified 1995), http://www.oefre.unibe.ch/law/icl/ir00000_.html #I000_.

[12] "Iran – Annual Report 2004" (Paris: Reporters Without Borders [RSF], 3 May 2004), http://www.rsf.fr/article.php3?id_article=9940&Valider=OK.

13 "Iran Report" (RFE/RL, 17 November 2003), http://www.rferl.org/reports/iran-report/2003/11/46-171103.asp.

14 "People Know the Facts," *Iran News,* 01 February 2004.

15 "Internet Under Surveillance, 2004: Iran" (RSF, 22 June 2004), http://www.rsf.org/article.php3?id_article=10733.

16 "Taghyirat-e Barnameh-ye Chaharom dar Majles Moshajareh Afarid" ("Changes in the Fourth Plan Generates Controversy in the Majlis"), *Iran,* 18 August 2004.

17 "Iran's Bloggers in Censorship Protest," BBC News, 22 September 2004, http://news.bbc.co.uk/1/hi/technology/3677984.stm.

18 "Director Accuses Iran of Film Ban," BBC News, 6 May 2004, http://news.bbc.co.uk/1/hi/entertainment/film/3690857.stm.

19 "Row Builds over Iran Cleric Film," BBC News, 11 May 2004, http://news.bbc.co.uk/1/hi/world/middle_east/3887311.stm; "Iran Anti-Cleric Film Withdrawn," BBC News, 15 May 2004, http://news.bbc.co.uk/1/hi/world/middle_east/3718275.stm.

20 Iranian Constitution, Art. 38, translated in A. Tschentscher, ed., "International Constitutional Law" (last modified 1995), http://www.oefre.unibe.ch/law/icl/ir00000_.html#I000_.

21 "Iran Report" (RFE/RL, 17 May 2004), http://www.rferl.org/reports/iran-report/2004/05/17-170504.asp.

22 "Namayandegan-e Majles Tarh-e Do Fawriyatiye Ehteram beh Azadiha-ye Mashru' va Hefz-e Hoquq-e Shahrvandi-ra Tasvib Kardand" ("Majles Deputies Approved Double-Urgency Bill on Respecting Lawful Freedoms and Citizens' Rights"), *Sharq,* 5 May 2004, 3.

23 "Judicial Justice and Respecting Human Rights," *Towse'eh,* 5 May 2004, 1.

24 "Iran: Torture Used to Suppress Dissent" (New York: Human Rights Watch [HRW], 7 June 2004), http://www.hrw.org/english/docs/2004/06/07/iran8774.htm.

25 "Like the Dead in Their Coffins: Torture, Detention, and the Crushing of Dissent in Iran" (HRW, 7 June 2004), http://hrw.org/campaigns/torture/iran/.

26 "Dossier Up in the Air; Reza Alijani, Hoda Saber, and Taqi Rahmani are Still Under Temporary Detention," Vaqaye-ye Ettefaghieh," 11 July 2004, 3.

27 Golnaz Esfandiari, "Iran: Rights Group 'Revolted' at Treatment of Ailing Journalist" (RFE/RL, 20 April 2004), http://www.rferl.org/featuresarticle/2004/04/f1e665b8-bff0-4d82-bc33-26f5041aa2f3.html.

28 "Preparing the New Penal Adjudication Law," *Hemayat,* 1 May 2004.

29 "Khatami: Freedom Means Security of Thought and Setting It Forth for Discussion," *Aftab-e Yazd,* 28 April 2004, 1, 2.

30 Editorial: "Note," *Hambastegi,* 3 May 2004.

31 Golnaz Esfandiari, "Judiciary Revokes Death Sentence for Blasphemy on Academic" (RFE/RL, 1 June 2004), http://www.rferl.org/featuresarticle/2004/06/64ceb28d-49b6-4be3-811c-d96d9ae80f1a.html.

32 Iranian Constitution, Preamble and Art. 20, translated in A. Tschentscher, ed., "International Constitutional Law" (last modified 1995), http://www.oefre.unibe.ch/law/icl/ir00000_.html#I000_.

33  "Iran Police in Fashion Crackdown," BBC News, 12 July 2004, http://news.bbc.co.uk/1/hi/world/middle_east/3887311.stm.

34  "Iran Report" (RFE/RL, 19 January 2004), http://www.rferl.org/reports/iran-report/2004/01/3-190104.asp.

35  "Iran Report" (RFE/RL, 15 March 2004), http://www.rferl.org/reports/iran-report/2004/03/10-150304.asp.

36  "2003 International Disability Rights Monitor Compendium Report," Iran (Chicago: Center for International Rehabilitation, 2003), http://www.cirnetwork.org/idrm/reports/compendium/iran.cfm.

37  "Government Action on Disability Policy: A Global Survey, " Iran (Stockholm, Sweden: Institute on Independent Living: 1997) http://www.independentliving.org/standard rules/UN_Answers/Iran.html.

38  "Iran Report" (RFE/RL, 6 September 2004), http://www.rferl.org/reports/iran-report/2004/09/30-060904.asp.

39  "Iran Report" (RFE/RL, 5 January 2004), http://www.rferl.org/reports/iran-report/2004/01/1-050104.asp.

40  "One Iranian Pastor Still in Custody," *The Christian Post,* 15 September 2004, http://www.christianpost.com/article/missions/1070/section/one.iranian.pastor.still.in.custody/1.htm.

41  "Longest Serving Baha'i Prisoners Released in Iran" (Washington, D.C.: Baha'is of the United States, Office of Public Information, 17 February 2004), http://www.wfn.org/2004/02/msg00131.html.

42  "Iran Report" (RFE/RL 5 January 2004), http://www.rferl.org/reports/iran-report/2004/01/1-050104.asp.

43  "Like the Dead in Their Coffins ..." (HRW, 7 June 2004), http://hrw.org/reports/2004/iran0604/8.htm#_ftnref157.

44  Ibid., http://hrw.org/reports/2004/iran0604/7.htm#_Toc73505656.

45  "Iran Report" (RFE/RL, 20 October 2003), http://www.rferl.org/reports/iran-report/2003/10/42-201003.asp.

46  "Iran Report" (RFE/RL, 10 November 2003), http://www.rferl.org/reports/iran-report/2003/11/45-101103.asp.

47  James Vick, "Low Turnout Tells Tale of Iranian Vote," *Washington Post,* 23 February 2004, A14.

48  "Iranian Postcards: Wrapped in Red Tape," BBC News, 13 February 2004, http://news.bbc.co.uk/1/hi/world/middle_east/3487249.stm.

49  Paul Klebnikov, "Millionaire Mullahs," *Forbes,* 21 July 2003, http://www.forbes.com/forbes/2003/0721/056_print.html.

50  "Penalty Notices in the Statoil Case" (Oslo: The Norwegian National Authority for Investigation and Prosecution of Economic and Environmental Crime, 29 June 2004), http://www.okokrim.no/aktuelt_arkiv/annet/290604_Statoil-forelegg-engelsk.htm); see also, "Iran Report" (RFE/RL, 10 November 2003), http://www.rferl.org/reports/iran-report/2003/11/45-101103.asp.

51  "Iran Report" (RFE/RL, 31 August 2004), http://www.rferl.org/reports/iran-report/2004/08/29-310804.asp.

52  "Numerous Questions: Who Is Accountable?," *Resalat,* 25 September 2004.

# LAOS

CAPITAL: Vientiane
POPULATION: 5.8 million
GNI PER CAPITA: $310

**SCORES**
ACCOUNTABILITY AND PUBLIC VOICE: 1.19
CIVIL LIBERTIES: 2.16
RULE OF LAW: 1.63
ANTICORRUPTION AND TRANSPARENCY: 1.51
(scores are based on a scale of 0 to 7, with
0 representing weakest and 7 representing
strongest performance)

*Carolyn Bull*

## INTRODUCTION

The Lao People's Democratic Republic is one of the world's few remaining Communist regimes. Since taking power in 1975, the Lao People's Revolutionary Party (LPRP) has favored the Chinese model of absolute one-party rule combined with gradual economic liberalization. Economic reform since 1986 under the New Economic Mechanism has not been matched by political or social transformation, although Lao society has gradually enjoyed greater freedom of movement, employment, and international interaction. The human rights situation has improved incrementally, but the government's record remains disturbing. The LPRP controls dissent tightly and acts harshly against those it perceives as threatening to itself or to social order.

Standards of government accountability in Laos are extremely poor. Laotians cannot change their government, as National Assembly elections are restricted to LPRP members and a few approved independents. Leadership change is determined by the LPRP, which dominates government at all levels. Neither the legislature nor the judiciary provides effective

---

**Carolyn Bull** is a PhD candidate in Politics at the Australian Defence Force Academy at the University of New South Wales.

315

checks against executive excess, and the civil service is politicized. The government views civil society as a threat to its monopoly on power and citizens have only minimal access to government information or consultation mechanisms. Restrictions on freedom of expression are severe. The government controls the local media, and slander of the state is proscribed through harsh penalties.

The state violates most international human rights standards. Violations have included restrictions on freedom of assembly and association, torture, arbitrary arrest and detention, and persecution of religious and ethnic minorities, particularly the Hmong. Laos has few functioning institutional safeguards against state abuse.

Having evolved only since the 1990s, Laos's constitutional and legal system is embryonic. The long absence of the rule of law has created an environment in which the authorities often apply the law arbitrarily and inhibit or violate the rights of citizens. The judiciary is subject to frequent executive, legislative, and LPRP interference, and the rights of the accused to presumption of innocence, defense, and a fair trial are severely curtailed. The military, which is highly influential in government policy making, operates outside civilian state control.

State corruption in Laos is pervasive, impeding reform. The politically powerful engage in a wide range of corrupt behavior, and the regulatory environment to protect against this is virtually nonexistent. Despite some accountability reforms, no effective legislative process exists to punish official corruption, nor are there effective internal or external audit systems for government. Government actions are generally nontransparent and secretive.

There are few signs that the current regime is open to change, and it continues to seek legitimacy through suppressing opposition. Over time, however, some reform may flow from increasing openness to external social, cultural, and political influences and the modernizing pressures of a younger, better-educated elite poised to benefit from accelerating reform. The progress of reform in neighboring states, particularly Vietnam, will be important.

## ACCOUNTABILITY AND PUBLIC VOICE – 1.19

Laos is a one-party Communist state that has been governed continuously by the LPRP since 1975. The 1991 constitution enshrines the

LPRP as the sole legal political party; thus there is no opportunity for rotation of power or alternative political activism.

The 109-seat National Assembly is elected every five years by secret ballot under universal adult suffrage.[1] Elections are multi-candidate, and although candidates are not required to be LPRP members, the party's vetting process ensures that the vast majority are. All candidates are nominated by party committees, government organizations, or state-owned enterprises and must be approved by the LPRP and the National Assembly.

The February 2002 National Assembly elections, with only one successful nonpartisan candidate, reaffirmed the LPRP's supremacy. The absence of opposition having eliminated the need for electoral interference, candidates had reasonable access to pre-election publicity, and the turnover of members was significant—60 percent were elected for the first time in 2002.[2] As international election monitors are not permitted in Laos and no effective indigenous monitoring capacity exists, it is difficult to gauge election conduct. Some irregularities in voting and tallying were reported by informal observers.[3]

The LPRP dominates government at all levels. General Khamtay Siphandone has been president of the party and state since 1998, and the prime minister, deputy prime minister, defense minister, and National Assembly chair are also politburo members. The president and vice president are appointed by the National Assembly. On the president's recommendation, the National Assembly elects the prime minister and other ministers, many of whom are not assembly members. In reality, all decisions regarding key leadership positions are determined by factional struggles within the LPRP and the military. There is little leadership movement; succession is often determined on the death or retirement of the incumbent. Nepotism and patronage are endemic within the party, the government, and the bureaucracy.

The LPRP's 10-member politburo and 52-member central committee determine most government policy; major decisions are taken at five-yearly party congresses, of which the last was held in 2001. Although the leadership has become gradually more open to economic reform and even to ethnic and gender diversity, it has shown very little appetite for political reform.

The National Assembly generally acts as a rubber stamp for LPRP decisions. It may consider and amend draft legislation, but the executive branch retains the authority to issue binding decrees. The absence of any opposition force, combined with the assembly's relative inexperience and lack of resources and skills, makes it an ineffective check against the executive. Some positive developments have taken place in recent years, including more active debate of draft laws and the establishment of a citizen complaints and petitions section. However, the quality of legislative drafting, debate, and public consultation remains extremely weak.

The government has made some progress in adopting laws to improve government administration, including through a provincial and district decentralization program. During 2004, the government continued to consider public management reform issues, including the questions of financial accountability and public consultation.

Civil service structures in Laos parallel those of the LPRP. Civil service recruitment is seldom transparent or based on merit. Promotion tends to be through seniority, clan ties, and political patronage. A significant ghost-worker problem reflects the absence of any system for registering or removing former civil servants from payrolls.[4] A new Civil Service Act passed in May 2003 provides for recruitment exams, job descriptions, assignment criteria, performance evaluations, and a reward system. Little progress has been made on its implementation, however, as is the case with plans to upgrade the Department of Public Administration and Civil Services. During 2004 the government made some limited progress in considering reforms to separate party and civil service structures.

Citizens have only minimal access to timely information about pending legislation, regulations, or government policy, nor are there established mechanisms for government consultation with civil society groups. Civic groups do not have opportunities to testify, comment on, or influence pending government policy or legislation.

Despite constitutional protections, Laotians are subject to severe restrictions on freedom of expression. The government controls all print and electronic media through the state news agency, Khaosan Pathet Lao. Media content is vetted by the Ministry of Information and Culture. A press law announced in 2001 that would allow limited private media ownership has not yet been adopted. If enacted, it would still impose strict controls, including the power to close publications deemed antigovernment.

Freedom of speech is also restricted by provisions in the penal code that forbid "slandering the state, distorting party or state policies, inciting disorder, or propagating information or opinions that weaken the state." Article 59 of the penal code sets a prison sentence of 1 to 5 years for antigovernment propaganda. Journalists who do not file "constructive reports" or who attempt to "obstruct" the work of the LPRP may be subject to jail terms of 5 to 15 years. Violators are believed to have incurred prison sentences of between 1 and 5 years.[5] The authorities have harassed the English-language press.

Lao citizens have easy access to the Thai broadcast media, international TV stations, and shortwave broadcasters, although some censorship occurs. Foreign publications are generally disseminated freely, but the government has been known to censor them and even insert its own articles.[6] Restrictions on publications mailed from overseas are loosely enforced. All domestic Internet providers are controlled by the state; e-mail is monitored sporadically, and some Web sites are blocked.

Laos restricts foreign journalists through onerous visa requirements and compulsory escorts. Restrictions on freedom of expression were highlighted in June 2003 when 12- to 20-year sentences were imposed on two European journalists, an American pastor of ethnic Hmong background, and at least three of their Lao assistants for reporting on the Hmong insurgency and for alleged involvement in the death of a security official. Although the foreigners were released in July 2003, at least two of the Lao remain in detention.[7]

The government limits the privacy rights of individuals and has an extensive surveillance network. Unlawful searches and seizures are common, while the government routinely ignores legal protections on privacy of mail, telephone, and electronic communications. Laos's isolation and curbs on freedom of expression have dampened artistic development, although this is not specifically restricted.[8]

*Recommendations*

- The government should open up National Assembly elections to multiple parties and take steps to ensure the conduct of free and fair elections.
- The government should expand the role of the National Assembly and match this with efforts to strengthen the assembly's legislative drafting, public consultation, and monitoring capacities.

- The government should step up efforts at public administration reform, such as implementing the Civil Service Act, separating party and civil service structures, and introducing a merit-based appointments system.
- The government should enact a new press law protecting press freedom and desist from interfering with and intimidating the media.
- The government should dismantle its surveillance network, including the monitoring of mail and telecommunications, and strengthen laws to protect the privacy of individuals from state interference.

## CIVIL LIBERTIES – 2.16

The constitution prohibits torture, arbitrary arrest, and detention without trial. Laos signed the International Covenant on Civil and Political Rights (ICCPR) and the International Covenant on Economic, Social and Cultural Rights (ICESCR) in 2000 but has continued to delay ratification. It has not signed the Convention Against Torture. Government understanding of these conventions, let alone implementation, is deficient; in addition, Laos has not met reporting requirements.

In practice, state actors routinely abuse the civil liberties protected under these instruments.[9] Limits on length of detention, while prescribed in law, are seldom met for court hearings or judgments. Individuals have been held for as long as 18 years without trial.[10] Individuals without money or connections can spend years imprisoned without trial, and prisoners who have served out their sentence but cannot pay their prison expenses are not set free. In some cases the government has applied national security laws to routine criminal actions to justify long periods of detention without trial. Illegal and incommunicado detention by security forces and the police is common.

Torture, shackling, and other sorts of ill-treatment by police and prison officials are widespread, especially with respect to detainees accused of insurgent or antigovernment activity. Access by prisoners to food and medical care is so restricted as to be life-threatening, particularly for those without family support. Money and personal connections are the only effective means by which detainees may obtain access to legal representation, prevent long-term detention without trial, and secure release.

Important safeguards, such as judicial oversight, independent monitoring, and a functioning court system are virtually nonexistent.

Laos has taken few steps to address international concerns about its nine known political prisoners,[11] including the uncertain fate of five student prisoners of conscience arrested in 1999.[12] Because the government refuses to admit any human rights abuses, it has not set up procedures for redress of such complaints.

With most political opposition stymied, the main threat to government authority comes from the long-running Hmong insurgency in the highlands. A crackdown on rebel groups by Laotian security forces during 2003 caused several hundred civilian casualties.[13] In turn, insurgent groups perpetrated fatal attacks on public transportation and in markets during 2003. In early 2004 the government launched a fresh offensive to eradicate these groups, renewing concerns about the impact on civilians in affected areas. At the same time, however, the government has made some effort to defuse the issue. Some Hmong appear to have been offered unofficial amnesties, while progress was made toward an agreement with the United States to resettle some 15,000 Hmong refugees sheltering in border camps in Thailand.

Within its limited capacity, the state acknowledges some issues affecting women, people with disabilities, and other distinct minority and interest groups, to the extent that these do not confront party interests. The state's ability and motivation to address these issues are limited by resource constraints, as well as by the issues' low profile in the absence of political opposition or civic groups able to pressure the government to take action. The government's efforts to address these issues have often been confined to facilitating the work of international nongovernmental organizations (NGOs). In the case of ethnic or religious minority groups, the government's motivation is further limited by a desire to ensure that these groups remain marginalized from the country's political life. Although 3 cabinet ministers and 28 National Assembly members belong to minorities, minority groups generally have little input into political affairs, which are dominated by the ethnic Lao.

The constitution protects equity for women and minorities, and the family code prohibits legal discrimination in marriage and inheritance. Laos has ratified the relevant international conventions,[14] although again it struggles with implementation. Gender discrimination is not generalized, but societal discrimination persists. Many urban women hold responsible positions in the civil service and private sector, drawing incomes commensurate with those of men. In contrast, women are significantly underrepresented in the party and government. Only 3 of 53 LPRP central committee members are women, with no female representation in the politburo or council of ministers. In the 2002 National Assembly elections, female representation increased from 20 to 22 of 109 members.

Domestic violence is illegal and not known to be widespread. Rape cases tried in court usually lead to convictions, although spousal rape is not illegal. The government has actively supported the Lao Women's Union and National Commission for Mothers and Children, as well as development assistance programs targeting women. Trafficking in women and children is a major problem, with an estimated 15,000 to 20,000 persons trafficked annually, mostly for prostitution. Although official involvement does not appear widespread, some local officials have been complicit in or profited from trafficking. Laos has made efforts to support international anti-trafficking endeavors, including through providing judicial and police training and in-kind support for NGOs such as office space and airtime. A draft anti-trafficking law is in progress.

The government is less proactive in promoting the rights of ethnic minorities. Ethnic Lao constitute approximately 40 percent of the population, with upland hill tribes, Vietnamese, Chinese, and south Asian groups comprising the remainder. Minorities experience some discrimination in mainstream society but tend not to suffer widespread government discrimination, with the exception of the Hmong. In this respect, the alleged torture and murder of five ethnic Hmong children by Lao soldiers in May 2004 is of concern.[15]

The 6.8 percent of the population with disabilities are seriously affected by limited education and training opportunities.[16] Government and donor support has focused on physical or medical rehabilitation, with little emphasis on employment or training. Homosexuality is illegal for men (and not mentioned in law for women), and although a more relaxed atmosphere has developed in recent years, police raids and arrests occasionally occur.

Approximately half the population practice Theravada Buddhism, and government support has given this religion an elevated status that brings with it relative freedom of existence. On the other hand, the government has incorporated Buddhist communities into the government structure and exerts a high degree of direction over the Buddhist clergy. Party requirements to integrate communist ideology into Buddhist teaching and for monks to attend party meetings appear, however, to be on the wane.

Article 9 of the constitution discourages acts that create divisions among religions and persons, and narrow interpretations of this article by the LPRP have emphasized the potential for religion to divide and destabilize. Accordingly, the freedom of minority religions is more restricted, particularly in the provinces. Animism is common among the hill tribes, and there are small numbers of Muslims, Christians, and Baha'is. Several Laotians have been imprisoned for proselytizing and other religious activities. Christians in particular attract government suspicion, partly due to their foreign connections. During 2003 at least 20 Christians were arrested, and although the number of detentions appears to be falling, official coercion of Christians to renounce their faith continues. In August 2004 a further four Christians were arrested.[17] Others were reportedly barred from worshipping or forced to renounce their beliefs, while some churches were closed.

In July 2002, the government promulgated a decree on religious practice that expanded the range of activities permitted to all religious practitioners, including for minority religions to proselytize and print religious material.[18] Its requirement that groups obtain advance permission for such activities proved restrictive in practice. In 2003, all such applications were rejected. However, freedom of religion appears to have improved slightly in 2003–2004, with the reopening of some churches and release of some religious property.

Freedom of assembly and speech are guaranteed in the constitution but not upheld in practice. The penal code prohibits participation in an organization for the purposes of demonstrations or other acts that cause "turmoil or social instability." Such crimes are punishable by sentences of up to 20 years, or in some cases, execution. Party membership is not compulsory but confers obvious political, economic, and social benefits.

Civil society is tightly controlled. Although a number of international NGOs operate in the country, Laos has very few indigenous civil society organizations. The government perceives them as threatening to its monopoly on power and discourages their establishment. There is no legal framework enabling the registration of civil society organizations, which in practice remains virtually impossible. Some professional and socially oriented NGOs are permitted, but all political associations and parties (except the LPRP) are banned, as is any organization that criticizes the government.

Informal nonpolitical groups meet relatively freely, but like much daily activity their meetings are subject to state surveillance. Although this appears to be diminishing, the security service continues to monitor the movements of vast numbers of Laotians, aided by networks of village militia and neighborhood/workplace committees.

Trade unions are permitted within the framework of the officially sanctioned Federation of Lao Trade Unions, which is controlled by the LPRP. The level of unionization is low, given that some 85 percent of workers are subsistence farmers. Trade unions have little voice and are largely restricted to the public sector. Workers do not have the right to bargain collectively. According to the labor code, disputes are to be resolved through workplace committees, with final authority resting with the Ministry of Labor and Social Welfare. Strikes are rare; while they are not prohibited by law, a ban on subversive activities and destabilizing demonstrations under the penal code acts as a disincentive.

Private enterprises now constitute about 80 percent of business activity in Laos, and business associations, while embryonic, have begun to develop. They are not independent, however; the 20 or so existing associations are formally linked to line ministries, and the party guides the fledgling Chamber of Commerce.[19]

Due to tight government control, demonstrations are extremely rare and have drawn excessive force. In October 1999 the first antigovernment demonstration since 1975 was quickly suppressed.

## Recommendations

- The government must genuinely commit itself to ending the impunity of state actors with respect to torture and ill-treatment of prisoners and to investing political and financial resources sufficient to promote radical change in state practice regarding the denial of individual civil liberties.
- The government should fully and promptly investigate allegations of state abuse of prisoners and implement practical preventive measures such as regular prison inspections and access to prisoners, including by international agencies. Correctional facilities need

urgent improvement to ensure that basic food, clothing, and health-care needs are met.

- The government should amend the penal code to remove punitive measures relating to freedom of association, remove restrictions on trade unions, and allow collective bargaining.

## RULE OF LAW – 1.63

The Lao judicial system consists of the People's Supreme Court; provincial, district, and municipal people's courts; and military courts. Although its independence is protected constitutionally, all levels of the judiciary experience frequent executive interference. Judicial appointments, including the president and vice-president of the People's Supreme Court and judges, are made by the National Assembly Standing Committee, which is controlled by the LPRP, as is the office of the public prosecutor.

There are no protections to prevent the use of state funding for the judiciary as an instrument of political control, although the opacity of funding disbursement and expenditure procedures makes it difficult to prove. In cases of political or personal interest, state authorities ignore judicial decisions with impunity or change them arbitrarily. The police, for example, have in some cases administratively overruled court decisions and continued to detain persons released by the courts. The police are not known to have been held to account for such behavior.

The judiciary is corrupt, and bribery of judges is of particular concern given that cases are decided by three-judge panels rather than juries. Since 1991 only one judge has been removed for improper behavior.[20] Trial outcomes are often predetermined.

The skill level of the judiciary is weak. Despite improvements introduced by development assistance programs and upgrades to the curriculum at the National University of Laos, judges and other legal officials lack sufficient legal training to handle the challenges of upholding law to international standards.

The constitution provides for open trials, with the exception of those relating to national security provisions, state secrets, minors, and some types of family law. However, the rule of law prevails in neither civil nor criminal matters. Laos does not have an extensive legal system and is primarily governed through the issuance of decrees. Although since 1989 the government has gradually strengthened the legal framework to a body of around 50 key laws, including a new constitution in 1991, it has generally proved reluctant to pursue legal reform. Implementation poses major challenges for poorly trained judges and administrators.

The 1989 Lao Law Concerning Criminal Case Proceedings sets out procedures for arrest, detention, and criminal prosecution, including measures to safeguard the right to be informed of charges, to present evidence, and to appeal. In practice, citizens are not guaranteed due process, and trials consistently fail to meet international standards of fairness. Although the presumption of innocence is guaranteed by law, trial judges usually determine the verdict in advance on the basis of police or prosecution reports. The emphasis thus falls on the presumption of guilt, making criminal conviction rates high.

Although accused persons have the constitutional right to defend themselves, and a Board of Legal Counselors is empowered to provide legal assistance, most defendants lack access to counsel and often do not know the charges laid against them. In practice the majority defend themselves. There is no legal aid system, and in 2004 there were only about 40 private lawyers in Laos. Even well-resourced defendants are not assured of a fair trial in cases that touch on powerful vested interests. A bar association exists but is not independent. Planned reforms announced in June 2004 would enhance its role in providing access to the law, including through a training scheme from early 2005 to increase the pool of publicly available solicitors.

The constitution provides for equal treatment for all citizens regardless of sex, social status, education, faith, or ethnicity. In practice, the government has sometimes acted to redress well-documented cases of discrimination, although Laos lacks a sufficiently developed legal mechanism under which citizens may bring charges. Noncitizens are discriminated against with respect to marriage.[21]

Security forces are highly influential in government policy making, although they play a less pronounced role than do neighboring Burma's. The president, vice president, and prime minister are senior ranking military officers, as are 7 of the 10 politburo members. The LPRP relies on its armed forces to maintain its grip on power, and the military exercises near total authority over state security policy. The police, military, and internal security apparatuses operate outside civilian state control. A military tribunal system exists, but judgments are not subject to civilian review by the Supreme Court. There is no political appetite for security sector reform, which is viewed in party circles as a threat to the supremacy of the vested interests underpinning their power base.[22]

The constitution protects state, collective, and private forms of ownership. There have been efforts since the mid-1990s to develop a land titling system for urban and peri-urban areas, including through a 1997 Land Law. However, security of tenure remains weak. The establishment in March 2003 of a National Land Policy Committee may over time promote progress.

Inequality in land and property ownership between ethnic groups and sexes persists; the economically deprived are vulnerable to land snatching by politically powerful groups, including the military. Land rights for farmers in highland areas remain insecure, with such groups often forcibly relocated without adequate compensation or support. A government Land and Forest Allocation Program has given villagers important collective rights to forest and agricultural land and improved resolution of conflicting claims. However, direct or indirect government pressure to resettle under the program has displaced up to 80 percent of villages in some areas, with the impoverished and ethnic minorities particularly affected.[23] Likewise, existing or planned government projects such as the Nam Theun Two dam threaten the forced resettlement of thousands of people.

## Recommendations

- The government should commit itself to ending all forms of interference in the judiciary and work to implement institutional protections to enforce this.
- Legal reform and development should be prioritized, including aligning key laws relating to criminal punishment and procedure with international standards, particularly regarding national security provisions.
- The government should allocate resources to reform judicial institutions and promote judicial professionalism, especially with respect to trial procedure. The establishment of legal defense services, including a legal aid system, should be given urgent priority.
- The government must separate the armed forces from state institutions and establish procedures for imposing civilian accountability

over the military, particularly by bringing the military under the jurisdiction of the Supreme Court.

## ANTICORRUPTION AND TRANSPARENCY – 1.51

State corruption in Laos is so pervasive that it impedes development at all levels. Graft began to escalate in the mid-1980s along with the growth of large-scale infrastructure projects, border trade, and foreign investment. State officials, the police, and the military regularly accept bribes for preferential treatment and are complicit in the narcotics trade. Formal state involvement in the economy has declined significantly since 1986, with 90 percent of state-owned enterprises now privatized, although some sensitive or particularly lucrative industries, such as wood processing, remain state controlled. However, the military and political elite have extensive commercial empires that take in forestry, construction, trade, and tourism interests. The police regularly demand payoffs, including for dropping criminal charges.

Any regulatory environment to protect against corruption is virtually nonexistent. Laos has no conflict-of-interest legislation or other mechanisms to enforce the separation of public office from the personal interests of officeholders. The quality, transparency, and attitude to reform of the bureaucracy vary between departments. Although some have taken advantage of economic reforms to adopt more dynamic processes, in general the Communist-inspired bureaucracy has adopted a reactionary approach designed to protect its resources and power. It is burdened by excessive, arcane regulations that impede reform and nurture corruption. Bureaucratic decision making is opaque and lengthy, discouraging public input. The concentration of decision-making power in the prime minister's office further expands possibilities for corruption.

In 2000 the prime minister issued an anticorruption decree targeting official abuses of power such as embezzlement, fraud, and bribe-taking. It applies to civil servants, the party, the military, police, and state-enterprise managers. The effectiveness of the decree has been undermined by the fact that it is not a law as such and does not define punishments. It has not evolved into an effective legislative process to prevent or punish official corruption, and the legal system has not begun to punish corrupt officials. Victims of corruption have no effective mechanism to pursue their rights. There is no open assets-declaration system for public officials or administrative processes that support this goal. The government is currently working on an anticorruption law. An anticorruption commission established in 1993 has proved ineffectual.

The government has no effective internal audit system to ensure accountability in expenditure and tax collection. Fiscal decentralization since the late 1990s has not been accompanied by accountability measures. The government has made some progress toward better public financial management, including the establishment in 2001 of a National Audit Office to inspect and audit the civil service. However, this body reports directly to the prime minister's office, is not independent, and has been largely ineffectual. Regulations were adopted in 2002 to enhance the financial accountability and transparency of government departments, requiring them to submit annual financial statements to the National Assembly,[24] but there is no ombudsman. More positively, management audits of key state-owned enterprises have occasionally resulted in top-level management changes. Financial reporting and procurement requirements for these enterprises were improved with the introduction of a new decree in 2002.

The National University of Laos in Vientiane is the country's only university. Informal preferential access is given to students with political connections or wealth, including through the selling of admission places and grades by academics seeking to supplement low wages. The appointments and promotions system for academic staff is also subject to political favoritism.

Whistleblowers and anticorruption activists have no legal protection, and tight restrictions on media freedom shield corrupt state or party officials from public exposure. State and party officials carry on corrupt practices with almost complete impunity.

Along with weak rule of law, lack of governmental transparency is one of the key impediments to development in Laos. Combined with a culture of secrecy, multiple layers of opaque and inefficient bureaucracy preclude timely public access to most forms of government information. Members of the public seeking information rely on personal connections and/or bribery, with the poor and disadvantaged thereby excluded. There is no freedom of information legislation or other mechanisms by which citizens may petition for information.

The budget-making process is not transparent. In contravention of constitutional provisions, the National Assembly does not receive adequate budget information, nor does it review extra-budgetary spending or government equity holdings, although it officially approves the budget. Budget documents have sporadically been made public since 1997 but do not conform to international standards for open budget preparation. Transparency has improved with the publication of the budget in the official gazette since 2002 and of the budget plan since 2003.[25] However, other key information such as extra-budgetary activities, tax exemptions, and fiscal reporting has not been made public.[26] Similarly, government accounts are incomplete. The Ministry of Finance has a financial inspection department, but this only inspects the accounts of those government organizations in which problems are known to have occurred.[27]

The awarding of government contracts is not transparent, and no legislative regime covers public procurement. Laos is heavily dependent on donor assistance, which is distributed freely. Corruption is rife in both sectors; the rigging of donor procurement processes to provide kickbacks to officials is common. A Procurement Monitoring Office was established in the Ministry of Finance in 2003 to oversee the implementation of better procurement processes, and revision of implementing regulations is currently under way.[28]

### Recommendations

- The government must implement systemic reform at all levels to address state corruption, nontransparency, and procedural inefficiency. It should enact conflict-of-interest legislation, an anti-corruption law, and legal protections for whistleblowers; establish an effective independent anticorruption commission; and consider developing an ombudsman institution.
- Public finance reform should be expedited, including establishing effective internal and external audit mechanisms, separating the National Audit Office from the control of the prime minister's office, improving budget transparency, and revising government procurement regulations.
- The government should work to reform cultures of secrecy and improve public access to information, including through enacting freedom-of-information legislation, strengthening information

infrastructure, and implementing processes by which citizens may petition for information. It should also take steps to improve information flow to and consultation with the National Assembly.

## NOTES

1 With the exception of citizens with mental disabilities or who have had their right to vote revoked by a court.

2 *The Parliamentary Centre Visits Lao PDR* (Ottawa: The Parliamentary Centre, 2004), http://www.parlcent.ca/asia/lao_pdr_e.php, accessed 6 September 2004.

3 Author interviews.

4 C. Westcott, *Summary of Lao PDR Governance Assessment* (Manila: Asian Development Bank, 2001), 26, http://www.adb.org/Governance/gov-publications.asp, accessed 2 September 2004.

5 *Question of the Violation of Human Rights and Fundamental Freedoms in Any Part of the World, Written Statement submitted by the South Asia Human Rights Documentation Centre (SAHRDC), a non-governmental organization in special consultative status* (Geneva: United Nations Commission on Human Rights, report no. E/CN.4/2004/NGO/127, 8 March 2004), 2.

6 *Laos – 2004 Annual Report* (Paris: Reporters Sans Frontieres [RSF], 2004), http://www.rsf.org/article.php3?is_article=10197, accessed 1 September 2004.

7 The two individuals believed to remain in detention are Thao Moua and Pa Phue Khang; see "Appeal for the release of the guides of Thierry Falise and Vincent Reynaud" (RSF, 25 July 2003), http://www.rsf.org/article.php3?id_article=7489, accessed 6 December 2004; see also, "ASEAN Summit – Foreign Press urged to expose lack of free expression in Laos and plight of jailed local guides" (RSF, 26 November 2004), http://www.rsf .org/article.php3?id_article=11959, accessed 6 December 2004.

8 S. Shaeffer, *Keynote Speech Delivered by Dr Sheldon Shaeffer, Director UNESCO, Bangkok, at the opening reception of aseanARToday Thailand and Cambodia, Laos, Myanmar 4 June 2002* (Bangkok: UNESCO, 2002), http://www.thavibu.com/articles/ATC21.htm, accessed 16 September 2004.

9 For more details see, "Lao Peoples Democratic Republic: The Laws are promulgated but have no impact on the people: Torture, ill-treatment and hidden suffering in detention" (London: Amnesty International [AI], 2002), http://web.amnesty.org/library/print/ ENGASA260042002, accessed 13 August 2004.

10 Ibid.

11 These include two officials from the pre-1975 government and two who served in the present regime before being jailed in 1990 for advocating multiparty politics. *Laos:* Country Reports on Human Rights Practices – 2003 (Washington, DC: U.S. Dept. of State, 2004).

12 For further details on political prisoners, see *Laos* (AI, 2003a), http://web.amnesty.org/ web/web.nsf/print/2004-lao-summary-eng, accessed 13 August 2004.

13 Ibid.; see also "Laos: Use of Starvation as a weapon of war against civilians" (AI, AI Index ASA 26/013/2003, 2003b; 2 October 2003), http://web.amnesty.org/library/print/ ENGASA260132003, accessed 13 August 2004.

[14] Laos ratified the International Convention on the Eradication of All Forms of Racial Discrimination in 1974, the Convention on the Elimination of Discrimination Against Women in 1981, and the Convention on the Rights of the Child in 1991.

[15] "Laos: Disembowelling and torture of children condemned as war crimes" (AI, 13 September 2004), http://www.amnesty.org.uk/news/press/15595.shtml, accessed 16 September 2004.

[16] "Study on Generating Employment through Micro and Small Enterprise and Cooperative Development in Lao PDR" (Geneva: International Labour Organisation [ILO], 2002), http://www.ilo.org/public/english/region/asro/bangkok/ability/msme_lao_summary.htm, accessed 2 September 2004.

[17] *Religious Freedom in Laos: Persecution Alongside Progress* (New Malden, Surrey: Christian Solidarity Worldwide, 2004), http://www.csw.org.uk/CSWnews.asp?item=492, accessed 7 December 2004.

[18] *Prime Minister's Decree 92 on the Administration and Protection of Religious Practice* (Vientiane: Government of Lao People's Democratic Republic, 2002).

[19] C. Westcott, *Summary of Lao PDR Governance Assessment*, 30.

[20] *Laos:* Country Reports on Human Rights Practices – 2003 (Washington, DC: U.S. Dept. of State, 2004).

[21] Citizens are required to obtain prior approval before marrying foreigners, and while such approval is generally given, it requires a lengthy and burdensome application process.

[22] T. Huxley, *Reforming Southeast Asia's Security Sectors* (London: Kings College London, Centre for Defence Studies, Conflict, Security and Development Group, 2001), 21–22.

[23] P. Vandergeest, "Land to some tillers: Development-induced displacement in Laos," *International Social Science Journal* 55, 175 (2003): 47–56.

[24] *Lao PDR: Economic Monitor: May 2004* (Vientiane: World Bank Office, 2004), 24.

[25] Ibid.

[26] C. Westcott, "Combating Corruption in Southeast Asia," in J. Kidd and F.-J. Richter (eds.), *Fighting Corruption in Asia: Causes, Effects and Remedies* (Singapore: World Scientific Press, 2003), 249, http://www.adb.org/Governance/combatting-corruption.pdf, accessed 2 September 2004.

[27] Marc A. Miles, Edwin J. Feulner, Jr., Mary Anastasia O'Grady, and Ana I. Eiras, "2004 Index of Economic Freedom: Laos" (Washington, DC: The Heritage Foundation, 2004), http://cf.heritage.org/index2004test/country2.cfm?id=Laos, accessed 6 September 2004.

[28] *Lao PDR: Economic Monitor* (World Bank).

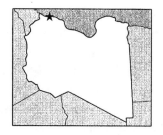

# LIBYA

CAPITAL: Tripoli
POPULATION: 5.6 million
GNI PER CAPITA: $5,944

**SCORES**
ACCOUNTABILITY AND PUBLIC VOICE: 0.56
CIVIL LIBERTIES: 1.17
RULE OF LAW: 1.12
ANTICORRUPTION AND TRANSPARENCY: 0.19
(scores are based on a scale of 0 to 7, with
0 representing weakest and 7 representing
strongest performance)

*Alison Al-Baddawy*

## INTRODUCTION

After coming to power in a coup in 1969, Libyan leader Colonel Muammar Al Qadhafi introduced a unique political, economic, and social system called the *Jamahiriyah* (state of the masses). This system was based on a mixture of Arab nationalism, socialism, and Qadhafi's own interpretation of Islam. He created a highly centralized state that relied heavily on the security services for its legitimacy and punished anyone who dared to challenge his control. Since then, he has successfully manipulated Libya's complex tribal relationships and imposed his own ideology on the population to the extent that he is in complete control of all aspects of Libyan life.

Following Colonel Qadhafi's announcement in December 2003 that he would abandon his weapons of mass destruction programs, Libya has been following a path of reintegration into the international

**Alison Al-Baddawy** is a research fellow at the International Policy Institute at Kings College London. She works primarily on security issues in North Africa with a particular focus on Libya. She has conducted several research projects on Libya that have entailed undertaking fieldwork there and has also published numerous articles on the country.

community. United Nations, European Union, and U.S. unilateral sanctions have for the most part been lifted since then, bringing high hopes that the Libyan regime would adopt a series of reforms to open up its tightly controlled society. However, while there have been signs of a new openness on the international front and some developments in the economic sector, there are no real signs of change on the political level. The country remains dominated by Qadhafi and his clique, and his children are currently consolidating their political and economic power.

Libyan citizens are still not able to influence politics or the political process in any meaningful way, and the state demands total conformity. Political parties are banned, and there are no genuinely independent civil society organizations, although a few individual voices are beginning to try to challenge the status quo. The media, like all other institutions, remain totally dominated by the state. Paralegal organizations such as the Revolutionary Committees Movement continue to spread fear among the population. Although their role has been somewhat sidelined to make way for the new reformist-minded faction who are able to engage with Western governments and actors, they are still a very important part of Qadhafi's power base.

Despite the adoption of a new discourse that promotes respect for human rights, the regime continues to commit human rights abuses, and anyone daring to challenge the regime is in danger of arrest, torture, or worse. The government continues to target Islamists in particular, and anyone suspected of belonging to or sympathizing with an outlawed politicized Islamic group is at risk. The judiciary is heavily influenced by the executive, and there is no guarantee of a fair trial for anyone suspected of a political offense.

Although some attempts have been made to open up Libya's tightly controlled economy, private sector activity remains limited, and bureaucracy is still highly problematic. Corruption is also a major problem, not only through the payment of bribes, but also because much of Libyan life still hinges on personal and tribal connections. Governmental transparency poses another problem, and the regime is slow to make even the most basic information readily available in the public domain. As a result, accessing reliable data and statistics on Libya is extremely difficult.

## ACCOUNTABILITY AND PUBLIC VOICE – 0.56

Qadhafi introduced Libya's unique political system, the Jamahiriyah, after coming to power in 1969. In theory this is a kind of direct democracy whereby every citizen over the age of 18 can participate at the local level in a series of Basic People's Congresses. The decisions reached at these congresses are then fed into the General People's Congress (parliament) and are implemented by the General People's Committee (cabinet). These congresses, however, are predominantly there to rubber stamp decisions that have been made by the regime; while in theory their members are free to express their opinions, anyone daring to criticize the regime or its policy decisions would be in an extremely dangerous position.

In reality, the Libyan people do not have the right to choose their own government and Libya remains a military dictatorship. Although Colonel Qadhafi has no official leadership role, preferring to refer to himself as "Brother Leader" or "Guide of the Revolution," all power rests with him, his informal clique of advisers, and increasingly his children.

Qadhafi has publicly declared on many occasions that Western-style democracy is highly flawed and that parliament is the "misrepresentation of the people."[1] Political parties are banned under a 1972 law, and membership in any illegal party is punishable by death. Despite the hopes of some that the new openness to the West would bring reforms in the domestic sphere, in a speech in May 2004 Qadhafi reiterated his intolerance of political parties, complaining that they were useless and outmoded and "belong in museums."

In theory the General People's Congress chooses the secretaries (ministers) who are appointed to the General People's Committee. However, in reality these posts are decided by Qadhafi, and he has kept many of the same few faces in positions of power over the past three decades, simply alternating their positions. The majority of the secretaries in the General People's Committee as of September 2004 have been in high-ranking governmental positions for many years. The current prime minister, Shukri Ghanem, however, is a relative newcomer to the Libyan political scene; Qadhafi appointed him in June 2003 largely at the behest of his son, Saif al-Islam. Although these secretaries have a degree of autonomy as to how to run their ministries, overall policy is dictated by Qadhafi.

Elections are held every four years to choose the members of the Basic People's Congresses, who represent their local region in the General People's Congress. Citizens can put themselves forward as candidates but must be approved by a special committee in order to stand. There is often a problem with finding enough candidates, as the general perception is that these congresses have no real purpose. In the July 2004 elections the regime introduced a new system that it claimed would increase transparency: It did away with the traditional voting booths, and instead every voter was forced to declare the name of his or her choice of candidate before a supervisory committee.

No effective mechanisms prevent those with economic privilege from having undue influence over the voting process, and no attempts are made to stop candidates from offering money and other goods in return for votes. In the July 2004 elections, candidates reportedly had set up tents to provide people with food, as well as offering cigarettes and money to try to attract voters.

Parallel to the formal political system, Qadhafi has also created a network of paralegal bodies that wield significant power and that carry with them the authority of the revolution. The most important is the Revolutionary Committee Movement, which was formed in the 1970s to "safeguard the revolution" and whose members act with almost total impunity. They spread intimidation and fear throughout the population and are currently used by Qadhafi to counterbalance the reformist trend that has been allowed to grow within the regime as a means of engaging with the West. They are given special privileges and have been allowed to dominate many sectors. In the reshuffle of the General People's Committee in March 2004, members of the Revolutionary Committee Movement were brought into the cabinet and given key posts by Qadhafi as a means of balancing the power of the reformist-minded prime minister.

The executive, legislative, and judicial branches of government are unable to oversee the actions of each other and are accountable to Qadhafi alone. It is he who determines how much influence each part of the government may have on any particular issue.

There are a number of powerful interest groups in Libya. In addition to the Revolutionary Committee Movement, important tribes play a key role in the functioning of Libyan society and political life. Libya remains a highly tribalized society and Qadhafi has succeeded in staying in power by playing the tribes against one another. As a result, tribes with links to Qadhafi's own tribal grouping, the Qadhafa, wield significant power. Qadhafi has placed key members of important tribes in certain positions of power.

Qadhafi's children are also highly influential in both the political and economic spheres. The most important of these is currently Qadhafi's son Saif al-Islam Qadhafi. Despite the fact that he runs a charitable foundation and claims to represent civil society, Saif is increasingly taking an active role in the political and economic running of the country. For example, during the course of 2004, he negotiated Libya's compensation deal with Germany for the 1986 La Belle disco bombing. Qadhafi's other children exercise influence in other spheres. Saadi Qadhafi, for example, controls Libyan football, and Mohamed Qadhafi controls the telecommunications sector as well as the Libyan Olympic committee. The increasing power given to Qadhafi's children, and to Saif al-Islam in particular, has prompted much speculation that the colonel is grooming his son to take over as leader.

The regime follows a socialist-style system in which the state is the main employer; as a result many people are guaranteed jobs in the public sector, although wages are not generally sufficient to live on and many people take second jobs to make ends meet. Selection for many jobs, especially high-ranking ones, is made on the basis of personal contacts and the degree of loyalty the applicant displays toward the regime. The government has repeatedly stated in recent months that it is intending to pare down the public sector to make way for more private-sector activity. However, as yet there is little indication as to how it plans to implement such policies. Moreover, the return of international businesses to Libya, especially in the energy sector, will see increased revenues coming directly into the hands of the state. As such there is less pressure on the regime to implement any meaningful reform in this respect.

All organizations must be sanctioned by the state and must conform to the ideals of the Libyan revolution. Thus, any such group is not in a position to make any genuine comment on or exert influence on government policy. As part of its recent attempt to revamp its image in the international community, the regime has increasingly tried to promote the façade of a civil society sector. The effort has been spearheaded by

Qadhafi's son Saif al-Islam. He runs the Qadhafi International Charitable Foundation, which carries out initiatives in its own right but also acts as an umbrella organization for affiliated bodies such as the Libyan Human Rights Society. Qadhafi's daughter Aisha Qadhafi also runs a charitable foundation, Watasimu, that claims to be independent. However, forming a genuinely independent organization would be considered anti-revolutionary and a threat to the interests of the state and therefore a punishable offense. It would also be impossible to secure funding for any such group, as there are no funders in Libya aside from the state, and any money given from abroad must be channeled through the authorities before it can be delivered.

The media is likewise entirely dominated by the state, and by the Revolutionary Committees in particular. The newspapers basically serve as propaganda tools for the regime. The television service is also state run, as are the radio and news agencies. Criticism of Qadhafi or the regime is not permitted. Qadhafi's son Saif al-Islam is currently experimenting with a series of alternative magazines, including *Al-Muatammar*. While these may express less revolutionary zeal than other publications, they still do not permit criticism of the Qadhafi regime and are generally in line with the regime's overall policies and thinking.

The state strictly controls publishing houses and printing presses. The main publishing house in Libya, Al-Ferjani, is privately owned but is in fact heavily linked to the state. Foreign newspapers are not generally available. In contrast, satellite television channels are readily accessible, although the regime tries to block some of them. The Internet is another fast growing information source in the country. Although the state prohibits access to some sites, including those of Libyan opposition groups based abroad, it appears that many Libyans are able to circumvent the restrictions and access these sites, which are rapidly growing in number.

Libel laws exist in Libya, and people have been taken to court in the past over allegations that have appeared in the newspapers. However, information in the public domain is limited, and everything is done within the framework of the regime. No ordinary citizen would dare to challenge what is in the media because these outlets are the mouthpiece of the state.

Cultural expression is restricted as well. Writers and artists are at risk of imprisonment if they produce what is deemed anti-revolutionary works of art. The Libyan Writer's Union, heavily dominated by the Revolutionary Committees Movement, is run by the cultural affairs secretary in the General People's Committee, Mehdi Emberish. In June 2004, Emberish allegedly confiscated the second issue of the Libyan cultural magazine *Arajeem,* which is published in Cairo, because it contained a number of articles about civil society in Libya.

In 2002, the regime announced that it was developing a new draft penal code. This has yet to be adopted; there are no indications as to when it will become legislation. However, despite the expectation of change, it appears that the new legislation will not be any less harsh on anyone daring to criticize the regime. For example, Article 164 of the draft imposes imprisonment on anyone who seeks to undermine the reputation of the goals of the revolution or defames its leader or insults public authorities or the Libyan people.[2]

### Recommendations

- The regime should lift the ban on political parties.
- Genuinely independent civil society actors should be allowed to operate and to make links with and receive funding from foreign nongovernmental organizations (NGOs).
- The regime should permit an independent press that fosters debate.
- A more transparent, merit-based process for entry into the public sector should be introduced.

## CIVIL LIBERTIES – 1.17

Libyan legislation prohibits the use of torture. However, torture remains widespread in Libya, and according to international human rights organizations is used regularly by the security services, especially to extract confessions from suspected regime opponents. Moves of late to address the issue have been largely rhetorical and appear to be aimed primarily at presenting a new image in the international community. The Qadhafi International Charitable Foundation ran an anti-torture initiative in 2003 that included a poster campaign condemning torture. Under the initiative Libyans who had suffered torture at the hands of the state were encouraged to record their experiences with the foundation. However, it appears that none of these cases has been followed up on, and no official has been brought to justice for any torture committed. In April

2004 Qadhafi gave a speech in which he condemned the practice of torture and declared that Libya would ratify international anti-torture conventions. However, as yet there is no evidence to suggest that anything is really changing on this front.

Prison conditions are generally poor, with newly built prisons often replicating the poor design of the existing prisons. There is serious overcrowding and inadequate washing, recreational, and medical facilities. In October 2003 the International Centre for Prison Studies was able to visit Libya to assess the state of the prisons. According to the center, occupancy rates in 2004 stood at 139.5 percent of official prison capacity.[3] Immigrants who have been imprisoned in Libya have complained of appalling prison conditions, as have the Bulgarian and Palestinian medics who were sentenced to death in May 2004 after they were convicted of deliberately infecting over 400 children in a Benghazi hospital with the HIV virus.[4]

Anyone expressing views that do not conform with those of the state is subject to punishment, including imprisonment and torture. For example, in March 2004, political prisoner Fathi el-Jahmi was released under U.S. pressure. After his release he gave a series of telephone interviews to the Arab media in which he criticized the Libyan regime for its use of torture and for its lack of democratic credentials. El-Jahmi and some of his family members were subsequently imprisoned, where, according to Amnesty International, he has been denied essential medical treatment.[5]

The security services operate with relative impunity and regularly carry out large-scale arrests of suspected regime opponents, whether they are involved in violent activity or not. There is no recourse against the state in such instances. Furthermore, the state appears to have no compunction about killing anyone it suspects of challenging its authority.

Long-term pretrial detention is very common in Libya. Laws explicitly limit how long a suspect may be detained, but they are not enforced. In July 2004, pretrial detention prisoners were estimated to make up 62.6 percent of the total prison population.[6] Moreover, prolonged incommunicado detention is widespread, whereby detainees, typically political prisoners, are held for in some cases many years without access to the outside world including their families. There are no effective mechanisms to protect against such treatment. All rights violations are carried out by the state, as there are no non-state actors powerful enough to carry out abuse.

The regime has attempted to introduce legislation to prevent discrimination against women. Qadhafi has actively championed women's rights as part of his progressive revolutionary ideology and encouraged women to take part in politics, providing this is done within the framework of the Jamahiriyah system. The state has encouraged women to participate in the Basic People's Congresses and to join the labor force as well as the armed forces. The government has also promoted women's education and has set up a Secretariat for Women's Affairs. Aside from some parts of family law, such as inheritance, marriage, and divorce, in which general Islamic principles of the Maliki school are practiced, Libyan legislation provides for the equal treatment of men and women. However, much of Libyan society remains very conservative and traditional, and discrimination persists. The state is the main employer, but legislation to prevent discrimination there is not enforced. More could be done to challenge existing customs and practices in order to improve things at the practical level.

Human trafficking is a problem, especially for women from sub-Saharan Africa who are being trafficked into Europe through Libya. Articles 415 and 420 of the penal code criminalize prostitution and prostitution-related activities, including sexual trafficking.[7] The state has arrested some of those involved, but there is little information on exactly what steps the regime has taken and how effective they have been. Those trafficking victims who are caught are punished, generally through imprisonment or deportation. However, Libya has begun working with foreign governments to tackle the problem. In 2003, Italy and Libya signed a bilateral agreement to patrol their waters jointly to try to prevent human trafficking. In February 2004, Libya extradited an Eritrean trafficker to Italy after Rome issued her arrest warrant.[8]

The Libyan regime does not recognize that it has any ethnic minorities despite the presence of Berbers and Tuareg in the country. As a result, there are no reliable statistics on the percentage of the population that these minorities make up. At a meeting of the United Nations Human Rights Committee in October 1998, the Libyan representative complained that the committee seemed to be constantly insisting that minorities existed in Libya when they did not. As a result of this policy

Berber is not recognized as an official language and any child given a Berber name cannot be registered and therefore is not entitled to schooling, health care, or other provisions.

Under a 1981 law, people with disabilities are entitled to various benefits including admission to specialized institutions if they need full-time care, care services at home, and exemption from income tax if they are working. However, the concept of equal opportunities for people with disabilities is not part of the regime's discourse. From the information available, it seems that no legislation has been introduced to protect people with disabilities from discrimination. Such people often face social stigma and are sometimes viewed as a source of embarrassment to their families. No special attempt is made to disseminate information to people with disabilities.

Libya is an Islamic country that broadly follows the Maliki school of Sunni Islam, although Qadhafi has developed his own personal interpretation of Islam to which everyone in Libya is expected to conform. The state is deeply concerned about politicized and especially militant forms of Salafi Islam. Anyone suspected of being involved in or sympathizing with outlawed religious groups risks heavy persecution. In addition, the Libyan regime has generally been intolerant of any outward displays of Islamic behavior that may be deemed excessive. In the 1990s even wearing a beard could bring harassment from the security services. Although there appears to be an increasing tolerance of Islamic dress in recent years, wearing the *niqab* (complete covering of the body and face) or sporting a long beard is still likely to attract suspicion.

The state has total control over the appointment of imams and other spiritual leaders, as well as over mosques and *khutbas* (Friday sermons). Any imam advocating an interpretation of the faith different from that prescribed by Qadhafi risks arrest. The regime also ensures that mosques remain open only for 15 minutes before and after prayer time in order to prevent potential Islamist opponents from gathering and creating a support base inside them. The International Islamic Call Society—a charity tasked with spreading Islam—was set up by Qadhafi in the 1970s and largely acts as a propaganda arm for the regime, although it claims to be independent.

Anyone professing a lack of belief in God is subject to severe social stigma. However, the government is broadly tolerant of other faiths, largely because they do not represent a threat. Those practicing other faiths may do so in their own homes, and a number of Christian churches are permitted to hold services.

Freedom of association is enshrined in Libyan legislation, and Article 6 of the Great Green Charter of Human Rights of the Jamahiriyan Era of 1998 states, "members of the Jamahiriya society are free to form associations, trades unions and leagues in order to defend their professional interest."[9] However, this activity must be channeled through the state. Article 173 of the draft penal code imposes the death penalty on anyone who calls for the establishment of any association or party that is against the Revolution or that aims to harm its public authorities or anyone who establishes, joins, administers, or funds such an association or party.[10]

The numerous trade unions in Libya are strictly controlled by the regime through the Labor Secretariat. All independent trade union activity is banned.[11] The notion of collective bargaining exists in law but is undermined by the fact that the government remains the most important single employer and therefore approves all collective agreements.[12] Assemblies, strikes, sit-ins, and demonstrations are all banned; anyone engaging in such events is liable to severe mistreatment. All Libyan workers are encouraged to join the National Trades Union Federation to show loyalty to the state. Students are expected to join the students' union movement.

Demonstrations and public protests are banned in Libya unless they have been orchestrated by the state in advance. When spontaneous protests do occasionally occur, the regime does not refrain from using excessive force. For example, in February 2004 a popular protest broke out spontaneously in the eastern town of Al-Bayda after a number of employees had not been paid their salaries for several months. According to the Libyan opposition in the United Kingdom, security services reportedly used violence to break up the demonstration and made a series of arrests.

### Recommendations

- Prison guards and security personnel need proper training, possibly with assistance from foreign governments, to teach them not to use torture or other degrading practices.
- The allegations of torture collected by the Qadhafi International Charitable Foundation should be followed up and the perpetrators brought to justice.

- Existing legislation protecting women from discrimination should be implemented and a grass-roots information campaign should be initiated to raise women's awareness of their rights.
- Information campaigns to encourage greater awareness of disability issues should aim to limit social stigma.
- Genuinely independent trade unions should be allowed to form and to make links with international trade union bodies.

## RULE OF LAW – 1.12

It is difficult to separate judicial decisions from the legislative, executive, and other parts of government, as all these institutions are tightly linked and work together in the interests of the revolution. Article 31 of the 1991 Promotion of Freedoms law states, "Judges are independent in their decisions and there is no authority above them apart from the law."[13] Under the law, all parties are treated equally before courts and tribunals. However, Qadhafi has ultimate control over the outcomes of important cases, especially those of a political nature. Moreover, judges and other lawyers are susceptible to bribery. Personal or tribal relationships also play an important part; if one has the necessary connections, it is possible to influence court decisions.

The Supreme Council for Judicial Authority, the administrative arm of the judiciary, is also tasked with studying legislation and improving the laws in accordance with the principles of the Jamahiriya.[14] Civil courts now employ Shari'a judges, who sit in regular courts of appeal and specialize in Shari'a cases (i.e., family cases).

A parallel People's Court system was set up in 1988 to try political offenses and crimes against the state. These courts have their own prosecution service with extensive powers and are heavily influenced by political considerations. Amnesty International has called for the abolition of this court system because it fails to comply with minimum international standards for fair trial.[15] Under this system, defendants cannot choose their own lawyers as these are usually appointed by the court, and hearings generally take place in closed sessions. Furthermore, unlike other courts, the People's Court system is not accountable to any higher judicial body. The future of the People's Courts is uncertain because Qadhafi declared in April 2004 that they should be abolished as they were no longer necessary. The Libyan leader also called for other legal reforms and for a more stringent application of Libyan law. However, as yet there has been no evidence of the implementation of any of these reforms.

The Supreme Council for Judicial Authority is responsible for appointing judges, although in many cases, having the right connections within the regime is the key to appointment. It is very rare for a judge ever to be dismissed in Libya. In order to practice law in Libya, citizens must complete a law degree and then train for two years with a legal firm, most of which have ties to the regime. To become a judge, Libyans must have several years' experience in the legal profession and also must be recommended by the Ministry of Justice.

According to Article 31 of the Constitutional Declaration of December 1969, defendants are presumed innocent until proven guilty. However, in many political cases, the results are predetermined. While there is little information in the public domain about criminal cases, it seems that ordinary citizens have access to fair and public trials, although not necessarily timely. However, in cases of a political nature, there is no guarantee of a fair, public, or timely trial. For example, the 152 members of the Libyan Islamic Group, who were arrested in 1998 on charges of belonging to an outlawed organization, were held incommunicado until April 2001, when the first hearing of their case took place. They were given lawyers appointed by the court. The case was subject to repeated delays, and the defendants were finally handed their sentences in February 2002; two received the death sentence and others long imprisonments. The men appealed but are still awaiting the verdict of the appeal, which has been postponed numerous times, most recently in April 2004.

Those being tried on political charges do not have the right to independent counsel and in many cases have had lawyers imposed upon them. Libyan lawyers have complained that in many cases, they receive the file for the case only in the first trial session. This leaves them insufficient time to review each case adequately.[16] In criminal cases, the government's Popular Lawyers Office provides legal representation for some who cannot afford to pay their own legal fees. However, this process is subject to corruption. Prosecutors can be directed by the executive, particularly in political cases. Public officials are on occasion prosecuted for wrongdoing if Qadhafi decides he wants to make an example of them, although the process appears to be arbitrary and driven primarily by political motives.

There is neither effective civilian control of the armed forces nor a defense ministry. Qadhafi has the rank of colonel, and all matters relating to defense are in his hands. He has created a multilayered and complex network of security services that are all answerable to him. He regularly carries out purges of the armed forces and security services to ensure that no power base that might act as a challenge to his authority may develop. He has drawn many of his security personnel from certain tribes, such as the Warfalla tribe, which is a member of the same confederation as Qadhafi's own tribe. Qadhafi's sons have also been able to wield influence within certain sections of the armed forces. The police, military, and security agencies are an organic part of the political process, their primary duty is to protect the regime.

In March 2004, in what was viewed by many as a positive step, the justice ministry was separated from the public security ministry. It was assumed that this was in order to allow for a number of judicial reforms under the reform-minded justice minister, Ali Omar Abu Baker. However, the appointment of regime hard-liner and Revolutionary Committee member Nasser al-Mabrouk to the post of secretary for public security signaled a continuing hard-line stance on security issues.

In a speech to the new graduates of the Public Security Services in April 2004, Qadhafi announced that the police would now take on a military role and become a military force to defend the country from terrorists. Their former duties would be taken over by the People's Congresses, who would be responsible for tasks such as traffic control. In the same speech, in a clear demonstration of who is in charge of such agencies, the leader announced that as with the armed forces, he would take personal responsibility for promoting police officers up the ranks.

Until 2004, Libya's property laws held that one could own property only to live in and that owning more than one property or renting property out was illegal. However, in May 2004, new legislation was passed to free up the property market. Law number 49 was passed, making it legal to buy property for investment and to rent out. Any Libyan national can own property. The state enforces property rights and contracts provided they are within the framework of the Jamihiryah system. However, it does not protect against confiscation of property or possessions.

In fact, confiscating property is one method used by the regime to intimidate and harass those it deems to have been disloyal. The Revolutionary Committees have been known in the past to bulldoze the houses of regime opponents and their families. No special provisions are made for Berber or Tuareg property customs.

*Recommendations*

- All citizens must have the right to independent counsel and be able to choose their own defense lawyer.
- The judiciary should be open to external scrutiny, and training courses should be set up for lawyers in issues such as human rights.
- Clear, concise, and easily accessible information sources should be produced to explain the country's laws and rights provisions to the population.
- Exceptional courts should be abolished.

## ANTICORRUPTION AND TRANSPARENCY – 0.19

Libya is steeped in bureaucracy and regulatory controls, providing ample opportunity for bribery and corruption, and both are rife. The state under Qadhafi has traditionally controlled all aspects of the economy. Most economic activity is based on the energy sector, with oil export revenues accounting for more than 95 percent of hard currency earnings and 75 percent of government receipts.[17] Moreover, Qadhafi's sons also have significant influence on the economy. The eldest son, Mohamed Qadhafi, is in charge of the telecommunications sector, while Saif al-Islam has his own investment company and plays an active role in the oil sector. Hannibal Qadhafi controls the marine transportation sector. Until recently, most private economic activity was banned. However, as part of its new openness to the international community, the regime has begun to open up Libya's economy. Still, private sector activity remains on a small scale for the time being, and it is necessary to have the right connections within the regime to be able to set up a private business.

There is little separation between private interests and public office. Many of those on the boards of important Libyan companies that profess to be private also hold important government posts. The elite in Libya is small and controls almost everything in the economic and political spheres. There are no financial disclosure procedures, nor is there any protection against conflicts of interest in the private sector.

Libya has legislation to deal with the problem of corruption; sentences for such offenses are severe. The penal code criminalizes bribery, and a series of laws criminalizes economic offenses, including corruption and favoritism; the laws require the reporting of illegal gains to the state. A Supreme Audit Institution reportedly promotes financial transparency and a Board of the General Peoples Control is tasked with suppressing corruption. A law was introduced in 1994 to fight financial corruption and black marketeering among other things, but it was enforced by the Purification Committees. These were set up in particular to root out corruption and were composed of members of the Revolutionary Committees tasked with safeguarding the revolution. The committees were primarily a political tool and used the legislation to spread further fear and intimidation among the population. Businessmen, traders, and shop owners were arrested arbitrarily in the mid-1990s on charges of corruption, dealing in foreign goods, and funding Islamist groups, and many businesses were closed. These committees are still in existence, although they are less active than in the past.

Despite the legislation, corruption remains a significant problem. Allegations of corruption by government officials are not investigated or prosecuted unless the leadership so dictates. Those with the right connections are able to act above the law. Qadhafi has imprisoned certain officials on charges of corruption or embezzlement, but this has been to make an example of them or to make a political point. Likewise, such allegations are only aired in the news media for political purposes. As a result, corruption and bribery permeate Libyan society. This extends to the oil sector; Transparency International has noted that in Libya "public contracting in the oil sector is plagued by revenues vanishing into the pockets of western oil executives, middlemen and local officials."[18]

There are no effective mechanisms to assist victims of corruption. It is very difficult and dangerous for an ordinary citizen to make a claim against someone in the regime or with links to the regime regarding corruption accusations or any other charges.

The higher education system is not immune from bribery. As with most of Libya's institutions, the Revolutionary Committee Movement has a significant influence within this sector.

The Libyan tax system is inconsistent and subject to change at short notice.[19] No effective internal audit systems ensure the accountability of tax collection. Like many sectors in Libya, the process is subject to inefficiency and corruption. Indeed, no effective auditing bodies free from political influence can report on the misspending and misuse of funds.

Public access to government information is very limited, and legal, regulatory, and judicial processes are not transparent. The regime makes little of its information public. This is partly due to excessive bureaucracy but also because Qadhafi uses this secrecy to maintain an atmosphere of orchestrated chaos to prevent any alternative power base from developing. Some improvements have been made in providing basic statistical information in recent years since the National Organization of Information and Documentation of the Planning Secretariat set up a web site that publishes data as well as books. The Web site is not updated regularly. Libyan legislation is difficult to access, although new laws that are passed by the General People's Congress are published in the newspapers and can sometimes be found in pamphlets on sale in the major bookshops.

Citizens do not have the legal right to obtain information about government operations or to petition for it. Anyone without the necessary connections would not be able to question or demand information about any part of the Libyan system, as this could have severe consequences.

Despite the fact that the budget is passed by the General People's Congress, its content is decided by Qadhafi and his advisers. The information filters down to the population as and when the regime sees fit. The budget is not subject to any review or meaningful scrutiny. Detailed expenditure accounting is not available, although some details are provided through the National Information and Documentation Office.

Government contracts are not awarded in any open, transparent way that ensures effective competition. All foreign assistance is prohibited unless it goes through government channels. No information is available concerning its administration and distribution.

### Recommendations

- The existing corruption law, which requires reporting of ill-gotten gains and provides for severe punishments for corrupt officials, must be applied more rigorously and without political prejudice.

- An independent study should be conducted to ascertain how much revenue is lost each year through corruption.
- An information campaign should be run to warn against corrupt practices and encourage and protect those who have been the victims of corruption to come forward with their grievances.
- More information should be readily available about government processes, legislation, and statistics, possibly through information centers. This information should not be used as a propaganda tool.
- Web sites should be set up to provide accurate information about the workings of the Libyan state as well as its laws.

## NOTES

[1] Muammar Al-Qadhafi, "The Green Book" (Tripoli: World Centre for the Study and Research of the Green Book, n.d.)

[2] "Libya: Time to Make Human Rights a Reality" (London: Amnesty International [AI], MDE 19/002/2004, April 2004).

[3] "Libya Prison Brief" (London: International Centre for Prison Studies, 14 December 2004), http://www.kcl.ac.uk/depsta/rel/icps/worldbrief/africa_records.php?code=28.

[4] "The Trial in Libya" (Bulgarian News Agency, 27 August 2002), http://www.bta.bg/site/libya/en/09hearings.htm.

[5] "Libya: Incommunicado detention/health concern" (London: AI, MDE 19/015/2004, 17 September 2004).

[6] "Libya Prison Brief" (London: International Centre for Prison Studies), http://www.kcl.ac.uk/depsta/rel/icps/worldbrief/africa_records.php?code=28.

[7] "Libya Country Report" (Washington, DC: Protection Project, 2002), http://www.protectionproject.org/human_rights/countryreport/libya.htm.

[8] *Trafficking in Persons Report* (Washington, DC: U.S. Dept. of State, Office to Monitor and Combat Trafficking in Persons, 14 June 2004), http://www.state.gov/g/tip/rls/tiprpt/2004/33200.htm.

[9] "Great Green Charter of Human Rights of the Jamahiriyan Era," 12 June 1988, http://www.geocities.com/Athens/8744/grgreen.htm.

[10] "Libya: Time to Make Human Rights a Reality" (London: AI, MDE 19/002/2004, April 2004).

[11] "Libya: Annual Survey of Violations of Trade Union Rights" (Brussels: International Confederation of Free Trade Unions, 2004), http://www.icftu.org/displaydocument.asp?Index=991219427&Language=EN.

[12] Ibid.

[13] "Libya: Time to Make Human Rights a Reality" (London: AI, MDE 19/002/2004, April 2004).

[14] "Libyans for Justice," http://www.libyans4justice.com (in Arabic).

[15] "Libya: Time to Make Human Rights a Reality" (London: AI, MDE 19/002/2004, April 2004).

[16] Ibid.

[17] "Libya: EIA Country Analysis Brief" (Washington, DC: U.S. Dept. of Energy, Energy Information Administration, January 2004), http://www.eia.doe.gov/emeu/cabs/libya.html.

[18] "Corruption is rampant in 60 countries, and the public sector is plagued by bribery, says TI" (Berlin: Transparency International, press release, 20 October 2004), http://www.transparency.org/pressreleases_archive/2004/2004.10.20.cpi.en.html.

[19] "Doing Business Libya" (London: UK Trade and Investment, undated), http://www.tradepartners.gov.uk/libya/doingbusiness/08_customs/customs.shtml.

# MAURITANIA

CAPITAL: Nouakchott
POPULATION: 3 million
GNI PER CAPITA: $280

**SCORES**
ACCOUNTABILITY AND PUBLIC VOICE: 2.00
CIVIL LIBERTIES: 2.39
RULE OF LAW: 2.12
ANTICORRUPTION AND TRANSPARENCY: 1.97
(scores are based on a scale of 0 to 7, with
0 representing weakest and 7 representing
strongest performance)

*Cédric Jourde*

## INTRODUCTION

Like many of its African counterparts, the Mauritanian regime is a hy-brid, combining democratic and authoritarian traits. On the one hand, Mauritania embarked upon a path of political liberalization in 1991, after 31 years of single-party and military rule. The 1991 constitution provided for a pluralist political regime and for the official recognition of universal human rights. For the first time since the year of indepen-dence (1960), the country has held an uninterrupted cycle of multi-party elections at the municipal, legislative, and presidential levels. Independent newspapers have flourished, allowing for an unprece-dented degree of public criticism of the government. New actors (i.e., local and transnational nongovernmental organizations [NGOs]) have entered the political field. In addition, the state's violent repression of non-Arabic-speaking minorities (Haalpulaar, Sooninke, and Wolof), which peaked in the 1989–1990 period, has been receding since the mid-1990s. In 2004, under pressure from international organizations,

---

**Cédric Jourde** is assistant professor at the University of Ottawa, School of Political Studies.

the Mauritanian government and civil society groups approved a "National Plan of Action for Human Rights," which the United Nations Development Program describes as "the most comprehensive document on the human rights situation in Mauritania to date."[1]

On the other hand, beyond these formal democratic reforms lies another reality. *Ancien régime* elites have maintained their privileged positions at the top of the state and have co-opted many opposition activists. They have successfully perpetuated authoritarian practices and skillfully manipulated the liberalization reforms. For instance, although elections have been organized on a regular basis, the regime has never put itself at risk: The incumbent president, who came to power through a coup in 1984, won all three presidential elections since 1992 in a process generally seen as unfair. Illustrative of such a process, in the most recent presidential election, in November 2003, security forces arrested the president's most serious opponent on the day before the election and again two days after. The government also cracked down on alleged Islamist leaders and organizations, while simultaneously harassing, arresting, and jailing opposition leaders and disbanding opposition parties. For their part, the presidential party and its smaller allies controlled 100 percent of the seats in the National Assembly in 1992, 99 percent in 1996, and 87 percent in 2001.

The public administration is highly politicized; the distribution of public offices and the management of public resources are influenced by loyalty to the regime and connections to powerful networks. Despite the civilian nature of the new constitution, the political (and financial) influence of top military and security personnel exceeds that of elected representatives and of most members of the cabinet. American and NATO support to the Mauritanian military, a consequence of Mauritania's allegiance to the "War on Terror," runs the risk of consolidating this regime and its allies in the security apparatus.

As the regime refuses to undertake substantive democratic reforms, it is more likely to witness radical forms of opposition. A failed coup occurred in June 2003, led by military officers who were frustrated by the government's foreign policy (*rapprochement* with the United States and Israel) and by its domestic military policy (perceived favoritism and discrimination based on regional identities). Two other coup attempts allegedly occurred in August and September of 2004.

## ACCOUNTABILITY AND PUBLIC VOICE – 2.00

In 1991, Mauritania adopted a constitution that provides for a pluralist political system. This led to an uninterrupted cycle of elections at the presidential, legislative, and municipal levels. In general, however, these elections have not been conducted fairly and freely. The only exceptions to this were the 2001 municipal and legislative elections.[2]

As the November 2003 presidential election approached, authorities pledged to replicate the conditions of the October 2001 legislative and municipal elections, including state funding for political parties on the basis of their representation in municipal councils;[3] the guarantee of fair media coverage; the establishment of a new computerized voters' list; and a new "unfalsifiable" identity card.[4] However, as in the previous elections, the government refused to create an independent electoral commission to organize and supervise the presidential election; it continued to rely upon the interior ministry to perform these functions. Opposition parties claimed that the presidency's formal and informal control over the public administration, and more specifically the interior ministry, prevented the organization of a fair election. In addition, foreign observers were not invited.[5]

As election day approached, unfair state interference increased. The main opposition candidate, Mohamed Khouna Ould Haidallah (who had been head of state until he was ousted in a coup by the current president), was specifically targeted. Security forces searched his house and those of his collaborators. Surprisingly, the chair of President Maaouya Ould Sid'Ahmed Taya's campaign staff—not an official representative of the state—showed the media a document allegedly found in Ould Haidallah's house that contained a plan to stage a coup. Security forces arrested Ould Haidallah's two sons a few days prior to the election. On election eve, Ould Haidallah and members of his organization were arrested. Ould Haidallah was released on the same day, possibly because the election would have been cancelled otherwise. But he was arrested again two days after the election, with 14 members of his campaign staff. Authorities accused him of plotting a coup and of receiving money from a foreign (i.e., Libyan) source.[6]

In addition to the arrests of the main candidate, newspapers reported that on election day, opposition parties' representatives at the voting sites were denied access to the voter list by interior ministry officials, were denied their right to compare each voter's identity card with the voter list, and had their mobile phones taken away.[7]

President Ould Taya won the election, for the third consecutive time, with 67 percent of the vote. His main opponent, Ould Haidallah, obtained 18.7 percent. The relatively fair campaigning opportunities of the 2001 legislative and municipal elections have not been replicated. These results confirmed the iron law of Mauritanian politics: Coups have been the *only* form of rotation of power at the top of the state since Mauritania became independent.

A month after the election, the criminal court gave Ould Haidallah and his staff members a suspended sentence of five years and stripped them of their civic and political rights, which means that they cannot run in elections.[8] Ould Haidallah's lawyers called upon the Supreme Court to annul the elections and, later on, to reexamine the accusations of the coup attempt and the deprivation of their client's political and civil rights; both demands were rejected.

In April 2004, Mauritania held elections for one-third of the Senate seats. The ruling party and one of its small allies won 15 seats and the opposition won 3 seats. The opposition denounced the administration's biased monitoring of the election, claiming for example that undue pressure was put on opposition municipal councilors to vote for the ruling party's candidate.[9]

More generally, as a Mauritanian legal expert explains, the 1991 constitution sanctions "the preeminence of the Head of State."[10] In effect, in theory *and* in practice, the state is highly centralized in the hands of the president, leaving the legislative and the judicial branches in a condition of political subordination. The president appoints and dismisses the government, and he can dissolve the National Assembly. In addition, he appoints three of the six judges to the Constitutional Council (including the court's president), whose task is, among other things, to validate electoral results (including the results of presidential elections); there is no oversight of these appointments. Also, the presidency is not subject to a term limit (Article 28). The power of the presidency is strengthened in practice by the fact that the president's party—the Parti républicain, démocratique et social (PRDS)—has always had control of the National Assembly and the Senate. The highest proportion of seats the opposition has ever had in the National Assembly is 13.5 percent

(11 seats out of 81), following the 2001 election. It won only one seat in 1996 and boycotted the 1992 legislative elections.

Opposition political organizations are regularly the target of unfair interference by the state. Over the past five years, the government disbanded some of the most popular opposition parties: Action pour le changement (AC) in January 2002; Union des forces démocratiques/ère nouvelle in October 2000; and At-tali'a in 1999. Opposition leaders have also been targeted: Ch'bih Ould Melainine (Front Populaire) was arrested in April 2001 and sentenced to five years in prison; he was eventually granted a presidential pardon.[11] Ahmed Ould Daddah (Union des forces démocratiques/ère nouvelle, before it was dismantled by the government) was arrested five times between 1998 and 2000.[12] State harassment of political opposition and the lack of political openness may lead political actors to opt increasingly for more violent forms of change, as illustrated by the failed coup of June 2003 and two alleged coup attempts in August–September 2004. However, opposition parties also have some responsibility for the ruling party's and incumbent president's permanent rule, as they have fought intense struggles among themselves, based partly on personal and factional rivalries and partly on ideological differences.[13]

The official centralization of power parallels unofficial forms of domination. Informal political relations connect the presidency to local rural leaders, powerful businessmen, and public servants. These patron-client relations provide a strong political base of support for the president and can help secure votes before, and irrespective of, electoral campaigns. This suggests that a narrow analytical focus on elections and electoral campaigning opportunities is not sufficient to understanding why a rotation of power through elections has not occurred since 1991.

The politicization of public institutions also weakens Mauritanian democracy. Appointments to, and management of, public offices are neither meritocratic nor transparent. Rather, they form a mechanism that rewards political loyalty to the regime and punishes political opposition. As one observer argues, the selection of public servants is determined less by formal education and diploma and much more by one's proximity to the top decision-making circle and by the president's informal policy of balancing among the different regions, tribes, and ethnic groups.[14]

No civic associations can operate without a formal interior ministry authorization, which can be denied or removed at any time. Past refusals to authorize NGOs were justified by these organizations' strong stand on issues such as slavery and human rights. In general, civic groups do not exert substantive influence on state policies and legislation. It must be said that the Mauritanian political system is not constituted only of formal organizations, such as NGOs and political parties. Political influence upon state policies emanates in large part from informal webs of networks and factions. These are based on various forms of loyalty, ranging from one's home region, lineage group, or religious brotherhood to childhood friendships. Some of these networks have survived for several years while others have changed and reformed at a fast pace.

Privately owned newspapers have flourished since 1992, before which only the state-owned daily was authorized. Yet, state censorship of independent media is frequent, not to mention the less quantifiable self-censorship. The state owns the only printing facility (Imprimerie nationale) in the country, and the ministry of the interior is entitled by Article 11 of the Law on the Press to censor any publication that "threatens the principles of Islam or the credibility of the State, or that threatens the general interest as well as public order and security." Newspapers, most of which are weeklies, must submit each issue to the ministry of the interior, which then authorizes or prohibits publication based on Article 11. (Two of the three daily newspapers are state-owned [in French and Arabic] and the third is relatively close to the government's position.) Article 11 has been used to censor the press when newspaper articles talk about (in no specific order) the Western Sahara dispute (in which Mauritania is officially neutral), Islamist organizations, corruption by public officials and/or big businesses, slavery, and bilateral relations with Israel.[15]

In October 2003, the government forbade publication of one issue of each of four newspapers because they included a pro-opposition advertisement. In May 2004, a journalist of *L'Éveil-Hebdo* was questioned by police forces after he had published an article that described daily police acts of intimidation and brutality against members of the local population.[16] In September 2004, the government shut down the newspaper *Al Jamahir;* no official reason was given other than that the shutdown was "in conformity with Article 11," although the fact that this newspaper is said to be ideologically and financially close to Libya, which the government accused of supporting coup plotters, could be an explanation.[17]

The state has never authorized the creation of national independent television and radio stations. However, both international shortwave radio stations and international television channels broadcast by satellite enjoy a wide audience in Mauritania. The boundaries of state censorship now seem to extend to opinions expressed on these foreign channels. For instance, on November 23, 2003, a Mauritanian professor at the University of Nouakchott was arrested because he had criticized the American invasion of Iraq on Al-Jazeera.

*Recommendations*

- The constitution should limit the number of terms a president can serve.
- Elections should be monitored by a fully independent agency to enhance the legitimacy of electoral results (and of the elections' winners). The relatively good conditions of the 2001 legislative and municipal elections should be replicated in future electoral contests, including for the presidential election.
- Limitations should be placed on the central state's power in rural areas, where the representatives of the interior ministry and of the defense ministry currently enjoy unchecked powers. Central government representatives should be at least partly accountable to local elected councils.
- Although the need to achieve a certain balance among the different regional groups is valid, effective control mechanisms are nonetheless needed to prevent the over-politicization of the public service. Appointments in the civil service should be based on merit.
- Article 11 of the Law on the Press should be abolished. Independent Mauritanian broadcast stations should be authorized.

## CIVIL LIBERTIES – 2.39

In theory, Article 13 of the Mauritanian constitution protects citizens from torture and from inhumane treatment in prisons. Article 91 proscribes arbitrary detention, and detention without trial cannot exceed 72 hours, with the exception of detention for crimes against the security of the state, in which case detention may last up to 30 days. A mediator of the republic (similar to an ombudsman) was established in 1993, both to investigate abuse of citizens by representatives of the public administration and to make recommendations to settle these *différends* (disputes). However, this legal framework does not match the empirical reality. When citizens seek to defend themselves they most often resort to informal mechanisms based on tribal, ethnic, and family-based connections.

In the aftermath of the failed coup attempt of June 8, 2003, about 130 members of the military were arrested, as well as members of their families.[18] On August 9, 2004, about 50 people, including military officers, religious leaders, and civilians, were arrested after the government allegedly uncovered another coup plot. About a dozen more military officers and civilians were arrested at the end of September 2004, including two leaders of the 2003 coup attempt. They were officially accused of "attempting to destroy and to change the constitutional order with the use of weapons . . . and to use armed groups to threaten the state."[19] Throughout these waves of arrests, defense lawyers have denounced several violations of the law. They asserted that the prisoners were illegally denied access to their family members and lawyers and that the duration of detention without trial exceeded the legal limit.[20] Human Rights Watch echoed these denunciations and stated that the "lack of access to the military officers that are in detention raises serious concerns about their treatment, given past reports of inhuman conditions of detention in Mauritania."[21]

The government has never authorized formal investigations of allegations of torture. The only measure it has taken recently was to let some foreign journalists talk to a selected number of prisoners. However, this took place in the presence of their guards, thereby making it difficult to determine the extent to which torture is practiced in Mauritanian jails. Official punishment of perpetrators is even less frequent.

Prison conditions depend on the detainee's status and political connections. Families are often expected to provide for prisoners' basic needs. Without such connections and family support, a prisoner's living conditions can be execrable. Limits on length of detention without trial are arbitrarily implemented, with the exception of high-profile prisoners, who enjoy strong media exposure and legal support.

Formal institutions are generally inadequate for protecting citizens against state and non-state abuses. Even the office of the mediator of the republic is powerless, given its lack of independence from the executive branch: The president appoints the mediator, its budget is drawn from the president's office, and its annual report is presented to the president only. Also, only deputies and mayors (elected representatives) can lodge a complaint with the mediator. Consequently, people often resort to informal networks of personal connections to express their grievances and to defend themselves when their rights are violated by state authorities. Most people are forced to plead for a personal favor in cases in which they should simply be able to secure a legal right.

No political assassination was reported in 2003–2004. However, up to this day, the state-sponsored killings of hundreds of Haalpulaar, Wolof, and Sooninke citizens and soldiers between 1989 and 1991 have never been investigated. The Amnesty Law of 1993 protects state officials involved in these human rights violations.

Slavery is both a highly controversial and complex issue. Historically, all four ethnic groups of Mauritania shared a relatively similar hierarchy based on social status, with groups such as religious scholars, warriors, artisans, freed slaves, and slaves. Although today these statuses no longer refer to actual professional occupations, generally speaking, high status continues to generate prestige and favoritism, and low-ranking people such as "freed slaves" face exclusion and discrimination.

The government and opposition groups are involved in a fierce battle over the issue of slavery. The government argues that only the after-effects of slavery remain, not slavery itself; after the official abolishment of slavery in 1980, a June 2003 law forbid trafficking in persons and the new labor code outlaws forced labor. The government also argues that poverty-reduction policies targeting vulnerable populations are addressing the after-effects of slavery, although the official discourse never explicitly mentions any of the low-ranking social groups. For their part, opposition parties and NGOs argue that slavery still persists among the *Bidhân* (Arabic-speaking communities), specifically outside the urban centers. They argue that the 1980 law has two major weaknesses: it does not specify any sanction for those who violate the law, and it provides for compensation only for former masters, not for former slaves. The government's arrest of activists (in 1998) and journalists (in 2005) and the disbanding of the AC in 2002, all on the basis of these parties' anti-slavery discourse and actions, reinforces the belief that slavery in some form has not completely disappeared.

Most analysts agree that the 1980 law in itself did not change anything.[22] Within the Arabic-speaking community, many *Haratin* (a contested social status that means "freed slaves") continue to be heavily dependent economically, socially, and politically on their social superiors. Studies suggest that changes are taking place, mostly due to socioeconomic transformations (urbanization, industrialization, and the rapid growth of the army following the Saharan war). The Haratin's dependency has been challenged in urban centers, and sometimes ended altogether. Even in such cases, however, the Haratin's extreme poverty persists.[23] As one of Mauritania's most reputable social scientists observes, the adoption of an anti-slavery legal framework is not "sufficient to abolish the status [of "former slaves" or "slaves"], which is inscribed in a complex web of economic, ideological and symbolic relations."[24] The constitution ordains the equality of all citizens but does not offer any specific guideline in cases of racial or ethnic discrimination. The Law of the Public Administration stipulates that there cannot be any discrimination against civil servants on the basis of their opinion, gender, or race (Article 15). In practice, however, citizens who feel they have been the subject of racial or ethnic discrimination in employment or occupation are left with few legal tools. No claims of racial discrimination have been filed so far, suggesting that individuals who feel that they are treated unfairly prefer to resort to personal and informal connections; unfortunately, not all citizens have access to such connections. State resources and appointments in the public service are informally distributed along tribal and ethnic lines.[25] However, these appointments generally benefit individual public servants and rarely the community to which they belong.

The State Secretary for Women's Condition is the main office through which the state seeks to promote women's rights in the country; international organizations—mainly UN branches—and local NGOs advise and put pressure on the office. For instance, in 2004 a local organization obtained the support of the imams of Nouakchott in their campaign against sexual harassment. In July 2001, the National Assembly adopted the personal status code, which put forward some legal improvements regarding women's rights. Husbands can no longer forbid their wives to study or to work outside the house, and wives can refuse polygamous weddings. But the personal status code confirms the husband's unilateral right to repudiate his wife, as authorized by Sharia. Marriage at an early age is common among Mauritanian women: In 2003, 23 percent of women between the ages of 20 and 29 were married before the age of 15.[26] The state's capacity and willingness to prevent and punish discrimination against women is relatively weak.[27] For instance, a UN report has documented the persistence of different forms of violence against women, including genital mutilation.[28]

Women's rights, as well as their socioeconomic and political conditions, are largely dependent on their ethnic, caste, and geographical (rural/urban) background. In the 2001 legislative election, three women were elected to the National Assembly, accounting for 3.7 percent of the total number of elected representatives. As of 2004, only three women were among the 54 members of the Senate. Women account for only 6.6 percent of the top positions in the public administration.[29] Hopefully the increasing rate of female school enrollment as well as the recent adoption of a compulsory education law (for boys *and* girls) will improve this situation, although this will also require that civil service appointments become transparent and merit based.

People with disabilities who wish to improve their living conditions and status in society cannot count on strong state support. They are usually cared for by their families, to the extent possible given the extreme poverty of most of the population. A special office of the Direction des affaires sociales (social affairs division) is in charge of providing educational and professional help to people with disabilities. The government asserts that its Social Affairs Secretary has "re-educated and provided [disabled people] with equipment" and that "300 physically handicapped children have been placed in elementary schools and 58 deaf or blind children are receiving special education. 218 handicapped adults are benefiting from a community-based reintegration project."[30] A group of local organizations formed the National Association for Disabled People in 1999 in an attempt to lobby for much greater changes. With the help of international organizations, people with disabilities recently called upon the state to adopt a legal framework and adopt measures that would protect their rights and promote their interests more substantially.[31]

Between 1989 and 1991, state officials directly and indirectly encouraged the assassination and expulsion from the national territory of citizens from the Haalpulaar, Sooninke, and Wolof ethnic minorities. Since then, gross violations have decreased in scope and number. However, less quantifiable (and recordable) forms of exclusion continue. For instance, individuals from these minorities are rarely appointed to strategic positions in the political and security apparatus. Tribal and regional identities within the Bidhân community can also be the source of discrimination. For instance, given that most of the alleged coup plotters in 2003 came from eastern Mauritania, many citizens from these regions were arrested or have lost their jobs, especially those at the top of the state administration and in the military.

The freedom of cultural expression of ethnic minorities has slowly improved since the aftermath of the 1989–1991 state-sponsored violence. The state has authorized the creation of associations that promote the Haalpulaar, Sooninke, and Wolof cultures. However, Arabic remains the only official language, whereas Haalpulaar, Sooninke, and Wolof are only national languages. Arabic and French are now the only two languages of public education, following the 1999 educational reform that abolished a special educational program in the Haalpulaar, Sooninke, and Wolof languages.

Mauritania is officially an Islamic republic. The state allows the few non-Muslims (Western expatriates and West African workers and refugees) to practice their religions. Since 1994, the government has increasingly controlled and repressed political activities that it defined as Islamist. This process has accelerated since the spring of 2003, when the government arrested high-profile Islamic figures while shutting down numerous Islamic associations. In June 2003 the council of ministers adopted a draft law that turned mosques into public facilities, thereby allowing the state to monitor sermons, control the mosques' sources of funding, and define imams' rules of conduct.[32]

The constitution guarantees citizens' right of association. However, this right is often violated in practice, as the state regularly interferes with the activities and even the existence of political parties, NGOs, and various associations, as illustrated by the numerous arrests and dismantling of opposition organizations and associations. Human Rights Watch claims that the arrests of religious leaders, opposition politicians, and social activists "have been justified in terms of the need to suppress terrorism, but appear rather to be designed to silence those who are critical of the government."[33] In addition, new parties and organizations have been denied official authorization. For instance, in October 2003, the government refused to authorize the creation of an Observatory for Democracy and Transparency, as requested by a group of citizens.[34] In

April 2004, the government refused to authorize a party created by supporters of Ould Haidallah, the Party of the Democratic Convergence. In May 2004, however, it authorized another party, Assawab, which also included supporters of Ould Haidallah. Although Mauritanians are allowed to join trade unions, two of the three main unions complain that the new labor code adopted in May 2004 further restrains their rights and activities.[35] Since the establishment of the 1991 constitution, Mauritanians are not compelled by the state to belong to any association. However, indirect incentives to join the ruling party do exist, given that the management and distribution of public resources are permeated by political clientelism.

In 2004, the streets of Nouakchott were relatively calm, and no major protests took place. However, police forces have severely repressed demonstrations in recent years, particularly when demonstrators protested against the Israeli government's handling of the second Intifada, against Mauritania's diplomatic relations with Israel, and against the war in Iraq.

*Recommendations*

- The Mauritanian state should both officially acknowledge and investigate the 1989–1991 human rights violations against citizens of Haalpulaar, Sooninke, and Wolof origins. This is the precondition for a real process of national unification.
- The government must authorize independent investigations of detention conditions and of allegations of torture and illegal arrests by state forces. This would simply confirm already existing constitutional rights.
- In order to end controversies about the existence of slavery in the country and in accordance with the existing law, the judicial system must proceed in a transparent and effective way when citizens report cases of slavery, trafficking of persons, and forced labor.
- State harassment of opposition political parties and opposition movements in general, and against organizations labeled as Islamic in particular, should cease.
- The government, with support from UN agencies and NGOs, should sustain and consolidate its new program of improving female enrollment at the secondary-school level. Measures would

include improved educational facilities and resources, especially in rural areas; financial support for teenage girls' families; awareness programs for parents and teachers; and enforcement of the compulsory education law for both boys and girls.

## RULE OF LAW – 2.12

The Mauritanian judicial system combines Western and Islamic (Malikite rite) legal traditions. The constitution guarantees the independence of the judiciary in theory (Article 89). An organic law also protects judges from undue influence (Law 94-012). However, the constitution as well as informal political practices point to the domination of the president over the justice system. The constitution enables the president to appoint three of the six members of the constitutional council, including its chair, whose voice predominates in case of a split vote. One of the constitutional council's tasks is to validate electoral results, including those of the presidential election. The president also appoints all five members of the high Islamic council, which advises the president on matters of Islamic law. The president presides over the Conseil supérieur de la magistrature (superior council of magistrates), whose tasks include the nomination of judges. In effect, the same politicization that prevails in the civil service also applies to the judiciary, both in terms of nominations and in terms of its inner working. As an independent newspaper argued, Mauritanian judges "in most cases do not respect the procedures and legal texts they are supposed to implement."[36]

In cases involving politically sensitive issues, the informal dominance of the presidency over the work of prosecutors and judges generally prevails, as the recent arrests of and charges against opponents suggest. In cases of lower political intensity, financial influences and political connections reduce the impartiality of the justice system. Attempts by the executive to influence the judiciary can also be seen in the recent dispute about the Mauritanian Bar. In June 2002, a lawyer close to the opposition, Mahfoudh Ould Bettah, claimed he had been elected as the *bâtonnier* (chair) of the Mauritanian Bar. The government, however, declared that it recognized the victory of another candidate, who happened to be a member of the presidential party. Since then, the latter has served as chair of the Bar. However, the international Union of Arab

Lawyers gave strong support to Ould Bettah by stating that they would only recognize his victory and that only he can represent Mauritania at the Union's meetings.[37] More generally, the contrast between the almost complete absence of legal investigation and condemnations of high-ranking civil servants, ruling party officials, and security and military personnel and the increasingly high number of arrests and condemnations of members of the political opposition and activists underscores the politicization of the judiciary.

Leading international organizations have highlighted the lack of adequate training of judges and of the personnel of the ministry of justice and have funded programs to tackle that problem.[38] However, formal legal training will have limited effects if informal political obstacles continue to block the real application of the law. Better training cannot eliminate political motivation.

A legal reform was passed in 1999 that, among other things, provides for better financial and legal support for poor citizens charged with an offense. No information on the actual effectiveness of this legal assistance is available. The constitution considers citizens innocent until proved otherwise.

The political power of the military began to rise when Mauritania fought the war in the Western Sahara in 1975. At the onset of the war, Mauritania had 2,000 troops; it had 18,000 troops three years later when it withdrew from the conflict.[39] Between 1978 and 1991, Mauritania was governed by various military juntas. The current president, Colonel Ould Taya, came to power in 1984 after he staged a coup against Ould Haidallah. Although the 1991 constitution provides for a civil form of government, in reality the military still is a key pillar of the regime. Its loyalty is secured through the distribution of significant political and economic advantages to top officers.[40] Security matters are the reserved domains of the military, as well as the internal affairs of the army. However, the failed coup of June 2003 and the alleged coup attempts of 2004 suggest growing frustration among segments of the military and breaches in its loyalty to the regime.

Article 15 of the constitution ensures the right to own property. The Law on Land Tenure, adopted in 1983, guarantees the private ownership of land. However, it does add that the state can evict citizens, with compensation, when "economic and social development needs" apply.

Communities that, in accordance with their communal customs, oppose the individualization and marketing of land must create cooperatives and officially register as associations.

In practice, however, many conflicts over property rights occur. In rural areas, de facto extortion of land by powerful agents with connections to high-ranking civil servants is frequent. In the Senegal River region—homeland of the Haalpulaar, Sooninke, and Wolof ethnic minorities—the implementation of the 1983 land tenure reform was seen by many in these minorities as a means to dispossess them of their land. This led to growing frustration, which eventually resulted in the state-sponsored killings and eviction of thousands of citizens between 1989 and 1991. Conflicts between Haratin and Bidhan masters also broke out in rural areas when the former claimed land ownership on the basis that they are the ones actually working the land. In urban centers, shantytowns have mushroomed, most often without any official delimitation of properties, and are the frequent targets of violent and sudden eviction by state officials. Some improvements took place recently: The Programme de developpement urbain, launched in 2002, aimed to delimit land occupation in Nouakchott's poorest neighborhoods, thereby providing the inhabitants with security of ownership.

*Recommendations*

- The constitutional independence of the judiciary must be applied in practice to provide for a universal and effective respect for the rule of law.
- Formal and informal reserved domains for the military and security agencies violate the civilian spirit of the 1991 constitution. The military must be effectively monitored and bounded by transparent and autonomous civilian forms of control.
- The government must implement transparent and effective procedures to prevent the arbitrary seizure of land in rural areas. Similarly, the sudden expulsion of poor urban squatters must be replaced with transparent mechanisms of property attribution.

## ANTICORRUPTION AND TRANSPARENCY – 1.97

In recent years, official state intervention in the economy has receded, as illustrated by the privatization of some state-owned enterprises. State intervention has also been more clearly defined through the adoption of an investment code (2002), a simplification of the tax system, and the elimination of many bureaucratic regulations in the economy. However, less state intervention does not mean better state intervention. Political clientelism, or the weak separation of public office from the personal and political interests of state officials, is widespread and nurtures corruption. The management of public resources, whether those generated from within or those channeled through international development aid, is strongly influenced by these political and private imperatives. The education system is also affected: high school and university exam results and grades are often said to be highly dependent on the student's personal connections.[41] As a consequence, state intervention in the economy, and in social affairs more generally (including the fight against poverty), has failed to serve the public interest.[42]

Public access to government information is both limited and unreliable. Even public institutions, such as the different commissions of the National Assembly, the Senate, and the Cour des comptes (comptroller and auditor general), face great difficulties in gaining access to government information and monitoring the policy-making process.[43] According to the IMF, the Mauritanian government argued that "instituting a financial disclosure law for high government officials [is] impractical . . . in a society where family and tribal links are predominant—thus making it possible for those officials to place their assets in the name of their relative tribesmen."[44] The government instead pledged to adopt and implement a code of ethics for public servants.

Private economic actors (individuals and firms) enjoy great economic freedom, so much so that they form an oligopoly with close family, clan, and personal ties to the presidency.[45] They control most sectors of the market economy, such as transport, banking, food-import, and construction, and they have little regard for the public good.

The government rarely cracks down on corruption at the highest levels of the state. Illustrative of this fact is the relative incapacity of the country's auditing body, the Cour des comptes, to fulfill its role. It has launched only two known investigations since its creation in 1993, one of which examined malpractices in the ministry of rural development and environment in February 2004.[46] Its lack of independence from the president, who appoints the Cour's chair, contributes to its relative weakness.[47] The accountability of tax collection is also hampered by weak human and material capacity. An IMF report pointed out, in diplomatic language, the possibility of "inadequate supervision by the revenue-collecting agencies" and that "revenue collection agencies are not obliged to provide annual reports to the legislature on their activities."[48] A government document promises that an audit of the tax collecting agency will soon be implemented.[49]

The IMF also noted that the budget-making process is weak. It states that "no annual accounts have been produced for over 30 years," which makes it difficult to determine how the annual budget is spent.[50] In addition, parliamentarians have neither the necessary training nor adequate access to information to provide oversight of the budget-making process.[51]

In theory, the mediator of the republic, the penal code (Article 124 and 128), and the constitutional right of expression should provide a safe legal environment for citizens who denounce cases of corruption. However, in reality the reliability of this framework is undermined by the institutional and empirical weakness of the mediator (see "Civil Liberties") and the judicial system's lack of independence. For their part, political activists and independent newspapers that attempt to publish detailed investigations of cases of corruption are subject to state censorship (see "Accountability and Public Voice"). In one case, four newspapers were brought to court after each had published articles on the corrupt practices of an ex-minister and leading figure in the presidential party.

The president made a much-publicized speech in July 2004 in which he stated that a major reform of the administration and of the management of public resources would soon be adopted. This reform would grant greater power to the agencies in charge of monitoring the management of public resources and would provide for a tougher legal framework to supervise the public service.[52] The approval of a General Framework of Good Governance by the government, civil society organizations, and international organizations in February 2004 points in the same direction. The major test for the regime consists in the effective implementation of public administration reforms and the democratization of state–society relations.

### Recommendations

- In the spirit of the presidential speech of July 2004, an effective mechanism must be set in place to investigate and condemn cases of private appropriation of public resources. This could be done by making the mediator of the republic fully independent of the presidency, by allowing all citizens (not just elected representatives) to lodge a complaint with the mediator and by providing the mediator with more human and material resources.

- In accordance with the above recommendation, Article 11 of the Law of the Press should be abandoned so as to allow media to investigate and publicize cases of corruption and state abuses more generally.

- The personnel of educational institutions should be given the means to resist undue pressures on their work in order to enhance the value of students' diplomas, as well as the overall quality of the civil service. This would include better salaries, better working conditions (including a lower student–teacher ratio and better class facilities), and the creation of an independent body to investigate illegal pressures by parents and by administrative superiors on teachers.

- In order to improve the management and control of public resources, internal and external auditing bodies (Inspection générale des finances and Cour des comptes) should be granted full independence from the presidency and must be protected against informal influences. They should be provided with the human and material means to undertake their mission.

## NOTES

[1] "Status Report No. 19" (New York: United Nations Development Programme [UNDP], Human Rights Strengthening Programme [HURIS], 25 May 2004), http://www.undp.org/governance/docshurist/statusrep19.doc.

[2] Hindou Mint Ainina, "La politique de censure des partis de l'opposition se consolide et le thème tabou de l'esclavage est au devant de la scène politique," *Annuaire de l'Afrique du nord 2000–2001* 39 (2001): 355. The author characterizes these elections as "surprisingly transparent."

[3] Ordinance on Political Parties (modified, February 2001), Article 20.

[4] Decree 028-2000 (19 March 2000) provided for the new identity card. See also "La carte infalsifiable, symbole de la 'transparence' des élections," Agence France Presse (AFP), 3 November 2003.

[5] "Derniers préparatifs," *Le Calame* 417, 5 November 2003.

[6] On the Ould Haidallah affair, see "Campagne électorale: le domicile de Ould Haidalla perquisitionné!" *L'Éveil-quotidien* 506, 5 November 2003; "Chronique de l'élection de tous les dangers," *Le Calame* 418, 12 November 2003.

7 "Chronique de l'élection de tous les dangers," *Le Calame* 418, 12 November 2003; "Rapport préliminaire relatif aux opérations du scrutin présidentiel du 07-11-03 en Mauritanie," *L'Éveil-hebdo* 508, 18 November 2003, 6.

8 La Cour suprême mauritanienne confirme le verdict contre Ould Haidalla, AFP, 20 April 2004.

9 See "Sénatoriales d'avril 2004: Interview du secrétaire général de l'UFP," *L'Éveil-hebdo*, 20 April 2004; "Le PRDS (au pouvoir) remporte le second tour des sénatoriales," AFP, 17 April 2004; "L'opposition dénonce la séquestration de conseillers après les sénatoriales," *Le Soleil* [Dakar], 20 April 2004.

10 Djibril Ly, "L'État de droit dans la constitution mauritanienne du 20 juillet 1991," *Revue mauritanienne de Droit et d'économie* 9 (1993): 50.

11 Hindou Mint Ainina, "La politique de censure . . . ," 352.

12 Ibid., 346.

13 See Zekeria Ould Ahmed Salem, "L'opposition dans l'imaginaire mauritanien: de la fronde au consensus mou," *Le Calame* 278, 20–26 April 2000, 8–9.

14 Abdel Weddoud Ould Cheikh, "Cherche élite, désespérément: évolution du système éducatif et (dé)formation des 'élites' dans la société mauritanienne," *Nomadic Peoples* 2.1 (1998): 235–51.

15 "Mauritania: Annual Report 2004" (Paris: Reporters sans frontieres [RSF], 2005), http://www.rsf.org.

16 "Mauritania Alert" (Legon, Ghana: Media Foundation of West Africa [MFWA], 18 June 2004), http://www.mfwaonline.org/en/updates/archives.php.

17 "Interdiction d'un hebdomadaire pro-libyen en Mauritanie,"AFP, 12 September, 2004.

18 "Nouvelle affaire du putsch: retour à la case départ," *Le Calame*, 435, 14 April 2004; "Enquête sur la nouvelle affaire du putsch: le chaînon perdu," *Le Calame*, 437, 28 April 2004.

19 Prosecutor of the Republic, cited in "Le procureur de la république lors d'un point de presse," *Horizons*, 23 September 2004; see also "Révélations: Ould Hannena entre les mains de la justice," *Le Calame*, 27 October 2004 and "Révélations sur la tentative de coup d'Etat manquée," Agence mauritanienne d'information, 27 August 2004.

20 "Présumées tentatives de putsch: réactions et prises de positions," *L'Éveil-hebdo*, 12 October 2004.

21 "Mauritania: Harassment of Opposition Undermines Free and Fair Elections: Open Letter to President Taya" (New York: Human Rights Watch [HRW], 3 September 2003), http://www.hrw.org/press/2003/09/mauritania090303.htm.

22 E. Ann McDougall, Meskerem Brhane, and Urs Peter Ruf, "Legacies of Slavery, Promises of Democracy: Mauritania in the 21st Century," in Malinda S. Smith, ed., *Globalizing Africa* (Trenton, N.J.: Africa World Press, 2003), note 7.

23 The best works in English on the condition of Haratin are those of Meskerem Brhane, "Narratives of the Past, Politics of the Present: Identity, Subordination and the Haratines of Mauritania," Ph.D. diss. (University of Chicago, 1997), and Urs Peter Ruf, *Ending Slavery: Hierarchy, Dependency and Gender in Central Mauritania* (Bielefeld: Transcript Verlag, Roswitha Gost, Sigrid Noke, 1999).

[24] Abdel Weddoud Ould Cheikh, "L'évolution de l'esclavage dans la société maure," in Edmond Bernus et al., eds., *Nomades et commandants* (Paris: Karthala, 1993), 192. See one such case, reported in "Problème d'esclavage ou de justice?" *Le Calame,* 427, 18 February 2004.

[25] The English word "tribe" is not used here as a synonym of "ethnicity." It is used as a translation of *qabila* (plural *qaba'il*), which refers to a lineage group that claims a common descent within the larger Arabic-speaking (or *Bidhân*) "ethnic" group. The Bidhân ethnic group is made up of numerous tribes (*qaba'il*).

[26] *Indicateurs de genre en Mauritanie,* (Calverton, Md., and Nouakchott, Groupe de Suivi Genre/Secrétariat d'État à la Condition Féminine, 2003), 49, http://www.unfpa.mr/docs/pdf/Indicateurs_Genre.pdf.

[27] See the criticisms expressed in "Programme d'appui à la mise en oeuvre du Programme national de Bonne Gouvernance" (UNDP, MAU/03/001, March 2003), 6, 17.

[28] *Rapport sur le progrès dans la mise en oeuvre des objectifs de développement du millénaire en Mauritanie* (Nouakchott: United Nations Development Group, December 2002), 16, http://www.un.mr/Pnud/publication/RAPPORT%20MDGs%202002.pdf.

[29] *Rapport sur le progrès . . .* (United Nations Development Group), 16.

[30] "State Party Report" (New York: United Nations, Committee for the Elimination of Racial Discrimination, CERD/C/330/Add.1, 26 October 1998), paragraphs 138–39.

[31] "Rapport Final, Atelier national de renforcement des capacités des OSC et lancement du réseau informel des ONG en Mauritanie" (UNDP, 7–8 April 2004), 20.

[32] See "Le conseil des ministres approuve une loi sur les mosquées," *Agence Mauritanienne d'Information* [AMI], 30 June 2003; "La Mauritanie adopte un projet de loi sur les mosquées," AFP, 30 June, 2003.

[33] "Mauritania: Harassment of Opposition Undermines Free and Fair Elections" (HRW, 3 September 2003), http://www.hrw.org/press/2003/09/mauritania090303.htm.

[34] "Observatoire pour la démocratie et la transparence: le pouvoir durcit sa position," *Nouakchott-Info,* 12 October 2003.

[35] "Révision du code du travail: timides réaménagements," *Le Calame,* 437, 28 April 2004, 1–4; "Réforme du code du travail: la CLTM exprime son opposition," *Le Calame,* 19 May 2004; "Code du travail: la grogne des syndicats," *L'Authentique,* 15 June 2004.

[36] "Conseil supérieur de la magistrature: en attendant que justice…" *L'Indépendant,* 57, 15 August 1999, 3.

[37] For the latest event on that issue, see "Barreau: l'UAA tranche en faveur de Me Bettah," *Nouakchott Info,* 692, 8 December 2004.

[38] For instance, see "Séminaire de formation au profit des magistrats et greffiers," *Horizons,* 26 July 2004.

[39] Philippe Marchesin, *Tribus, ethnies et pouvoir en Mauritanie* (Paris: Karthala, 1992), 153.

[40] Zekeria Ould Ahmed Salem, "La démocratisation en Mauritanie: une 'illusio' postcoloniale ?" *Politique africaine,* 75, October 1999, 140--41.

[41] For instance, "Népotisme et favoritisme," *L'Éveil-hebdo,* 539, 6 July 2004, 5.

[42] See, for instance, the criticisms expressed in "Programme d'appui . . ." (UNDP), 5.

43   As reported in "Report on the Observance of Standards and Codes—Fiscal Transparency Module" (Washington, DC: International Monetary Fund [IMF], Country Report No. 02/268, December 2002); and in "Groupe Technique Thématique, 'Gestion Ressources Publiques,' Rapport Provisoire" (Nouakchott: Islamic Republic of Mauritania, February 2004), 7; "Country Financial Accountability Assessment," World Bank and the Islamic Republic of Mauritania, Report No. 27065, Volume 1, November 2003), 46–47; "Programme d'appui . . ." (UNDP), 63.

44   "Article IV Consultation" (IMF, Country Report No. 03/314, October 2003), paragraph 42, 20.

45   "Project Performance Assessment Report" (World Bank, Report No. 29615, 1 July 2004), 25.

46   "La Cour des Comptes épingle des fonctionnaires du MDRE: la fin de l'impunité?" *Le Calame*, 426, 11 February 2004, 1–3; "Affaire du MDRE: faux lampistes," *Le Calame*, 428, 25 February 2004.

47   "Report on the Observance of Standards and Codes" (IMF, Country report 02/268), 13–14.

48   Ibid., 7–8, 14.

49   "Gestion Ressources Publiques" (Islamic Republic of Mauritania), 8.

50   "Report on the Observance of Standards and Codes" (IMF, Country report 02/268), 8, 11.

51   "Programme d'appui . . ." (UNDP); "Country . . . Assessment" (World Bank and the Islamic Republic of Mauritania).

52   Ould Taya, speech in Kiffa, 15 July 2004, transcribed in AMI, 15 July 2004.

# MOZAMBIQUE

CAPITAL: Maputo
POPULATION: 19.2 million
GNI PER CAPITA: $200

**SCORES**

ACCOUNTABILITY AND PUBLIC VOICE: 4.13
CIVIL LIBERTIES: 4.49
RULE OF LAW: 3.39
ANTICORRUPTION AND TRANSPARENCY: 2.78
(scores are based on a scale of 0 to 7, with
0 representing weakest and 7 representing
strongest performance)

*Robert B. Lloyd*

## INTRODUCTION

In the space of 15 years, Mozambique has undergone rapid change toward political and economic liberalization. The year 2004 marks the 10th anniversary of Mozambique's first multiparty democratic elections under a 1990 constitution that guarantees a broad array of political and civil rights. The nation's political life is in transition as President Joaquim Chissano prepares to leave office in December 2004 after 18 years in power. Chissano is the leader of the ruling Front for the Liberation of Mozambique party (known by its Portuguese acronym FRELIMO), which came to power when the nation gained independence 1975, and he maintained his rule through the 1994 and 1999 presidential elections.

While the country he has led has changed greatly, deep distrust remains between FRELIMO and the opposition Mozambican National Resistance (known by its Portuguese acronym RENAMO). RENAMO

**Robert B. Lloyd** is an assistant professor of international relations and chair of the international studies and languages division at Pepperdine University in Malibu, California. He worked in Mozambique in the 1990s with SIL, a nongovernmental educational organization, and has since maintained close ties with the country. He has published numerous articles on conflict resolution and democratization in Southern Africa.

is composed of politically disenchanted rebels, drawn largely from the central part of the country, who were supported by Rhodesia and later South Africa in their fight against the FRELIMO government. The two sides fought one another in a bloody civil war that began in 1977 and formally ended at the signing of the General Peace Accord in Rome in October 1992.

The outcome of the negotiation process between the two parties led to a number of surprising developments, especially given the country's violent past. The habit of negotiations forced by the dynamics of a stalemated and traumatic civil war, the adoption of a new and democratic constitution in 1990, and the eventual emergence of RENAMO as a viable political party have combined to create a fragile democracy with a competitive two-party system. Representation in the 250-member National Assembly, where FRELIMO maintains a slight majority, has fostered debate and accountability that reflect the broader interests of the citizens. Within this new political dispensation, the media and civil society have actively participated in spirited public debates on issues facing the country. However, neither political party has consistently been tolerant of the freedom of expression guaranteed by law.

Mozambique's constitution and legal framework establish safeguards for all citizens' civil rights and liberties, but the treatment of individuals who are arrested or detained remains a concern. In addition, prison conditions are substandard, and trafficking of children and women has increased.

Developing the legal and judicial capacity of the state has been a major challenge for the government. Accusations that the judiciary is poorly trained and incompetent are common. The government has been moving toward reform of the judiciary but has been hampered by lack of resources and disputes between FRELIMO and RENAMO over the details of such reforms. Judicial shortcomings undermine property rights in the country, negatively affecting a generally favorable investment climate for domestic and foreign businesses.

Corruption, well covered by the media, remains the major challenge for the country. While the state has been dismantling the state-control legacy of its Marxist-Leninist years, ample opportunities still exist for private gain at public expense. The government has responded by introducing new taxation and customs systems, divesting state-owned companies, and developing more thorough government auditing systems, but further reforms are still needed.

Mozambique's economic and political transformation needs to be supported by a strengthening of the judiciary, the professionalizing of the police and security forces, and a reduction in the opportunities for corruption. While Mozambique has made rapid progress since 1990, its future growth and stability will be undermined if it does not address these challenges.

## ACCOUNTABILITY AND PUBLIC VOICE – 4.13

Mozambique's constitution was ratified by the Mozambican parliament in October 1990. This replaced a 1975 constitution based on Marxist-Leninist principles, which FRELIMO wrote and approved just five days before officially assuming power from the departing Portuguese colonial government. The 1990 constitution—widely circulated throughout the country for debate—introduced a multiparty system, universal suffrage, an independent judiciary, and freedom of assembly, religion, and speech. Although FRELIMO, which has exercised power continuously since 1975, had pointedly not included RENAMO in constitutional talks, the document reflected many of the latter's demands.

The new constitution guided the historic 1994 national and provincial elections that marked the first multiparty democratic vote in Mozambique's history. Importantly, the elections included RENAMO. The 1994 and subsequent elections in 1998, 1999, and 2003 were conducted by secret ballot, monitored by independent electoral authorities, and generally considered by independent observers to broadly reflect voter will. RENAMO, however, has made consistent allegations of electoral irregularity at each election and in fact boycotted the 1998 local elections. Since then the country's electoral law has been periodically revised in response to opposition objections as well as the experiences of each election. FRELIMO won the presidential elections in 1994 and 1999. Despite its concerns over the integrity of the electoral process, RENAMO regularly receives about 40 percent of the national vote, making it the only viable opposition party.

The state attempts to ensure that citizens' political choices are not dominated by parochial interests. The constitution requires that political parties be national in scope, uphold national interests, and refrain from advocating violence (Articles 31–43). The large size of the country, whose length is equivalent to that of the east coast of the United States, combined with the lack of efficient transportation and communication links, makes it difficult for parties to expand beyond regional bases. Although both RENAMO and FRELIMO draw voters from every province in the country, the political parties still tend to reflect regional and ethnic interests. RENAMO's leadership and constituency is pulled from the Ndau and Sena groups in the central part of the country. FRELIMO's leadership and base is among the Shangaan in the far south.

In theory all parties seeking local, provincial, and national office have equal campaigning opportunities. In practice, FRELIMO enjoys a decided advantage because it has access to state resources not available to opposition parties. RENAMO has an advantage over smaller opposition parties because of its size, resources, and national reach. Recognized political parties are small, vary in number from election to election (at latest count 25), and are able to receive campaign funds from the government.[1] Given the relative poverty of Mozambique, broad voter support for individuals and parties is limited. Thus, economic elites have a financial advantage over other participants in the political process. Foreign interests, largely European and American nongovernmental organizations (NGOs)—often with their government's financial support—influence the political process through grants and technical assistance to parties.

In the most recent legislative elections, in 1999, 12 parties competed on a party-list system. The parties represented a range of political interests and policy options. FRELIMO and RENAMO, however, were the only two parties to garner more than 5 percent of the vote. FRELIMO and RENAMO accuse each other of physically harassing one another's supporters in political strongholds, with some evidence to support their claims.

Democratic competition is strong in Mozambique. In the 1999 presidential elections the RENAMO candidate, Afonso Dhlakama, received 47.71 percent of the vote compared to 52.29 percent for the FRELIMO candidate, President Joaquim Chissano. In the November 19, 2003, local elections, RENAMO took control of the northern cities of Beira, Nacala, Angoche, and Ilha. This was the first time that any elected body was not controlled by FRELIMO. In another city, Marromeu, the elected mayor is a member of RENAMO but the majority of the elected municipal assembly are FRELIMO party members.[2]

[*Editor's note:* As of February 2005, the results of the third democratic elections held in early December 2004 show the FRELIMO presidential candidate Armando Guebuza won the election with 63.74 percent of the vote. His rival, RENAMO candidate Afonso Dhlakama, came in second with 31.74 percent of the vote. RENAMO challenged the election results, citing evidence of voter fraud. The Constitutional Council subsequently turned down the appeal on the grounds that it was filed after the official deadline. Independent observers noted serious irregularities in the vote, particularly the vote tabulation process, but stated that these would not have altered the outcome. In the parliamentarian elections, FRELIMO won 160 seats and RENAMO won 90 seats. RENAMO initially contested these results, but eventually seated its 90 deputies.]

The 1990 constitution provides for the separation of the executive, legislative, and judicial branches. However, FRELIMO has not always distinguished between the various branches of government, or even between party and state. The constitution establishes a strong presidency, but the legislative branch—which is nearly evenly split between RENAMO and FRELIMO—has acted to influence executive policy. The executive branch tends to dominate the judicial branch, in part due to its ability to select judges. Thus, a system of checks and balances is as yet incomplete.

The civil service is selected on the basis of open competition and merit. In practice, however, relatively low pay, inadequate resources, and a lack of training undermine its efficiency and professionalism. Reports of corruption are common.[3] The government is currently undertaking reforms of the civil service system. The long-term plan is to double the number of civil servants, place an increasing number at the district level, and place many of the new employees in the education and health sectors.[4]

Civic groups are able to discuss pending policy with government officials but are not major players in the policy-making process. Beginning in the early 1990s, the government began to encourage the development of NGOs, both domestic and international. This policy led to a rapid proliferation of NGOs. While some NGOs have complained about the length of time required for registration with the government, none have reported being denied registration. Foreign-based NGOs, such as the Summer Institute of Linguistics, operate freely throughout the country. There are no reports of state pressure on financial patrons of civic organizations and public policy institutes, even when they are involved in politically sensitive issues.

The government owns and operates the primary print, radio, and television media. The vast majority of Mozambicans receive news from state-owned Radio Mozambique.[5] *Notícias,* the major newspaper in the capital, is state managed. In recent years, however, private media have begun operating in urban areas. These include media owned by foreign television and radio corporations. The BBC World Service, for example, is available on the FM band in the major cities. In addition, a number of privately owned newspapers are available, although their circulation numbers are low and market area limited.

While the state-owned media are the major sources of information, the Committee to Protect Journalists states that they do have editorial freedom. The organization particularly commends Radio Mozambique, the only Mozambican station that broadcasts throughout the country, for its nonpartisan coverage.[6] RENAMO, however, argues that some media coverage is biased in favor of the ruling party. A European Union Observer Mission study of the radio and print media for the 2003 elections concluded that Radio Mozambique showed no bias in reporting, but that print media indirectly controlled by the government did indeed have a pro-FRELIMO bias.[7]

Article 105 of the constitution guarantees "freedom of the press, and the independence of the media." There have been no reports of government restriction on cultural expression, which is constitutionally guaranteed. There is no direct censorship of the media. Journalists report a generally open environment for press freedom, except for issues relating to corruption of government officials. The 2000 murder of the Mozambican journalist Carlos Cardoso, who was investigating a case of bank fraud, has caused greater caution in reporting on such cases (see "Anticorruption and Transparency"). Journalists assert that they feel free to criticize the government or opposition policies but avoid investigative reporting regarding political corruption and organized crime.[8] Reporters Without Borders ranks Mozambique 64th of 167 countries in its most recent press freedom index. This score, which lies midway between a "good situation" and "very serious situation," means that Mozambique has "noticeable problems."[9] There continue to be reports of party and government officials threatening and detaining journalists.[10]

Libel laws restrict some press freedoms. The constitution provides a fundamental right to defend one's honor, good name, and reputation. In August 2004 the governor of Tete province and the director of the Zambezi Valley Planning Office threatened a libel suit against *Zambeze,* a weekly newspaper. The paper had printed an unsigned article based on an interview with a RENAMO member of parliament, Ossufo Momade, who claimed the two men were organizing death squads against RENAMO supporters.[11]

In several instances journalists have been detained by the police. For example, the Media Institute of Southern Africa and the Niassa provincial branch of Mozambique's journalists' union charged that the provincial chief attorney had unlawfully ordered the arrest of correspondent Fabião Mondlane on May 15, 2004. Mondlane was released after 10 hours. The chief attorney claims Mondlane defamed him in an article on corruption in the attorney's office that was published in the independent Niassa paper *Faisca.* The director of the prison released Mondlane, telling him his detention was illegal.[12]

The constitution guarantees free artistic expression and intellectual property rights. There have been no reports of government restriction on cultural expression.

### Recommendations

- Mozambique should subject itself to a formal review under the newly developed African Peer Review Mechanism of the New Partnership for African Development (Nepad). This self-assessment questionnaire should serve as the basis for a public discussion on good governance, with representatives from civic groups and political parties included.
- The National Assembly should consider legislation that shields journalists from libel lawsuits arising from reporting on public officials.
- *Notícias* should be fully privatized. The government should have no editorial or financial stake in the paper. The government should also encourage the development of private broadcast radio stations that cover the entire country.

## CIVIL LIBERTIES – 4.49

Article 82 of the constitution allows citizens the right of recourse for any act that violates constitutional guarantees. The constitution prohibits torture and cruel or inhumane treatment. The Mozambican Human Rights League, however, has accused the police of torture of prisoners. These allegations have not resulted in investigations, trials, or prosecution of wrongdoers.[13]

There are a number of reports of inhumane conditions in prisons. The Mozambican Human Rights League charges that prisons are overcrowded, health and sanitation conditions are poor, sick prisoners are left untreated, and children under the age of 16 are also incarcerated in these substandard facilities; under Mozambican law, children under 16 may not be accused of a crime.[14] Amnesty International reported that six prisoners had been left in chains for four days. After inspecting the prisoners accompanied by a representative of the Mozambican Human Rights League, the attorney general, Joaquim Luis Madeira, ordered that the chains to be removed, stating there were no legal grounds for the restraints.[15]

The death penalty is illegal. However, there are reports of execution of individuals detained by the police. The Mozambican Human Rights League alleges that on November 1, 2003, the police took four detainees from a town outside the capital and shot them. The police state the four men were trying to escape.[16] The media did not report any further investigation into this matter.

Article 101 of the constitution limits detention. Details concerning the length and conditions of such detention are set by law. Detainees have the right to judicial review of their detention. However, human rights groups argue that citizens' constitutional rights are restricted by the fact that police and judicial officials are unfamiliar with the penal process code governing detentions, and the accused are often held in detention for extended periods of time. Police reportedly randomly arrest citizens and foreigners on the street who fail to produce required identity documents and do not pay bribes.

Since the beginning of multiparty democracy in 1994, there has been no systematic and widespread abuse of citizens by private/non-state actors. The political tension and distrust between RENAMO and FRELIMO, however, remain as a legacy of a bloody civil war. In one reported incident, RENAMO members and sympathizers seized and detained Salvador Januario, a journalist working with Radio Mozambique, in their offices in the city of Montepuez, in the northern province of Cabo Delgado, in November 2003. Januario had been investigating reports of RENAMO supporters removing election posters of competing political parties and intimidating market vendors.

Article 67 of the constitution states, "Men and women shall be equal before the law in all spheres of political, economic, social, and cultural affairs." The assembly approved a revision of the colonial-era civil code on August 24, 2003, such that it no longer assumes the husband is the head of household or representative of the family. One spouse may not restrict the right of the other to work, and the wife no longer needs permission to obtain business or contract debts.[17] But these provisions are not always upheld. There are reports of the abuse of women and children, although detailed research into its extent is not available.[18] Traditional African customs do not always hold the same views on the roles of men and women as state law or international norms. Thus, it is not clear, particularly in the rural areas, how much of an impact government laws have on practices such as polygamy.

The government mandates that at least 30 percent of the National Assembly and cabinet must be women. On February 17, 2004, President Joaquim Chissano appointed Finance Minister Luisa Diogo as prime minister; she is the highest-ranking woman in government and the first to hold this position.[19]

The constitution prohibits forced labor. Prostitution is illegal. Mozambique is also a signatory to the International Labor Organization Convention on the Abolition of Forced Labor, the Protocol to Prevent, Suppress, and Punish Trafficking in Persons, Especially Women and Children, and the Convention Against Transnational Organized Crime. Despite these legal safeguards, Mozambique is a source country for human trafficking, both domestically and internationally. The South African National Prosecuting Authority task force and a group of NGOs called the War Against Trafficking Alliance stated that South African–based crime syndicates procure children from Mozambique for sexual exploitation or labor.[20]

There is also evidence of organ trafficking. It is thought that organ trafficking is used both for medical transplants and for *muti* (traditional medicine). In one case, a Mozambican women and her two-year-old son were found murdered in Nampula province. The woman's genitals had been removed.[21] The Human Rights League has presented evidence of organ trafficking as well, including in children.[22] The European Commission recently promised €10 million to help investigate these allegations.

Mozambique's population of approximately 18 million people speak a total of 39 languages. Ethnolinguistic diversity has been a source of tension in the country. Addressing this issue, the constitution guarantees equal rights before the law, regardless of ethnic origin or religion, and outlaws discrimination based on these criteria. While Portuguese is the official language, the government actively promotes the development of Mozambique's nearly 40 indigenous languages.[23] Recently, for example, the government announced a major reform of the educational curriculum that would use mother tongue languages instead of Portuguese as the medium of instruction in primary schools.[24]

Most Mozambicans practice some form of traditional religion. These modes of worship are headed by traditional religious leaders called *curandeiros*. About 30 percent of the population is Christian, with Catholics slightly more numerous than Protestants. Muslims—located in the north, largely along the coast—comprise about 20 percent of the population. Many Muslims and Christians also practice some form of traditional African religion.[25] The government, with the introduction of the 1990 constitution, made major efforts to abolish laws and practices that discriminate against ethnic and religious groups. Article 9 of the constitution, while proclaiming a secular state, nevertheless "recognizes and values" religious groups. In some cases, however, the government has passed legislation that is inconsistent with traditional ethnic or religious practices in the interest of supporting citizens' civil rights. For example, the recently approved Family Law allows a wife to work and incur debt without her husband's permission, places civil unions on the same level as religious ones, and changes existing law that assumed the male was head of household.[26]

The state protects the rights of nonbelievers and adherents of minority religious faiths and movements. The government has permitted the opening of Christian and Muslim schools, returned most religious property expropriated during the Marxist era, and sought good relations with religious groups. The government is continuing to negotiate the return of remaining church property seized by the state. Foreign missionaries are regularly granted residence visas. These policies are in marked contrast to those that prevailed in the Marxist era when religious groups were severely suppressed. Religious institutions are required to register with the government, but the government refrains from interference with religious organizations. The state prohibits religious groups from forming political parties, and political parties, for their part, may not sponsor religious groups. Current law forbids political campaigning at religious sites. FRELIMO has recently accused Muslim religious leaders of allowing mosques in the northern city of Angoche to be used for local campaigning for the RENAMO opposition.[27]

Article 68 of the constitution states that people with disabilities have the same rights and responsibilities as other citizens. The constitution also guarantees the right to assistance in the case of disability. In practice, given the deep poverty in the country, addressing the issue of individuals with disabilities, including disabled veterans from the war, has not been a high priority for the government. A major study sponsored by the British Department for International Development noted that, as in many other developing nations, public transportation is generally inaccessible to the physically disabled, leading to unemployment, under-education, and lack of access to government and private services that could help improve their lives.[28]

The government's Marxist past has heavily influenced government policy with respect to work. The constitution guarantees work, just payment, safe working conditions, the right to form unions and strike, and paid holidays. Employment discrimination based on sex is prohibited.

The constitution guarantees freedom of association. There are a number of religious, business, human rights, and political groups in the country. Civic, business, and political organizations are permitted to organize, mobilize, and advocate for peaceful purposes, although there are some reports of their meetings being disrupted. Citizens are not compelled by the state to belong to any association, either directly or indirectly. During the Marxist era citizens had to belong to neighborhood political associations, but these have since been abolished. The constitution specifically provides for the right to form and join a trade or labor union, but in general, unions are not strong in Mozambique. There have been reports in recent years of the police using excessive and lethal force against RENAMO supporters and striking workers.[29]

The police, in direct violation of the constitution, have banned street marches and demonstrations of *majermanes* (Mozambicans who used to work in former East Germany) at an open area in central Maputo. The workers have demonstrated in public places to demand government compensation for pensions they argue had been transferred from East Germany to Mozambique.[30] The government has stated it was not at fault but has agreed to meet in part their demands for pensions.

### Recommendations

- The prison system should be reformed, including mandatory posting of laws governing detention and prison conditions, expanded police training programs to increase professionalism and awareness of legal responsibilities, increased police pay so as to reduce the temptation for corruption, and the construction of additional prisons to alleviate overcrowding.
- Mozambique should ratify and begin active implementation of the provisions of the United Nations Convention Against Transnational Organized Crime and its related protocols. Specific priorities include implementing security and border controls to detect and prevent trafficking and securing technical assistance programs for law enforcement and judicial training.
- The government should develop a comprehensive public/private orphanage system to respond to the projected increase in the number of AIDS orphans. This will also help protect children from sexual exploitation and trafficking.
- Mozambique should mount an official and comprehensive investigation into reports of organ trafficking.
- The government should abolish the requirement that citizens and foreigners carry identification papers when in public.

## RULE OF LAW – 3.39

The judiciary is charged with guaranteeing and strengthening the rule of law and promoting the rights and freedoms of citizens. The courts may not act contrary to the constitution. Their decisions take precedence over decisions of other branches of government. President Chissano noted in May 2004 that establishing the rule of law and a "healthier legal system" remained a challenge for the government. He also stated that foreign donors had faulted the government on this issue but were nevertheless supportive of government reform.[31]

If one party controls both the assembly and the presidency, that party can exercise substantial political influence over the Supreme Court, the highest judicial body. The president, who is from FRELIMO, chooses *professional* judges to the court. These must be ratified by the assembly. The assembly votes on *elective* judges to the court. As FRELIMO has a majority of the votes in the parliament, and given the political polarization between FRELIMO and RENAMO, these judges may be possibly perceived as more sympathetic to FRELIMO policies.

Mozambique also has a constitutional council, which assesses whether or not legislation is consistent with the constitution, resolves conflicts between branches of government, and oversees elections. This body, like the Supreme Court, is chosen by the president and assembly. Institutional clarity between these two bodies is lacking. Since 1990, the Supreme Court has been responsible for some of the duties of the council due to legal disputes over constitutional provisions governing the council.[32]

As yet, the court has not ruled against the executive on any major legislative or executive decision. Thus, it is not clear whether the government would comply if and when a court does rule against it. In one case—the recent Family Law legislation—the president requested a revision from the assembly on the grounds that he thought it would be ruled unconstitutional by the court. This shows some sensitivity to the possible impact of court decisions on the legislation.[33]

The constitution states that judges should be obedient to the law, impartial, and disinterested. However, the selection of judges from the executive and legislative branches reflects political considerations, and appointments are not for life. There is no evidence that judges are removed for not adhering to the views of politicians. Judges often do not have adequate training before assuming the bench. There are also allegations that prosecutors are influenced by political officials, although concrete evidence is not available to support these charges.

RENAMO claims that the FRELIMO government chooses incompetent judges. This, it states, leads to a public perception of a collapsed judicial system. RENAMO also asserts that the Supreme Court's unanimous rejection of RENAMO's appeal of the 1999 election results constitutes political bias against the party. One FRELIMO parliamentarian, reflecting the strong emotions still present from the civil war, argues that RENAMO itself is not interested in a strong judiciary for fear it would hold the party responsible for illegal actions.[34]

Everyone charged with a crime is presumed innocent until proven guilty. There are a number of reports that the accused are often held in detention for extended periods of time. Furthermore, the judges presiding over the cases may lack proper training, causing the accused to be deprived of legal rights. Citizens do have a right to independent counsel. The constitution also guarantees legal counsel for those who lack financial resources for defense, although in practice funds are limited.

There is no evidence of widespread bias against ethnic, religious, or gender groups seeking equal treatment from the court. The administration of justice has been frequently criticized, but alleged lack of equal protection may relate more to the general incompetence of the courts than to any particular animus against individuals.

Military, security, and police forces fall under the jurisdiction of the president. The assembly has the ability to review domestic and foreign policies, as well as budgetary considerations. Police, military, and internal security services are generally free from the influence and direction of non-state actors. There have been a number of allegations, however, of organized crime rings in the country, and such groups could not function without at least some degree of influence on security forces.[35]

In line with its tensions with and distrust of the government, the opposition RENAMO believes that the police interfere in the political process. It cites the death in November 2000 of scores of RENAMO supporters in the northern city of Montepuez who suffocated to death while in the custody of the police.[36] Showing the continuing tension, in September 2004 approximately 150 ex-rebel forces guarding RENAMO leader Afonso Dhlakama's house in the central Sofala province clashed with the police. The police argue that the bodyguards were in violation of the 1992 peace accord that required police and military forces of the two sides to be integrated. RENAMO argues that the police are not nonpartisan. One reporter noted that after the December 2004 elections the police would withdraw from strategic parts of Sofala and RENAMO would control these areas.[37]

The constitution guarantees the right to ownership of property. Reflecting its Marxist history, however, the state owns the land. Furthermore, the state owns natural resources in or under the land, and extending out into territorial waters. Property title is historically an important issue due to the expropriation of the property of Portuguese settlers and religious organizations during the Marxist era. Under the current constitution the state may expropriate property only in accordance with law, for the public interest, and with just compensation. The state has been gradually returning property to religious groups in the country. The state promotes the private sector, encourages foreign investment, and guarantees the right of inheritance. The lack of judicial capacity is one issue that the government has acknowledged as a constraint on the enforcement of property rights.

Traditional law with respect to real estate property views the land as communal and allocated by the chief. Disputes over FRELIMO policies in the Marxist era regarding traditional land tenure were a source of dispute that RENAMO championed. The civil war led to widespread displacement of people into refugee camps in the country and abroad. Demand for land grew through post-war resettlement of the country by former refugees, the general growth of the population, and requests for land by farmers from neighboring South Africa and Zimbabwe led to a revision of land policies. The 1997 Land Law clarified land title, fostering greater access to land for farmers (including communities and women), permitting claims for title based on use of the land for ten years and allowing these claims to be made based on oral testimony rather than written documentation. The legislation was broad, reflecting compromises with NGOs seeking guaranteed access for all Mozambicans and those wanting clear and unrestricted property rights. This has led to a number of continued disagreements over the application of the law.[38]

*Recommendations*
- The government should increase funding and continue judge-training programs to fill the critical need for qualified judges.
- The Constitutional Council must be fully staffed and institutionalized to address constitutional and election disputes and entrench the principle of judicial oversight. Efforts should be undertaken to clarify the relationship of these two bodies in terms of legal jurisdiction.
- All government officials should be required to disclose all land leases or allocations.
- Clearer guidelines for land tenure should be established for the 1997 Land Law.
- The government should also examine procedures for the possible future privatization of land title, longer-term leases of the land, and stronger property rights for urban areas.

## ANTICORRUPTION AND TRANSPARENCY – 2.78

The state has been pursuing a policy of privatization for several years. The South African Institute for International Affairs noted that, while the investment climate is generally favorable, corruption and bureaucratic inefficiency are key impediments to South African investment in Mozambique. Smaller businesses investing in the country reportedly face more red tape than larger companies.[39] Recently, the government has been seeking to reform the bureaucracy to reduce the time and simplify paperwork associated with the business registration process.[40]

Mozambique has a number of state-owned firms. The state is a minority shareholder in some private enterprises as well, such as the new Maputo Port Development Company, which gained control of the port in 2003.[41] The close relationship of the government with for-profit activities increases the opportunities for rent-seeking behavior by government officials. Allegations persist that high-level officials use public office to further personal interests. Assets declarations of public officials are not open to public and media scrutiny or verification.

The World Bank stressed in an October 2003 report that Mozambique needs to reform its legal system to foster transparency and effectiveness. This would assist enterprises in resolving disputes and reduce incentives for corruption. The report also called for the government to withdraw from the financial sector and assume a supervisory role to help avoid conflicts of interest with the private sector.[42]

Transparency International's 2003 Corruption Perceptions Index score for Mozambique was 2.7, on a scale on which 10 is a clean score.[43] Legislative and administrative safeguards to prevent, detect, and punish corruption of public officials are weak. There are frequent allegations of high-level corruption among government officials but there have been no prominent prosecutions. In Maputo, the FRELIMO candidate for mayor in 2003 made an anticorruption stance a central plank of his platform. He stated that the municipal police had been squeezing money from informal traders and implied that some civil servants had been dishonest. His comments suggest that this had been the situation for the past five years.[44] The FRELIMO candidate later won 75 percent of the vote in the November 2003 municipal elections, trouncing RENAMO and other political party candidates. Maputo, however, is a

FRELIMO stronghold, so it is unclear the role that partisan loyalty or popular dissatisfaction with corruption played in his easy victory.[45]

The state provides mechanisms by which victims of corruption may pursue their rights, but these are not always effective. For example, in the case of police corruption, proving a case would be extremely difficult. Lack of capacity in the judiciary can impede the ability to pursue a claim in a timely and effective manner.

In the period covered by this report, there were no specific media, government, or NGO reporting on the existence or pervasiveness of corruption in the primary, secondary, and tertiary educational sectors. However, given the relatively low level of salaries paid to teachers, it would not be surprising to discover the types of corrupt practices reported in some other African countries, including paying bribes or exchanging sexual favors to gain school admission or higher grades.

Government reforms of the administration of customs and tax (value added tax) have increased transparency. The Office of General Inspector of Finance, based in the Ministry of Planning and Finance, audits state-owned enterprises, provinces, and externally funded projects.[46] In December 2003, the assembly of the republic began considering reform on taxation that separates the body responsible for collecting taxes from the one hearing appeals to the taxes. The new finance minister, Luisa Diogo, appointed in February 2004, noted that this allows taxpayers to appeal administrative decisions on taxation to a separate and impartial tribunal.[47]

Mozambique has an Administrative Tribunal, an independent auditing body administratively and financially independent from the executive. This body must examine and certify the government budget and its management. Departments must respond to questions posed by the tribunal. The long-term effectiveness of this auditing body is still to be determined. The government conducts internal audits but lacks capacity to audit government agencies effectively. The attorney general is tasked with investigating allegations of wrongdoing. It is not clear how free from political influence these bodies are, but there is legislative oversight, and parliamentarians do inquire as to the status of investigations.

Citizens became increasingly aware of corruption at high levels of government through a highly publicized murder trial for the death of Carlos Cardoso, a Mozambican investigative journalist in November 2000.[48] At the time of his death Cardoso had been investigating allegations of fraud at two banks: the state-owned Commercial Bank of Mozambique and the then-private Austral Bank. Shortly after Cardoso's death, Mozambique's central bank seized control of the troubled Austral Bank. The government appointed a central bank official, Antonio Siba-Siba Macacua, to oversee the sale of the bank. Siba-Siba, who had also been exposing cases of wrongdoing at the bank, was murdered in August 2001. At that time, President Chissano voiced his lack of confidence in the "impartiality and integrity of the Mozambican police."[49] After three years the case remains unsolved.[50]

Six men, three of them linked with the Commercial Bank of Mozambique, were charged and convicted in January 2003 with Cardoso's murder. One, accused of being the leader of the hit squad, twice escaped prison—apparently with the assistance of the police and unnamed political officials. He was recaptured mostly recently on May 25, 2004, at the Toronto, Ontario, airport.[51] During the trial three of the accused stated that the president's son, Nyimpine Chissano, had ordered and bankrolled the murder, citing evidence of checks signed by Chissano. This charge was strongly denied by the younger Chissano, who claimed the checks were for collateral on a loan to a business partner. Whether by design or incompetence, the investigation by the police of the Cardoso murder did not meet high standards of professional conduct in that the crime scene was not secured, leading to key evidence being compromised. The murder, investigation, and trial received widespread and extensive media attention. In the trial phase, the presiding judge, after some hesitation, allowed live broadcasts.[52] The trial revealed evidence of government corruption, but there is insufficient evidence to state categorically that the murders were indeed ordered by high-level government officials to cover up bank fraud. The case clearly damaged FRELIMO's reputation among many in the public.

Other, smaller-scale allegations of police corruption appear in the media as well.[53] However, as a result of the Carlos Cardoso case, members of the media do not feel completely secure about investigative reporting. The murder of Antonio Siba-Siba Macacua has undoubtedly depressed the willingness of citizens to report wrongdoing as well.

The International Monetary Fund (IMF) reported in 2001 that Mozambique had made enormous strides in transparency in the budget-making process. They also stated that government involvement in the banking and private sectors had been reduced. State and local management responsibilities are generally clear. The government's annual budget must be approved by the legislature. The IMF report expressed concern over the need for greater auditing detail, inclusion in government reports of central and provincial extra-budgetary items, and more timely reporting.[54] Since then the government has worked to continue the reform process.

Public sector information is published regularly. The annual Government General Accounts Report is published after its approval by the assembly. The budget and budgetary legislation are available on the internet. The *Bulletin of the Republic* also publishes government information. The Ministry of Planning and Finance makes available additional reports that relate to budgetary matters.

Citizens have a legal right to this information. In practice, however, this right has been undermined by a lack of bureaucratic capacity and cost-efficient methods of disseminating the information to the broader public. Government efforts focus on the broad and timely dissemination of information.

The state attempts to ensure transparency, open bidding, and effective competition in the awarding of contracts. The IMF reports that procurement and bidding rules for the purchases of goods and services are regulated by rules that set tendering procedures. Purchases of goods and services costing above a certain threshold require bids. However, the IMF notes that these rules are not always observed.[55]

Mozambique is a poor country and the central government is heavily dependent on foreign assistance to meet its budget. This has allowed foreign donor agencies and intergovernmental agencies such as the World Bank and IMF to exert considerable influence on government administration and distribution of foreign assistance. The reporting requirements have required greater financial transparency for funding programs. Nevertheless, corruption is still present in the donor process.[56]

## Recommendations

- The government should continue privatization policies to reduce opportunities for private gain from public resources. This should be done in an open and transparent manner in order to avoid political elites using influence for personal gain. The new owners must be required to disclose financial assets for a period of time after acquiring former government assets. Furthermore, any politician or civil servant should be ineligible to purchase state assets.

- Allegations of political corruption should be thoroughly investigated and punished.
- The government should establish an investigative unit, similar to South Africa's "Scorpions," that will look into high-level corruption and organized crime.
- Auditing standards of government transactions must be improved, particularly for transactions that involve cash.
- Police protection should be provided for journalists (and their families) investigating corruption.

## NOTES

[1] "Raul Domingos Establishes a New Party," *The Economist*, 22 March 2004.

[2] *Mozambique Political Process Bulletin* 29 (Amsterdam: European Parliamentarians for Africa [AWEPA], December 2003).

[3] "Mozambique: Constitution and Institutions" (London: Economist Intelligence Unit, 18 June 2004).

[4] "State Reform will Require More Staff" (interview with Adelino Cruz, director of the government's Public Sector Reform Technical Unit, as reported in *Notícias*, 3 September 2004), Mozambique News Agency, *AIM Reports* 283 (16 September 2004).

[5] "Newspaper Runs Remain Tiny," Mozambique News Agency, *AIM Reports* 278 (22 June 2004).

[6] "Attacks on the Press 2003: Mozambique" (New York: Committee to Protect Journalists, 2004), http://www.cpj.org/attacks03/africa03/moz.html.

[7] "European Union Praises Mozambican Elections" (Maputo: Agência de Informação de Moçambique, 21 November 2003), http://allafrica.com/stories/200311210044.html.

[8] Ibid.

[9] *Mozambique—2004 Annual Report* (Paris: Reporters Without Borders, 5 March 2004), http://www.rsf.org.

[10] Ibid., http://www.rsf.org/print.php3?id_article=10185.

[11] "Libel Suit Threatened Against Weekly Paper," Mozambique Information Agency/All Africa Global Media via COMTEX, 26 August 2004.

[12] "Provincial Attorney Orders Journalist's Arrest for Defamation," BBC, 25 May 2004.

[13] "Police Accused of Summary Executions," AllAfrica.com, 23 December 2004, allafrica.com; see also http://venus.niu.edu/~archives/ABOLISH/rick-halperin/mar04/0906.html.

[14] Ibid.

[15] "Mozambique: Further Information on Torture or Ill-Treatment/Medical Concern, Prison Conditions" (New York: Amnesty International, Public AI Index AFR 41/002/2003, 18 December 2003), amnesty.org/library/Index/ENGAFR410082003?open&of=ENG-MOZ.

[16] "Police Accused of Summary Executions," AllAfrica.com, 23 December 2003, allafrica.com; see also http://venus.niu.edu/~archives/ABOLISH/rick-halperin/mar04/0906.html.

[17] "Family Law Passed," Mozambique News Agency, *AIM Reports* 282 (3 September 2004), http://www.poptel.org.uk/mozambique-news/newsletter/aim282.html.

[18] "Mozambique: Abuse of Women and Children in the Spotlight" (United Nations Integrated News and Information Networks, IRINNews.Org, 16 April 2004), http://www.irinnews.org/report.asp?ReportID=40622.

[19] "Luisa Diogo Appointed Prime Minister," Mozambique News Agency, *AIM Reports* 270 (18 February 2004), http://www.poptel.org.uk/mozambique-news/newsletter/aim270.html.

[20] "Southern Africa: Conference on Human Trafficking Opens," IRINNews.Org, 22 June 2004, http://www.irinnews.org/report.asp?ReportID=41817.

[21] "Government Slammed on Organ Scandal," News24.com, as reported in *Notícias,* 3 April 2004, http://www.news24.com/News24/Africa/News/0,,2-11-1447_1507682,00.html.

[22] Gavin du Venage, "Mutilated to Supply Trade in Human Flesh," *The Australian,* 25 August 2004.

[23] "Ethnologue" (Dallas, Tex.: SIL, Inc., May 2004), http://www.ethnologue.com/show_country.asp?name=Mozambique.

[24] "Education Minister Explains New Curriculum," Mozambique News Agency, *AIM Reports* 263 (23 October 2003), http://www.poptel.org.uk/mozambique-news/newsletter/aim263.html.

[25] "The World Factbook," Mozambique (Springfield, Va.: U.S. Central Intelligence Agency [CIA], 30 November 2004), http://www.cia.gov/cia/publications/factbook/geos/mz.html#People.

[26] "Family Law Passed," Mozambique News Agency, *AIM Reports* 282 (3 September 2004), http://www.poptel.org.uk/mozambique-news/newsletter/aim282.html.

[27] "Muslim Clerics Accused of Backing Opposition's Election Campaign," BBC Monitoring, source Mozambique Information Agency, 14 November 2003.

[28] *Enhanced Accessibility for People with Disabilities Living in Urban Areas* (Wokingham, UK: TRL Ltd. in coordination with CSIR Transportek and other agencies, 2002), 2–3.

[29] "Mozambique Review," Janet Matthews Information Services, *World of Information Country Report,* 27 February 2004.

[30] "Majermanes Want Independent Commission," Mozambique News Agency, *AIM Reports* 280 (27 July 2004), http://www.poptel.org.uk/mozambique-news/newsletter/aim280.html.

[31] "Deputy President of Supreme Court Sworn In," Mozambique News Agency, *AIM Reports* 276 (24 May 2004), http://www.poptel.org.uk/mozambique-news/newsletter/aim276.html.

[32] "Mozambique: Election Process is Being Questioned," IRINNews.Org, 29 October 2004, http://www.irinnews.org/report.asp?ReportID=37205.

[33] "Family Law Passed," Mozambique News Agency, *AIM Reports* 282 (3 September 2004), http://www.poptel.org.uk/mozambique-news/newsletter/aim282.html.

[34] "RENAMO Objects to Supreme Court Appointments," Mozambique News Agency, AIM Reports 275 (6 May 2004), http://www.poptel.org.uk/mozambique-news/newsletter/aim275.html.

[35] Peter Gastrow and Marcelo Mosse, "Mozambique: Threats Posed by the Penetration of Criminal Networks" (Pretoria: Institute for Security Studies, 18–19 April 2002), http://www.mol.co.mz/analise/crimes/mosse05.html.

[36] "Mozambique Review," Janet Matthews Information Services, *World of Information Country Report,* 27 February 2004.

[37] "Mozambique: Polls 'not Endangered' by Political Rivalry," IRINNews.Org, 29 September 2004, http://www.irirnews.org/report.asp?ReportID=43421.

[38] "Mozambique: Women Still Struggle for Land Rights Despite New Law," IRINNews.Org, http://www.irinnews.org/webspecials/landreformsa/Mozambique.asp.

[39] "Mozambique–South Africa: Investment Climate Generally Favorable—New Report," IRINNews.Org, 2 June 2004, http://www.irirnews.org/report.asp?ReportID=41385.

[40] "Government Simplifies Company Registration," Mozambique News Agency, AllAfrica.com, 23 October 2004, http://www.allafrica.com/stories/printable/200410250163.html.

[41] "Mozambique Privatizes Maputo Port," BBC News, 25 March 2003, news.bbc.co.uk/go/pr/fr/-/1/hi/business/2885683.stm.

[42] "Donors Promise Mozambique $790 Million," Mozambique News Agency, *AIM Reports* 262 (9 October 2003), http://www.poptel.org.uk/mozambique-news/newsletter/aim262.html.

[43] *Corruption Perceptions Index 2003* (Berlin: Transparency International, 7 October 2003), http://www.transparency.org/pressreleases_archive/2003/2003.10.07.cpi.en.html.

[44] "Comiche Promises to Wage War Against Corruption," Mozambique News Agency, *AIM Reports* 264 (6 November 2003), http://www.poptel.org.uk/mozambique-news/newsletter/aim264.html.

[45] Bonifacio Antonio, "Mozambique: Ruling Frelimo Claims Majority Win in Local Elections," Southern African News Features, Southern Africa Research and Documentation Center, http://www.sardc.net/Editorial/Newsfeature/electionsmz.htm.

[46] *Report on the Observance of Standards and Codes (ROSC): Mozambique* (Washington, DC: International Monetary Fund [IMF], 22 February 2001), http://www.imf.org/external/np/rosc/moz/fiscal.htm.

[47] "Bill on Fiscal Tribunals Passed," Mozambique News Agency, *AIM Reports* 267 (5 January 2004), http://www.poptel.org.uk/mozambique-news/newsletter/aim267.html.

[48] Yves Sorokobi, "The Murder of Carlos Cardoso: A Special Report from the Committee to Protect Journalists" (New York): Committee to Protect Journalists, 2002. http://www.cpj.org/Briefings/2002/moz_may02/moz_may02.html.

[49] Ibid.

[50] "Mozambique Urged to Punish Killers of Banker," *China View,* 11 August 2004, http://news3.xinhuanet.com/english/2004-08/12/content_1764166.htm.

[51] "Canada/Mozambique: Cardoso Killer Arrested in Canada After Escape from Prison" (New York: Committee to Protect Journalists, 3 June 2004), http://www.cpj.org/news/2004/Moz03june04na.html.

52 "Fight for Justice: Carlos Cardoso Murder Trial," *Carte Blanche*, 2 February 2003, http://www.mnet.co.za/CarteBlanche/Display/Display.asp?Id=2156.

53 "Police Drug Traffickers Arrested," Mozambique News Agency, *AIM Reports* 265 (21 November 2003), http://www.poptel.org.uk/mozambique-news/newsletter/aim265.html.

54 ROSC: Mozambique (IMF).

55 Ibid.

56 "Abuse of Swedish Funding Suspected," Mozambique News Agency, *AIM Reports* 271 (4 March 2004), http://www.poptel.org.uk/mozambique-news/newsletter/aim271.html.

# PARAGUAY

CAPITAL: Asuncion
POPULATION: 6 million
GNI PER CAPITA: $1,170

**SCORES**
ACCOUNTABILITY AND PUBLIC VOICE: 4.10
CIVIL LIBERTIES: 4.06
RULE OF LAW: 3.92
ANTICORRUPTION AND TRANSPARENCY: 3.28
(scores are based on a scale of 0 to 7, with
0 representing weakest and 7 representing
strongest performance)

*Peter Lambert*

## INTRODUCTION

After 35 years as dictator, General Alfredo Stroessner was overthrown in February 1989 in a putsch led by his erstwhile military ally, General Andrés Rodríguez. Keen to attract national and international support, Rodríguez ushered in a democratic opening in Paraguay. In May of that year, Rodríguez and the same Colorado Party that had been the political backbone of the Stroessner regime emphatically won presidential and legislative elections. The ensuing democratic transition has been limited, elite led, and ongoing, with the Colorado Party successfully retaining power through four consecutive presidential elections. However, despite such apparent party hegemony, the transition to democracy has not been smooth, and attempted military coups in 1996, 1999, and 2000 have underlined the precarious nature of the democratic process.

The constitution of 1992 represented a high point of progressive reform in the Paraguayan transition. It is thorough, inclusive, and progressive, seeking to guarantee basic freedoms to all Paraguayans. This framework has been built upon by various codes and laws that further

**Peter Lambert** is a senior lecturer in Latin American studies at the University of Bath, UK. He has written extensively on different areas of Paraguayan politics.

seek to enshrine rights and freedoms. Recent examples are the establishment of a Human Rights Ombudsman in 2001 and a Truth and Reconciliation Committee in 2003, as well as the very real legal gains in women's rights over the past decade. However, there is a gulf between democratic legal and constitutional frameworks and the reality of Paraguay, in which corruption thrives and many basic freedoms are violated with impunity. This can be attributed not only to the legacies of the dictatorship of General Alfredo Stroessner (1954–89), but also to a series of governments during the democratic transition that have been characterized by inefficiency, economic mismanagement, and rampant corruption.

Among the most significant limits to freedom in Paraguay are the high levels of poverty and inequality, which adversely affect the exercise of civil and political rights and individual freedoms. Paraguay is among the most unequal countries in the world (with a Gini index rating of 57.7), as well as among the poorest.[1] The prolonged recession and stagnation since 1996 have resulted in a decline in per capita income by over a third in the past 10 years to just $1,019 in 2003. Meanwhile, according to the government's own figures, the portion of the population living below the poverty level has increased steadily from 32 percent in 1995 to 48.8 percent in 2003, of whom 24.7 percent live in absolute poverty.[2] These figures are exacerbated by rising unemployment, underemployment, and the growth of a vast informal economy in a country in which between 60 percent and 70 percent of workers earn less than the established minimum wage (approximately $160 per month).[3] Combined with widespread corruption and illicit enrichment—principally in the form of contraband—these factors have led to a growing disillusionment with the limited progress of the political transition, reflected in a level of commitment to democracy that is almost the lowest in the region.[4]

However, since he assumed power in August 2003, President Nicanor Duarte Frutos has focused on attacking corruption and improving the quality of public management, correctly identifying these as the key governance issues. He has introduced major progressive tax reforms, cut tax evasion, and reduced corruption in customs and the Ministry of Finance, while also improving macroeconomic performance and clearing arrears with international creditors, thus preventing a widely forecast economic collapse. Nevertheless, while such progress has been highly encouraging, it must be recognised that Duarte is the first president since the transition to democracy began who has dared to even begin to tackle such issues in a serious manner and against such powerful vested interests.

## ACCOUNTABILITY AND PUBLIC VOICE – 4.10

The 1992 constitution provides citizens with the right to elect a government through regular, free, and fair elections held every five years, on the basis of universal suffrage for adults over 18 years of age. The ballot is secret, and independent authorities, as well as national and international observers, monitor elections. In principle there is the opportunity for effective rotation of power among different political parties, although in practice the Colorado Party has won all four presidential elections since 1989 and has held power since 1947. It maintains tight control of government and the state, and participation in power-sharing by the opposition has been limited to two brief and unsuccessful periods (1995 and 1999–2002) when members of the opposition party were offered cabinet posts in Colorado governments. The Colorado Party did narrowly lose an extraordinary vice-presidential election in 2000, called after the collapse of the previous administration, to the opposition Partido Liberal Radical Auténtico (PLRA). However, the incoming PLRA vice president, Julio Cesar Franco, made little impact and resigned in 2002.

The presidential elections of 2003, considered broadly free and fair by a range of international observers, were won by Nicanor Duarte Frutos of the Colorado Party. However, although the Colorado Party won the most seats in the Congress (37 out of 80 seats) and Senate (16 out of 45 seats), it failed to secure an absolute majority in either. Five other parties won seats in the Senate and four in Congress, representing a reasonably wide political spectrum.

The constitution provides for separation of powers guaranteeing the independence of the executive, legislature, and judiciary, as well as a system of checks and balances enabling them to oversee the actions of one another and prevent excessive exercise of power. However, in practice, the system of checks and balances has proven inadequate, failing to ensure public accountability of the executive and the legislature. The independence of the judiciary has been compromised, due both to the legacy of political intervention under the Stroessner dictatorship and to a political power-sharing arrangement reached by the major parties in 1995 (see "Rule of Law"). Concerns have been expressed over President Duarte's public statements regarding the need to reform the 1992 constitution with the aim of strengthening the executive, further reforming the judiciary, and reforming the electoral law—including to allow for consecutive re-election of the president. While the necessity for some reform is widely recognized, there is fear that if not handled appropriately, such changes could alter the power balance between executive, legislature, and judiciary in favor of the first.

Legislation on party campaign financing does not ensure fairness. Limited state funding for party campaigns is based on the number of votes received by each party in the previous election. The bulk of party finances is therefore private. Parties are prohibited from receiving donations from public bodies, international organizations, or state employees, and they cannot use state resources for party campaigns. However, they are not required to reveal their sources of funding, and few effective checks and balances are in place. As a result, misuse of public funds and state resources for electoral campaigns is common among all parties, especially the ruling Colorado Party. Such lack of controls also enhances the propensity toward clientelism and undue influence wielded by economically privileged interests in politics. Private wealth and financial contributions have become major criteria in the allocation of positions on party electoral lists and to public office.[5] As a result, several groups, including Transparency International, have successfully pressed the government to look into reform of financing of political parties, although to date no concrete progress has been made.

While civil servants are officially selected on the basis of merit and are expected to serve the public rather than any partisan political interest, in practice, personal and especially political ties remain important factors in civil service appointments. Moreover, the civil service as a whole remains highly politicized: Closely tied to the ruling Colorado Party, it is a bastion of its electoral support.[6]

Civil society was severely repressed and controlled under the 35-year dictatorship of General Alfredo Stroessner. However, the past 15 years have seen dramatic growth in Paraguay's civic sector, which is increasingly active and independent. Nongovernmental organizations (NGOs) are able to operate without government interference, free from legal impediments, state pressures, or onerous registration requirements. The government allows them to receive funding freely from the international donor community and to participate in international forums. The NGO community has taken an active role in promoting policy reform on a broad range of issues including human rights, government transparency and accountability, citizens' (including women's and indigenous peoples') rights, compulsory military service, and protection of the environment.[7]

The government widely upholds freedom of the press, although there have been a number of cases of intimidation of journalists, threats and attacks by non-state actors. Problems occur especially at moments of political crisis, such as at the time of the attempted coup d'etat of 1999, and surrounding investigations into corruption and smuggling, which often result in physical assault, threats, and harassment.[8]

Broad protection of freedom of expression is guaranteed under Article 26 of the constitution. Furthermore, Paraguay is one of the few Latin American countries that do not have *desacato* laws, which criminalize offensive expression directed at public officials. However, freedom is limited by the constitutional requirements that information must be "accurate, responsible and even-handed" (Article 28) and that expression does not "exceed the bounds of acceptable criticism" (Article 151), the wording of which in practice has led to a degree of self-censorship in the press.

The media are independently owned and both freely criticize the government and discuss opposition viewpoints. The Paraguayan Union of Journalists (SPP) complains that private ownership of the media is highly politicized and that journalists who do not conform to the political views of their proprietors are often censored by their employers. Indeed, newspapers in particular are often used to defend personal, political, and economic interests rather than promote objective reporting, while free press is limited by indirect measures of non-state censorship, harassment, and the threat or use of legal action against journalists.[9]

Community radio is thriving and free. However, there have been frequent complaints that there is little transparency in the granting of licenses, which is often based on political and economic criteria rather than on the merits of individual local projects or in response to the needs of local communities. This has forced many community radio stations to operate illegally. As a result, in July 2004, the National Communications Commission (CONATEL), which regulates air frequencies, pledged to grant special licenses to more than 100 such stations. In addition, CONATEL has also requested the cooperation of UNESCO to make the current broadcasting legislation more democratic, effective, and transparent.

*Recommendations*

- Professionalization of the state sector should be based on the introduction and promotion of merit-based systems of appointments and promotions.
- Thorough reform of party campaign financing is required to prevent vested interests from buying congressional seats. This should include tighter controls on misuse of public and private funds for electoral campaigns, greater transparency in party accounts, and publication of all private party donations.
- Political parties should be encouraged to promote a higher proportion of women candidates in elections. Measures should also be taken to ensure the greater presence of women candidates in the upper echelons of party lists, including through reform of the Electoral Law.

## CIVIL LIBERTIES – 4.06

Article 12 of the constitution guarantees the right to individual liberty and, in conjunction with Article 239 of the penal code, restricts occasions on which a person may be detained. In practice, laws are frequently disregarded. Arbitrary arrest and detention are persistent problems, people are detained without a judicial order or other requirements established in the law, and they are often held in detention for excessive periods of time.[10] The use of torture is prohibited under the constitution and the penal code, although the classification omits certain elements of the UN Convention on Torture and is not fully in line with UN definitions and procedures. In practice, torture remains a recurrent problem in prisons and in police stations, employed with the aim of extracting information or simply for intimidation or punishment. In 2003 the Office of the State Prosecutor received 43 accusations of torture and use of excessive force by the security forces, but it is believed that most cases are simply not reported.[11] The issue is generally downplayed by the authorities and is exacerbated by internal problems in the security forces, including an authoritarian cultural legacy dating back to the dictatorship, a lack of appropriate training, and widespread impunity.

According to the World Prison Brief, in 1999, 92.7 percent of prisoners had not been convicted of any crime.[12] This reflects a deep-rooted problem of excessively long preventive detention, with some prisoners serving years without trial. However, since the introduction of a new penal code in 2000, progress has been made; the backlog has been reduced and trials speeded up, resulting in a drop of 75 percent in average trial duration.[13]

A further problem is poor and deficient prison conditions, including overcrowding, lack of sanitation, and insufficient medical facilities, with the poorest sectors suffering the worst conditions of overcrowding and lack of basic necessities. Tacumbú, the largest prison in Asuncion, was built for 800 prisoners but in 2003 held as many as 2,470, while other prisons also hold up to three times the appropriate number of inmates. On a national level, 5,063 inmates are held (of which 33 percent have been convicted) in a system with a capacity of 2,836.[14]

The legal basis for the protection of the individual against infringements by the state is in place but is not always adequate. For example, in 2003 and 2004 there were no politically motivated killings by the state, but two peasants were killed by police in January 2004 through use of excessive force, bringing the overall number of peasant activists killed by state forces or paramilitary groups since 1989 to 81.[15] According to major peasant organizations, peasant demonstrations and land occupations resulting from the recent growth of land disputes continue to elicit excessive force from the police and security staff, while reports indicate that landowners are increasingly using privately organized paramilitary forces against landless peasants, with the acquiescence of the government forces.[16]

Accusations continue of enforced conscription for military service, especially in rural areas. However, since 1993 approximately 120,000 conscripts have been recognized as conscientious objectors, and a strong campaign continues with the aim of abolishing compulsory military service.[17] Although mistreatment of military conscripts has been reduced through regular inspections of barracks and steps to eliminate recruitment of minors, reports continue, and no progress has been made in investigations into the deaths of more than 94 young conscripts since 1989.[18]

In November 2001, a human rights ombudsman (*Defensor del Pueblo*), was created to promote the defense of human rights as well as to investigate human rights abuses under the Stroessner dictatorship. However, although a few cases did result in prosecutions and compensation to victims, the ombudsman has been was criticized for slow progress in investigations, for a lack of political will in promoting human rights, and for being appointed as part of a political compromise (the ombudsman is from the Colorado Party, while the vice-ombudsman is from the opposition PLRA). In a major advance in September 2003, the Congress passed legislation to create a Truth and Justice Commission to investigate abuses committed under the dictatorship and hence replace the work of the ombudsman in this field. The commission is currently investigating more than 330 lawsuits. It has its own state-allocated budget and contains members of civil society and government, including victims of human rights abuses.[19] It is widely seen as having the political will to make progress where the ombudsman failed.

There are no legal impediments to women's participation in government, and participation in elections is only marginally lower among women. However, women remain under-represented in politics, with little access to political or judicial decision-making circles. The results of the 2003 elections produced just 5 female senators out of 45, 8 female national deputies out of 80, and one female departmental governor (the first to attain such a position). In the new cabinet 4 out of 17 members are women, including the minister for foreign affairs. Although the electoral code requires that 20 percent of party candidates must be female, the results of the 2003 elections reflect the common practice of placing male candidates higher up the party electoral lists, thus giving them precedence under the system of proportional representation. A bill to increase the quota of women to 50 percent, including measures to ensure greater presence of women in the upper levels of party lists, is currently before Congress.

The constitution recognizes full equality of women and men and includes measures to promote policies to prevent domestic violence and ensure equality in the workplace. In recent years the state has adopted major legal reforms to protect women's rights and eliminate discrimination, including the penal code (2000), which characterizes domestic violence as a criminal offense; the labor code; and the electoral and civil codes, all of which include clauses to further gender equality. A Secretariat for Women's Affairs (1993), the Plan for Equal Opportunity for Women (1997–2001), and the National Plan of Equality of Opportunity (2003–2007) have also helped achieve significant legal advances to ensure greater gender equality and fuller enjoyment of civil and political rights, as well as to reduce discrimination.

However, although much progress has been made in creating a more favorable legal framework, in practice some major legal discrepancies still exist and discrimination is widespread. For example, women receive lower pay, poorer training opportunities, and fewer chances for promotion in the workplace. This is especially the case in the unregulated informal sector, which accounts for over 40 percent of the workforce. Within this, domestic service, in which approximately 25 percent of the female workforce is employed, has minimal standards for pay and conditions.[20] In addition, domestic violence is widespread and often unreported. According to a survey in 2003, 49 percent of interviewees were aware of cases of domestic violence in their own homes and 30 percent admitted to being victims.[21] Under law, however, domestic violence must be habitual before being recognized as a crime and is then only punishable by a fine.

The constitution specifically prohibits trafficking in people, and in 1995 Congress established a temporary moratorium on international adoptions in an attempt to stamp out the growing illegal baby trade. However, trafficking for sexual exploitation remains a problem and is becoming more visible. In 2003 two cases of international trafficking for prostitution in Spain were uncovered, involving 10 and 18 Paraguayan women respectively.[22] To date, however, there have been no prosecutions against traffickers.

The constitution mandates that the state provide people with disabilities with health care, education, and professional training. However, there is no appropriate legislation to establish such programs, and in practice people with disabilities are not sufficiently provided for in these areas. Many people with disabilities face significant discrimination in terms of public attitudes, access to the labor market, public transport, and inaccessibility of public and private buildings.[23]

The 17 indigenous ethnic groups in Paraguay represent approximately 1.5 percent of the population and remain the poorest and most marginalized sector, largely unassimilated and neglected by the state. Despite cultural recognition and a favorable legal and constitutional framework, the protections contained therein are routinely circumvented or ignored. Indigenous people are largely excluded from political and economic participation due to a lack of adequate access to land and resources and social services such as education and health care. Although they are entitled to vote, and their participation has increased over the past decade, no indigenous people have been elected to either Congress or the Senate, and indigenous people are not represented in public office. Indigenous people suffer from routine violation of basic labor rights and protection in the workplace, especially in terms of extremely low or nonexistent pay and unacceptable working conditions.[24] Deep-rooted and institutionalized discrimination is reflected in economic, social, and cultural marginalization. For example, illiteracy rates are approximately 64 percent for indigenous people compared with 6 percent for the population as a whole[25]; approximately 95 percent of the indigenous population lives under the poverty line.[26]

The constitution provides for freedom of religion, which is respected in practice. The rights of atheists and minority faiths are protected, and the state ensures free practice of religion, with no undue state interference or restrictions. The Catholic Church freely criticizes the government, especially over issues of poverty, corruption, and inequality. Conscientious objection is recognized under the constitution, although there is no legal framework for treatment of those claiming such status. The constitution protects freedom of association, including the right to form and join trade unions in both the public and private sectors (with the exception of the armed forces and the police). Citizens exercise this right in practice. No citizens are compelled to belong to an association, although the public sector in general retains strong links with the ruling Colorado Party, and there have been repeated complaints of undue exercise of political power during elections. Freedom to demonstrate is observed by the government, although some groups have criticized limitations on the timing of demonstrations and access to parts of the capital, Asuncion. The government has also frequently been criticized for permitting excessive use of force by the police and army in response to demonstrations, especially when they involve peasants.

Although the process for registering unions is highly bureaucratic, nearly all unions do eventually receive recognition. However, union activity remains highly unprotected by the state, and harassment of union organizers occurs in the private sector, mainly through the firing of recognized union activists in violation of the labor code. Indeed, from 1989 to 2003 more than 1,965 workers were sacked for involvement in union activity.[27] Fear of reprisal, together with factors such as economic decline, rising unemployment, the growth of the informal sector, and internal crises within the different union federations has resulted in a situation in which unionism is weak and in decline, with only 6.4 percent of workers unionized compared to 13 percent in 1992.[28]

*Recommendations*

- The police need appropriate training in the principles of democracy, the observance of human rights, and public order. Cases of torture, impunity, and excessive use of force should be dealt with expeditiously and transparently. The penal code must be fully implemented, with special attention to minimizing the duration of preventive detention and speeding up judicial processes.
- Prison conditions should be improved with special attention to overcrowding and lack of basic health care and sanitation.
- The constitutional rights of indigenous people must be fully implemented, including greater legal protection of individuals and labor rights, and provision of funds to guarantee basic social welfare.
- The government should ensure the payment of all reparations designated by the ombudsman in cases of violation of human rights under the dictatorship. The government should also agree to abide by the commission's recommendations and widely disseminate any reports once they are released.
- The penal code should be reworded to classify torture in strict accordance with the definition in the UN Convention on Torture, fully adopting its conventions on procedures including investigation, prosecution, punishment, and compensation.

## RULE OF LAW – 3.92

According to the constitution, separation of powers, as well as a system of checks and balances, guarantee the independence of the executive, legislature, and judiciary. Members of the Supreme Court of Justice are to be selected through due process (by the Council of the Judiciary and the Senate) on the basis of merit. In practice, however, selection of officials in the judiciary is highly political. Since a political agreement between the major parties in 1995, Supreme Court judges and members of the Council of the Judiciary have been negotiated by different parties in accordance with the number of seats held in Congress, on grounds of political allegiance rather than merit. This in turn can have a ripple effect throughout the judiciary, as the Supreme Court is central in confirming and dismissing lower-court judges, and well as overseeing judicial decisions. Thus, appointments lower down the judiciary are likewise based on political allegiance over merit.[29] Furthermore, both the legislature and the executive frequently criticize judicial decisions to the press, adding to the factors that compromise the independence and impartiality of the judiciary.

In October 2003, President Duarte launched a popular campaign to clean up (or "pulverize" in his words) the Supreme Court, which was widely associated with institutional corruption.[30] With support from Congress, he forced first impeachment proceedings and then the removal of 6 out of the 9 members of the Supreme Court on the grounds of corruption. The major political parties subsequently negotiated choice of the new members of the Supreme Court on political grounds, a process that was widely criticized by civic organizations for compromising the independence of the judiciary. Corruption in the Supreme Court may have been reduced, but the lack of independence and high level of political interference have been reinforced.

Although reform has been ongoing, the judiciary is widely seen as inefficient, corrupt, underfunded, and unable to combat corruption and impunity or protect citizens' rights. Local judges and prosecutors often lack adequate training and are subject to undue pressures from local economic and political elites. Despite a project funded by the Inter-American Development Bank (IADB) under the auspices of the UNDP to improve the efficiency, transparency, capacity, and technology of the judicial system in 1999, the system is overloaded and subject to long delays. One result of this is long-running cases, which until May 2004 were dropped after the three-year period stipulated by the statute of limitations, leading to accusations of impunity. Such was the case in October 2003 when charges against 68 members of the armed forces accused of involvement in the March 1999 killings of at least seven students were dropped after the time period stipulated for their trial expired.[31] In May 2004 the statute of limitations was extended to four years. No limitations, however, are applicable to cases of abuses committed under the dictatorship, which have an exceptional status guaranteed under the constitution.

The law grants access to independent counsel but in practice the government lacks resources to provide it to the vast majority of defendants. Although real progress has been made over the past few years, there are still fewer than 150 public defenders in the country, with the result that most Paraguayans are forced to rely on private finance, thus limiting defense to those who have the requisite financial resources.[32] Furthermore, the national police are inadequately funded and staffed, as well as poorly trained in all aspects of police work from public order to investigative procedure. In practice, criminal investigations are usually carried out by lawyers, who are privately employed by the injured party, provided sufficient personal finances are available.

The police are also widely perceived as institutionally corrupt and there is evidence of continued police involvement in crime (a legacy of the dictatorship) and links to national mafias. As a result, distrust of the police is high—over 83 percent of the population do not trust the police—and less than 5 percent of crimes are reported in Asuncion.[33] The perception is widespread that police protect local vested interests and enjoy a high level of impunity in terms of corruption, abuse of human rights, and excessive use of violence. Reform of the national police has mainly focused on improvements to equipment, although the new administration has promised a program of large-scale retirements and transfers to reduce corruption as part of its public sector anticorruption campaign.

Between 1954 and 1989 the armed forces were a central pillar of the Stroessner dictatorship, highly politicized and closely linked to the ruling Colorado Party. Since the beginning of the transition in 1989, serious violations of the prohibition on military involvement in politics have taken place, especially in the period 1992 to 1996 when supporters of ex-General Lino Oviedo within the armed forces repeatedly made political comments to the press and even political speeches at rallies organized by the Colorado Party. Sectors of the armed forces and the police supporting Oviedo were involved in unsuccessful coup attempts in 1996, 1999, and 2000 (Oviedo is currently in prison awaiting trial). Overall, however, the security forces have been noticeably depoliticized in the past decade; they no longer play an overt role in politics, remaining instead under the effective control of civilian authorities. Since 1989 efforts have been made to sever the Colorado Party–armed forces links through the 1990 Electoral Law, the constitution, and replacement and rotation of personnel. Troops are still widely used in issues of public order, especially in land disputes and occupations, and in 2003 the government was widely criticized for twice briefly sending troops onto the streets of Asuncion in response to a perceived rise in criminal behavior. Impunity and a lack of public accountability are still widely seen as characteristics of the armed forces.

The constitution guarantees full protection of property rights. However, due to the highly unequal distribution of land, the high level of landlessness among the rural population, and the lack of land reform over the past 15 years, land occupations and conflicts continued to escalate throughout 2003 and 2004. In some cases (such as in that of a land dispute and peasant occupation of agricultural lands near Asuncion that led to the founding of the Marquetalia peasant settlement in 2003) the government has intervened in favor of landless peasants. However, generally security forces have viewed such conflicts as questions of public order and intervened on behalf of landowners. In mid-2004, following a strong resurgence in peasant land occupations, President Duarte entered into negotiations with the two major peasant organizations to end the land conflict and introduce a long-overdue land reform programme. However, Duarte found himself under pressure from two irreconcilable forces—peasant organizations and landowners—and hence with little room to progress. As a result, progress stalled, and land conflicts continued throughout the latter half of 2004.

Indigenous communities have frequently complained regarding non-recognition of titles and invasion of lands by private individuals, groups, and companies. There is no adequate state protection of indigenous habitat, and the state is failing in its constitutional duty to protect communities from uncontrolled and increasing deforestation and ecological degradation. Moreover, while the property interests of indigenous people are protected, they are not fully codified, with the result that in practice, police or legal protection is insufficient to prevent illegal occupations of indigenous land. INDI, the government ministry for indigenous peoples, has the authority to purchase land for communities and to expropriate land, but a combination of under-funding, non-delivery of promised funds, a lack of fulfillment of obligations, and institutional corruption have limited their effectiveness. Of 56 land claims made by indigenous people since 1989, only 17 have been resolved and none of these since 1998.[34] Significantly, there is no state budget for land acquisition, and no political party has a policy on indigenous peoples.

*Recommendations*

- A comprehensive and transparent system of merit-based selection and promotion of judges should be established and adhered to.
- Political influence in the judiciary needs to be eradicated, by agreement of all political parties and at all levels.
- A clear judicial complaints system needs to be established, including guarantees of the anonymity and protection of the plaintiff, transparency of any investigation, and a set framework of investigative and disciplinary procedures.
- Greater resources are needed to improve the role of public defenders and to provide training to improve police investigative capacity.
- The government must comply with its commitment to introduce a thorough and long-overdue land reform program to defuse rising tensions and conflict in the countryside. This should form part of its commitment to direct the maximum resources available to improve basic social services, including the provision of funds to guarantee adequate land, and protection of the environment.

## ANTICORRUPTION AND TRANSPARENCY – 3.28

Corruption is both endemic and systemic in Paraguay. This is in great part due to the rampant corruption of the Stroessner dictatorship, which permitted and was involved in a wide variety of illegal and corrupt activities, including drug trafficking, contraband, and arms smuggling, as mechanisms of political control and support. However, during the transition corruption has escalated, pervading all sectors of government, in a seemingly endless list of scandals.[35] Paraguay is now renowned as a regional center for organized crime, the influence of which has reached the highest government levels. The governments of Rodríguez (1989–93), Wasmosy (1993–98), Cubas Grau (1998–99), and González Macchi (1999–2003) were all heavily involved in different aspects of corruption, representing the different faces of military and civilian involvement. Meanwhile, over the course of the transition, powerful economic groups have routinely been able to use their influence to buy congressional votes. Despite promises to tackle corruption, successive governments have lacked the political will to implement the necessary measures. Indeed, of Paraguay's four ex-presidents in the transition, one (Cubas Grau) is in prison, and two, Wasmosy and González Macchi, are currently facing criminal proceedings for corruption and are barred from leaving the country. The fourth, Rodríguez, heavily implicated in international contraband, died in 1997.

Despite being a partner in U.S.-sponsored hemispheric initiatives to combat narcotics, money laundering, trafficking in people, contraband, and intellectual property rights, Paraguay remains a major regional center and conduit for narcotics and arms smuggling, contraband, money laundering, counterfeiting, and pirated goods from East Asia (leading to growing pressure from the United States over infringements of intellectual property rights). This reflects both weak laws (in the case of copyright, for example) and minimal implementation of existing laws. The result of years of high-level tolerance of corruption in both the public and private sectors has resulted in an appropriately poor international image. According to Transparency International, Paraguay was the third most corrupt country in the world in 2002 and fourth most corrupt in 2003—in both cases ranking as the most corrupt country in Latin America.[36] Much of the corruption is due to a lack of internal government transparency, with little independent scrutiny of the executive, legislature, or public sector.

Corruption is rampant in a public sector that remains highly bureaucratic, inefficient, and unreformed. Indeed, the state is institutionally and structurally corrupt, characterized by a lack of real controls and oversight and the overlapping of authority and functions. It is also highly politicized and strongly linked to the ruling Colorado Party. Efforts to reduce excessive, and loss-making, state involvement in the economy through privatization have been slow and widely discredited due to the lack of procedural transparency and the extent of corruption and inefficiency involved in the few completed transfers to the private sector. The lack of transparency in terms of those officials responsible for state assets is exacerbated by poor internal auditing systems that are often subject to corruption. There is no legislation providing for public financial disclosure for government personnel or effective legislation concerning appropriate ethical standards or establishing clear boundaries between public and personal interests. As a result, abuses of public office and trust are commonplace. Corruption in the awarding of government contracts is widespread. Despite an active media, which does seek out and report cases of corruption (providing there is no political conflict of interest with the media proprietors), the effectiveness of prosecutions is severely hindered by the inefficiency, politicization, and corruption within the judiciary. Many citizens fear coming forward as witnesses or plaintiffs due to the risk of reprisals.

Since coming to power in August 2003 President Duarte has identified the struggle to purge institutionalized corruption as the central governance challenge in Paraguay and a major program of his presidency. In 2003 he began a highly successful campaign to reduce corruption in tax collection—evasion was estimated by the International Monetary Fund (IMF) at approximately 70 percent.[37] This included the rotation and isolation of corrupt officials and a reduction in the number of officials and departments dedicated to corruption controls—ironically also a source of widespread corruption—including a 250-person special unit for investigation into Paraguay's largest company taxpayers.[38] As a result, in the first year tax receipts were up by over 40 percent.[39] The government has also shown itself keen to clamp down on illegal activities in the border region between Paraguay, Brazil, and Argentina, closing more than 50 illegal businesses in Ciudad del Este thought to be involved in contraband and narcotics.

Duarte has also carried the anticorruption campaign to the police, leading to a purge of high-ranking officers in October 2003. He removed the director of customs, the head of social security, and the president of the state oil company, Petropar, and his own interior minister, Roberto Gonzalez, all on corruption-related charges. Long overdue reform of the public sector has begun with the Ministry of Finance, which under the independent finance minister, Dionisio Borda, is fast becoming seen as an island of integrity in its struggle against public-sector corruption, especially due to its improvements in internal auditing and accountability. This concept has been successfully exported to the key area of customs, which was previously a center of corruption. Under pressure from watchdog groups, the government is beginning to promote reforms on a range of key issues, such as publication of interests and finances of politicians, combating conflicts of interest and nepotism in the public sector, and promoting merit-based appointment and promotion in the public sector. In addition, Duarte has tightened up significantly on public procurement, a traditional source of kickbacks, by introducing a more transparent system of tendering for the public sector and an independent watchdog to monitor the process.

Paraguay is one of the few countries in the hemisphere to have complete legislation regarding habeas data (the right of all to personal information in public and private records), although in practice bureaucracy and red tape tend to make access extremely difficult. In 2001 efforts were made to pass a law to ensure greater access to information, but it remains in Congress, with little hope of progressing in the near future. President Duarte has repeatedly signaled that he is in favor of greater government transparency and access to information. The Ministry of Finance has been at the center of this policy, and it has made great strides in increasing internal transparency and accessibility of information, including through the publication of budgetary information on its Web site.

However, the scale and pervasiveness of corruption and illegal financial and economic activities makes reform a difficult and long-term task. Corruption is present at the highest levels of state and government. Hence, reform would involve a high level of political risk, as it would bring Duarte into conflict with members of his own party and perhaps of his own cabinet and risk upsetting the already delicate balance of political power in Congress. It would also be a dangerous task, involving taking on powerful groups operating outside the law, which allegedly exercise a considerable degree of influence over the legislature and the judiciary. However, with corruption representing a major obstacle to development, justice, and democracy in Paraguay, reform is a key task for the current administration.

*Recommendations*
- Appropriate funds and political and judicial support should be devoted to investigating and punishing alleged corruption, especially among politicians, members of the public sector, and the security forces.
- Efforts to promote democratic public sector reform should focus on reducing (Colorado Party) political influence in the state sector. Great care should be taken with any plans for privatization to ensure a high level of transparency and legitimacy and to minimize corruption. Reform efforts should also seek to emulate and promote

as good practice the significant progress already made in the Ministry of Finance in terms of internal auditing, transparency, publication of budgets via the Web, and anticorruption strategies.

- Work with international partners should continue against the illegal international trade in narcotics, arms smuggling, money laundering, and contraband.
- A bill should be introduced to strengthen, regulate, and protect in practice and under law the right to information, as a basic tool to strengthen democracy.
- The government should consider the creation of an independent anticorruption ombudsman to play a public role in investigating and denouncing abuses and promoting reforms, as well as the creation of an independent Office of the Inspector General in all key ministries.

## NOTES

[1] For an in-depth analysis of poverty and inequality in Paraguay, see E. Gacitúa Marió, A. Silva-Leander, and M. Carter, "Paraguay: Social Development Issues for Poverty Alleviation," Social Development Papers no. 3 (Washington, DC: World Bank, 2004).

[2] *Indicadores de Bienestar: Porcentaje de Población por Status de Pobreza* (Asuncion, Paraguay: Dirección General de Estadísticas, Encuestas y Censos [DGEEC], 2003), http://www.dgeec.gov.py/indicadores/2003/ind_bienestar.htm#5.

[3] L. Moliner, "Análisis Económico," in *Informe Derechos Humanos en Paraguay 2003,* Coordinadora de Derechos Humanos del Paraguay (CODEHUPY) (Asuncion: Litocolor, 2003, 25).

[4] "Informe Resumen Latinobarómetro" (Santiago, Chile: Latinobarómetro Corporation, 2004), http://www.latinobarometro.org/Upload/InformeLB2004Final.pdf.

[5] E. Gacitúa Marió et al., "Paraguay," 25.

[6] R. A. Nickson and P. Lambert, "State Reform and the Privatised State in Paraguay," *Public Administration and Development* 22 (2002): 163–174.

[7] For an in-depth analysis of civic action, see C. Soto, L. Bareiro, Q. Riquelme, and R. Villalba, "Sociedad Civil y Construcción Democrática en Paraguay," in M. Albuquerque, *La Construcción Democrática desde abajo en el Cono Sur* (Sao Paolo: Instituto Polis, 2004), 135–193.

[8] Paraguay: Annual Report (Paris: Reporters sans frontières [RSF], 2004), http://www.rsf.org/article.php3?id_article=10059AND//Valider=OK.

[9] Sindicato de Periodistas Paraguayos (SPP), "No disminuyen obstáculos para el acceso a la información pública," Informe . . . (CODEHUPY), 2003, 165–172.

[10] *Third Report on the Situation of Human Rights in Paraguay* (Washington, DC: Organisation of American States [OAS], IACHR, 2001), http://www.cidh.oas.org/countryrep/Paraguay01eng/TOC.htm.

[11] H. Valiente, "Tortura: Impunidad Garantizada," *Informe* . . . (CODEHUPY), 2003, 37–48.

[12] *Reporte Anual sobre los Sistemas Judiciales en las Américas* (Santiago, Chile: Centro de Estudios de Justicia de las Américas [CEJA], 2003), http://www.cejamericas.org/reporte01ed/rep01-paraguay.pdf.

[13] Ibid.

[14] Figures calculated from *Informe Anual de la Dirección General de Institutos Penales 2003* (Asunción, Paraguay: Dirección General de Institutos Penales, 2003).

[15] M. L. Rodríguez, "Análisis de la coyuntura sociopolítica," *Informe* . . . (CODEHUPY), 2003, 16.

[16] "Nuestra Opinión," Informativo Campesino, Centro de Documentación y Estudios (Asuncion, Paraguay, August 2004), 2.

[17] C. Soto et al (2004), 163.

[18] *Report on Paraguay* (New York: Amnesty International [AI], 2004), http://web.amnesty.org/report2004/pry.

[19] For a breakdown of responsibilities, powers and composition of the Commission, see Law no. 2225, http://www.tni.org/pin-docs/law2225.pdf.

[20] O. Martinez and M. González, "Igualdad de las Mujeres y los Desafios ante el Nuevo Gobierno," *Informe* . . . (CODEHUPY), 2003, 109.

[21] H. Soto, M. González, and M. Elias, *Encuesta Nacional sobre la Violencia Doméstica e Intrafamiliar* (Asunción: Centro de Documentación y Estudios, 2003), 5.

[22] O. Martínez and M. González, *Informe* . . . (CODEHUPY), 2003, 106.

[23] C. Pacheco and M. Horvath, "La Situación de las Personas con Discapacidad en las Políticas Sociales Nacionales," *Informe* . . . (CODEHUPY), 2003, 147–51.

[24] *Third Report* (OAS, IACHR, 2001), 106.

[25] *Educación para Todos* (Asuncion: Ministerio de Educación, 2000), 32.

[26] E. Gacitúa Marió et al., "Paraguay," 10.

[27] R. Villalba, "El Movimiento Sindical: Aun Mucho por Resolver" *Informe* . . . (CODEHUPY), 2003, 206.

[28] Ibid., 202.

[29] L.E. Escobar Faella, "Estalla la crisis del sistema del Justicia" *Informe* . . . (CODEHUPY), 2003, 61–70.

[30] Latin American Weekly Reports (LAWR), 1 March 2004, 4.

[31] *Report* (AI, 2004).

[32] *Reporte Anual* (CEJA, 2003).

[33] M. L. Rodríguez, "Análisis de la Coyuntura Sociopolítica" *Informe* . . . (CODEHUPY), 2003, 16.

[34] A. Ramirez, "Indígenas; pocos avances para los pueblos indígenas" *Informe* . . . (CODEHUPY), 2003, 377.

[35] R. A. Nickson, "Corruption and the Transition" in P. Lambert and R. A. Nickson, *The Transition to Democracy in Paraguay* (Basingstoke: Macmillan, 1997), 24–46.

[36] See "Corruption Perceptions Index" 2002 and 2003 (Berlin: Transparency International), http://www.transparency.org.

37 *Latin America Monitor:* Southern Cone 19, 9 (September 2002): 7.

38 R. A. Nickson, "Development Prospects for Paraguay Under the Government of Nicanor Duarte Frutos," *Análisis del Real Instituto,* Madrid, July 2004.

39 *Realidad, Económica Nacional* (Asuncion: Ministerio de Hacienda, 2004), 14.

# PERU

CAPITAL: Lima
POPULATION: 27.5 million
GNI PER CAPITA: $2,020

**SCORES**
ACCOUNTABILITY AND PUBLIC VOICE: 4.65
CIVIL LIBERTIES: 4.64
RULE OF LAW: 3.84
ANTICORRUPTION AND TRANSPARENCY: 3.21
(scores are based on a scale of 0 to 7, with
0 representing weakest and 7 representing
strongest performance)

*Martin Edwin Andersen*

## INTRODUCTION

After more than 10 years of harsh authoritarian rule and guerrilla violence that had undermined Peru's civilian democratic institutions and
the rule of law, the 2001 election of Alejandro Toledo raised the bar of
public expectations for political, economic, and social reform. When
Toledo took office, the resistance from the Shining Path guerrillas—who
led an ultra-left campaign of terror centered in the Indian highlands during the 1980s and part of the 1990s—had been decisively beaten.[1] Still,
the iron-clad control that Toledo's predecessor, Alberto Fujimori, had
maintained on the press, courts, congress, military, and police left serious challenges for the president.

**Martin Edwin "Mick" Andersen** has served as Director of Latin American and Caribbean
programs for the National Democratic Institute for International Affairs (NDI), as a
member of the professional staff of the U.S. Senate Foreign Relations Committee, and
as a Senior Advisor for Policy Planning at the U.S. Department of Justice. As a *Newsweek*
special correspondent, in 1981 Andersen was one of the first non-Peruvian journalists
to cover the Shining Path guerrillas from their mountain stronghold in Ayacucho.

Toledo—who received a Ph.D. from Stanford and is the Americas' first Native American chief executive since colonial times—has presided over an enviable period of economic growth, and his government is credited with great strides in rebuilding Peru's tattered democratic institutions. Reforms, some initiated by a caretaker government before he took office, have produced important although largely incomplete changes: greater independence for the press and the judiciary, new congressional checks on the executive, greater accountability by the military and security services to independent public bodies, and deepening policies aimed at consolidating a market economy.

The Toledo government, together with opposition parties and independent civil society leaders, also created an *Acuerdo Nacional* (National Agreement) designed to promote a consensus agenda for additional far-reaching reform. The proposed changes included constitutional reform, improvements in public services, the overhaul of the country's tax system, and the modernization of its judicial sector. In 2002, much-heralded decentralization of political power, and with it the promise of far greater accountability from officials, occurred when elections took place for 25 newly created regional presidencies. Most of those elected, however, had little or no administrative experience; their limited real powers and resources confounded local expectations even further. In 2004, congress debated plans for a new constitution.

Continuing governance challenges, weak and still over-centralized institutions, and growing public skepticism about the country's political elite, together with popular disenchantment with Toledo's erratic and unchaste governing style, including allegations of corruption reaching into the heart of his family circle,[2] have all contributed to political disputes that brought the groundswell for reform to a standstill. The weakness of Toledo's ruling coalition, together with his shaky leadership skills, were exacerbated when his Peru Posible party lost control of the presidency of the congress in July 2004 and two of its founding members resigned from the party, reducing its congressional representation to 36, 9 fewer than in 2001.

A country of largely of peasant farmers and underemployed shantytown dwellers, Peru has a relatively modern sector on the coastal plains and a mostly subsistence sector in the mountains of the interior and in the jungle region made more remote by poor transportation and communications linkages. The largely dual nature of the economy, and its political consequences, are reflected in the facts that traditionally economic power has been in the hands of a European-descended elite centered in Lima and that income distribution is highly unequal.

Public corruption remains endemic; the many reforms have been juxtaposed with a string of scandals that have shaken Toledo's government at the highest levels. Questions persist about the government's ability to address problems of social and economic inequality. A general strike called in July 2004, although only partially successful, had a marked anti–free enterprise bias. It was supported by what public opinion surveys say is one of the strongest candidates to succeed Toledo in 2006—former president Alan Garcia, whose failed term in office (1985–1990) was marked by economic collapse, hyperinflation, social unrest, and an upswing in the guerrilla insurgency.

By late 2004, it seemed likely that the country had, at least for the medium term, escaped the specter of a constitutional challenge to Toledo's government resulting from its declining legitimacy. This was due largely to Peru's strong economic performance—July 2004 marked the economy's 37th month of expansion—and the fact that the political opposition was not much more popular than Toledo. Because anti-Toledo forces are in effective control of congress, they have been at pains to show the electorate their own institutional responsibility in preparation for the 2006 national elections.[3]

## ACCOUNTABILITY AND PUBLIC VOICE – 4.65

Peruvians can change their government through free and fair elections. Elections since 2001 have been characterized by universal and equal suffrage, conducted by secret ballot and monitored by independent electoral authorities.

In preparation for the 2001 vote, congress reformed the constitution, replacing a single nationwide district for congressional elections with a system of multiple districts. This provided fair representation for the almost 50 percent of the population who live outside the four largest cities and guaranteed them some attention from the state and from political parties, which traditionally had ignored them. Still, Peru's large indigenous population remains reluctant to participate in the political process as Native Americans representing their own communities' rights to land, resources, and respect for their culture, in large degree due to long-standing patterns of social and economic marginalization, as well as the effects of the Shining Path insurgency and the military's brutal counterinsurgency campaign.

A law approved in October 2002 was designed to promote transparent political party financing by requiring candidates to provide within 60 days of an election the sources and amount of financing they received during a campaign. The law's a posteriori character, vague requirements on the disclosure of financing sources, and lack of real sanctions mean it has little genuine impact. No regulations control Peruvian or foreign expenditures effectively in political campaigns. For example, in 2001, the international financier George Soros donated $1 million to the Toledo campaign.[4] A political party law passed by the Peruvian congress in late 2003 sought to enhance the parties' internal transparency and democracy. During 2004, the parties assessed their statutes and implemented financial controls in order to comply with the new law.

The executive, legislative, and judicial branches of government, which are independent of each other according to the constitution, can oversee one another's actions and on occasion have held each other accountable for excessive exercise of power. The president's cabinet is composed of 15 ministers under the functional direction of a premier. The finance minister controls the budgets of all other ministries, thus exercising important oversight functions on the operations of the executive branch.

Political interference in public administration, patronage, and nepotism continue to be serious problems; the example of Toledo's immediate family raises questions about his government's commitment to merit-based principles. Allegations include his wife's failure to declare significant income by using foreign bank accounts; a brother's involvement in influence trafficking in the case of a contract awarded to a telephone company; and Toledo's sister's masterminding of the mass forgery of petition signatures for his 2000 presidential campaign for election as head of Peru Posible.[5] Transparency International has pointed out that, because many public entities are bound by more flexible private sector labor laws, "many job vacancies are filled and contracts awarded without public advertisement. The beneficiaries are often government officials, legislators or their relations." Such official steering of jobs had been reported at the ministry for women, the national food distribution agency, the airport administration, and the state-owned oil company, among others.[6]

A large gap remains between government rhetoric and actual performance with respect to the ability of civic groups to testify about, comment on, and influence pending government legislation. While opportunities to comment have been expanded, civic leaders say the practical effect of their input is often vitiated by official inertia and inter-party gridlock. Nongovernmental organizations (NGOs), including human rights monitors, operate freely in Peru and are not subject to either legal impediments or onerous registration requirements.

The government protects individuals from imprisonment for the free expression of their views. Under Fujimori, both state-run and private media that had received secret payments were unrelentingly pro-government, with little coverage given to opposition views. Independent journalists were harassed and subject to detention, death threats, and serious physical mistreatment. Under Toledo and his interim-president predecessor, Valentine Paniagua, the climate of press freedom has improved significantly. The primarily privately owned press offers a wide spectrum of political and social views. In 2004, the Supreme Court's judicial oversight office began internal investigations to ascertain if any court rulings infringed upon the right to freedom of speech. There are both public and private radio—still the most important source of news and information in many rural areas—and television stations. The government does not limit access to the Internet, and the state provides broad freedom for cultural expression.

However, some problems persist. Libel is considered a criminal offense, and charges are often brought against journalists seeking to expose official corruption, particularly when it concerns illegal narcotics. Although the number of threats against journalists has fallen from their epidemic level under Fujimori, the practice still persists, particularly in the provinces, including death threats. There have been allegations that the government has played too intrusive a role in steering the outcomes of legal proceedings concerning control of media outlets. Officials have also been accused of trying to induce favorable coverage by inviting media owners to social events or by taking them on all-expenses-paid business trips; by giving them tax breaks for the import of necessary equipment; and by subsidizing certain publications through official advertisements.[7]

Peru's judicial branch appears unable to provide the guarantees necessary for full press freedom, in part because of high levels of public and private corruption.[8]

The anticorruption court handed down its first sentences in 2004 against reporters, publishers, and media outlets charged with accepting government bribes in return for their support for the Fujimori regime. Three television executives went into hiding in Argentina rather than appear at their final hearing on a Peruvian extradition request.[9] Somewhat paradoxically, the jailing of a handful of media executives on bribery charges contributed to an even further decline in the public's trust of the media.

*Recommendations*
- Political party financing laws and regulations should be strengthened, including the establishment of enforceable penalties for their violation and rules for the transparent expenditure of foreign money in campaigns.
- A civil service system that is effectively based on merit principles should be implemented for the public sector. Stricter laws on nepotism and patronage, including meaningful penalties for those who violate them, should be enacted.
- Greater opportunity should be afforded to civic groups to testify about, comment on, and influence pending government legislation by holding greater numbers of publicized hearings and other official meetings outside the capital.
- Libel should be restricted to civil law, and penalties should be balanced between the need to maintain protections for individuals' honor and the requirements of a free press in an open society.

## CIVIL LIBERTIES – 4.64

Since the fall of the Fujimori government, Peruvians have been protected from state terror and unjustified imprisonment. Although under Toledo many abuses of civil liberties still occur in a variety of forms, few are of the kind of politically motivated acts that characterized the Fujimori government or the rule of Alan Garcia. A series of laws passed in early 2003 addressed the problem of arbitrary detention, and the practice has notably diminished. However, although the constitution and the law prohibit torture and inhumane or humiliating treatment, security forces continue to torture and abuse both individuals in police custody and inmates in prison, as well as military recruits. In response to torture complaints, security force actions have been increasingly addressed through the civilian court system.

Following nationwide road blockages by striking teachers and agricultural workers in May 2003, Toledo declared a state of emergency that suspended some civil liberties and empowered the military to enforce order in 12 departments. In 2004, the state of emergency was reduced to only areas where Shining Path guerrillas were known to be operating. That year, human rights groups criticized the Toledo government for failing to implement the recommendations of the truth and reconciliation commission concerning reparations for victims of the violence and the prosecution of those guilty of human rights crimes. On August 24, the Constitutional Tribunal ruled that during states of emergency military authorities could not assume political functions and that military violations of human rights must be tried in civilian courts rather than by military tribunals.

The office of the human rights ombudsman in Peru, funded by the Peruvian and foreign governments, has both investigative independence and the ability to report its conclusions and recommendations to the public without interference. Human rights activists say the office has actively and effectively investigated cases of alleged government abuse. However, the ombudsman, who is chosen by at least a two-thirds majority of votes in congress and serves a five-year term, lacks a mechanism to enforce the office's findings.[10]

The 2002 reform of Peru's highly centralized political structure, designed to improve government accountability, was intended in part to address complaints that the hyper-concentration of decision making in Lima resulted in the inability of citizens living outside the capital to receive effective petition and redress rights. However, the government has been slow to devolve power and financial resources to the regions, citing a lack of local administrative and technical experience and capabilities. This, in turn, has meant that the ability of people in the regions to petition and redress rights effectively remains hampered.

The national prison institute controls most of Peru's penal facilities, where conditions range from poor to extremely harsh, the latter in particular in maximum-security facilities in the highlands; the largest facilities are run by the national police. In addition to meager budgets, lack of sanitation, poor nutrition and health care, and severe over-crowding, prisoners are victimized routinely by prison guards and by their fellow inmates.

In August 2003, a truth and reconciliation commission reported on the scope and origins of the political violence that had wracked Peru from 1980 to 2000. It found that the Maoist Shining Path guerrilla group was the "principal perpetrator of the human rights violations," which included 69,000 people killed—double the previously accepted figure. The commission also accused the military and security forces of serial gross atrocities. Nearly three-fourths of the victims in the conflict were Indian peasants living in rural areas, long the object of neglect at the hand of the central government.[11]

To the extent that it can, the government protects citizens from abuse by private and non-state actors. However, the poorly paid Peruvian national police are not effective in general; with the exception of a few special units, their professionalism is substandard, sometimes egregiously so. Since Toledo assumed power, no politically motivated killings by government agents have been reported, although allegations persist about unlawful or unwarranted killings by police, often focused on the excessive use of force against protesters.

A 2000 law allows suspects in corruption investigations to be detained for up to 15 days without arraignment and permits authorities to impede suspects from traveling abroad. Terrorist suspects may be detained for a maximum of 15 days and held incommunicado for the first 10 days. Although the prison system continues to be plagued by sentencing delays, the government has sought to remedy these by streamlining court procedures and providing more public defenders. Prisoners continue to wait excessively long times between the end of their trial and their sentencing.

The constitution, the Employment Promotion Law, and other laws concerning marriage, divorce, and property rights prohibit discrimination against women, but racial and sexual discrimination in employment and education continues. Spousal abuse is perhaps the greatest problem facing women in Peru today, although recently the government has taken some steps to address the issue. For example, the ministry of women and social development's Women's Emergency Program addressed the legal, psychological, and medical problems facing women and children who were victims of domestic violence, with greater public education efforts. Forced labor, including child labor, exists in the gold-mining region of the Amazon. Cases of international trafficking in persons are rare, but domestic trafficking is common, particularly to bring young women from the Amazon region or the highlands into the cities or mining areas to work as prostitutes. The problem of trafficking, particularly that of minors, has received increasing government attention. In an effort to combat the domestic sex trafficking of adolescent girls, in 2003 the ministry of the interior signed an agreement with the Foundation for Missing Peruvians, a nongovernmental group, making that organization the official registry for missing persons in the country. A 2000 law stipulates that at least 30 percent of each party's congressional candidates, and at least 25 percent of those for municipal elections, be women, and women constitute about one-sixth of the members of congress. Women have also served as cabinet ministers and in the Supreme Court.

Racism against Peru's large Indian population has been prevalent among the middle and upper classes, although the Fujimori government made some effort to combat it. Indigenous people living in the Andean highlands speak Quechua and Aymara, which are recognized as official languages. Between 200,000 and 300,000 indigenous persons live on the eastern side of the Andes and in the tropical lowlands that feed into the Amazon basin. Afro-Peruvians, who live in communities concentrated mostly along the Pacific coast, are among the poorest groups in Peru and, like their Indian counterparts, face strong discrimination and social prejudice. The election of Toledo, who boasted of his indigenous heritage, initially gave hope to Peru's indigenous and other minority communities. However, the discontent with his government characteristic of all strata of Peruvian society includes the country's Native American and Afro-Peruvian groups. Indigenous representation in congress remains extremely low, as does that of Afro-Peruvians, who at senior levels of the executive branch are virtually nonexistent.

The constitution prohibits discrimination against persons with disabilities. In addition, a 1998 law establishing the National Council for the Integration of People with Disabilities set down rights, allowances, programs, and services; prohibited discrimination; and provided for the appointment of a disability rights specialist in the human rights ombudsman's office.[12] A 1998 law also mandates that public spaces be barrier-free and that buildings be architecturally accessible to people with disabilities. In 2003 the Toledo government kicked off a campaign in which people with disabilities could register themselves and receive benefits. A national Equal Opportunity Plan for Persons with Disabilities approved that same year focused on improving the quality of life of disabled persons by targeting antidiscrimination measures, priority care, prevention, and the strengthening of existing services. However, in practice the government has dedicated few resources to persons with disabilities.[13] Little has been done to implement the regulations, and accommodations such as interpreters for the deaf in government service offices and Braille or recorded versions of the constitution do not exist.[14]

Peru's constitutional provisions for freedom of religion and the separation of church and state are generally respected in practice. The Roman Catholic Church is acknowledged as "an important element in the historical, cultural, and moral development of the nation" and receives preferential treatment, including state benefits and beneficial tax laws. Roman Catholicism is a mandatory subject in primary and secondary schools, but all faiths may establish places of worship, train clergy, and proselytize. Official registration of religious denominations or churches is not required.

The constitution provides for the right of peaceful assembly, and the authorities generally respect this right in practice. The government permits numerous NGOs dedicated to monitoring and advancing human rights to operate freely. In contrast to previous years, these groups reported no harassment or other attempts by the authorities to hinder their operations in 2003. Citizens are not required, either directly or indirectly, to belong to state-sanctioned associations in order to receive indispensable benefits.

In 2003, a bill was presented in congress that would establish, in accordance with the constitution, the right of everyone to ask for and receive complete and truthful information from all NGOs. Under its provisions, all NGOs would be required to create a Web page, which would contain a transparency portal.[15]

Only about 5 percent of the formal sector workforce belongs to organized labor unions. The Fujimori era exacerbated an already steep decline in labor's fortunes, which also suffered from cuts in the public

sector labor force, more flexible labor laws, and other free market policies. In July 2004, national labor unions called the first general strike in
Peru since 1999, in part to demand an investigation of alleged public
corruption. The strike received the support of the country's largest opposition party. In response, the government called out several hundred
troops that it said were needed to guard key government buildings. Critics charged that the involvement of the army increased the chances for
confrontation; the strike itself received only partial support in major
cities around the country.

*Recommendations*
- The decentralization of power should receive priority status from
  the central government, at the Council of Ministers level, so that
  greater accountability and the effective redress of grievances can
  be made available to the greatest number of Peruvians.
- The recommendations of the truth and reconciliation commission
  concerning reparations for victims of the 1980–2000 violence and
  the prosecution of those guilty of human rights crimes should be
  enacted. The government should also extend full protection to
  witnesses in human rights prosecutions.
- Greater efforts, including devotion of a larger share of public
  resources and greater engagement by the executive branch, should
  be made to enforce laws and regulations concerning gender equity
  issues and the rights of ethnic, religious, and other distinct groups.
- Civilian police forces should receive modern training, equipment,
  and pay adequate to fulfill their duties in a professional manner.

## RULE OF LAW – 3.84

Although the constitution provides for an independent judiciary, in fact
the legal system enjoys the smallest degree of public confidence of any
government institution. The judiciary is corrupt, inefficient, and subject to political and economic influences, although some improvements
have been made since Fujimori left the presidency. After Toledo assumed
office, the ministry of justice began to put into place a broad anticorruption effort. The number of provisional judges, whose positions were
dependent on the executive and therefore were unduly susceptible to
pressure, decreased markedly. However, popular perceptions remain that

the justice system is an inefficient, overloaded bureaucracy riddled with political influence and greed.

In January 2003 the government had to restart the judicial restructuring process in response to several scandals in which the executive itself was accused of exerting undue influence over a number of judges, including through bribes. Toledo publicly expressed his concern about judicial decisions that exonerated Fujimori-era officials of charges of rights violations and corruption.[16] Most of Peru's judges are overworked and underpaid as a result of scant resources. In 2004, the judicial branch petitioned the Constitutional Court for operational budgetary autonomy equal to that enjoyed by the executive and legislative branches.

Prosecutors generally follow orders from the government, which names them and pays their salaries. Those who show real independence rarely survive in office; despite the Toledo government's pledges to reform the system, the political subordination of the judiciary remains a problem. In general, legislative, executive, and other governmental authorities do comply with judicial decisions. Through the middle of 2004, the vast majority of public officials prosecuted for wrongdoing had served in the Fujimori regime, despite apparently well-founded charges of increasing corruption within the Toledo government.[17]

Citizens are afforded public trials in Peru, but the timeliness of their hearings, as well as the competency, impartiality, and independence of the tribunals in which they are held, is frequently in doubt. The backlog of cases is a particular impediment, with more than 1 million cases recorded in 2003. The judicial system is rife with instances of class-based and political favoritism, as well as discrimination against the country's indigenous population. Moreover, fully one-third of the population—those who are most marginalized from the dominant society—are outside the effective reach of the courts. This has led to isolated incidents of vigilante justice.[18]

Judicial training continues to be a problem and, in the case of military judges, a significant number are active-duty officers with little or no professional legal training. Although defendants have the right to counsel, the public defender system often fails to provide indigent defendants, including those accused of serious crimes, with qualified attorneys.

In general, the country's military and security forces are considered to be under effective civilian control. However, Peru lacks the codified distinction between national defense and internal security that is characteristic of more modern democratic states; responsibility for internal security is shared between the military and the Peruvian national police. Both Toledo and his interim-president predecessor successfully cashiered numerous high-ranking military and police officials associated with the Fujimori regime, and military judges no longer try civilians. However, many complaints arise about police abuse, mostly centered on acts of corruption.

In August 2002, the Supreme Court decided that the military court system should have jurisdiction in the trial, on charges of extrajudicial killings, of 120 military commandos who had rescued 74 hostages held by members of the Tupac Amaru Revolutionary Movement (MRTA) at the residence of the Japanese ambassador in April 1997. The court also found that four others, including former Intelligence Service Director Vladimiro Montesinos, were subject to civilian criminal court. This case helped to fortify civilian oversight in internal security.

In September 2003, Toledo fired the head of the national intelligence service, a retired admiral, after it was discovered the spy agency had tapped the president's phone line and leaked the tape to a scandal-driven television program.[19] In March 2004, the government announced that it was dissolving the national intelligence service after the seventh head of the National Intelligence Council under Toledo resigned because he was under investigation for alleged corruption.[20]

In general, the state does attempt to enforce property rights and contracts and protect citizens from both arbitrary and unjust deprivation of their property. Still, problems exist. In the Peruvian countryside, there are few formal property rights, as much of the land has not been surveyed and thus technically does not belong to anyone. Traditionally, an important deterrent to economic development in both rural and urban areas has been the lack of land titles for impoverished families—which keeps them from using the land as collateral for loans to start businesses or improve their homes. In 1996, the Fujimori government initiated an innovative program that awarded land titles to mostly urban people living in shantytowns. As a result, the government's Commission to Formalize Informal Property handed out more than 1.4 million urban property titles. Because of commercial bank reluctance to finance home improvements made by the new owners, since 2000 the government commission has established a private partnership that has lent a total of $728 million to 296,000 new titleholders at low rates.[21] However, the improper registry of land titles continues to be a major problem due to a lack of administrative resources, poor survey work, conflicting claims, and the absence of title insurance.[22]

The 1993 constitution and subsequent laws offer less protection for native lands than earlier legislation, which had more explicit guarantees about the inalienability and non-marketability of native lands for the indigenous peoples of the Amazon region. Current laws only preserve the concept that the land is "unassignable," meaning that the title to such lands cannot be reassigned to a non-indigenous tenant by right of tenure. However, the land can be bought and sold.[23]

*Recommendations*
- The judicial branch should have operational budgetary autonomy comparable with that enjoyed by the executive and legislative branches.
- Efforts at judicial training should be accelerated, with a thorough vetting that includes the elimination of all trainees who do not meet minimum standards.
- A distinction should be made in law between national defense and internal security, with exclusive jurisdiction for law enforcement assigned to civilian police forces in all cases save grave national disorders.
- Traditional law should be codified for use in indigenous communities in all cases not typified as major crimes, so that native peoples have greater access to the justice system while preserving elements of their heritage and cultures.
- The authorities should take steps to promote the proper registry of land titles, and more explicit guarantees about the inalienability and non-marketability of native lands should be given the force of law.

## ANTICORRUPTION AND TRANSPARENCY – 3.21

Although independent observers consider corruption under Fujimori—which included bribery, extortion, and racketeering—to have been systemic and many magnitudes greater than that under Toledo—whose government's main problem in this area appears to be nepotism—in 2004 the country seemed to be returning to a prior state of generalized institutional corruption. By mid-2004 one public opinion poll showed that 70 percent of those surveyed felt the president himself was corrupt.[24] At the same time, Peru's score in Transparency International's Corruption Perceptions Index dropped from 3.7 to 3.5 (on a scale of 1 to 10, with 10 being the most favorable ranking possible). The 2004 score put the country just half a point above the level Transparency International considers to indicate grave and uncontrollable corruption problems. By 2004, popular concerns about resurgent official corruption involved both the president and his family. Toledo was accused of taking a bribe from a Colombian brewing company, a charge he denied, while his wife, sister, and several political associates were also linked to unsavory financial and political deals.[25]

Toledo has suggested that media accusations of corruption against his government are the handiwork of Fujimori aide Montesinos, who continues to influence the media even though he is in jail.[26] Some observers, including Peruvian media watchdogs, also point out that part of the problem was not of Toledo's making: The press, newly liberated from the controls and corruption of the Fujimori era, has engaged in *denuncialogia*—an obsession with denunciations—that trivializes investigative journalism and helps to poison both political debate and public confidence.[27] Throughout 2004 a debate took place about the degree to which the press covered alleged government corruption; whether the coverage was appropriate for the seriousness of the misconduct uncovered; and whether the government might be pressuring journalists in order to influence their coverage.

An inefficient bureaucracy, characterized by excessive red tape, remains a major stumbling block in Peru, adding to the costs of doing business in the country and providing numerous opportunities for official corruption. For example, entrepreneurs still face considerable difficulties when trying to start a business or register a company in Peru.[28] The American Chamber of Commerce in Peru has reported that the "biggest obstacles" arising from government intervention come from regional and municipal governments, which are farther from the reach of the central government's efforts to promote market reforms. It has also complained that the National Institute for the Defense of Competition and Intellectual Property and other regulatory bodies, "which long ago used to enjoy greater independence, now are subject to strong political pressures."[29]

The Peruvian civil code prohibits family members of the president from participating in negotiations in which the interests of the state are at stake. In general, however, the state does not adequately enforce the separation of public office from the personal interests of public officeholders. In many cases, the purchase of goods or the execution of works is done with officials who disguise their personal stake by using either family members or testaferros (third parties).[30]

Senior public officials are normally required to file financial disclosure forms designed to prevent conflicts of interest. In practice, these are frequently fraudulent or distorted. In August 2004, 12 of 15 cabinet ministers decided to follow Toledo's personal example and exempted themselves from banking secrecy laws in what they said was an effort to improve public transparency. Opposition leaders Alan Garcia and Lourdes Flores took similar actions.[31] But critics called the move irrelevant under Peruvian law; personal accounts cannot be reviewed without the opening of a formal investigation, which had not taken place in the cases of any of those who exempted themselves from the banking secrecy shield. In 2003, a law regulating lobbying was approved, establishing that all activity meant to influence the decisions of public officials and members of congress must be made publicly available. The state does exercise some control over conflicts of interest in the private sector.

The Peruvian state is a primary victim of corruption; its still weak regulatory and enforcement framework leaves it vulnerable and unable to protect its interests. According to the Coordinadora Nacional de Derechos Humanos, a notable lack of progress in public corruption investigations, including the small number of convictions, is in part due to the need to create a subsystem of police, prosecutors, judges, and special anticorruption courts untainted by the mafia-like corruption of the judicial branch under Fujimori. The slowness of the judicial process, strikes by judicial personnel, political instability, threats, and lack of support are other factors. By September 2004, 143 public corruption cases had been pursued against 1,453 people; yet, despite the repatriation of some $151 million in funds stashed by the Montesinos network in U.S. and Swiss banks, only 14 cases had been concluded.[32]

Prosecutions continue to be hindered by a lack of effective anticorruption statutes that allow for timely resolution of cases and swift punishment.[33] Public corruption commonly receives light sanction, usually limited to house detention or restrictions on foreign travel. Jail terms are rare.[34] In the fall of 2004, it was reported that 27.5 percent of the members of Peru's unicameral congress had had formal complaints lodged against them before that body's ethics commission. Of the 41 cases, however, only one resulted in an effective sanction.[35] In a positive development, the congressional ethics committee has drafted a new ethics code and procedures manual designed to ensure effective handling of complaints and multiparty representation.[36] Peruvian institutions of higher learning are less susceptible to corruption and graft than other institutions, but favoritism is common and sometimes "grease payments" are necessary to gain admission.

The national superintendency of tax administration (SUNAT) is effective in tax collection among medium and lower-income people, but it has the reputation of being complacent with the rich and powerful, allowing tax delinquency among the upper-income brackets to be treated with leniency. Because the SUNAT's investigations are conducted in secrecy, it is difficult to establish whether it acts correctly in enforcing tax laws.

The independent special anticorruption prosecutors' investigations of former officials of the Fujimori government were carried out following the same rules used in other cases, with defendants having full access to attorneys and all the norms of due process followed. By the beginning of 2004 allegations were increasing that the cases against official corruption centered almost exclusively on deeds committed by members of the Fujimori regime, with little attention given to alleged misdeeds conducted during the Toledo period. That changed significantly when the lead special prosecutor announced early in 2004 that his unit would also investigate alleged corruption within the Toledo government, including members of Toledo's own family. However, although Toledo pledged publicly that even his own family was not exempt from examination, senior government officials routinely began to question the work done by the prosecutors, saying it would evaluate the work of the independent special unit, and floated the names of possible replacements.[37]

Official hostility to the independent special anticorruption prosecutors increased as probes into the current government progressed. The lead anticorruption prosecutor reported: "There is a sector in this regime that is very uncomfortable with the independence that we demonstrate each time we talk in favor of ending the corruption in this government, which is doing very little to promote the combat against it." He added that he had evidence that his e-mail and telephone communications were being monitored. The conflict between the government and the anticorruption office worsened in September, when a special prosecutor charged that Toledo's brother was involved in corrupting public officials. Nevertheless, in late September 2004 it was announced that the contracts of the special prosecutors' office's 3 assistant prosecutors, 18 lawyers, and their support staff had been extended.[38] In the summer of 2004, the parliamentary anticorruption commission committed to extending whistleblower protection to persons appearing before it; however that promise has not yet been formalized, thus reducing the willingness of many Peruvians to come forward.

The 1993 constitution set out extensive freedom of information rights, and in August 2002 the Law on Transparency and Access to Public Information went into effect, giving every individual the right to request information in any form from any government body or private entity that offers public services or executes administrative functions without having to explain why. The law establishes procedures for disciplining government employees who do not release public information, although there are not yet any known cases of any public official being sanctioned.[39] The government has had difficulty in implementation because of the complexity of the system and the cost of monitoring, particularly at the regional and local levels.[40]

The law requires government departments to establish Web sites and to regularly publish information on their activities, budget, costs of the acquisition of goods and services, official activities of high-ranking officials, regulations, and salaries. Detailed public finance information must be published on the Web site of the ministry of economics and finance every four months.[41] In practice, however, compliance with these requirements varies according to agency, and the effectiveness of the measure is often determined by the amount of public and media interest in the particular information.

A local group, Transparencia, maintains a useful Web site, Datos del Congreso, tracking various congressional topics relating to good government issues. The government puts little or no restriction on the administration and distribution of foreign assistance.

## Recommendations

- The independence of the special anticorruption court should be reinforced by the issuance of stable work contracts to its employees and the opening of additional tribunals, as needed, to facilitate the timely consideration of cases.
- New whistle-blower protection laws should be enacted to protect both public and private employees from reprisal for bearing witness against waste, fraud, and other abuses of power.
- Effective anticorruption statutes allowing for quicker resolution of cases and swift punishment should be enacted.
- Serious efforts should be made to improve the dissemination of government information at the regional and municipal levels; consideration should be given to tying those efforts to the provision of greater resources in the decentralization process.

### NOTES

[1] According to former law enforcement minister Fernando Rospigliosi, "the enormous weakness of the state—political discontinuity, frequent changes in ministers and the lack of interest on the part of Peruvian society"—is the biggest problem preventing the formation of long-term plans to eliminate the remnants of the guerrillas. *Latin America Weekly Report*, 27 July 2004.

[2] Among the allegations of corruption or misconduct against members of Toledo's inner circle are claims that members of his family falsified signatures to register his Peru Posible party for the 2000 elections; ironically,election fraud was one of the major charges candidate Toledo made against Fujimori.

[3] "Peru: Country Profile 2004" (London: Economist Intelligence Unit [EIU], 2004).

[4] "Global Corruption Report, 2004" (Berlin: Transparency International [TI], 2004), 232; "Few Count Out Contender for Peruvian Presidency," *Miami Herald*, 6 May 2001; "Peru: Rising Uncertainty Ahead of Elections," *LatinFocus*, May 2001; for a slightly different take on Soros's involvement in Peru, see Adrian Karatnycky, "Messianic Billionaire: Soros Funded Freedom Where It Was Lacking," *The Philanthropy Roundtable*, September/October 2002.

[5] "Denuncian en Peru a un hermano de Toledo," *La Opinion*, 12 September 2004.

[6] "Global Corruption Report, 2004" (TI), 235; personal communication (name withheld by request).

[7] Personal communication with Peruvian journalist (name withheld by request).

[8] "Peru" (Miami: Inter American Press Association [IAPA], October 2004).

[9] Ibid.

10  For a list of the Ombudsman's powers and faculties, see the sections "Que es la Defensoria del Pueblo?" and "Nuestra competencia," on their Web site, http://www.ombudsman.gob.pe.

11  "Peru Truth Commission Says Battle with Insurgents Killed Nearly 70,000,' *San Francisco Chronicle*, August 28, 2003; "Peru: Country Profile 2004" (EIU).

12  "Americas 2004 Report – Peru," *International Disability Rights Monitor*, 24 August 2004, http://www.cirnetwork.org/idrm/reports/americas/countries/peru.html.

13  See Consejo nacional para la integracion de la persona con discapacidad (CONADIS), http://www.conadisperu.gob.pe; "Americas 2004 Report – Peru," *International Disability Rights Monitor*.

14  Ibid.

15  "Privacy and Human Rights 2003: Peru" (London: Privacy International [PI], November 2003), http://www.privacyinternational.org/survey/phr2003/countries/peru.htm.

16  "Global Corruption Report, 2004" (TI), 233.

17  "Informe Anual de Derechos Humanos 2003," (Lima: Coordinadora Nacional de Derechos Humanos del Peru, 2004), 60.

18  "Informe Anual" (Coordinadora Nacional), 65.

19  According to "Privacy and Human Rights 2003: Peru" (PI), http://www.privacyinternational.org/survey/phr2003/countries/peru.htm, in 2002 a new law was passed regulating the interception of communications and private documents.

20  "Peru spy body scrapped," BBC News World Edition, 23 March 2004.

21  Tyler Bridges, "Land titles give poor a chance to advance," *Miami Herald*, 4 April 2004.

22  Tyler Bridges, "Land records are a tangled web," *Miami Herald*, 4 April 2004.

23  "Peru: Property Issues; General; Displaced Indigenous Populations Deprived from Access to Their Traditional Lands" (Geneva: Global [Internally Displaced Persons] IDP Project Database, 2004), http://www.db.idpproject.org/Sites/idpSurvey.nsf/wViewCountries/E04AF659CE5A9D4EC12567D80059B0F0.

24  *ViewsWire* (EIU), 12 July 2004.

25  "Peru: Talk of Corruption Trails Toledo" *Miami Herald*, 27 July 2004; *Proetica* (Lima), January 2004, http://www.transparency.org/surveys/dnld/proetica_survey_peru.pdf.

26  Montesinos received at least $10 million from the CIA ostensibly for counter-narcotics purposes but diverted the money to other, illegal activities.

27  "Peru Politics: Troubled Toledo" (EIU, 12 July 2004); on "denuncialogia," see Jason Felch, "Have Peru's Press Heroes Gone Too Far?" *Columbia Journalism Review* (July/August 2004).

28  "Doing Business: Snapshot of Business Environment—Peru" (Washington, DC: World Bank, 2004).

29  "Benefitting from the FTA—The Urgency for Improving the Business Climate," *Contact*, June 2004. The business group attributed the regional and local problems in part to "the process of decentralization and the consequent transfer of responsibilities from the Central Government to the regions."

30  "Denuncian . . .," *La Opinion*, 12 September 2004.

31  "Ministros peruanos se autolevantan secretos bancarios," *El Mercurio*, 2 August 2004.

32  "Lucha anticorrupcion bajo la lupa en Peru," *El Nuevo Herald*, 10 September 2004.

[33] "Informe Anual" (Coordinadora Nacional), 59–60.

[34] "Informe Anual" (Coordinadora Nacional), 60, notes, for example, that of 1,326 people accused of corruption, only 15 percent were jailed.

[35] "Global Corruption Report, 2004" (TI); "Transparencia," *Datos del Congreso* 27 (October 2004).

[36] "Latin America and the Caribbean: Peru," (Washington, DC: National Democratic Institute for International Affairs, 2004).

[37] "Denuncian . . .," La Opinion; "Toledo won't end probe that may target him," *Miami Herald*, 1 October 2004; "Lucha . . .," *El Nuevo Herald*.

[38] "Informe Anual" (Coordinadora Nacional), 60; "Advierten peligro en la lucha anticorrupcion," *El Comercio*, 14 September 2004.

[39] "Peru" (IAPA, 2004), http://www.sipiapa.org/pulications/report_peru2004o.cfm.

[40] "Global Corruption Report, 2004" (TI), 232.

[41] "Privacy and Human Rights 2003: Peru," (PI), http://www.privacyinternational.org/survey/phr2003/countries/peru.htm.

# PHILIPPINES

CAPITAL: Manila
POPULATION: 83.7 million
GNI PER CAPITA: $1,030

**SCORES**
ACCOUNTABILITY AND PUBLIC VOICE: 4.46
CIVIL LIBERTIES: 3.92
RULE OF LAW: 3.30
ANTICORRUPTION AND TRANSPARENCY: 3.50
(scores are based on a scale of 0 to 7, with
0 representing weakest and 7 representing
strongest performance)

*Gabriella R. Montinola*

## INTRODUCTION

In May 2004, the Philippines held its third set of general elections since the restoration of democracy in 1986. The exercise demonstrated the progress the country has made in terms of ensuring democratic accountability. Voter turnout was relatively high; a multitude of parties contested elections; hundreds of thousands of volunteers monitored the polls on election day, and the public accepted the results with few objections. However, the conduct of elections also highlighted a number of issues that need to be addressed if citizens are to be fully represented through the electoral process. First, the continued absence of coherent party platforms makes it difficult for voters to determine what various parties represent and thus precludes meaningful electoral choice. Second, current campaign finance laws perpetuate the undue influence of economically privileged interests. Finally, the institution charged with the administration of elections, the commission on elections, is too weak to ensure the integrity of the electoral process.

**Gabriella R. Montinola** is associate professor of political science at the University of California, Davis. Her current research interests center on the quality of democratic governance in developing countries. She has written several articles on the causes of corruption and the conditions that undermine the rule of law in the Philippines.

These persistent weaknesses in the electoral process limit voters' ability to hold elected officials accountable and have implications for the government's performance in other respects. One serious implication is the persistence of corruption at almost every level of government. While successive administrations have taken steps to reduce opportunities for corruption since 1986, these have not been sufficient to control corruption, largely because elected officials have not shown sufficient political will to enforce anticorruption laws. Like previous administrations, the current government has introduced a number of anticorruption initiatives. Although many of them provide grounds for optimism, it is too early to evaluate their impact.

The picture in terms of civil liberties is similarly mixed. On the one hand, the government has taken legal steps to ensure that citizens enjoy the rights protected in the 1987 constitution. On the other hand, many of these constitutional and legal provisions have not been fully implemented. Hence, while the constitution guarantees citizens due process and protection from torture, cases of arbitrary arrest, disappearances, and torture of suspected insurgents and their sympathizers persist. Similarly, while citizens are free to join groups and mobilize for peaceful protests, government forces do not always exercise restraint when dispersing demonstrators. This civil rights record suggests that the government does not have adequate control of its security forces. Notably, the performance of security forces in protecting citizens from each other is also lacking. While violent crime has been decreasing since 1986, homicides, physical injury, theft, and rape occur with sufficient regularity to be of concern.

The government has enacted many laws promoting women's rights, and their presence in top government positions indicates that they have achieved some degree of equity. In contrast, minority groups, specifically Muslims and groups identified by the government as indigenous peoples, continue to perceive that their rights to land and economic opportunities are not respected. This perception underlies the current armed conflict between the government and Muslim insurgents and the recent clashes that have occurred between the government's security forces, on one hand, and indigenous peoples and their sympathizers on the other.

The Philippine judicial system is currently undergoing comprehensive reforms to increase its capacity to uphold the rule of law. The reforms are designed to enhance the judiciary's independence, efficiency, and impartiality. The judicial system shows signs of improvement in the former two goals. The Supreme Court recently demonstrated its independence by rendering high-impact rulings against the executive's interest; court delays have decreased slightly over the past five years. But it is still too early to determine whether the reforms will produce an impartial judicial system.

Lack of civilian control of the military is another obstacle to establishing the rule of law in the Philippines. In 2003, a group of junior officers and enlisted men attempted to overthrow the civilian government. While the rebels were eventually persuaded to return to the barracks peaceably, and the likelihood of a successful coup is extremely low given the record of rebellious military officers since 1986, such incidents are reminders of the weakness of the Philippine state. A state that is unable to resolve the grievances of the military and deter coup attempts once and for all is unlikely to be strong enough to uphold the rule of law.

## ACCOUNTABILITY AND PUBLIC VOICE – 4.46

The Philippines is a republic with a bicameral presidential system. As stipulated in the present constitution, adopted in 1987, the president and vice president are elected by popular vote for single six-year terms. Members of the upper house, the Senate, are also elected nationwide by popular vote. Members of the lower house, the House of Representatives are elected in two ways: 80 percent are elected by plurality vote from single-member districts, and the remainder are elected from party lists under a closed-list proportional representation system. No party is permitted to have more than three seats of those allotted under this system. President Gloria Macapagal-Arroyo was elected in May 2004 after having served out the remainder of her predecessor's presidential term. Arroyo received 40 percent of the popular vote, a narrow victory over her closest contender. Arroyo's ruling party alliance currently holds 58 percent of seats in the Senate and 70 percent of seats in the House.

In the May 2004 elections, 74 percent of the more than 43 million registered voters went to the polls. The voters included over 230,000 overseas Filipino workers who, until the Overseas Absentee Voting Act was enacted in 2003, did not have the right to vote while out of the country.[1] The elections demonstrated the continued commitment of Filipinos to democracy. However, they also highlighted issues that need to be addressed if citizens are to be effectively represented through the electoral process.

One serious issue is the continuing weakness of Philippine political parties. Due in large part to electoral rules that encourage personality politics and the three-seat maximum for parties running under the party-list system, a dizzying array of parties contests elections in the Philippines. As in previous elections, the 2004 contest revolved around personalities rather than ideological platforms. Campaign rallies provided little information on parties' or candidates' policy positions. The absence of coherent platforms makes it difficult for voters to determine what various parties represent and thus precludes meaningful electoral choice.

A second issue concerns inequities in the financing of political parties and candidates. Although all parties and candidates have equal campaigning rights, the prohibitive cost of campaigns privileges wealthy candidates. The 1985 omnibus election code prohibits campaign contributions from specific individuals and entities, including financial institutions, public utility operators, government contractors, government civilian and military personnel, and foreigners and foreign corporations. But there are no limits on the size of contributions from individuals or entities not covered by the prohibition. Moreover, the code specifies limits on expenditures for election purposes, but enforcement of such limits is doubtful. Thus, economic elites continue to influence election results disproportionately.

A third issue concerns the weakness of the institution charged with administering elections: the commission on elections (COMELEC). The COMELEC's weakness was evident in its failure to fulfill three critical tasks. First, the COMELEC mishandled the automation of the country's voting system as specified in the Election Modernization Act of 1997. In May 2003, the COMELEC awarded the automation project to a technology firm without observing technical and legal requirements. The decision was challenged in court and ultimately nullified by the Supreme Court.[2] With no time to repeat the bidding process, the elections had to be held using the existing write-in ballot and manual vote-counting system. The manual system is extremely vulnerable to fraud, and as in previous elections, fraud was alleged during the tallying and shortly after the proclamation of the 2004 results. In the event, the electorate peaceably accepted the results, but only because nongovernmental organizations (NGOs) monitoring the elections expressed confidence in the results' validity.

Second, the COMELEC failed to ensure the accuracy and timely posting of voters' lists. The COMELEC received 1.2 billion pesos' (around US$21 million) worth of new technology to ensure that only those entitled to vote in the 2004 elections could do so. But on the eve of the elections, the COMELEC had not completed the voter validation process. The result was the disenfranchisement of voters whose names were missing from lists in precincts where they expected to vote. While this confusion did not result in "massive disenfranchisement," at least according to the officially designated nongovernment election-monitoring organization,[3] it does raise concerns about the COMELEC's capacity to administer elections effectively.

Finally, the COMELEC failed in its obligation to ensure the security of candidates and voters during the election period. While police records show that there were fewer incidents of poll violence—174 in 2004 as opposed to 267 in the previous general election—they also note that the number of deaths increased by 30 percent.[4] Moreover, the insurgent National People's Army (NPA) was reportedly extorting permit-to-campaign fees in the areas that it controlled.[5] While most election-related violence occurred in provincial towns or rural areas and may not have affected the results elsewhere, voters in areas where violence or the threat of violence existed were not free to make informed political choices and were thus effectively disenfranchised.

In sum, the country needs more programmatic parties, better enforcement of campaign finance regulations, and a more effective election monitoring commission if citizens are to be fully represented through the electoral process. That said, meaningful elections are only one component of democratic performance. It is also crucial that political actors be held accountable between elections. In this regard, the Philippines appears to have made considerable progress.

The Philippines' democratic accountability between elections is reinforced by the ability of each branch of government to check the abuses of power of the others. During the dictatorship of Ferdinand Marcos (1972–1986), neither the legislative nor the judicial branch could limit the power of the executive. Since then, both branches have demonstrated their ability to check the executive as well as each other. In December

2000, the legislature initiated impeachment proceedings against then-President Joseph Estrada for corruption, betrayal of the public trust, and culpable violation of the constitution. Twice in 2003 it initiated impeachment proceedings against the Supreme Court chief justice for misuse of funds under his control. None of these proceedings resulted in Senate convictions. Ultimately, street demonstrations and the military's loss of confidence in Estrada compelled him to leave the presidential palace (see "Rule of Law"), while the proceedings against the chief justice were aborted. Nonetheless, the legislature's actions indicate that it has the capacity to expose and thereby limit abuse of power by other branches of government.

Another positive feature of the Philippines' democracy is its vibrant and politically engaged civil society. Civil society in the Philippines is strong largely for two reasons. First, the state does not subject NGOs and other civic organizations to onerous registration requirements, nor does the state harass donors and funders of these organizations. Second, since 1986 the government has not only tolerated input from civic groups but has actively incorporated civil society organizations into decision-making processes. The local government code adopted in 1991 mandates that representatives of accredited NGOs sit on local development councils and school boards. More recently, in 2003, the president signed into law a Government Procurement Act, which mandates that NGO and private-sector representatives sit on executive department bids and awards committees (BACs).[6] With funding from the European Union, the government is starting to train volunteers from accredited civil society organizations to participate in these BACs. The increasing engagement of civil society in decision-making processes has promoted government accountability between elections.

Finally, democratic accountability in the Philippines is supported by active media. The media are free from direct state censorship. Allegations of corruption are given wide and extensive airing in news reports. Libel is considered a crime, but libel laws are not so onerous as to impede open criticism of state officials. State officials have reportedly attempted to control media content through informal contacts with journalists and editors, but these contacts appear not to have cowed the media.

This freedom of expression, however, is not as well protected by the state in rural areas as it is in the national capital region. Violence against journalists is not uncommon in provincial towns. Local government officials, local police, and military forces deployed in rural areas are often suspected of perpetrating this violence. In 2004 alone, 11 journalists were murdered after exposing government officials and security forces for corruption and other human rights violations.[7] The Philippines ranks among the top five countries in terms of journalists killed in the line of duty between 1995 and 2004.[8] To date, there have been few arrests and no convictions for crimes against journalists committed in past years.[9] Such violence constitutes a form of indirect censorship and suggests that government officials are less accountable in the country's rural areas.

*Recommendations*

- The government should encourage the development of programmatic parties by increasing the proportion of party-list seats in the House of Representatives and eliminating the three-seat limit per party.
- The government should follow through on the automation of the vote-tallying process prior to the next elections.
- The government should hold political parties responsible for election-related violence committed by their party members, ensuring prompt investigation, prosecution, and punishment.
- A clear set of qualifications for COMELEC commissioners should be drawn up, and the appointment process for commissioners should be more transparent and open to the public.
- The government should respond promptly to summary executions of journalists and ensure appropriate prosecution and punishment of perpetrators.

## CIVIL LIBERTIES – 3.92

The Philippine constitution, which guarantees citizens extensive rights, was adopted in 1987. Since then, the government has taken additional legal steps to ensure that citizens enjoy these rights. While most Filipinos enjoy the rights in practice, constitutional and legal provisions are sometimes contravened in cases of suspected insurgents and their sympathizers, minority groups, and the poor due to the administration's weak control over the country's security forces.

The constitution guarantees protection against deprivation of liberty without due process and against torture. Indeed, as stipulated in the constitution, a Commission on Human Rights was created in 1987 with the power to investigate, on its own or upon complaint, violations of these protections as well as other civil and political rights. Yet arbitrary arrests, long-term detention without trial, and even torture persist, primarily in cases of suspected insurgents and their sympathizers.[10] For example, in October 2003, a court ordered the release of 14 Muslim Filipinos who had been arrested in 2001 for sympathizing with a Muslim insurgent group. They had been illegally arrested; further, they alleged that they were tortured during detention. Yet no charges were filed against the alleged military perpetrators.[11] The case is not an aberration. From January to September 2004, 17 cases of torture involving 41 individuals were documented by the NGO Task Force Detainees of the Philippines (TFDP). In 2003, 20 cases were documented and the year before, 16.[12] These documented numbers are in all likelihood smaller than the actual incidence of torture. Legal impediments protect violators rather than victims. Torture victims must fulfill relatively strict evidentiary requirements in order to pursue their cases through the courts. Penalties provided for in existing laws fail to reflect the crime's grave nature. Few criminal cases have been filed against accused public officers, and conviction rates are extremely low.[13]

The government has also been deficient in responding to abductions and killings of peaceful activists, especially in regions where the government's security forces are in conflict with armed opposition groups. Many activists have been abducted or summarily executed by these armed groups, but by one estimate, more such crimes are perpetrated by the government's security forces or their vigilante supporters.[14] From January to September 2004, TFDP documented 7 cases of summary executions and 12 cases of "disappeared" individuals. The victims had been vocal in their criticism of government policy.[15]

Citizens whose rights are violated by the state can legally petition for redress through the judicial system. But the judicial system, while in the process of reform, is still biased against those of little means (see "Rule of Law"). The poor majority often do not have the education and financial resources to help them navigate the legal system.

Prison conditions are cause for concern. The prison population has increased by 50 percent since 2002—due in large part to harsher drug laws—but the resources of the penal system have remained the same. The result has been overcrowding and insufficient provision of basic necessities for prisoners.[16] Moreover, despite many laws designed to protect children in custody, children continue to be detained with adults in these overcrowded facilities and are thus vulnerable to abuse by other prisoners.[17] According to one children's rights group, at least 36 children per day are arrested and detained with adult prisoners.[18] Women in detention also continue to be vulnerable to rape and sexual abuse. In 1997, the government examined plans to improve the conditions of women in detention, including separate facilities for female offenders supervised by female staff and an institutionalized monitoring mechanism including NGO visits to police stations and jails. To date, these plans have not been implemented.

The constitution enshrines the right to form associations for purposes not contrary to the law as well as the right to mobilize and advocate for peaceful purposes. The state does not compel citizens directly or indirectly to belong to particular associations. The wide array of organizations in the country indicates the substantial freedom of association that Filipinos enjoy. In 2003, over 20 percent of the total number of paid employees in the country belonged to trade unions.[19] By one estimate, the country has over 70,000 NGOs actively advocating different causes,[20] although these NGOs are notably concentrated in Manila.

While citizens are free to join groups and mobilize for peaceful protests, the government often fails to exercise restraint when dispersing demonstrators. In July 2004, demonstrators called on the government to secure the release of a Filipino hostage in Iraq by recalling Philippine troops. Although the government ultimately responded to the demands of the demonstrators, more than 500 individuals were reported to have been hurt that day as security forces tried to disperse the crowd.[21]

The government has a relatively strong record with respect to freedom of conscience and belief. The vast majority of Filipinos are Roman Catholic (83 percent); Protestants make up 9 percent, Muslims 5 percent, and other faiths the remainder. While Catholics predominate in government, the state does not interfere in the appointment of religious leaders or the internal activities of other peaceful faith-related organizations, nor does it place restrictions on religious observance, religious ceremony, or religious education.

While they are free to practice their religion, Filipino Muslims' rights to land and economic opportunities generally have not been respected by successive governments. This history of discrimination underlies the current armed conflict between the government and Muslim groups, which essentially began in 1972. In an effort to address Muslim concerns, the architects of the 1987 constitution provided for the creation of an autonomous region in Muslim Mindanao (ARMM). But the establishment of ARMM did not end the insurgency because many Muslims as well as Christians in the region were dissatisfied with the way the region's boundaries were set and the region's lack of fiscal autonomy. Since then, successive governments have alternated between conciliatory and aggressive military tactics in dealing with the armed insurgents.

There are two distinct Muslim organizations whose stated goal is to establish an independent Islamic state in the southern Philippines: the Moro Islamic Liberation Front (MILF) and the Abu Sayyaf. Both are offshoots of the Moro National Liberation Front (MNLF), an older secessionist organization. Numerous times over the past decade, the MILF, which is estimated to have as many as 15,000 armed members,[22] and the government have agreed to cease hostilities—but each time, fighting resumed shortly thereafter. This is in part due to the contradictory policies of the government. For example, even as the government advocated peace talks, the army attacked an MILF base in February 2003. Negotiations have also been complicated by revelations that members of an Indonesia-based group with links to al-Queda, Jemaah Islamiah (JI), have trained in MILF camps, despite statements by MILF leaders to the contrary. In February 2004, the parties met to discuss conditions for formal peace talks. As of September 2004, peace talks had not resumed (formal talks had occurred—and failed—in October 2001).[23] Meanwhile, militarization of the area due to the conflict has created many opportunities for violations of the rights of peaceful residents, both Muslim and Christian, in the area.

The Abu Sayyaf is estimated to have only a few hundred members. The government considers them nothing more than bandits—the organization is infamous for its use of piracy and ransom kidnapping to finance its activities—and has refused to negotiate with the organization. In part due to the Abu Sayyaf's past links with al-Queda, in 2001 the United States offered the Philippine government nearly US$100 million in military aid to eradicate them.[24] U.S. forces have also been deployed on two separate occasions between 2002 and 2003 to train, advise, and assist Philippine troops in their fight against the Abu Sayyaf. In April 2004, the government claimed to be close to eradicating the organization, but as of September 2004, the group's leaders remained at large.

Muslims are not the only group in the Philippines to perceive discrimination by successive governments. Between 15 percent and 20 percent of the population belong to distinct groups identified as indigenous peoples.[25] Until 1987, indigenous peoples' rights to their communal landholdings were not legally recognized, and the people were progressively dispossessed of their lands. Since then, the government has tried to accommodate indigenous peoples' concerns. The 1987 constitution recognizes indigenous communities' rights to their ancestral lands. In 1997, the government enacted the Indigenous Peoples Rights Act (IPRA), which created a commission—the National Commission on Indigenous Peoples—to implement the rights guaranteed in the constitution. The constitution and the IPRA provide a solid framework for the promotion of indigenous peoples' rights, including to their ancestral lands. However, the state's commitment to protecting indigenous peoples' rights is questionable. The titling of ancestral land has occurred at a snail's pace.[26] Moreover, the government continues to promote mining projects that would displace indigenous peoples or degrade the environment surrounding their ancestral lands.[27]

In contrast, the government has a reasonable record in the promotion of gender equity. Many laws promoting women's rights have been enacted since 1986. One of the most significant is the 1991 Women in Development and Nation-Building Act, which ensures that a substantial portion of official development assistance from foreign governments and multilateral organizations is set aside for agencies and programs that promote women's rights. The national government also employs policies, including relatively flexible time schedules and maternity leave, that promote recruitment and retention of women in the civil service.[28] While implementation of laws promoting women's rights could be more forceful, women have achieved some degree of equity in the Philippines. Two of the four presidents in the post-Marcos period have been women, although both were related to powerful men. The current president has appointed several women to head key executive departments and constitutional commissions. Among Filipino senators 17 percent are women, as are 14 percent of the members of the incoming 13th House of Representatives.[29] Filipino women constitute over 50 percent of civil service employees. Women continue to be underrepresented, however, at the higher levels of the civil service: They fill only 30 percent of positions at the executive/managerial level.[30]

During 2003 to 2004, two new laws protecting the interests of women were enacted. The Anti-Violence Against Women and Their Children Act criminalizes violence against domestic partners and their children. The Anti-Trafficking in Persons Act establishes institutional mechanisms for the protection and support of trafficked persons, mainly women and children. It stipulates penalties not only for offenders, but also for legal officers and medical practitioners who fail to protect the privacy of trafficking victims.[31] It remains to be seen whether the new laws will be implemented in such a way as to deter these crimes.

The Philippine government formally recognizes people with disabilities as a sector of society that has traditionally been disadvantaged in terms of access to basic services, in large part due to their extreme poverty. In an effort to address the concerns of the country's poor majority, including people with disabilities, the government established a National Anti-Poverty Commission (NAPC) in 1998. The NAPC, which is composed of representatives from national government agencies, local governments, and basic sectors of society identified as traditionally disadvantaged, meets regularly to develop and review government anti-poverty projects, including those specifically targeted at people with disabilities. While some progress has been made in integrating these people into mainstream society—in large part due to the efforts of NGOs—they continue to face problems of access to basic social services, housing, education, and employment.[32]

## Recommendations

- Allegations of torture and violations of due process should be investigated promptly and fully, and the government should ensure appropriate prosecution and punishment.
- Laws designed to protect children in custody should be strictly enforced. Female offenders should have separate facilities supervised by female staff.
- Peace talks between the government and the MILF should be resumed, and the autonomous region of Muslim Mindanao should be given genuine fiscal autonomy.

- The titling of indigenous peoples' lands should be expedited. Guidelines should be established for compensating indigenous peoples whose titles are revoked for governmental use.
- Training for law-enforcement personnel should include techniques on negotiating with demonstrators in order to reduce the use of force. Law enforcement personnel determined to have used force indiscriminately should be appropriately punished.

## RULE OF LAW – 3.30

The Philippines' performance in rule of law, including an independent, impartial, and well-functioning judicial system and civilian control over the military, is mixed. The Philippine judiciary's vulnerability to political influence is a persistent concern. The source of this influence varies at different court levels. At the highest levels, such as the Supreme Court, the Sandiganbayan (Anti-Graft Court), and the Court of Appeals, politicization occurs during the appointment process. Justices and judges are appointed by the president, who must choose from a list of at least three individuals nominated by a judicial and bar council (JBC). The JBC is composed of four *ex officio* members—the chief justice, the secretary of justice, a senator, and a member of the house—and four regular members from the Integrated Bar of the Philippines (IBP), the official organization composed of all lawyers in the country. The inclusion in the appointment process of professional lawyers from the IBP was intended to limit the influence of politicians over judicial appointments. But because IBP members in the JBC are appointed by the president with the consent of the commission on appointments, which is composed of members of each congressional house, it is unclear whether this goal has been achieved. Thus, while almost all justices and judges nominated by the JBC and ultimately appointed by the president meet generally accepted minimum qualifications, the judiciary, especially justices at the higher-level courts, are vulnerable to charges of political influence when they rule on high-profile cases.

Politicization of lower-court decisions is typically due not to the appointment process but to local courts' lack of resources. Because of the meager budget of the judicial branch, salaries of local court personnel, including judges, are not competitive with those of similar positions in the private sector. To compensate for this problem, local government units are authorized to augment the salaries of local court personnel. As these allowances are disbursed at the discretion of local governments, the latter have the opportunity to place undue pressure on judges.

These concerns notwithstanding, high-court justices are evidently able to resist political pressures. In November 2003, the Supreme Court declared the second impeachment case initiated by a group of legislators against the high court's chief justice unconstitutional (see "Accountability and Public Voice"). Although this case may have been politically motivated, the action by the Supreme Court was a genuine demonstration of its independence, and the legislature accepted the decision.

High-court justices have also been able to resist political pressures from the executive branch. In 2004, the Supreme Court declared null and void several substantial contracts between government agencies and private corporations.[33] In addition, the high court dismissed a petition to disqualify Fernando Poe Jr. from the presidential race of 2004. Poe was incumbent president Gloria Macapagal-Arroyo's strongest rival for the presidency. These examples demonstrate both the ability and the willingness of the judiciary to limit the powers of other branches of government. Moreover, recent developments suggest that lower-court judges should be better able to resist pressures from local government officials. In 2003, Congress enacted a bill, the Judiciary Compensation Act, that increased local court judges' salaries and allowances.

A more serious problem in the administration of justice is the inability of courts to resolve disputes in a timely manner. Delays in case resolution deny the affected parties justice and discourage victims from seeking redress. A study performed in 2002 showed that criminal cases can take as long as five and a half years to be decided, while cases involving corruption of government officials take over nine years.[34] It should be stressed that these delays are generally not due to the incompetence of judges; they are largely due to the high rate of judge vacancies vis-à-vis the increasing number of cases filed and the primitive case-flow management systems and poor equipment used by courts.

In 2001, the current Supreme Court chief justice launched a comprehensive reform program designed, among other goals, to improve the efficiency of the judicial system. While the reforms have not yet been fully implemented, courts are already showing some improvement in their disposition of cases. Although the total number of cases filed each year is increasing, the average number of cases disposed of as a percentage of total cases filed in all courts around the country increased from 59 percent in 1999 to 70 percent in 2003.[35]

The most serious problem of the Philippine judicial system is its lack of impartiality. In general, the system favors individuals with political connections or wealth. The problem is particularly acute because of the extremely unequal distribution of wealth and power in the country. Prosecution of high-ranking government officials is rare; conviction is even rarer. As the current ombudsman acknowledges, no "big fish" has been successfully prosecuted in at least 15 years.[36] In a 2004 survey, only 40 percent of respondents agreed with the statement: "Whether rich or poor, people who have cases in court generally receive equal treatment."[37] There is some basis to the majority's perception. People of higher economic status run less risk of being arrested, prosecuted, and convicted of crimes. They have the resources to hire top lawyers and/or bribe legal officers. In criminal trials, while all those prosecuted are presumed innocent until proven guilty and are provided with counsel if it is beyond their means, implementation of these rights depends on the accused's knowledge and ability to assert his or her rights. Poor defendants with little education and/or a weak command of English are often unable to understand their counsel, who generally use legal terms and speak in English.[38] The chief justice's comprehensive reform program currently under way is designed to address this problem, but it is still too early to tell if they will do so.

Lack of civilian control of the military is also an obstacle to establishing the rule of law in the Philippines. Since 1972, the military has engaged periodically in overt political activity. For example, in 2001, besieged by demonstrators calling for his resignation, Estrada decided to abandon the presidential palace when senior military officers made clear their intention to support Vice President Arroyo as the new head of government. As recently as July 2003, a group of junior military officers organized a rebellion to overthrow the government. While the rebels were eventually persuaded to return to the barracks peaceably, the incident indicates the state's vulnerability to military intervention. A fact-finding commission created to investigate the incident found that the coup attempt had involved months of planning, which had occurred under the noses of senior military officers and civilian officials. Notably, the commission also discovered that groups identified with former president Estrada and former senator and retired colonel Gregorio Honasan supported the rebels.[39] This suggests that elements in the military may be influenced by non-state actors as well.

While the government generally refrains from infringing on individuals' property rights, the time it takes to resolve civil cases, which typically involve disputes over property, renders these rights relatively insecure. According to a World Bank study, on average more than a year is required to enforce a contract and more than five and a half years to resolve bankruptcy disputes through the courts.[40]

*Recommendations*

- More resources should be devoted to ensure that poor defendants are provided with appropriate counsel, and that citizens in rural areas have easier access to courts.
- Salaries of judges should be increased in order to attract sufficient numbers of qualified individuals to fill judge vacancies.
- Alternative dispute resolution mechanisms should be promoted in order to alleviate the backlog of cases in court dockets.
- Non-state actors and/or civilian political leaders suspected of promoting and supporting rebellion among military ranks should be vigorously investigated and prosecuted.

## ANTICORRUPTION AND TRANSPARENCY – 3.50

Since the restoration of democracy in 1986, the Philippines has experienced major changes that theoretically should have reduced opportunities for corruption. One significant change has been the reduction in the state's role in the economy. Since 1986, nearly 500 state-owned enterprises have been privatized, and several critical sectors of the economy have been deregulated. Nominal tariff rates are now within ceilings set by the World Trade Organization.[41] Another important change has been the increased transparency of government decision-making processes, including the executive budget-making process. While the legislature may only reduce appropriations recommended by the executive, the budget now requires legislative approval and is routinely subjected to meaningful review. Congressional budget committee hearings and plenary debates are open to the public and are regularly attended by the media. Furthermore, expenditure accounts are available to citizens on written request.

Despite these positive longer-term developments, both high-level and petty corruption remain pervasive, largely due to weak enforcement of anticorruption laws. The reasons for this failure vary across different auditing and investigative bodies. The internal audit division of the country's tax collection agency, the bureau of internal revenue (BIR), is highly inefficient. From January 2001 to May 2004, 140 corruption charges were filed against 136 BIR personnel. As of June 2004, the division had resolved only 20 cases.[42] This slow pace in processing charges, whatever the reason, contributes to the perception that BIR officials can engage in corruption with relative impunity. In public opinion surveys, the BIR consistently ranks as one of the most corrupt departments within government.[43]

In contrast, the personnel of the commission on audit (COA), the independent body charged with auditing government expenditures, are generally considered highly competent. In 2003, the current COA chairman was selected to be a member of the United Nations Board of Auditors, and 36 veteran COA auditors were selected to be part of the UN auditors pool.[44] But COA's authority is limited to exposing anomalies. The commission does not have the authority to punish or prosecute corrupt officials.

The main agency charged with prosecuting as well as investigating corruption cases is the office of the ombudsman (OMB). The constitution guarantees the OMB's political independence: The ombudsman serves a seven-year, fixed term of office with no possibility of reappointment and is removable only by impeachment. However, the OMB's record indicates that institutional independence does not guarantee efficacy in the fight against corruption. Under the leadership of the first ombudsman (1988–1995), the OMB was notoriously inefficient. By the end of 1994, the office had a backlog of 14,652 cases.[45] The second ombudsman's record (1995–2002) was no better. Indeed, confidence in his integrity dropped so low that impeachment proceedings were initiated against him for bribery and betrayal of the public trust.

In response to these persistent problems, several steps the current government has taken to combat corruption provide grounds for optimism. First, between 2003 and 2004, the government increased the OMB's budget, allowing the agency to double the number of its prosecutors. While no big fish have yet been convicted, the OMB has used the additional resources to investigate mid-level government officials more thoroughly. This appears to have improved the OMB's performance: The agency's conviction rate rose from 6 percent in 2003 to 14 percent in 2004.[46] This suggests that the OMB is capable of combating corruption, given committed leadership and adequate resources.

Second, Arroyo has established a novel anti-graft institution: a "Lifestyle Checks Coalition," composed of the heads of government departments, intelligence-gathering units, prosecuting agencies including the OMB, and representatives of civil society organizations. The most innovative aspect of this initiative is the institutionalization of the public's role in identifying government officials whose lifestyles appear inconsistent with their officially declared income and assets. With funding from the European Union, the government has been training volunteers from accredited NGOs to perform these lifestyle checks. Notably, there does not appear to be a shortage of volunteers willing to join the coalition, despite the fact that they can expect no compensation from the government for their services and the country has no whistle-blowers act to protect those who expose corrupt officials.

Third, the government is continuing to reduce bureaucratic regulations and registration requirements, thereby further reducing opportunities for corruption. Over the past two years, it has streamlined review and approval procedures for government contracts, reduced the number of signatories required for licenses and permits, and reduced the number of documentary requirements to participate in government-sponsored programs.[47]

Finally, the government is taking steps to increase transparency further. Two main developments stand out. First, in 2000, the government launched an online system for procurement. As of June 2004, more than 7,000 suppliers and 2,500 government units had registered with the system, and more than 45,000 new bid notices and 7,000 awards had been posted online. The second phase of this project—actual online bidding and trading—is expected to be operative by September 2005.[48] With the establishment of an online record of all bids and awards, this measure should make it easier to monitor the competitiveness of the procurement process.

Second, in 2004, the government secured funding from foreign donors to create a publicly available data bank of public officials' statements of assets, liabilities, and net worth.[49] Although citizens have a constitutional right to view such statements, the latter are currently difficult to obtain. Record-keeping practices of the different government agencies vary; in some agencies, documents are available only haphazardly, and if government agencies choose to withhold or delay access to information, the only recourse is to petition the Supreme Court for redress of an unconstitutional act. By facilitating access to public officials' financial statements, the data bank will eliminate the need to go to court and facilitate detection and prevention of corruption.

## Recommendations

- The government should ensure appropriate prosecution and punishment of high-ranking government officials by devoting more resources to the office of the ombudsman contingent on continued improvement in the agency's performance.
- A law providing legal protections for whistle-blowers should be adopted.
- A freedom of information act providing clear penalties for the unlawful denial of access and destruction of records should be adopted.

## NOTES

[1] Ellene A. Sana, "The OAV Law: Defend and Amend, Guarantee Its Continued Exercise," *Kasama* 18, 2 (2004), http://www.cpcabrisbane.org/Kasama/2004/V18n2/OAV.htm.

[2] Information Technology Foundation of the Philippines et al. v. Commission on Elections et al. (Philippine Sup. Ct. No. 159139, 13 January 2004).

[3] National Citizen's Movement for Free Elections (NAMFREL). In the same report, NAMFREL estimates that "disenfranchisement may have run as high as two million voters." "The Terminal Report to NAMFREL Operation Quick Count 2004" (Manila: NAMFREL, 30 June 2004).

[4] Christina Mendez, "Political Groups Are Closely Watched for Destabilization," *Philippine Star,* 20 May 2004, http://www.newsflash.org/2004/02/hl/hl100384.htm.

[5] Christian V. Esguerra, "PNP fears bloody polls; 125 private armies identified," *Inquirer News Service,* 18 March 2004, http://www.inq7.net/nat/2004/mar/18/nat_1-1.htm.

[6] "SONA Updates: As of 30 June 2004," (Manila: State of the Nation Address [SONA] Updates), http://www.gov.ph/sona/SONAUpdates_30June2004.pdf.

[7] Sonny Evangelista, "We Want Concrete Actions to Stop the Killing of Journalists, Media People Tell President Arroyo," *AsiaNews.it,* 17 November 2004.

[8] "Journalists Killed in the Line of Duty: Statistics for 1995–2004" (New York: Committee to Protect Journalists, n.d.), http://www.cpj.org/killed/Ten_Year_Killed/stats.html.

[9] "Philippines – 2004 Annual Report" (Paris: Reporters Without Borders, 5 March, 2004), http://www.rsf.org/print.php3?id_article=10089.

[10] "Philippines: Torture Persists: Appearance and Reality within the Criminal Justice System" (London: Amnesty International [AI], 24 January, 2003), http://web.amnesty.org/library/Index/ENGASA350012003?open&of=ENG-PHL.

[11] "2004 Report: Philippines" (AI), http://web.amnesty.org/report2004/phl-summary-eng.

[12] "Cases of Torture Under the Arroyo Government" (Manila: Task Force Detainees of the Philippines, n.d.), http://www.tfdp.org/resources/1statistics.htm.

[13] "Philippines: Torture Persists" (AI), 28–31, http://web.amnesty.org/library/Index/ENGASA350012003?open&of=ENG-PHL.

[14] "Human Rights Record of the Philippines: Spectacular on Paper" (New Delhi: Asian Centre for Human Rights, 2003), 7–9.

[15] Aurora Corazon A. Parong, M.D., "Martial Law, 32 Years Hence: Lessons from Our Past, Challenges for Our Present" (Manila: Philippine Human Rights Update, June 2004), http://www.tfdp.org/resources/ar_martiallawspeechsept04.pdf.

[16] Sonny Evangelista, "A prison system on the verge of collapse," *Asianews.it*, 22 October 2004, http://www.asianews.it/view.php?l=en&art=1747.

[17] "2004 Report: Philippines" (AI), http://web.amnesty.org/report2004/phl-summary-eng.

[18] "Philippines: Alternatives to Jail Sought for Kids [News]" (Hong Kong: Asian Human Rights Commission), Asia Child Rights *Weekly Newsletter* 3, 3 (21 January 2004), http://acr.hrschool.org/mainfile.php/0162/261.

[19] "Extent of Unionism" (Manila: Philippine Department of Labor and Employment), *Labstat Updates* 8, 13 (October 2004).

[20] Caroline Hartnell, "The Philippines: Self-Regulation on Trial," *Alliance* 8, 4 (December 2003), http://www.allavida.org/alliance/alliancehome.html.

[21] See House Resolution No. 75, introduced by six members of the House of Representatives, http://www.bayanmuna.net/legislation/reso/HR_75.htm.

[22] "Southern Philippines Backgrounder: Terrorism and the Peace Process," Asia Report no. 80 (Singapore/Brussels: International Crisis Group, 13 July 2004).

[23] "Mindanao Peaceweaves call for the formal resumption of peace talks" (Davao City, Philippines: Initiatives for International Dialogue, 27 September 2004), http://www.iidnet.org/adv/mda/2004/peaceweavers_ontalks.htm.

[24] "Terrorism in the Philippines: The Jolo Conundrum," *The Economist*, 22 November 2001.

[25] The Philippine Indigenous Peoples Rights Act (IPRA) defines indigenous peoples as "homogeneous societies identified by self-ascription and ascription by others, who have continuously lived as organized community on communally bounded and defined territory, and who have, under claims of ownership since time immemorial, occupied, possessed and utilized such territories, sharing common bonds of language, customs, traditions and other distinctive cultural traits, or who have, through resistance to political, social and cultural inroads of colonization, non-indigenous religions and cultures, become historically differentiated from the majority of Filipinos."

[26] "Indigenous Issues" (New York: United Nations Economic and Social Council, Commission on Human Rights, 5 March 2003, http://www.unhchr.ch/huridocda/huridoca.nsf/e06a5300f90fa0238025668700518ca4/568f8e64e2800006c1256cf7005d2593/$FILE/G0311521.pdf.

27  See, for example, "Mindoro Nickel Project MPSA Reinstated" (London: Mines & Communities, 24 March 2004), http://www.minesandcommunities.org/Action/press300.htm; Ma. Elisa P. Osorio, "High Court upholds mining law," *Manila Times*, 2 December 2004.

28  Assistant Commissioner Mary Ann Z. Fernandez, "Diversity Policies and Practices in the Civil Service: The Philippine Experience" (Chicago, Ill.: International Public Management Association for Human Resources, Annual Conference, 9–13 September 2003).

29  Calculated by the author from lists of Senate and House members available on the Web sites for each house of congress.

30  Mary Ann Z. Fernandez, "Diversity Policies . . ." (International Public Management Association for Human Resources).

31  "Prioritizing Women's Issues: 12th Philippine Congress" (Pasig City, Philippines: Center for Legislative Development), *Legislative Women's Watch*, May 2004.

32  Foundation for International Learning, "Identifying Disability Issues Related to Poverty Reduction: Philippines Country Study" (Manila: Asian Development Bank, 2002).

33  "High Impact Supreme Court Decisions" (Manila: Transparent Accountable Governance, n.d.), http://www.tag.org.ph/judiciaryWatch/high_impact.htm.

34  Rosemary Hunter, "Philippines Case Decongestion and Delay Reduction Project" (Washington, DC: World Bank, 2002), http://www1.worldbank.org/publicsector legal/CDDRPpresentation.ppt.

35  "Statistics on Public Order, Safety and Justice" (Manila: National Statistical Coordination Board, 1 July 2004), http://www.nscb.gov.ph/secstat/d_safety.asp.

36  "Ombudsman's Briefing Paper on its Anti-Corruption Program," presentation by Simeon V. Marcelo at the Combatting Corruption Conference, Makati, Philippines, 22 September 2004.

37  Mahar Mangahas, "A Public Opinion Survey on the Courts: Philippines 2003" (Manila: Asian Development Bank, International Symposium on Judicial Independence, 7 August 2003).

38  "Report on RETA 5856: Legal Literacy for Supporting Governance—'Legal Empowerment: Advancing Good Governance and Poverty Reduction'" (Manila: Asian Development Bank, 2001).

39  "The Report of the Fact Finding Commission," pursuant to Administrative Order No. 78 of the President of the Republic of the Philippines" (Manila: Information Site on Philippine Politics and Government, 30 July 2003), http://www.i-site.ph/Record/ FFFC-Report/FactFinding%20AO78%20Report%20-%20Part%201.PDF.

40  "Snapshot of Business Environment—Philippines" (Washington, DC: World Bank, 2005), http://rru.worldbank.org/DoingBusiness/ExploreEconomies/BusinessClimate Snapshot.aspx?economyid=153.

41  "Country Commerce: Philippines" (New York: Economist Intelligence Unit, 2004).

42  "SONA Updates: As of 30 June 2004" (SONA), http://www.gov.ph/sona/SONA Updates_30June2004.pdf.

43  Social Weather Survey, annual public opinion surveys performed by Social Weather Stations (Quezon City, Philippines: Social Weather Stations), http://www.sws.org.ph.

44  "PICPA Installs Chair Carague in Accountancy Hall of Fame" (Manila: Commission on Audit), *COA News* 4, 8 (November–December 2003).

[45] Cecile C. A. Balgos, "Ombudsman," in Sheila S. Coronel, ed., *Pork and Other Perks: Corruption and Governance in the Philippines* (Metro Manila: Philippine Center for Investigative Journalism, 1998).

[46] "Anti-Corruption" in *Medium-term Philippine Development Plan 2004–2010* (Metromanila, Philippines: Philippines National Economic and Development Agency, 2004), 249–53.

[47] "SONA Updates: As of 30 June 2004" (SONA), http://www.gov.ph/sona/SONA Updates_30June2004.pdf.

[48] Ibid.

[49] "Philippines, World Bank Ink Grant to Support Ombudsman's Anti-Corruption Activities" (World Bank, Press Release, 21 October 2004), http://www.worldbank.org.ph/WBSITE/EXTERNAL/COUNTRIES/EASTASIAPACIFICEXT/PHILIPPINESEXTN/0,,contentMDK:20270207~menuPK:333002~pagePK:141137~piPK:141127~theSitePK:332982,00.html.

# RUSSIA

CAPITAL: Moscow
POPULATION: 144.1 million
GNI PER CAPITA: $2,130

**SCORES**

ACCOUNTABILITY AND PUBLIC VOICE: 2.88
CIVIL LIBERTIES: 3.72
RULE OF LAW: 3.41
ANTICORRUPTION AND TRANSPARENCY: 2.79
(scores are based on a scale of 0 to 7, with
0 representing weakest and 7 representing
strongest performance)

*Michael McFaul with Sanja Tatic*[1]

## INTRODUCTION

The end of communism did not lead smoothly to the beginning of democracy in most of the states that emerged from the collapse of the Soviet Union in 1991. For most of the 1990s, the regime in Russia appeared trapped somewhere between dictatorship and democracy. On the one hand, the autocratic institutions of the Soviet *ancien regime* had collapsed and were replaced by the basic elements of an electoral democracy. Throughout the 1990s, major political leaders came to power through the ballot box in semi-competitive elections. The constitution, adopted in 1993, remained the highest law of the land, and by the end of the decade, few political leaders or organizations remained committed to overtly anti-democratic programs or extra-constitutional tactics. On the other hand, this political system lacked most of the elements of a liberal democracy, such as a powerful legislative check on executive power, an independent courts system, or a vibrant party system and civil

---

**Michael McFaul** is the Peter and Helen Bing Senior Fellow at the Hoover Institution, and an associate professor of political science at Stanford University. He is also a non-resident associate at the Carnegie Endowment for International Peace. He is the author and editor of several monographs. **Sanja Tatic** is a researcher at Freedom House.

society. The Russian polity nonetheless seemed stable and typical for the region.[2]

In the last several years, regimes have begun to move out of the post-Soviet gray zone between autocracy and democracy. Serbia, Georgia, and Ukraine have experienced a second wave of democratization jump-started by societal mobilization to thwart falsified elections. Under the rule of President Vladimir Putin, Russia has moved in the opposite direction. Putin did not inherit a consolidated democracy when he became president in 2000, and he has not radically violated the 1993 constitution, cancelled elections, or arrested hundreds of political opponents. Russia today remains much freer and more democratic than the Soviet Union. However, although the formal institutions of Russian democracy remain in place, the actual democratic content of these institutions has eroded considerably in the last few years. Putin has systematically weakened or destroyed every check on his power, while at the same time strengthening the state's ability to violate the constitutional rights of individual citizens. He has weakened the power of Russia's regional leaders, the independent media, the business community or oligarchs, both houses of parliament, the Russian prime minister and his government (as opposed to the presidential administration), independent political parties, and genuine civil society. At the same time, he has increased the role of the federal security service (FSB, the successor to the KGB) in governing Russia and arbitrarily wielded the power of state institutions such as the courts, the tax inspectors, and the police for political ends. Furthermore, throughout his time in office, Putin has waged an inhumane war in Chechnya against citizens of his own country.

Today, decision-making authority is more concentrated in the office of the president than at any time in Russia's post-Soviet history. The Russian polity has considerably less pluralism in 2004 than it did in 2000, and the human rights of individual Russian citizens are less secure. Russia's 1993 constitution established a set of formal rules that facilitated Putin's campaign to consolidate power in the presidency.[3] Moreover, the anarchy and uncertainty during the regime of his predecessor, Boris Yeltsin, created a demand for political order and stability within society. Putin has succeeded in undermining pluralism because he has remained popular, while societal actors and individuals within the state have proven reluctant or incapable of preventing these democratic rollbacks. In public opinion surveys, most Russians continue to express support for democratic practices and values.[4] However, the majority is also reluctant to fight for the defense of these principles. Putin has remained popular even as public support for his policies—including the protracted war in Chechnya, the elimination of direct elections of governors, and structural economic reforms—has waned. The autocratic turn in Russia was not inevitable or determined by the weight of Russian history or culture or demanded by the people; after all, this same history and culture preceded Soviet and then Russian democratization, which began two decades ago. Rather, Putin is the main driver of Russia's recent authoritarian drift.

In the long run, the forces of internal modernization and international integration will push Russia in a democratic direction. In the short run, however, the prospects for renewed democratization in Russia look uncertain. Putin now faces no serious opposition. Those willing to criticize the president—human rights activists, a handful of print journalists, a few former senior government officials, and a smattering of individual politicians in the State Duma (parliament) and regional assemblies—have little or no power. This new balance of power within the Russian polity offers Putin and his allies the possibility to rule Russia for a long, long time. He most certainly can amass the support to amend the constitution and extend his time in office, currently now limited by the constitution to two terms. Under more dire circumstances, he probably has the power to suspend the constitution altogether.

The real question for the short term, therefore, is what kind of political system Putin ultimately does desire. So far, he has demonstrated little tolerance for criticism or checks on his power. At the same time, he has demonstrated no proclivity for resurrecting full-blown dictatorship. He has not taken more extreme steps of canceling elections or arresting hundreds of political opponents. Even in his persecution of dissident forces, he has used the law, not brute force. It is an arbitrary use of the law for political purposes, but it is not open defiance of the law or democratic procedures altogether. Putin most certainly has not articulated an alternative ideology or project in opposition to democracy. In this sense, he must be distinguished from those communists, fascists, and extreme Islamists from the past and present who have openly challenged democracy as a political practice. However, whether Potemkin democracy, or "managed democracy" as Kremlin loyalists euphemistically call it, facilitates the future development of meaningful democratic practices or not is an open question. Today, we know one thing for sure: that for Putin and Putin alone to decide what kind of political regime Russia should have is a bad sign for the future of Russian democracy.

## ACCOUNTABILITY AND PUBLIC VOICE – 2.88

Competitive elections are the most dramatic institutional change that distinguishes the new Russian political system from the old Soviet dictatorship. During the Soviet period, elections occurred on a regular basis but lacked any real political consequences. In 1993, Boris Yeltsin used force to crush the Russian parliament and thereafter fiat into place a new constitution and electoral system. Though the process of establishing these procedures was not democratic, the new rules did stick. Between 1993 and 2003, national elections occurred on time and under law. Incumbents, especially President Yeltsin when seeking reelection in 1996, enjoyed tremendous advantages over challengers. In parliamentary votes, some parties and individuals were barred from competing in the electoral process, and falsification did occur. However, the basic rules of the game prevailed, campaigns were competitive, and the outcomes of national elections were not predetermined by those sitting in the Kremlin.

Over the last two electoral cycles, the political implications of elections have changed considerably. In particular, under President Putin, the outcomes of elections have become more certain, less competitive, and therefore less meaningful in Russian politics. As Yeltsin's prime minister and chosen successor, Putin became president in March 2000 elections after Yeltsin's resignation the previous December. In combination with the 1999 legislative victory of state-supported Unity, this marked the beginning of the Kremlin's dominance over national electoral politics in Russia.

After a decade of chaotic revolutionary change, Russian citizens yearned for stability. With the exception of the ongoing war in Chechnya, Putin delivered. The Russian economy grew more in each year of Putin's first term in office than in all of the previous decade. Whether or not this growth was due to Putin's economic reforms, the public gave Putin the credit.

It is not surprising, therefore, that Putin and his allies won again in the 2003 parliamentary elections and the 2004 presidential elections. In December 2003, his party—United Russia (the latest incarnation of

Unity)—won a major victory. They captured more than a third of the popular vote on the party list, which determined 50 percent or 225 of the seats in the Duma, and won more than 100 of the 225 single-mandate contests. Two other parties close to the Kremlin also performed well beyond expectations: the Liberal Democratic Party of Russia (LDPR) and Rodina (Motherland). After independents lined up behind different factions in the Duma, United Russia and its allies controlled the two-thirds majority needed to pass amendments to the constitution.

While the pro-Kremlin parties surged in 2003, the main opposition parties on both left and right faltered. On the left, the Communist Party of the Russian Federation (CPRF) lost half of its party-list vote from 1999. As a result, the CPRF faction in the Duma fell to 52 seats in 2003. Liberal opponents of the Kremlin fared even worse. Both Yabloko and the Union of Right Forces (SPS) failed to cross the 5 percent threshold required to hold seats in the parliament, raising real questions about their long-term futures.[5] In the single-mandate contests, Yabloko won only four seats, while candidates affiliated with SPS won three seats. Thus, to varying degrees, all three parliamentary parties that have increased their share of the popular vote since the last election supported Putin and enjoyed state support. Moreover, amendments incorporated into the new law on political parties make it considerably more difficult for new political parties to form.

The overwhelming victory of United Russia in the Duma elections made it clear that Putin would win the March 2004 presidential ballot without any difficulty. Indeed, Putin's reelection was so certain that none of the party leaders who competed in the December parliamentary vote ran as presidential candidates. Putin won on the first ballot, capturing 71.3 percent of the popular vote.

Given the president's popularity, it is hard to imagine how Putin and his surrogates could have lost free and fair elections in 2003 or 2004. Nevertheless, the elections in December 2003 and March 2004 did not take place on a level playing field. First, Putin controlled all significant national media, and he had almost complete support from major regional media outlets. This contrasted with the last national electoral cycle in Russia, when opposing points of view were represented in the national electronic media.

Second, and again in contrast to the previous electoral cycle, Putin and the Kremlin enjoyed nearly universal loyalty among regional leaders in 2003–2004. Wielding carrots and sticks, the Kremlin eliminated the serious divisions among regional elites that had created the main drama of the 1999 parliamentary elections. These regional executives deployed their local resources to support United Russia candidates in single-mandate district races.

Third, the Putin regime cracked down on Russia's tycoons (or oligarchs). Very early in his term, Putin made clear that these billionaires could no longer treat the state as simply another tool to be used for their personal enrichment. Instead, Putin implied that the oligarchs had to get out of politics altogether. Eventually, he arrested or chased into exile three major oligarchs—Boris Berezovsky, Vladimir Gusinsky, and Russia's richest man, Mikhail Khodorkovsky, head of the business conglomerate Yukos. All three had previously played significant roles in funding and supporting political parties and individuals not deemed loyal to the Kremlin. The downfall of these three sent a chilling message to other tycoons. In the 2003 parliamentary campaign, oligarchs continued to contribute significant resources to political campaigns, but only as sanctioned by the Kremlin. Compared to the previous electoral cycle, big business in 2003 was relatively united in backing United Russia and other pro-Kremlin candidates. In 2004, everyone backed Putin.

The absence of independence and division within media, regional elites, and oligarchic ranks reduced the freedom to maneuver for opposition political parties and candidates. Before the legislative balloting, the Organization for Security and Cooperation in Europe (OSCE) issued its first-ever critical preliminary report on a Russian election, stressing that the run-up to the State Duma elections "failed to meet many OSCE and Council of Europe commitments for democratic elections."[6] Although none of Russia's previous national elections were wholly free and fair, the most recent round have been the least so.

An equally alarming trend over the past four years has been the arbitrary interference by the central authorities in regional elections. For example, Chechens voted for a president, a parliament, and a referendum on continued membership within the Russian Federation. However, several candidates were forced to withdraw in both parliamentary and presidential races, while massive fraud tainted all electoral outcomes.

In September 2004, in the wake of the horrific slaughter of innocent children by terrorists at a school in Beslan, Putin went one dramatic step further by announcing a proposal to abolish direct elections of all governors of *oblasts* (provinces) and presidents of republics. Instead, Putin will appoint these regional leaders himself. The appointment of governors directly strengthens the power of the Kremlin and weakens the autonomy of regional governors. Putin also recommended that all, not just half, of Duma members should be chosen through proportional representation. Indirectly, the introduction of proportional representation for all seats in the parliament will make it easier for the Kremlin to control the Duma, as the previous electoral system allowed regional elites to play the central role in determining the winners in single-mandate districts.

Since coming to power, Putin has moved systematically and successfully to weaken political pluralism within the state. His first move was to weaken the power of the regional governors. In a decree on May 13, 2000, Putin overlaid seven super-regions (federal districts), accountable to Moscow, on the 89 units of the federation. Each was to be headed by a plenipotentiary who would be appointed by the president personally and would sit on his Security Council.[7] The envoys have writ over all federal agencies in the regions other than the military and thus have access to officials in the most politically sensitive and influential positions, such as those in the treasury, tax inspectorate, procuracy, FSB, and regular police. Their mission is to oversee the activities of the bureaucracy and to report to the president's office on any regional noncompliance with the constitution or laws of Russia.

Other changes accompanied the advent of the super-regions. A law passed in July 2000 authorized the president to suspend elected governors accused of wrongdoing by the procurator-general's office. Inasmuch as criminal proceedings could drag out indefinitely (especially if it suited the president), the law was tantamount to a presidential right to fire governors, a power that has been used only sparingly but has been an effective threat for either obtaining cooperation of a once-resistant regional executive or for convincing an uncooperative governor to step down "voluntarily." Putin can also dismiss any regional legislature that passes laws contravening federal laws or the constitution. In addition, Moscow has pushed through a more centralized allotment of tax receipts, with more reaching Moscow from the regions. Finally, the Kremlin has played a very aggressive role during regional elections to oust or tame independent governors. The campaign to force former Ingush president Ruslan Aushev not to stand for reelection in 2003 was the most audacious, but by no means the only example of Kremlin manipulation of local elections as means to secure local loyalty.

Putin also emasculated the Federation Council, the upper house of Russia's parliament, by removing governors and heads of regional legislatures from this chamber and replacing them with appointed representatives from the regional executive and legislative branches of government. This new method for constituting the Federation Council has undermined its legitimacy and essentially turned it into a rubber stamp. Many members, in fact, are Muscovites with patronage ties to Putin who acquired their seats with his administration's backing and have put the Kremlin's interests ahead of those of their constituents.[8] The new setup also makes it more difficult for regional leaders to take collective action vis-à-vis the central government. As the Duma deputy Vladimir Lysenko stated in 2001, "The president had managed to get rid of one of the strongest and most authoritative state bodies in the country. It provided the function of check and balance on the other branches of power, especially the executive."[9] Putin's changes to the Federation Council did not formally transgress the democratic rules of the game outlined in Russia's constitution, which allows such dramatic changes in the way politics are organized to occur without amendments or changes in the formal rules.[10] Nor was the prior method of constituting the upper house perfect, as it blurred the lines of separation between executive and legislative authority. A more democratic reform, however, would have been direct election of senators, as occurred from 1993 to 1995.

After the December 2003 election, the Duma also evolved into a loyal supporter of Kremlin initiatives due to the supermajority of pro-Kremlin parties. The Kremlin initiates almost all new draft laws, which are then quickly passed by the Duma. The non-democratic flavor to executive–legislative relations in Putin's Russia comes not from the president's desire to have a parliamentary majority but from the way the majority has been achieved: through parliamentary elections in which pro-Kremlin candidates were given an unfair advantage.

At the same time, informal networks not accountable to the people have gained influence in ruling Russia. Even though elected officials do still control the highest levels of the Russian state, non-elected officials from the FSB have assumed an increasing role in the federal government since Putin became president.[11]

After reaching a peak of popular mobilization and political influence in 1991, Russian civil society struggled to survive throughout the 1990s. By one estimate, more than 200,000 nongovernmental organizations (NGOs) formed during this decade,[12] yet when Yeltsin left office, Russian civil society was weak, atomized, apolitical, and heavily dependent on Western assistance for support. Nonetheless, Putin believes that NGOs are still a threat to his power. By enforcing new registration procedures and draconian tax laws, Putin's administration has forced thousands of NGOs to close,[13] and NGO leaders considered too political are harassed and jailed.[14] Pro-Kremlin members of parliament have introduced legislation that would tighten state control over the distribution of grants from foreign donors.[15] To force independent NGOs to the margins of society, the Kremlin has devoted massive resources to the creation of state-sponsored and state-controlled NGOs. State transfers to and cooperation with the nongovernmental sector have been targeted only to those NGOs supportive of state policy or not involved in politics at all.

Western civil society groups are not immune from Russian state harassment. Putin's government has tossed out the Peace Corps, closed down the office of the OSCE in Europe in Chechnya, declared *persona non grata* the AFL-CIO's field representative in Moscow, and raided the offices of the Open Society Institute (which eventually exited Russia) and the National Democratic Institute.

In June 2001, Putin met with representatives of more than 30 NGOs. The organizations Putin chose to invite to the meeting, however, were far from the most influential NGOs and included stamp-collecting, gardening, educational, cultural, and sports organizations. Similarly, in November 2001 the Russian Press Institute's Vitaly Ignatenko, the National Association of Television and Radio Broadcasters' Eduard Sagalayev, and new Media Union head Aleksandr Lyubimov created a new journalists' union, Mediasoyuz, sanctioned by the Kremlin, to counterbalance the "oppositionist" Russian Journalists' Union. This new union consists of journalists working for state-owned or state-loyal mass media.

The weakening of the State Duma as an independent political institution has had negative consequences for civic engagement of the state, as this institution has traditionally been more open to interaction with civic groups than the presidential administration. Civic chambers have been established at the regional level to serve as listening posts for societal complaints and suggestions, but most NGO leaders see this institutional innovation as nothing more than another method of cooptation.

Putin has also tightened the state's grip on the mass media, especially national television.[16] When Putin came to power, only three networks had the national reach to really count in politics—ORT, RTR, and NTV. By running billionaire Boris Berezovsky, the de facto owner of ORT, out of the country, Putin effectively acquired control of the channel with the biggest national audience. RTR was always fully state owned, and so it was even easier to tame. Putin's administration leaned on prosecutors to investigate reputed past misdeeds of NTV owner Vladimir Gusinsky, and state-controlled Gazprom called in a large loan to NTV. In the space of several months in 2001, Gazprom's media holding company took over NTV, Gusinsky fled abroad, the staff of the weekend newsmagazine *Itogi* was fired, and the daily newspaper owned by Media-Most, *Segodnya* (*Today*), was shut down; the latter two were once owned by Gusinsky. Gazprom purged NTV a second time in January 2003, removing Boris Jordan, the Russian-American director it had appointed in 2000. Many of NTV's best journalists and producers migrated to two other stations, TV6 and then TVS, both of which were shut down by June 2003.

Print media have greater autonomy from the state, at both the national and regional levels. The state still controls several print outlets, but independent newspapers publish critical coverage and analysis of Kremlin activities. All of these so-called national publications, however, have limited readership in Moscow and very little reach into the rest of Russia. Moreover, during crises the state has intervened to shape the content of print journalism. For instance, when the newspaper *Izvestiya* tried to ask questions about the state's failures in response to the inept performance of Russia's security forces in the Beslan standoff in 2004, the newspaper came under heavy pressure. The editor in chief of *Izvestiya*, Raf Shakirov, eventually was forced to step down.[17] One independent journalist was detained when trying to reach Beslan, while another was allegedly poisoned to deter her from reporting from the scene of the terrorist attack. Dozens of newspapers and Web portals that have remained independent offer a platform for political figures of all persuasions, but none of these enjoys mass audiences.

The independence of electronic media has also eroded at the regional level. Heads of local state-owned television stations continue to follow political signals from regional executives, and most regional heads of administration stood firmly behind Putin in the last electoral cycle. The flow of information is most confined in Chechnya, where governmental agencies have severely restricted access to the territory by Russian and foreign correspondents and have arrested and intimidated several print journalists whose war stories they found inconvenient. Criminal prosecution by the national and regional authorities as well as the strict enforcement of libel laws have also been widely utilized as ways to deter critical reporting.

More generally, Putin has changed the atmosphere for doing journalistic work. His most vocal media critics have lost their jobs, have been harassed by the tax authorities or by sham lawsuits, or have been arrested. Several Russian journalists and one American journalist have been killed during the Putin era, and no one has yet been convicted of these crimes.[18] In its Media Sustainability Index for Europe and Eurasia, International Research and Exchanges (IREX) reported serious backsliding in Russia's freedom of speech, the access of its citizens to a variety of independent news sources, and the quality of news and information its citizens receive.[19]

*Recommendations*
- Direct elections for governors should be reinstated.
- Direct elections for members of the Federation Council should be reinstated.
- The mixed electoral system for the State Duma, first adopted in 1993, should be reinstated, including the 5-percent threshold on the PR ballot.
- Channel 1 (ORT) should be privatized and Channel 2 (RTR) should be transformed into a public television station, complete with an independent board to help safeguard against political interference.

## CIVIL LIBERTIES – 3.72

Russia's 1993 constitution provides comprehensive guarantees for defending the civil liberties of all Russian citizens. In practice, however, not all rights are guaranteed to the same degree. In particular, residents of the southern republic of Chechnya enjoy few civil liberties. For statists like Putin, the anarchy in Chechnya was and remains the most embarrassing testament to Russia's weakness. At the time of the rebirth of Russia as an independent country in 1991, the leaders of Chechnya also declared Chechnya's independence from the Russian Federation. Throughout most of the 1990s, Kremlin authorities acquiesced to Chechnya's de facto autonomy. The initial use of force against invading Chechen rebels in 1999 was legitimate, as Russia was defending its borders and was obliged to address the lawlessness that enveloped Chechnya. But the way in which Putin's army has fought this war—a full-scale military reoccupation, bombardment of civilian urban centers by heavy weaponry, and indiscriminate arrest and abuse of civilians—has demonstrated Putin's weak commitment to defending the rights of Russian citizens.

Accusations of rights abuses in Chechnya, corroborated by several monitoring groups, include arbitrary detention and arrest, disappearances, torture, killings, and rape.[20] Russian federal authorities have even kidnapped family members of Chechen rebels as a means to fight "terrorism." The most notorious of these actions are state sponsored, carried out either by the so-called Kadyrovtsi, the Putin-backed Chechen "police" force, or the Russian federal forces.[21] The abuse of human rights is especially acute for internally displaced persons in Ingushetia and within Chechnya. By some estimates more than a quarter of Chechnya's population have perished since this war began, while experts reckon that another 400,000 refugees have been displaced by the fighting.[22] In 2002, a plan was drawn up to force the return of internally displaced people to Chechnya through closure of camps in Ingushetia and elsewhere. This plan of "normalization" is now enforced by the Russian authorities.[23]

In order to force displaced persons in Ingushetia to return to Chechnya, vital utilities have been cut off at camps, making living conditions even more unbearable. Moreover, camps that have not yet been closed were removed from aid lists, cutting off those in need from supplies and medical attention, while creating the impression that the numbers of the displaced Chechens had been reduced. Many Chechens were unable to obtain new documentation after their Soviet documentation, including birth certificates, expired in 2003. Moreover, Chechens are barred from holding international passports, which would allow them to seek refuge outside Federation territory. Thus, those endangered by continuing warfare are forced to remain either in squalid conditions in their former homes or displaced within Russia.[24]

Those who monitor and defend human rights in Chechnya are themselves increasingly subject to attacks.[25] Victims include activists and lawyers from prominent organizations, journalists, community leaders, applicants to the European Court of Human Rights, and their family members.[26] According to the International Helsinki Federation for Human Rights, federal forces are suspected of involvement in 108 of 141 cases of recorded abuse against human rights defenders and their families in 2004.[27] In an extreme case, the office of the Russian-Chechen Friendship Society has been raided several times and its director kidnapped 15 times and subjected to torture more than once. Since February 2004, the ministry of interior and FSB have distributed leaflets fingering as terrorists several doctors working in Ingushetia and openly seeking their arrest.[28]

In addition, the Russian state has not convicted anyone in the murder of Yuri Shchekochikhin, a member of the State Duma and head of the State Security Committee who was critical of the war and was investigating corruption associated with it. Mystery also still surrounds the bombings of apartment buildings in Moscow in the fall of 1999.

In Chechnya, the military is allowed to operate brutally and with impunity. According to Human Rights Watch, Russia has resisted establishing a meaningful accountability process for crimes its forces commit, and in most cases officials have not begun genuine investigations despite hundreds of criminal investigations opened by the procuracy. "As a result, most investigations remained unsolved and almost none were sent to the courts."[29] To date, only one person—Colonel Yuri Budanov—has been held accountable for an extrajudicial killing, and this lone conviction was nearly overturned in late September 2004.[30]

Although not to the same extent, individuals and groups outside Chechnya also have experienced the loss of their civil liberties. Starting in the later 1990s under Yeltsin but then more intensively under Putin, the FSB has dramatically increased the number of arrests of Russians accused of treason and espionage. The All-Russian Public Movement for Human Rights has compiled a list of such politically motivated arrests under the guise of security threats, which includes journalists, professors, scientists, lawyers, businesspeople, and others.[31] Many of these alleged spies have been held for years without being notified of their alleged crimes and without being tried.[32] Many human rights groups and politicians now consider Russian billionaire Mikhail Khodorkovsky and his colleagues from the oil company Yukos and its parent company Menatep to be political prisoners.[33]

Drafted soldiers are another group in Russia that continues to endure cruel treatment. Although inhumane initiation practices within the armed forces have received public attention, the Russian government has enacted few reforms to address the problem.[34] As a symptom of the endemic violence within the military, the Mothers of Soldiers social movement has become one of the largest and most vocal in the country.

Prisoners in Russia constitute another constituency whose treatment remains well below international standards.[35] Torture and abuse are common. According to sociologist Yuri Levada, who has conducted public opinion surveys on the subject, "The scale of this phenomenon proves that this is not mere arbitrariness on the part of certain irresponsible individuals, not singular occurrences, but a general rule."[36] In a survey conducted in 2003, a quarter of all respondents believed that their rights had been violated by the police or courts over the past year.[37] Russian law does not list torture as a crime, so police officers accused of torturing prisoners or those held in detention receive only minor sanction.[38] More generally, prisons are overcrowded and unsanitary and therefore filled with life-threatening diseases. With nearly 1 million people behind bars, Russia has one of the highest per capita rates of incarceration in the world, but with little capacity. Cells intended for eight often house nearly two dozen.[39] Overcrowding also breeds violence among inmates. Protests, including self-infliction of wounds and especially hunger strikes, have become common methods used by inmates to demand more attention to their pitiful conditions.[40]

Formally, equal rights for women and men are secured in Russia's constitution and other legislation, although actual equality between men and women is still a distant goal. Despite numerous initiatives for new legislation, domestic violence is still not recognized as a distinct crime.[41] In 2002, Russian state authorities reported to the UN Committee on the Elimination of Discrimination against Women (CEDAW) that 14,000 women die every year at the hands of their husbands or other relatives.[42] Russia is also a major source of human trafficking. Putin has given some attention to this issue, but the state itself has done little to address the problem systematically.[43]

The constitution provides for religious freedom, and most religious, ethnic, and cultural groups can express their views openly and organize to promote their interests. However, some religious organizations enjoy wider rights and more autonomy than others. The Russian Orthodox Church succeeded in pressing for a law in 1997 that gave it, along with Buddhism, Islam, and Judaism, official status, while denying this status to all others. In February 2002, the Russian Constitutional Court ruled that religions registered before 1997 should not lose their legal status, a major victory for religious freedom. Nonetheless, some denominations, including the Jehovah's Witnesses, Pentecostals, the Mormons, and other Protestant sects, report discrimination and harassment, though chiefly by local officials and not the national government.[44] Visas at times are denied to foreign religious leaders traveling to Russia. Recently, the state also has become more directly involved in selecting leaders within religious groups, especially in Jewish and Orthodox Old Believer communities.[45]

Russians with disabilities are protected by the social security law, which guarantees financial support to those whose disabilities prevent them from working. The 1995 Federal Law on Social Protection of People with Disabilities prohibits discrimination in employment, education, and housing; public buildings and mass transportation are required to be wheelchair accessible.[46] The state also developed special publications and recordings that provide information about government services. In practice, however, state services for the disabled are limited, and many citizens living in rural areas have no access to assistance. Some experts report that employers often discriminate against the disabled, finding it more cost-effective to pay fines than to make accommodations for workers with disabilities.[47]

The Russian constitution guarantees freedom of association, and the government generally respects this right. NGOs do face harassment, however (see "Accountability and Public Voice"). Trade union rights are legally respected, but the power and activity of these groups is limited in practice. Discrimination against union members and the punishment of those who participate in worker strikes is not uncommon. The largest labor federation is closely aligned with the state. When trade unions voiced their dissatisfaction with the new draft labor code in 2002, Putin's government chose to reach out to the larger Soviet-era Federation of Independent Trade Unions of Russia (FNPR) rather than to the independent trade unions to work on the draft with state officials.

*Recommendations*

- A political process for resolving the conflict in Chechnya must begin with a cease-fire, followed by high-level negotiations and specific confidence-building measures. Talks must include representatives appointed by the survivors from the last freely and fairly elected government in Chechnya, must involve international mediation, and should focus on the withdrawal of Russian Federal and FSB forces and disarmament of Chechen rebel factions. Specific measures should include a declaration by both sides to adhere to the statutes of the Geneva Convention, full media and aid access to Chechnya, and the cessation of harassment of internally displaced persons in Chechnya and the north Caucasus.
- To provide for stability in the North Caucasus as a whole, the Russian government must provide for more local autonomy of regional governments and greater local representation within these governments.
- The Russian government should allow greater international and domestic monitoring of human rights abuses in Chechnya.
- Russia should aim to reduce abuse of soldiers by transforming the military into an all-volunteer force. In the interim, those drafted should be allowed to serve in nonmilitary jobs.
- Religious organizations should not be subjected to state interference in their internal governance affairs.

## RULE OF LAW – 3.41

A disconnect between formal laws and law in practice permeates Russia's legal system. For example, in December 2001 Putin's administration won parliamentary approval for a new criminal code.[48] At the same time, three other laws on the legal system were also passed, ensuring the security of judicial tenure, which lessened the potential for political interference; increasing judicial salaries; and providing for greater judicial input in the administration of courts. On paper, the new code is a revolutionary document. As Russia expert Leon Aron describes it, "A number of articles in the new Criminal-Procedural Code spell a major victory for the rights of the defendants and human rights."[49] Anecdotally, there seem to be some positive trends in the development of an independent judiciary since these reforms were introduced. Russia's experiment with jury trials, for instance, has produced some unexpected outcomes in which the will of ordinary citizens trumped the preferences of the state.[50] Nevertheless, although most judges and juries are trained to administer justice as bound by the new code, evidence shows that the prosecution still receives an unfair advantage in the higher courts. For example, in two Moscow district courts, judges heard more than 4,000 cases between January 2003 and September 2004 without making a single acquittal.[51]

The new criminal code also guarantees the accused the right to legal counsel and that a judge will hear the case within 24 hours of arrest. If a citizen charged with a serious crime cannot afford a private attorney, the state is required to provide independent counsel. However, many lawyers are reluctant to work as public defenders because the government often fails to pay them. Furthermore, public defenders are commonly victims of harassment and intimidation by the police, who frequently act to cover their own unlawful conduct.[52]

Many judges have resigned over the past four years because they refused to carry out illegitimate verdicts ordered by the head of the court, who is closely associated with Putin's chief of staff.[53] When the Kremlin clearly expresses an opinion in a legal matter, Russian courts almost always comply. [*Editor's note:* In October 2004, the Russian judiciary suffered a major setback when the upper house of parliament, with Putin's support, voted to increase the role of the president in appointing judges.[54]]

All persons in Russia are not treated equally before the law. For example, Russian public officials suspected of crimes are not commonly prosecuted, although exceptions do exist. Instead of being charged following an abuse of power, corrupt bureaucrats are usually required to resign from their old positions and are later appointed to other high-ranking jobs. For example, Vladimir Yakovlev, former governor of St. Petersburg, was forced to resign after he allegedly misspent 1 billion rubles (about $330 million) in federal funds but was later appointed as minister in charge of housing reform.[55] The investigation into his abuse of power ended after he received the new position.

In the summer of 2003, Menatep officials Platon Lebedev and Alexei Pichugin were arrested. On October 25, 2003, Russian authorities arrested Khodorkovsky on charges of fraud and tax evasion. Khodorkovsky's lawyers have issued reports documenting how his and his associates' constitutional rights have been violated.[56] The Russian state has refused to respond. Three members of Khodorkovsky's legal defense team have also been detained. External evaluations of the case have concluded that the arrest of Khodorkovsky and his colleagues was motivated first and foremost by politics, not the enforcement of the rule of law. According to the Parliamentary Assembly of the Council of Europe, the arrests "put into question the fairness, impartiality and objectivity of the authorities [in Russia]. . . . [T]he interest of the State's action in these cases goes beyond the mere pursuit of criminal justice, to include such elements as to weaken an outspoken political opponent, to intimidate other wealthy individuals and to regain control of strategic assets."[57]

The arrest, detention, and prosecution of Mikhail Khodorkovsky is the best-known example of Russia's judiciary enforcing the law arbitrarily for political purposes, but others have faced a similar fate. For instance, Russian media magnate Vladimir Gusinsky was arrested in 2000. However, he succeeded in leaving the country, achieving refugee status in the United States, as did the former head of Gusinsky's NTV television network, Igor Malashenko. Likewise, senior executives at Vimpelcom, a Russian telecommunications firm, have been targeted for investigations for tax fraud that many consider to be politically motivated.

In most of these cases, while the accused may in fact be guilty of committing economic crimes, it is not the enforcement of the law that is troublesome but the arbitrariness and selectivity of its use. Oligarchs considered loyal to the Kremlin have not been investigated. Even the decisions of juries have been overturned arbitrarily when the Kremlin seeks a different outcome.

The military, police, and internal security forces, with the notable exception of the Chechen rebels, are controlled by the president and the executive branch. These security organs remain plagued by deep-rooted corruption and are frequently swayed by the criminal underworld. In the most tragic instance, armed hostage takers allegedly were able to bribe local police officers to get past security checkpoints before seizing the school in Beslan. Eyewitnesses report that driving through a checkpoint in war-torn Chechnya can be negotiated for a mere $2.[58]

Property rights in Russia are protected under Article 23 of the Russian constitution. Millions of Russian citizens became owners of their apartments following the privatization laws adopted in 1991. In 1996 Boris Yeltsin strengthened the right to control and own agricultural land. The Russian government, however, continues to enforce contracts and property rights in commercial settings only weakly, making lack of enforcement one of the top impediments to foreign investment in Russia.

The rights of ownership in Russia can be terminated against the will of the owner in only a few instances: if the owner commits a crime for which the penalty calls for property confiscation, when a transaction is intentionally made contrary to legal order, and when the owner fails to satisfy ownership obligations.[59] The current law forbids any form of nationalization of privately owned property.

*Recommendations*
- The arbitrary use of the law for political purposes must end.
- Courts must become more autonomous from state control, perhaps through direct elections of court judges.
- Judges should be paid higher salaries to give them a greater capacity to resist corruption.

## ANTICORRUPTION AND TRANSPARENCY – 2.79

Vladimir Putin has vowed to tackle systemic corruption within Russian politics and in the government, the economy, and the judiciary.[60] In 2003 he called for legislation prohibiting bureaucrats from engaging in entrepreneurial activities and restricting those who leave civil service jobs from working in areas formerly under their supervision. To date, however, these proposals remain little more than affirmations of intent.

Russia continues to rank low in comparison with other countries in surveys on corruption. The World Economic Forum's Global Competitiveness Report 2004–2005, which uses corruption as a benchmark in its assessment, ranked Russia at 70 out of 104 nations.[61] Transparency International's Corruption Perceptions Index 2004 ranked Russia at 90 out of 146 countries, with a score of 2.7 (10 being "highly clean" and 0 being "highly corrupt").[62]

Russia has a uniquely high level of major corruption (as opposed to petty bribes), which is closely associated with the oil and gas industry and other exported natural resources. Putin and his government have moved systematically to place oil and gas companies under greater state control.[63] The state's seizure of Yuganskneftegaz, the most profitable asset of the Yukos oil company, and its subsequent transfer into Kremlin-friendly hands was the most notorious corrupt act sanctioned by the state in 2004. Senior officials in Putin's presidential administration now serve as board members in major oil and gas firms. This fusion of the state and the most profitable industries in Russia is an obvious recipe for corruption and graft, and high oil prices have created incentives for greater state interference in this strategic sector of the economy. Furthermore, Russia does not have adequate regulations requiring officials to disclose their assets and income, making it even easier for the bureaucrats to hide illegal profiteering.

Although Russia has many laws that safeguard against corruption, their application is selective and politically motivated. This is not surprising given that most investigative and auditing bodies are aligned with the government and afflicted by political pressures. In addition to Khodorkovsky, the state has also filed criminal charges against former railroads minister Nikolai Aksenenko and several top police officers involved in corrupt activities. At the time of these arrests, the government benefited from numerous media stories that portrayed the state's determination to root out corruption, even at the highest levels. Yet, independent journalists who investigate cases of corruption, outside of what is being handed to them by officials, often face serious threats. In both 2002 and 2003 a reporter from *Tolyatinskoye Obozreniye*, a paper specialized in reporting on graft and organized crime, was murdered, most likely because of their investigations of underhanded corporate deals.[64]

General business regulations and procedures in Russia remain complex and unwieldy, creating a breeding ground for corruption. To assist the business sector in adhering to state-imposed regulations, government bureaus are permitted to create their own "consulting agencies," which provide advice for a fee.[65] Companies that opt to pay the government for such services receive preferential treatment, limiting fair market play. In contrast, Russia has eased registration and licensing requirements. The new Law on Registration has had a positive effect by simplifying the procedure for starting a business, although it has made the process more costly.[66]

The Russian constitution gives immunity from prosecution to members of the Council of Federation and deputies of the State Duma while in office. Deputies cannot face any kind of criminal investigation, detainment, questioning, or surveillance without the consent of a majority in parliament. In the 1999 parliamentary elections, 1,000 of the 6,700 candidates vying for 450 Duma seats had criminal records, according to information released by the Russian interior ministry.[67] The list of candidates included a Moscow Mafioso who had spent over two years in Swiss prisons for money laundering, a businessman who allegedly ordered the killing of eight city officials and rival businesspeople, and a person who had spent seven years in prison for the attempted assassination of former Russian president Mikhail Gorbachev. Moreover, a 2001 law guarantees lifetime immunity for Russian presidents, creating even less incentive for honest dealings at the highest levels of administration.

Corruption has also been a dominant problem in Russian institutions of higher education. In a recent poll, over half of the families surveyed admitted to paying bribes in an effort to guarantee university admissions and "fix" their children's report cards.[68] In 2004, about 900 new court cases were opened concerning alleged corruption in education.[69]

The Russian taxation system is still plagued by a complex tax code and a culture of tax evasion. Since the 1998 financial crisis, the government has introduced several important reforms, including a flax income tax, a lower corporate tax, new rules for tax audits, penalties for tax violations, and well-defined rights for participants in the tax system.[70] These have substantially increased tax collections and compliance while moving the country closer to international standards.[71] At the same time, the state continues to pursue tax evaders selectively for political purposes.

Russia does not allow for thorough public access to government information. Although freedom of information is guaranteed in Article 29 of the Russian constitution, Russians do not have appropriate channels through which they can request such information. The government does not publicize state expenditures, although the federal budget is subject to approval by the Duma.

Russia does not have a competitive national procurement system based on fair, transparent, and open competition. Only about half of public expenditures on the purchasing of goods, public works, and services in 1999 were determined by open tendering; even then, a substantial proportion of procurement bidding was restricted by requirements such as limitations on where a bidder could be located.[72] Yet, the government has made progress with advertising public procurement opportunities in the "Competitive Bidding" bulletin, thus improving the access of bidders to information on tendering opportunities.

Russia has received substantial funds through grants and loans designed to assist the Russian political and economic transition following the end of communism. Corruption in foreign aid assistance became apparent in the late 1990s after it was discovered that more than $6 billion, some of which was part of an IMF assistance package, had been laundered through a Swiss bank account associated with organized crime. High-ranking bureaucrats are suspected to have cooperated with Russian crime groups to channel this money for their private use.[73]

### Recommendations

- Senior government officials should not be allowed to serve in management capacities in companies owned by the state.
- All government expenditures and revenues, including transfers between regional and federal authorities, must be made public and preferably posted on the Web.
- Anticorruption NGOs must be granted greater access to government procedures and information. A serious freedom of information law must be passed and enforced.
- Creating more permissive conditions for the expansion of both a free press and powerful opposition parties are reforms necessary for more effectively fighting corruption in Russia.

### NOTES

[1] Many thanks to Erin Mark for her research assistance.

[2] On the weakness of Russian liberal institutions, see Michael McFaul, *Russia's Unfinished Revolution: Political Change from Gorbachev to Putin* (Ithaca, N.Y.: Cornell University Press, 2001), chapter 9.

[3] M. Steven Fish, "The Dynamics of Democratic Erosion," in Richard Anderson, M. Steven Fish, Stephen Hanson, and Philip Roeder, eds., *Postcommunism and the Theory of Democracy* (Princeton, N.J.: Princeton University Press, 2001), 54–95.

[4] Henry Hale, Michael McFaul, and Timothy Colton, "Putin and the 'Delegative Democracy' Trap: Evidence from Russia's 2003–04 Elections," *Post-Soviet Affairs* 20, 4 (Fall 2004): 285–319.

[5] See http://www.fairgame.ru.

[6] "Statement of Preliminary Findings and Conclusions, Russian Federation State Duma Elections, 7 December 2003" (Vienna: Organization for Security and Cooperation in Europe/Parliamentary Assembly [OSCE/PA], International Election Observation Mission, December 2003), http://www.osce.org/documents/odihr/2003/12/1629_en.pdf.

[7] Natal'ya Zubarevich, Nikolai Petrov, and Aleksei Titkov, "Federal'nyye okruga-2000," in Nikolai Petrov, ed., *Regiony Rossii v 1999 g. [The regions of Russia in 1999]* (Moscow Carnegie Center, 2001), 190.

[8] Aleksei Makarkin, "Sovet Federatsii: novyi sostav, novyye problemy," in Rostislav Turovskii, ed., *Politika v regionakh: gubernatory i gruppy vliyaniya [Politics in the regions: governors and interest groups]* (Moscow: Tsentr politicheskikh tekhnologii, 2002), 53–75.

[9] Vladimir Lysenko, "The Federation Council Fails to Become a House of Lords," in Yuri Senokosov and John Lloyd, eds., *Russia on Russia: Administrative and State Reform in Russia*, no. 5 (Moscow School of Political Studies, June 2002), 20.

[10] For a strong statement to this effect, see Vladimir Ryzhkov, *Moscow Times*, 11 December 2002, 10.

[11] On the rise of the FSB in Russian state structures, see Olga Kryshtanovskaya, "Rezhim Putina: liberalnaya militokratiya?" [Putin's Regime: Liberal Militacracy?] (unpublished manuscript, 2002).

[12] *The 1999 NGO Sustainability Index* (Washington, DC: U.S. Agency for International Development), http://www.usaid.gov.

[13] *Russian Authorities Force Organizations to Become Underground* (Moscow: Glasnost Public Foundation, 2004), http://www.glasnostonline.org/eng_projects/registration.htm.

[14] Sarah E. Mendelson, "Russians' Rights Imperiled: Has Anybody Noticed?" *International Security* 26 (Spring 2002), 39–69.

[15] Anfisa Voronina, "A Filter for Grants: The state will decide which donors are acceptable," *Vedomosti*, 23 July 2004, translated and redistributed by WPS Monitoring Agency.

[16] For details, see Masha Lipman and Michael McFaul, "Putin and the Media," in Dale Herspring, ed., *Putin's Russia: Past Imperfect, Future Uncertain*, 2d ed. (Lanham, Md.: Roman & Littlefield, 2005), pp. 55–74.

[17] "Izvestia's Chief Editor Raf Shakirov Fired over Hostage Drama Coverage," *Moscow News*, 6 September 2004.

[18] "Annual Report, 2004" (Paris: Reporters Without Borders [RSF]).

[19] *Media Sustainability Index 2003* (Washington, DC: International Research and Exchanges Board, 2004).

[20] See for instance, Dr. Charlotte Granville-Chapman, "Rape and Other Torture in the Chechnya Conflict: Documented Evidence from Asylum Seekers Arriving in the United Kingdom" (London: Medical Foundation for the Care of Victims of Torture, April 2004); "No Happiness Remains: Civilian Killings, Pillage, and Rape in Alkhan-Yurt, Chechnya" (New York: Human Rights Watch [HRW]), *Russia/Chechnya* 12, 5 (April 2000): 1–33; "February 5: A Day of Slaughter in Novye Aldi" (HRW), *Russia/Chechnya* 12, 9 (June 2000): 1–43; "The 'Dirty War' in Chechnya: Forced Disappearances, Torture, and Summary Executions" (HRW), Russia/Chechnya 13, 1 (March 2001): 1–42; "Burying the Evidence: The Botched Investigation into a Mass Grave in Chechnya" (HRW), *Russia/Chechnya* 13, 3 (May 2001): 1–26. *Chechnya Weekly* (Washington, DC:

Jamestown Foundation) also provides full coverage of the war, including human rights violations. There is also extensive discussion of human rights abuses in Chechnya in Anna Politkovskaya, *A Small Corner of Hell: Dispatches from Chechnya* (Chicago: University of Chicago Press, 2003); and Matthew Evangelista, *The Chechen Wars: Will Russia Go the Way of the Soviet Union?* (Washington, DC: The Brookings Institution, 2002).

21   Murad Magomadov, "New Methods, Same Old Abuses," *The Observer,* 6 February 2004; "The Trauma of Ongoing War in Chechnya: Quantitative assessment of living conditions, and psychological and general health status among war displaced in Chechnya and Ingushetia" (Amsterdam, Netherlands: Medecins Sans Frontieres [MSF], Report, August 2004); *The Situation of IDP's in Ingushetia after the Armed Incursion of 21/22 June 2004* (Vienna: International Helsinki Federation for Human Rights [IHF-HR], 4 August 2004).

22   See "Statistical Yearbook 2003: Trends in Displacement, Protection, and Solution" (Geneva: United Nations High Commissioner on Refugees [UNHCR], June 2004); "Russsian Federation: Governmnent Ignores Its Obligations towards IDPs" (Geneva: Norwegian Refugee Council [NRC], Global IDP Project Database, last updated December 2004), http://www.db.idpproject.org/Sites/IdpProjectDb/idpSurvey.nsf/wView SingleEnv/Russian+FederationProfile+Summary; "IDP Estimates" http://www.idpproject .org/statistics.htm; "Asylum Levels and Trends: Europe and non-European Industrialized Countries, 2003" (UNHCR, 24 February 2004), http://www.unhcr.ch.

23   See "The Coerced Return of Chechen IDPs from Ingushetia" (IHF-HR, Report, March 2004); "Briefing to the 60th Session of the UN Commission on Human Rights" (HRW, 29 January 2004), http://hrw.org/english/docs/2004/01/29/Russia7248.htm.

24   Ibid.; see also, "The Trauma of Ongoing War in Chechnya" (MSF); "Report from Seminar on IDPs from Chechnya" (NRC, European Council on Refugees and Exiles [ECRE], Moscow, 30–31 August 2004); "Statistical Yearbook 2003" (UNHCR, June 2004).

25   "The Silencing of Human Rights Defenders in Chechnya and Ingushetia" (IHF-HR, Norwegian Helsinki Committee [NHC] Report, 15 September 2004).

26   Archana Pyati, *The New Dissident: Human Rights Defenders and Counterterrorism in Russia* (New York: Human Rights First, 2005).

27   "The Silencing of Human Rights Defenders . . ." (IHF-HR, NHC), 6, 26; see also *From the Conflict Zone* (Moscow: Human Rights Center [HRC] "Memorial," Bulletin, December 2004), http://www.memo.ru/eng/memhrc/texts/4bul12.shtml.

28   "Ingushetia: Doctors Employed by International Medical Corps Wrongly and Repeatedly Exposed as Suspected Terrorists" (IHF-HR, press release, 27 September 2004).

29   "Briefing to the 60th Session of the UN Commission on Human Rights" (HRW, January 2004), http://hrw.org/english/docs/2004/01/29/russia7248.htm.

30   Egor Belous, "Pomiluet li Putin Budanova?" *Pravda,* 20 September 2004, http://www .politics.pravda.ru/politics/2004/1/1/1/18068_BUDANOVPOMIL.html; "Russian Who Murdered Chechen No Longer Seeks Pardon," Reuters, 21 September 2004, http://www.hrvc.net/news2004/22-9-04.html.

31  *Black Book of Russian Justice: Political Repressions and Politically Motivated Persecutions in Today's Russia* (Moscow: All-Russia Public Movement "For Human Rights" [ARPM], 2004).

32  "Russia's 'Spy Mania': A Study of the Case of Igor Sutyagin" (HRW, briefing paper, October 2003).

33  Author's interviews with several senior Russian politicians, none of whom agreed to be identified, February 2004; "Chronicle of Political Persecution in Present Day Russia" (Moscow: Za Prava, January 2005), 11.

34  *The Wrongs of Passage: Inhuman and Degrading Treatment of New Recruits in the Russian Armed Forces* (HRW, October 2004).

35  Jonathan Weiler, *Human Rights in Russia: A Darker Side of Reform* (Boulder, Colo.: Lynne Rienner, 2004).

36  "Rights Groups Concerned over Police Torture," Mosnews.com, 29 June 2004, http://www.mosnews.com/news/2004/06/29/tortures.shtml.

37  Nick Patton, "Torture now routine for Putin's police: Corrupt force extracts confessions with 'elephant mask' and beatings," *The Observer*, 19 October 2003, http://observer .guardian.co.uk/international/story/0,6903,1066223,00.html.

38  Ibid.

39  Maria Danilova, "Rights groups report human rights violations in Russian prisons and call for international community to step in," Associated Press, 28 April 2004.

40  Ibid.; Aleksandr Kolesnichenko, "Rebellion – A Wave of Actions of Insubordination Sweeps Through Russia's Penal Institutions," *Noviye Izvestia*, 28 April 2004, 2.

41  "Violence against Women in the Russian Federation" (London and New York: Amnesty International [AI], n.d., http://www.amnesty.org/russia/womens_day.html.

42  "Action Appeal" (AI, 4 June 2003), http://web.amnesty.org/pages/rus-050603-action-eng.

43  "Trafficking in Persons Report, Country Narrative: Europe and Eurasia" (Washington, DC: U.S. Dept. of State, 14 June 2004).

44  "Annual Report of the United States Commission on International Religious Freedom" (Washington, DC: U.S. Commission on International Religious Freedom, May 2004), 56–60, http://www.uscirf.gov.

45  Lawrence A. Uzzell, "Russia: Religion on a leash," *International Religious Freedom Watch*, issue 2004-05-04.

46  "2003 Compendium Report: Russia," *International Disability Rights Monitor* (Chicago: Center for International Rehabilitation, 2004), http://www.cirnetwork.org/idrm/reports/ compendium/russia.cfm.

47  Denise Roza and Kotov Vyacheslav, "Innovative Employment Initiatives in Russia," *Disability World*, December 2004-February 2005, http://www.disabilityworld.org/12-02_05/employment/russia.shtml.

48  Leon Aron, "Russia Reinvents the Rule of Law," *AEI Russian Outlook*, 20 March 2002.

49  Ibid., 9.

50  Seth Mydans, "Rare Russian Jury Acquits Scientist in Spy Case," *New York Times*, 30 December 2003, A7.

51  Peter Finn, "Fear Rules in Russian Courtrooms," *Washington Post,* 27 February 2005, http://www.washingtonpost.com/ac2/wp-dyn/A56441-2005Feb26?language=printer.

52  Mark Kramer, "Rights and Restraints in Russia's Criminal System" (Washington, DC: Center for Strategic and International Studies [CSIS], Program on New Approaches to Russian Security [PONARS], Policy Memo 289, 2003).

53  "Dismissed Judge Tells Putin His Staff Are Pressurizing Judiciary" *Moscow News,* 11 March 2005, http://www.mosnews.com/news/2005/03/11/oustedjudge.shtml.

54  Daniel Treisman, "Is Russia's Experiment with Democracy Over?" (Los Angeles: UCLA Center for European and Eurasian Studies, paper, 21 October 2004).

55  "Audit Chamber Makes Good on Promise to Seek Criminal Prosecution of St. Petersburg Officials," Radio Free Europe/Radio Liberty [RFE/RL] *Newsline,* 10 June 2003.

56  Platon Lebedev and Alexei Pichugin, "Constitutional and Due Process Violations in the Khodorkovsky/Yukos Case," White Paper prepared by the defense lawyers on behalf of Mikhail Khodorkovsky (Washington, DC: APCO Worldwide, November 2003).

57  "The circumstances surrounding the arrest and prosecution of leading Yukos executives" (Strasbourg: Council of Europe Parliamentary Assembly, Committee on Legal Affairs and Human Rights, Do. 100368, 29 November 2004).

58  Kim Murphy, "Russia May Pay for Bribes in Lives," *Los Angeles Times,* 11 August 2004, http://www.ncsj.org/AuxPages/110804LATimes_bribes.shtml.

59  Evgueny Sukhanov, "The Right of Ownership in the Contemporary Civil Law of Russia," *McGill Law Journal* 44 (1990): 301.

60  Vladimir Putin, Speech for the Fight against Corruption (First Session of the Council under the President, 12 January 2004), http://www.president.kremlin.ru/eng/speeches/2004/01/12/2044_59046.shtml.

61  *Global Competitiveness Report 2004–2005* (Geneva: World Economic Forum, October 2004), xiii.

62  *Corruption Perceptions Index – 2004* (Berlin: Transparency International [TI]), http://www.transparency.org/cpi/2004/cpi2004.en.html.

63  Peter Baker, "Putin's Kremlin Asserting More Control of Economy," *Washington Post,* 9 July 2004, A14.

64  "Cases 2003" (New York: Committee to Protect Journalists [CPJ], 13 October 2004), http://www.cpj.org/cases03/europe_cases03/russia.html.

65  *Administrative Barriers to Investment within Subjects of the Russian Federation* (Washington, DC: Foreign Investment Advisory Service, September 2001).

66  Ibid.

67  Ian Traynor, "Welcome to the safest club in town," *The Guardian,* 16 December 1999, www.guardian.co.uk/yeltsin/Story/0,2763,194985,00.html.

68  Bryon McWilliams, "Russia's Big Test," *The Chronicle of Higher Education,* 1 October 2004.

69  "Nine Hundred Cases Opened Over Bribery in Education," ITAR-TASS, 26 October 2004, http://www.tass.ru/eng/level2.html?NewsID=1390300&PageNum=0

70  "The Russian Tax System: Surprises and Prospects" (Moscow: Institute of Economics and Canada: University of Western Ontario, Department of Economics, Centre for the Study of International Economic Relations, joint research project, January 2002).

71  Ibid.

72  "Russian Federation: Final Country Procurement Assessment Report" (Washington, DC: The World Bank, February 2001).

73  Preston Mendenhall, "Russian crime creeps into Kremlin," MSNBC, http://msnbc .msn.com/id/3071652.

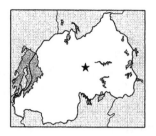

# RWANDA

CAPITAL: Kigali
POPULATION: 8.4 million
GNI PER CAPITA: $230

**SCORES**
ACCOUNTABILITY AND PUBLIC VOICE: 1.48
CIVIL LIBERTIES: 2.21
RULE OF LAW: 1.22
ANTICORRUPTION AND TRANSPARENCY: 1.97
(scores are based on a scale of 0 to 7, with
0 representing weakest and 7 representing
strongest performance)

*Sara Rakita*

## INTRODUCTION

The year 2004 marked the 10th anniversary of the Rwandan genocide, in which more than half a million Tutsi and moderate Hutu were slaughtered and Rwanda was devastated in just three months. Rwanda has since made enormous progress in bringing stability and development to the country. Nevertheless, the regime remains repressive, allowing very little space for independent voices.

President Paul Kagame and the Rwandan Patriotic Front (RPF)–dominated legislature were elected by a landslide in historic elections ending the country's post-genocide transitional phase in 2003. However, the elections were marred by bias and intimidation, which precluded any genuine challenge to the RPF. The legislative and judicial branches of government have not done much in the way of counterbalancing the executive. In practice, power remains concentrated in the hands of a small inner-circle of military and civilian elites known as

---

Sara Rakita is a New York–based attorney and consultant. She has lived in Rwanda and travels frequently to Africa.

the *akazu*. Critical voices in civil society and the media have been silenced.

The government states that genocide prevention is one of its main priorities. While Rwanda's Hutu, Tutsi, and Twa—all of whom share a common language and culture—have achieved a substantial measure of peaceful coexistence, ethnic divisions remain a concern. The government established a parliamentary commission to investigate what it calls a growing trend of divisionism and genocidal ideology throughout the country and has attempted to identify those responsible and stop them in their tracks. The 2001 Law on Discrimination and Sectarianism establishes stiff criminal penalties for those accused of divisionism, which is defined only in broad and vague terms,[1] opening the concept up to abuse and political manipulation. Politically motivated accusations of divisionism can carry criminal penalties and have been used to attack civil society organizations, political parties, and individuals. Accusations of divisionism or genocidal ideology are among the most effective tools for silencing critics in Rwanda.[2]

The justice system remains overwhelmed by the enormous backlog of detainees awaiting trial on charges that they were involved in the genocide. In an effort to speed up the process of the trials, the government established courts loosely based on *gacaca* (a traditional justice mechanism in which residents of a community gathered to discuss and resolve a conflict within the community) to try the bulk of genocide cases. Previously, gacaca had been used only for community-level problems, such as theft of livestock. In 2002, the government granted the new courts criminal jurisdiction over genocide cases in the hope that their participatory nature would contribute to reconciliation. However, the gacaca courts had yet to begin trials by September 2004. Transitional justice has been largely one-sided in Rwanda; gacaca will not be used to prosecute revenge killings or war crimes by the RPF. These crimes are not nearly of the same scale as crimes of genocide, yet failure to address them adequately has led to perceptions of victors' justice. Meanwhile, the country's conventional courts did not function during much of 2004, awaiting implementation of an overhaul of the system aimed at improving the professionalism of the judiciary.

The government had yet to finalize a land law and policy by September 2004. As a result, property rights remained ambiguous. Cases of citizens being arbitrarily denied their property continued. Many families still depend on plots of land too small to support them.

Rwanda has a reputation for being less corrupt than many other African countries. During the year, Rwanda took important steps to weed out corruption, but much remains to be done.

## ACCOUNTABILITY AND PUBLIC VOICE – 1.48

In 2003, Rwanda adopted a new constitution, held historic parliamentary and presidential elections, and swore in leaders of a new government, bringing to a close the official phase of transitional government that had lasted for nine years after the genocide. The elections, which resulted in a landslide victory for President Kagame and the RPF, were remarkable for the high voter turnout, low levels of violence, and impressive administrative efficiency. The draft constitution was approved with 93 percent support in a national referendum, Kagame won the presidency with 95 percent of the vote, and the RPF won nearly 74 percent of the votes in parliamentary elections.

While the elections were a step forward for the country in many ways, Rwanda still falls short of international standards guaranteeing people's right to participate in their governance. The environment in which the elections and electoral campaign took place was extremely restrictive and precluded opposition politicians from mounting an effective challenge. The European Union election observation mission concluded that the election laws had improved in some respects since the constitutional referendum earlier in 2003 but remained deeply flawed, that the impartiality of the National Electoral Commission was not guaranteed, and that the Supreme Court failed to exercise effective oversight.[3]

The elections took place in a climate fraught with fear and intimidation. Numerous supporters of opposition candidate Faustin Twagiramungu were arrested and two received death threats. Pasteur Bizimungu—a Hutu who used to belong to the RPF and was president for six years after the genocide—along with seven associates, remained in pretrial detention throughout the electoral period (see "Rule of Law"). The government failed to investigate a number of high-profile disappearances (the victims included a member of parliament, three former military officers, a businessman, and a student). Large numbers of citizens were coerced to join the RPF,[4] and people were made to fear that electing the opposition candidate could lead to renewed violence, which, in the Rwandan context, was interpreted as a threat. Three political parties, including the largest Hutu party and two new parties, were effectively banned in the run-up to the elections.

Throughout the transition period, the RPF had strictly controlled political party activity, allowing other parties to operate only on a national level in an RPF-dominated Political Forum. Most parties endorsed the RPF prior to the elections, and only parties that endorsed Kagame in the presidential race won seats in the parliament. The forum of political parties was institutionalized in the 2003 constitution. While this forum can play an important role in fostering dialogue among political parties, it has demonstrated its potential to impose RPF-dominated consensus, rendering the multiparty system ineffective.[5]

Media gave disproportionate coverage to the RPF candidates, while some journalists were harassed for covering opposition politicians. The governmental subsidies for campaign finance provided for in the 2003 constitution were not distributed prior to the election.[6]

Despite the unfair playing field, the RPF landslide victory has largely been interpreted as a strong mandate for the ruling party. Yet, in effect, the elections resulted in even less political pluralism than existed during the transition phase.[7]

The executive, supported by a small group of military and civilian insiders known as the *akazu,* continues to dominate government policy. The legislature and judiciary have largely gone along with the executive's agenda and have rarely seized on opportunities to stem excessive exercise of power.

The 2003 constitution mandated establishment of a Public Service Commission to centralize the appointment and recruitment of public servants as well as civil service reform. However, legislation to establish this body had not yet been enacted by September 2004, and questions remained as to how the commission would function. Many Rwandan citizens believe that civil service positions are awarded through patronage.

Civic groups have been able to influence government policy and pending legislation to a limited degree on issues including promotion of women, the Poverty Reduction Strategy, and transitional justice. However, input is not always taken into account, and some policy analysts have observed that the government often knows what it wants to do and solicits outside views only as window-dressing.

Rwandan nongovernmental organizations (NGOs) typically organize within collectives or umbrella groups to improve coordination. A byproduct of this is that the collectives, which tend to be dominated by pro-government organizations, serve to silence critical views. For example, these collectives declined to lobby against the very restrictive 2001 Law on Non-Profit Associations. This law provides for so onerous a process of registration that, three years later, most still have only provisional legal status and some have been denied registration altogether. The result is uncertainty and a lack of legal protection. Moreover, final guidelines on implementation of the law have not been promulgated, thus deepening NGOs' legal limbo.

The Rwandan government has encouraged formation of an NGO Forum to enhance coordination between the government and NGOs on development issues. Some fear that this forum could be used by the government to monitor and control civil society activity. Civil society organizations are largely dependent on foreign funding and have been accused of representing foreign interests.

Although the constitution and the Press Law of Rwanda state that the press is free, serious concerns remain about freedom of the press in practice. Independent journalists complain of harassment, especially when they report on sensitive subjects such as corruption, the military, and government abuses against dissenting voices. Self-censorship has been common since the genocide, and harsh penalties for divisionism served to aggravate this.

The state maintains economic control of newspapers. The New Times, which owns a publishing house and an English-language newspaper, is supported by the state. The Rwanda Independent Media Group, the next-largest publishing society, struggles to meet its costs. State agencies and state-controlled companies, the largest group of would-be advertisers, generally do not advertise in independent newspapers. Private companies advertise in pro-government papers so as not to offend the government.

There is currently one independent newspaper, Kinyarwanda-language *Umuseso*. *Umuseso* journalists have suffered continual harassment. The paper's first three managing editors fled the country during the paper's three-year history, as have several of its journalists. Journalists and editors are routinely called in for questioning, detained, asked to divulge their sources, and threatened. Issues of the newspaper, which is printed in Uganda, have been confiscated at the border when they contain controversial stories. The vice president of parliament has filed a defamation suit against *Umuseso*. Newsline, an English-language newspaper run by the same company as *Umuseso*, was banned in 2002 and briefly resumed operations in June 2004, then stopped.

Radio is by far the most effective medium for reaching the population. Independent radio was banned in 1994 after the independent station Radio-Television Libre des Mille Collines (RTLM) used the airwaves to incite genocide. However, a 2003 law set the stage for non-state stations to apply for licenses, although critics have complained that fees are prohibitively high. Six stations' applications for licensing were approved in January 2004, and four of these have started to broadcast. The stations that have begun to operate have pledged to avoid politics; Radio-10 (a popular music channel) uses news presented on government broadcasts. Foreign radio services do broadcast in the country, some in local languages. The parliamentary commission report on divisionism (see "Civil Liberties") made accusations against several foreign radio stations. The state maintains a monopoly on television.

In July 2004, Rwandan officials arrested César Balume Wetemwami, a Goma-based Congolese photojournalist who crossed the border from the Democratic Republic of Congo (DRC) on an assignment. After a statement by the DRC-based Journalistes en Danger and international media reports, Rwandan officials handed Wetemwami over to Congolese authorities, and he was released on July 18.

*Recommendations*

- The electoral laws should be amended to ensure greater transparency in the electoral process (including registration of voters and candidates), the independence of the electoral commission, and freer campaigning. In order for such amendments to pave the way for free and fair elections in practice, however, the government must also open up space for independent political thought.
- RPF dominance over other political parties must end. The Political Forum should be used only to share views and not to impose consensus. New parties should be established, and parties or party

members should not be accused of divisionism without proof of incitement of violence.

- The government should stop interfering with civil society and the media and should encourage these groups to exercise their roles as independent monitors of government policy by taking proactive steps to end self-censorship, such as recognizing critical views and acknowledging the role of NGOs as independent from government policy.
- The government must stop intimidating journalists who report on controversial topics.
- The government should address economic inequalities that privilege pro-government media by advertising in all media and refraining from confiscating newspapers that contain critical articles.

## CIVIL LIBERTIES – 2.21

Ten years after the end of the genocide, survivors and families of those who were killed have yet to receive any compensation. Large numbers of survivors, especially women—many of whom were raped during the genocide and suffer from AIDS—live in extreme poverty.[8] Many Rwandans continue to suffer the effects of trauma. The government has established a Fund for Assistance to Genocide Survivors that provides some support to defray the costs of education and health care. However, no genocide victims have received compensation, and a draft law on reparations was never finalized.

A detailed report released by the Parliamentary Commission on Genocidal Ideology in mid-2004 documents instances of killings, threats, and discrimination as well as interference with the justice process. The report also alleges that plans are under way for further killings.[9] The report names some individuals, organizations, and religious institutions that are allegedly responsible for these acts, but it does not substantiate its allegations in all cases. More than 20 members of parliament abstained from voting on the report, but none voted against it. The government endorsed the report in September 2004.

The International Criminal Tribunal for Rwanda (ICTR), based in Tanzania, is in the process of trying a handful of the most serious genocide offenders. The ICTR has been criticized for its slowness and inefficiency.

The vast majority of genocide suspects are to be tried in Rwandan courts. To date, approximately 10,000 people have been tried, with a conviction rate of approximately 80 percent. The first genocide trials in the country began in 1996, and the pace of trials increased steadily until 2001. With more than 100,000 detainees, it quickly became evident that it could take more than 100 years to complete the trials. Thus, the government introduced gacaca courts in 2002 to try the bulk of genocide cases. Gacaca courts have been established on a pilot basis in some areas, where they have completed lengthy pretrial phases. However, as of September 2004 the first actual trials were scheduled to take place no earlier than 2005, and much remained to be done in terms of preparing for the trials and training of judges. Since 2002, conventional courts have handled fewer cases as the gacaca law abolished Specialized Chambers, which had been created to hear genocide trials, and prosecutors turned their attention to preparing files for gacaca. Only 450 genocide suspects were tried in 2003.[10] Observers say that even fewer were tried in 2004, as the government suspended most judicial operations to allow for an overhaul of the judicial system (see "Rule of Law").

Preliminary gacaca proceedings have resulted in large numbers of new accusations, leading analysts to predict that gacaca courts may ultimately face the prospect of trying 500,000 suspects or more. This is ironic, given that gacaca was supposed to expedite completion of the process rather than increase the work to be done. And it is clear that Rwanda's justice system lacks the capacity to try such a large number. For the time being, the government has not been arresting those newly accused, save in exceptional cases.

The government has barred gacaca from hearing cases of war crimes and revenge killings committed against Hutu, leading many to perceive it as victors' justice. Regular and military tribunals have tried few cases of this nature, and most of these resulted in only nominal penalties. The ICTR has also been accused of one-sided justice, as it has declined to investigate allegations of war crimes by the RPF.

Because the criminal justice system has been so overwhelmed by the genocide caseload, it has lacked resources to deal adequately with those accused of common crimes. The law protects against lengthy periods of detention without charge, but this is rarely respected in practice, for genocide or common crimes. Allegations of physical abuse at the time of arrest and interrogation are common. There are reports of torture in military detention facilities. Street children and itinerant traders are frequently subjected to arbitrary arrests.[11]

During the first three years after the genocide, military and judicial authorities conducted widespread arbitrary arrests of genocide suspects. The country's prisons and jails quickly filled beyond capacity. Overcrowding reached epic levels, with the prison population swelling to more than 130,000 at its peak, and some 11,000 prisoners died of preventable diseases, malnutrition, and poor sanitation between 1994 and 2001. There were also reports of death in custody due to physical abuse by prison officials. While conditions have continued to improve over the past several years and overcrowding has become slightly less severe, conditions remain far below internationally recognized standards.[12]

In January 2003, the president decreed that more than 20,000 pretrial detainees be released, including those who had confessed and had already been detained for the length of their presumed sentences. However, they were still to be tried in gacaca. A substantial minority of those released were rearrested after new accusations surfaced. These releases marked the end of an earlier policy of releasing detainees against whom prosecutors had no concrete evidence, and the government is planning to try those who maintain their innocence after those who have confessed.

Local Defense Forces (LDFs), an armed civilian militia operating throughout the country, remain poorly trained and unpaid and have been accused of a number of abuses. LDFs accused of rape are rarely prosecuted and, if they are jailed, are often released within a few days.[13] The National Police and Rwanda Defense Forces have reportedly taken measures to improve professionalism among their ranks.

A former member of Rwanda's external intelligence service, David Kiwanuka, was shot dead in Kenya in February 2004. It was thought that his killing was a targeted assassination to prevent him from speaking out about the downing of President Juvenal Habyarimana's plane in 1994, which sparked the genocide. The crime has yet to be solved.[14]

Four genocide survivors were murdered in Gikongoro in 2003 and 2004, reportedly to prevent them from testifying in gacaca. Seventeen people accused of the killings were convicted and sentenced to death or life in prison. However, news of the killings led to fear, especially among genocide survivors, that there could be reprisals for testifying in gacaca.

Although the government dealt with these accusations in an exemplary fashion, it is possible that they could have a chilling effect on potential witnesses in gacaca. The parliamentary commission on divisionism cited these killings as contributing to a spread of genocidal ideology in the country.

The National Human Rights Commission (NHRC), an institution created in 1999 and established in the 2003 constitution, has some power to help individuals whose rights have been violated. However, the commission tends to concentrate its efforts on promotion, rather than protection, of human rights. The NHRC congratulated the government on administration of the 2003 elections without criticizing disappearances, arbitrary arrests, and other acts of intimidation. The office of the ombudsman, created in the 2003 constitution, also has the power to help citizens aggrieved by the state. In the first months of its operation, the office was inundated with complaints from hundreds of citizens; it has already intervened with government agencies to solve some of their problems.

The Rwandan government has made significant progress in promoting gender equality in law and policy. The 2003 constitution reflects gender equality, as do most new laws, and the government is in the process of amending existing laws to eliminate gender discrimination. The constitution states that a minimum of 30 percent of government positions must go to women. Rwanda now leads the world in terms of representation of women in parliament, with women holding 48.8 percent of seats in the National Assembly.[15] Women's groups have been particularly effective in lobbying the government to address historic and systematic patterns of discrimination against women at a policy level. Women also play a prominent role in the business community.

It has proven more difficult to overcome gender-based discrimination in practice, especially at the local level. Important gaps remain in legal protections, especially to prevent violence against women. The penal code fails to define rape as a crime. The government has made a priority of prosecuting individuals accused of raping young children, a phenomenon that has been on the increase since the genocide, but has not had sufficient resources to address the problem adequately. Few genocide prosecutions have included charges of sexual violence, despite recognition that egregious crimes against women were widespread. Trafficking of women and children is a crime, but due to lack of resources it remains a serious problem, especially trafficking carried on for the purpose of prostitution.

The Rwandan government has a policy that Rwandans should consider themselves first and foremost Rwandan, rather than as Hutu, Tutsi, or Twa. The logic behind this policy, which was first articulated by the National Unity and Reconciliation Commission during the transition period, is that the three ethnic groups, which make up the entire Rwandan population, have a common language and culture and, to a certain degree, ethnic divisions were imposed by foreigners whose influences were in part to blame for the genocide. While some observers question the wisdom of top-down enforcement of a single national identity, the Rwandan government maintains that its intention is to prevent discrimination and that this is the best way to prevent another genocide. As such, ethnicity has become something of a taboo in Rwandan society.

There is no longer explicit discrimination against members of ethnic groups, and laws and policies reflect this. However, some Tutsi genocide survivors, indigenous minority Twa, and members of the Hutu majority continue to complain that they are victims of discrimination in many aspects of government and society. Addressing these complaints of ethnic-based discrimination can be extremely difficult, as advocacy on behalf of any of these groups is often interpreted as promoting divisions within society and is thus illegal.

The constitution allows the president to appoint eight members of the senate to ensure representation of historically marginalized communities, a phrase widely considered to refer to the indigenous Twa. However, while the president has appointed four senators under this provision, he had yet to appoint a Twa as of September 2004. The ban on divisionism has made it difficult for Twa associations to protect their interests. The Community of Indigenous Peoples of Rwanda (CAURWA)—which has worked for more than a decade to address persistent societal inequalities against the Twa, including insufficient access to land, education, and employment—was denied the right to register on the grounds that its name and purpose promote divisionism and are contrary to the constitution.[16]

A new member of parliament (MP) represents the interests of people with disabilities. While the post is primarily a symbolic step forward, the MP says he intends to use his position to overcome societal attitudes that disabled persons are "a lost cause."[17]

The constitution recognizes freedom of association, but this right is curtailed in practice. The 2001 Law on Non-Profit Associations gives government authorities the power to control projects, budgets, and hiring of personnel so that NGOs will restrict themselves to supporting government efforts in development and service provision, not policy. Critical views expressed in policy dialogue have led to civil society organizations being accused of political activity and opposition to the government.[18] Belief that the proper role of civil society is to support the government is so widespread that some NGOs have even condemned fellow groups for being critical of the government. Police have denied human rights organizations permission to hold meetings on a number of occasions. A human rights activist forced to flee Rwanda in 2004 cynically remarked that, if human rights groups did not report any meetings being broken up that year, this is because the organizations have been afraid to discuss topics the government does not approve.

The parliamentary report on genocide was highly critical of the Rwandan League for the Promotion and Defense of Human Rights (LIPRODHOR), Rwanda's only independent human rights organization, and three other community-based organizations, recommending that they be banned and some of their members prosecuted. LIPRODHOR was not given a chance to defend itself, and many observers felt the accusations were unfounded. A number of its leaders and employees fled the country.[19] The report has had a chilling effect on independent voices, compounding the self-censorship already prevalent among human rights defenders and others.

Some trials of religious personnel have proven that a number of churches, including the Catholic Church, failed to protect Tutsis during the genocide. Since then, a number of smaller churches and sects have been established, and the government has accused some of these of political activities. Some have encountered difficulties in registering with the government.

In early 2002, the government banned a faith-based organization working on reconciliation. The organization was authorized to resume activities in 2004 after intervention by the ombudsman. In past years, the government had been accused of interfering in the internal affairs of religious organizations, including the appointment of religious leaders.

Relations between labor unions and the government have been strained since 1996 but are reportedly improving. Unions are able to advocate for the interests of their members to a limited degree. However, union membership is low, as a large percentage of the working population is involved in small-scale agriculture.

*Recommendations*

- A law guaranteeing compensation for genocide victims should be passed.
- The law governing NGOs should be amended to protect their autonomy and freedom of association. NGOs should be able to register with minimal hassle, the rules should be clear to avoid arbitrary abuses, and the government should not control project objectives or budgets.
- Government actions to root out genocidal ideology and divisionism should incorporate due process and human rights standards. The government should not publicly accuse individuals or organizations of these offenses without thorough investigation of facts and without giving them a chance to defend themselves. The definitions of these offenses should be made clear.
- Historically marginalized groups, such as the Twa, should be allowed to organize to advocate for their interests in accordance with the law, so long as there is no criminal intent or behavior.
- Genuine prosecutions of military and civilian personnel accused of revenge killings and war crimes should take place.

## RULE OF LAW – 1.22

The challenges faced by the Rwandan judiciary have no parallel anywhere in the world. Participation in the genocide was on an unprecedented scale, and in its wake, the judiciary was decimated. Many lawyers and judges had been killed, had fled the country, or were themselves accused of being involved in the killing. The judiciary is still struggling to rebuild itself and deal with the massive undertaking of holding those responsible for genocide accountable.

The constitution of 2003 guarantees judicial independence, but in practice the judiciary is subject to influence by the executive and by members of the political, military, and economic elite. This has been apparent in some genocide trials, on which there have been credible reports that the executive dictated how judges should rule. The government, especially at the local level, has failed to ensure enforcement of judicial decisions in many cases, and the judiciary lacks sufficient authority to insist that its judgments be executed. In a number of instances, police rearrested individuals who were acquitted on genocide charges.

Since early 2004, the judiciary has functioned only in exceptional cases while awaiting implementation of planned judicial reform. In June 2004, the government implemented a sweeping overhaul of the judicial system aimed at increasing professionalism. More than 500 judges who lacked professional qualifications were fired, and 223 new judges were sworn in. Many of the new judges had only recently completed university. It is too soon to predict whether the new measures will be sufficient to overcome the weaknesses of the system. Some fear that the firing of magistrates signaled an intention to ensure that magistrates remain susceptible to influence by the RPF. Some observers say that the conditions that allowed the pre-genocide government to control the judiciary have essentially remained in place.

It is common for civil and criminal disputes to be handled outside the formal judicial system. Local officials often intervene in cases of accusations of rape to encourage the parties involved to resolve the matter amicably, in part to protect the victims from the stigma of being known as a rape victim. Street children arrested for petty theft are often beaten, jailed for one or two days, and then released without ever seeing a courtroom.[20] This is due in large part to how overburdened the court system is. The 2003 constitution established mediation committees to help resolve certain disputes at the local level before the parties go to court. However, the mediators are unpaid, which has led to some fears of corruption.

Lack of capacity among magistrates led to instances of corruption prior to the recent judicial reform. By some accounts, it was standard practice to give a gift or payment to a magistrate to ensure that one's case would be heard in a timely fashion or that it would be decided in one's favor.

The presumption of innocence is protected in the constitution but is essentially absent in many criminal cases, especially genocide cases. The government publishes a list of suspects accused of the most heinous genocide crimes. While individuals must still be tried, the list leads others in Rwandan society to view those named as guilty and can result in a loss of civil rights, such as suffrage. Moreover, some versions of the list were found to have a significant number of errors.[21] There are also concerns about the broadcasting on radio of the names of some of those accused of divisionism.

The 2003 constitution guarantees the right to independent counsel, a right that was not previously assured. In genocide trials in conventional courts, various national and international initiatives have attempted to provide defense counsel for indigent defendants. However, in genocide and common criminal trials defendants do not always have access to defense as there are only approximately 120 qualified lawyers in the country, and few Rwandans have the means to hire a lawyer. Societal perceptions that defense lawyers were aiding the perpetrators of genocide, prevalent in the first years after the genocide, have largely been overcome.

The trial of former President Pasteur Bizimungu, the former minister of transportation, and six others ended in 2004. Bizimungu was sentenced to 15 years in prison and the others to 5 or 10 years. They had been charged with threatening state security after they attempted to create a political party in 2001. There were numerous irregularities at the trial, including reports that some evidence used at trial had been obtained using torture, and one prosecution witness recanted, claiming his testimony had been made under police duress. Bizimungu's defense lawyer was also briefly detained by the judge for contempt of court.[22]

The gacaca system is separate from the rest of the Rwandan judiciary. Gacaca has been heavily criticized in its pilot phase, and it is not clear whether it can meet its objectives. Given the high number of potential defendants and the fact that the start of trials has been delayed by years, it is failing in its objective to speed up trials. In response to difficulties in obtaining quorums for pilot phases, attendance at gacaca is now mandatory under law for all community members, which some interpret as inconsistent with its professed participatory nature.

The accused are not allowed to be assisted by defense counsel in gacaca. Rwandan lawyers called on the government to amend the gacaca law to bring it into compliance with the new constitution and allow counsel, but the government has said that this would not be practicable and would bog down gacaca courts.[23] Furthermore, gacaca courts sometimes operate outside the parameters of the law, as some judges lack basic understanding of legal principles. Gacaca judges have received very little training, and observers have found that what training judges did receive has often been inconsistent from one training site to the next.

Senior military officials continue to play an important role in the government and akazu. While security forces have become more profesional in recent years, they continue to commit abuses in many cases. For example, police and military intelligence were responsible for much of the intimidation and abuse in the run-up to the elections (see "Accountability and Public Voice"). Rwanda has also been criticized for maintaining stability within the country by launching a brutal and exploitative occupation of the DRC. There have been credible reports of Rwandan troops in the country again since the official withdrawal in 2002, although the Rwandan government publicly denied this.

Land was one of the root causes of the genocide, and access to land remains a volatile issue, as Rwanda is a densely populated country. In 1959, hundreds of thousands of Tutsi refugees fled to neighboring countries in the wake of ethnic violence, abandoning their land to Hutu who remained. In 1994, the genocidal government used this in its propaganda, warning Hutu that the Tutsi were going to take their land back and inciting the Hutu to kill the Tutsi enemy before this could happen. In the immediate aftermath of the genocide, a huge number of Hutu refugees fled the country at the same time as the 1959 refugees returned to Rwanda. Many of the 1959 returnees occupied houses and land that had been left vacant by those who fled more recently, averting tension until the new-caseload refugees returned in massive waves of (forced) repatriation in 1997–98.

In an effort to find a solution for the old-caseload refugees, who were not supposed to claim the homes or land they had left decades ago, and to avoid further conflict, the government and donors built settlement villages. The government later adopted a national policy of villagization, which required all Rwandans to move to these villages, instead of the traditional, dispersed habitats. From 1998 to 2000, villagization was carried out on a large scale, sometimes by force or coercion. Many farmers lost their land in the process or had their houses destroyed, and many families were obliged to share their land with old-caseload refugees.[24]

Approximately 90 percent of Rwandans depend on subsistence agriculture to make their living. As families have grown and more people are living off smaller plots, the government has sought ways to better utilize the land. In a number of cases, senior government and military officials or important businessmen assumed control of large plots of land to use as commercial farms. Families who were displaced from the land rarely had access to due process or compensation for their loss.

The 2003 constitution guarantees the right to own private property individually or collectively. The government has been working on a revised land law and land policy, in part to grant individuals full ownership rights over the land they farm. A number of elements of the draft could be problematic. The Poverty Reduction Strategy requires that all plots of less than one hectare be eliminated, yet it is not clear what compensation would be provided for families who depend on them. The draft also threatens to eliminate the traditional property system, *ubukonde,* which grants rights to the lineage group of those who first cleared the land and is still used in some parts of the northwest of the country. The policy would revert to villagization but does not address problems with its earlier implementation, including forced relocation and decreased agricultural productivity. The draft would also confirm the state's power to determine whether land is being used productively and, if not, expropriate it.[25]

A 1999 law mandated that girl children be allowed to inherit land on an equal basis with boys, but this provision is not always implemented, as cultural practices often prevail.[26] The draft land law fails to address some of the societal realities that discriminate against women with respect to property ownership.

The municipal government of Kigali has been working on transforming the capital city to make it more cosmopolitan. In order to accomplish this, city authorities have closed down the central market to make room for construction of a shopping mall, demolished large numbers of business kiosks from city streets in 2004, and forced itinerant traders away from the city center. Those affected have had little access to due process or compensation for loss of property and livelihood.

*Recommendations*

- The government must expedite training of gacaca judges in basic legal principles—including the presumption of innocence and protection of genocide survivors—and proper procedures so that the implementation of gacaca trials can begin without further delays.

- The judiciary should make sure that courts continue to hear cases during implementation of judicial reform to minimize the unacceptable delays that exist.
- The government should accelerate passage of the land law and policy after making substantive changes to ensure that compulsion is not used to enforce the new law and avoid increasing the number of landless Rwandans. The law and policy should not promote forced relocation, should not allow for people to be dispossessed of their land without due process and compensation, and should go further than previous legislation to enforce women's property rights in practice.

## ANTICORRUPTION AND TRANSPARENCY – 1.97

Rwanda enjoys the reputation of having relatively low corruption as compared to many other African countries, and it has instituted tough new anticorruption measures in the past year. However, corruption does remain a problem in the bureaucracy. The government has professed commitment to privatization, but the state retains control of many of the country's largest companies. Senior government and military officials maintain substantial business interests.

Pursuant to the national policy objective of promoting foreign investment, Rwanda has attempted to root out corruption.[27] Government institutions to fight corruption include the auditor general (which audits government finances), the National Tender Board (which is supposed to ensure that government contracts are awarded fairly), and the semiautonomous tax agency, the Rwanda Revenue Authority. President Kagame was recently quoted as saying that the bottom line in fighting corruption is political will and that institutions such as a strong parliament, independent judiciary, free media, and civil society are less important.[28] President Kagame has also indicated that the independent newspaper *Umuseso* performs a useful role in curbing corruption,[29] although this has not protected its journalists from arrest and intimidation by authorities for reporting on corruption (see "Accountability and Public Voice").

The 2003 constitution mandates that the budget process be transparent and that the parliament oversee that process. However, parliament has yet to assert this power in practice, and many questions remain, including how responsibility for budget oversight should be divided between the two houses of the assembly.[30] Under the government's decentralization program, Rwanda's 106 districts are theoretically to be responsible for their own budgeting; but, given lack of capacity of local government structures and the difficulty of raising tax revenues in poor communities, it remains to be seen how this will be implemented. Within the ministry of finance, the Central Projects and External Finance Bureau (CEPEX) is mandated with overseeing the national budget and administration of foreign assistance but is not independent and has been criticized as a weak institution.

The office of the ombudsman has powers to root out official corruption, in addition to its mandate to help citizens who have been aggrieved by the state (see "Civil Liberties"). It remains to be seen whether the government will grant the new institution of ombudsman the resources and autonomy to do its job. One of the ombudsman's first tasks was to request all government officials (including President Kagame) to declare their wealth, and it is currently investigating those declarations. In 2004 the government fired 139 police officers accused of corruption. Similarly, the government removed 47 district mayors and 5 governors apparently linked to allegations of corruption.

The auditor general's office audited 10 ministries in 2002, including defense. Its report, released in March 2004, documented irregularities in the public procurement process in several ministries and parastatal companies resulting in millions of dollars in losses for the government. The report also found mismanagement of some revenue sources, such as visa fees collected abroad and deposited in private accounts.[31] However, there were also concerns that the auditor general may not have sufficient autonomy to be an effective watchdog. The 2003 constitution, which provides for the role of the auditor general, does not require that the auditor general's report be made public, and the constitution grants the president alone the power to remove an auditor general.[32]

Government officials accused of abuse of power are rarely prosecuted. The former attorney general resigned in disgrace in early 2004 when allegations surfaced that he had engaged in corrupt activities. His resignation was touted as a sign that such impunity would no longer be tolerated, but he has not been prosecuted. In April 2004, a former minister who was dismissed in 1997 amid corruption allegations was appointed to run the state-owned coffee company.[33]

A UN panel of experts investigating the nexus between illegal resource exploitation and the war in the DRC accused Rwandan troops of illegally benefiting from Congo's substantial wealth in natural resources. The Rwandan government dismissed the panel's reports as biased and has failed to carry out a serious investigation into the allegations. Nevertheless, wealth obtained from the Congo is clearly visible in Kigali, and analysts report that economic activity in Rwanda is far larger than what the Rwandan economy alone could support.

Rwanda was one of the first countries to volunteer for the African Peer Review Mechanism under NEPAD, an apparent sign of its commitment to transparency. Rwanda began its self-assessment, the first step in the process, in June 2004. However, the government's crackdown on LIPRODHOR occurred just days after a high-level NEPAD mission visited the country, raising questions about Rwanda's commitment to NEPAD's goals of transparency and good governance.

Government policies are often lacking in transparency and inaccessible to the general public. No law guarantees public access to government information. The primary means the government uses to impart information to the public is through National Radio broadcasts and so-called sensitization meetings organized by local officials. These meetings are sometimes billed as soliciting popular feedback, but most Rwandans view them as forums for the government to provide information without allowing the people to express differing points of view. In this way, the government is able to control when and to what information the public has access.

## Recommendations

- The government should afford institutions such as the ombudsman and the auditor general the autonomy necessary to exercise their functions.
- The government must refrain from harassing journalists and others who report cases of corruption.
- The government should follow up with investigations and prosecutions to ensure that government officials and members of the elite accused of corruption are not above the law.
- The government should conduct an independent investigation into illegal resource exploitation in the DRC, institute measures

to ensure that business activities of Rwandan military and other citizens in DRC are conducted in accordance with the laws, and prosecute those alleged to have committed criminal acts.

## NOTES

[1] Law on Discrimination and Sectarianism, Law No. 4/72001, 18 December 2001.

[2] "Silence in the Court of King Paul – Rwanda," *The Economist*, 30 October 2004.

[3] *Rapport Final sur l'élection présidentielle et les élections législatives* (Brussels: European Union, Mission de L'Observation Electorale de L'Union Européenne Rwanda [EU Mission], 2003), 4.

[4] "Preparing for Elections: Tightening Control in the Name of Unity" (New York: Human Rights Watch [HRW], Backgrounder, 8 May 2003); "Rwanda: Run-up to presidential elections marred by threats and harassment" (New York: Amnesty International [AI], 21 August 2003).

[5] *Rapport Final* (EU Mission), 9.

[6] Ibid., 17.

[7] Ibid., 12.

[8] "Rwanda: Broken Bodies, Torn Spirits Living with Genocide, Rape and HIV/AIDS" (Kigali and London: African Rights [AR], 15 April 2004; "Marked for Death, Rape survivors living with HIV/AIDS in Rwanda" (AI, 5 April 2004); "Struggling to Survive: Barriers to Justice for Rape Victims in Rwanda" (HRW, 30 September 2004).

[9] "Rapport de la Commission Parlementaire Ad Hoc, Cree en date du 20 janvier 2004 par le Parlement, Chambre des Députés, pour Analyser en Profondeur les Tueries Perpétrées dans la Province de Gikongoro, L'Idéologie Génocidaire, et Ceux qui la Propagent Partout Au Rwanda" (Kigali: Chamber of Deputies of Rwanda, June 2004), unofficial translation from Kinyarwanda into French.

[10] "Rwanda" in *AI Report 2004* (AI), http://web.amnesty.org/web/web.nsf/print/2004-rwa-summary-eng.

[11] See, e.g., Robert Walker, "Rwanda Struggles with Street Children," BBC News, 3 February 2004.

[12] "Rwanda: The enduring legacy of genocide and war" (AI, 5 April 2004).

[13] Ibid.

[14] John Swain, "The Riddle of the Rwandan Assassins' Trail," *The Sunday Times*, 4 April 2004.

[15] "Rwanda Leads World Ranking of Women in Parliament" (Geneva: Inter-Parliamentary Union, 22 October 2003).

[16] "Rwanda: Atteinte à la liberté d'association/menaces," (Paris: Fédération Internationale des Ligues des Droits de l'Homme, 2 December 2004).

[17] Marcellin Gasana, "Rwanda's Disabled: A Legacy of the Genocide," *Internews*, 1 April 2004.

[18] "Searching for Sense and Humanity: Civil Society and the Struggle for a Better Rwanda," draft report provided to author, Kituo Cha Katiba [East African Center for Constitutional Development], Kampala, 2004, 89.

[19] "Rwanda: Parliament seeks to abolish human rights group" (HRW, 2 July 2004).

[20] *Lasting Wounds: Consequences of Genocide and War for Rwanda's Children* (HRW, April 2003).

[21] *Leave None to Tell the Story* (HRW, March 1999), 752.

[22] "Rwandan trial 'bad for democracy,'" BBC News, 8 June 2004.

[23] "Lawyers Call on Government to Harmonize Gacaca Law with Constitution," IRIN News, 30 December 2003.

[24] *Uprooting the Rural Poor* (HRW, June 2001).

[25] Herman Mushara and C. Huggins, "Land Reform, Land Scarcity and Post Conflict Reconstruction: A Case Study of Rwanda," *Eco-Conflicts* (Nairobi: African Centre for Technology Studies) 3, 3 (October 2004): 2.

[26] Jennie E. Burnet, *Culture, Practice, and Law: Women's Access to Land in Rwanda* (Kigali: Rwanda Initiative for Sustainable Development [RISD], 2001).

[27] "Rwanda: Protect Investors," *New Times,* 13 September 2004.

[28] Andrew Mwenda, "Political Will is Central to the Fight Against Corrupt Institutions," *The Monitor,* 1 September 2004.

[29] "Country Report: Rwanda," *The Economist Intelligence Unit* 15, November 2004, 12.

[30] Ian Lienert, "Choosing a Budget Management System: The Case of Rwanda" (Washington, DC: International Monetary Fund [IMF], Working Paper, WP/04/132, July 2004).

[31] Arthur Asiimwe, "Rwanda Unearths Tendering Scam," *The East African,* 15 March 2004; "Rwanda: Audit unearths irregularities in use of state funds," IRIN News, 5 March 2004.

[32] Lienert, "Choosing a Budget Management System" (IMF), 14–15.

[33] "Former Minister Appointed Director of Coffee Company," *New Times,* 21 April 2004.

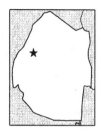

# SWAZILAND

CAPITAL: Mbabane
POPULATION: 1.2 million
GNI PER CAPITA: $1,240

**SCORES**
ACCOUNTABILITY AND PUBLIC VOICE: 1.85
CIVIL LIBERTIES: 2.98
RULE OF LAW: 1.45
ANTICORRUPTION AND TRANSPARENCY: 1.85
(scores are based on a scale of 0 to 7, with
0 representing weakest and 7 representing
strongest performance)

*John Daniel*

## INTRODUCTION

There is no tradition of democracy in the Swazi polity. Since its emergence in the early 19th century, the Swazi state's political culture has been authoritarian with power centralized in a hereditary monarchy. The late colonial period and early years of independence introduced an element of choice and party-political competitiveness into the polity but this ended in 1973 with the suspension of the independence constitution and the proscribing of political parties.

Swaziland's political regime is not one of straightforward monarchical domination. It is a complex diarchic one with two distinct but interrelated sets of institutions—those of the Swazi nation (the monarchy and its key advisory institutions, the Liqoqo, Libandla, and Tinkhundla) and of the Swazi government, comprising cabinet, parliament, and the judiciary. It was in the latter that Britain vested constitutional authority at independence in 1968. However, then–King Sobhuza II was able to circumvent this dilution of his traditional authority by forming a

---

**John Daniel**, a former professor of political science at the University of Swaziland, is currently a research director in the democracy and governance program of South Africa's Human Sciences Research Council.

political party—the Imbokodvo National Movement—and contesting and winning all parliamentary seats in two pre-independence elections. Thus, even though not a member of parliament, Sobhuza was able to ensure that the body enacted no legislation of which he did not approve. The king's domination of the post-independence power arrangement was articulated by the then–prime minister, Prince Makhosini Dlamini, who stated "It is the king, not I, who leads the people."[1] This is the central principle of Swazi political life, and to challenge it is regarded by the ruling elite (if not by the letter of the law) as sedition.[2]

This period of post-independence one-party rule gave way to no-party rule in 1973 when Sobhuza reacted to an opposition grouping's winning of 3 seats out of 28 in the first elections held after independence and a successful high court challenge of controversial immigration legislation by abrogating the constitution. A state of emergency was declared (which persists today, more than 30 years later), a detention-without-trial provision was introduced, parliament was dissolved, and all political parties, even the pro-monarchy Imbokodvo Movement, were banned. In an address to the Swazi people, Sobhuza justified his actions by declaring that the independence constitution was incompatible with Swazi tradition as it had "permitted the imposition into our country of highly undesirable political practices, alien and incompatible with the way of life in our society, and designed to disrupt and destroy our own peaceful and constructive and essentially democratic method of peaceful political activity."[3]

What Sobhuza was targeting as "undesirable" and "alien" was the political party as an institution. His words remain salient today; they essentially inform the view of his successor, Mswati III, and his advisers. They regard political parties as un-Swazi, institutions incompatible with their concept of tradition. Therefore, to concede to the Swazi people the right freely to organize themselves politically would necessitate an ideological paradigm shift on the part of the monarchy as well as open up the possibility of an effective challenge to its continued political and economic dominance.

Since 1973, Swaziland has functioned as a near-absolute monarchy. In 1978, a two-chamber parliament was reconvened with a mix of members nominated by the king (40 out of 90) and elected on a no-party basis. In 1996, the king appointed a constitutional review commission that five years later reported without supporting evidence that the Swazi nation preferred no change to the political and legal status quo.[4] The king then appointed a group headed by one of his brothers to draft a new constitution. This was unveiled in 2004, proposing a continuation of the monarchy's supreme executive, legislative, and judicial powers as well as the ban on political parties.

In 2002, all the judges of Swaziland's highest court, the court of appeal, resigned in protest at the government's refusal to implement two rulings whose effect would have been to overturn previous state measures. In September 2004, the Commonwealth Secretariat brokered a settlement under which the government agreed to be bound by the orders of the kingdom's courts. As of September 2004 this settlement had not been implemented.

In addition to a crisis over the rule of law, Swaziland is confronted by a human disaster of epic proportions in the form of one of the highest—and possibly the highest—HIV/AIDS prevalence rates in the world. According to the Swazi Minsistry of Health, the rate in 2002 for adults aged between 15 and 49 years was 38.6%. For those in the age brackets 20–24 and 25–29, the rates were 45.4% and 47.7% respectively. By 2004, it was estimated that one in two Swazis in their twenties would be HIV positive. In the period 1980–2005, life expectancy for Swazis almost halved from 60 years of age to 34. By 2010, it is projected that it will have fallen to 27 years of age. Furthermore, by then it is estimated that 12 percent of the population—some 120,000 children—will have been orphaned.

## ACCOUNTABILITY AND PUBLIC VOICE – 1.85

Politically, Swaziland is an absolute monarchy with effective executive, legislative and increasingly judicial powers vested in the king although there is a partially elected but thoroughly subordinated parliament.

Parliamentary elections are held every five years. These are conducted in terms of a traditional *tinkundhla* system: Candidates run only as individuals and not as representatives of any party or grouping. The number of candidates per constituency is limited to three, and their nomination is subject to a local screening process. This is conducted in public by the local chiefs in the area by a show of hands. The franchise is open to all adults over the age of 18, and votes are cast by secret ballot. No cases of fraud and intimidation were reported in the elections of 1998 and 2003.

Despite the democratic form of this electoral process, it does not conform fully to the now widely accepted "free and fair" criteria for democratic elections. First, the ban on party political activity limits the range of political choice. So too does the local screening process, which inevitably has the result that the majority of candidates are linked, or sympathetic, to the royalist power structure. Finally, balloting is for only 55 of the 95 parliamentary seats. This means that 42 percent of legislative seats are nominated, mostly by the king himself. Thus, even in the unlikely case that a majority of elected members turn out to be reformists, their capacity for change would be neutralized by the nominated bloc of royalist-aligned members of Parliament. According to the Economist Intelligence Unit's (EIU) 2004 Country Profile of Swaziland, "the ban on political parties and the boycotting of elections by progressive groups mean that political debate in parliament is inconsequential."[5] There are no effective campaign finance laws. Under current circumstances, therefore, a change in power in Swaziland is very unlikely. Given that the executive branch of government, in the form of the monarchy, conceptualizes itself as not being subject to statutory laws, there are obvious limitations on the capacity of the judicial and legislative branches to oversee the executive branch (see "Rule of Law").

Recruitment into the civil service is largely by merit, and a high proportion of public servants hold university degrees and/or appropriate technical qualifications. At entry level, women applicants appear not to be discriminated against, and a high proportion of upper-level civil servants are women with distinguished academic records. This is offset by the fact that the top posts in the civil service tend to be filled by males regarded by the traditional authorities as politically reliable. These are often princes of the dominant Dlamini clan.

Civil society in Swaziland is neither strong nor well developed. This is not because the government makes it especially difficult for this sector to operate. Civil groups are able to comment upon and attempt to influence policy and legislation. They are not subject to onerous registration requirements. Nor is there evidence that their funders are subject to state pressure. The disability they face is the overwhelming political apathy of the Swazi majority and the continued internalization of a political culture that demands of the Swazi people unquestioning subservience to the wishes and whims of the traditional royalist and chieftancy authorities.

The position is quite different in regard to the media. Freedom of speech and of the press in Swaziland is not legally protected, and the government has frequently acted against the media especially to discourage critical coverage of the royal family. This has included closing down newspapers and magazines and detaining and then harassing journalists and broadcasters. There are two daily newspapers in Swaziland, one of which is government owned. The state has a monopoly over television and radio ownership. In 2003, a censorship policy for the state-owned Swaziland Broadcasting and Information Services was imposed to prohibit the dissemination of negative information about the government. Libel laws and detention have been used by the government to intimidate journalists. The state is more tolerant in the realm of cultural expression, in part because this is not a particularly active area of expression and also because what there is largely reflects traditional values.

*Recommendations*
- All political offices should be opened to free and competitive elections under an independent election commission. The ban on political parties should be lifted, and all candidates should have the opportunity to campaign openly.
- The government should take all necessary steps to ensure that the draft constitution currently under consideration is consistent with Swaziland's international and regional human rights treaty obligations, and a vigorous and independent legal reform process should be instituted to facilitate such incorporation into domestic law.
- Ongoing training should be provided to all state officials on the professional and other implications of these obligations.
- An enabling environment should be created for the vigorous expression of views and opinions by, inter alia, freeing the press and broadcast media from all forms of censorship, as well as through the creation of an independent media authority to ensure a non-partisan state media.

## CIVIL LIBERTIES – 2.98

Swazi law does not prohibit the use of torture, and there have been credible reports in recent years of the use of torture by security officials. While the Prison Act provides for the prosecution of officials suspected of torture or degrading treatment, there have been no reports of any such cases being mounted. Prison conditions are on a par with basic international standards. However, a lack of basic hygiene and unsafe sexual practices contribue to the spread of HIV/AIDS among prisoners. By contrast, conditions in pre-trial detention facilities are overcrowded, a fact exacerbated by the introduction of non-bailable provisions for a range of offenses (see "Rule of Law").

No members of the political opposition or activists have been killed in Swaziland in recent years. While repressive, political life in Swaziland since the 1973 declaration of a state of emergency has not been characterized by high levels of brutality and terror. The exception to this was the period 1981 to 1989, when the Swazi security forces actively collaborated with the South African security forces, and in some cases participated in, the killing and abduction of South Africans engaged from Swaziland in the struggle against apartheid.[6]

Swazi law prohibits arbitrary arrest and detention, and the government generally respects these prohibitions. There is currently no provision for detention without trial for a period beyond 48 hours. No evidence suggests that the state does not protect its citizens from abuse by private or non-state actors. On the other hand, citizens do not have effective means to petition for the redress of their rights.

In March 2004 Swaziland acceded to four core international human rights treaties, including the UN Convention on the Elimination of all Forms of Discrimination Against Women (CEDAW). With one of the poorest international human rights treaty records in sub-Saharan Africa, Swaziland seemed in the view of most commentators to be attempting to mend its negative human rights image internationally. No attempt has been made to incorporate CEDAW's provisions into domestic law, nor is one expected. This is because many of the convention's provisions would undermine key tenets of Swazi law and custom.

Men and women clearly do not occupy equal status in Swazi society. Women are subordinate in both civil and traditional marriages. Wives are treated as legal minors, although women married under civil law can attain the status of an adult through a signed pre-nuptial contract. In the absence of such an agreement, women generally must have the permission of their spouses to open bank accounts, acquire passports, travel abroad, purchase land, and undertake a host of other acts that men take for granted. In terms of customary law, Swazi men can practice polygamy while women cannot. While not common, there are cases where young Swazi teenage girls—many of them still school-going—are forced into marriages with members of the royal family, the king included. One of Mswati's more recent marriages involved the abduction in 2002 of a teenage schoolgirl from her home.

There is a long history of violence directed against women and girls in Swaziland. The disproportionately high incidence of HIV/AIDS among Swazi women (by contrast with that of Swazi males) reflects their generally unequal status socially and their disempowered sexual status in particular. There are no reports of trafficking in women and children, although it may occur given that evidence does exist of a trade in children in particular in South Africa. The proposed draft constitution for Swaziland advocates a prohibition of discrimination on grounds of gender. In an analysis of the draft, Amnesty International stated that this was too weak and too general a position and that what was required was "a clear prohibition on the grounds of sex and marital status."[7] Only in this way could girls and young women be protected sufficiently against such abuses as forced marriages.

Legislation and general practice in Swaziland are not sensitive to the needs of people with disabilities. While all new government buildings must provide ramps and easy-access facilities to disabled persons, no attempt has been made to convert existing public buildings for this purpose.

Given that Swaziland is largely homogeneous ethnically, issues of ethnic discrimination or disadvantage do not arise. Nor is there any sustained record of religious disadvantage. While there is no formal legal provision for religious freedom in Swaziland, the government generally respects freedom of religion in practice and respects the rights of non-believers and the beliefs of minority religious groupings. The one exception is the Jehovah's Witnesses, against whom state action has from time to time been directed. For example, in June 2003 a teacher and three school pupils were expelled from a primary school on grounds of their membership in this faith. New religious groups must register with the government, and state permission is required for the construction of religious buildings. There is no record of refusals in regard to these two requirements. On occasion, however, prayer meetings have been disrupted or banned because they were considered political gatherings.

Freedom of association is not guaranteed in Swaziland and is actively restricted. Police permission is required and routinely refused for meetings and demonstrations of a political nature. Where such gatherings or marches do occur, they are invariably broken up by force with the use of tear gas, baton charges, rubber bullets, and water cannons. Despite this antipathy to gatherings of a political nature, the government does respect the right to form and join trade unions. This has, however, not protected trade unionists from state action; the detention and general harassment of pro-democracy trade-union leaders is common.

### Recommendations

- The provisions of the CEDAW treaty should be incorporated fully and without any qualifications into Swazi domestic law. In addition and as a means of strengthening the law, the government should accede to both the Optional Protocol of the CEDAW so that Swazi women can lodge complaints with the UN treaty-monitoring body established under the Protocol and to the Protocol to the African Charter on Human and Peoples' Rights on the Rights of Women in Africa.
- Measures need to be taken to strengthen the rights of Swazi children, particularly to ensure that they are freed from all forms of violence, including sexual violence and corporal punishment in schools and homes.
- Citizens should have the right to form political and other associations in support of their interests.
- Laws requiring prior permission for meetings and protests should be repealed, and the use of force against peaceful demonstrators should be banned.

## RULE OF LAW – 1.45

Swaziland operates a dual court system comprising traditional courts, in which presiding chiefs apply customary law, and a Roman-Dutch system of magistrate courts, a high court, and a Court of Appeal. The latter is not a permanent body but one currently staffed by retired South African judges that convenes in Swaziland two to three times per year. All judges, including those from South Africa, are appointed by the king, and their appointments are not subject to parliamentary approval or scrutiny. In the late 1990s Prime Minister Sibusiso Dlamini unilaterally scrapped the commission originally set up to make recommendations for judicial appointments and replaced it with a special committee on justice composed of certain cabinet ministers, the attorney-general, the director of public prosecutions, the commissioner of police, heads of the security services, the chief justice, and some palace advisers—all these officials are appointed by the king and are consequently subject to dismissal by him. Its brief goes well beyond judicial appointments and involves close scrutiny of the workings of the entire justice system. It meets weekly; hence the widespread popular reference to it as the "Thursday Committee." According to Amnesty International, this group has very intrusively and broadly interfered with judicial decisions.[8]

The coexistence of two legal traditions with fundamentally different conceptions of rights lies at the core of the political crisis that has afflicted Swaziland since the early 1970s. It began with the declaration of a state of emergency in 1973, which was triggered in part by the fact that the high court had acted to overturn the legislative will of parliament, which functioned then as the handmaiden of the monarchy. Its latest manifestation took the form of the 2002 resignation en bloc of the appeal bench, stemming from the monarchy's refusal to implement decisions with which it did not concur.

The political and legal crisis stemming from this action on the part of the monarchy severely compromised the independence of the judiciary and threw the administration of the judicial system into disarray. Throughout the 2003–2004 reporting period Swaziland remained without a court of appeal. This resulted in a continued violation of the rights of those favored by the court's November 2002 decisions (see the concluding paragraph of this section for fuller details of these two cases), as well as those of numerous individuals whose civil and criminal cases were at the appeal stage and therefore could be neither heard nor concluded. In one case, the imposition of a death sentence was being appealed.

What the last three decades of Swazi political life have revealed is that in any clash between the two legal systems, it is the view of the Swazi king and his advisers that the law of custom prevails. What this means politically is that even in this age of democratization, an unelected and unaccountable monarchical order refuses to accept any constitutional or legal limits to its rule—a modern manifestation of the ancient notion of the divine right of kings. The primary casualties of this ideological worldview have been the Swazi democratization process, the rule of law, the administration of justice, and perhaps above all, the economic and social development of the people.

The collective body of judges—local and expatriate—that has since 1968 served in the high and appeal courts of Swaziland have developed a strong reputation as able and competent judicial officials. This applies also to the current serving justices. While many local judges have lacked the experience and seniority of most of their foreign colleagues, they have all been trained legal practitioners with appropriate graduate qualifications in law. The good reputation of the Swazi bench is based not solely on the fact that it has always attempted to apply the law fairly and consistently but also on the fact that it has strongly resisted attempts by the state and traditional authorities to influence decisions through intimidation. In a July 2004 report on Swaziland, Amnesty International cited numerous instances of the abrogation of the rule of law by the government. These included "the repeated ignoring of court rulings, interference in court proceedings, intimidating judicial officers, manipulating terms and conditions of employment to undermine the independence of the judiciary, the effective replacement of the Judicial Services Commission with an unaccountable and secretive body . . . and the harassment of individuals whose rights had been upheld by the courts."[9]

According to the "saved provisions" of the 1968 independence constitution, a high court judge can be removed from office only on grounds of an "inability to perform the functions of his office, whether arising from infirmity of body or mind or any other cause or for misbehaviour."[10] This provision is supposed to be invoked only after the chief justice has requested the king to investigate the conduct of the judge in question, which must occur through a tribunal appointed by the king. None of these requirements had been met when in April 2003 Justice Thomas Masuku was "transferred" from the high to the industrial court. This de facto removal from the bench was challenged in the high court by the Swazi Law Society. During the course of the hearing on the matter, counsel for the government stated that the government "can be pushed around [only] a certain point."[11] Despite this implied threat, the high court ruled in May 2004 that the dismissal of Judge Masuku was unlawful and reinstated him in his post.

In the past decade, the presumption of innocence until proven guilty, a cardinal legal principle, has been undermined in Swaziland through the passage in 1993 (with subsequent amendments) of the Non-Bailable Offences Order. According to this legislation, Swazi courts are prohibited from granting bail to persons charged with one or more so-called scheduled offenses. These include murder, rape, robbery, and offenses referred to in public order and anti-subversion laws. In 2001, the appeal court struck down the order, describing it as "draconian" and "inconsistent with the presumption of innocence and an . . . invasion of the liberty of the subject." In the face of this rejection, the government issued decree Number 3 of 2001 reimposing the provisions of the 1993 order. Challenges to this decree were launched by two pre-trial detainees denied bail, resulting in November 2002 in a second appeal court's ruling striking down the legislation. In response, the then–Prime Minister Sibusiso Dlamini announced that the act would remain in force and that all government agencies had been instructed to ignore the appeal court's ruling. Significantly, he described their judgment as an attack on the powers of the king.

Citizens have the right to independent counsel of their choice. For most Swazis, however, this is a nominal right, given that 40 percent of them are living below the poverty line, and 34 percent of the potential labor force are unemployed. There is no state system of legal aid for those unable to afford counsel.

In recent years prosecutors and state judicial officials have in some cases been subjected to political pressure. For example, in late 2002 the mother of an 18-year-old schoolgirl whom King Mswati wished to marry claimed that the girl had been abducted from the family home and petitioned the high court to order that she be restored to the mother's custody. While the matter was pending, considerable pressure was exerted on the judges of the high court. This included a meeting between the chief justice and his two fellow judges and the attorney-general accompanied by the chiefs of the army, police, and prison services at which an instruction from the palace to discontinue the hearing or resign was conveyed to the judges. Their refusal to withdraw from the case resulted in a letter from the attorney-general in which they were informed that unless their resignations were submitted, the attorney-general's office had been instructed "to submit the relevant instruments for your removal from office." Amnesty International described these acts of intimidation as illustrative of how difficult it was in Swaziland "to protect the internationally recognized human rights of women and girls, particularly where their rights were violated by unaccountable authorities and in a context of longstanding discrimination and subordination of women."[12]

The chief justice (a foreign national) lodged a complaint stating that the attorney-general's letter amounted to a threat to and interference in judicial functions. The director of public prosecutions (another foreign national) then charged the attorney-general with sedition and attempting to defeat the ends of justice. The Thursday Committee, meeting in emergency session, instructed the director to withdraw the charges. His refusal resulted in several acts of intimidation, including his being twice locked out of his office, as well as a burglary of his office in which video footage showed that the attorney-general had participated. On persisting with the case, the director was then charged in regard to an alleged misdemeanour that had occurred some years earlier. At this point he resigned and left the country. Three months later, the chief justice followed suit. The case against the attorney-general lapsed.

The above events illustrate both the anarchic and the politicized nature of the administration of justice in Swaziland. While some public officials and ruling party actors are charged before the courts, cases are brought selectively and usually only involve those who fall foul of the traditional authorities. All Swazis do not experience an equal application of the law despite the best efforts of the Swazi high and appeal courts.

Any civilian state control of the security services by the judicial and legislative branches of government is ineffective, as the services essentially function as an enforcement arm of the traditional authorities in the executive branch. They consequently do not refrain from interfering in the political process. They are, however, free from the influence of non-state actors.

The issue of property rights in Swaziland is complex. There is a dual land system with distinct freehold and leasehold sectors. This roughly corresponds with the urban–rural divide of the country. For those with freehold rights, all residents of the country have an equal right—though obviously not an equal capacity—to property ownership. This sector operates under normal market conditions, and the state adequately enforces and protects property rights and contracts. A very different situation prevails in the communal leasehold sector, in which the majority of Swazi citizens reside. In these areas, land cannot be bought and sold, and the tenure rights of the occupants are dependent on the goodwill of the chiefs who administer the land on behalf of the king. This situation can be manipulated for political and other reasons; there is a long history in Swaziland of the precarious nature of tenure rights being used as a means to pressure or discipline the commoners resident in the leasehold sector. In short, those who do not with their chiefs' orders can have their land taken from them and forcible eviction of families or whole communities is not uncommon.

The most politically significant case in recent years involved 120 residents of the KaMkhweli and Macetjeni communities who were forcibly evicted from their homes by the police in October 2000, along with their chief, when they refused to accept the appointment of one of the king's brothers as their new chief.[13] The evictees have on several occasions taken their case to court, and in all but one instance their right to return to their homes has been upheld. Finally, in November 2002, the court of appeal made such an order, and the government publicly stated it would not obey. This led to the resignation of the appeal bench. In its ruling the court also upheld an earlier high court decision to jail the commissioner of police for contempt because he had not implemented earlier rulings allowing the residents to return to their homes. This order has never been implemented, and the commissioner in question is still in office.

*Recommendations*

- An urgent commitment is required on the part of the executive to respect and protect the independence and impartiality of the judiciary by, inter alia, stating in public its resolve henceforth to respect and implement the judgments of the courts of Swaziland.
- Steps need to be taken to restore the presumption of innocence to judicial and administrative practices by restoring to the courts the discretion to decide on matters of bail.
- The government must ensure in law and in practice that all residents of Swaziland are protected from forced evictions from their homes.

## ANTICORRUPTION AND TRANSPARENCY – 1.85

Corruption is endemic and pervasive in Swaziland. This is especially true in the monarchy and the institution of the Swazi nation where expenditure is lavish and rarely accounted for. For example, in recent years, the king has sought state funds to purchase an executive jet for his personal use. In June 2004, he announced a decision to construct new royal palaces for his 10 wives and 2 fiancees at a cost of $14 million. In April 2004 he spent $600,000 on a party in the national stadium to celebrate his 34th birthday. This occurred at a time of severe strain in the economy prompted by a fourth consecutive year of drought; some 40 percent of Swazis are living below the poverty line, and a similar percentage is living with AIDS. The EIU in its 2004 country profile noted that "most corruption seems to emanate from the traditional system of government, with its in-built nepotism and cronyism."[14]

Corruption in Swaziland is not a result of excessive bureaucratic regulations or registration requirements. Its stems, rather, from the undemocratic nature of the political order. For example, in the mid-1990s the Swaziland Development and Savings Bank went bankrupt largely because a series of large loans to members of the royal family and chiefs were never repaid. No action was taken against the loan defaulters nor were the funds recovered.

The Swazi economy is a capitalist one. Foreign investment is sought and encouraged, and there are few controls on the repatriation of profit. There is, however, considerable state involvement in the economy in the form of royalist-controlled investment corporations. The largest of these is the Tibiyo Take Ngwane Fund. At independence, control over Swaziland's mineral rights and royalties were vested in the Swazi nation and not the government. To administer the concession, the king established Tibiyo. Headed by a board whose majority are princes (male relatives of the king) and answerable only to the monarchy, Tibiyo pays no taxes, is not required to publish an annual statement (although it has done so for the last 10 years), and is not answerable to parliament. According to the EIU, "Tibiyo is a controversial institution that has some high-profile equity holdings in Swaziland, ostensibly made in the national interest, although some people have made accusations that its revenue is appropriated by the royal family."[15]

Over the years, Tibiyo has developed into a major corporation and a source of wealth for the royal family and those close to it, as well as a means to rapid upward mobility. Funds were initially used to buy back freehold land from non-Swazis, much of which was developed into royally owned maize and dairy estates. Tibiyo then moved into the retail sector, establishing butcheries, liquor stores, and taxi routes. Ultimately, the fund generated sufficient capital to begin acquiring equity (usually in the range of 40 percent to 49 percent) in practically every foreign company active in the economy. These have included huge agro-industrials in the sugar, timber, citrus, and fruit processing industries, large wholesalers, and banking, mining, manufacturing, and tourist companies. In this way, Tibiyo has spread its net into all sectors of the economy, establishing a solid partnership with foreign capital, the dividend payments from which have become Tibiyo's largest source of revenue. It has also been the means by which the Swazi aristocracy has acquired for itself a considerable material base in the modern economy, complementing their control of the traditional agrarian sector, which is achieved through its monopoly over the right to allocate and withdraw land tenure rights. In other words, the Swazi aristocracy—the royalist lines within the Dlamini clan—is not just a privileged elite but a modestly wealthy capitalist class for whom a regime change, or even a significant democratization of the system, could have negative consequences.

The state does not enforce effective legislative or administrative processes either to promote professional integrity or to prevent and detect corruption. No adequate financial disclosure procedures prevent or minimize conflicts of interest among either public officeholders or those in the private sector. No asset register exists to record the business and other interests of, or gifts to, public officials.

Tax collection is efficient and accountable in the formal (that is, outside the institutions of the Swazi nation) sector of the economy and in regard to ordinary citizens/commoners. Swaziland has no independent auditing office such as an auditor-general or ombudsman. Bribes are not necessary to gain admission to higher education, although in some cases pressure was applied successfully on the authorities of the University of Swaziland to admit members of the royal family lacking the necessary admission criteria.

Other than the courts, victims of corruption have no means to pursue their rights or seek redress. Allegations of corruption directed at members of the royal family and other figures in the traditional sector (like chiefs) are rarely investigated—and even more rarely acted upon. There is no legal environment to protect whistle-blowers. While for some years in the 1990s the press gave extensive, even gleeful, coverage to allegations of scandal, the state crackdown on the media in recent years has effectively silenced it, with journalists and editors largely succumbing to self-censorship.

The public has little access to state information, and no legal mechanisms facilitate it. The process of awarding government contracts and tenders is public, but it is susceptible to corruption.[16] The executive budget-making process is not transparent, although parliament does exercise a watchdog role over the budget and government expenditure. It has at times undertaken this function to good effect by reining in, for example, reckless spending on the part of some government ministries. The government does provide an enabling environment for the distribution of foreign assistance.

## Recommendations

- An independent auditing watchdog in the form of an auditor-general's office should be established, as well as an independent complaints directorate in the form of an ombudsman's office.
- Legislation should be enacted to guarantee the public's right to both official state information and their individual personal records held by the state.
- The Tibiyo Fund and other such royalist-controlled private corporations should be converted into public corporations and required to operate in terms of relevant company laws. This would include subjecting their financial records to public scrutiny as well as rendering them taxable.

## NOTES

[1] See Johnson Vilane and John Daniel, "Swaziland: Political Crisis, Regional Dilemma," *Review of African Political Economy* 35 (May 1986).

[2] A leader of an opposition grouping, Mario Masuku, was charged with sedition in 2000 after calling in a public speech for the relegation of the Swazi monarch's position to that of a constitutional or symbolic one. After several months on bail, Masuku deliberately broke his bail conditions in order to be arrested. This was to force the judicial/political authorities to decide whether to try him or drop the charges. They tried him. Up until this point in time, they had resorted to repeated postponements rather than going to trial and presenting what in legal terms was a flimsy case. It took nearly a year for the case to come to trial. The end result was an acquittal.

[3] Cited in Vilane and Daniel, p. 56.

[4] The Constitutional Review Commission's *Final Report on the Submissions and Progress Report on the Project for the Recording and Codification of Swazi Law and Custom* (Mbabane: 2001) contained numerous vague and unsubstantiated assertions, such as, "the nation recommends that rights and freedoms which we accept must not conflict with our customs and traditions as the Swazi nation"; and "an overwhelming majority of the nation recommends that political parties remain banned."

[5] *Country Profile: Swaziland* (London, Economist Intelligence Unit [EIU], 2004), 6.

[6] In 1981, King Sobhuza II entered into what was then a secret security agreement with the government of apartheid South Africa under the terms of which South African security forces and their agents were given an unfettered right to undertake operations against opponents of the apartheid. Throughout the 1980s, the South African forces conducted numerous cross-border incursions into Swaziland resulting in the deaths and abductions of numbers of South Africans and some Swazis.

[7] See *Swaziland: Human rights at risk in a climate of political and legal uncertainty* (London: Amnesty International [AI], 2004), 11.

[8] AI, 20.

[9] Ibid.

[10] At the time of the suspension of the independence constitution in 1973, King Sobhuza decided that some of its provisions would remain in force. These, which included provisions for the appointment of judges, became known as the "saved provisions."

[11] Ibid., 33. Soon after making this statement, the lawyer in question sent a letter of apology to the Registrar of the High Court in which he stated that he had acted under pressure from his clients, who were people in positions of authority over him.

[12] Ibid., 28, in regard to both quotes used in this paragraph.

[13] A full account of this case has been provided in AI, 36–63.

[14] *Country Profile* (EIU), 14.

[15] Ibid., 18.

[16] Ibid., 14.

# SYRIA

CAPITAL: Damascus
POPULATION: 18 million
GNI PER CAPITA: $1,130

**SCORES**

ACCOUNTABILITY AND PUBLIC VOICE: 1.29
CIVIL LIBERTIES: 2.04
RULE OF LAW: 2.13
ANTICORRUPTION AND TRANSPARENCY: 1.70
(scores are based on a scale of 0 to 7, with
0 representing weakest and 7 representing
strongest performance)

*David Lesch*

## INTRODUCTION

On June 10, 2000, Hafiz al-'Asad, the president of the Syrian Arab Republic since an intra-Ba'ath party coup in November 1970, died after a long illness. The next day his eldest surviving son, Bashar al-'Asad, was unanimously chosen by the ruling Ba'ath party as the only nominee for president. The parliament quickly amended Article 83 of the Syrian constitution to decrease the minimum age for the president of the republic from 40 to 34, Bashar's age at the time. On June 24, he was elected secretary-general of the Ba'ath, in effect the head of the party, at the Ninth Regional Congress meeting, the first such gathering of the Ba'ath party to be held in 15 years. The meeting had already been scheduled prior to Hafiz al-'Asad's death; in the aftermath, however, the meeting clearly gained increased importance by providing a timely imprimatur

**David W. Lesch** is Professor of Middle East History at Trinity University in San Antonio, Texas. Among his publications are: *Syria and the United States: Eisenhower's Cold War in the Middle East; The Middle East and the United States: A Historical and Political Reassessment* (3rd edition); *1979: The Year that Shaped the Modern Middle East*; and the upcoming (2005) political biography of President Bashar al-'Asad, *The Next Lion of Damascus? Bashar al-'Asad and Modern Syria.*

for Bashar. Three days later the Syrian parliament voted "yes" to the nomination, and in a nationwide referendum on July 11, Bashar received nearly all of the votes in support of his presidency. Bashar al-'Asad officially took the constitutional oath of office and delivered his inaugural speech on July 17, 2000.

Bashar al-'Asad has been called the reluctant president, someone who was untested, inexperienced, and maybe even ill prepared to lead the country in what is a very difficult and often dangerous domestic and regional environment. Bashar is a licensed ophthalmologist who had been engaged in advanced studies at the Western Eye Hospital in London before he returned to Syria in January 1994, soon after his elder brother, Basil al-'Asad, was killed in a car accident. Throughout the 1990s Hafiz al-'Asad was reported to have been in ill health, and Basil was commonly thought to have been the anointed successor, as his official responsibilities and profile had increased in the years before his death. Subsequently, Bashar assumed most of Basil's official positions and rose through the ranks in the military; again, it was putatively assumed that Bashar was being groomed to succeed his father. It seemed to be a race against time to build up Bashar's credentials and support base within Syria to the point where he could successfully and smoothly succeed his father when the moment came.

The 'Asad family are Alawis (Alawites), members of a minority Islamic sect who make up approximately 11 percent of Syria's population. Long an underprivileged minority in Syria, Alawis came to dominate the military after the First World War and then entered politics through an alliance with the rising Ba'ath party after independence. They have a preeminent power base in Syria, including most of the important positions in the military and *mukhabarat* (security/intelligence) apparatus, and they are determined not to give this up.

In the end, while the transition seemed to be devoid of any overt political struggle—thus indicating the path had indeed been cleared adequately—a number of questions remained regarding Bashar's readiness and ability to rule as well as reign. In particular, questions arose with respect to the string of regional and international events that occurred soon after he came to office and that have directly affected his position: the beginning of the Palestinian *intifada* in September 2000, the events of 9/11 and the U.S. war in Afghanistan in 2001, and, finally, the U.S. war against Iraq in 2003 and the subsequent instability in Syria's neighbor to the east. Thus, President Bashar was forced to get his feet wet in Middle East politics very quickly.

Because of Bashar's relative youth as well as the fact that he was an ophthalmologist, computer nerd, and avowed modernizer, it seemed to many in and outside Syria that he might help the country break away from the ossified and stagnant political and economic system he inherited from his father. There were some immediate positive signals in the first six months or so of his tenure, the so-called Damascus Spring. However, since then there has been a period of retrenchment—the so-called Damascus Winter—that harkens back to his father's time in power. This has led to the vexing question of whether Bashar really does have the willingness and/or ability to implement the type of political and economic reforms many expected when he came to power, or whether Syria will continue to muddle along as it has done in the past while the regional and international context in which it finds itself continues to deteriorate.

## ACCOUNTABILITY AND PUBLIC VOICE – 1.29

According to the 1973 constitution, Syria is a Socialist Popular Democratic Republic. However, in actuality it is an authoritarian regime with only some of the trappings of democracy. Article 2 of the constitution states that Syria's "system of government is republican and sovereignty is exercised by the people," but in practice the people have no avenue or recourse to change the government, and candidates for election are vetted by the party and government. While the constitution technically allows for a multiparty pluralist system, Syria is in effect a one-party authoritarian structure.

The constitution establishes the executive, legislative, and judicial branches of government. The unicameral parliament consists of 250 representatives elected by popular vote every four years. The parliament proposes the candidacy of the president, proposes and votes on laws (which are generated by the executive branch and/or the Ba'ath party), discusses cabinet policy, and approves the budget. The constitution mandates that the Ba'ath party receive at least one-half of the parliamentary seats. Currently the ruling coalition, the National Progressive Front (NPF)—which is dominated by the Ba'ath party and includes six other leftist and communist parties—holds 167 seats while non-NPF independents, all of whom are vetted by the government, hold 83 seats. The last parliamentary elections were in 2003.

The president is elected to a seven-year renewable term after nomination by the Regional Command of the Ba'ath party and the parliament. The president, the party, and the cabinet can issue legislation whether or not the parliament is in session. The late President Hafiz al-'Asad was confirmed by unopposed referenda five times, usually garnering 99 percent approval. Bashar ran unopposed following his father's death and received 97.29 percent of the vote in a national referendum. Political opposition to the president is not tolerated, except for that of the so-called loyal opposition within the parliament. The parliament provides no check on the president.

The 21-member Regional Command of the Ba'ath party retains decision-making authority over the cabinet and the ministries. Several members of the cabinet are also in the Regional Command. This includes President Bashar, who is the head of the party as secretary-general. Bashar is trying to transform the party into a more advisory body within the government rather than an entity that interferes with and dictates government policy, as has often been the case in the past. In late 2000 Bashar decided that the 21 members of the Regional Command should be elected by Ba'ath party membership rather than appointed, although all candidates must be approved first by the secretary-general of the party (i.e., Bashar). In July 2000, in addition to Bashar, 11 new members were elected to the Regional Command, most of whom were considered to be technocrats and supporters of change. However, all had been long-time party cadres, and the prime stalwarts of Hafiz al-'Asad's regime— the so-called old guard—retained their positions, so it appears that the body is not as reformist as many had hoped at first.

Decree No. 39 of 1958, Syria's Law of Association, requires every civil organization to register and obtain a license from the Ministry of Social Affairs. In the months following Bashar's assumption of the presidency, hundreds of civil society organizations, most operating from within the homes of the organizers, received licenses. Today, registration is approved only for those groups that have official support. An organization cannot receive funds from foreign donors unless it is officially recognized by the government; as a result, many organizations suffer from lack of funds. Asma al-'Asad, the president's wife, is very active in advocating the growth of nongovernmental organizations in Syria. In particular, she has taken a leading role in the Fund for the Integrated Rural Development of Syria (FIRDOS), a group that facilitates rural development in Syria.[1] Nevertheless, civil society has little opportunity to influence policy.

During the Damascus Spring after Hafiz al-'Asad's death, Bashar al-'Asad promoted freer and more pluralistic media in Syria. For the first time in 40 years private newspapers were licensed and public criticism of the regime was permitted, even from state-controlled entities. Although publications that criticized the government—including the hugely popular satirical weekly *al-Dumari* (The Lamplighter), which ceased publication in April 2003 due to government pressure—have since struggled against the restrictions of the regime, the fact that such criticism was permitted for some time indicates that there may be some cracks in the armor of political repression.

The crackdown on journalism became evident with Decree 50 of 2001. This law enables privately owned newspapers, magazines, and other periodicals to seek licenses to publish, but they essentially do so only at the discretion of the government. The prime minister's office can deny licenses for reasons "related to the public interest." In addition, the decree prohibits articles and reports about "national security, national unity, and details of secret trials." It also established harsh criminal penalties for publishing "falsehoods and fabricated reports."[2] In effect, editors oppose regime policies only when they have official instructions to do so.

The state runs the Syrian media. Lebanese newspapers and pan-Arab satellite news channels such as al-Jazeera, both widely available in Syria, allow open political discussion and criticism of the government to continue. In addition, the Syrian government has allowed a good bit more criticism of the Ba'ath party in 2003–2004; in fact, the editor of the party newspaper wrote a series of articles severely criticizing the party. [*Editor's note:* In October 2004 this editor became the new minister of information, a sign that Bashar wants to revamp the party and its role.] And although the government is the sole official internet provider and restricts access to politically sensitive material, President Bashar's aggressive push to bring Syria into the computer and Internet age has meant that the flow of information into Syria from the outside has further widened; many Syrians go online with a Lebanese Internet service provider and have unbridled access to the Worldwide Web.[3]

*Recommendations*

- The dominant role of the Ba'ath party in Syria needs to be reduced by allowing real opposition parties to participate in the national assembly and accelerating the current program of transforming the party apparatus toward a more advisory capacity. This will facilitate the transition to a truly pluralistic democratic society based on free and fair elections of parliamentary members as well as the president.
- Press and media freedoms need to be re-instituted as they existed during the period of the Damascus Spring, especially freedom for independent private newspapers, an end to censorship, and freedom of association for civil society forums and their allied publications. In the long run, this will provide an effective institutionalized voice of criticism and opposition.
- Bashar al-'Asad needs to exercise more leadership in the short term to accelerate positive change in the economic, social, and political spheres by explicitly laying out his vision for democratic reform. He should encourage the formulation of systematic development plans and programs in general and in specific ministries for comprehensive economic and institutional reform and remove from their positions elements that oppose his reform efforts.

## CIVIL LIBERTIES – 2.04

Bashar al-'Asad's inaugural speech was, by Syrian standards, a remarkably enlightened one that even criticized certain past policies. However, the new reformists in the government were more technocrats than pro-democracy elements, tasked by Bashar with modernizing Syria, implementing administrative reform in the ministries, and devising ways to improve the moribund state of the economy. They did not enact political reform to advance civil liberties.

One of the regime's prime weapons against internal dissent has been Decree No. 51 as amended and promulgated on March 9, 1963, one day after the Ba'ath party came to power in Syria. It declared a state of emergency that was ostensibly designed to thwart the military threat emanating from Israel but instead has been used to stifle and eliminate internal challenges to the regime. The Syrian leadership considers the decree a fundamental right as recognized in the International Covenant on Civil and Political Rights, which allows states to violate its provisions "in time of public emergency which threatens the life of the nation and the existence of which is officially proclaimed."[4] Under this provision, the martial law administrator (the prime minister) and his deputy (the minister of interior) are empowered to issue wide-ranging written orders restricting freedom in all areas of life. President Bashar al-'Asad has admitted that mistakes have been made with Decree 51 and that government officials have abused the law for their own purposes. While not committing himself to lifting the law once and for all, he has told journalists and others that it should be used to genuinely protect the people and not to abuse them.[5] However, given the current international environment and the uncertainty regarding the stability and strength of the regime, Decree 51 is likely to remain in place for the foreseeable future. Arbitrary arrests, detention, imprisonment, and lack of due process still occur, although not as much as under Hafiz al-'Asad.

One of the hallmarks of the Damascus Spring was the November 2000 closing of the infamous Mezzeh prison and the release of some 600 political prisoners, reportedly the first time the Syrian government acknowledged holding prisoners for political reasons.[6] Over the next two years, a number of leading political activists, many of whom had been in and out of prison for two decades and some of whom had been released during the Damascus Spring, were again arrested in a sporadic fashion, including the parliamentarians Riyad Seif and Ma'mun al-Humsi. Most of the activists arrested were again sent to prison, although under less harsh terms and in less severe conditions than during their previous stays. This may be because of increased international scrutiny in addition to the less overtly repressive nature of Bashar al-'Asad's regime as compared with his father's. In July 2004, President Bashar decreed an amnesty for more than 250 political prisoners who would be released in stages to mark the fourth anniversary of his accession to power.[7] However, almost all of those who were incarcerated during the crackdown on the Damascus Spring are still imprisoned.[8]

Article 25 of the constitution stipulates that citizens are equal before the law, and various articles of the penal code prescribe penalties for discrimination.[9] However, civil society organizations regularly demand equal treatment of women in their statements and manifestos, suggesting that the protection of women's rights and minority groups lags behind constitutionally mandated prescriptions. Syria supports women's rights to a greater degree than most Middle East states. Labor Act No. 91 of 1959 enshrines gender equality in the workplace, and Legislative Decree No. 4 of 1972 confirms equal remuneration between men and women. The Electoral Law promulgated in Decree No. 26 of 1973 grants women the right to vote in public elections and to stand as candidates in elections to the parliament, where they currently constitute over 10 percent of the total membership. Women have held a small number of ministerial positions over the years and are represented in the cabinet. Nevertheless, a number of discriminatory laws and practices remain in place, especially in personal status issues that fall under the Shari'a courts. For example, women are discriminated against in initiation of divorce proceedings and child custody rights. In the case of the more constructive laws that are in place, the primary reasons for their failure are police deficiencies, lack of enforcement provisions, and a reluctance on the part of victims to report discrimination.

Syria's 1.5 million to 2 million Kurds do not publicly seek an independent state. They demand the right to teach their language, which is denied them by law, as well as full citizenship, which is required for state education and employment, for some 290,000 Kurds classified as stateless based on a 1962 survey.[10] Tensions between Arabs and Syrian Kurds have been ongoing. In March 2004 Kurdish riots and demonstrations took place, apparently sparked by events in Kurdish areas in neighboring Iraq. The July 2004 amnesty included about 100 Kurds who had been arrested after clashes with security forces in which 40 people were killed after a soccer match in Qamishli.

Syria is the only Arab country other than Lebanon whose constitution does not establish Islam as the state religion, although it does require the president to be a Muslim. The secular philosophy of the ruling Ba'ath party as well as the fact that the government is controlled by a minority Islamic sect, the Alawis (Alawites), ensures better protection of religious freedom, as well as women's rights, than in most Arab countries. Generally speaking, the country's Christian minority groups (about 10 percent of the population) and small Jewish enclave have been free to practice their religion without government restrictions and interference.

On July 19, 2004, the president enacted a new law to protect the rights of disabled Syrians and to provide them with education, job training, and financial support. Currently, very few government buildings and public areas are accessible to people with disabilities, and the Ministry of Social Affairs has yet to issue detailed instructions on what sort of accommodations will be required under the new law. The Syrian government provides free medical care and social services to people with disabilities, but nearly all of those resources are available only in Damascus, far from most affected people. The government also operates rehabilitation facilities for victims of land mines in Syrian Golan.[11]

In February 2001, the ministry of social affairs announced that political forums (discussion groups, often with guest speakers) could not meet without its permission (as opposed to receiving licenses), which would only be granted if specific information was provided as to the location of the meeting and who was attending. Demonstrations are permitted only with the permission of the government, and often they are arranged by the government for public show. There are no free trade unions, but there is a government-controlled labor union.

Civil society activists have been more circumspect in their actions since the Damascus Spring, but they have also continued to maintain pressure on the regime. The fear factor that existed under Hafiz al-'Asad seems to have dissipated. While Syria may not be more politically open than it was before Bashar came to power, it is less ruthlessly authoritarian.

*Recommendation*
- It is imperative for the Syrian regime to eliminate the state of emergency and afford its citizens their full range of rights.
- The Syrian government should increase its efforts to abolish human rights violations, including arbitrary arrests of political activists as well as the mechanisms of torture and political repression, by safeguarding the rights of individuals to due process and representation as articulated in the constitution.
- The formation of civil society organizations and political forums should not be restricted by the government.
- The government must implement existing and new laws on freedom of association, freedom of speech, and the right to due process to protect political freedoms.

## RULE OF LAW – 2.13

The Syrian legal system is primarily based on civil law, heavily influenced by the French during the mandate period from 1923 to 1946, when the French were the supervisory power and controlled the central governing administration. It is also drawn in part from Egyptian law—particularly as a result of Syria's merger with Egypt to form the United Arab Republic from 1958 to 1961—and Islamic law (Shari'a). Syria has separate secular and religious courts. Civil and criminal cases are heard in secular courts. The Shari'a courts handle personal, family, and religious matters in cases involving Muslims and between Muslims and non-Muslims. Doctrinal courts hear cases involving primarily members of the Druze Islamic sect, and spiritual courts settle personal status cases for Christians, Jews, and other non-Muslims.

The State of Emergency Act (Decree No. 51) as amended in March 1963 is an exceptional constitutional regime (see "Civil Liberties"). Under the act, Supreme State Security Courts (SSC) were implemented by decree in 1968 and in principle follow the procedures of the ordinary courts. The SSC consist of two divisions, in each of which three judges preside, one of whom is a military judge. Their judgments are considered final but are not enforceable until they have been ratified by the president, who has the right to annul the ruling, order a retrial, or reduce or commute the sentence. Defendants—who are almost exclusively political prisoners—appearing before the SSC are guaranteed the same right of defense that they would enjoy before ordinary courts, but rarely have defendants been accorded these rights, especially as the trials were off-limits to public scrutiny. However, a number of the trials of activists in the SSC were opened to certain journalists and representatives of foreign embassies between 2001 and 2004. A number of Kurds arrested in the March 2004 disturbances were tried in the SSC under cloak of secrecy and reportedly not allowed to see their families; visits from lawyers were carefully monitored.[12]

The judicial system is generally corrupt and inefficient. Guilt must be proven in the normal legal process, but this does not hold in the SSC. Citizens have the right to counsel in all courts but often do not have access to one in the SSC, and in the normal judicial process they often have incompetent or corrupt counsel because of the nature of the system. In most cases independent counsel is appointed, except, again, in the SSC, in which someone may be appointed only to give the pretense of meeting the citizen's supposed right to counsel.

Article 131 of the constitution stipulates that "The judiciary shall be independent, its independence being guaranteed by the President of the Republic with the assistance of the Higher Council of the Judiciary." Administrative authority of the judiciary is vested in the Higher Council of the Judiciary, which has power of appointment, promotion, and transfer of judges. The council is presided over by the minister of justice and includes the president. The highest constitutionally ordained judicial body in the country is the Supreme Constitutional Court, to which the five justices are appointed by the president for four-year terms. This court rules on the constitutionality of laws and election disputes and can try officials of the state, including the president, for criminal offenses.[13]

In practice, there is very little judicial independence, especially above the lower-court level. Particularly with Decree 51 in place, the executive branch wields far too much power over the judiciary, and judges' appointments and decisions at all levels are ultimately subject to the approval of the executive branch and/or martial law representatives. In the lower-level courts, corruption is rampant, with the size of payments made to intermediaries representing judges dependent on the offense. Business and government connections play a major role in determining guilt or innocence, or even whether charges should be filed. At lower levels prosecutors have some independence depending upon the case; in the higher courts and more high-profile cases prosecutors can come under considerable government pressure or even pressure from powerful families. Capital crimes, especially murder, are less susceptible to corruption except in cases that involve a powerful figure or powerful family. Public officials and ruling party actors are prosecuted for abuse of power and corruption but almost always at the behest of the executive for political reasons rather than driven by the judiciary. The educational system overall in Syria is extremely lacking in skills training, and lawyers and judges are for the most part ill prepared. Judges are often chosen based on loyalty to the regime and/or the Ba'ath party. Thus, the system generates a vicious cycle of judicial incompetence and lethargy.

Governmental authorities generally comply with judicial decisions unless they run up against the policies of the government; however, this usually does not happen as the verdicts in cases of note are determined a priori, thereby precluding the need for the executive to waive or reverse a decision. Overall the system is weak, corrupt, and inefficient, by default leaving real judicial powers to the executive branch of government.

The military/security apparatus has tremendous influence over the judicial and legislative branches and even at times over the executive branch, which it essentially serves. It has a kind of symbiotic relationship with private business interests in Syria, creating avenues of influence and enrichment extending in both directions and discouraging the emergence of an independent business class. The military is intimately involved in the political process, often vetting candidates in and outside the Ba'ath party for elected and appointed positions.

The presence of between 13,000 and 16,000 Syrian troops in Lebanon has also created something of a sinecure for the military/security apparatus. The troop presence has been used to enrich certain elements in the military and in the government while providing some relief to Syria's unemployment problems, as there are an estimated one million Syrian workers in Lebanon. Although it has supplied an element of stability in Lebanon for more than twenty years, it is not uncontroversial. [*Editor's note:* The assassination of former Lebanese Prime Minister Rafiq Harriri in February 2005 brought the Syrian presence in Lebanon into question even more. Many believe that even if Syria was not directly responsible for the slaying, its presence in Lebanon contributed to the situation. As such, local, regional, and international calls for Syria to remove its troops from Lebanon have grown louder.]

The right to own property is guaranteed in the constitution. The state protects property rights and contracts fairly adequately once they are consummated; the process leading up to this point, however, is often fraught with corrupt practices. Under martial law, the state reserves the right to confiscate property and holdings. It presumably addresses discrepancies on these issues in a way that best serves its interests rather than according to official property law. Stateless Kurds cannot own property.

*Recommendations*

- The state security courts must be abolished through revocation of the State Emergency Law. This would scale back the mechanisms of control emanating from the military-security apparatus, de-link the executive from the judiciary branch, and begin to protect Syrian citizens from the arbitrary power of the government.

- President Bashar al-'Asad needs to reinforce the independence of the judiciary by encouraging legislation that will remove the office of the president from the Higher Council of the Judiciary and make his appointments to the Higher Council and the Supreme Constitutional Court subject to approval by an independent parliament.
- Syria needs to vastly improve its training of lawyers and judges, starting with education reform in the universities beyond technological modernization.

## ANTICORRUPTION AND TRANSPARENCY – 1.70

Syria is well known for its corrupt business environment. The Transparency International Corruption Perceptions Index of 2004 gave Syria a 3.4 score on a 10-point scale, according the country a rank of 71 out of 146 countries.[14] As in most countries where the public sector plays a dominant role in the economy, the opportunities for corruption are numerous.

The most common form of corruption is through what is called *wasta,* or the use of influence and/or connections to consummate business deals and other types of favors. It is almost an accepted form of doing business in Syria, but it establishes prescribed entrances into the Syrian economy that dampen any free market tendencies. One cannot enter into a private or public sector business situation of any significance without local mediators (who some have called the 5-percenters), who often multiply as the business relationship deepens; indeed, the mediator provides access to decision makers for those who would not otherwise have it. In reality, wasta is an additional form of control by the state, fragmenting bourgeois and upper bourgeois classes who might in its absence coalesce into a recognizable pressure group. In addition, it spreads the wealth to certain classes, supplements the income of government officials tied into the 5-percenter organizations, and gives more people an interest in maintaining the current regime.

The public sector in Syria, as a creation of the Ba'athist socialist doctrine of the 1960s, is dominant in the country in most industries and as such creates consistent opportunities for corruption. Licensing, bureaucratic regulations, and the like are oppressive, inefficiently applied, and subject to bribes. The black market economy, especially the portions that have become intertwined with Lebanese business transactions, competes with the legal economy in terms of overall domestic product.

The state has launched a program to promote integrity and honesty in Syrian society in an attempt to weed out corruption as a socially accepted practice, but so far legislative progress has been limited. A number of ministries are now hiring based on merit rather than connections, but the process is far from being judged successful at this time. There are anticorruption laws on the books, but they are applied selectively by the regime only when cronies behave in an irresponsible, abusive fashion or to destroy someone politically through often-fabricated charges. The arbitrary and selective application of anticorruption drives tends to keep regime elements within accepted parameters. Individuals involved in high-profile corruption cases cannot feel secure, as their fate—good or bad—is ultimately left to the discretion of the regime, the military-security apparatus, and/or the predetermined judicial or martial law system. Human Rights Watch reported in 2002 that people who protested against nepotism and corruption in Syria faced unfair trials on charges that included "endangering state unity" and "trying to change the constitution by illegal means."[15] Corruption allegations are often accompanied by media coverage, although the latter, as it is state controlled, is usually orchestrated by the government to legitimate its charges and reinforce its anticorruption campaign.

Allegations of widespread cronyism and nepotism abound in Syria. Under the regime of Hafiz al-'Asad, the price for the unswerving loyalty of his inner circle of subordinates was allowing them a virtual free hand to enrich themselves through mostly corrupt methods of controlling business opportunities in Syria. Wealth was funneled into the hands of some very powerful families who were either in or well connected to the government. Ba'ath party members and sons or daughters of high-level officials and rich families have received preferential treatment in higher education, although the current regime is trying to raise the standards for Ba'ath party cadres incrementally before they are automatically accepted into the university.

Bashar al-'Asad came into office known as someone who was decidedly against corruption, having headed a well-publicized anticorruption campaign in the year or so before ascending to the presidency (although his critics contend this was as much an attempt to help clear the path for his succession by removing potential adversaries on charges of corruption as a vehicle to stamp out unsavory business practices). Some reports suggest that overt corruption has receded in Syria since Bashar came to power, but corruption via cronyism still exists at the highest levels. This centers primarily around the powerful Makhluf family, in particular Rami Makluf, who runs SyriaTel; Bashar's mother is from the Makhluf family. Syrians have generally embraced anticorruption campaigns by the government, but Bashar's progress in this area has been hindered. This is in part because he has yet to secure the unquestioned legitimacy and support base that would allow him to adopt such tough measures. From all indications, he is incrementally attempting to create a critical mass of support in the government and in the party that will allow him to implement judicial reform and anticorruption policies.

The tax administrator does not implement an effective internal audit. Tax collection is inefficient and subject to political interference. There is no auditing body outside the executive branch for this purpose. Some regulatory committees with supervisory capacities exist, but they are largely subject to corruption and government pressure.

Transparency in the Syrian judicial and business environments is minimal. The current regime, with French and British assistance, is attempting to put in place some mechanisms in the judicial and financial sectors (with the recent establishment of the first four private banks) that will create more transparency in order to build a more business-friendly environment for foreign investment and the return of expatriate capital. Citizens can petition for information, but often their petitions are ignored or fall victim to the bloated and inefficient bureaucracy.

The budget-making process is officially subject to both parliamentary approval and the input of the Ba'ath party Regional Command and as such appears comprehensive. However, in practice the parliament acts as a rubber stamp for the party and the executive on this issue. The government does not publish accounting expenditures in a timely fashion on a coordinated basis; however, expenditures are detailed periodically through the state-controlled media. The state officially has an open bidding process and promotes a competitive environment, but these are hindered by the influence of political connections and under-the-table payments.

Foreign assistance from international institutions is minimal in Syria; therefore, the state's obligation to administer and distribute this aid legally is under very little scrutiny. Private assistance and grants from foreign countries to the government are more the norm and are distributed at the discretion of the government. Funds are generally put toward the most pressing needs at any given time, but sometimes they are put toward projects that are run by elements in the regime.

## Recommendations

- President Bashar al-'Asad needs to mobilize popular sentiment against corruption to continue his anticorruption campaigns in a more systematic fashion.
- Judicial reform is required to prosecute corruption fairly, particularly to make the justice system truly independent of the executive branch and the Ba'ath party.
- A more open, regulated, and transparent bidding process is required for international contracts.
- The government should submit to international arbitration in disputed business cases.

## NOTES

[1]   Interview with Asma al-'Asad, Damascus, Syria, 3 June 2004.

[2]   "Attacks on the Press 2003" (New York: Committee to Protect Journalists, Middle East and North Africa, March 2004), http://www.cpj.org/attacks03/mideast03/syria.html.

[3]   For instance, the World Bank Development Data Group estimates that the number of Internet users in Syria increased from close to none in 1995 to 60,000 by 2001, a figure that almost certainly has at least doubled since then.

[4]   "International covenant on civil and political rights: Consideration of Reports Submitted by States Parties under Article 40 of the Covenant; Second periodic report of States parties due in 1984 – Syrian Arab Republic" (Geneva: United Nations, Human Rights Committee, 19 January 2000), http://www.hri.ca/fortherecord2001/documentation/tbodies/ccpr-c-syr-2000-2.htm.

[5]   Interview with President Bashar al-'Asad, Damascus, Syria, 26 May 2004.

[6]   "Syria: U.S. Relations and Bilateral Issues" (Washington, DC: Congressional Research Service, Issue Brief for Congress, 15 November 2002), 10.

[7]   The Jordan Times, 21 July 2004.

[8]   Ibid.

[9]   "International covenant" (UN, 19 January 2000).

[10]   The Jordan Times, 30 August 2004.

[11]   "Landmine Monitor Report 2004: Syria" (New York: International Campaign to Ban Landmines, 2004), http://www.icbl.org/lm/2004/syria.

[12]   Ibid.

[13] Ibid.

[14] "Corruption Perceptions Index 2004" (Berlin: Transparency International, July 2004).

[15] *World Report 2002* (New York: Human Rights Watch, February 2003).

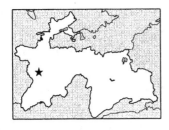

# TAJIKISTAN

CAPITAL: Dushanbe
POPULATION: 6.6 million
GNI PER CAPITA: $180

**SCORES**

ACCOUNTABILITY AND PUBLIC VOICE: 1.77
CIVIL LIBERTIES: 2.74
RULE OF LAW: 2.84
ANTICORRUPTION AND TRANSPARENCY: 1.40
(scores are based on a scale of 0 to 7, with
0 representing weakest and 7 representing
strongest performance)

*Adam Smith Albion*

## INTRODUCTION

Tajikistan is an impoverished, clan-ridden state whose institutions, infrastructure, and social fabric were wrecked by a brutal civil war. The accords that ended hostilities in 1997 brought peace but not much harmony between the rival factions, and the country is still dealing with the legacy of the war. President Imomali Rakhmonov accepted a power-sharing agreement with his opponents that brought an Islamic-oriented party into the government, initially winning him plaudits for vision and openness. However, the intervening years have brought increased authoritarianism as Rakhmonov has consolidated power in the name of stability and centralization. In parallel, a narrow elite from the president's native region has worked its way into the state's top positions. His opponents have been systematically pushed out of government, marginalized, and repressed. Freedom of the press has been steadily curtailed, especially in the run-up to the February 2005 parliamentary elections.

The regime has generally ignored (and on occasion may have authorized) violations of civil liberties, including arbitrary arrest and torture at the hands of law enforcement officials. The legislative framework

---

Adam Smith Albion is Director of Critical Areas Research for World Monitors Inc.

regarding pretrial detention and a defendant's right to counsel is unsatisfactory. Human trafficking, a serious problem since the war, has yet to be addressed properly, although the government has belatedly begun to elaborate a national action plan.

Grinding poverty annually drives a sixth of the population to seek work abroad as migrant laborers. Poverty also feeds corruption. Corruption has spread into all spheres of life in Tajikistan, crippling effective government and distorting the administration of justice. Desperately needed foreign investment and business development have been stunted by the prevalence of graft and cronyism. The level of corruption is making international donors think twice about providing aid and assistance.

## ACCOUNTABILITY AND PUBLIC VOICE – 1.77

Although Tajikistan became independent in 1991 when the Soviet Union collapsed, the contours of political life today can be traced back to June 1997. That date marks the general peace agreement concluded between the government and the United Tajik Opposition (UTO) that ended a devastating five-year civil war. At its core was a battle between regional elites and clans for power and privileges. Broadly speaking, the pro-government faction—ex-Communists identified with the Kulob region—stood for Soviet-style rule and the status quo. The UTO, a loose grouping of interests that drew support from the center and east of the country, was more ambitious for change and partially colored by an Islamist agenda. In 1999 the UTO disbanded its forces and broke up into its constituent parts. The backbone of the UTO, the Islamic Renaissance Party of Tajikistan (IRPT), has endured as the main opposition party. Current developments are rooted in this background of regionalism, warlordism, and tension between secularism and Islam.

Notwithstanding the adoption of a democratic constitution in 1994, Tajikistan has made little progress in moving from Soviet-style authoritarianism to open, accountable government. Power is concentrated in the hands of President Imomali Rakhmonov, a native of the Kulob region. Kulobi-dominated forces engineered the rise of the former collective-farm director to national leadership in November 1992 during the first days of the civil war. Rakhmonov subsequently consolidated his position in seriously flawed presidential elections in 1994 and 1999. In the latter election Rakhmonov officially won 97 percent of the vote, running against a single opponent whose candidacy was allowed by the authorities only days before the election. Other potential candidates were unable to meet onerous registration requirements, such as collecting large numbers of supporters' signatures under unreasonable time pressure. By contrast Rakhmonov had access to the resources of the state, which he fully mobilized to his advantage right up to election day, when observers reported multiple instances of official interference in the casting and tabulation of ballots.

As the law stood at the time, Rakhmonov's victory in 1999 won him a single, nonrenewable seven-year term. But prospects of a rotation of power faded in June 2003, when a hastily organized national plebiscite presented citizens with 56 constitutional amendments, which they were obliged to accept or reject as a single package by voting yes or no. The key revision (to Article 65) gave the president the right to serve two seven-year terms instead of one. The public was poorly informed about the substance of the proposed amendments, the texts of which were hard to obtain and did not feature on the ballot papers. The referendum passed officially with 93 percent in favor. The Organization for Security and Cooperation in Europe (OSCE) and other international watchdogs refused to monitor the referendum, citing insufficient time to prepare missions and criticizing its provisions and lack of transparency. Adjusting the law on the president's tenure in office has significantly strengthened Rakhmonov's grip on power. It licenses him to start afresh when his current term ends in 2006, making it possible for him to remain in office until 2020. By that time Rakhmonov would be 68 years old and would have led the country for 28 years.

A key condition of the 1997 peace accords was a power-sharing agreement whereby 30 percent of government posts went to the UTO. Yet the promise of political pluralism in Tajikistan implied by the provision has never been adequately realized. Violating the spirit if not the letter of the agreement, Rakhmonov has steadily maneuvered to push his opponents out of government; by the start of 2004, the opposition's share of posts had fallen from 30 percent to 5 percent.[1] Concurrently, an ever-tighter inner circle of Kulobis (often natives of Rakhmonov's home town of Danghara) has come to dominate the regime.[2] In the past few years the president has felt strong enough to turn against erstwhile allies when he sensed a threat. The indictments of Yakub Salimov, a former interior minister, and Ghaffor Mirzoev, a former commander of the presidential guard, on charges ranging from corruption and tax evasion to treason and murder, were key political events in Tajikistan in 2004. As both men reportedly had political ambitions of their own, their arrests conveniently removed them from the scene while warning off any other would-be challengers.[3]

The only remaining figure with the stature to stand up to Rakhmonov is the mayor of Dushanbe and National Assembly speaker Mahmadsaid Ubaydulloev. Ubaydulloev is frequently touted as a potential adversary to Rakhmonov in the 2006 presidential elections. Ubaydulloev is a close ally of Mirzoev, however, and the latter's fall is likely to weaken him. Many analysts speculate that in targeting Mirzoev, the president's real aim has been to undermine his most dangerous rival, Ubaydulloev.

Rakhmonov deserves credit for working to ensure peace and stability after the civil war, reining in warlords and bolstering the authority of state structures. But instead of building on his achievements to create an open and inclusive political process, he has performed a jealous accumulation of power for himself and a narrow elite, which can only lead to less transparency in public affairs and fresh resentment among regional competitors.

A second crucial stipulation of the 1997 peace accords was the legalization of opposition parties. Of the six parties that contended in parliamentary elections in 2000, two derived from the UTO. But opposition parties have never been permitted to compete on a level playing field with Rakhmonov's highly centralized People's Democratic Party of Tajikistan (PDPT): In particular, they are regularly denied coverage by state-controlled mass media. The bicameral parliament, called the Supreme Assembly, consists of the Assembly of Representatives (lower chamber of 63 members, elected by popular vote to five-year terms) and the National Assembly (upper chamber of 33 members, indirectly elected or appointed by the president to five-year terms). In the 2000 election the Islamic Renaissance Party of Tajikistan (IRPT), the main opposition party, won only two seats in the lower chamber. Otherwise the PDPT and its allies swept the vote, which was judged neither free nor fair by international monitors.

Dominated by deputies who follow Rakhmonov's lead, the legislature has functioned as a pliant appendage of the executive branch. The prime minister and his cabinet serve at the president's behest and have shown themselves similarly devoid of real authority or autonomy. Despite constitutional requirements for transparency and public access to information, the processes of developing legislation and making political decisions are extremely secretive and rarely open to citizen input. However, some nongovernmental organizations (NGOs) have succeeded in influencing draft legislation.[4]

The results of February 2005 parliamentary elections were widely regarded as a foregone conclusion, with the PDPT expected to sweep the board again. Opposition parties complained of harassment by the authorities to stymie their chances, including politically motivated lawsuits. For example, in early 2004 the deputy chairman of the IRPT was sentenced to 16 years' imprisonment for alleged criminal activities, polygamy, and murder. Only months later, a second senior member of the IRPT (an elderly man who had performed the Hajj pilgrimage to Mecca) was sentenced to nine years for allegedly being part of a gang that raped underaged girls.[5] The nature and timing of these charges have led some observers to doubt their veracity. The government's motives for repeatedly refusing to register an opposition party, Taraqqiyot (Progress), have also been questioned. Taraqqiyot's application supposedly failed on technicalities. It is suggestive that the party leader, Sulton Quvvatov, is a prominent Kulobi politician who sought to run for president in 1999 but was barred from the race. By autumn 2004 both Quvvatov and his deputy had been charged with "insulting the honor and dignity of the president" (a crime in Tajikistan carrying a five-year jail sentence) as well as inciting ethnic, racial, and religious strife.[6]

Opposition parties are also put at a disadvantage by the election law. Over their protests, in June 2004 the law was amended to require parliamentary candidates to put up a security deposit equal to 200 times the minimum monthly wage, or about $500 (Article 32.1). The deposit will be returned only if the candidate wins a seat in parliament. Furthermore, the new law requires political parties to pay the same $500 deposit for each candidate fielded on their party lists (rather than, as before, a lump sum for the whole list irrespective of the number of candidates). The parties get their money back only if they clear a 5 percent threshold in the elections. The IRPT warned in a press release that the deposits could make it too expensive for 80 percent of citizens to run in elections. The new provisions clearly favor the well-funded PDPT.[7] Other election law amendments, such as the appointment of independent members to local election commissions and the outlawing of armed men at polling stations, were uncontroversial and should improve the voting.

Nepotism is a problem throughout the country—a function of massive unemployment intersecting with a culture of extended family obligations. Entry and promotion in the state bureaucracy are dominated by nepotism and cronyism. Efforts to combat them were initiated in February 2004 when the parliament passed a series of amendments to the labor code prohibiting the directors, vice-directors, accountants, and cashiers of agencies to be related to one another. The labor ministry planned to extend the legislation to NGOs as well.[8] All too often, family ties are the primary criterion for employment at NGOs.

As a rule, NGOs have been able to operate without excessive government intervention, and the atmosphere has generally been welcoming, especially for organizations focusing on humanitarian and refugee assistance. The government is more obstructive toward NGOs dealing with democratization or human rights. The process of registering an NGO in Tajikistan is time-consuming and swathed in red tape, but registration costs were lowered in 2001, encouraging more local groups to form and apply.

There are hints that the November 2003 Rose Revolution in Georgia has prompted the government to rethink its attitude toward civil society. Reports from the Open Society Institute and other NGOs in Tajikistan in 2004 indicate that their activities and finances have attracted closer scrutiny by the authorities. The examinations may herald tighter control in 2005.

Tajik law enshrines the principles of free expression and media independence. The only national TV station is state-run Tajik Television, but Tajikistan has a small number of independent newspapers and radio stations that sometimes criticize the regime. However, they are continually subject to persecution by tax inspectors, lawsuits for defamation, allegedly random violence at the hands of faceless attackers, and indirect censorship in the form of state control of the licensing process and the capital's printing houses. Government outlets ignore bad news and promote the president's image and policies with Soviet-style slavish propaganda.[9] Few people have access to or can afford the Internet; nevertheless the government blocks the only opposition Web site (http://www .tajikistantimes.ru), which is posted from Europe. It was launched in spring 2003 by Dododjon Atovulloev Atovulloev, editor-in-chief of *Charogi ruz* (Light of the Day), an opposition newspaper that is also published abroad.

The country's first independent radio station, Asia-Plus, started broadcasting in September 2003 after a four-year wait for a license.[10] During 2004 independent newspapers experienced a pattern of harassment practically indistinguishable from a crackdown. After the state printing house refused on various pretexts to print two popular newspapers—*Ruzi Nav* (New Day) and *Nerui Sukhan* (Power of Words), both with a reputation for exposing government corruption—they took their business to Jiyonkhon, an outmoded but serviceable private printing press. Five other independent papers were forced to follow. In August 2004 Jiyonkhon was shut down by the authorities, allegedly for tax evasion, decimating nongovernment newspapers in the run-up to parliamentary elections: The IRPT paper *Najot* had also been printed on its presses.[11] Furthermore, the founder and editor of *Ruzi Nav,* Rajabi Mirzo, was beaten up twice in the course of the year by unidentified assailants. The Committee to Protect Journalists describes "an escalating campaign of intimidation and harassment against independent and opposition journalists in Tajikistan."[12]

## Recommendations

- For the sake of pluralism and political stability, instead of favoring one regional clique, the government should make more genuine efforts to include and promote other regional voices and interests into its structures and decision-making processes.
- Taraqqiyot should be granted registration as a legal political party, and all legal opposition parties should be permitted to hold meetings, campaign for support, and have adequate access to the media to get their messages out without fear of harassment or reprisals from the authorities.
- Foreign and domestic NGOs, notably those devoted to strengthening democracy and civil society, should be permitted to function without government harassment. The registration requirements for NGOs should be simplified. Government personnel, including parliamentarians, should provide for more NGO input into the policy-making and legislative processes by making their offices more accessible to NGO representatives and inviting them to participate in working groups.

- The government should stop its campaign of intimidation of the independent media and should refrain from blocking independent newspapers' access to printing houses.

## CIVIL LIBERTIES – 2.74

The Tajik constitution and the criminal execution code contain strong prohibitions against torture, and Tajikistan ratified the UN Convention against Torture in 1995. Yet Tajik security officials are reported to resort systematically to beatings, electric shocks, and sexual abuse while interrogating detainees or to extract confessions. Among those who have reportedly received such treatment are accused members of the banned Islamist group Hizb ut-Tahrir (Party of Liberation) and IRPT Deputy Chairman Shamsiddin Shamsiddinov. Many detainees have told Amnesty International they were tortured even before being charged.[13] Torture goes on with impunity. There is no public record of the government putting any suspected torturer on trial or any Tajik court demonstrating appropriate concern about allegations of pretrial torture. As Amnesty International says, "On the contrary, confessions reportedly elicited through torture have been used to convict numerous prisoners who have been sentenced to death."[14] However, perhaps in partial recognition of this problem, the president signed into force a moratorium on capital punishment in July 2004, replacing the death penalty with a 25-year prison term.[15]

The authorities have been similarly lax about investigating political killings, most notoriously the murders of between six and seven dozen journalists during the civil war. Many are believed to have been killed by pro-government leaders who tracked them down in revenge for stories that appeared in print. Only three of the murders have been solved by the police, despite cases in which the killer's identity was an open secret or easily inferred. However, in early 2004 a new commission was established within the prosecutor-general's office to re-launch a belated quest for justice. There are worries that prosecutors, after years of dragging their feet, may now indict innocent people in their eagerness to clear up cases.[16]

Arbitrary arrests by procurators and police, especially of suspected Islamists, continue without visible efforts by the regime to stamp out abuses. The law permits police to detain persons without a warrant for three days (and the procurator's office to do so for 10 days) before charges must be filed. Pretrial detention can last up to 15 months, or longer in circumstances poorly defined by the law. There is no presumption of liberty under Tajik law and no provisions for bail, although detainees in criminal cases may be given the option of awaiting their trial under house arrest.[17] Tajikistan has seven prisons, the physical conditions of which are privately reckoned by the International Red Cross, which was permitted to visit Tajik prisons in 2003, to be among the worst in the world. Inmates face disease and maltreatment in overcrowded and unsanitary facilities; some die of hunger.

Tajik citizens have few means of recourse or redress if the state violates their rights. To sue the authorities is considered a hopeless venture when the judiciary identifies so closely with the government (see "Rule of Law"). There are two offices—the presidential Office for Constitutional Guarantees of Citizens' Rights, and the Commission on Fulfillment of International Human Rights Commitments, chaired by the deputy prime minister—that are supposed to receive and answer citizens' complaints and, when appropriate, forward them to the relevant ministries. It is unclear what meaningful remedies either commission can afford its petitioners. Certain rights of complaint feature in the tax code, but few complainants or inspectors are familiar with the procedures.[18]

Legally, women share equal civil and political rights with men, including the right to equivalent pay. In practice, discrimination in all areas is a problem. Under the USSR, Tajik women accounted for a high percentage of the workforce, but war and poverty have prompted a reassertion of traditional social, cultural, and religious norms that preferentially situate women in the home and subservient to their menfolk. In competition with men for shrinking resources, women are being squeezed out of jobs and education, pushed to marry young and stay at home, particularly outside the cities. On the other hand, women increasingly must fend for themselves in a country where men are scarce; as many as 25,000 male heads of households died in the war, and an estimated 1.2 million Tajiks go abroad every year in search of work.[19] The government has done little to help women—although a woman has served as minister of labor and a parliamentary committee exists on social issues, family, women, health protection, and ecology—beyond sending them to the plantations to handpick cotton for miserable wages. It has been left to NGOs and local civic organizations to step in with projects to create women's support groups or train female entrepreneurs. Over a third of Tajik NGOs are headed by women.

Anecdotal evidence suggests that domestic violence is on the rise. Wife-beating or rape tend to go unreported or be treated by the police as private matters for the family to sort out; there are no special police units for handling rape cases. Patriarchal voting, with the male head of a household casting ballots for the whole family, is relatively common in rural areas. In August 2004 Tajikistan's religious leaders banned women from attending mosques, arguing that the sexes must pray apart, while most mosques lacked the necessary separate facilities. The edict, which outraged popular opinion, was upheld by the government.[20]

Trafficking in persons, primarily for prostitution, has been a significant problem in Tajikistan since the civil war, when it flourished along with other smuggling operations run by warlords. With the average monthly wage around $10, traffickers continue to snare many victims with false offers of work abroad. The government largely ignored the issue until amendments to the criminal code in 2003 made human trafficking punishable with prison and confiscation of property. Currently the government is seeking to toughen measures and develop a national action plan. For the moment, however, preventive information campaigns and relief programs for victims are almost exclusively the province of local NGOs and the International Office for Migration's bureau in Dushanbe.[21]

Tajik is the state language in Tajikistan, and Russian has remained the official language of interethnic communication. Concentrated in the north and mostly supportive of the regime, Uzbeks are Tajikistan's largest ethnic minority, constituting a quarter of the population. Discrimination based on ethnicity and language is prohibited by law. Nonetheless ethnic Uzbeks, Russians, and Pamiris face bias in Tajik-controlled government bodies, where an institutional culture has now developed of promoting the titular majority over minorities. Minorities such as Uzbeks and Pamiris have been excluded from any important government positions, although four ethnic Uzbeks did serve as members of parliament. The prevalence of nepotism also tends to favor co-ethnic kin, as mixed marriages are relatively rare. (By the same token, ethnic Tajiks face discrimination in institutions or networks dominated by Uzbeks in the north of the country or Pamiris in the east.) All non-

Kulobis are currently at a disadvantage in state structures. Much of the ethnic Russian population has emigrated in search of better economic and societal opportunities. Schooling in the Uzbek language does remain available, although schools everywhere in Tajikistan lack such basic resources as teachers and textbooks.

People with disabilities also suffer from widespread discrimination in daily life and high unemployment. This is despite their large numbers due to the civil war as well as ongoing injuries from stepping on landmines. The law does not require employers to provide physical access for people with disabilities, public transport makes no provisions for them, and public places lack basic technology, including wheelchair ramps, to help them.

An estimated 95 percent of Tajik citizens regard themselves as Muslims, although only a minority are regularly observant. Almost all are moderate Sunnis. Among the Pamiri peoples living in Gorno-Badakhshan (the mountainous southeast of the country) is a concentrated community of some 350,000 Shi'ite Ismailis, who revere the Aga Khan as their spiritual leader. The government (which nominally includes members of the religiously oriented IRPT) promotes a policy of aggressive secularism. While freedom of religion is generally respected and constitutionally guaranteed, the government vigorously patrols against any suspected adherents of religious extremism or political Islam. Mosques and religious communities require registration to function, and the law authorizes no more than one mosque per 15,000 residents in a given geographic area. The hiring and firing of preachers depends on the Council of Ulema (Islamic scholars), a body technically separate from the government but in actuality controlled by the State Committee on Religious Affairs. Imams often include a prayer of wellbeing for Rakhmonov in their Friday sermons.

The government increased pressure on suspected Islamists in the wake of the September 11 terrorist attacks. The radical Hizb ut-Tahrir, which advocates the nonviolent overthrow of secular regimes in Central Asia and their replacement by an Islamic state, has been banned in Tajikistan since 2001. The group's base is among ethnic Uzbeks in northern Soghd province, but support is spreading to Kulob and other ethnically Tajik, economically desperate areas. About 150 accused members of Hizb ut-Tahrir have been imprisoned on charges of subversion, usually for no more than possession of the group's propaganda leaflets.[22] Visiting Soghd in summer 2002, Rakhmonov inveighed against the excessive number of mosques in the region. Soon afterward, local imams were forced to sit examinations on their knowledge of Islam. Fifteen failed and were removed from their positions, and more than 30 mosques and a *madrasa* (religious school) were shut down. Local observers claimed that the tests were used to depose certain religious figures who were especially outspoken politically.[23]

Government statistics show that 90 percent of the workforce is organized into trade unions, most of them gathered under the roof of one giant federation of trade unions, a legacy of Soviet centralization. In practice, many enterprises represented by the unions are moribund, and the unions are becoming hollow shells in a country where one-fifth of the population are labor migrants, mostly in Russia. The authorities curtail freedom of assembly and association, especially if they are of a political nature, often by withholding the official permits that are required to stage public meetings or by intimidating would-be organizers. Consequently demonstrations are rare in Tajikistan. In 2003, the capital witnessed its first spontaneous street protests in a decade when a company running a pyramid investment scam collapsed, leaving tens of thousands of Tajiks out of pocket or destitute. Police brutally dispersed the crowds outside the presidential palace, attacking with truncheons and water cannons.[24] In political life, the president's PDPT is dominant, and it is hopeless to seek advancement in government structures without being a member.

## Recommendations

- The government should demonstrate its intolerance of torture by its police and security services by condemning it unreservedly, vigorously investigating allegations of its practice, and trying and punishing offenders in open courts.
- The government should condemn the ban on women attending mosques and ensure it is rescinded.
- A national action plan against human trafficking should be adopted and implemented that cracks down on gangs involved in trafficking, introduces improvements in border control, and widely disseminates information to warn potential victims about the dangers.

- De facto curbs on freedom of assembly and association should be eliminated; groups espousing views different from those of the government should be allowed to meet unmolested, and peaceful demonstrations should receive the necessary permissions to go forward.

## RULE OF LAW – 2.84

On paper the judiciary is a separate and equal branch of government. In reality it operates largely as an extension of the executive, and the courts provide citizens neither justice nor protection from the state in the political or economic realms. Judges of the Constitutional Court, Supreme Court, and Supreme Economic Court are elected by the legislature on the president's recommendation. Given that the parliament is packed with Rakhmonov's supporters—and the fact that the president personally appoints and dismisses the remaining judges and state prosecutors—the opportunities for influence and abuse are manifest. Important decisions are vetted in advance or discreetly telephoned in from the presidential palace. Meanwhile, constitutional provisions conflict regarding court jurisdiction and supremacy to interpret and enforce the law.[25]

Tajiks' faith in judicial integrity and the rule of law has never really recovered from the trauma of the civil war, when it was public knowledge that certain factions or militias existed above the law. The general amnesty of 1997, which pardoned all but the most serious crimes committed by combatants, was crucial to securing peace, but it established the principle that politics trumps justice. In today's Tajikistan members of the power elite are no longer above the law—but that is because Rakhmonov and his faction in government have embarked on a purge of potential rivals and are using the judiciary to do it. Some of the mightiest figures in Tajikistan fell in 2004, accused of abuse of power, corruption, treason, or murder. Sometimes the charges are lurid but not implausible in view of the defendants' warlord pasts. However, all the wartime commanders doubtless have skeletons in their closets. The selectivity of the targeting indicates that the driving motive is to shore up power rather than mete out justice.

Cash also can trump justice. Criminal groups are said to have forged links with all tiers of the justice system. Bribery of prosecutors and judges is standard practice. Otherwise, judges rarely remain impartial and often side with the prosecution automatically. A common complaint of defendants and lawyers is that the majority of cases result in guilty verdicts. The constitution (Article 20) and the criminal code (Article 4) guarantee the presumption of innocence until proven guilty in court. Furthermore, Tajikistan has ratified and is legally bound by the International Covenant on Civil and Political Rights. However, in everyday practice the Tajik court system tends to follow the Soviet approach, which presumed the defendant's guilt, and state officials and media routinely proclaim high-profile defendants guilty before their trials have even started. Judges at all levels are poorly trained and lack basic legal reference materials, although an examination system now manages to screen out the most hopeless candidates for the bench. The creation of a National Association of Barristers in March 2003 is a step forward in professionalizing the justice system.

The law stipulates that cases must go to court within four weeks once entered for trial, yet in some instances cases have been delayed for months. A defendant's right to a public trial is restricted by the catch-all proviso that if national security is involved, the trial is heard behind closed doors. Defendants have the right to independent counsel, but only after they have been fully interrogated and indicted, a process that can take months. Many detainees have reportedly been refused access to an attorney altogether. The state is supposed to appoint a defense lawyer for citizens who cannot afford one. However, counsel is chosen by the official investigating the offense, who has an incentive to appoint ineffective and inexperienced defense attorneys.[26]

Neither the legislature nor the judiciary has effective oversight of Tajikistan's army or police, which are headed by Rakhmonov loyalists and report directly to him. Rakhmonov has the militia and armed forces of the ministries of interior and defense well under his control and relies on them to govern. He demonstrated less confidence in his presidential guard, sacking its commander in early 2004, only to face a near-rebellion when about 200 officers threatened to resign and rumors spread of a coup in the offing.[27] Crisis was averted, but since then the presidential guard has been reorganized into a national guard commanded by a Kulobi from Rakhmonov's native town of Danghara. There have been instances when army personnel have abused their power and the state has cracked down on them. In autumn 2004 nine senior military officials were fired for press-ganging unfit or underage boys into the army to meet recruitment targets.[28] The government has been less active about reining in local police who have taken it upon themselves to detain and intimidate members of the opposition, apparently on their own initiative rather than as state policy.[29]

Tajikistan is the poorest nation of the former Soviet Union, with 80 percent of the population living below the poverty line. Thus, few people own much property beyond their house in the village and a family cow. Recently the government has pressed ahead with a land reform scheme, due to be completed in 2005, designed to create a class of private farmers. Yet as the state is the sole landowner according to the constitution, this "privatization process" actually amounts to leasing state land to individuals or associations, usually for 99 years.[30] Moreover, the government does not actually respect (or appreciate) the difference between rent and usufruct: Although leaseholders are theoretically free to handle the land as they choose, the authorities continue to decree cotton plans for them and draft in harvesters to ensure the targets are met. Rakhmonov has also ordered farmers to clear their debts with private investors for seeds, fertilizers, and fuel.[31]

Property rights and politics have come into conflict as the result of a provision of the 1997 peace agreement that requires a right of return to all refugees and internally displaced persons. The government began in 2000 to implement a scheme to restore homes to those forced to flee during the war. Thousands of houses were returned to their original owners, usually entailing the eviction of families occupying them. Many buildings had merely been seized as spoils of war. Yet in some instances families moved in with a reasonable expectation that the property had been abandoned and made improvements; still others actually bought the houses and have now been evicted with minimal compensation. Explaining a Supreme Court ruling that supported eviction in such cases, a spokesman said, "the court was guided not only by the legislation, but . . . the interests of those who suffered the most during the civil war."[32]

## Recommendations

- The law should be amended to ensure that prisoners are given the presumption of liberty. The practice of government officials and state press of publicly pronouncing defendants guilty before trial must cease.

- The law should be amended to ensure that prisoners are granted access to an attorney at the beginning of their detention and that if the state assigns counsel, the appointment is made by the court, not a prosecutor.
- As a prerequisite for the emergence of an independent judiciary, the system of selecting judges must be reformed to make them less dependent on and beholden to the executive. More money and effort should be devoted to training a more professional cadre of judges.
- The government should better respect the letter and spirit of its own land reform program by ceasing to interfere in the planting and harvesting decisions of lease-holder farmers.

## ANTICORRUPTION AND TRANSPARENCY – 1.40

Tajikistan is one of the most corrupt countries in the world. It was ranked 133 out of 146 countries in Transparency International's 2004 Corruption Perceptions Index with a score of 2 on a scale from 10 ("highly clean") to 0 ("highly corrupt").[33] Bribes are paid to pass exams at university, to buy airplane tickets, or to secure a bed in a hospital. Traffic police opportunistically flag down cars for imaginary infractions. Graft pervades the judiciary and the civil service. The tangled bureaucracy provides ample means for corruption; bureaucrats' minuscule salaries provide motive. According to an April 2004 survey by the International Finance Corporation, 98 percent of Tajik businessmen have paid bribes to state officials. In the higher echelons of government, positions are bought and sold.[34]

The government regularly assures journalists and donors that it is aware of the problem, but it has been sluggish in addressing it. Tajikistan passed detailed legislation against corrupt practices in 1999 but has barely implemented it. It has yet to sign the OSCE's Convention on Combating Bribery. Rakhmonov has sacked some high-profile officials—the tax committee chief and national border guard commander in 2002, two ministers and several deputy ministers in 2003—supposedly to root out corruption in his administration. But the purity of his motives is subject to doubt given that corruption probes most commonly target his political rivals. Various lower-level officials, including two judges, have been indicted on corruption charges. Yet no one has faced serious jail time except Dushanbe's former deputy mayor, who was sentenced to 16 years for embezzlement. In sum, the regime's spasmodic acts of punishment fall far short of any systematic plan to tackle corruption. The citizenry hears of these when stories appear in independent newspapers or when the arrest of a government opponent calls forth a vituperative exposé of his financial misdeeds in the state-controlled media.

The state does not involve itself excessively in the economy as a whole, but this is because much of the economy is beyond state control. Half the country's revenues are generated abroad by labor migrants, the vast majority of whom work illegally in Russia. Remittances from Tajik labor migrants in 2003 were estimated at $240 million, roughly equal to the Tajik government's budget revenues.[35] Perhaps a quarter of the gross national product is generated in a gray economy into which businesses and traders have been driven by mountains of red tape, sticky-fingered officials, and a tax system that has been described as "officially sponsored extortion."[36] Tax evasion is ubiquitous, sometimes helped along by the willingness of tax collectors and inspectors to strike private arrangements with the establishment in question. Businesspeople have little legal recourse against persistent harassment by the authorities. Small businesses have the option of a complaints hotline, set up by the State Anti-Monopoly Commission, but this has little impact.[37]

Tajikistan was poorly industrialized under the USSR, and its infrastructure was wrecked in the war. The government privatized some of its light industry and enterprises in the second half of the 1990s. Rigged auctions, nontransparent tenders, and phony valuations of assets meant that many state holdings went to government insiders and their friends at knock-down prices. Heavy industry, especially the Tursunzoda aluminum factory (another mainstay of the economy) remains predominantly in government hands. The state has not done enough to loosen its hold on agriculture, especially cotton production, where it continues to set and enforce targets; cotton is the country's main export. Russian companies have signaled interest in buying into Tajikistan's national electricity company and hydropower plants. It is fair to assume that such deals would bring significant personal benefit to relevant government officials. There is no adequate legislation requiring public officials to disclose their financial assets or conflicts of interest and poor enforcement of the laws that do exist.

Tajikistan's chronic poverty and a foreign debt of $1 billion have apparently focused some minds in the government on the need to tackle corruption if the country is ever to get on its feet. They have become aware that the key to Tajikistan's development is to attract foreign investors, who have mostly steered clear of the country as a quagmire of corruption. In May 2004 Rakhmonov signed into law a package of business-friendly legislation, including fresh tax and customs regulations. It remains to be seen if the legislation really will spur broader improvements in the overall climate in which businesses operate.

Corruption also threatens flows of international aid and assistance to Tajikistan. In 2003 international donors pledged $900 million to support Tajikistan's poverty-reduction strategy, but only a fraction of that sum has been disbursed, due in large part to major donors' concern about the lack of progress in combating corruption and introducing more transparent government. Millions of dollars have already disappeared from World Bank projects in Tajikistan, prompting Rakhmonov to fire two of his officials administering them.[38]

The trustworthiness of the information sporadically released by the government about its funding and expenditures (and by the same token, the accuracy of statistics or estimates offered in this report) is compromised by the secrecy of its budgets, which are not subject to public scrutiny or independent auditing. Funding priorities, or even the rationale behind budgetary allocations, are barely debated by the legislature, which effectively rubber-stamps the executive's submissions. Most of the information gathered at the state statistical agencies is classified as secret and impossible for the public to obtain. In any case government agencies massage their data to head off possible criticisms of their operations or results.

## Recommendations

- As a step toward reducing the temptations of bribe-taking in state structures, the salaries of public servants should be raised and the number of public servants should be cut.
- With the participation and input of NGOs and businesspeople, a "Reinventing Government"–type initiative should be launched to excise unnecessary regulations and bureaucratic bottlenecks—especially those that commonly require bribes to negotiate. The streamlined procedures should be published with the government's authoritative backing and made generally available to ensure that

both civil servants and petitioners know their rights and responsibilities.

* Laws should be enacted that require public officials to disclose their financial assets or conflicts of interest.

* Information on state revenues and expenditures, including a reasonable breakdown of the national budget, should be made public and accessible to petitioners.

## NOTES

[1] "Tajikistan: President Reshuffles Government" (Prague and Washington DC: Radio Free Europe/ Radio Liberty [RFE/RL], 22 January 2004), http://rferl.org/features/features_article.aspx?id=DA297BBD-4C51-45E4-90D4-9DB1DE6F4155&m=1&y=2004.

[2] *Tajikistan's Politics: Confrontation or Consolidation?* (Dushanbe/ Brussels: International Crisis Group [ICG], Asia Briefing, 19 May 2004), 5, http://www.icg.org/home/index.cfm?id=2757&l=1.

[3] "Moscow Extradites Controversial Tajik Politician" (London: Institute of War and Peace Reporting [IWPR], 27 February 2004), http://www.iwpr.net/index.pl?archive/rca/rca_200402_268_3_eng.txt; "Tajikistan: Fall of Praetorian Guardsman" (IWPR, 10 August 2004), http://www.iwpr.net/index.pl?archive/rca2/rca2_306_1_eng.txt.

[4] An American legal NGO pioneered a successful civic initiative project to influence the drafting of new criminal legislation: see "Participatory Government: A New Reality Slowly Emerges in Tajikistan" (Chicago and Washington, DC: The American Bar Association Central European and Eurasian Law Initiative [CEELI], 12 March 2004), http://www.abanet.org/ceeli/countries/tajikistan/success_story_taj_participatory_government.html. The OSCE had some success with a working group to propose changes to the election law: see *Tajikistan's Politics* (ICG), 12. Also, the Council of Ministers has formally consulted with trade unions before presenting some draft laws on welfare and worker rights.

[5] "Islamic Party Official Jailed" (RFE/RL Central Asia Report, 19 January 2004), http://www.rferl.org/reports/centralasia/2004/01/3-190104.asp.

[6] "Odd Goings-on at Tajik Party" (IWPR, 3 September 2004), http://www.iwpr.net/index.pl?archive/rca2/rca2_311_2_eng.txt; "Newsline" (RFE/RL, 17 September 2004), http://rferl.org/newsline/2004/09/2-TCA/tca-170904.asp.

[7] For an English text of the election law (adopted 10 December 1999, amended 16 June 2004), see http://www.legislationline.org/view.php?document=61978. Also, "Tajikistan: Parliament Passes Amendments to Election Code" (RFE/RL, 17 June 2004), http://www.rferl.org/featuresarticle/2004/6/A98F5F57-2E9E-4C9F-B26B-98A7F57A660F.html; *Tajikistan's Politics* (ICG), 13. [*Editor's note:* The 2004 minimum monthly wage of 7 somonis ($2.50) was increased to 12 somonis ($4.30) starting 1 January 2005.]

8 "Newsline" (RFE/RL, 27 February 2004), http://www.rferl.org/newsline/2004/02/2-TCA/tca-270204.asp.

9 *Europe and Central Asia: Attacks on the Press 2003* (New York: Committee to Protect Journalists [CPJ], 12 March 2004), http://www.cpj.org/attacks03/europe03/tajik.html.

10 *Tajikistan – Annual Report 2003* (Paris: Reporters Without Borders [RSF], 5 February 2003), http://www.rsf.org/article.php3?id_article=6540.

11 "Independent Press Subjected to Printing Obstructions, Threats and Assault" (RSF, 24 August 2004), 1, http://www.rsf.org/print.php3?id_article=11222; "Media Pressure Intensifies" (IWPR, 13 October 2004), http://www.iwpr.net/index.pl?archive/rca2/rca2_320_2_eng.txt.

12 "Tajikistan: CPJ Calls for End to Intimidation Campaign" (CPJ, 31 August 2004), http://www.cpj.org/protests/04ltrs/Tajik31aug04pl.html.

13 *Tajikistan: Deadly Secrets. The Death Penalty in Law and Practice* (London and New York: Amnesty International [AI], 30 September 2002), 5, http://web.amnesty.org/library/Index/ENGEUR600082002?open&of=ENG-TJK.

14 Ibid., 1, 6.

15 *Belarus and Uzbekistan: The Last Executioners* (AI, 4 October 2004), http://web.amnesty.org/library/Index/ENGEUR040092004?open&of=ENG-BLR.

16 "Memories of Journalist Killings Revived" (IWPR, 27 January 2004), http://www.iwpr.net/index.pl?archive/rca/rca_200401_260_1_eng.txt; "Tajikistan: Media See Gains, Setbacks" (RFE/RL, 8 January 2004), http://www.rferl.org/featuresarticle/2004/01/ac3d9727-aa9c-4c35-acfc-2fddd5c2457e.html.

17 *Tajikistan: Deadly Secrets* (AI), 9–12.

18 *Tajikistan: A Roadmap for Development* (Osh/Brussels: ICG, Asia Report No.51, 24 April 2003), 12, http://www.icg.org/home/index.cfm?id=1447&l=1.

19 "Tajik Migrants Face New Threat" (IWPR, 27 August 2004), http://www.iwpr.net/index.pl?archive/rca2/rca2_310_3_eng.txt.

20 "Tajikistan: Women Challenge Mosque Ban" (IWPR, 6 October 2004), http://www.iwpr.net/index.pl?archive/rca2/rca2_318_3_eng.txt.

21 *Trafficking in Persons Report* (Washington, DC: U.S. Dept. of State, June 2003), http://www.state.gov/g/tip/rls/tiprpt/2004/33192.htm; "Tajikistan: Human Trafficking a Growing Concern" (RFE/RL, 22 April 2004), http://www.rferl.org/featuresarticle/2004/04/4f5d68ec-514a-46b1-ba00-245544d329e9.html.

22 "Central Asia: State Policy Towards Muslims in Central Asia" (Oslo: Forum 18 News Service, 16 February 2004), http://www.forum18.org/Archive.php?article_id=253.

23 *Tajikistan: International Religious Freedom Report 2003* (U.S. Dept. of State), 2, http://www.state.gov/g/drl/rls/irf/2003/24437.htm; Tajikistan's Politics (ICG), 9.

24 "Tajiks Stung by Investment Scandal" (IWPR, 2 September 2003), http://www.iwpr.net.

25 "Legal Information for Tajikistan" (CEELI), 1, http://www.abanet.org/ceeli/countries/tajikistan/legalinfo.html.

26 *Tajikistan: Deadly Secrets* (AI), 11.

27 *Tajikistan's Politics* (ICG), 2.

28 "Tajik Army Abuses Tackled" (IWPR, 5 November 2004), http://www.iwpr.net/index.pl?archive/rca2/rca2_324_2_eng.txt.

29 *Tajikistan's Politics* (ICG), 7.

30 *Tajikistan's Land Reform Programme: Sowing the Seeds of a Brighter Future* (Vienna: OSCE Secretariat), OSCE Magazine, July 2004, 4, http://www.osce.org/documents/ sg/2004/07/3343_en.pdf; *Tajikistan, A Roadmap for Development* (ICG), 3.

31 "Tajik Cotton Harvest in the Balance" (IWPR, 19 October 2004), http://www.iwpr.net index.pl?archive/rca2/rca2_322_2_eng.txt.

32 "Tajikistan: Wartime Property Dispute" (IWPR, 26 November 2004), http://www .iwpr.net/index.pl?archive/rca2/rca2_328_2_eng.txt.

33 *Corruption Perceptions Index* (Berlin and London: Transparency International, 2004), http://www.transparency.org/cpi/2004/cpi2004.en.html#cpi2004.

34 *Tajikistan: A Roadmap for Development* (ICG), 14.

35 "Newsline" (RFE/RL, 4 February 2004), http://rferl.org/newsline/2004/02/2-TCA/tca-040204.asp.

36 "Tajikistan: Clock Ticking on Corruption" (IWPR, 15 June 2004), http://www.iwpr.net/ index.pl?archive/rca/rca_200406_293_3_eng.txt.

37 *Tajikistan: A Roadmap for Development* (ICG), 7.

38 Ibid., 26, note 135; "Tajikistan: Donors Meeting Following Up On Dushanbe's Promises to Fight Poverty, Corruption" (RFE/RL, 9 February 2004), http://www.rferl.org/ featuresarticle/2004/02/7cc553b5-81c3-4e0f-a361-9fb5b0fab892.html.

# THAILAND

CAPITAL: Bangkok
POPULATION: 63.8 million
GNI PER CAPITA: $2,000

**SCORES**
ACCOUNTABILITY AND PUBLIC VOICE: 4.04
CIVIL LIBERTIES: 3.72
RULE OF LAW: 4.22
ANTICORRUPTION AND TRANSPARENCY: 3.48
(scores are based on a scale of 0 to 7, with
0 representing weakest and 7 representing
strongest performance)

*Duncan McCargo*

## INTRODUCTION

The adoption of a relatively liberal constitution in 1997 was a defining moment in Thailand's recent political history. The new constitution sought to improve the quality of electoral politics, introducing a range of independent agencies (such as the Election Commission and the National Counter Corruption Commission [NCCC]) so as to build checks and balances into the political system and broaden popular participation.

The 1997 constitution was unfinished business dating from the political crises of 1991 and 1992. This troubled period began with a military coup in February 1991, followed by an attempt by the coup leadership to commandeer parliament through the manipulation of the March 1992 election. The turbulence culminated in the 1992 May events, which saw massive street demonstrations in central Bangkok and the shooting dead of scores of unarmed protesters. Subsequently, the military reluctantly withdrew to the barracks, leaving the governance of

**Duncan McCargo** is professor of Southeast Asian politics at the University of Leeds, UK. His books on Thailand include *Politics and the Press in Thailand: Media Machinations* (Routledge, 2000), *Reforming Thai Politics* (edited) (NIAS, 2002), and *The Thaksinization of Thailand* (with Ukrist Pathmanand) (NIAS, 2005).

573

Thailand to a series of unstable coalition administrations based on alliances between professional politicians, business interests, technocrats, and prominent criminals. Liberal elements of the elite, pressing for a cleaner and more responsive political order, led the political reform movement that culminated in the 1997 constitution.

In addition to the promulgation of the new constitution, 1997 also saw the onset of the Asian financial crisis, which began in Bangkok. The economic crash followed almost three decades of strong growth and rapid social change in Thailand. Ironically, just as the reformist agenda of the 1997 constitution was coming into its own, Thais began to embrace alternative ideas: nationalism (the IMF and World Bank were widely criticized for their role in addressing the crisis), reduced dependence on the global economy, and strong government. In 1998, billionaire telecommunications magnate and ex-policeman Thaksin Shinawatra founded his Thai Rak Thai (Thais Love Thai) Party (TRT). TRT capitalized upon the changed popular mood, Thaksin's own financial successes (his businesses had emerged from the crisis virtually unscathed), and the constitutional provisions that favored the emergence of a small number of stronger political parties. After TRT won a decisive victory in the 2001 elections by gaining 248 of the 500 seats (control of almost half of the seats in parliament by a single party was unprecedented in Thailand's multi-party system), Thaksin proceeded to demonstrate his disdain for the causes espoused by the liberal reformers of the 1990s.[1] He sought to neutralize the new independent governance agencies, to achieve total dominance over party politics by creating a grand coalition under his own control, and to move Thailand in a more authoritarian direction.

Thailand is now in a paradoxical position. On paper, it has a rather liberal set of governance arrangements, a vibrant civil society, and progressive stances on many human rights issues. Yet in practice, the spirit and the letter of the 1997 constitution are frequently ignored by the ruling party. Thaksin has made himself a "CEO" (chief executive officer) prime minister, assuming immense personal power and creating an elaborate support network among elements of the private sector, the military, and the police. Most alarmingly of all, the Thaksin government has engaged in a range of human rights violations, notably by apparently sanctioning extrajudicial killings in a 2003 war on drugs. Growing political violence in the Muslim-dominated southern border provinces has been fueled by the use of torture, disappearances, and excessive harshness by the security forces. Thaksin's critics have argued that there are conflicts of interest between his political position and his family businesses, something he strongly denies. Leading social activist Wanida Thantiwithayaphitak has argued that the 1997 constitution is now bogged down in interest-group politics.[2] [*Editor's note:* TRT won a landslide victory in the February 2005 election, winning around 75 percent of all parliamentary seats. Thaksin's party was decisively rejected in the southern region, however.]

## ACCOUNTABILITY AND PUBLIC VOICE – 4.04

Thailand has a rather open political order, and power has rotated among a number of political parties in recent years. Most parties, however, do not represent genuine ideological or policy alternatives but rather are little more than interest groups closely associated with powerful political faction bosses and cliques. Political choice has contracted since 2001, given the merger of smaller parties with the ruling TRT. Parties are equally free to campaign, but the overwhelming dominance of TRT now gives the incumbent considerable advantages.

Under the 1997 constitution, a powerful Election Commission (EC) was established, with extensive powers to manage, oversee, and regulate the electoral process. The EC adopted a highly interventionist approach to both the 2000 Senate elections and 2001 lower house elections. In response to complaints of electoral abuses—mainly in the form of vote-buying—the EC handed out hundreds of soccer-style yellow cards (forcing reruns) and red cards (also compelling reruns but debarring problematic candidates from standing). In total, 78 reruns were ordered after the initial 200 Senate races and 62 reruns for the lower house. Some Senate elections went through as many as seven reruns.[3] However, despite the existence of campaign finance laws and state support for political parties via the EC, much campaign spending goes toward vote-buying and other illegal activities that are never declared. Accordingly, candidates with strong financial backing are at a considerable advantage. The EC has made little serious attempt to monitor spending by political parties.

Although very keen on pursuing rogue candidates, the EC has been less interested in monitoring electoral manipulation by government officials. As filing a complaint with the EC is essentially cost-free, many complaints are filed as face-saving ploys by losing candidates (or even by losing gambling syndicates), and repeated reruns have the effect of undermining the legitimacy of the electoral process. After May 2001, the original team of five national election commissioners was completely replaced. Their successors appeared far less independent-minded, and members of Parliament (MPs) dropped their calls for a pruning back of the EC's powers.[4] The real test of the EC will come when there is a close-run general election, which currently seems a distant prospect.

The 1997 constitutional arrangements were deliberately constructed to create a system of checks and balances, primarily through a nonpartisan Senate (whose members are barred from party affiliation) and a range of independent agencies, including the Election Commission, Constitutional Court, Administrative Court, and a National Counter Corruption Commission. Unfortunately, the reality is rather different. The Senate is full of the wives, children, and associates of politicians, as well as a large contingent of former government officials, many with close personal and financial ties to party leaders and cliques of MPs.[5] Only a handful of Thailand's 200 senators consistently perform the kind of monitoring role envisaged by the constitution.

Similar problems characterize many of the post-1997 independent agencies. There is ample evidence that the government has sought to politicize the process of appointments to these agencies, and TRT has been consistently critical of them. Given the weakness of the Senate and other bodies, dominant power interests such as the ruling TRT are exposed only to limited critical scrutiny. Most civil service posts are gained through open appointments procedures, though some processes—notably for the police and the interior ministry—have been tainted by persistent reports of cheating.

Civic groups are able to comment freely on policy issues and legislation, and many have been very influential. At the same time, formal mechanisms for consultation remain weak—despite a recent vogue for public hearings, the government has tended to rely on ad hoc consultation structures, which produce arbitrary outcomes. After initially seeking to co-opt nongovernmental organizations (NGOs) by adopting progressive rhetoric, the Thaksin government has demonstrated a growing reluctance to listen to critical views from civil society bodies: For example, the outspoken Thailand Development Research Institute

(TDRI), a technocratic think tank employing many of the country's top economists, has been marginalized for refusing to accept the TRT line. In May 2003, the government planned to put pressure on foreign donors to reduce funding for certain NGOs, but the plan was not implemented.[6] The Thaksin government has also put pressure on major funders of civic organizations, including the progressively inclined Thai Health Fund, which derives its income from a hypothecated excise tax on alcohol and tobacco products. Because there are demanding requirements for NGO registration under legislation dating from 1942, most NGOs are not formally registered with the interior ministry. In practice, legal registration is not required, and Thailand has one of the most vigorous NGO communities in Southeast Asia. However, the Thaksin government sought to discourage political activity by NGOs and organized a clampdown on NGO protests at the time of the October 2003 Asia-Pacific Economic Cooperation (APEC) meeting in Bangkok.

Electronic media are largely controlled by the state and have always been subject to considerable political interference. Radio frequencies remain dominated by the military, supposedly for reasons of national security, but in practice because they are a lucrative source of revenue. Thailand has a long tradition of vigorous and critical print media, with a parallel tradition of press manipulation and cooptation by power-holders. The Thaksin government has been widely criticized for putting pressure on critical media voices—such as the English-language daily *The Nation* and the small but outspoken Thai-language daily *Thai Post*—and for using a combination of sticks and carrots to promote more favorable coverage. In the case of *The Nation*, its editors were subjected to an investigation by the Anti-Money Laundering Organization in 2002, while in 2003, a prominent Thaksin associate bought a significant share in the newspaper group.[7] To date, however, *The Nation* remains broadly critical of the government. Print media are not directly funded by the state, but the Thaksin government has ensured that pro-government newspapers carry the bulk of state-funded advertising. Media ownership in Thailand is also a problematic issue; there are persistent rumors that prominent figures close to the government have acquired formal or informal ownership of elements in the print media.[8]

Thai libel laws are deeply problematic: Those charged with libel may face immediate imprisonment if they are unable to produce the large sums typically required for bail. Politicians and their associates have not hesitated to harass critics through use of these punitive laws. One particularly disturbing case occurred in 2003, when Shin Corporation (owned by Thaksin's family) sued Supinya Klangnarong, secretary-general of the small NGO Campaign for Media Reform, along with the *Thai Post,* for the staggering sum of 400 million baht—around US$10 million. Supinya had asserted that there were conflicts of interest between Thaksin's business activities and his political position.[9] The controversial trial was deferred by the courts until July 2005, well after the election scheduled for the beginning of the year.

Although there is considerable freedom of cultural and political expression in Thailand, a notable exception lies in lese majesty laws, which outlaw all criticism of the royal family. While technically applying only to the current king, the queen, and the heir-apparent, these laws formed a justification for the 1999 banning of the Hollywood film *Anna and the King,* which deals with the great-great-grandfather of the present monarch. Two Western journalists for the *Far Eastern Economic Review* were threatened with deportation in 2002 for alleged violation of lese majesty laws, although ultimately they were allowed to remain in Thailand.

*Recommendations*
- The government should respect the spirit and the letter of the 1997 constitution by resisting temptations to interfere in the workings of independent agencies.
- The constitutionally mandated commission to allocate radio frequencies should be established without further delay, and the commission should ensure that control of radio frequencies is completely removed from the military.
- Thailand's libel laws should be urgently overhauled so that those accused of libel do not face imprisonment and cannot be forced to pay disproportionate levels of damages. Meanwhile, leading public figures could set an example by refraining from suing individuals for libel without a compelling justification.

## CIVIL LIBERTIES – 3.72

Despite constitutional injunctions (Article 243) there is persistent evidence of torture and abuses of pretrial prisoners by both police and military agencies, especially in relation to rural protest movements and alleged drug offenders. Punishment of state officials for such abuses is very rare. Pretrial detention for up to 84 days is widely used in criminal cases, and extensions may be requested for complex cases. Thai prisoners are kept in poor conditions: They must pay for a space to sleep (even on the floor) and need money from outside in order to obtain reasonable food.[10] International monitors claim that prisoners are often shackled in leg irons, despite the fact that this is illegal; and trusted convicts are sometimes allowed to beat fellow prisoners.[11]

Murders of local politicians, journalists, and activists occur regularly in Thailand. Amnesty International has expressed concern about the violent deaths of human rights defenders, including six environmental activists in 2001 and five community leaders in 2002 whose deaths were not comprehensively investigated.[12] The arbitrary arrest of demonstrators is a widespread practice. Citizens may be at risk from non-state actors—in two recent cases, commercial areas in central Bangkok were violently cleared, apparently by landowners operating with the collusion of the police and military. In the January 27, 2003, incident, around 600 men, many of them soldiers, demolished dozens of bars and tourist shops in Sukumvit Soi 10 using bulldozers and cranes. A market area was similarly cleared in 2004.[13] Thaksin's support for the U.S.–led war on terror was reflected in his August 2003 promulgation of tough antiterrorism laws by executive decree, laws that were subsequently passed by parliament. Critics argued that these laws could be abused to crack down on political dissent and that provisions for detention without trial undermine the human rights of Thai citizens.[14]

The most serious assault on civil liberties in modern Thai history was the 2003 war on drugs, an apparently officially sanctioned policy of extrajudicial killing that involved some 2,275 deaths in its initial three months.[15] While the authorities implausibly claimed that most of these killings resulted from drug dealers turning their weapons on each other, there was ample evidence of widespread official collusion in numerous murders. Blacklists of suspected drug dealers in each district formed the basis of the murders, yet many of those on the lists apparently had no connection with the drug trade; others were users rather than dealers. Prime Minister Thaksin personally initiated the drug war and strongly criticized both international bodies such as the United Nations and members of the National Human Rights Commission for their public expressions of concern. Yet even Thailand's revered king expressed reservations, and in December 2003 he called upon the national police chief to account for the large number of deaths.[17] Local Thai-language media carried little critical or investigative coverage of the drugs war, although one outlet did coin the phrase silent killing (*kha tat ton*) to describe the extrajudicial deaths.

This dark episode undermined Thailand's claims to a good human rights record, nullifying many of the country's recent reforms. To date, no proper investigation of the war on drugs has taken place, and no list of its victims has been published. The policy drove many heroin addicts underground, making it more likely that intravenous drug users would resort to the dangerous practice of sharing needles—thus ultimately leading to further deaths from HIV infection.[18] Amnesty International is said to have scaled down its own investigation of the drugs war because of fears for the safety of its local staff.[19]

A further area of grave concern relates to the government's handling of political violence in the southern border provinces during 2004. Around 80 percent of the population of Pattani, Yala, and Narathiwat provinces are Malay Muslims, whose first language is not Thai. This region has been characterized by longstanding yet sporadic separatist violence. The Thaksin government dismantled the existing security command structure in May 2002, placing the police in charge of maintaining order. Tensions mounted following a large-scale attack on an army base on January 4, and a spate of shootings and small explosions followed. Martial law was subsequently imposed in these provinces. By September 2004 around 200 Muslims had been killed by the security forces or had disappeared, while more than 140 security personnel and civilians—including Buddhist monks and one judge—had met violent deaths, many apparently at the hands of Muslim extremists.[20]

The National Human Rights Commission received complaints of beatings and abductions associated with heavy-handed raids on Muslim communities, including Islamic boarding schools, or *pondok*. Somchai Neelaphaijit, an activist lawyer from the area, accused the police of torturing five suspects charged with involvement in the January army base raid, a claim that was verified by the Commission. On March 12 Somchai disappeared. A remark by Deputy Prime Minister Chavalit Yongchaiyudh two weeks later revealed that the authorities knew he was already dead.[21] The five suspects whom Somchai had defended were released on May 18, 2004, for lack of evidence.[22] No action has been taken against those accused of using torture. The Asian Human Rights Commission stated that "The authorities in Thailand have abandoned any pretence that they are trying to resolve the disappearance" of Somchai,[23] although five police officers were charged with his abduction.

On April 28, 108 Muslim men and 5 police officers were killed when groups of lightly armed militants launched a coordinated attack on security positions. The day's events culminated in a siege of the historic Krue Se mosque in Pattani, where 32 Muslim men were killed by commandos, allegedly at point-blank range. Although an investigation found that the military had used excessive force, the prime minister refused to accept the resignation of General Pallop Pinmanee, the officer who ordered this attack.[24] Pallop responded by publishing a best-selling book defending his actions.[25] [*Editor's note:* Matters worsened considerably when 84 Muslim protesters died in events arising from a demonstration on October 25 outside a police station in Tak Bai, Narathiwat province. The authorities claimed that 78 of the deceased had died as a result of suffocation after they were arrested and piled into army trucks. The events triggered an international outcry, partly because of Thaksin's inept handling of the issue and failure to apologize properly for the deaths.]

The 1997 constitution gives citizens the right to petition the president of the Senate for the removal of national politicians or high-ranking officials accused of corruption or abuses of power (Article 304), but the procedure has been little invoked, partly because 50,000 signatures are required. Citizens may also bring complaints to independent agencies such as the Counter-Corruption or Human Rights commissions, both of which have large backlogs of cases. The National Counter-Corruption Commission saw a big increase in reports of alleged corruption in local government bodies, from 501 complaints in 2000, 629 in 2001 to 852 in 2003.[26]

Under the constitution, the state is committed to promoting equal rights between men and women (Article 80) and to supporting individuals with disabilities and underprivileged people. In practice only around 10 percent of MPs and senators are female, and less than 6 percent of ministers.[27] A small number of women are now serving as district officers (8.9 percent) and provincial governors (2.6 percent), positions previously reserved for men.

A number of constitutional provisions support gender equality, but changes in both legislation and practice are needed in relation to issues such as rape and domestic violence, which are often not taken seriously or handled sensitively by the police. According to a Labor Ministry survey, women are paid around 17 percent less than men—a figure that compares favorably with those in many developed countries. Despite legislation forbidding trafficking in people, Thailand is a major nexus for human trafficking, notably from Burma, Cambodia, China, Laos, and to a lesser extent Vietnam. Much of this trafficking involves placing women and children in the lucrative Thai sex industry, though some of those trafficked are employed in sweatshops, agriculture, construction, and fisheries.

Racial discrimination is also prohibited by the constitution (Article 30), but there is no specific mention of ethnic minorities. This reflects the official view that all Thais are simply Thai and a persistent tendency to deny the significance of ethnic difference. Chapter 3 of the 1997 constitution is explicitly entitled "Rights and liberties of the Thai people," thereby excluding all noncitizens. As one informant told Amnesty International, "The Thai constitution does not apply to me, because I am an ethnic minority."[28]

Many ethnic minority peoples in the northern highland areas of Thailand are not Thai citizens and have been subject to persistent discrimination; similar problems apply in the case of Burmese refugees and illegal workers from Cambodia. The estimated half million Karen or other so-called hill tribe people lack Thai citizenship and are effectively stateless. Many are unable to prove that they were born in Thailand, while others are similarly unable to claim Burmese citizenship. Like Burmese migrants working illegally in Thailand, these groups are vulnerable to arbitrary arrest.[29] In the early 1970s, a military regime arbitrarily revoked citizenship for all those descended from Vietnamese fathers who had immigrated to Thailand before 1972, but that decision was reversed in 2004.[30] Many Thai Muslims, especially in the southern border provinces, have a poor command of the central Thai language, which compounds their limited economic opportunities. The Thai state has been slow to recognize the need to address issues of discrimination on racial and ethnic grounds; for many local government officials, minority groups are stereotyped as sources of insecurity, crime, and social problems, to be dealt with by forceful incorporation into Thai cultural norms.[31]

Discrimination against people with disabilities is illegal under the constitution, but widespread in practice, and many public buildings lack proper access. In one widely publicized recent case, a law graduate who suffered some slight disabilities from childhood polio was barred from sitting for the examination to become a judge. The government has a poor record of making information available to people with disabilities, for example through braille or audio versions of important documents. On the positive side, sign language is widely used to accompany television broadcasts. Overall, the government's record on enforcing equality issues is mixed.

In theory Thais enjoy freedom of religion, and religious observance is not restricted. However, the Thai state exercises control over the *sangha* (Buddhist order) and has moved to exclude dissident religious groups from the officially sanctioned order. In other words, the state has arrogated to itself the right to determine what does and does not constitute true Buddhism.[32] The sangha has recently been thrown into crisis by the serious illness of its aging head,[33] while Prime Minister Thaksin has been criticized for intervening in the leadership of the Buddhist order. Since 2002, Islamic, Christian, and other religious groups have been overseen by the Department of Religion (part of the Ministry of Culture), while a National Office of Buddhism is located in the office of the prime minister.

Freedom of association is broadly respected in Thailand, although levels of unionization remain low (at less than 2 percent of the total workforce) except in state enterprises, where more than half of employees are union members. Although people are free to join unions, there is evidence that some employers have dismissed union leaders or executive members. When such cases were brought to government-backed tribunals, the union activists received back pay but employers were not otherwise penalized. The Thaksin government has so far failed to fulfill its 2001 election pledges to ratify ILO conventions 87 and 98 on freedom of association and collective bargaining.

There is no evidence of citizens being forced by the state to join particular associations. The right to peaceful organization and mobilization is generally widely practiced and respected, but the state has supported harsh repression of certain kinds of protest movements, particularly anti-development movements by the Forum of the Poor and other rural-based groups. This included repression of protests surrounding the Pak Mun Dam in the northeastern province of Ubon in December 2002[34] and violent suppression of protests against the Thai-Malaysian gas pipeline in the same month.

*Recommendations*
- Thailand should immediately hold a full public inquiry into the circumstances surrounding the war on drugs of 2003 and the extrajudicial killings associated with it.
- Those suspected of involvement in any extrajudicial killings, including senior officers, should be brought to trial.
- Firm action should be taken against state officials allegedly responsible for human rights abuses, torture, and disappearances in the south, including criminal trials where appropriate.
- Full citizenship rights should be granted to all members of Karen and so-called hill tribe minority groups who are long-term residents of Thailand.

## RULE OF LAW – 4.22

Thailand's judiciary is generally independent but also somewhat corrupt. This skews the justice system toward the suspect's ability to pay bribes, leading to structural inequalities and often allowing the guilty to walk free. A national survey in 2000 found that a third of those who had been involved in court cases had been asked to pay bribes to secure a favorable outcome. Around half of these requests came from public prosecutors.[35] In 2002, Supreme Court Chief Justice Santi Thakral laid down detailed guidelines intended to curtail patronage and corruption in the judiciary, including rules concerning expenses on transportation, meals, and entertainment.

The Economist Intelligence Unit suggests that government interference in the judiciary is increasing. Despite a series of widely publicized fraud cases in the 1990s—such as the collapse of the Bangkok Bank of Commerce, in which a number of prominent politicians were implicated—not a single conviction had been achieved by the end of 2002.[36] High-profile criminal cases such as the 2004 acquittal of a politician's son on charges of murdering a policeman have undermined public confidence in the judicial system.[37] The Appeal Court—sometimes referred to as "the money court"[38]—is especially problematic. The Central Bankruptcy Court has also been criticized for making politicized decisions that undermined the confidence of foreign investors.[39] However, Thailand's strict contempt-of-court laws—which apply outside the courtroom—make open discussion of the judicial system very difficult. This in turn curtails critical reporting where abuses in the legal process may be widely suspected.

All career judges must be qualified as barristers, have no less than two years of legal experience, and pass a difficult and competitive examination before being appointed as trainee judges for a trial period of one year. There is no jury system, and verbatim transcripts of court proceedings are not made. Judges are generally held in high regard in Thai society. However, a senior judge from the Central Labor Court has claimed that appointments as associate judges were manipulated by an organized gang that charged candidates 400,000 baht (around US$10,000) per appointment.[40]

Article 33 of the constitution specifies that criminal suspects are presumed innocent until convicted. Citizens have the right to a fair trial with independent counsel. Despite these provisions, in the case of the 2003 war on drugs, extrajudicial killings did take place. Those accused of serious crimes are provided with lawyers by the state if they cannot afford to pay for their own defense. However, these court-appointed lawyers are often recent graduates with little experience in conducting a defense.[41] Thammasat University runs an active legal aid and legal literacy program.

Leading politicians (including the current prime minister and the former secretary-general of the ruling Democrat Party) and senior officials have been tried on corruption-related charges by the Constitutional Court, although its judgments have been criticized as erratic.[42] One of the most controversial decisions was the acquittal of Prime Minister Thaksin Shinawatra on charges of assets concealment in 2001. Thaksin escaped conviction on technical grounds by 8 votes to 7, although only four of the judges hearing the case actually found him innocent. The retiring president of the Constitutional Court declared in 2002 that he had "witnessed many subtle attempts by politicians to sway judges" and had "felt strong pressure from the pro-Thaksin mob."[43] Full written judgments have sometimes not been published for up to a year after Constitutional Court decisions, thereby undermining the credibility of the court.

The Thai military (mainly the army) has staged numerous coups and coup attempts since the end of the absolute monarchy in 1932 and until the violence of May 1992 was a prominent and outspoken participant in the political processes of the country. Since 1992, the military has returned reluctantly to the barracks, maintaining a low profile but retaining various economic privileges. Despite much talk of security sector reform, no substantive reforms have been enacted. Civilian politicians remain wary of interfering with the military's internal workings, despite general recognition that the armed forces are bloated (with an estimated 1,400 generals) and of doubtful military competence. The Thaksin government has pursued a policy of co-opting the military, and relatives and former classmates of the prime minister have been appointed to numerous key positions.[44] As an ex-police officer himself, Thaksin has enjoyed good relations with the police force, enlisting it in support of various government initiatives. Both the military and police enjoy close relationships with a range of actors engaged in legal and illegal business activities. Longstanding rivalries between the police and the military may have contributed to the deteriorating security situation in the South.

Property rights are recognized in law, although in practice the system of land title deeds is complex, and many poor people do not have proper ownership of the land they farm. Many hold so-called Sor Tor Kor deeds, or usufructuary land licenses.[45] Abuse of land and contractual rights by local elites and corrupt officials is widespread in rural areas, and structural corruption in the legal system often disempowers the poor. The Economist Intelligence Unit describes Thai courts as "generally competent and effective in enforcing property and contractual rights," but notes that "extra-legal means" may complicate cases involving wealthy or powerful individuals.[46] Problems are exacerbated by legal provisions that allow people to sell land provisionally yet retain the right to redeem it. Many sell their land in this way, only to discover that in practice their redemption rights are almost impossible to exercise.[47] The Sor Pho Kho 4-01 land reform program in the 1990s resulted in many local elites improperly obtaining lands that were supposed to be allocated to poor farmers. Local traditions of common land usage have been widely overridden by the state; the Kho Jo Ko program of the 1980s and early 1990s saw many poor farming communities forcibly evicted from lands designated as reserve forest areas, despite their having lived on them for decades or even generations.[48]

*Recommendations*

- A special investigative team should be created to identify corrupt judges and prosecutors, who should be swiftly suspended and then dismissed from office.
- A substantive program of security sector reform is needed, first concentrating on the core objective of reducing the number of generals—a problem that underpins a culture of military privilege.
- A new agency should be created to police the police, with an emphasis on identifying and removing officers deeply involved in the illegal economy.
- Land tenure needs to be reformed so that wherever possible those who actually farm the land own the land, and laws rewritten to allow farmers to borrow money without having to hand over their land to predatory creditors and local elites.
- The Constitutional Court should promptly publish full written judgments by all judges, and judges who have not attended all hearings should not be allowed to pass judgment on the case concerned.

## ANTICORRUPTION AND TRANSPARENCY – 3.48

Thailand is a legalistic and bureaucratic state in which opportunities for official corruption are legion. The state is extensively involved in the economy, notably through numerous state enterprises, including the Electricity Generating Authority of Thailand, the Petroleum Authority of Thailand, the State Railway, Thai Airways International, and the Thailand Tobacco Monopoly. Privatization of state enterprises has been much discussed, but progress has been slow. Given the current structure of the economy, it seems likely that greater privatization would simply allow privileged elites further opportunities for self-enrichment.

Under Article 110 of the constitution, MPs are not permitted to hold state concessions or contracts, but in practice such regulations are readily subverted. Thaksin has nominally transferred most of his considerable business assets to his family and his servants. In 1996, two of Thaksin's maids were listed as the 12th and 13th richest people in Thailand, and his driver the 49th richest.[49] Assets declarations are required from all cabinet members, MPs, senators, and other senior elected officials. Those made by ministers (including the prime minister) are open to public and media scrutiny, but the assets declaration system has so far failed to stop endemic conflicts of interest between politicians and the business sector. Concessions allocations in Thailand typically reflect a culture of benefit sharing rather than the public interest, or the interests of individual consumers. The award of government contracts has never been open and transparent in Thailand: Whatever formal procedures are observed, these processes are widely seen as vitiated by structural corruption.

Transparency International rates Thailand number 64 out of 146 countries assessed in its 2004 Corruption Perceptions Index, with 3.6 out of a possible 10 points.[50] Victims of corruption may lodge complaints with the NCCC, which has extensive powers to investigate corruption by state officials. However, the 2003 appointment of new commissioners widely seen as government-friendly meant that the NCCC was effectively neutralized.[51] Access to higher education is generally open, although scandals concerning alleged abuses of the entrance examination system surface regularly.[52]

Collection of income taxes is uneven. In 2004 there were 6.27 million taxpayers (including corporate and value-added taxpayers), a figure the Revenue Department hopes to increase to 20 million by 2009.[53] The Revenue Department has been encouraging taxpayers to pay online, as this reduces scope for bribery. The Economist Intelligence Unit suggests that up to 100 billion baht (or one-fifth of potential revenue) may be lost annually through tax evasion. The State Audit Commission and the auditor general have extensive authority to monitor the proper use of public funds, but in the past their effectiveness has been hampered by lack of timely cooperation on the part of the police, and lack of power to implement their findings. Auditor General Jaruvan Menthaka was ousted in controversial circumstances in 2004, with some senators alleging that her removal reflected her critical stance concerning various mega-projects backed by leading ministers.[54]

The most notable success of the NCCC has been the conviction of Sanan Kachornprasart on asset-declaration charges in March 2000. As secretary-general of the ruling Democrat Party and interior minister, Sanan was among the three or four most powerful men in Thailand, and his five-year ban from serving in any political office was an impressive achievement for the NCCC. While Prime Minister Thaksin Shinawatra avoided a similar ban in controversial circumstances in 2001, the

Constitutional Court did convict a minister of fraud in 2003. Sanan organized a petition to impeach four of the judges who failed to convict Thaksin on asset declaration charges, but his attempts foundered because fewer than 50,000 of the signatures he raised were found to be genuine.[55] [*Editor's note:* In December 2004 former foreign minister Prasong Sunsiri successfully defended a defamation action brought by eight constitutional court judges who had "acquitted" Thaksin in 2001; allegations of political interference and the offering of incentives to judges in the case resurfaced.[56]] Issues concerning corruption by politicians are widely aired in the media, although the electronic media rarely offer critical perspectives on current power-holders. Whistleblowers do not feel secure; as media activist Supinya Klangnarong told the *New York Times,* there is a hierarchy of punishment in Thailand: "If you act too much, you'll be killed. If you talk too much, you will be sued. If you're an academic, you might be discredited."[57]

Thailand has enacted freedom of information legislation. In principle, it affords extensive rights to citizens, although to date its provisions have been little used. In principle, the national budget is open to scrutiny by the legislature—and dozens of senior officials attend annual parliamentary sessions for this purpose—but given the current dominance of the ruling TRT party in the House of Representatives, this scrutiny is necessarily limited. Foreign assistance can be freely distributed in Thailand, although the relatively high level of economic development means that apart from long-standing support from Japan and from the Asian Development Bank, Thailand is not a major aid recipient country.

*Recommendations*

- New legislation to regulate potential conflicts of interest between politicians and business concerns is urgently needed.
- More rigorous regulatory mechanisms are needed to protect the interests of consumers, especially in areas such as telecommunications.
- Current loopholes allowing serving MPs and ministers to transfer their business assets to relatives and servants should be closed.
- The Revenue Department should be strongly supported in its attempts to increase the tax base and curtail tax evasion.
- New legislation should be enacted to protect whistleblowers from dismissal or harassment.

## NOTES

1. See Pasuk Phongpaichit and Chris Baker, *Thaksin: The Business of Politics in Thailand* (Chiang Mai: Silkworm, 2004), 89.

2. Wanida Thantiwithayapithak, "The Weak People's Constitution," *Thailand Human Rights Journal* 1 (2003): 221.

3. Sombat Chantornvong, "The 1997 Constitution and the Politics of Electoral Reform," in Duncan McCargo (ed.), *Reforming Thai Politics* (Copenhagen: Nordic Institute of Asian Studies [NIAS], 2002), 207–09; "Thailand's house elections of 6 January 2001: Thaksin's landslide victory and subsequent narrow escape," in Michael H. Nelson (ed.), *Thailand's New Politics: KPI Yearbook 2001* (Bangkok, White Lotus, 2002), 395.

4. Pasuk and Baker, Thaksin, 174–75.

5. Sombat, "The 1997 constitution," 108.

6. *Thailand: Grave Developments: Killings and Other Abuses* (London: Amnesty International [AI], ASA 39/008/03, November 2003), 2.

7. *Thailand 2004 Annual Report* (Paris: Reporters without Borders [RSF]), http://www.rsf.org. According to Matichon (25 May 2004), relatives of TRT secretary-general Suriya Jungrungruangkit hold 19.97 percent of the Nation Group's shares.

8. On problematizing received concepts of media ownership in the Thai case, see Duncan McCargo, *Media and Politics in Pacific Asia* (London: Routledge, 2003), 7–11.

9. The original article appeared in *Thai Post*, 16 July 2003. For details of the case, see the Web site of Forum Asia (http://www.forumasia.org) and also *The Nation*, 6 September 2004.

10. *Thailand Guide* (London: Prisoners Abroad, n.d.), 36–39, http://www.prisonersabroad.org.uk..

11. *Thailand: Widespread abuses in the administration of justice* (London: AI, ASA 39/003/2002, 2002), 1.

12. *Thailand: Grave Developments* (AI), 15–17.

13. For details on the first of these, see "PM condemns 'mafia,'" *The Nation*, 28 January 2003; "Heavies received Bt20m," *The Nation*, 29 January 2003.

14. Shawn W. Crispin and Jeremy Wagstaff, "The terror war's next offensive," *Far Eastern Economic Review*, 28 August 2003.

15. "Not enough graves: The War on Drugs, HIV/AIDS, and Violations of Human Rights," (New York: Human Rights Watch [HRW]), 16, 8 [C], 1.

16. "Not enough graves" (HRW), 7–19.

17. *The Nation*, 6 December 2003.

18. "Not enough graves," *HRW*, 1–3.

19. "Amnesty's concerns about Thai probe," *Far Eastern Economic Review*, 2 October 2003.

20. "Disappearance of a human rights defender and disappearance of justice in Thailand" (Hong Kong: Asian Human Rights Commission [AHRC], 18 June 2004), http://www.ahrchk.net. Exact numbers of politically related deaths are difficult to establish, as Thailand has a high murder rate, and some of the killings may have been the outcome of "ordinary" business or personal conflicts.

21. Pasuk and Baker, *Thaksin*, 236.

22 "Submission to UN Sub-Commission on the Promotion and Protection of Human Rights" (Bangkok: Asian Forum for Human Rights and Development [AFHRD], August 2004), http://www.forumasia.org.

23 "Disappearance" (AHRC).

24 "Submission to UN" (AFHRD).

25 Pallop Pinmanee, *Phom phit ru? thi yut Krue Se!* [Was I wrong to storm Krue Se?] (Bangkok: Good Morning Publishing, 2004). The book is completely unapologetic, arguing that any military in the world would have responded similarly. Pallop explains how he ordered 12 commandos to throw 8 hand grenades into the mosque before opening fire through the windows (39–41).

26 *Prachachat Thurakit*, 27 September 2004.

27 *Monitoring the Pulse of the Nation: Indicators of Good Governance and Development in Thailand* (Nonthaburi: King Prajadhipok's Institute [KPI], 2003), 100–03.

28 *Thailand: Grave Developments* [AI], 11.

29 *Thailand: Grave developments* (AI), 23.

30 "Battle over: citizenship restored to Vietnamese descendants," *The Nation*, 4 August 2004.

31 Pinkaew Laungaramsri, "Constructing marginality: The 'hill tribe' Karen and their shifting locations within Thai state and public perspectives," in Claudio Delang (ed.), *Living at the Edge of Thai Society: The Karen in the highlands of Northern Thailand* (London: RoutledgeCurzon, 2003), 31. Pinkaew points out that the term "hill tribe" is pejorative and inaccurate with respect to the Karen.

32 Duncan McCargo, "Buddhism, democracy and identity in Thailand," *Democratization* 11, 4 (2004): 164–67.

33 "Buddhist reform is long overdue," editorial, *The Nation*, 20 July 2004; "Thaksin to monastic plan critics: Pipe down," *The Nation*, 22 July 2004.

34 Protesters' camps were destroyed under suspicious circumstances. *Thailand: Grave developments* (AI), 18–19.

35 Pasuk Phongpaichit, Nualnoi Treerat, Yongyuth Chaiyapong, and Chris Baker, *Corruption in the Public Sector in Thailand: Perceptions and Experience of Households* (Bangkok: Chulalongkorn University, Political Economy Centre, 2000), 58–59.

36 Siriporn Chanjindamanee, "White collar crime: Ten years on, not one conviction," *The Nation*, 12 December 2002.

37 "Insufficient, contradictory evidence clears Duang," *The Nation*, 27 March 2004; "Twenty Pub murder: Wife lodges appeal over Duang ruling," *The Nation*, 26 May 2004; "Prosecutors say no to Duang appeal," *The Nation*, 6 July 2004.

38 *Thailand* (Prisoners Abroad), 26.

39 Shawn W. Crispin, "Courts under the spotlight," *Far Eastern Economic Review*, 4 September 2003.

40 "Top judge exposes appointments scam," *The Nation*, 5 April 2002.

41 *Thailand* (Prisoners Abroad), 20.

42 For detailed discussion see James R. Klein, "The battle for the rule of law in Thailand: the role of the Constitutional Court," in Amara Raksataya and James R. Klein, *The Constitutional Court of Thailand: The Provisions and Workings of the Court* (Bangkok: Constitution for the People Society, 2003), 76–78.

[43] "Retiring president warns court's impartiality at risk," *The Nation*, 4 October 2002.

[44] Duncan McCargo and Ukrist Pathmanand, *The Thaksinization of Thailand* (Copenhagen: NIAS Press, 2004), 121–57.

[45] Philip Hirsch, *Political Economy of the Environment in Thailand* (Manila: Journal of Contemporary Asia, 1993), 60–61.

[46] "Thailand risk: legal and regulatory risk country briefing," Economist Intelligence Unit *RiskWire*, 7 October 2004.

[47] Vitit Muntarbhorn and Charles Taylor, *Roads to Democracy: Human Rights and Democratic Development in Thailand* (Bangkok and Montreal: International Centre for Human Rights and Democratic Development, 1994), 37.

[48] Somchai Phatarathaananunth, *Civil Society in Northeast Thailand: The Struggle of the Small Scale Farmers' Assembly of Isan* (Leeds: University of Leeds, unpublished PhD thesis, 2001), 85–86.

[49] Klein, "The battle," 93.

[50] "Corruption Perceptions Index" (Berlin: Transparency International, 2004).

[51] Pasuk and Baker, *Thaksin,* 175.

[52] See, for example, "Exam test scandal—Adisai distorted report: Sumet," *The Nation,* 5 June 2004.

[53] "Thailand Tax Regulations Country Briefing," Economist Intelligence Unit *ViewsWire*, 10 February 2004.

[54] "Senate votes to seek Jaruvan's replacement," *Bangkok Post,* 2 November 2004.

[55] See *The Nation,* 17 March 2004, and 1 July 2004.

[56] "Defamation Case: Prasong Wins," *The Nation,* 3 December 2004.

[57] Jane Perlez, *New York Times,* "Thai Activist is sued by Thaksin, and can't wait for court," *Cambodia Daily,* 9 July 2004.

# TUNISIA

CAPITAL: Tunis
POPULATION: 10 million
GNI PER CAPITA: $1,990

**SCORES**
ACCOUNTABILITY AND PUBLIC VOICE: 1.65
CIVIL LIBERTIES: 3.08
RULE OF LAW: 2.79
ANTICORRUPTION AND TRANSPARENCY: 3.53
(scores are based on a scale of 0 to 7, with
0 representing weakest and 7 representing
strongest performance)

*Michele Angrist*

## INTRODUCTION

Tunisia is an ethnically and religiously homogeneous nation with a strong tradition of political identity and unity. In the past half century, its leaders have pursued a modernizing, Westernizing political trajectory that has firmly entrenched civilian rule and substantially improved the status of women. More recently, Tunisia has abandoned statist economic policies for liberal ones, generating a substantial private capitalist sector as a result. Today it boasts a low poverty rate, a large middle class, and high education and literacy rates for the developing world. Yet despite these trends, which should bode well for the establishment of pluralism, since independence in 1956 Tunisia has been ruled by a hegemonic political party, currently known as the RCD (Rassemblement Constitutionelle Démocratique). Indeed, Tunisia's is one of the world's oldest authoritarian one-party regimes, one that impinges greatly on citizens' political and civil rights.

---

**Michele Angrist** is assistant professor of political science at Union College. Her research and publications focus on questions of political development and democratization in the Middle East and the Third World.

President Zine el Abidine Ben Ali and the executive branch control the public sphere in Tunisia. A weak legislature does little more than rubber-stamp legislation despite the presence of token opposition party members within its ranks. Elections are multiparty but not competitive due to fraud and because the regime bans truly popular and thus politically threatening political parties—most notably the Islamist en-Nahda. It also tightly constrains the activities of civic and religious groups as well as the media, which are moribund. The executive branch uses the security services under its command to ensure that expression of political voice and dissent in the public sphere is minimal. That which is forthcoming emanates from only the most courageous activists, who suffer serious retribution from the state for their actions. The judicial branch of government is arguably as weak as the legislative. The executive controls judges' careers, interferes in their courtrooms, and often dictates their verdicts. The accused generally do not enjoy fair trials, nor do they have substantial recourse in the likely event that their rights are violated by the state. Impunity also reigns regarding the practice of state terror: Political detainees are routinely tortured, prison conditions are inhumane, and very rarely are state agents held accountable for these circumstances.

The state performs better outside the realm of politics. To a large extent the civil service is competent, well remunerated, and free of corruption. This has facilitated the achievement of the long-held state goal of economic development, pursued in recent years through liberalization, privatization, and deregulation. The state has made substantial progress here. Property rights are relatively secure. While burdensome bureaucratic controls on business and lingering illiberal trade practices remain, the state is no longer excessively involved in the economy and has created increasing prosperity that is comparatively widespread. Procedures for holding public officials accountable for wrongdoing arguably function better when the accusations concern financial and other more mundane abuses than when human rights abuses are alleged; still, these procedures could be strengthened, and they do not hold those at the commanding heights of the government accountable. The government administers effective poverty relief programs and is forthcoming vis-à-vis people with disabilities. Finally, though more needs to be done to further their cause, women enjoy important legal and socioeconomic rights in Tunisia.

## ACCOUNTABILITY AND PUBLIC VOICE – 1.65

In Tunisian politics, the leader of the RCD occupies the presidency and uses the power of the executive branch and the party's political supremacy to dominate all aspects of public life. Party structures parallel the state's administrative apparatus, and the president dominates both through broad powers of appointment.[1] In May 2002 President Ben Ali abolished term limits on the presidency (which he himself had established after taking office in 1987) and raised the age limit for presidential candidates. He may now remain in office until at least 2014.

The authority of the government is minimally based upon the people's will. Elections are held every five years under universal and equal suffrage. The October 1999 presidential elections were the first to see more than one candidate compete. However, Ben Ali hand-picked his opponents by passing a constitutional amendment that limited potential presidential candidates to individuals who for five consecutive years had headed a legal opposition party with at least one seat in parliament. Two men met these conditions. The incumbent officially received 99.4 percent of votes cast, while his challengers received 0.3 percent and 0.2 percent respectively. There is no secret ballot. Candidate ballots are differentiated by color, and voters must return unused ballots to election officials. No independent observers were reported to have monitored the 1999 elections. Ballots are counted in secret, and the final tallies released by the interior ministry are regularly characterized by critics of the regime as inflated.

[*Editor's note:* Tunisia held presidential and parliamentary elections on October 24, 2004. President Ben Ali retained the presidency with 94 percent of the vote, while his three challengers each garnered between 1 percent and 4 percent of the vote. The RCD won every parliamentary seat save those reserved for the legal opposition parties. Of the latter, two of seven boycotted the election; the remaining five acquired 37 of 189 seats. The only independent observers who monitored the election were 10 Arab League representatives; domestic human rights groups' requests to do so were denied. Critics of the regime accused it of falsifying the results.]

Majoritarian electoral rules designed to overrepresent large parties help the RCD monopolize the legislature. The regime sets aside approximately 20 percent of parliamentary seats for the opposition (34 of 182 seats in the 1999 elections), to be distributed in proportion to parties' relative national vote-getting success. The seven legal opposition parties are token and weak, while truly popular opposition bodies (most notably the Islamist en-Nahda party) remain illegal. The legal opposition parties have scant financial resources, a significant portion of which come from government subsidies. Their newspapers thus are not critical of the incumbent. During campaign periods the opposition is allotted tiny amounts of radio and television airtime relative to the media attention the ruling party commands. A 2003 law put opposition parties at a further disadvantage by prohibiting privately owned domestic or foreign broadcast media from taking a position on electoral candidates. Government repression and intimidation also dissuade citizens from supporting even the legal opposition organizations.

The executive branch dwarfs the legislature. Cabinet members are appointed by and responsible to the president, not parliament. The legislature is in session just six months a year; when it is not, the president may rule by decree. Members of parliament have neither office space nor professional staffs. While they may in theory draft legislation, presidential initiatives have priority. The executive can count on the legislature to ratify laws because 80 percent of its seats are held by ruling-party representatives. While on paper the legislature has the right to vote down legislation proposed by the president and exercise no-confidence votes against his cabinet, it never does either. Members of parliament can question ministers and raise concerns about bills during parliamentary sessions, where policy debates can be vigorous. Still, the legislature cannot alter legislation in substantial ways.[2]

The government must consult the Economic and Social Council (ESC) on laws affecting social and economic affairs. The ESC has 100+ members, including representatives of unions, public enterprises, civic groups, local government, the RCD, and the legal opposition parties, as well as independents and intellectuals. ESC debates are lively, but its recommendations are submitted only to the president and parliament and are not made public. At the end of the day, the opinions of the ESC seem to be heard but not heeded; it is not thought to be an influential actor in the legislative process.[3]

There is no judicial review of legislation.[4] In 1987 Ben Ali decreed the creation of a Constitutional Council to evaluate the constitutionality of proposed legislation, but lawmakers' decision to submit a bill to the council was optional. In 1990 it became mandatory that all constitutional amendments and laws affecting rights and liberties be vetted by the council. A 1998 constitutional amendment made the council's decisions binding on all branches of government. However, as council members are appointed by and beholden to the president, they do not constitute an effective check on governmental action.

Rural elites and the urban bourgeoisie comprise the regime's social anchors. These groups have benefited from the privatization of both industrial and agricultural capital that has taken place in recent years.[5] However, they are not the sole beneficiaries of state policies. While many have observed that Ben Ali only places into top offices bureaucrats who faithfully carry out his vision and support his presidency,[6] Tunisia is generally acknowledged to have a capable bureaucracy, in part because civil servants are hired based on their performance on a competitive exam. Development policies have generated impressive growth rates and increasing prosperity that is widespread (70 percent to 80 percent of Tunisians own their own homes, for example), and the state is quite attentive to the needs of poor and marginalized populations. The state is also rather admirably engaged in women's issues. The Ben Ali regime has allowed multiple women's organizations to form, established a new ministerial post for women's and family affairs and a new party secretary for women's affairs, and created a women's research center.[7] Currently, 43 of 189 parliamentary seats are held by women. The state prioritizes people with disabilities in the distribution of public services and makes provisions for their care, training, and integration into society. The state facilitates handicapped access to sidewalks and public buildings.

While the state does not cater exclusively to its main constituencies, the state system leads to domination by the specific interests of the ruling party as well as the economic elites that support it by refraining from (and ensuring that those they influence refrain from) challenging the regime. They have, in effect, traded the right to prosper for institutionalized political and civil rights. Rich elites do not fund parties in search of post-election policy favors because the victor in elections is never in doubt and because the ruling party's control over state coffers means it does not need their contributions to function. Individual-to-individual lobbying is a more effective and commonly used mechanism for the pursuit of government favors by private elites.[8] Meanwhile, the law that governs state subsidies for the opposition parties requires the latter to submit to the state's account court itemized listings of the sources and amounts of private financial contributions to party activities. Knowing their donations are not anonymous, private actors shy away from financing the opposition for fear of state retribution.[9] All nongovernmental organizations (NGOs) that receive state subsidies must reveal this information as well, bringing the same prospect of state pressure down upon these actors.

There is little opportunity for civic groups to function freely in the public arena and weigh in on policy matters. The state routinely imprisons its critics. Journalists, human rights activists, and opposition politicians are the main victims of this practice, and their family members also often suffer from physical and bureaucratic harassment at the hands of the state. Ordinary citizens know not to speak their mind about politics in public. The regime also carefully regulates NGOs and creates obstacles to their free functioning. Associations must have interior ministry permission to function legally and can be shut down if they offend the authorities. The Law of Associations stipulates that persons found guilty of participating in an illegal organization can be imprisoned and fined. The Tunisian Human Rights League has been closed down on more than one occasion and had portions of its funding blocked by the regime. The regime refuses to grant legal status to several other rights organizations.[10]

Press freedoms are similarly constrained. In 1998, 1999, 2000, and 2001 the Committee to Protect Journalists (CPJ) named Ben Ali to its list of the "10 Worst Enemies of the Press" (2001 was the last year it produced such a list). In 2004 Reporters without Borders' press freedom index ranked Tunisia 152nd out of 167 countries.[11] Until recently, the government monopolized radio and television broadcasting and thus directly controlled content on those media. The country's first privately owned radio station began operations in November 2003; it is run by a former journalist close to the regime, however, and airs mostly music. The government encourages Internet usage but routinely blocks Web sites critical of it. While those of Amnesty International (AI) and many French papers can be accessed, many other sites cannot.[12] The government carefully controls Internet service providers in Tunisia, regulates and monitors Internet cafés, and monitors subscribers' e-mail accounts. Those convicted of creating or surfing banned Web sites receive long jail sentences.

Newspapers are privately owned, although they are licensed by the government. Tunisia's press code affirms the freedom of the press but holds that journalists may not commit defamation or libel or disturb the public order. Because these crimes are not clearly defined in the legislation, their interpretation is the prerogative of the interior ministry, which tends to equate them with criticism of state policies.[13] Journalists who transgress may be fined, suspended from the profession, and/or imprisoned; publications found to be in breach of the law may be fined, confiscated, and/or banned. Critical journalists routinely experience substantial extralegal state punishments, including the denial of accreditation, police surveillance, physical assaults, restriction of freedom of movement, and torture during imprisonment. In May 2000 journalist Riad Ben Fadhel suffered multiple gunshot wounds after he published an article critical of the government in a foreign newspaper; there is no evidence that the government conducted a serious investigation into the attack. Thus, many journalists have resorted to intensive self-censorship.

Other less draconian measures help control content as well. One-half of newspapers' correspondents must be graduates of the government-run Institute of Journalism. The regime limits the information sources newspapers can draw on to the Tunisian wire service and government press conferences. A copy of all printed materials must be presented to the interior ministry and a receipt obtained before they can be legally distributed (the *depot legal* process); these receipts are withheld from troublemaking publications. The depot legal requirement extends to all printed matter, and while there is no specific policy, creative works that are explicitly political and critical of the regime are likely to be suppressed. The government also blocks crucial advertising business from publications that displease it. Foreign publications containing content critical of the government do not reach the newsstand.

## Recommendations

- The Rassemblement Constitutionelle Démocratique's organization should be separated from the state administration to ensure that public funds cannot be used to finance the operations of the party in power.
- The principle of the secret ballot should be ensured in elections, and independent international election monitors should be invited to oversee the balloting process.

- All nonviolent political parties that seek to operate in the political arena should be legalized.
- The government should act on its publicly stated commitment to a free press by rewriting the press code so that it cannot be used to prosecute critical journalists and by dispensing with both the licensing and *depot legal* processes for printed materials.
- The government should stop blocking what it considers sensitive Internet sites.

## CIVIL LIBERTIES – 3.08

The government's record on matters of state terror, unjustified imprisonment, and torture is not good.[14] In the early 1990s Islamic activists associated with en-Nahda were arbitrarily arrested by the hundreds. Mass arrests no longer occur, yet the arbitrary arrest and detention of peaceful opponents of the regime—while prohibited by law—is still routine.

Although laws protecting against the practice have improved, state agents routinely torture political prisoners. Prison conditions are inhumane in other respects as well, including prolonged solitary confinement, inability to communicate with others and pray freely, insufficient medical care, denial of the right to work and study, poor hygiene, and overcrowding. Political prisoners receive harsher treatment than ordinary criminals, but a majority of both endure poor prison conditions that fail to meet standards established in Tunisian law. New laws have increased prisoners' rights and provided for judicial inspection of prisons; however, the former are not always implemented and the latter does not include a requirement that prisons implement judicial recommendations. No domestic or international nongovernmental organizations have access to Tunisian prisons. Meanwhile, citizens have next to no redress in the face of state abuses. While a few violators of human rights have been punished, state agents as a rule are not held accountable for their actions.

The experience of some prisoners suggests that pretrial detention can be problematically lengthy, though this practice does not appear to be systematic. The outright killing of political opponents or other peaceful activists is rare. The primary ways in which public officials have been responsible for wrongful civilian deaths in recent years are through torture and medical neglect in custody. Abuse by private/non-state actors generally is not a concern in Tunisia.

Tunisia is among the most progressive Arab regimes when it comes to women's rights.[15] Women cannot be married against their will, and women can marry without the presence of a male guardian. Polygamy is forbidden. Women have many more divorce rights than those provided in Islamic law. Family planning is facilitated by the state. Abortion is legal. Girls attend primary school in almost equal percentages with boys. With few exceptions, women also have the right to work without discrimination regarding employment or pay, and anecdotal evidence suggests that this occurs in practice. Maternity leave laws protect women's jobs. Tunisian women have the right to vote, and the constitution explicitly defines all citizens as equal. There remains room for improvement, however. Women's rights and achievements lag behind men's in areas such as inheritance law, marriage to non-Muslims, nationalization matters, literacy, and contract and property disposition. In addition, patriarchal social mores mean that progressive laws are not always fairly applied by the judicial system. The constitution fails to ban sex-based discrimination, and the language of laws concerning women depicts them as inferior beings and emphasizes their maternal role—in so doing, implicitly denigrating their participation in the workforce.[16] Trafficking in women and children is not a significant problem in Tunisia. In 2003 the government introduced measures designed to criminalize elements of the practice.[17]

People with disabilities seem not to face significant obstacles in employment. Tunisian law bans discrimination against the disabled with respect to employment, education, and public services and requires that at least 1 percent of public- and private-sector positions be allotted to citizens with disabilities. The government has funded several NGO-run educational and vocational assistance programs for citizens with disabilities. The most egregious employment practice targets political prisoners who, upon release, are often prevented by the administration from pursuing their studies or returning to their careers.[18]

With a population that is 98 percent Arab and 98 percent Muslim, Tunisia has no large minorities to speak of and no politically significant ethnic or linguistic divides. Religious affairs can be more tendentious. The constitution states that all citizens possess the same rights and duties and that all are equal before the law. It further asserts that the state protects the free exercise of beliefs, with the caveat that this shall not disrupt public order. Christians appear to concern the regime the least. Tunisia welcomed a papal visit in 1996, and the Ben Ali government contributed funds for repairs of a cathedral in downtown Tunis. Tunisia's various Christian denominations function and worship freely although proselytizing is forbidden and groups have not been allowed to establish new churches. Also, converts to a faith other than Islam have had passport applications denied.

Jews are treated decently, although the government exerts more control over Jews than over Christians (probably due to the sensitivity of the Arab–Israeli conflict in the sentiments of Tunisia's Muslim majority). The physical security of the Jewish community, which is concentrated primarily on Djerba island, is overseen solicitously by the government—although a suicide bomber struck the historic Ghriba synagogue there in 2002. Reporting following the attack suggested that Jews felt basically comfortable, secure, and integrated into society.[19] The government allows Djerba's Jewish children to split their time between secular public schools and private Jewish religious schools, and it encourages Jewish expatriates to return for an annual pilgrimage to Ghriba. Still, the government pays the salary of the Jewish Grand Rabbi and subsidizes many synagogues, a fact that facilitates political control.

The government reserves its harshest controls for Islam, as the most potent threat to the Ben Ali regime emanates from the Islamist corner. Most Tunisians are Sunni Muslims and are severely constrained in terms of their freedom of belief. The government trains, appoints, and pays the salaries of all prayer leaders and other religious officials, who must toe the administration's line. Individuals showing signs of special religiosity (e.g., those who pray frequently, men wearing full beards, and women wearing headscarves) invite harassment from security personnel.[20] Political parties based on religion are not permitted; en-Nahda failed to receive recognition for this reason. Baha'is—whom the government perceives as a heretical sect of Islam—can worship only privately. Finally, reflecting the government's ongoing efforts to quash political Islam, in 2003 AI expressed concern that antiterrorism legislation being considered in parliament would become an additional tool with which the regime would restrict freedom of belief. [21]

The right of association is only selectively granted. Trade unions played a pivotal role in the Tunisian independence movement; as a result of this legacy, the constitution guarantees the right of unionization, and the state respects this right in practice. For other types of associations, the constitution guarantees the right of association within "conditions defined by the law." The government denies legal registration to political parties based on political orientation (e.g., the Communist Party). Several human and legal rights organizations have also been denied legal status. Moreover, the government places substantial obstacles in the way of civic, business, and political associations organizing, mobilizing, and advocating for peaceful purposes. The regime's repertory of control tactics includes subsidizing groups so as to undercut their political autonomy, infiltrating potentially threatening organizations with party loyalists in order to control them from within, and founding duplicate organizations that dilute their counterparts' influence.[22] Rights organizations experience particularly pernicious forms of government repression: Their funds have been blocked, their property damaged or taken, their activists harassed and imprisoned, and their meetings and elections disrupted. Organizations must obtain interior ministry permission to hold public meetings, rallies, or demonstrations. This requirement, combined with the regime's well-known aversion to public expressions of dissent, means that demonstrations and public protests are a rare occurrence. Press reports of the few protests that did occur in 2003 and 2004 suggest that police responses by and large avoided the excessive use of force.

The RCD bureaucracy appears to be politically neutral in its treatment of business people, thus refraining from pressure to join the ruling party.[23] At the same time, analysts commonly disclose anecdotal information that belonging to the ruling party can yield preferential treatment, for example, in terms of the allocation of bank loans, waivers on zoning restrictions, and scholarships and housing preferences for university students.[24]

*Recommendations*
- The government should ensure that all allegations of torture by state agents are fully investigated and vigorously prosecuted.
- Prison conditions should be brought in line with accepted international standards by ending solitary confinement, improving

hygiene, providing adequate medical care, and addressing over-crowding.

- The state tradition of progressiveness vis-à-vis women's affairs should be honored and carried forward by rewriting remaining statutes that discriminate against women, particularly with respect to inheritance law. Also, judges should be monitored to ensure that women enjoy full protection under and fair application of existing laws.

- Controls on and restrictions of citizens' freedom of belief should be lifted. Authorities should cease the harassment of citizens whose physical appearance (e.g., beards and headscarves) reflects their religiosity. Mosques and their staffs should function free of state constraints and oversight.

- All peaceful civic organizations should be granted legal recognition and the right to function autonomously.

## RULE OF LAW – 2.79

While the constitution holds that the judiciary is independent and subject only to the law of the land, in practice there is little independence, impartiality, or nondiscrimination in the administration of justice—and seemingly none where sensitive political and human rights cases are concerned. Executive pressures on judges are manifold. AI notes "a pattern of executive interference with the administration of justice,"[25] and there seem to be minimal adequate protections against the practice. Former senior magistrate Mokhtar Yahyaoui, who was fired from the bench in 2001 after publishing an open letter to President Ben Ali criticizing the lack of judicial independence in Tunisia, asserted that the government dictates verdicts to judges and intimidates and coerces them into pronouncing those verdicts (rather than their true legal convictions) in part by placing plainclothes informants in their courtrooms.[26] When positive inducements (e.g., an offer to make him ambassador to Lebanon) failed to convince Yahyaoui to abandon his public campaign, Yahyaoui's phone, e-mail, and mail communications were monitored and tampered with; his chambers were repeatedly ransacked; he has been physically assaulted and barred from leaving the country; and his family has been subject to extensive harassment.[27] Presumably, other judges have similarly been deterred from speaking out.

Judges must be university graduates and pass an exam to gain entry into the Magistrate High Institute (MHI), where they pursue a two-year course of study. However, this gateway to judgeship is state run and thus likely shapes judges' training in ways that suit the regime. The executive branch presides over judicial appointments, career paths, and dismissal through the High Council of the Judiciary. The president presides over the council and appoints the vast majority of its members; he also personally selects judges to fill top-ranking positions in the judicial system (such as the president of the appeals court). There is substantial evidence that executive management of judges' careers is not carried out in a fair and unbiased manner. The fate of Yahyaoui is only the most glaring case in point. In addition, lawyers who run afoul of the government are similarly placed under surveillance, harassed, and physically assaulted.

Given this environment, judicial decisions against the executive branch are rare. In the 1990s, courts ruled twice to protect the Tunisian Human Rights League against government interference. However, evidence suggests that such decisions, as well as the choice by the executive branch to heed them, are driven as much by sensitivity to international criticism and political expediency in general as they are by principle and respect for the rule of law.[28] No other such challenges to the executive have been reported.

Tunisia possesses an administrative tribunal to which private citizens and firms may appeal all executive and administrative decisions (save presidential decrees), including cases of abuse of power. However, when they encounter political pressures, not all tribunal judges faithfully defend the laws and annul improper decisions taken by public institutions. Political pressures on the tribunal undoubtedly bear down when human rights and other politically sensitive charges are being brought by citizens, and in these situations justice is rarely done.[29]

According to the constitution, Tunisians charged with a criminal offense are presumed innocent until proven guilty. However, this provision is not upheld.[30] Citizens as a rule do not enjoy fair trials. Detainees do not have a right to legal counsel prior to arraignment. For the post-arraignment phases of judicial proceedings, although the state provides free legal assistance to poor defendants, in sensitive political cases defendants often are not notified of their right to legal representation. The court process often is slow. Prosecutors often prevail in verdicts despite having produced insufficient evidence for conviction, while the rights of defense lawyers and their clients are severely curtailed: Confessions extracted under torture are admitted into evidence without investigation; defendants have been tried more than once for the same crime; the defense (particularly in political trials) may not even be able to address the court; and, often in "terrorism" cases, civilians are tried before military courts.[31]

Currently, civilian authorities are in firm control of the Tunisian police, military, and internal security services, which are fully free from the influence and direction of non-state actors. However, under Ben Ali, whose career was launched in the military and security forces, the security apparatus has quadrupled in size and become increasingly operationally capable.[32] This apparatus is more pivotal to Ben Ali's rule than it was to his predecessor, and it enjoys substantial prestige and privileges as a result. Some observers are concerned that the military or security forces could move against Tunisia's civilian leadership if they felt that their position was becoming undermined.[33] Civilian direction of the security apparatus is far from democratic. Here again the executive branch dominates. Plainclothes security agents play an intimidating role in courtrooms, and the security services are intimately involved in a regime-directed process of repressing political dissidents through the practices of surveillance, harassment, and torture. Save for the most courageous of individuals, Tunisians as a whole have been forced into complete silence in the public sphere by the actions and ubiquitous presence of the security forces.

Article 14 of the constitution confers the right to own property "exercised within the limits established by the law." In its 2004–2005 Global Competitiveness Report, the World Economic Forum gave Tunisia a fairly strong score of 5.14 (on a scale of 1/worst to 7/optimal) for the performance of its public institutions; local business executives' opinions on whether "[p]roperty rights, including over financial assets, are clearly defined and well protected by law" represented one-eighth of the total weight of the score.[34] Citizens have no substantial concerns about property rights, with the important caveat that those who incur the political wrath of the regime have been retaliated against in this domain. Citizens judged to be politically threatening allegedly "run the risk of . . . abusive tax reprisals if they are industrialists, artisans, merchants, or members of the professions."[35] In addition, the government deprived thousands of Islamists of their identification cards in the early

1990s, which effectively blocked them from making major financial transactions such as purchasing a car or signing for a loan.

### Recommendations

- Separation of powers should be augmented by removing the executive branch from the processes that govern the appointment, promotion, and dismissal of judges.
- Judges should be unconstrained in their ability to render verdicts consistent with the law.
- Citizens' guarantees to a fair trial—including counsel in all cases, an impartial civilian tribunal, and protection against torture—should be upheld.
- The activities of the security services should be redirected exclusively to defense against external attack and violent domestic groups.

## ANTICORRUPTION AND TRANSPARENCY – 3.53

Since the 1980s, Tunisia has been engaged in economic liberalization—deregulating, privatizing, and encouraging foreign investment. As it has made considerable progress, the Heritage Foundation's 2004 Index of Economic Freedom assigned Tunisia a score of 2.5 on the question of government intervention in the economy on a scale of 1 to 5 where 5 is most repressed. The Heritage Foundation assigned Tunisia a 3.0 on the issue of regulation, noting the bureaucracy's slowness and lack of transparency. The bureaucracy has a long tradition of seeking to license and monitor all aspects of business affairs; it confronts entrepreneurs with substantial controls and paperwork requirements. At the same time, Tunisia's civil service is characterized by "decent remuneration, secure employment . . . specialized training . . . esprit de corps and security of tenure."[36]

In this environment, corruption is a problem at both the highest and lowest levels of government, but not in its main ranks. In the World Economic Forum's Global Competitiveness Report, one-half of Tunisia's score of 5.14 was determined by indigenous business executives' answers to questions regarding the pervasiveness of bribery.[37] In Transparency International's 2004 Corruption Perceptions Index, Tunisia received a score of 5.0 on a scale of 1 to 10, with 10 being "clean."[38] Industrialists report that businesses do not have to pay bribes in order to succeed and that what corruption exists is petty, taking place at the lowest levels of the bureaucracy.[39] In contrast, many would add that President Ben Ali appears to be using his office illegally to benefit his extended family financially. As University of Exeter Lecturer Larbi Sadiki has pointed out, "Bin Ali's in-laws all have been linked to corrupt activities, including the illegal appropriation of prime real estate, and acquisitions of formerly State-owned companies at substantially depreciated prices."[40]

Reports of nepotism surrounding the presidency suggest that the state does not adequately ensure transparency, open bidding, and effective competition in the awarding of government contracts. Furthermore, in June 2004 opposition party leader and former presidential candidate Abderrahmane Tlili was found guilty on several charges of abuse of power while at the helm of Tunisia's Civil Aviation and Airports Bureau. One charge was that he awarded contracts to cronies, and his defense lawyers pointed out that, as the head of a public company, Tlili would have required "the direct approval" of government officials in order to carry this out.[41]

The Tunisian state has long adhered to a developmentalist ethos, and the priority it currently places on generating strong economic growth through liberalization means that the state has a core interest in ensuring that public institutions support that objective. Thus, while state agents may commit human rights abuses essentially with impunity, the same cannot be said for more quotidian financial and other nonpolitically sensitive abuses and acts of corruption. Financial disclosure regulations are in place to prevent conflicts of interest among public officials. The Cour des Comptes (Audit Office) is charged with verifying the correctness of all public sector actors' books, and the IMF reports that this institution generally produces high-quality work.[42] The Disciplinary Financial Court is in charge of sanctioning when financial laws and regulations are violated by public authorities.[43] The World Bank reports that this court renders on average 20 condemnations annually; these are made public and punished, typically with fines.[44] Given that corruption is not a major problem in the main ranks of the bureaucracy, these processes appear to have some substantial effect.

Less encouraging is the fact that the Cour des Comptes is not independent of the executive branch.[45] The executive can interfere with this body's functioning, a practice that probably occurs in order to deter scrutiny of the corruption that allegedly takes place at the very top of the party-state system. Allegations and findings of corrupt behavior are not widely aired in the news media, given the cowed and docile nature of the press and the regime's determination to cultivate a public image of Tunisia as an investment-friendly state. Finally, investigation and punishment of wrongdoing sometimes have political motivation. Tlili's long career in the public sector and his status as leader of an opposition party suggest that the case brought against him, albeit legal, is punishment for having crossed a red line vis-à-vis the regime.

The budget is carefully developed in the executive branch. Tunisia's rubber-stamp parliament then examines and discusses it extensively. Genuine debates about the budget, as with all other legislation, occur in secret during parliamentary committee sessions that are closed to journalists, and whose proceedings are not made public.[46] Moreover, even in these sessions parliament has done little more than review;[47] it cannot substantially alter the proposed budget's provisions. Information regarding politically sensitive matters, such as human rights, is not made publicly available. For example, the findings of a committee created in December 2002 to investigate prison conditions were not publicized. There is only limited provision of budgetary and audit information to the public.[48] The government does a better job when it comes to information regarding more mundane issues and public services. Many ministries post information on accessible Web sites, for instance.[49] There is no freedom-of-information legislation.

Corruption and graft in the higher education system are not pervasive. The large plainclothes security presence on campuses deters questionable actions such as the bribing of faculty for good grades. Instead, association with the ruling party is more likely to make a difference vis-à-vis gaining admission to preferred universities.

No information indicates that the state places obstacles in the way of the legal administration and distribution of foreign assistance. It does not, however, tolerate foreign assistance targeted at human rights organizations, political parties, or other nodes of civil society perceived as threatening to the regime.

## Recommendations

- Bureaucratic controls over businesses and other private initiatives should be streamlined, and guidelines detailing all requisite procedures made publicly available.

- The independence of the Cour des Comptes from the executive branch should be guaranteed by law and respected in practice.
- Parliamentary deliberations over the budget should be opened to the public and to the press.
- The state should make a much more comprehensive array of information and statistics from its key departments and agencies publicly available, via Web sites and other mediums.

## NOTES

[1] Susan E. Waltz, *Human Rights and Reform: Changing the Face of North African Politics* (Berkeley and Los Angeles: University of California Press, 1995), 60.

[2] Michele Penner Angrist, "Parties, Parliament and Political Dissent in Tunisia," *Journal of North African Studies* 4, 4 (Winter 1999): 89–104, 98.

[3] Ibid., 100.

[4] Yath Ben Achour, "Tunisia," in Herbert M. Kritzer, ed., *Legal Systems of the World: A Political, Social, and Cultural Encyclopedia* (Santa Barbara: ABC-CLIO, 2002), 1651–1657, 1654.

[5] Stephen J. King, *Liberalization Against Democracy: The Local Politics of Economic Reform in Tunisia* (Bloomington: Indiana University Press, 2003).

[6] "Tunisia 2004: Manifesto of Progressive Tunisian Democrats," issued 20 March 2001, Journal of Democracy's Documents on Democracy, 12, 3 (2001): 183–186, 184. See also Emma Murphy, "Ten Years On—Ben Ali's Tunisia," *Mediterranean Politics* 2, 3 (Winter 1997): 114–122, 119.

[7] Emma C. Murphy, "Women in Tunisia: Between State Feminism and Economic Reform," in Eleanor Abdella Doumato and Marsha Pripstein Posusney, eds., *Women and Globalization in the Middle East: Gender, Economy, and Society* (Boulder: Lynne Rienner, 2003), 169–194, 178–180.

[8] Eva Bellin, *Stalled Democracy: Capital, Labor, and the Paradox of State-Sponsored Development* (Ithaca: Cornell University Press, 2002), 56–57, 80.

[9] Angrist, 95.

[10] "Human Rights Lawyers and Associations Under Siege in Tunisia" (New York: Human Rights Watch, 17 March 2003), http://www.hrw.org/backgrounder/mena/tunisia 031703.htm.

[11] "Worldwide Press Freedom Index" (Paris: Reporters without Borders), http://www.rsf .org/article.php3?id_article=11715.

[12] Neil MacFarquhar, "Tunisia's Tangled Web Is Sticking Point for Reform," *New York Times*, 25 June 2004, A3.

[13] Larbi Sadiki, "Bin Ali's Tunisia: Democracy by Non-Democratic Means," *British Journal of Middle Eastern Studies* 29, 1 (2002): 57–78, 71.

[14] Unless otherwise noted, the data contained in the next three paragraphs were drawn from "Tunisia: The Cycle of Injustice" (New York: Amnesty International [AI], 10 June 2003), http://web.amnesty.org/library/print/ENGMDE300012003.

15 Unless otherwise noted, the material in the next two paragraphs is drawn from Laurie A. Brand, *Women, the State, and Political Liberalization: Middle Eastern and North African Experiences* (New York: Columbia University Press, 1998), 207–214.

16 Ibid., 209–210.

17 *Victims of Trafficking and Violence Protection Act of 2000: Trafficking in Persons Report* (Washington, DC: U.S. Dept. of State, June 2004).

18 "Tunisia: The Cycle of Injustice" (AI).

19 Associated Press, "5 Killed as Truck Crashes Into Tunisian Synagogue," *New York Times,* 12 April 2002, A4; Donald G. McNeil Jr., "Tunisian Jews at Blast Site: A Stalwart Remnant," *New York Times,* 15 April 2002, A3.

20 Jonathan G. Farley, "Tunisia: Forty Years on from Independence," *Contemporary Review* 270, 1574 (March 1997): 125–131, 127.

21 "Tunisia: New Draft 'Anti-Terrorism' Law Will Further Undermine Human Rights" (AI EU Office, 30 September 2003), http://web.amnesty.org/library/print/ENGMDE 300212003.

22 Eva Bellin, "Civil Society in Formation: Tunisia," in Augustus Richard Norton, ed., *Civil Society in the Middle East,* Vol. 1 (Leiden: E. J. Brill, 1995), 120–147, 139–141.

23 Bellin, 2002, 77.

24 See, for example, Sadiki, 68, and U.S. Dept. of State, 12.

25 "Tunisia: The Cycle of Injustice" (AI).

26 Judge Mukhtar Yahyaoui, "Open Letter to President Ben Ali, 6 July 2001" (New York and Washington, DC: Human Rights First), http://www.humanrightsfirst.org/middle_east/tunisia/hrd_tun_1.htm.

27 "Tunisian Judge Blows Whistle on Judicial Tampering" (Human Rights First), http://www.humanrightsfirst.org/middle_east/tunisia/hrd_tun_1.htm.

28 See discussion in Emma C. Murphy, *Economic and Political Change in Tunisia: From Bourguiba to Ben Ali* (New York: St. Martin's Press, 1999), 206.

29 "Tunisia: Breaking the Cycle of Injustice—Recommendations to the European Union" (AI), http://web.amnesty.org/library/print/ENGMDE300142003.

30 "Tunisia: The Cycle of Injustice" (AI).

31 Ibid.

32 "Behind the Beaches," *The Economist,* 13 January 1996, 40–41; Michel Camau and Vincent Geisser, *Le syndrome autoritaire: Politique en Tunisie De Bourguiba à Ben Ali* (Mayenne, France: Presses des Sciences Po, 2003), 203.

33 Christopher Alexander, "Back from the Democratic Brink: Authoritarianism and Civil Society in Tunisia," *Middle East Report* 205 (October–December 1997), 34–38.

34 "Global Competitiveness Report" (Geneva: World Economic Forum, 2004), http://www.weforum.org/site/homepublic.nsf/Content/Global+Competitiveness+Programme%5CGlobal+Competitiveness+Report.

35 "Tunisia 2004: Manifesto of Progressive Tunisian Democrats."

36 Bellin, 2002, 79.

37 "Global Competitiveness Report" (World Economic Forum), http://www.weforum.org/site/homepublic.nsf/Content/Global+Competitiveness+Programme%5CGlobal+Competitiveness+Report.

38 "Corruption Perceptions Index 2004" (Berlin: Transparency International), http://www
.transparency.org/cpi/2004/cpi2004.en.html.

39 Bellin, 2002, 77–78.

40 Sadiki, 69.

41 "Tunisian Opposition Leader Jailed for 9 Years for Abuse of Power," Agence France
Presse, 3 June 2004.

42 "Experimental IMF Report on Observance of Standards and Codes: Tunisia" (Washington, DC: International Monetary Fund [IMF]), http://www.imf.org/external/np/
rosc/tun/index.htm.

43 Ben Achour, 1655–1656.

44 "Republic of Tunisia Development Policy Review: Making Deeper Trade Integration
Work for Growth and Jobs" (Washington, DC: World Bank, Report No. 29847-TN,
October 2004), 63.

45 "Experimental IMF Report . . . Tunisia" (IMF), http//www.imf.org/external/np/rosc/tun/
index.htm.

46 Angrist, 98.

47 Waltz, 63–64.

48 "Republic of Tunisia Development Policy Review" (World Bank), 62–63.

49 "Experimental IMF Report . . . Tunisia" (IMF).

# TURKEY

CAPITAL: Ankara
POPULATION: 71.3 million
GNI PER CAPITA: $2,490

**SCORES**
ACCOUNTABILITY AND PUBLIC VOICE: 4.35
CIVIL LIBERTIES: 3.98
RULE OF LAW: 4.18
ANTICORRUPTION AND TRANSPARENCY: 3.43
(scores are based on a scale of 0 to 7, with
0 representing weakest and 7 representing
strongest performance)

*Sarah Repucci*[1]

## INTRODUCTION

The current Turkish government of Recep Tayyip Erdogan has pursued
a vigorous reform agenda in preparation for the December 2004 meeting of European Union (EU) leaders, at which the EU has promised to
consider whether Turkey can begin membership negotiations. Turkey
has passed a string of constitutional amendments and reform packages in
recent years, and the government has taken serious steps toward ensuring their implementation. Turkey hopes that a positive response in
December will help consolidate and expand reforms and improve business investment as well.

The modern Turkish republic was founded by Kemal Mustafa Ataturk
in 1923. Ataturk was a visionary who wanted to form a modern state.
He separated Islam from the state and banned such external signs of religion as the fez and the headscarf. He also created a Turkish identity and
a nationalism that had not existed under the Ottoman Empire. Although his party ruled uninterrupted for more than 25 years, an important legacy of his rule is the republican institutions that he helped put
in place.

---

**Sarah Repucci** is a researcher at Freedom House and an analyst of Turkey.

In 1980 Turkey experienced the most recent of three military coups that temporarily took power from the elected civilian government. The military-led government wrote a new constitution that Turkey's citizens approved in a 1982 referendum. This constitution strengthened the role of the military and restricted many fundamental freedoms. Soon afterward, fighting began in the southeast that ultimately developed into a 15-year guerrilla war between Turkish forces and Kurdish separatists.

A ceasefire was declared after the capture of separatist leader Abdullah Ocalan in 1999. In the same year, the EU accepted Turkey as an official candidate in response to its initial application in 1987. As a final turning point, Turkey's financial system collapsed in 2001 and the IMF stepped in to help with restructuring. These three events combined to spark a new era of rights and reforms in Turkey.

In November 2002 elections, the new Justice and Development Party (AKP) came to power. AKP had grown out of the remnants of the Welfare Party—an Islamic-oriented party that had been banned after it was pressured out of power by the military in a soft coup (the military did not subsequently assume power) in 1997—but AKP had publicly renounced any intentions to change Turkey's secular orientation, and many of their supporters voted for change, not religion. Because Erdogan, AKP's leader, had been banned from politics due to a prior conviction for reading an allegedly Islamic poem in public, he was not permitted to become a member of parliament. After AKP won a majority of parliamentary seats (a rare event in a country that has almost always been led by fragile coalitions), Abdullah Gul served as prime minister until the party used its majority to change the constitution and pave the way for Erdogan's leadership. Erdogan became prime minister in March 2003.

Despite the amendments, Turkey's constitution lacks the inclusiveness, the clearly defined rights, and the limitation on state power that are crucial for democracy in a multicultural society. The reforms thus far have been largely imposed from the outside, with little grassroots effort from Turkey itself. Turks have great faith in the state's ability to serve their best interests, and a culture of freedom and democracy has yet to be fully instilled throughout the population. Education reform is required to improve opportunities for the poor and develop the popular basis for the full consolidation of reforms. With time, Turkey will ultimately need to draft an up-to-date civil constitution as well.

## ACCOUNTABILITY AND PUBLIC VOICE – 4.35

Turkey is a parliamentary democracy. A president, elected by parliament (the Turkish Grand National Assembly, or TGNA), is head of state but is not formally involved in policymaking. The current president, Ahmet Necdet Sezer, was elected in 2000 for a non-renewable seven-year term. The TGNA is composed of 550 deputies elected by universal suffrage to five-year terms. The prime minister is technically chosen by the president, although in practice he/she is the leader of the party in power.

Turkish laws establish a framework for democratic elections generally in line with international standards, although with certain restrictions. In January 2003 new legal amendments loosened regulations on party names and candidates and narrowed the grounds for closure of a political party. However, a party can still be shut down if its program is not in agreement with the constitution, and this can be widely interpreted to include support for Kurdish insurgents and opposition to government pillars such as secularism and the military. Limits on campaign donations are not enforced, and party financing is not transparent.[2]

In addition, a so-called double barrier impedes entry to the TGNA: In order to win seats a party must be organized in at least half of the Turkish provinces and one-third of their districts, and it must also obtain at least 10 percent of the votes cast nationwide. The effect of this provision has been that many parties with considerable support are not represented in the TGNA, particularly if their base is regional.

The last TGNA elections, in November 2002, were widely judged both domestically and internationally as free and fair. A large number and variety of parties participated in active campaigning, the ruling parties lost, and opposition parties won seats in the TGNA, thus attesting to the ability of the electorate to precipitate change. Only two parties passed the 10-percent threshold—AKP and the Republican People's Party (CHP)—and AKP, which won significantly more seats than any other party, won just 35 percent of the total vote, a stark demonstration of the limitations of these election rules. As of September 2004 AKP holds an overwhelming 367 seats in the TGNA, while the CHP holds 172. The True Path Party also has four seats after as many parliamentarians resigned from their former party affiliations. The remaining seats are held by independents.

One of the most prominent restrictions imposed during the 2002 election campaign was Erdogan's own inability to run. Turkey's Supreme Electoral Board had banned Erdogan's candidacy under a constitutional provision prohibiting convicted criminals from running for public office. The ban was generally believed to have been an attempt to inhibit the momentum of AKP, of which the Turkish establishment disapproved due to AKP's roots in the religious, previously banned, Welfare and Virtue parties. After AKP established its resounding TGNA majority it voted to amend the constitution, thus paving the way for Erdogan's leadership. Significantly, the military did not intervene despite its own reservations about the election of AKP.

The old guard saw a sharp drop in support in 2002 amid widespread public discontent with official corruption and inept handling of the economy (manifested in particular by the 2001 financial crisis), and its parties have not yet recovered. In local elections in March 2004, AKP won a commanding victory across the country. Instead of from a traditional opposition, most parliamentary challenges to government policies come from inside AKP itself.

The extent to which AKP has abandoned its former Islamist aspirations is unclear. Although the party has supported some loosening of restrictions on religious activity, such as the bans on headscarves and on the admission of students from religious schools to secular universities (see "Civil Liberties"), it has not made any serious attempt to undermine Turkey's secular underpinnings. The AKP government has thus far been defined by its push for reform with the goal of EU entry, not an underlying Islamic agenda. However, concerns remain about what AKP might support in the future.

Although no parliamentary system has complete separation of powers, legislative oversight of Turkey's executive branch is especially weak. Very little legislation actually originates in the TGNA; instead, it is drafted by the government for review by parliamentarians. The party leader wields great power, and most decisions are made by the prime minister and a small group of advisers. Civil servants in Turkey are officially hired on the basis of examinations, but patronage undeniably plays a large role in practice.[3]

The Turkish establishment traditionally mistrusted civic groups and controlled them tightly. However, as these groups have gained strength since the 1980s and state-societal relations have developed more recently through encouragement by the EU, civic groups have become more engaged in public policy. EU harmonization reforms in 2002 and 2003 have eased restrictions on the establishment of associations, and a draft Law on Associations, pending as of September 2004, would go even further. Still, the government is selective about which groups gain full disclosure of draft laws, and many groups accuse it of listening but not taking responsive action.[4] Limitations on so-called partnerships with foreign groups will remain in place, and the vagueness of the term "partnerships" could allow the government to require permission for a wide range of activities involving groups abroad.[5]

While Turkey's constitution establishes freedom of the media (Articles 28–31) and EU harmonization reforms have included many measures to reduce political pressure on the media, including a new Press Law in 2004, in practice major impediments remain. The media are mostly privately owned. They, and journalists specifically, have been the victims of the penal code's provisions against aiding and abetting an illegal organization and insulting the state and state institutions, among others, despite recent reforms limiting their scope. Fines, arrests, and imprisonment are the punishments regularly allotted to media and journalists who, for example, criticize the military or portray Kurdish activists in too positive a light. In one instance, the pro-Kurdish newspaper *Yeniden Ozgur Gundem* was forced to close in February 2004 due to fines amounting to hundreds of thousands of dollars.[6] Further changes were made in the 2004 penal code reform, but their effect remains to be seen. Moreover, Turkey's Supreme Council of Radio and Television (RTUK) has the authority to sanction broadcasters if they are not in compliance with the law or its expansive 23 broadcasting principles. Thus, a local television station was shut down for a month in April 2004 after broadcasting songs in Kurdish, a language that has traditionally been banned in public. Cultural expression is also limited by similar effects of these laws, although the number of banned books, journals, and newspapers decreased in the first half of 2004.[7]

Censorship is not explicit, but censorship and self-censorship occur at the levels of both editors and journalists, who are concerned about violating the many restrictions.[8] Furthermore, media organizations are nearly all owned by giant holding companies with interests in many sectors beyond media, and they therefore influence news to serve their own business interests, in addition to allegedly trading positive coverage for political favors. As the strength of these media groups continues to grow unchecked, they could become a bigger obstacle to press freedom than the state.[9] The quality of the Turkish media is low.

Some very positive steps have been taken to expand media freedom. As part of the ninth EU adjustment package, passed in June 2004, a member of the military will no longer be part of the RTUK. The government has issued statements instructing the RTUK to implement the new regulations. More significantly, new laws were instituted allowing broadcasts for the first time in minority languages, including Kurdish. The legalization of these broadcasts was a major step for Kurdish rights (see "Civil Liberties") and freedom of expression. After considerable delay (the initial law was passed in August 2002), the first broadcast in Bosnian took place on June 7, 2004, followed two days later by the first broadcast in the most widely spoken Kurdish dialect. The broadcasts have been criticized for being too short and being limited to the national station, and liberalization still has a long way to go.[10] However, the significance of the changes cannot be overstated. Further opening of the media policy will enable Turkey to provide full freedom of expression to its people.

*Recommendations*
- To allow more political pluralism in the TGNA, the 10-percent threshold should be reduced, perhaps to 5 percent.
- The grounds for sanctions of political parties should be restricted to only those expressions that provoke violence, and dissolution of political parties should be a last resort.
- The RTUK should be restructured to include members chosen by civil society in addition to those chosen by the government, and its authority should be limited from the current broadcasting principles.
- Press offenses should not be punishable by imprisonment, and the context of offending statements rather than just their content should be considered when sentencing takes place.

## CIVIL LIBERTIES – 3.98

Many of the EU harmonization reforms that Turkey has passed since 2001 have been specifically geared toward protection of civil liberties, including increased minority and women's rights, broadened freedom of association and religion, stronger measures to protect against and prosecute torture, and a more democratic penal code. Turkey signed a European convention protocol abolishing the death penalty in January 2004 and made relevant legal changes over the summer. Moreover, the government is watching implementation closely. It has set up rights-monitoring boards such as a Reform Monitoring Group, created in September 2003, and thousands of police, judges, and public prosecutors have participated in human rights training. In June 2004 the Council of Europe decided to end its monitoring of Turkey due to the country's progress in human rights. Nevertheless, problems remain, particularly (although not entirely) with implementation.

Torture and ill-treatment by officials continue to be an issue in Turkey. The Erdogan government has declared a zero-tolerance policy toward torture, and it appears to be backing up its position with new detention laws and, as of April 2004, a policy forbidding police from entering the room when doctors examine alleged torture victims. Recent legal amendments have limited the initial custody period after arrest to 24 hours, a measure widely believed to reduce opportunities for torture. A Council of Europe Committee for the Prevention of Torture investigation found that this period was respected in practice, and proper procedures were followed when an extension was necessary.[11] The cumulative result of these policies has been a marked decline in torture cases in the past couple of years.[12]

Turkey now needs to implement safeguards and legal amendments to ensure prosecution in accordance with the law. Human rights groups continue to cite instances of torture (the Human Rights Association of Ankara cited 692 cases in the first half of 2004), trials are excessively long and often drag on beyond the statute of limitations, and official immunity continues to pervade the system.[13] In one case in spring 2004, a 12-year-old girl reported receiving threats after she lodged a complaint against police who had beaten her.[14] The trend is positive, but more still needs to be done.

Prison conditions are harsh in some facilities, including treatment such as solitary confinement and medical neglect.[15] Most controversial are the so-called F-type prisons, which isolate their prisoners. An especially contentious imprisonment is that of Abdullah Ocalan, former leader of the Kurdish guerrilla movement, who is serving a life sentence in solitary confinement on an island off the Turkish coast and allegedly has not had adequate access to his lawyer or to visitors.[16]

The government is unable to prevent non-state violence. Traditionally, such violence has come from Kurdish separatists in the southeast. Their organization, formerly the Kurdistan Workers' Party (PKK) and recently renamed Kongra-Gel, ended its five-year ceasefire with the government on June 1, 2004, due to dissatisfaction with continued government operations against its fighters. In the first half of 2004, 61 people were killed on both sides combined.[17] Rights violations by government forces have reportedly increased since the ceasefire ended as well, potentially including extrajudicial killings.[18]

Women's rights in Turkey are not fully realized in the cities and are observed even less in rural districts. Although constitutional amendments in the spring of 2004 included a provision granting women full equality before the law, building on earlier changes in the civil and penal codes, progress has not been significant. A 2004 report by Amnesty International on violence against women found that up to half of all women in Turkey are subject to violence. The report also documents forced marriages, deprivation, and lack of access to justice, which, it says, are tolerated and even endorsed by community leaders and government officials.[19] UNICEF has determined that more than half of all girls under age 15 in some rural provinces do not attend school,[20] a fact the government attributes to economic barriers and a patriarchal culture. Women are also discriminated against in certain professions. Their participation in the formal workforce decreased from 34 percent in 1990 to 26 percent in 2001, in part due to families leaving agriculture for the cities, where uneducated women cannot find work.[21] Although women have had the right to vote and run for office since 1934, they are drastically underrepresented in government and do not have equal access to decision-making positions.

Honor crimes, including killings—in which family members punish women who are considered to have brought dishonor on their family through situations such as pregnancy while unmarried or having been raped—are a serious problem among traditional Kurdish families. In February 2004, the government instructed prayer leaders to state that honor killings are a sin against God, and the 2004 revisions to the penal code included an end to sentence reductions for these crimes, among other provisions to improve women's rights. On the other hand, AKP leaders attempted to include a law criminalizing extra- and pre-marital sex in the penal code amendments, which, although it was ultimately excluded, raised fears of Islam in politics and a disproportionate negative effect on women. Turkey is a destination country and, somewhat less so, a transit country for trafficking in women and girls, although the government has been taking steps to reduce all forms of human trafficking.[22]

Most of Turkey's population is Muslim, and many people are devout. While the constitution protects freedom of religion, the Turkish republic was set up on the premise of secularism, in which state and religious affairs are separated. In practice, this has meant considerable government control of religion; most prominently, the Directorate of Religious Affairs regulates the country's mosques and employs their imams, who are civil servants in Turkey and are occasionally instructed on what to say by the government. Perhaps most contentiously, external signs of piety are banned in public institutions, which means that women are not allowed to wear headscarves in public universities and government offices, and observant men are dismissed from the military.[23] There are periodic protests against the headscarf ban, although the European Court of Human Rights ruled in June 2004 that it is legal, and AKP dropped its attempt to introduce an easing of the ban in the 2004 penal code reforms. A much higher-profile controversy erupted in spring 2004 over an AKP proposal to allow graduates of vocational schools—including Islamic imam hatip schools, where many parents dissatisfied with state education send their children—to enroll in state universities. After the president vetoed the bill, AKP allowed it to drop.

Under the revised penal code, discrimination on the basis of personal characteristics is illegal. Minorities in Turkey are defined by religion, and only Jews (about 25,000 of whom live in Turkey), Greek Orthodox Christians (3,000), and Armenian Orthodox Christians (50,000) are recognized.[24] These groups are not integrated into the Turkish establishment. Although their rights are generally respected, freedom of religion is difficult for non-Muslims. Moreover, many other groups that do not belong to the dominant Sunni Muslim sect have less protection. Other Christian and Muslim groups—including Alevis, who practice a combination of Islam and pre-Islamic religion—as well as mystical religious-social orders have no legal status, and some of their activities are banned. Jewish sites were the targets of terrorist attacks in November 2003, and a Masonic lodge was targeted in March 2004.

The Kurds are the largest group of non-ethnic Turks in Turkey, estimated at about 10 to 12 million people.[25] Many are well integrated and
suffer no problems. However, the legacy of the 15-year guerrilla war in
the southeast, in which more than 35,000 people were killed,[26] as well
as Ataturk's emphasis on Turkishness over multiculturalism, has left the
Kurds facing restrictions on their language, their culture, and their freedom of expression. The situation has improved with the EU harmonization reforms; in addition to the start of Kurdish-language broadcasts
(see "Accountability and Public Voice"), 2003 regulations allow for
classes in Kurdish and Kurdish names for children. But the classes have
faced bureaucratic obstacles, and a ban on the letters q, w, and x (which
are used in Kurdish but not Turkish) has undermined the reform's
intent. More significantly, Kurds suffered severe human rights abuses
during the insurgency, and up to 4.5 million were displaced from their
homes.[27] About 125,000 have been authorized to return since June
2000, and Kurds have clearly benefited from broader human rights reforms. But village guards—a civil defense force put in place by the central government in the southeast during the insurgency—continue to
be insufficiently accountable, and Kurdish freedom of expression still
needs greater protection.

The Kurdish population and other ethnic minorities continue to face
political roadblocks as well. The Kurdish Democratic People's Party
(DEHAP) is accused of being the political arm of the Kongra-Gel—
which is considered a terrorist organization by the Turkish government
as well as the EU and the United States—and has therefore faced continual legal battles and arrests. Still, DEHAP does not represent the interests of most Kurds, who, when living outside the southeast, are generally
more integrated and participate in mainstream politics.

The interests of people with disabilities are addressed by the High
Council of Disabilities, which brings public officials together with nongovernmental groups. The council has admirable aims and even conducted a thorough survey of people with disabilities in 2002 in order to
address problems better. Nevertheless, the needs of such people continue
to exceed the limited services provided.[28] There are efforts to integrate
children with disabilities into mainstream education through improved
accessibility and staff training, but very few can take advantage of their
supposed right to education. Thus, most people with disabilities are
unskilled. Employers are required to reserve 3 percent of their workforce

for employees with disabilities, but few comply, while others hire workers with disabilities to fill the quota, only to fire or retire them soon afterward. The government is starting vocational programs, but discrimination is widespread.[29] Information about government services and regulations is not readily available in formats accessible to people with disabilities.

The constitution protects freedom of association, but broad language in laws leaves room for restrictions despite some tightening through recent reforms. Some local officials exploit bureaucracy to prevent registration of demonstrations, and police regularly disperse peaceful public gatherings, often using excessive force.[30] Regulation of the activities and membership of nongovernmental organizations (NGOs) has relaxed with recent reforms, but limitations remain. NGOs are often fined, thus making their work difficult and at times financially unfeasible, although imprisonment of members has decreased.[31] Demonstrators and human rights defenders who refer to Kurdish rights or Abdullah Ocalan are particular targets. In June 2004 the interior ministry issued a circular confirming that small informational gatherings do not require government notification.

Employees have the right to join trade unions and cannot be discriminated against for doing so, although fines for discrimination are too small to act as a deterrent.[32] Unions face restrictions on assembly similar to those of civic groups, and public employees do not have the right to strike. While the constitution protects citizens from being forced to join an organization (Article 33), certain fields have compulsory membership in professional organizations.

### Recommendations

- The government should establish a commission independent of security forces to perform comprehensive monitoring of police stations and gendarmeries in order to ensure respect for human rights, and findings should be reported to the government and made public.
- All human rights violations must be promptly and thoroughly investigated and prosecuted, and officials under investigation should be suspended from duty.
- Restrictions on public gatherings should be limited to those mandated by the European Convention on Human Rights.

- The principle of multiculturalism needs to be embraced, perhaps through constitutional amendment, to ensure that all religious, ethnic, and cultural groups are treated equally.

## RULE OF LAW – 4.18

Turkey's judicial system is characterized by the opposing pulls of, on the one hand, the enlightened reforms passed since 2001 and, on the other, the more traditional attitudes of the court system and especially the judges. While the reforms have increased judicial independence, seriously curbed the role of the military in the justice system, and fundamentally revised the penal code, the judges, prosecutors, and ministry of justice continue to be dominated by pre-reform ideas about defending national integrity, governmental institutions, and Turkish identity. Thus, as in other areas, implementation is the major stumbling block, although not the only one.

According to the constitution (Article 15), everyone has a right to be presumed innocent until proven guilty. Recent reforms give all detainees the right to see a lawyer immediately, free of charge, and according to Human Rights Watch, legal counsel has improved markedly since they were passed.[33] However, some rights groups have reported attempts to circumvent proper procedures, and a September 2003 visit by the Council of Europe found that only 3 percent to 7 percent of those detained had seen a lawyer, either because they were unaware of their right or because of concern about how it would impact their cases.[34] Trials can drag on excessively, although the portion of this that is due to overburdened court dockets (as opposed to purposeful neglect in cases of human rights abuses) should be reduced by the establishment of appellate courts as envisioned in a law enacted in September 2004. In order to improve implementation of new reforms, judges and prosecutors have been receiving training in human rights and other values that has continued into 2004.

The Turkish constitution provides for an independent judiciary, but the court system is not in fact entirely separate from the executive. The executive plays a strong role in judicial training, appointment, promotion, and financing. Training of judges is inadequate, and because there is no proper review of cases, many of those that end up in the courts result in acquittal due to lack of merit. Public prosecutors in Turkey have a status very close to that of judges, both functionally and symbolically, thus placing the defense in an inferior position. Prosecutors are sometimes pressured by the ministry of justice to pursue cases without merit, and the government issues circulars instructing public prosecutors on how to interpret certain laws.

The constitution grants immunity to all legislators and cabinet ministers, and AKP has reneged on a pre-election promise to end immunity. Furthermore, permission is required from the superiors of public officials (or the TGNA in the case of ministers) to open investigations against them. Some officials have been tried after leaving office, but often the statute of limitations has expired before a case can legally be brought against them.

In late September 2004, just ahead of a crucial report on Turkey's progress from the EU Commission, the TGNA approved the first major overhaul of the penal code since it was written 78 years earlier. The new code introduces fundamental changes, such as attempting to make explicit what actions are considered crimes and stating that no other acts are punishable, as well as institutionalizing the concept that punishments should be in proportion to the crimes committed. The revisions fill many of the gaps in the system and were considered essential in order for the commission to recommend that Turkey begin EU negotiations. There are, however, accusations that residual ambiguities still allow judges to interpret some laws at will. More generally, unequal treatment under the law remains a problem, as discrimination against the poor in the administration of justice is common.

Another major change to the justice system has been the May 2004 abolition of State Security Courts. These courts, comprising both civilian and military judges, tried cases against the integrity of the state and had been accused of human rights abuses and an absence of due process. They ruled on such high-profile cases as those involving Ocalan and Erdogan before he was prime minister. The cases formerly under their jurisdiction have been passed to other courts. The end of the State Security Courts is widely considered to be positive, although it remains to be seen whether the types of cases formerly tried in them will be any better served by the new system.

The case in the Turkish system with the most international renown in recent months has been that of Leyla Zana and three other Kurdish former parliamentarians, who were convicted of belonging to the PKK in 1994. The four are widely considered to have been targeted as a result of their (peaceful) pro-Kurdish views, and the European Court of Human Rights in 2001 ruled that their trial was unfair. Their sentences were upheld by a State Security Court in April 2004 in a trial that was criticized by the EU and rights groups, but they were released in June pending an appeal that was ongoing as of September 2004. The trial is considered emblematic of both Turkey's flawed judicial system and the push for Kurdish rights.

The military holds a special place in the Turkish republic. Since Turkey's first military coup, in 1960, it has acted as the guarantor of Turkey's secularism, territorial integrity, and government functioning. While it has never stayed in power long, it used the first and subsequent coups, in 1971 and 1980, to increase its autonomy and enhance its role during civilian rule. In particular, the power of the National Security Council (NSC)—which was dominated by the military—to influence civilian governments was increased. Turkish generals have expressed opinions on everything from judicial decisions to draft bills in the TGNA to EU membership, and those opinions have seldom been ignored. After an Islamic party came to dominate the ruling coalition in 1996, leading to increased fundamentalism, the military forced its removal. During the state of emergency declared in most of the southeast during the guerrilla war in the 1980s, the military wielded particular power in the region.

Reducing the political influence of the military has been a prime concern of the EU. Beginning with the 2001 constitutional amendments, Turkey has confined the NSC to an advisory role with, as of August 2004, a civilian at its head; it has removed the military members from the higher education council and RTUK; and it has increased transparency and parliamentary oversight of military expenditures. The military is still not entirely subservient to the ministry of defense, and its budget remains disproportionately high. The military continues to voice an opinion on political issues (such as the recent controversy over religious schools). However, it is significant that the military did not intervene in situations in which previously it would have been likely to play a role—for example, when the TGNA voted against allowing U.S. troops access to Iraq through Turkish territory in 2003, or when the Turkish government supported the reunification of Cyprus. Public trust in the military is strong, and military schools are among the best in the country, thus contributing to the continued power and prestige of this institution.

Property rights are generally respected in Turkey, although in some areas societal biases impede women from owning property. The most significant property rights problem in Turkey is that of tens of thousands of people who were driven from their homes by government forces during the conflict in the southeast. The government has initiated a project to compensate these people and return them to their villages, and more than 100,000 have returned so far, according to official figures. Some of those displaced have adjusted to their new residences and do not wish to return. However, village guards have allegedly used intimidation and violence to prevent others from returning to their homes.[35]

*Recommendations*

- Governmental immunity must end so that official wrongdoing can be prosecuted properly.
- Members of the judiciary require training in the provisions of the new penal code, particularly to ensure that punishments are commensurate with the gravity of crimes committed and to ensure that all people are treated equally under the law.
- Symbolic and literal signs of equality between public prosecutors and judges should be replaced by greater equality between prosecutors and the defense.
- The village guard system must be abolished to ease the return of displaced people and build trust between the government and the people in the southeast.

## ANTICORRUPTION AND TRANSPARENCY – 3.43

Turkey struggles with substantial corruption in government and in daily life. The AKP rose to power despite (or perhaps because of) being relatively unknown in part due to the corruption and economic mismanagement of previous governments. In the last year alone Turkey has signed a series of international corruption conventions, including the Group of States Against Corruption (GRECO), the UN Convention against Corruption, and the European Convention on the Fight against Corruption. However, AKP's commitment to fighting corruption has been halfhearted at best. Perhaps even more so than with other reforms aimed at EU membership, the anticorruption framework has not translated into individuals changing their behavior.

Upon taking office AKP instituted an urgent action plan that included corruption measures, but it never formed the relevant committee nor has it passed an anticorruption law it drafted. Bureaucracy pervades the system, and regulations are a burden for businesses. The government has made increasing efforts to streamline regulations since the 2001 financial crisis; but although a considerable privatization program is in place to reduce the number of state-owned enterprises, the AKP has lacked the political will required for its implementation. Many government officials have business interests that conflict with their public service duties.[36] All must file asset-disclosure forms, but these forms are inaccessible to the public and are not generally used for investigative purposes. Conflicts of interest in the private sector are regulated by laws in each sector, not by a single piece of legislation. The 2001 crisis sparked the disclosure of the huge conflicts of interest that existed in the financial sector, and new scandals continue to emerge. Conversely, corruption in the education sector is not a serious problem.

Corruption is severely punishable under Turkish law, but many of those cases that make it to court result in acquittal or light sentences.[37] Corruption investigations have served more to publicize corruption than to punish it and can be influenced by political agendas. All legislators and ministers have immunity from prosecution (see "Rule of Law"), despite significant allegations of legislative corruption. Many former ministers have faced corruption charges in recent months, although none were allies of AKP. Most prominently, former prime minister Mesut Yilmaz was accused of interference in the privatization of Turkbank; charges were dropped against Yilmaz in July 2004 due to procedural flaws, but the case is expected to be revived by the TGNA.

The media report widely on such cases and have also revealed lower-level corruption, but journalists risk imprisonment for investigations of those still in office as well as censorship by the business interests that own their outlets.[38] An electrical engineer was killed, allegedly by state agents, in October 2002 after he exposed corruption in the energy sector, but such extreme measures are rare. Citizens do not have an impartial intermediary with whom they can file complaints about corruption;

while they can go to the police, the bureaucracy required to pursue a claim tends to be more of a hassle than it is worth.

A court of accounts conducts annual audits of revenues and expenditures of public bodies on behalf of the TGNA, but the irregularities it reveals are rarely investigated.[39] The government has proposed abolishing the central inspection board, which already lacks coordinating powers, without a plan for a new central institution. Tax auditing currently is performed by several different units of the ministry of finance at the national and local level and is largely ineffective, although, in partnership with EU consultants, the ministry of finance has been evaluating the current tax system in order to increase efficiency of tax administration and collection, as well as to implement a new audit system.

A new law ensuring budget transparency went into effect in January 2004, with some provisions to be effective in January 2005, the combined effect of which will improve financial transparency in public institutions through extending the scope of budgets. The law will be enhanced by a new draft law that will reclassify budgets according to international standards and ensure that revenue and expenditure are stated in publicly available budgets. Such measures were required by foreign donors to ensure accountability.

The government launched a reform of the public procurement system in the aftermath of the financial crisis to ensure transparency and accountability, culminating in a new law adopted in 2002. However, AKP overturned certain provisions, leaving room for corruption once again. A law on freedom of information went into effect in April 2004, but implementation has been slow. Civil servants remain reluctant to provide governmental information, in part due to vague provisions in the law exempting state and trade secrets, although some reportedly will respond to bribes.[40]

## Recommendations

- An independent, central anticorruption agency should be created to ensure that corruption is consistently and systematically punished.
- The government must repeal government officials' immunity and prosecute governmental corruption.
- To reduce the opportunity for bribes, asset disclosure for all public officials should be improved so that information is available to the public and irregularities are investigated.

- A political ethics law for government officials would establish a model for the general population to follow.
- Public awareness of the impact of corruption must be increased, including through the education system to target citizens at an early age.

## NOTES

[1]  I would like to thank the Turkish branch of Transparency International (TSHD), the Eurasia team at the National Democratic Institute, and the staff at the Turkish Economic and Social Studies Foundation (TESEV) for their valuable input on this report.

[2]  Yilmaz Esmer, "Turkey," *Global Integrity Report* (Washington, DC: Center for Public Integrity, 10 September 2004), www.publicintegrity.org/ga/country.aspx?cc=tr; "Response of Toplumsal Saydamlik Hareketi Dernegi to EC's Questions about Corruption and Transparency in Turkey" (Istanbul: Toplumsal Saydamlik Hareketi Dernegi [TSHD-TI Turkey], 5 July 2004), www.saydamlik.org/haber.html.

[3]  Esmer, "Turkey."

[4]  Author interviews, October 2004.

[5]  Author interview, 14 October 2004; "Turkey: Restrictive Laws, Arbitrary Application— The Pressure on Human Rights Defenders" (New York: Amnesty International [AI], 12 February 2004).

[6]  "Turkey Annual Report" (Vienna: International Helsinki Federation for Human Rights[IHF-HR], 23 June 2004).

[7]  "Turkish Human Rights Details Alleged Abuses in First Half of 2004," BBC Worldwide Monitoring, 18 July 2004.

[8]  Esmer, "Turkey"; author interview, 26 October 2004.

[9]  L. Dogan Tilic, "Media Ownership Structure in Turkey" (Ankara: Progressive Journalists Association, January 2000); author interviews, October 2004.

[10]  Author interview with Human Rights Association (Ankara), 28 October 2004.

[11]  "Report to the Turkish Government on the Visit to Turkey Carried out by the European Committee for the Prevention of Torture and Inhuman or Degrading Treatment or Punishment (CPT) from 7 to 15 September 2003" (Strasbourg: Council of Europe, 18 June 2004).

[12]  "Turkey: Rights Progress Marred in Key Year for EU Bid" (New York: Human Rights Watch [HRW], 3 March 2004); Senem Aydin and E. Fuat Keyman, "European Integration and the Transformation of Turkish Democracy" (Brussels: Centre for European Policy Studies, EU–Turkey Working Papers no 2, August 2004).

[13]  "Turkish Human Rights . . .," BBC Worldwide Monitoring, 18 July 2004; "Eradicating Torture in Turkey's Police Stations," (New York: HRW, September 2004); "Turkey: Prime Minister Erdogan must convert his political promise of human rights into reality" (New York: Amnesty International, press release, AI Index EUR 44/008/2004, 13 February 2004); Aydin and Keyman, "European Integration . . ."

14 "Turkey: Ill-treatment/fear for safety" (New York: Amnesty International, Urgent Action, AI Index EUR 44/019/2004, 19 May 2004).

15 "Turkey Annual Report" (IHF-HR).

16 "Report to the Turkish Government on the Visit to Turkey Carried out by the European Committee for the Prevention of Torture and Inhuman or Degrading Treatment or Punishment (CPT) from 16 to 17 February 2003" (Strasbourg: Council of Europe, 25 February 2004).

17 "Turkish Human Rights . . .," BBC Worldwide Monitoring, 18 July 2004.

18 Author interview with Human Rights Association (Ankara), 28 October 2004.

19 "Turkey: Women Confronting Family Violence," Stop Violence against Women series (New York: Amnesty International, June 2004).

20 Vincent Boland, "Lack of Opportunity for Girls Could Affect Turkey's EU Hopes," *Financial Times*, 25 May 2004.

21 "Response of the Republic of Turkey to the Questionnaire on Implementation of the Beijing Platform for Action" (Ankara: Republic of Turkey Prime Ministry, April 2004).

22 Ibid.; *Victims of Trafficking and Violence Protection Act of 2000: Trafficking in Persons Report* (Washington, DC: U.S. Dept of State, June 2004).

23 Levent Korkut, "Country Report: Turkey," *Report on Measures to Combat Discrimination in the 13 Candidate Countries* (Brussels: Migration Policy Group, May 2003).

24 Aydin and Keyman, "European Integration . . ."

25 Ibid.

26 Ibid.

27 "Profile of Internal Displacement: Turkey" (Geneva: Norwegian Refugee Council/Global IDP Project, 5 April 2004.

28 Irem Cosansu Yalazan, "Disability Culture: An Overview of Services for People with Disabilities in Turkey," *Access Press*, 13, 2 (10 February 2002); author interview, 28 October 2004.

29 Yalazan, "Disability Culture"; Korkut, "Country Report: Turkey"; author interview, October 2004.

30 "Turkey: Continuing Restrictions on Freedom of Assembly," letter to Abdullah Gül (New York: Human Rights Watch, 28 April 2004); "Turkey Annual Report" (IHF-HR); author interview with Human Rights Association, 28 October 2004.

31 "Turkey: Restrictive Laws . . ." (AI); author interview with Human Rights Association, 28 October 2004; author interview with Mazlumder (Ankara), 28 October 2004.

32 "Turkey: Annual Survey of Violations of Trade Union Rights" (Brussels: International Confederation of Free Trade Unions [ICFTU], 2004).

33 "Turkey: Rights Progress Marred . . ." (HRW).

34 Ibid.; "Turkey: Ill-treatment . . ." (AI); "Report to the Turkish Government on the Visit to Turkey Carried out by the European Committee for the Prevention of Torture and Inhuman or Degrading Treatment or Punishment (CPT) from 7 to 15 September 2003" (Strasbourg: Council of Europe, 18 June 2004).

35 Aydin and Keyman, "European Integration and the Transformation of Turkish Democracy"; "Turkey Annual Report" (IHF-HR).

[36] "Response of Toplumsal Saydamlik Hareketi Dernegi to EC's Questions about Corruption and Transparency in Turkey" (TSHD-TI Turkey), www.saydamlik.org/haber.html.

[37] Ibid.

[38] Ibid.; author interview, 26 October 2004.

[39] Esmer, "Turkey"

[40] Esmer, "Turkey"; David Banisar, "The Freedominfo.org Global Survey: Freedom of Information and Access to Government Record Laws around the World" (Washington, DC: Freedominfo.org, May 2004).

# ZAMBIA

CAPITAL: Lusaka
POPULATION: 10.9 million
GNI PER CAPITA: $340

SCORES
ACCOUNTABILITY AND PUBLIC VOICE: 3.85
CIVIL LIBERTIES: 4.57
RULE OF LAW: 4.26
ANTICORRUPTION AND TRANSPARENCY: 3.39
(scores are based on a scale of 0 to 7, with
0 representing weakest and 7 representing
strongest performance)

*David J. Simon*

## INTRODUCTION

In December 2001, Levy Mwanawasa became only the third president of Zambia in 37 years. He had defeated 11 rivals for the post but garnered just 29 percent of the vote—only two percentage points more than his nearest rival. With the resulting weak mandate in hand, Mwanawasa assumed control of a state plagued by corruption and inefficiency and of a country deeply mired in debt, rife with poverty, and facing a devastating AIDS crisis.

Both of Mwanawasa's predecessors, Kenneth Kaunda and Frederick Chiluba, often displayed authoritarian tendencies. Kaunda banned all political parties other than his own United National Independence Party (UNIP) for 17 years. Upon that ban's repeal, Chiluba and the newly created Movement for Multiparty Democracy (MMD) swept into office in a landmark general election in 1991. Despite his party's name, however, Chiluba's government often resembled his predecessor's. For example, Chiluba paved the way for his reelection with constitutional changes that prohibited Kaunda from standing on the dubious grounds of the latter's

---

**David J. Simon** is lecturer in political science at Yale University.

parentage. Toward the end of his second term, Chiluba aggressively—but unsuccessfully—pursued another constitutional change that would have overturned a prohibition on serving a third term in office.

Chiluba then hand-picked Mwanawasa to be his successor. Many expected Mwanawasa to stay true to Chiluba's illiberal democracy pattern. Although he had been a vice president early in Chiluba's tenure, Mwanawasa had not had a high political profile since he competed for the party presidency in 1995 and was said to have suffered physical and mental damage in a 1992 car accident.[1] A leading independent newspaper, the *Post of Zambia,* alleged the president-elect to be Chiluba's puppet-designate—"of Chiluba, by Chiluba, and for Chiluba."[2] Indeed, his electoral victory was primarily a result of the party infrastructure Chiluba bequeathed him and of the way in which his opportunistic opponents (most of whom had defected from the MMD either in opposition to Chiluba's third-term overtures or out of disappointment at not having been selected successor themselves) neatly split the remaining 71 percent of the votes, rather than any positive attribute ascribable to Mwanawasa.

Nonetheless, Mwanawasa had consistently sounded governance and anti-poverty themes in his campaign and continued to do so once in office. Most remarkably, Mwanawasa surprised many by targeting Chiluba in an anticorruption campaign. Although saddled with a petition challenging the validity of the 2001 election, Mwanawasa has frequently sought to transcend interparty tensions—including taking the unprecedented (and, to some parties, unwelcome) step of inviting some opposition parliamentarians into his cabinet.

Mwanawasa has not put the challenges facing either his rule or his agenda behind him. Indeed, the electoral petition—still under consideration after two and a half years—has revealed that Mwanawasa himself benefited from corrupt electoral practices during the 2001 campaign. High-profile anticorruption efforts have encountered more setbacks than even minor victories. On some fronts, Mwanawasa's programs resemble those of his predecessors. Pervasive—and not unwarranted—distrust of the state on the part of civil society poses yet another challenge to Mwanawasa's governance agenda. And debt, poverty, and AIDS remain unyielding, continuing to present perhaps the greatest challenges to the majority of the Zambian people and to the country itself.

## ACCOUNTABILITY AND PUBLIC VOICE – 3.85

The 2001 concurrent presidential, parliamentary, and local elections illustrate both the promise and the shortcomings of the electoral mechanism in Zambia. On one hand, voters had several options from which to choose. Election Day itself featured a high turnout relative to the previous general election (67 percent of registered voters) and peaceful behavior by all. The MMD carried a narrow plurality in parliament (converted to an outright majority in subsequent by-elections), which helped that body emerge from having been relegated to rubber-stamp status during most of the Kaunda and Chiluba years. On the other hand, logistical issues such as the late delivery of ballot boxes apparently prevented many who wished to vote from doing so, and the procedure of counting ballots lacked transparency in many instances.[3] In winning, Mwanawasa earned the support of less than 30 percent of registered voters and barely 15 percent of eligible voters. Moreover, the campaign that preceded it was highly tainted: All major parties favored food and clothing giveaways as a campaign tool, the incumbent party exploited state resources and media to its advantage, and several like-minded candidates effectively canceled out one another's earned votes.[4]

Mwanawasa's small plurality and narrow victory primarily reflect the self-defeating proliferation of opposition contenders. Candidates such as Michael Sata (of the Patriotic Front) and Benjamin Mwila (Chiluba's uncle, of the Zambia Republican Party), who had been fixtures in Chiluba's cabinet for most of the preceding decade, failed to win a single constituency and frequently finished in the bottom three of all candidates outside the MMD's traditional strongholds. Anderson Mazoka of the second-place United Party for National Development (UPND) and Lt. General Christon Tembo of the Forum for Democracy and Development (FDD), in contrast, performed the strongest in areas outside the MMD strongholds. Accordingly, these parties may have represented true alternatives to the MMD (even though Tembo was himself a former vice president to Chiluba and a long-time cabinet member). That the UPND and FDD both performed most strongly in many of the same areas, however, illustrates their redundancy as political alternatives. It proved to be the political undoing for both of them, to the detriment of those voters who sought an end to MMD rule.

The election spawned numerous court challenges. Most significantly, Tembo, Miyanda, and Mazoka jointly filed a Supreme Court petition challenging the presidential result, citing (most prominently) widespread abuse of government resources. While the courts have tended to resolve lesser election petitions expeditiously (even, on a few occasions, overturning the result), the presidential petition remained tied up in court through September 2004. In the meantime, public testimony by former Chiluba officials (including Sata, as well as former minister of finance Katele Kalumba) has lent credence to the petitioners' claims: Kalumba, for example, testified that after release of 50 million kwacha (approximately US$25,000) of indeterminate origin for campaign purposes in one province, some of the proceeds were devoted to buying off leading members of the opposition.[5] Although Mwanawasa has been in no hurry to accelerate the pace of the trial, he has pledged to abide by the court's judgment.

The petition illustrates that campaign-related violations are not subject to redress until after the election and the violations' effects have taken place. The electoral commission lacks enforcement powers and resources. Moreover, campaign transgressions are specifically spelled out only in the electoral code of conduct—an essentially unenforceable administrative document. Furthermore, aside from prohibitions against the abuse of state resources, even that code has little to say about the origin, declaration, and extent of campaign finance. A recent study by the Sweden-based Institute for Democracy and Electoral Assistance (IDEA) found no evidence of any campaign finance regulation on the books in Zambia.[6]

Throughout the multiparty era, Zambian elections have been plagued by low voter participation.[7] Turnout in the 2001 election stood at 67 percent of registered voters, which was almost 10 points higher than the 1996 level and over 20 points higher than that of the transitional 1991 election. However, for each election, barely half of the estimated population of eligible voters had registered. A cumbersome registration process, which must be undertaken anew prior to each national election (and therefore well before the presidential campaign even begins), is largely to blame. Poverty exacerbates the problem, as many poor Zambians find the time and monetary costs of going through the registration process prohibitive. Finally, politicians frequently fail to interact with the constituencies they represent, even to mobilize participation.

The executive—and the president in particular—historically has dominated the legislative branch. In the single-party era there was a premium on loyalty, which bound even back-benchers not to oppose (or even question) the president's initiatives. These norms have persisted into the multiparty era, bolstered by practices such as the presidential appointment of the speaker of parliament. The larger size of the opposition since 2001 has made for more vocal parliamentary opposition to Mwanawasa than his predecessors ever had to contend with. However, parliament remains underresourced and underinformed on many issues, preventing it from providing effective oversight of the executive branch.

Ideally, local government could make the Zambian state more accountable to its people. However, local councils generally have few resources at their disposal, so that basic services such as local road maintenance or garbage collection are beyond their means. That the vast majority of Zambians live without any connection to public utilities infrastructure may further undermine the potential of local government to serve a meaningful role in people's lives. Thus, the announcement in 2004 that local government elections would not be held upon the expiry of local councilors' three-year terms due to a lack of electoral funding seemed to upset few.

The controversies emanating from the 2001 election have made the government sensitive to the weaknesses of its electoral processes. With a view toward electoral reform, the government of Zambia commissioned an Electoral Reform Technical Committee (ERTC) in late 2003. After soliciting input from a wide range of governmental and nongovernmental actors, the ERTC proposed a wide-ranging set of reforms in 2004. The most radical (vis-à-vis the current system) include a recommendation that 40 additional parliamentary seats be allocated on the basis of a party list system and a call for run-offs in contests in which no candidate attains a majority of the votes.[8] As of September 2004, neither the cabinet nor parliament had considered the recommendations.

Mwanawasa has also convened a Constitutional Review Commission (CRC) to consider constitutional changes beyond electoral reform. The CRC comprises both governmental and nongovernmental representatives. Many of the latter who were initially invited declined to join, perhaps wary of the 1996 precedent, in which a review commission's work was largely ignored in favor of the MMD's own proposals. Although the commission reportedly received 13,900 submissions,[9] the major opposition parties refused to cooperate. Their most prominent concern is Mwanawasa's refusal to convene a constituent assembly—a constitutional convention of sorts, at which the ruling party would have less procedural control—to determine the final form of the new constitution. Civil society groups and opposition parties made similar demands on the MMD in 1995 and 1996, to no avail.

Evident in the CRC–constituent assembly controversy is the emerging power of civil society in Zambia, as well as the tensions it brings to the political sphere. In 2004, civil society groups met, organized, and agitated freely for a wide range of objectives. Some groups, such as Transparency International–Zambia, the Foundation for the Democratic Process, and the Catholic Centre for Justice, Development, and Peace, frequently and professionally scrutinize the government's activities. Civil society organizations regularly participated in the formulation of Zambia's Poverty Reduction Strategy Paper (PRSP), a medium-term economic planning tool required under the Heavily Indebted Poor Country (HIPC) debt relief initiative. They often did so at the invitation of the government, most notably at a National Summit on Poverty convened in October 2001. The most prominent civil society organizations have demonstrated a willingness to engage with the state while retaining an ability to remain independent and critical. The Societies Act requires nongovernmental organizations (NGOs) to register with the state, which retains the prerogative to revoke their registration at any time. In November 2003, for example, the Ministry of Home Affairs de-registered 198 organizations.[10] Since the Chiluba era, MMD officials have frequently criticized NGOs for being partisan or for being beholden to foreign interests. Many governance-oriented NGOs are largely funded by grants from foreign donors seeking to promote democracy in Zambia.

Another sphere exhibiting conflicting tendencies is freedom of the media. Reversing decades of state monopoly, new opportunities for media freedom emerged throughout the Chiluba years. The widely read and internationally acclaimed *Post of Zambia* has been almost reflexively critical of the Chiluba and Mwanawasa governments. Independent radio stations and, more recently, independent television stations have appeared on the scene, developments that would have been unthinkable during the Kaunda years. Zambia now has multiple Internet service providers, although Internet usage remains highly concentrated in urban areas.

However, like its predecessor, the Mwanawasa regime has exhibited a tendency to undermine press freedom. A plan to convert the state-owned media into the public media—with greater independence from the state—faltered when the government decided to retain what amounts to editorial control of its television, radio, and newspaper outlets. In November 2003, the government banned a televised morning show (running on the government-owned and operated ZNBC) that featured a review of the day's newspaper headlines. The government also occasionally cracks down on the media it does not control directly. A recent analysis on investigative journalism in Zambia concluded that "libel laws have been used with such frequency that journalists are increasingly shunning stories which are likely to lead to costly litigation."[11] In June 2003, Masautso Phiri, editor of the independent *Today*, was threatened with arrest for reporting on an opposition parliamentarian's challenge to the appointment of a new vice president. In November 2003, the government banned the independent Omega television station, which was owned by a former Chiluba aide, allegedly for violating the terms of its license.[12] In early 2004, the government attempted to deport a British columnist for the *Post* for "insulting the president" in a column based on George Orwell's *Animal Farm;* the high court blocked and then overturned the deportation order.[13] Under Section 53 of the penal code, the president retains the power to ban publications (a power Chiluba used in 1996 to ban an issue of the *Post*). The press has been banned from covering several recent events, including the ongoing presidential petition hearings and an October 2003 inter-party meeting.

*Recommendations*

- Presidential and parliamentary elections should require winners to receive a majority of votes cast, with a second-round run-off in the event that no candidate does so in the first round.
- Electoral reforms should provide for the continuous maintenance of voter registration rolls, guaranteed budgetary and operational independence for the electoral commission, and an electoral code of conduct featuring a mechanism for its independent enforcement.
- The constitutional revision process should accommodate the participation of the citizens of Zambia in both the design and enactment phases. Steps might include a constituent assembly

(with well-defined responsibilities and limits) and/or a referendum on the passage of the final document.

- The revised constitution should enshrine protections for the freedom of the media and should repeal the president's power to ban publications under Section 53 of the penal code.

## CIVIL LIBERTIES – 4.57

At the highest level, the Mwanawasa regime has established a strong commitment to the protection of Zambians' civil liberties. The constitution provides for extensive protections for civil rights, including the rights of the accused. Zambia's shortcomings regarding civil liberties lie primarily at the local level, where constraints such as resources, cultural practice, and long-established patterns of behavior can serve to undermine the positive features.

Section 15 of the constitution provides that "No person shall be subjected to torture, or to inhuman or degrading punishment or other like treatment." During the Chiluba era reports of inhumane treatment were not uncommon. Under Mwanawasa, neither political imprisonment nor accusations of torture have been an issue. Nevertheless, the police are known to apply excessive force in detaining suspects. Governmental bodies such as the Human Rights Commission and the Police Public Complaints Commission Authority hold the power to investigate claims of such violations but lack enforcement powers.

The Zambian prison system is overcrowded, resulting in inhumane conditions as a matter of course.[14] Health concerns abound, with high HIV/AIDS infection rates among the prison population, as well as elevated vulnerability to infectious diseases such as malaria, tuberculosis, and cholera.

Mwanawasa has taken a strong stance against the imposition of the death penalty, for which the constitution provides. He has pledged not to sign any orders of execution during his tenure in office,[15] and he has commuted the death sentences of 60 prisoners since assuming office, including 22 who had been convicted of attempting to overthrow the Chiluba government in a 1997 coup attempt. In 2004, Mwanawasa released one of the alleged masterminds of the plot, Captain Jack Chiti, who was terminally ill at the time and died a few weeks later.[16]

The Mwanawasa era has not witnessed any major politically motivated assassinations. Mwanawasa's anticorruption efforts have targeted
political figures, although the most prominent—Chiluba and associates—
are former allies of the president rather than opponents. Moreover, the
corruption charges on which such prosecution rests are generally credible
and have been construed as politically motivated only by those subjected
to them (or who might potentially be subjected to them in the future).

Crime in Zambia is very common, especially in urban areas. Police
appear powerless to prevent car-jacking and violent home raids, which
occasionally victimize well-known individuals. Beyond this, the state is
generally able to provide protection from the infringement of liberties
by non-state actors. The campaigns for the 2001 elections, as well as
recent parliamentary by-election campaigns, witnessed flare-ups of partisan violence. However, even in 2001, incidents tended to be isolated
rather than widespread. Future flare-ups remain a possibility.

People with disabilities are not included among the groups protected
from discrimination under the constitution. As a result, the electoral
code do not explicitly provide for the right of access to voting facilities
for people with disabilities or for accommodations for deaf or blind people. Indeed, access and accommodations for people with disabilities in
most cases do not exist.[17] In addition, the Electoral Act states that no
person "adjudged or otherwise declared to be of unsound mind" can
register to vote, a clause that could be used to disenfranchise people with
mental disabilities. Zambia's Persons with Disabilities Act (1996) does
provide protections for people with disabilities against discrimination
in employment or access to education, although the extent of their enforcement is unclear.

The rights of religious and ethnic minorities are generally respected
in Zambia. According to one of the amendments to the constitution in
1996, Zambia is officially a "Christian Nation." Hindus and Muslims,
among others, are nonetheless generally able to practice their religion
without obstruction. Zambia has not experienced religiously motivated
violence.

Officially, 72 African ethnic groups compose the greater part of Zambian society, none large enough to dominate any of the others. Partially
due to the legacy of Kaunda's conscious efforts to prevent ethnic divisions
from emerging, ethnic violence is rare. More than 100,000 people of

European or Asian descent also permanently reside in Zambia, many of them citizens.[18] Although people of non-African descent are occasionally subject to political or social scapegoating, infringements on personal liberty are rare. Indeed, whites and Asians hold parliamentary seats and have held cabinet seats in the past. In recent years, Zambia has welcomed white farmers and entrepreneurs fleeing persecution and property seizure in neighboring Zimbabwe.[19]

On paper, Zambia embraces gender equality as a core principle. The constitution grants "fundamental freedoms and rights of the individual" regardless of sex and marital status. Civil society groups (including Women for Change and the NGO Coordinating Committee) and government officials commonly pay lip service to the need to be sensitive to gender issues in public policy.[20] Yet poverty, cultural practice, and the absence of legal instruments to enforce constitutional protections make Zambia a particularly poor place to be a woman. One recent survey of more than 5,000 Zambian women found a widespread expectation, as well as acceptance, of the practice of spousal abuse.[21] Spousal rape is not explicitly criminalized.

In particular, women's inheritance rights are frequently abrogated. When a husband dies, his original family commonly repossesses all of his property, leaving his widow in a vulnerable, potentially destitute position. A deceased man's brother frequently takes on guardianship of the children, a situation in which daughters in particular are subject to sexual abuse. In an age of AIDS, orphans whose parents have died of AIDS must frequently fend for themselves. Girl-children in such scenarios sometimes turn to prostitution. AIDS-infected men find young girls desirable for sex, based on the myth that sex with virgins can rid the man of the disease.[22]

Zambia is both a source and a destination country for trafficking in women and children, primarily for sexual purposes. There is no single law against trafficking, although several trafficking cases have been prosecuted in recent years under laws against kidnapping, promoting prostitution, or sex with a minor.[23] The criminal justice system is poorly equipped to handle spousal or sexual abuse issues. Police departments remain male-dominated, with little experience with or understanding of gender-sensitive issues. The police are reluctant to intervene when perpetrators justify their acts in the name of cultural practice.

Zambia's civil society is vibrant (see "Accountability and Public Voice"). Trade unions—which played a leading role in the formation of the MMD (Chiluba was a union leader himself)—are active. In 2003–04, teachers, telecommunications workers, civil servants, and health clinic workers were among those who went on strike. Although pledged to remain nonpartisan, unions have been vocal critics of the government and its economic policies.

For its part, the government frequently tries to rein in the capacity of civil society to influence politics. Informal groups face potential barriers to collective action. Although the Mwanawasa administration has not relied upon it as much as the Chiluba regime, the Public Order Act allows the state to license—and thereby restrict—public demonstrations. The act effectively enables the state to prohibit and criminalize certain public gatherings, if it so chooses. The police, under regional commanders, bear primary responsibility for maintaining order around public demonstrations. They have been willing to break up demonstrations when a decision—usually politically motivated but justified legally in a technical sense—is made that a given demonstration is illegal. When they do, they frequently resort to the use of tear gas but have not had a major incident involving lethal force since 1997, when Kenneth Kaunda and another opposition politician were shot and injured at a rally in Kabwe. In 2003–04, there were few demonstrations and riots that might have prompted a heavy police or military response, and almost no record of the application of lethal force. One exception was a market riot in the border town of Nakonde that left one woman dead, apparently from a police officer's gunshot.

## Recommendations

- To reduce prison crowding, the government should upgrade the Zambian prison infrastructure and explore wider use of non-custodial means of punishment.
- The government should build on Mwanawasa's refusal to use capital punishment and abolish the death penalty altogether.
- The police should become better prepared to handle sexual abuse cases. Possible measures include comprehensive police training on domestic violence and sexual assault laws, the creation of a dedicated anti-domestic violence task force, and the hiring of more female officers.

- To mitigate against the social devastation of the AIDS epidemic, the government should employ protections of the property of widows (including sanctions against those who attempt to deprive widows of their property) and devise a strong safety net for orphans with a focus on deterring the incidence of drug use and prostitution.
- The revised constitution should enshrine protections for the rights of Zambians to associate with one another. Laws that may contradict those rights, such as the Public Order Act, should be revised so that they are consistent with fundamental protections.

## RULE OF LAW – 4.26

The Zambian judiciary has exhibited laudable independence from political pressures, even during the most illiberal phases of the Chiluba administration. The constitution mandates that the president may remove a judge of the High Court or Supreme Court only after obtaining the recommendation of a specially designated tribunal convened to investigate the ability of the judge in question to perform the duties of the office. The avenue has not been pursued in recent years. Moreover, although several prominent judges were UNIP-era holdovers, Chiluba never attempted to pack the courts. Mwanawasa has continued the tradition of respecting the judiciary's independence.

Mwanawasa did draw criticism in early 2004 for firing the director of public prosecutions, Mukelabai Mukelabai, for meeting with Xavier Chungu, a co-defendant of Chiluba's in an ongoing corruption trial. An investigatory tribunal rejected the charges and recommended Mukelabai's reinstatement.

Corruption remains an issue for Zambia's judiciary. Most notably, in 2003, Chief Justice Matthew Ngulube resigned after a tax tribunal found that he had accepted over $10,000 in gifts from President Chiluba between 1998 and 2000.[24] Perhaps more damaging to the pursuit of justice is corruption in trial courts. In April 2004, two Lusaka magistrates were suspended for petty corruption. The sitting home affairs minister, Ronnie Shikapwasha, has claimed that corrupt judges bear some responsibility for Zambia's high crime rate, with criminals able to bribe their way out of conviction.[25]

The judiciary system as a whole suffers from insufficient staffing and a lack of resources. It is consequently overwhelmed by its caseload. Cases—including hearings on the petition challenging the 2001 presidential vote—commonly adjourn on account of insufficient court personnel. Despite constitutional protections to the contrary, suspects sometimes languish for years in custody awaiting trial in the overburdened system.

According to the constitution, individuals have a right to representation by a counsel of their choosing. However, the constitution does not provide for a publicly funded defense counsel, even in the case of an indigent defendant accused of a felony. Poorer Zambians thus cannot expect equal treatment before the judiciary.

Under Mwanawasa, the government has been more aggressive in investigating and prosecuting allegations of abuse of power by members of the ruling party. Most notable is the case of former President Chiluba (see "Anticorruption and Transparency"). However, sitting judges, members of parliament, and cabinet members have been charged with crimes and prosecuted as well. Most prosecutions are related to corruption charges—although in the case of Justice Ngulube cited above, a tax violation provided the occasion for investigation and prosecution.

It is uncommon for the military to participate in—or even comment upon—civilian politics. The military has generally been respectful of the rule of law. Even in the case of a notorious exception—the 1997 coup attempt by dissident officers—the rank and file as well as most of the military's leadership structure remained loyal to the republican president.

The Zambian constitution provides for protection from deprivation of property, although the enumeration of 27 exceptions, including "in terms of any law vesting any such property or rights in the President," and "in execution of judgments or orders of courts," suggests that the protection is somewhat weak. The court system handles cases involving the enforcement of contracts, including those implicating the state. Their resolution does not appear to be systematically biased but does remain subject to the inefficiencies of the court system discussed above.

In urban areas, many residents live in townships—called compounds in Zambia—without title to their dwellings or the land on which the dwellings sit. These townships are technically illegal, as the state owns the land and may dictate its use. Indeed, during the Kaunda era, the government occasionally bulldozed them. However, they have grown to accommodate such a significant portion of the population that similar actions would be unthinkable today. During the Chiluba administration, the government undertook a program of granting private ownership to urban residents who had hitherto rented their property from local government councils. The program promoted ownership, although the councils resented the loss of an income source.

Ownership of land is a source of controversy. According to the Land Act, land in Zambia is vested in the president, who lets it to occupants in 99-year leases. In practice, 80 percent of the land is leased to traditional rulers, who then allocate it among subjects and others. As a result, most rural residents are twice removed from actual ownership of their land. Either the government or the traditional ruler may effectively expropriate residents' land, which results in both insecurity and a potential for corrupt exploitation.[26] The individuals most likely to lose property are widows (see "Civil Liberties").

*Recommendations*
- The government should transparently and vigorously investigate corruption at all levels of the judiciary.
- The courts, which should be better funded, should institute human resource policies to prevent the rampant absenteeism that results in delayed and slow trials.
- The revised constitution should mandate the provision of legal counsel if a defendant is unable to hire one on his or her own.
- The government should extend its promotion of individual housing and land ownership to semi-urban and rural areas, while remaining sensitive to interests of traditional rulers in order to make such a program politically feasible.

## ANTICORRUPTION AND TRANSPARENCY – 3.39

According to the Anti-Corruption Act (last amended in 1996), "abusing a public position for a personal (family, party, sectional, tribal, and so on) advantage or interest over those of the many" is a criminal act. Nevertheless, corruption is a dominant concern in Zambia, which ranked 14 out of the continental 28 Sub-Saharan countries listed in Transparency International's 2004 Corruption Perceptions Index.[27]

Since taking office, President Mwanawasa has prioritized anticorruption efforts, including the creation of an anticorruption task force that has investigated more than 500 companies and individuals. The highlight of these efforts has been the prosecutions of ex-president Chiluba and several of his associates. One of Mwanawasa's first moves as president was to push for the removal of the immunity from prosecution to which ex-presidents had been entitled. He succeeded through an act of parliament, which was later upheld by the Supreme Court.[28] In February 2003, a day after the court's decision, Chiluba was arrested and charged with 66 corruption-related counts.[29] By December, Chiluba was facing two trials—one for abusing a slush fund and another for stealing from suspended accounts in the Zambia National Commerce Bank—featuring 233 separate charges against him and his associates and relating to more than US$44 million worth of allegedly stolen funds.[30]

Since the initial arrests, however, politics and scandal have plagued the prosecution of Chiluba. By September 2004, the Chiluba trials had yielded no convictions. The highest-profile defendants among his co-accused—former Intelligence Director Xavier Chungu and former Ambassador to the United States Attan Shansonga—had jumped bail. Mwanawasa tried unsuccessfully to dismiss the prosecutor in charge of the case after the latter was alleged to have consorted with the accused. By September 2004, only Chiluba and two lesser-known aides remained on trial. Charges relating to the slush fund case have been dropped, and the remaining case involves just $500,000.[31]

Although Mwanawasa's anticorruption campaign has focused a high level of media attention on Zambia's corruption problems, critics have claimed that the resources devoted to the Chiluba prosecution would have been better spent on broader anticorruption efforts, such as those of the longer-standing Anti-Corruption Commission.[32] Along with Mwanawasa's Taskforce on Corruption, the Anti-Corruption Commission and the auditor general also have mandates to detect, prevent, and seek the punishment of public officials accused of corruption (in the latter case, by recommending prosecution before a court of law). These latter institutions, however, have been beset by resource constraints.[33]

Each is dependent upon the will of the executive to varying extents. Salaries of the offices in question are constitutionally protected, but their operating budgets are determined by the president. Allegations of corruption implicating those close to the president may therefore receive a less-than fair hearing. Whistle-blowers filing complaints under the parliamentary and ministerial code of conduct may be further deterred by legislation that provides for a sentence of imprisonment in cases in which the complaint in question is not proven.

The lack of success in the Chiluba case has overshadowed other developments. In 2003, Mwanawasa dismissed his vice president, Enoch Kavindele, in the wake of allegations of irregular contracting procedures tied to the campaign for the 2001 elections.[34] Other ministers and officials have also been forced out.[35] Meanwhile, Mwanawasa has been on the defense as well. Many of his current opponents were MMD members until recently and have testified that Mwanawasa benefited from the abuse of state resources during the 2001 presidential campaign.[36]

Mwanawasa's anticorruption focus has involved few efforts to change the underlying environment, in which corruption is endemic. Despite more than a decade of privatization efforts, the state's involvement in the economy provides ample opportunities for corruption. The bureaucracy is rife with licensing requirements and bureaucratic controls. Widespread poverty and low formal-sector wages lead many public sector employees to top off income with corrupt practices out of necessity.

The fact that many of the richest and most successful individuals in Zambia are current or former government ministers raises perceptions of corruption. A recent survey found that 71 percent of Zambians believed that their politicians entered politics in pursuit of their self-interest rather than the public good.[37] Indeed, recent corruption scandals—such as that which forced Kavindele to resign—have originated in alleged efforts by public office holders to use their position for private gain. Although it has improved in recent years, the government still does relatively little to promote transparency in its actions and those of its leaders. No law compels government officials to declare their assets or to declare potential conflicts of interest with the private sector. The enactment of a freedom of information bill, which the government introduced in 2002, would be a strong move in that direction by reducing government officials' protection from having to disclose personal information. However, the government pulled the bill for further comment after its initial introduction, and the law remained unpassed as of September 2004.[38]

The education system is not immune from corruption. The ministry of education has, at times, been plagued by theft and sale of exam questions, although few incidents along those lines have been reported recently. In November 2003, the principal and three other officials at Mulungushi College in Kabwe were arrested on corruption charges.[39] No other corruption scandals drew widespread notice in 2003–04.

Citizens have a right to information about government's ordinary activities. However, information on bills under consideration, legislation, and judicial opinions is hard to come by. The weekly *Government Gazette* reports on a wide range of government activities but is expensive and, in practice, narrowly available. The independent *Post* newspaper has occasionally taken the initiative to publish legislation and court opinions *verbatim*. Government Internet sites are poorly maintained and thus usually well out of date.

Recent events have improved the transparency of the activities of parliament. The current balance of political parties is far more competitive than at any other time in Zambian history, presenting opportunities for opposition members to serve a more effective watchdog role. The budgeting process has also been more transparent and inclusive in the wake of the PRSP experience, which has the added benefit of bringing donor flows more directly into public view. However, data on actual expenditures are generally not released in a timely manner.[40] Expenditures not authorized by parliament are not required to come to light until 30 months after they have taken place.[41] Matters relating to borrowing and debt fall entirely under the jurisdiction of the ministry of finance and are therefore not subject to parliamentary oversight. In 2004, budget transparency took a step backward with the suspension of the HIPC Tracking and Monitoring Team, a quasi-NGO that had originally been established by the ministry of finance.[42] The team had identified several instances of alleged abuse of HIPC-related funds.[43]

The Zambia National Tender Board (ZNTB) is, according to Transparency International–Zambia, well designed but greatly abused and lacking discipline in practice.[44] Avenues of appeal regarding the ZNTB's decisions are not sufficiently independent of the board itself. A Web site established in 2004 provides more information about open tenders (and the tender process) than was previously available but does not contain data on successful and unsuccessful bids on closed tenders.[45]

## Recommendations

- The government should continue efforts to prosecute former president Chiluba, although it should be careful not to neglect other anticorruption efforts—particularly those combating petty corruption—as it does so.
- The Anti-Corruption Commission should be provided with more financial and human resources. Oversight and operational support for the Commission should be vested in parliament (with guaranteed opposition or civil society participation), rather than in the president.
- The ministry of finance should be accountable to parliament for its borrowing and debt-service activities. The ministry of finance and the ZNTB should regularly release to the public information on their activities in a widely accessible format.
- The government should reintroduce and parliament should enact the freedom of information bill. Security-based exceptions to the bill's disclosure provisions should be narrowly tailored.
- The PRSP process should be regularized beyond the life of the HIPC program to provide for institutionalized transparency regarding mid- and long-term planning, the annual budgeting process, and the flow of foreign assistance.

## NOTES

[1] For a profile of Mwanawasa, see "Profile: Zambia's New Leader," BBC News Online, 8 January 2002, http://news.bbc.co.uk/1/hi/world/africa/1748595.stm.

[2] As reported in "Verdict divided on Zambia's poll," BBC News Online, 4 January 2002, http://news.bbc.co.uk/1/hi/world/africa/1742676.stm.

[3] "Observing the 2001 Zambia Elections – Final Report" (Atlanta: Carter Center, October 2002), 37, 41, http://www.cartercenter.org/documents/1135.pdf (accessed 14 December 2004).

[4] "Interim Report on the 2001 Tripartite Elections" (Lusaka: Foundation for Democratic Process [FODEP]), http://www.fodep.org.zm/intrep1.htm.

[5] Webster Malido, "We Used Money To Buy Off Opposition —Katele," *The Post* (Lusaka, Zambia), 15 February 2003.

6  "Handbook on Funding of Political Parties and Election Campaigns" (Stockholm: Institute for Democracy and Electoral Assistance [ IDEA], 2004), 191, 195, 199, 207, 218, http://www.idea.int/publications/funding_parties/index.cfm#tableofcontents.

7  Michael Bratton, "Political Participation in a New Democracy," *Comparative Political Studies* 32, 5 (August 1999): 549–78.

8  "Interim Report" (Lusaka: Electoral Reform Technical Committee [ERTC], 6 August 2004), http://www.ertc.gov.zm/images/ERTC%20INTERIM%20%20REPORT.pdf.

9  Nakubiana Mumbuna, "Draft constitution to be ready this year," *Times of Zambia* (Ndola), 28 August 2004.

10  "198 Societies De-Registered," *Times of Zambia*, 4 November 2003.

11  Leonard Kantumoya, "Investigative Journalism in Zambia: A Practitioner's Handbook" (Lusaka: Transparency International–Zambia [TI–Z] and the Friedrich Ebert Stiftung, 2004).

12  "Zambia: Attempt to close down TV station poses threat to media freedom," IRINNews (UN Office for the Coordination of Humanitarian Affairs), 5 November 2003, http://www.irinnews.org/report.asp?ReportID=37658&SelectRegion=Southern_Africa&Select Country=ZAMBIA.

13  Portions of this paragraph draw heavily from Henry Macha, "Zambia: 2003 World Press Freedom Review" (International Press Institute [IPI], 2004), http://www.misa.org/sothisisdemocracy/zambia/zambia.html.

14  In June 2002, one report held that the prisons were at 259% capacity. See "World Prison Brief: Zambia" (London: International Centre for Prison Studies, Kings College, n.d.), http://www.kcl.ac.uk/depsta/rel/icps/worldbrief/africa_records.php?code=52.

15  "Mwanawasa declines the job of chief hangman," *The Post* (Lusaka), 28 February 2004.

16  "Captain Chiti is dead," *The Post,* 19 August 2004.

17  See "Report on the IFES sponsored election monitoring project for the 2001 tri-partite elections" (Frome, UK: Action on Disability and Development [ADD] – Zambia Programme, January 2002), http://www.ifes.org/disabilities/publications/news/02_01_Zambia_Report.htm.

18  The 100,000 figure comes from extrapolating from the 2000 census, which counts 10.3 million Zambians, of whom 1.3 percent are of non-African descent. See Government of Zambia, Central Statistics Office, "Census of Population Housing and Agriculture" (Lusaka: Government Printers, 2004).

19  "Zambia: Zimbabwean farmers increase tobacco production," IRINNews, November 2003.

20  See, for example, "Levy's a gender sensitive president," *Times of Zambia*, 14 May 2004.

21  See "Zambia: Culture of Silence over Gender Violence," IRINNews, 1 December 2003.

22  See "Suffering in Silence: The Links between Human Rights Abuses and HIV Transmission to Girls in Zambia" (New York: Human Rights Watch, 2002), http://www.hrw.org/reports/2003/zambia/.

23  *Trafficking in Persons Report* (Washington, DC: U.S. Dept. of State, 14 June 2004).

24  See "Former chief justice Ngulube loses appeal," *Times of Zambia*, 24 July 2004.

25  See "Shikapwasha saddened by judiciary corruption," *Times of Zambia*, 31 March 2004.

[26] These issues are discussed at length in "Land Tenure Systems and Sustainable Development in Southern Africa" (Addis Ababa: UN Economic Commission for Africa, ECA/SA/EGM.Land/2003/2, December 2003).

[27] "Corruption Perceptions Index" (Berlin: TI, 2004), http://www.transparency.org/cpi/2004/cpi2004.en.html#cpi2004. In this statement, "continental Africa" includes Madagascar but excludes Seychelles and Mauritius.

[28] See "Chiluba loses immunity appeal," BBC News Online, 19 February 2003, http://news.bbc.co.uk/1/hi/world/africa/2779615.stm.

[29] "Zambia ex-leader on theft charge," BBC News Online, 24 February 2003, http://news.bbc.co.uk/1/hi/world/africa/2794441.stm. Additional charges were made in August of 2003: see "Charges against Chiluba mount," BBC News Online, 5 August 2003, http://news.bbc.co.uk/1/hi/world/africa/3125601.stm.

[30] "Zambia's matrix of plunder," BBC News Online, 9 December 2003, http://news.bbc.co.uk/1/hi/world/africa/3302419.stm.

[31] "Chiluba corruption case cut back," BBC News Online, 14 September 2004, http://news.bbc.co.uk/1/hi/world/africa/3654612.stm.

[32] "Zambia: Anti-corruption body under attack," IRINNews, 10 May 2004, http://www.irinnews.org/report.asp?ReportID=41088&SelectRegion=Southern_Africa&SelectCountry=ZAMBIA.

[33] See, for example, "Manpower shortage hampers ACC—OPS," Times of Zambia, 24 July 2004; and "Increase funding to auditor general's office plead MPs," Times of Zambia, 17 February 2004.

[34] "Zambia: Anti-corruption campaign claims VP," IRINNews, 2 June 2003, http://www.irinnews.org/report.asp?ReportID=34476&SelectRegion=Southern_Africa&SelectCountry=ZAMBIA.

[35] See, for example, the case of Matthew Ngulube, noted above.

[36] See, for example, "We Used Money To Buy Off Opposition —Katele," as well as "Zambian leader survives sack bid," BBC News Online, 14 August 2003, http://news.bbc.co.uk/1/hi/world/africa/3149871.stm.

[37] "Police service tops TIZ's survey on corruption," The Post (Lusaka), 19 December 2002.

[38] The draft legislation is available online at http://www.humanrightsinitiative.org/programs/ai/rti/international/laws_papers/zambia/foi_bill_2002.pdf.

[39] "Mulungushi college principal arrested," Times of Zambia, 14 November 2003.

[40] "Austerity without injuring the poor: 2004 post-budget statement" (Lusaka: Catholic Commission for Justice, Development, and Peace [CCJDP], February 2004), http://www.sarpn.org.za/documents/d0000749/P843-CCJP2004.pdf.

[41] Mulela Margaret Munalula, "A position paper on the effectiveness of government watchdog institutions in Zambia" (TI–Z, August 2002), http://www.tizambia.org.zm/watch_doc.doc.

[42] "Zambia: NGOs to continue monitoring HIPC fund spending," IRINNews, 10 May 2004, http://www.irinnews.org/report.asp?ReportID=40973&SelectRegion=Southern_Africa&SelectCountry=ZAMBIA.

[43] "Call for more transparency in loan agreements," IRINNews, 10 May 2004, http://www.irinnews.org/report.asp?ReportID=41769&SelectRegion=Southern_Africa& SelectCountry=ZAMBIA.

[44] Munalula, "Watchdog Institutions," 43; see also K. Lolojih, "Report on Government Procurement Systems" (TI–Z, November 2003), http://www.tizambia.org.zm/admin/ docs/Report%2014%20on%20Government%20Procurement%20Systems%20-%20 Nov%202003.pdf.

[45] Zambia National Tender Board Web site: http://www.tenderboard.gov.zm/index.php.

# SURVEY METHODOLOGY

The Freedom House *Countries at the Crossroads* survey provides a comparative evaluation of government performance in four touchstone areas of democratic governance: Accountability and Public Voice, Civil Liberties, Rule of Law, and Anticorruption and Transparency. This survey examines these areas of performance in a set of 30 countries that are at a critical crossroads in determining their political future.

The timeframe for events covered is October 1, 2003, through September 30, 2004. In addition, for this baseline survey authors were asked to reference any defining events, major reforms or setbacks, or critical trends prior to October 1, 2003, that helped to illuminate the current state of affairs.

The 2005 edition is the second in the *Countries at the Crossroads* series. It examines 30 countries distinct from those in the 2004 edition. In cooperation with a team of methodology experts, Freedom House designed a methodology that includes a questionnaire used both to prepare analytical narratives and for numerical ratings for each government. The survey methodology provides authors with a transparent and consistent guide to scoring and analyzing the countries under review and uses identical benchmarks for both narratives and ratings, rendering the two indicators mutually reinforcing. The final result is a system of comparative ratings accompanied by narratives that reflect both governments' commitment to passing good laws and also their records on upholding them.

The survey's methodology was created for the 2004 edition by a committee of senior advisers from the academic and scholarly communities. Its members were Larry Diamond, Hoover Institution; Adrian Karatnycky, Freedom House; Paul Martin, Columbia University; Rick Messick, the World Bank; Ted Piccone, Open Society Institute; Louise Shelley, American University; Jay Verkuilen, University of Illinois, Urbana-Champaign; Ruth Wedgwood, Johns Hopkins University; and Jennifer Windsor, Freedom House. In consultation with the committee, the Freedom House staff revised and updated the methodology for

2005. Most notably, a new subsection on property rights has been included under the Rule of Law section.

Freedom House enlisted the participation of prominent scholars and analysts to author the survey's country reports. In preparing the survey's written analyses with accompanying comparative ratings, Freedom House undertook a systematic gathering of data. Each country narrative report is approximately 6,000 words. Expert regional advisers reviewed the draft narrative reports, providing written comments and requests for revisions, additions, or clarifications. Authors were asked to respond as fully as possible to all of the questions posed when composing the analytical narratives; thus, the country narrative reports help inform the numerical scores.

For all 30 countries in the survey, Freedom House, in consultation with the report authors and academic advisers, has provided numerical ratings for the four thematic categories listed above. Authors produced a first round of ratings for each subcategory by evaluating each of the questions and assigning scores on a scale of 0–7, where 0 represents weakest performance and 7 represents strongest performance. The regional advisers and Freedom House staff systematically reviewed all country ratings on a comparative basis to ensure accuracy and fairness. All final ratings decisions rest with Freedom House.

Scores are assigned on a scale of 0–7, where 0 represents weakest performance and 7 represents strongest performance. These ratings allow for comparative analysis of reform among the countries surveyed and are valuable for making general assessments of the level of democratic governance in a given country; they should not be taken as absolute indicators of the situation in a given country.

In devising a framework for evaluating government performance, Freedom House sought to develop a scale broad enough to capture degrees of variation so that comparisons could be made between countries in the current year, and also so that future time series comparisons might be made to assess a country's progress in these areas relative to past performance. These scales achieve an effective balance between a scoring system that is too broad—which may make it difficult for analysts to make fine distinctions between different scores—and one that is too narrow—which may make it difficult to capture degrees of variation between countries and therefore more difficult to recognize how much a given government's performance has improved or eroded over time.

Narrative essays and scoring were applied to the following main areas of performance, which Freedom House considers to be key to evaluating the state of democratic governance within a country:

## ACCOUNTABILITY AND PUBLIC VOICE

- Free and fair electoral laws and elections
- Effective and accountable government
- Civic engagement and civic monitoring
- Media independence and freedom of expression

## CIVIL LIBERTIES

- Protection from state terror, unjustified imprisonment, and torture
- Gender equity and minority rights
- Freedom of conscience and belief
- Freedom of association

## RULE OF LAW

- Independent judiciary
- Primacy of rule of law in civil and criminal matters
- Accountability of security forces and military to civilian authorities
- Property rights

## ANTICORRUPTION AND TRANSPARENCY

- Environment to protect against corruption
- Existence of laws, ethical standards, and boundaries between private and public sectors
- Enforcement of anticorruption laws
- Governmental transparency

In addition to the main subject matter areas, authors were asked to prepare an Introduction, giving a brief history of the country and outlining key issues in its development. At the end of each of the four major category sections, the authors provide succinct recommendations for the regime to take with respect to areas of most immediate and pressing concern.

## Scoring Range

The *Countries at the Crossroads* survey rates countries' performance in each of the four major subject areas on a scale of 0 to 7, with 0 representing the weakest performance and 7 the strongest. The scoring scale is as follows:

**Score of 0–2** Countries that receive a score of 0, 1, or 2 ensure no or very few adequate protections, legal standards, or rights in the rated category. Laws protecting the rights of citizens or the justice of the political process are nonexistent, rarely enforced, or routinely abused by the authorities.

**Score of 3–4** Countries that receive a score of 3 or 4 provide few or very few adequate protections, legal standards, or rights in the rated category. Legal protections are weak and enforcement of the law is inconsistent or corrupt.

**Score of 5** Countries that receive a score of 5 provide some adequate protections, legal standards or rights in the rated category. Rights and political standards are protected, but enforcement may be unreliable and some abuses may occur. A score of 5 is considered to be the minimally adequate performance in the rated category.

**Score of 6–7** Countries that receive a score of 6-7 ensure nearly all adequate protections, legal standards, or rights in the rated category. Legal protections are strong and are usually enforced fairly. Citizens have access to legal redress when their rights are violated, and the political system functions smoothly.

# METHODOLOGY QUESTIONS

## 1. Accountability and Public Voice

### 1.a. Free and fair electoral laws and elections

1.a.i)   Is the authority of government based upon the will of the people as expressed by regular, free, and fair elections under fair electoral laws, with universal and equal suffrage, open to multiple parties, conducted by secret ballot, monitored by independent electoral authorities, with honest tabulation of ballots, and free of fraud and intimidation?

1.a.ii)   Are there equal campaigning opportunities for all parties?

1.a.iii)   Is there the opportunity for the effective rotation of power among a range of different political parties representing competing interests and policy options?

1.a.iv)   Are there adequate regulations to prevent undue influence of economically privileged interests (e.g.effective campaign finance laws)?

### 1.b. Effective and accountable government

1.b.i)   Are the executive, legislative, and judicial branches of government able to oversee the actions of one another and hold each other accountable for any excessive exercise of power?

1.b.ii)   Does the state system ensure that people's political choices are free from domination by the specific interests of power groups (e.g.the military, foreign powers, totalitarian parties, regional hierarchies, and/or economic oligarchies)?

1.b.iii)   Is the civil service selected on the basis of open competition and by merit?

659

1.b.iv)  Is the state engaged in issues reflecting the interests of women; ethnic, religious, and other distinct groups; and disabled people?

### 1.c.  Civic engagement and civic monitoring

1.c.i)  Are civic groups able to testify, comment on, and influence pending government policy or legislation?

1.c.ii)  Are nongovernmental organizations free from legal impediments from the state and from onerous requirements for registration?

1.c.iii)  Are donors and funders of civic organizations and public policy institutes free of state pressures?

### 1.d.  Media independence and freedom of expression

1.d.i)  Does the state refrain from direct and indirect censorship of the media?

1.d.ii)  Does the state oppose onerous libel laws that would impede open criticism of state officials?

1.d.iii)  Does the state protect individuals from imprisonment for the free expression of their views?

1.d.iv)  Does the government otherwise refrain from determining or controlling media content (e.g.through direct ownership of media, distribution networks, or ownership of printing facilities; prohibitive tariffs; selective investigation; or intimidation)?

1.d.v)  Does the state refrain from funding the media in order to propagandize, primarily provide official points of view, and/or limit access by opposition parties and civic critics?

1.d.vi)  Does the state protect the freedom of cultural expression (e.g., in fictional works, art, etc.)?

## 2. Civil Liberties

### 2.a. Protection from state terror, unjustified imprisonment, and torture

2.a.i)   Is there protection against torture by officers of the state, including through effective punishment in cases where torture is found to have occurred?

2.a.ii)  Are prison conditions humane and respectful of the human dignity of inmates?

2.a.iii)  Does the state effectively protect against or respond to killings of political opponents or other peaceful activists?

2.a.iv)  Are there effective protections against arbitrary arrest, including of political opponents or other peaceful activists?

2.a.v)   Is there effective protection against long-term detention without trial?

2.a.vi)  Does the state protect citizens from abuse by private/nonstate actors?

2.a.vii)  Do citizens have means of effective petition and redress when their rights are violated by state authorities?

### 2.b. Gender equity and rights of ethnic, religious, and other distinct groups

2.b.i)   Does the state ensure the equal right of men and women to the enjoyment of all civil and political rights?

2.b.ii)  Does the state take measures to prevent trafficking in women and children?

2.b.iii)  Does the state take measures, including legislation, to modify or abolish existing laws, regulations, customs, and practices that constitute discrimination against women?

2.b.iv)  Does the state ensure that persons belonging to ethnic, religious, and other distinct groups exercise fully and effectively all their human rights and fundamental freedoms (including ethnic, cultural,

and linguistic rights) without discrimination and
with full equality before the law?

2.b.v)  Does the state take measures, including legislation,
to modify or abolish existing laws, regulations, customs, and practices that constitute discrimination
against ethnic, religious, and other distinct groups?

2.b.vi)  Does the state make a progressive effort to modify
or abolish existing laws, regulations, customs, and
practices that constitute discrimination against
disabled people?

2.b.vii)  Does the state make reasonable efforts to protect
against all forms of discrimination in employment
and occupation?

### 2.c.  *Freedom of conscience and belief*

2.c.i)  Does the state protect the rights of nonbelievers
or adherents of minority religious faiths and
movements?

2.c.ii)  Does the state refrain from interference in the
appointment of religious or spiritual leaders and in
the internal organizational activities of faith-related
organizations?

2.c.iii)  Does the state refrain from placing restrictions
on religious observance, religious ceremony, and
religious education?

2.c.iv)  Does the state otherwise ensure the free practice
of religion?

### 2.d.  *Freedom of association*

2.d.i)  Does the state recognize every person's right to
freedom of association?

2.d.ii)  Does the state respect the right to form and join
trade unions?

2.d.iii)  Are citizens protected from being compelled by the
state to belong to an association, either directly or
indirectly (e.g.because certain indispensable benefits
are conferred on members)?

2.d.iv)  Does the state effectively protect and recognize the rights of civic associations, business organizations, and political organizations to organize, mobilize, and advocate for peaceful purposes?

2.d.v)  Does the state refrain from excessive force in dealing with demonstrations and public protests?

## 3. Rule of Law

### 3.a. Independent judiciary

3.a.i)  Is there independence, impartiality, and nondiscrimination in the administration of justice, including from economic, political or religious influences?

3.a.ii)  Are judges and magistrates protected from interference by the executive and/or legislative branches?

3.a.iii)  Do legislative, executive, and other governmental authorities comply with judicial decisions, which are not subject to change except through established procedures for judicial review?

3.a.iv)  Are judges appointed and dismissed in a fair and unbiased manner?

3.a.v)  Do judges have adequate legal training before assuming the bench?

### 3.b. Primacy of rule of law in civil and criminal matters

3.b.i)  According to the legal system, is everyone charged with a criminal offence presumed innocent until proven guilty?

3.b.ii)  Are citizens given a fair, public, and timely hearing by a competent, independent, and impartial tribunal?

3.b.iii)  Do citizens have the right and access to independent counsel?

3.b.iv)  Does the state provide citizens charged with serious felonies with access to independent counsel when it is beyond their means?

3.b.v)  Are prosecutors independent of political direction and control?

3.b.vi)  Are public officials and ruling party actors prosecuted for the abuse of power and other wrongdoing?

3.b.vii)  Are all persons treated equally before the courts and tribunals?

### 3.c. Accountability of security forces and military to civilian authorities

3.c.i)  Is there effective and democratic civilian state control of the police, military, and internal security forces through the judicial, legislative, and executive branches?

3.c.ii)  Are police, military, and internal security services free from the influence and direction of nonstate actors?

3.c.iii)  Do police, military, and internal security services refrain from interfering in the political process?

### 3.d. Protection of property rights

3.d.i)  Does the state give everyone the right to own property alone as well as in association with others?

3.d.ii)  Does the state adequately enforce property rights and contracts?

3.d.iii)  Does the state protect citizens from the arbitrary and/or unjust deprivation of their property (e.g.Does the state unjustly revoke property titles for governmental use or to pursue a political agenda?)?

3.d.iv)  Does the state adequately address discrepancies between official and traditional (e.g.aboriginal) property laws?

## 4. Anticorruption and Transparency

### 4.a. Environment to protect against corruption

4.a.i  Is the government free from excessive bureaucratic regulations, registration requirements, and/or other controls that increase opportunities for corruption?

4.a.ii)  Does the state refrain from excessive involvement in the economy?

4.a.iii)  Does the state enforce the separation of public office from the personal interests of public officeholders?

4.a.iv)  Are there adequate financial disclosure procedures that prevent conflicts of interest among public officials (e.g.Are the assets declarations of public officials open to public and media scrutiny and verification?)?

4.a.v)  Does the state adequately protect against conflicts of interest in the private sector?

## 4.b. Existence of laws, ethical standards, and boundaries between private and public sectors

4.b.i)  Does the state enforce an effective legislative or administrative process designed to promote integrity and to prevent, detect, and punish the corruption of public officials?

4.b.ii)  Does the state provide victims of corruption with adequate mechanisms to pursue their rights?

4.b.iii)  Does the state protect higher education from pervasive corruption and graft (e.g.Are bribes necessary to gain admission or good grades?)?

4.b.iv)  Does the tax administrator implement effective internal audit systems to ensure the accountability of tax collection?

4.b.v)  Is there an auditing body outside of the executive and free from political influence (e.g.an auditor general or ombudsman) that has wide-ranging authority to report on instances of funds being unlawfully or unwisely spent?

## 4.c.Enforcement of anticorruption laws

4.c.i)  Are there effective and independent investigative and auditing bodies created by the government and do they function without impediment or political pressure?

4.c.ii)  Are allegations of corruption by government officials at the national and local levels thoroughly investigated and prosecuted without prejudice?

4.c.iii)  Are allegations of corruption given wide and extensive airing in the news media?

4.c.iv) Do whistleblowers, anticorruption activists, investigators have a legal environment that protects them, so they feel secure about reporting cases of bribery and corruption?

### 4.d. Governmental transparency

4.d.i) Is there significant legal, regulatory, and judicial transparency as manifested through public access to government information?

4.d.ii) Do citizens have a legal right to obtain information about government operations, and means to petition government agencies for it?

4.d.iii) Does the state make a progressive effort to provide information about government services and decisions in formats and settings that are accessible to disabled people?

4.d.iv) Is the executive budget-making process comprehensive and transparent and subject to meaningful legislative review and scrutiny?

4.d.v) Does the government publish detailed accounting of expenditures in a timely fashion?

4.d.vi) Does the state ensure transparency, open-bidding, and effective competition in the awarding of government contracts?

4.d.vii) Does the government enable the legal administration and distribution of foreign assistance?

# ABOUT FREEDOM HOUSE

Founded in 1941 by Eleanor Roosevelt and others, Freedom House is the oldest non-profit, non-governmental organization in the United States dedicated to promoting and defending democracy and freedom worldwide. Freedom House supports the global expansion of freedom through its advocacy activities, monitoring and in depth research on the state of freedom, and direct support of democratic reformers throughout the world.

**Advocating Democracy and Human Rights:** For over six decades, Freedom House has played an important role in identifying the key challenges to the global expansion of democracy, human rights and freedom. Freedom House is committed to advocating a vigorous U.S. engagement in international affairs that promotes human rights and freedom around the world.

**Monitoring Freedom:** Despite significant recent gains for freedom, hundreds of millions of people around the world continue to endure dictatorship, repression, and the denial of basic rights. To shed light on the obstacles to liberty, Freedom House issues studies, surveys, and reports on the condition of global freedom. Our research is meant to illuminate the nature of democracy, identify its adversaries, and point the way for policies that strengthen and expand democratic freedoms. Freedom House projects are designed to support the framework of rights and freedoms guaranteed in the Universal Declaration of Human Rights.

**Supporting Democratic Change:** The attainment of freedom ultimately depends on the actions of courageous men and women who are committed to the transformation of their societies. But history has repeatedly demonstrated that outside support can play a critical role in the struggle for democratic rights. Freedom House is actively engaged in these struggles, both in countries where dictatorship holds sway and in those societies that are in transition from autocracy to democracy. Freedom House functions as a catalyst for freedom by working to strengthen civil society, promote open government, defend human rights, enhance justice, and facilitate the free flow of information and ideas.